# active voice

## 2nd edition

Edited by

**W.H. New and
W.E. Messenger**

*University of British Columbia*

Prentice-Hall Canada Inc. *Scarborough, Ontario*

*Canadian Cataloguing in Publication Data*

Main entry under title:
Active voice

Includes index.
ISBN 0-13-003724-9

1. College readers.   2. Exposition (Rhetoric).
I. New, William H., 1938-     II. Messenger,
William E., 1931-

PE1122.A26 1985        808'.0427        C85-099450-0

©1986 *by Prentice-Hall Canada Inc.*
*Scarborough, Ontario*

*All rights reserved. No part of this book may be reproduced*
*in any form or by any means without permission in writing from the publisher.*

Prentice-Hall Inc., Englewood Cliffs, *New Jersey*
Prentice-Hall International, Inc., *London*
Prentice-Hall of Australia Pty. Limited, *Sydney*
Editora Prentice-Hall do Brasil, Ltda., *Rio de Janeiro*
Prentice-Hall of India Private Limited, *New Delhi*
Prentice-Hall of Japan, Inc., *Tokyo*
Prentice-Hall of Southeast, Asia Pte. Ltd., *Singapore*
Whitehall Books Limited, Wellington, *New Zealand*
Prentice-Hall Hispanoamericana, S.A., *Mexico*

ISBN 0-13-003724-9

Production Editor: Bruce Erskine
Design: Gail Ferreira Ng-A-Kien
Production: Sheldon Fischer

Typesetting: Skymark Graphics

Printed and bound in Canada by Webcom

1 2 3 4        89 88 87 86

# CONTENTS

# A Note to the Reader

No book on its own can answer all your questions about writing or tell you once and for all how to write. People learn to write only by writing— by finding out what does reach readers and what does not. There are no rigid rules, no certain shortcuts, no guarantees of success, and for that matter, no inevitable pitfalls. But there are models. By reading attentively, and by responding—sympathetically, analytically, and inquiringly—to other writers' efforts to communicate, you can increase your understanding of the ways that writers and readers connect, and you can learn some of the practical strategies that successful writers use.

Active Voice gives you a cross-section of such models. It shows a variety of twentieth-century writers (Canadian, American, British, Australian, South African) dealing with a variety of subjects (science, history, language, medicine, politics, the arts, economics, psychology, race, sport, philosophy, nature, gender, the media, travel, food, mathematics, personal experience) in a variety of styles and forms (formal, informal, experimental; personal narrative, journal, interview, letter, editorial, review, investigation, argument, explanation, entertainment). But the thematic and the technical are only the most obvious among the many avenues of approach offered you here. For example, asking if Americans write differently from Canadians, or women from men, or writers of the 1920s from writers of the 1970s, might lead to an informed discussion on the biases of culture, sex, and fashion that sometimes colour a writer's attitude or affect the premises on which an argument rests. Exploring the nature of rhythm might lead to a greater understanding of the importance of sound to an essay's effect on a reader. Seeking the relation between technique and meaning might lead to a greater understanding of the nature of liter-

1

acy and a greater appreciation of the need for verbal accuracy in all kinds of communication. Examining expository essays alongside poems and narratives, and even beside prose forms conventionally considered nonliterary, might help develop an appreciation for literary endeavour in general. Much depends on your willingness to invest effort and imagination in the process of reading. By asking questions, suggesting possibilities, affirming the open-endedness of literary inquiry, and giving some indication of the range of twentieth-century stylistic excellence, the readings in this book give you models to follow and places to begin learning about writing.

The essays and categories isolated here are not meant to impose limits on your powers of invention. Whatever the examples in this collection might imply, not all letters have to be argumentative, nor all reviews sarcastic or humorous. It is important to emphasize that language is flexible, to assert again and again that the forms of composition overlap and that the categories by which we describe the varieties of prose form are not mutually exclusive. Many of the examples in this book have more than one aim: to explain *and* persuade, for example, or to describe *and* amuse. And many, with some difference of emphasis, could be classified differently: Haig-Brown's essay could be considered explanatory, Orwell's essay persuasive, Woolf's letter humorous,  and so on. Keep in mind that the organization of any anthology of essays is essentially an arbitrary structuring device, one which the good reader will both use and transcend.

The particular organization that we have adopted for *Active Voice* is meant to draw your attention to three features of the strategy of writing essays:

1. The large or overall purpose that motivates a writer to write (to tell a story, to explain a problem, to convince someone of something). This element of form governs the division of the book into its six sections. Section I stresses the importance of observing closely, actively, and personally; all the essays show what the authors themselves see, hear, do and remember. Section II stresses the art of indirect communication. The good interviewer, for example, can induce people to reveal the character that lies behind their public mask, or to demonstrate the set of values that governs their judgments and their behaviour; other essays can be personally revealing, or can adapt the revelatory techniques of the interview and the journal to more conventional essay forms. The writers of such essays address one subject on the surface, even apparently neutrally, but all the while they are drawing attention to their real subject (which lies at some tangent to the other) and implying a different (and often more judgmental) interpretation of the details they are assembling. Sections III and IV explore the tasks of persuasion, explanation, and instruction; they show how these apparently abstract enterprises can also be subjectively organized, sometimes

deliberately and sometimes unconsciously—the art of persuasion being the most open to personal bias, and the art of explanation being the most neutral. The last two sections, V and VI, isolate particular formal problems—humorous writing and experimentation—for practical consideration, and encourage apprentice writers to experiment intelligently as they practise their way toward their own personal style. In section VI, too, there appear examples of fable and other narrative, adaptations of form which call attention to the fine line separating some essays from fiction, and which return the book full circle to the world of personal experience.

2. The immediate purpose—the sense of audience—that governs the writer's choice of form (letter, recipe, reminiscence, editorial, review, feature article, research essay, *jeu d'esprit*). These forms range across the general categories; you will find other kinds of form—advertisement, poem, anecdote—also used as examples in various parts of the book, and you may find it instructive to compare the conventions of prose with other, often more exclusively visual or aural, conventions of communication.

3. The specific techniques by which writers develop and express their ideas. The principal methods of development, what we here call *internal strategies,* are
   definition;
   classification and division (analysis);
   comparison and contrast;
   process analysis; and
   cause and effect.
An essay may seem to have one or another of these as its overall purpose. "How to Bone a Duck, Turkey, or Chicken" (section IV), for example, is strictly a process; but its *purpose* is to inform, to give instructions. Both Woolf's and Jenkins's pieces (section III) are largely exercises in definition, but both have argument or persuasion as their overall purpose, and both use other strategies internally, as well. Gorman's "Man, Bytes, Dog" (section V) is an exemplary piece of comparison and contrast, but its governing intention is to entertain, to amuse. Nearly every piece of writing will use one or more of these internal strategies in order to develop its idea, to realize its overall purpose. Forster's essay (section I), for example, depends largely on analysis and cause and effect, Mitford's (section IV) on explaining a process, Baker's (section IV) on classification. If you examine almost any essay in this book, or any essay you are engaged in writing, you will find these techniques at work in the service of an overall purpose.

Even narration and description, which we treat in section I as overall purposes, commonly function as internal strategies. A description of a person or a scene, or a brief illustrative anecdote, often works toward achieving a larger purpose. Any process analysis, for example, is necessarily narration; Roueché's expository essay (section IV) depends heavily on narration. And the most common internal strategy of all, the supplying of *illustrations and examples*, of *details*, to explain or support a thesis, is so broad as to be all-embracing; that is, the illustrations and examples themselves are often made up of bits of narration, description, cause-and-effect, classification, and so on—though of course they may also be simply lists of concrete particulars illustrating a generalization. As you read and study the essays in this book, look for examples of these strategies at work.

The introductions to each section establish this triple context. Rather than analyze the essays that follow or prescribe procedures for reading them, however, they suggest some of the terms of reference within which different kinds of analysis and discussion can take place. They do this in part by definition and discussion, and in part by technical example. Direction, like meaning, often lies in form. The introduction to section IV, for instance, concerns the need for explanations to be clear, which is a commonplace that will raise little argument and little cheering. How actually to write clearly is another question. The essays in this section provide examples of some successful techniques: using a precise vocabulary, making comparisons between unfamiliar and familiar things, telling illustrative anecdotes, and adopting an informal, person-to-person tone. The introduction at once generalizes about these methods and uses at least some of them in the process of talking about them. Hence it begins anecdotally in order to discuss the effect of anecdotal beginnings, and uses the vocabulary of its own anecdote as part of its process of exploring the language of explanation. Meaning and method unite. You will discover analogous techniques in the other introductions as well: an ironic quotation, quoted ironically, forms part of the commentary on humorous writing; sentence fragments appear in a section that asks if it is acceptable to break standard rules of composition; rhetorical questions and other deliberate devices— litotes, chiasmus, simile, antithesis—appear both as strategies for argument and as examples for analysis.

Some of these terms and techniques—such as litotes (the "negative positive": "not unusual") and chiasmus (an X-shaped structure: "He had a talent for making the easy difficult and the difficult easy")—will not be familiar to all readers. Some of the essays, too, might seem unusually difficult. To add to what the introductions can do to illuminate them, therefore, *Active Voice* provides at the end of each section some brief accounts of relevant terms and some suggestions for study, discussion, and composition. Like the introductions, these study sections neither assert easy answers nor suggest that all answers come easily; part of the function of this book is to encourage a little overreaching, for real learning seldom takes place without it. Wrestling with something difficult can be frustrating, of course. But if you consult not only the resources within yourself but also those provided by our questions and suggestions, you can return to your challenging subject with more of the tools you need in order to master it. Such a procedure can prove far more stimulating than simply making do with the knowledge and skills you already have.

Similarly, because your ability to express yourself depends partly on the words you can command, each study section begins with a list of words selected from the essays in that section—not technical, foreign, coined, or otherwise special words, but words that can be useful in your general vocabulary. You may know many of them already, but ask yourself whether they are part of your *recognition* vocabulary rather than your *working* vocabulary. That is, you may understand a word when you read it in a context; you may even be able to define it; but can you *use* it naturally and confidently in your own writing? To increase your ability as a reader and your power as a writer, stretch your vocabulary. Keep your own list. Include not only words from our lists but also any others you encounter that you aren't thoroughly at home with. Even if you think you know a word, look it up: it may have uses you weren't aware of; try *tonic*, for instance, or *confer*. And don't be surprised if you have to look up other than "big" words: for example, are *shun, akin, loath,* and *wry* in your working vocabulary? Look your words up in a good dictionary; write out their definitions if necessary. But don't stop there. In order to make words part of your active vocabulary you must practise using them. Make it a point to incorporate some words from your list in whatever you find yourself writing. Compose sentences using them; if a word has more than one meaning or usage, write a sentence for each. If a word has derivatives or forms that function as different parts of speech, practise with all of them. Don't stop with *bigot*; use *bigotry* and *bigoted* as well. When you learn *facile,* learn *facility, facilely,* and *facilitate.* Try *heresy, heretic,* and *heretical; evoke, evocation, evocative,* and *evocatively; prudent, prudence, prudently, prudential,* and *prudentially; derided, derision, derisive,* and *derisively; dogma, dogmatic,* and *dogmatism;* and so on. And use some words figuratively as well as in a narrowly limited literal sense, as when Baker (section IV) writes of a "hypotenuse of sunlight," or Thurber in his essay in section III writes of "our moribund vocabulary" and "elephantiasis of cliché," and says that "synonym atrophied." Finally, when you look up a word look at its *etymology;* knowing a word's origin often makes it more interesting and memorable: consider for example the etymologies of *abject, candid, curfew, scrupulous,* and *subjugation.* Your dictionary should provide the sources and histories of words as well as their current definitions; if it doesn't, get a better dictionary, or consult an etymological dictionary such as Eric Partridge's *Origins.*

Throughout, *Active Voice* emphasizes the extent to which form embodies meaning. In particular, this idea is the central concern of the essays in the last section, which therefore constitutes a kind of formal and argumentative coda to the book as a whole. But, depending on one's approach, this section could provide as forceful a beginning as it does an end. The essays offer variety and hence a variety of places to start. Most of all, they are enjoyable in their own right, whether as models for the apprentice writer or as inquiries and diversions for people who just like to read.

To conclude this introductory note, here are some terms that you should be familiar with at the outset:

*Diction* The choice and use of words. "Good diction" means the use of correct and specific words. The term "levels of diction" refers to formal, informal, colloquial, and slang usage.

*Idiom* A combination of words that constitutes the accepted way of saying something in a particular language, even though it may not be entirely grammatical or make literal sense. For example we say (informally) "There is loads of time," treating *loads* as if it were singular, like *plenty*. Certain verbs and other words take certain prepositions: *agree on*, *agree to*, and *agree with* have precise but different usages, as do *differ from* and *differ with*, *compare to* and *compare with*, *wait for* and *wait on*, and *part from* and *part with*; one can have mastery *of* something but mastery *over* someone; one is *convinced of* something but *persuaded to* do something; one can be *capable of* doing something but *able to* do it; something can be redolent *of* something but not redolent *with* it. The word *idiom* also refers to expressions like *by and large*, *all but* (as in "all but finished," where the seemingly equivalent *except* will not work in place of *but*), *all in* (*worn-out*), and *shut up!* which work in defiance of logical or literal sense. Others, like *give the high sign*, *be on edge*, *take the lion's share*, *go the whole hog*, *bottle up*, *switched on* (*with it*), *wet blanket*, *get in high gear*, *here and now*, *hit-and-miss*, *lay of the land*, *go to the dogs*, *a dog's breakfast*, and *as the crow flies*, show that many idioms are metaphorical and that some can be classified as slang or cliché, or both. Clearly many idioms cannot be translated literally into another language, though some do have equivalents. For example a *brown study* would in French be a *sombre rêverie*; but the French also say *broyer du noir*, which wouldn't work translated into English even though it overlaps in meaning with "to be in a brown study." *Battre les buissons* means much the same as our "beat the bushes," but it also works as a counterpart of our "beat around (or about) the bush." Where we would say "Ay, there's the rub" or "You've hit the nail on the head," the French would probably say "C'est là que gît le lièvre" and Germans either "Da liegt der Hase im Pfeffer" or "Da liegt der Hund begraben." (For more on idioms, see Hornyansky's essay in section VI.)

*Cliché*  A trite expression, one worn-out from overuse (a bolt from the blue, last but not least, pretty as a picture, nothing new under the sun, it's a small world).

*Abstract, concrete*  Basically, an abstract word denotes something intangible, such as an idea, quality, or condition (honour, beauty, laziness, patriotism, sorrow), and a concrete word denotes something tangible, perceivable by one or more of the senses (chair, fir tree, hyena, flame, raindrop). Poetry works mainly with the concrete; philosophical discussion, in contrast, can be relatively abstract. Much amateur writing is weak because it lacks concreteness.

*General, specific*  Relative terms, different from abstract and concrete terms with which they partly overlap. A *general* term denotes a class (for example *art*) which has subclasses named by *less general*—or *more specific*—terms (*painting, literature, music,* etc.). The term *literature* can be further subdivided into the less general or more specific classes of *poetry, fiction, essays,* etc., until you get to a single, indivisible, concrete item such as the novel sitting on your desk or the book you are reading right now. Generalizations are necessary ("There seems to be a violent streak in human beings"), for we could scarcely communicate without them; but they are seldom of much use unless supported by specifics ("Two of the players started a fight over an imagined insult, but fortunately they cooled off before anyone got hurt").

*Syntax*  The arrangement of words; the grammatical relations among words in phrases, clauses, and sentences. *Grammar* is simply the systematic study and description of the way a language works.

*Active voice, passive voice*  Grammatical terms describing two ways some verbs (transitive ones) can work. A verb in the active voice acts upon an object: A woman *bought* the green sports car this morning. When a verb is in the passive voice, what would otherwise be the object of the verb becomes the subject of the sentence: The car *was bought* by a woman this morning. (The *by*-phrase is not always present: The car *was bought* this morning. The verb is nevertheless still in the passive voice.) Verbs in the passive voice are generally weaker than verbs in the active voice, though they are sometimes useful in controlling emphasis and in constructing sentences when the agent or actor is unknown or unimportant. (The title of this book does not refer only to this grammatical principle; there we also use the term figuratively, to suggest that good writers actively and consciously choose their style, their "voice," rather than passively letting the style do the choosing.)

**Fragment**   A group of words lacking a subject or a verb, or both. A fragment that is acceptable, that is satisfactorily complete because of context (as would be a brief answer to a question), is sometimes referred to as a *minor sentence.*

**Point of view**   The angle or perspective from which an author writes, which governs the way a reader receives information. Technically, for example, the author of a narrative may use first-person point of view ("I did so and so") or third-person point of view ("She, he, they did so and so").

**Metaphor**   A figurative use of language in which things not usually thought of as alike or even related are identified with each other; that is, a word or phrase usually applied to one thing is applied to something quite different, as in "The ship *ploughed* through the rough sea." At the end of the first paragraph of "Living Like Weasels" (section I), Dillard refers to a weasel as "socketed" into a man's hand. A metaphor often not only helps clarify meaning but also provokes a sharp reappraisal of the subject. A metaphor usually forces a reader to perceive one thing as if looking at it through the filter of the other: the weasel with its teeth partakes of the qualities of the two-pronged plug gripping its socket; or "socketed" may suggest merely something firmly and tightly pushed in. Slang is a prolific source of metaphor: *ace in the hole, square, coffin nail, heel.* So is a poet's imagination: "tongues of consuming fire" not only suggests the shape and movement of flames ("licking," often) but also enforces the idea of consuming as an act of eating, devouring. And some metaphors are buried deep in the language: "daisy" is a collapsed form of "day's eye." A *simile* is a form of metaphorical language that states a similarity explicitly, usually with *like* or *as*: "His voice was *like thunder.*" A metaphor would condense the likeness, for example into a verb, adjective, noun, or adverb: "He (or his voice) *thundered*"; "In his *thundering* voice"; "The *thunder* of his voice"; "He spoke *thunderously.*" An *extended metaphor* (or simile) is one in which an implicit (or explicit) comparison is continued, like an analogy, beyond a single statement: "His voice thundered. When he spoke, the clouds parted and the lightning of his wit flashed through. The resulting deluge of information and entertainment floated the audience's spirits." Extended metaphors can be dangerous in that they sometimes get out of control or distract by becoming too much of a good thing, drowning out the point being made.

**Image**   A verbal representation, either literal or figurative, of something concrete, usually something visual. Metaphors often create figurative images. An image can also be aural, olfactory, gustatory, tactile, or kinesthetic.

**Symbol**   An image that not only represents a concrete, empirical reality but also makes that reality stand for something else, usually something more abstract. A flag, for example, not only represents a country but also symbolizes, for many people, their country's political or ethical virtues. The word *rose* not only represents an actual flower but also, in many poems, symbolizes feminine beauty or the Virgin Mary. Don't confuse the verbs *symbolize* and *represent.*

***Allusion***  An indirect or casual reference to something, usually something outside an immediate context. Writers often allude to figures and events from literature and other arts, from history, and from contemporary popular culture. When Forster in his essay "My Wood," for example (section I), alludes to particular passages in the Bible, he intends to call up in his readers' minds a wide array of associations that bear on what he is directly saying. When Dylan Thomas in his second paragraph (section I) rattles off a catalogue of well-known children's books, he expects it to help you conjure up memories of your own childhood Christmases and thus become more attuned to the mood and content of his essay. (But if you haven't read, or don't remember, *Struwwelpeter* and *Black Beauty* and the rest, you may have to do some homework in order to climb all the way aboard his memory-train.)

***Tone***  An author's attitude toward his or her subject and audience. Tone is manifested by various stylistic qualities of a piece of writing. Tone can be formal, informal, relaxed, playful, serious, condescending, insulting, ironic, sarcastic, bitter, questioning, matter-of-fact, and so on. It is related to the general sense of point of view.

***Rhythm***  The movement or cadence in an arrangement of words, sentences, or paragraphs; the movement one feels when reading (even if one is not reading aloud). Is there a regular, rhythmical, metrical beat from the patterns of stress on the syllables? The preceding sentence, for example, is anapestic. Besides the anapest ( / ∪ ∪ ), the standard metrical feet are the iamb ( ∪ / ), the trochee ( / ∪ ), the dactyl ( ∪ ∪ / ), and the spondee ( / / ). Though regular metre is relatively rare in prose, other kinds of rhythm are not. For example is there a rising— or a falling—inflection to the words? Does a string of words move quickly, or does it, instead, move rather heavily, sluggishly, slowly? (Punctuation of course affects rhythm in a sentence.) Is there enough variety of sentence and paragraph length to prevent a monotonous rhythm?

***Sound patterns***  The flow of prose can also be affected by such patterns of sound as *alliteration* (repetition of the same sound at the beginning of nearby words), *assonance* (similarity of vowel sounds within nearby words), *consonance* (similarity of consonant sounds within nearby words), and even *rhyme* (the same or similar sound at the ends of words, beginning with the last stressed vowel: n*ight* fl*ight*, du*tiful* and b*eautiful*, the salv*ation* of the n*ation*). Such patterns often occur accidentally, of course, but they can be controlled.

*Style* The overall make-up and arrangement of sounds, words, phrases, sentences, and paragraphs in a piece of writing. Style consists of everything having to do with the *way* a writer writes something. Styles do not fall into absolute categories; styles are as individual as good writers. Style is affected by fashion and taste, by regional and cultural variations, by changing standards of usage, by the development of new words and new meanings in the language, and by the fertility of an author's imagination. A good style is one that most aptly chooses and arranges words to convey the particular tone and the particular shades of meaning—to produce the precise effect— that an author intends.

If you want further explanation of these and other terms defined in this book, or if we have not provided definitions of terms you don't know, you should consult a good standard dictionary. Better yet, there are many dictionaries or glossaries of literary terms that will help you even more. Here are the names of a few of them, just to get you started:

M.H. Abrams, *A Glossary of Literary Terms*
C. Hugh Holman, *A Handbook to Literature*
Lee T. Lemon, *A Glossary for the Study of English*
Harry Shaw, *Concise Dictionary of Literary Terms*

Once the terms are familiar to you, apply them to the essays and to your other reading, practise using the techniques yourself, and ask yourself how useful and effective they are for shaping your ideas in prose and for reaching your chosen reader.

# Introduction:
# Audience and Purpose

To begin, here are six examples of how some people actually talk:

1. "How are *we* today?"
2. "It has come to a point where the Prime Minister must begin to face matters and recognize that an election must be called forthwith."
3. "You have *no idea* how difficult it's been to arrange everything for this afternoon."
4. "Cold out by the bluff today, eh?"
5. "There's still a real relationship between him and I, irregardless of what he done."
6. "The organization metatalk of this is offered in terms of the recognition that composition situations will be met down the road, and persons without a game plan, on the basis of the correlation interface between their multivalent experimental factors and their societal age-group factors, will be quantified institution-wise."

Each utterance conveys a message—though the sixth example deeply buries it—and each conveys clearly the character of the speaker. Interestingly, however, the message that the speaker intends and the public face that he or she wishes to display often differ from the message an audience actually hears and the face it perceives. Consider again the six examples:

1. The first is the classic utterance of the stereotypical primary school teacher. She—and one makes a biased, presumptive leap identifying the gender here—appears to want to assert her oneness with her class. But how effective is the utterance if she uses it with a group of fifteen-year-olds instead of five-year-olds, or with a group of parents or school inspectors? The adult audience merely cringes politely, with some degree of pity for someone who can no longer separate herself from "her" children. The fifteen-year-olds, by contrast, bristle, for they indignantly reject what they hear as condescension, what they interpret as the speaker's refusal to recognize how much they have grown up. Given a difference in the age of the audience or a difference in milieu, this communication breaks down.

2. The second utterance, clearly political, just as clearly comes from the mouth of someone not on the governing party's side. It will scarcely be effective. Compare it for a moment with the standard slogans of actual election campaigns: "Hold the Vote Now!" "Vote Them Out!" "Time for a Change!" The bluntly monosyllabic slogans appeal directly—hence personally—to the listener: "*You* vote them out." But any utterance that begins wordily (*It has come to a point where*), continues with vague words (*matters, forthwith*), and closes with a passive evasion (*must be called*—by whom???) dooms itself. No one will take it seriously. No one will hear the overt message; they will hear a waffling covert message instead, something like: "I know this is futile but the party requires me to make a mechanical gesture." The emphasis falls, finally, on the futility and the sense of obligation.

3. The third example, too, offers a personal glimpse of the speaker. Ostensibly it's about *you* ("You have no idea"), but really it's about *I*, the speaker. "It's been *difficult*, for me," the speaker is saying. "Admire *me* because *I've* done something difficult; *I've* put *myself* out." The message contains at least two further notions. The first —"I'm a martyr"—is a curiously perverse sort of self-aggrandizing. The second—"and it's *your fault*"—implies that the afternoon's event is less than successful. This last twist emerges because the message (*"no idea," "difficult"*) is essentially negative. It occurs only when there's a problem. And whose problem is it? The speaker's, perhaps—certainly not *yours*—but the speaker has difficulty admitting to it. In any case, an afternoon event that's proceeding well will call forth an utterance more like "There was a lot to do, but *we* had a *good* time doing it." It is at once less defensive and less shrill.

4. The fourth example reveals no problem of personality. It's a colloquial fragment of conversation, informal in tone, designed not

so much to impart or to ask for information—despite the fact that it's cast as a question—as to give a kind of ritual voice to a chance encounter. "How do you do?" offers a more formal parallel. Try to imagine yourself replying, "I do do well." The exchange is a social convention, varying according to the social circumstances. The speaker who says "Pleased to meet you" may not be. The speaker who says "Charmed, I'm sure" conveys the distinct impression that he isn't, and that he's stuffy to boot. What we know of the speaker who uses *bluff* and *eh?* has more to do with his nationality than his social status. He's likely Canadian. But there's another geographic variable here, for if he's a prairie speaker, *bluff* means a *grove of trees*, not a *cliff*. Without a context, the utterance is ambiguous.

5. In a conversational context, a sentence fragment—as in example number four—is perfectly acceptable. Provided it grows directly out of a previous utterance, its meaning will usually be clear. But the fifth example contains a grating combination of plain and fancy mistakes. Among some occupations and in some environments, grammatical errors do constitute a norm, of course; in such settings, correctly spoken English would sound curiously stiff. But in an environment where grammatical correctness is valued, an ungrammatical speaker sounds either boorish or ill-educated. Whether the simple mistakes in this example—mistakes of diction (*irregardless*) and of grammar (*what he done*)—derive from lack of education or from regional or cultural norms of usage would be hard to tell were it not for the presence of the more elaborate mistake (*between him and I*). The overcorrection here—which erases *me* even when syntax demands it—suggests some acquaintance with grammar and a conscious desire to appear "proper." But the ultimate effect is the same as that of tawdry paintings: of elegance wanted, and elegance still wanting.

6. The final example shows what happens when inflated notions of elegance and preciseness take over. The result is inelegance and impreciseness. Long words do not intrinsically sound better than short ones, nor do they somehow mean better. Yet these assumptions seem to lie behind every outburst of such bafflegab. Relying on the passive voice allows the speaker to evade responsibility for everything he says; relying on clichéd stock phrases (*game plan*), vague reference (*this*), noun clusters (*composition situation*), long words and invented words (*multivalent, metatalk*) allows him to create the illusion of complexity and great intelligence even when both are lacking. Listeners cannot just absorb a communication like this one; they have to decode it. And the message they decode is often crashingly pedestrian.

These examples draw attention to many of the points of connection between speakers and their audiences. Age, education, occupation, social standing, nationality, region, time, and taste can all bring speaker and listener together or irrevocably separate them. Speakers who condescend, either through the tone they adopt or by oversimplifying their subject, cause listeners to respond, at the very least, unsympathetically. Similarly, overestimating an audience's ability to handle the complexity of a subject or a certain level of vocabulary will estrange speakers from the people they are trying to reach. Waffling, evading the responsibility for thought, speaking too quickly, and speaking too slowly or quietly all interfere with the act of communicating. An audience distracted by a speaker's dress or gestures, by a strange or strained pitch of voice, by a failure to look at them (or at the television camera), or by a series of verbal tics (*er, um, y'know, like*) is not listening to the words. It is more likely counting the *ums*. Such speakers parody themselves, but may never realize it, nor recognize how much they are dissolving before their audience's eyes.

Other speakers, knowledgeable about body language, can cleverly manipulate their audience through their gestures rather than through their actual words. The earnest crease in the forehead, the expansively open gesture of the arms, the honest raising of the eyebrows or widening of the eyes: speakers can falsify their emotions as easily as they can leave them on display. The informed audience learns how to distinguish between the trustworthy and the deceptive, between the actual and the acted, between the event and the advertisement for the event. The social psychology of the relation between speaker and listener is far more complex than this simple declaration suggests, but the ability to recognize some of the links between them is increasingly necessary as North American culture comes to rely more and more on pictorial and oral communication.

The relation between writer and reader is not the same as that between speaker and listener. It is similar, but the act of writing things down has the effect of limiting an audience in further ways. Education, whether formal or informal, remains an issue, for writers almost always write to an audience that values the act of reading. Writing for a person who can't read is self-contradictory; writing for a person who won't read is probably futile. One might argue, therefore, that writing is essentially a middle-class act, and that the spoken rhetoric of the street, the wharf, the hustings, and the television set can reach a greater range of people than books, and reach them more directly. That may or may not be so; but what is undeniable is that writers, like speakers, face problems of reaching and holding their chosen audiences. And they are subject to many of the same variables of style. Tone, directness, accuracy, level, and movement all matter acutely if a writer intends to win a receptive audience. Merely writing things down, in the first words that come to mind and in whatever order they occur, will not suffice. An economics argument in current slang would not convince the people attending a businessmen's luncheon; producing a simile like "as barren as a plant sale reduced to its lowest common cactus" is not likely to amuse gardeners, especially cactus fanciers.

Writers write; but they write with both a purpose and a reader in mind. Knowing *why* they want to write and *what* they want to say, they make a series of decisions: to write a letter or an essay or a book, for children or adults, for a specialized group or the general public. Then, as they plan and write and revise, the fine rhetorical choices follow, and in making them, writers shape what they say until they are as sure as they can be that they have matched their intention with their audience. They have to consider the age, education, biases, ability, and expectations of their readers. They have to decide if they want to be funny or serious or neutral or sad. They have to decide whether they want to entertain or instruct or argue or describe or reveal. They have to decide if they want to announce their subject directly or to draw their readers into deducing conclusions. They have to know their subject and their grammar well enough to be accurate and clear. They have to decide whether to be personal, informal, and conversational, or distant and formal and objective. And they have to decide how to shape their rhetoric: whether to make it flow grandly or step in staccato phrases, to ring eloquently or murmur laconically, to dazzle with metaphor or convince by plain speaking. Only when they have made these decisions are they close to a strategy for writing effectively on a given occasion.

Whether consciously or unconsciously, writers question their choice of words (are they monosyllabic or polysyllabic? abstract or concrete? easy or difficult? objective or slanted? formal or informal? general or precise?), syntax and structure (are the sentences short or long? simple or complex? varied or unvaried? fragmentary or whole?), and the organization of their whole work (is it coherent? unified? clear? is the emphasis appropriate? do the paragraphs flow?). If they are true stylists they worry also about the sound and the cadence and the freshness of the arrangements they have devised. In short, they address themselves actively to their audience in their own voice and in a form they choose. The choices they make do not derive from some secret set of absolutes. There is no hidden writer's chart somewhere that reveals to a chosen few that polysyllables are "good" and informality "bad".

Nor do writers usually set out, as textbooks often imply, to tackle as vague a project as a "comparison-and-contrast essay." They do not begin with a structural device; rather they have subjects to explore, and they know that substance and style are intrinsically related. They have audiences to satisfy, and they have particular tasks to do—letters to write, explanations to provide, stories to tell, arguments to deliver. In carrying out these tasks as articulately as possible, skilled writers can use an extraordinary variety of verbal techniques, even to the point of making deliberate errors to achieve particular effects. In the process they will demonstrate not only some of the many creative ways in which words work, but also the individuality that can invigorate all prose forms. Their work reveals the force of writing both for an audience and with a purpose in mind.

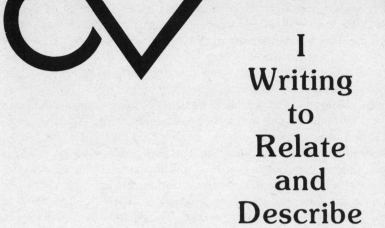

# I
# Writing
# to
# Relate
# and
# Describe

"Once upon a time…" and "Have you heard the one about…" are two of the most familiar ways in the language to begin a story. And they invite particular responses. The first, either part of a child's tale or else adopting the form of one, asks readers to suspend empirical judgments for the moment and to accept the possibilities of fantasy. The other nudges clearly toward the salacious bar-room jest or the simple corny joke. Like other preludes, they seize and settle the people in the tale-teller's audience and establish the likely mood of the story to follow. These particular preludes, moreover, invite audiences to expect an ensuing narrative rather than an explanation or an argument. Only highly sophisticated writers manage to use such an opening for a different end.

Story, or narrative, rarely appears in as undiluted a form as it does in joking anecdotes. Even when constructed with a careful plot, as in novels and short stories, narratives contain more than the basic narrative elements of event, time, and sequence. Stories can, however, also appear in contexts other than purely narrative ones. The personal narrative, for example, contains a story, or stories, and conveys an individual personality. But it is not plotted. White, Thomas, Fisher, Haig-Brown, and Mukherjee, writing narrative memoirs and relating a variety of internal anecdotes, use an identifiable chronology and create individual characters. Plot, however, relies on causal relationships among episodes. One event makes another one happen, and part of the reader's task with a plotted narrative is to unravel how and why. In these essays, the writers focus primarily on something other than cause and effect. The events they write about may join to achieve a consistent single effect, therefore, but they do not connect into a plot. Fisher writes about food and family, Haig-Brown about the art of fishing and the temptations of pride, Mukherjee about familiarity, place, and the politics of privilege and custom. Characteristically, moreover, the narrative essayist employs descriptive as well as narrative techniques, and it is sometimes a moot print whether the essay that results should properly be called narrative or descriptive. In the long run, naming a proper category matters less than appreciating the essay itself, with its blend of techniques and the skilful balance which each author individually contrives.

Description begins in concrete observations; it delights in adjective and verb, and depends upon exact detail: smooth and elongated pebbles, squawking chimpanzees, lurching home late, the flash of jade-green thumb-nails, the muted thunder of my uncle's breathing. John Updike's verbal snapshot of Central Park is really an orchestration of just such details as these, cumulatively arranging an effect. And George Johnston's journal of a trip to the Faroe Islands builds observed detail into a brief but graphic account of the spirit of a place and a people. But description, like narration, usually appears as an "impure" form. Narrative emphasizes temporal sequence but incidentally observes settings and records dra-

matic conversational exchanges; description emphasizes visual placement—direction, size, texture, and general appearance—but often for other
than simply pictorial purposes. Hence in personal memoirs—and even in
much fiction—descriptive passages frequently occur. They can heighten a
reader's sense of both the place and the event a writer is recreating, intensify the mood that the writer is striving to convey, and often illustrate
or epitomize, concretely and clearly, the writer's ideas. This excerpt from
an 1883 feminist novel, Olive Schreiner's *The Story of an African Farm*,
employs descriptive details for just such purposes:

> It was eight o'clock when they neared the farm-house: a
> red-brick building, with kraals to the right and a small or-
> chard to the left. Already there were signs of unusual life
> and bustle: one cart, a waggon, and a couple of saddles
> against the wall betokened the arrival of a few early guests,
> whose numbers would soon be largely increased. To a Dutch
> country wedding guests start up in numbers astonishing to
> one who has merely ridden through the plains of sparsely-
> inhabited karroo.
>
> As the morning advances, riders on many shades of
> steeds appear from all directions, and add their saddles to
> the long rows against the walls, shake hands, drink coffee,
> and stand about outside in groups to watch the arriving carts
> and ox-waggons, as they are unburdened of their heavy
> freight of massive Tantes and comely daughters, followed by
> swarms of children of all sizes, dressed in all manner of print
> and moleskin, who are taken care of by Hottentot, Kaffir,
> and half-caste nurses, whose many-shaded complexions,
> ranging from light yellow up to ebony black, add variety to
> the animated scene. Everywhere is excitement and bustle,
> which gradually increases as the time for the return of the
> wedding party approaches. Preparations for the feast are
> actively advancing in the kitchen; coffee is liberally handed
> round, and amid a profound sensation, and the firing of
> guns, the horse-waggon draws up, and the wedding party
> alight. Bride and bridegroom, with their attendants, march
> solemnly to the marriage chamber, where bed and box are
> decked out in white, with ends of ribbon and artificial flow-
> ers, and where on a row of chairs the party solemnly seat
> themselves. After a time bridesmaid and best man rise, and
> conduct in with ceremony each individual guest, to wish suc-
> cess and to kiss bride and bridegroom. Then the feast is set
> on the table, and it is almost sunset before the dishes are
> cleared away, and the pleasure of the day begins. Every-
> thing is removed from the great front room, and the mud
> floor, well rubbed with bullock's blood, glistens like polished
> mahogany. The female portion of the assembly flock into

the side-rooms to attire themselves for the evening; and re-issue clad in white muslin, and gay with bright ribbons and brass jewellery. The dancing begins as the tallow candles are stuck up about the walls, the music coming from a couple of fiddlers in a corner of the room. Bride and bridegroom open the ball, and the floor is soon covered with whirling couples, and everyone's spirits rise. The bridal pair mingle freely in the throng, and here and there a musical man sings vigorously as be drags his partner through the Blue Water or John Speriwig; boys shout and applaud, and the enjoyment and confusion are intense, till eleven o'clock comes. By this time the children who swarm in the side-rooms are not to be kept quiet longer, even by hunches of bread and cake; there is a general howl and wail, that rises yet higher than the scraping of fiddles, and mothers rush from their partners to knock small heads together, and cuff little nursemaids, and force the wailers down into unoccupied corners of beds, under tables, and behind boxes. In half an hour every variety of childish snore is heard on all sides, and it has become perilous to raise or set down a foot in any of the side-rooms lest a small head or hand should be crushed. Now, too, the busy feet have broken the solid coating of the floor, and a cloud of fine dust rises, that makes a yellow halo round the candles, and sets asthmatic people coughing, and grows denser, till to recognize any one on the opposite side of the room becomes impossible, and a partner's face is seen through a yellow mist.

To create the effect she wants, Schreiner chooses precise terms, often in Afrikaans (*kraal, karroo, Tantes*), specific numbers and colours (*one* cart, *brass* jewellery), exact and evocative details (*half-caste* nurses, *artificial* flowers, *bullock's blood*, and *John Speriwig*), and a whole array of verbs, both active and passive. The variety of adjectives lends colour and texture to the scene, but it is the verbs that give the passage its life. Schreiner marshalls the active verbs to contrive an illusion of speed and commotion: riders *appear, add, shake*, and *drink*, the wedding company *flock, reissue, mingle, sing, drag, shout*, and *applaud*; mothers *rush, knock, cuff*, and *force*. Such verbs help her to perceive and define movement exactly and therefore to describe scenes effectively. She uses static verbs (*is, seem, appear*) sparingly. But somewhat surprisingly, she does use a number of verbs in the passive voice (coffee *is handed round*, the dishes *are cleared away*, everything *is removed* from the table), which ordinarily would have a dampening effect on the action; here, under creative control, they manage to generalize from the specific event, to imply that the events and relationships described never change in this society: the women, who are doing the work, disappear into the passive structures. It is not difficult, then, to see the relation between form and meaning, to see how the author makes the activity itself inherently misleading, and how she makes the paragraphs form part of her novel's general attack upon the static roles and relationships which society opens to women.

Essayists, like novelists, can use prose rhythm and precise detail evocatively. Thomas's attempt to capture the Welsh vernacular, Mukherjee's anecdotal representations of Indian speech, and MacLennan's choral invocation of the Québécois *ouais* all illustrate the effectiveness of rhythmic control. Forster's, White's, Eiseley's, and Dillard's mastery of simple verbs, their talent for metaphor, and their eye for significant detail all contribute to their transformations of experience into art. Good writers know, of course, that not all metaphors are valid. Many are inappropriate, clichéd, irrelevant, and unnecessary; and no good writer would be drawn into writing a mixed metaphor—as in the sentence "He's buttered his bread, and now he must lie in it"—without being aware of the ludicrous image it is likely to create. If the writer's intention is to amuse, or if the established situation is a little bizarre, the mixed metaphor's incongruity might reinforce the effect; but otherwise it will jolt a reader abruptly out of an essay. Good writers know, too, that not all details are significant. Much of the art of good writing is knowing when to leave things out. The wrong details, or too many or too few, will cause the reader to respond unfavourably or not at all. But leaving out the right things at the right time—as Eiseley does in his rhythmic account of the way the mind remembers and discovers—can at once intensify the effect of the remaining details and add to the suspense of the narrative memoir and the surprise of its conclusion.

Perhaps most important, because narrative tries above all else to interest and entertain, good writers know that not every personal experience intrinsically fascinates every reader; it is the *telling* of a story that is fascinating. When writers subtly transform experience, the process may appear effortless, but the transformations only appear subtle and easy because the writers have been so skillful at selecting and arranging details that the reader is willing to watch along with them, the listener willing to hear.

# Central Park

## John Updike

(March 1956)

On the afternoon of the first day of spring, when the gutters were still heaped high with Monday's snow but the sky itself was swept clean, we put on our galoshes and walked up the sunny side of Fifth Avenue to Central Park. There we saw:

Great black rocks emerging from the melting drifts, their craggy skins glistening like the backs of resurrected brontosaurs.

A pigeon on the half-frozen pond strutting to the edge of the ice and looking a duck in the face.

A policeman getting his shoe wet testing the ice.

Three elderly relatives trying to coax a little boy to accompany his father on a sled ride down a short but steep slope. After much balking, the boy did, and, sure enough, the sled tipped over and the father got his collar full of snow. Everybody laughed except the boy, who sniffled.

Four boys in black leather jackets throwing snowballs at each other. (The snow was ideally soggy, and packed hard with one squeeze.)

Seven men without hats.

Twelve snowmen, none of them intact.

Two men listening to the radio in a car parked outside the Zoo; Mel Allen was broadcasting the Yanks–Cardinals game from St. Petersburg.

A tahr (*Hemitragus jemlaicus*) pleasantly squinting in the sunlight.

An aoudad absently pawing the mud and chewing.

A yak with its back turned.

Empty cages labelled "Coati," "Orang-outang," "Ocelot."

A father saying to his little boy, who was annoyed almost to tears by

Copyright ©1956 by John Updike. Reprinted from *Assorted Prose*, by John Updike, by permission of Alfred A. Knopf, Inc. Originally appeared in *The New Yorker*.

the inactivity of the seals, "Father [Father Seal, we assumed] is very tired; he worked hard all day."

Most of the cafeteria's out-of-doors tables occupied.

A pretty girl in black pants falling on them at the Wollman Memorial Rink.

"BILL & DORIS" carved on a tree. "REX & RITA" written in the snow.

Two old men playing, and six supervising, a checkers game.

The Michael Friedsam Foundation Merry-Go-Round, nearly empty of children but overflowing with calliope music.

A man on a bench near the carrousel reading, through sunglasses, a book on economics.

Crews of shinglers repairing the roof of the Tavern-on-the-Green.

A woman dropping a camera she was trying to load, the film unrolling in the slush and exposing itself.

A little colored boy in aviator goggles rubbing his ears and saying, "He really hurt me." "No, he didn't," his nursemaid told him.

The green head of Giuseppe Mazzini staring across the white softball field, unblinking, though the sun was in its eyes.

Water murmuring down walks and rocks and steps. A grown man trying to block one rivulet with snow.

Things like brown sticks nosing through a plot of cleared soil.

A tire track in a piece of mud far removed from where any automobiles could be.

Footprints around a KEEP OFF sign.

Two pigeons feeding each other.

Two showgirls, whose faces had not yet thawed the frost of their make-up, treading indignantly through the slush.

A plump old man saying "Chick, chick" and feeding peanuts to squirrels.

Many solitary men throwing snowballs at tree trunks.

Many birds calling to each other about how little the Ramble has changed.

One red mitten lying lost under a poplar tree.

An airplane, very bright and distant, slowly moving through the branches of a sycamore.

# The Site at Kvivik

**Pages From a Journal:
Torshavn, Stremoy,
Faroe Islands 1967**

## George Johnston

At about half-past two Bjarni was coming up the driveway to the house. We were expecting Hanus to take me to the north end of this island, Stremoy, on his way to fetch Sverri from a site up there; I was sleepy and had gone off into a snooze when they said Here comes Bjarni. I looked out the window. In his Faroese cap. Then voices at the end of the house: Sverri and Hanus. So we meet Sverri. There is a plan: we are to drive in Hanus's car to Kvivik, roughly forty-five kilometres across the island, to see an old Viking and a site there. Into the house for a quick *snaps*. The men would not sit down, and soon we were off. The weather had been clear until noon, then snow flurries. We followed a road that climbed behind the town and gave us a changing view as though from an ascending aircraft, then across into the fells.

There were driving snow flurries, and the high places were white. On top of the highest fell were domes of a NATO early-warning base. The slope was full of tunnels and rooms, they said. Beside the road was a handsome long low building, living quarters for the base, with an outlook down Kaldbaks Fjord. Three or four buildings at the inner end of the fjord, green fields and a creek with straight stretches and acute angles. The fjord was deep and had deep, rounded sides. We cross a barren stretch heavy with snow, drop to sea level again, then drive alongside Kolla Fjord till we cross a stone bridge into a brightly painted village, Hamar. Eastward the slopes were not so steep; we could see Eysturoy and beyond that the white peaks of Bordoy, both smaller islands, under clouds and patches of falling snow. Inland the slopes were steep and high

From *Views from the North*, ed. Karen Mulhallen (Erin, Ont.: Porcupine's Quill, Inc., 1984).

and green, ridged by sheep walks and bulging with thick strata of dark grey basalt. Along the top, snow. Black, grey and brown sheep everywhere, singly or in groups of two or three, trotting along with their lambs.

Sverri wants us to see the church. He is the senior of two archaeologists in the islands, a stubby man with a thick face and short legs, thick, soft, curly hair, built like Bjarni, another typical Faroe man. Both gentle, rather erratic and good-natured. Hanus is gentle too, and good-natured, patient, lean rather than stubby, and handsome. Sverri is wearing a grey-green parka, and as he goes up the road to find the house that has the key to the church, he looks like a piece of the countryside. The wind blows his coat but hardly moves him. The church is a plain wooden building tarred outside. A green-capped, stubby belfry rises diagonally out of it. The inside is all a bright natural wood; Sverri says it has been scrubbed with sand and soap and left so, unfinished. There is a choir screen, but the space it encloses is too small to be meaningful except as decoration; it is of thin wood with simple floral and cruciform patterns cut out of it, the inner edges of the cut-outs painted a pale blue. Pale blue is the only colour painted in the church, and it has been used sparingly, in thin bands, to outline the wood panelling. The pulpit rail is covered in royal-purple velvet. Sverri disapproves of the electric fixtures along the walls, imitation candle-holders, and he especially dislikes the fuse box behind the screen. The priest's robing room is tiny but it has to hold the vacuum cleaner. The altar decoration is a plain painting of a country lass holding a baby at arm's length above a manger, a realistic painting, without aureoles or external marks of religiousness. A black model Faroe boat with oars and sail hangs above the aisle, just outside the choir screen, and high above the other end of the aisle, before a small gallery, hangs an elaborate candelabrum, four gilt hoops in an open sphere, with candles around the equator on lazy-tong brackets. It had been made by a parishioner about a hundred years ago.

Up into the fells again, and across the island to Kvivik. This village is not in a fjord but looks straight out on the open sound between Vagar and Stremoy towards the steep islands of Koltur, Hestur and Sandoy. No harbour, only a stone jetty, which would be good for small boats. Several streets, all climbing and twisting; almost no level ground, houses at every height. Two rivers run through the village, one through the centre under a wooden bridge and a basalt bridge. The houses, as in Torshavn and Hamar, are partly or entirely poured concrete, painted in bright colours. In some the lower half has been left unpainted; in others, the lower half is unpainted concrete and the upper half wood, usually dark, with vertical battens. Older houses are of wood, painted bright colours or else tarred and trimmed with bright colours. Many roofs are of sod. One or two older buildings are of basalt, a dark-grey stone with iron and copper tints in which the mortar pointing shows up clearly. Looking at a village from any angle one gets an impression of triangles and rectangles, bright paint, turf, stone, and the steepness of the green slopes rising on all sides.

We stop on a grade beside a stone wall, and opposite us, so close that a truck would have to pass carefully between, is a small red wooden house, the old Viking's house. He is not in it, so off go Sverri and Bjarni in search, and when they come back we get out on the road and are introduced. Warm sunshine for a moment. The old man's best room feels warm for a while too, from the warmth of everyone's mood. Bjarni has brought him a bottle of Norwegian *snaps*, a treasure in the islands, and his speech of acceptance is translated for us. He says that the Vikings would drink their drinks straight down, and everyone from the same cup. We agree that this is proper. The host drinks first, to show that there is no poison. Agreed. Very good. He does not quite drain his first glass and turns it upside-down on some sort of printed paper on his table. He is very old. Nobody knows exactly what his age is but it is perhaps ninety, perhaps eighty-six; Sverri has it written down somewhere, he thinks it must be at least eighty-five, very old, *gamli mann*. He is brought into the discussion, and although no figure is established he agrees that he is old, too old, not much good any more. Hard to say how Jeanne and I understand, but we do somehow, there is enough Danish in it. No complaint in his tone, and his manner is proud and friendly, but one can feel the sadness of old age as well as his warmth and the brightness of his eye. Bjarni thinks he may be persuaded to sing us a song, or part of one.

His best room is small, he and the five of us fill it. It is a cube with an alcove. Upholstered furniture, large round table, crocheted table-cloth and a vase with yellow paper roses in the middle. Many pictures on the walls, mostly photographs of poets and important people, and family photographs. The largest picture was not a photograph but a silk-screen portrait in four shades of brown of a poet of Kvivik who had died young and not long ago. There was a large photograph of a twelve-year-old girl with a big, old-fashioned hair ribbon. She was a favourite daughter who had died soon after the photograph was taken. Over the door hung a text in bright-blue Gothic letters, *Harrin Signi Heimid* ('God Bless Our Home').

The *snaps* glass had been around three times and the *gamli mann* had fetched us family photographs to look at and now he brought his guest book to be signed. It was a birthday book, printed in Torshavn, and it gave a stanza from a Faroese poem or hymn for each day. Many birthdays were recorded in it, from Scandinavia mostly, but also from other parts of the world. While we were writing our names in his book, Gragas was persuaded to sing and he agreed to two verses and we were to dance with him. So we joined hands around the table. His face expressed great pleasure. It was a solid block of a face, well-shaped but hardly protruding nose, Hapsburg lower lip and a bristly, drooping moustache. His hair was grey, still thick, cut short and combed down over his forehead. He was dressed in the national dark knee breeches and dark socks, a dark-brown knitted pull-over that came up to his neck and the Faroese dark-brown woven jacket over this, a longish jacket, without lapels, held together just under the throat by a short chain with small pewter buttons at each end. He has been a famous singer, and his voice is still strong and sweet, he sings three verses and Bjarni and Sverri and Hanus sing the choruses; we dance the stately ancient dance, three steps forward, two steps back, around the table; then after three verses it is over, Gragas looks breathless and there is more talk of his age. We put our coats and hats on and go out.

The weather had become miserable, cold wind and sleet. We went down the hill to a site on a bit of level ground at the mouth of one of the rivers. Sverri had worked it and uncovered the stone foundations of a house and byre from the Viking Age. The walls were only about two feet high, at least a foot lower than they had been built, Sverri said, and the seaward ends had been eroded by the, couldn't think of the English, *brim*, what's that? Surf. That's right, surf. I remember from *The Faroe Islanders' Saga* that there had been *brim* at the island when Sigmund Brestisson reached it after his heroic swim. The site was untidy, bits of scrap paper and two heaps of swept-up dirt down by the seaward end of the byre. It was not like this when Gragas was in charge, Gragas had been to the site every day, but he is too old now. One would have liked to know how the house had aged before it was abandoned at last. Had it been derelict for a while, with a few pieces of derelict furniture, perhaps a derelict human being? That was hundreds of generations of buried memories ago. When did these walls finally disappear under the ground? Sverri is convinced that there is another house beneath a level cobbled piece right next door, if he could only get at it. Everyone is cold and wet. We move off with Bjarni and Gragas, and before long there is another *snaps*, but we do not take our coats off because we are going up the road in a moment to a son's place. Sverri is till attending to something at the site.

The son's house is warm. A bright room with garish wall-paper and much furniture. A beautiful fair-haired young woman with a sweet patient manner and not much to say waits on us. She had laid out many different kinds of bought cakes and cookies; we sit down to them, Gragas at the end of the table, and she brings us coffee as we want it, but does not sit down herself. Occasionally I realize that the conversation has been mostly in Faroese; much of it seems to be good-natured, vigorous argument. I have learned to distinguish a few expressions. A good one is *hald kaft*, pronounced chafft; literally translated, it means something like hold your jaw or shut up, but in practice it mostly means just go on or you don't say. It has been as frequent as argument in this afternoon's talk. But we are not trying to make anything of the conversation now, and I am eating as many of the cakes and cookies as I think will not seem greedy, quite a few.

The sky breaks and white sunlight falls into the room. It is time to go, we shake hands with the young woman and with another young man who has come in, perhaps her husband. The sun is patchy on the fells and islands, and it shines full down on us as we stand in the walk with the old man. I have discovered that his name is Gregorius. I find myself in his best room again with Bjarni and we are having a *gonga snaps*, one for the road. I regret the damage we have done to his precious bottle but I am told that drinking is to be done with friends and when the occasion offers, especially if you are an old man.

To whom one must say goodbye. Gragas is dignified and serious, every move he makes is both ceremonious and friendly. We shake hands and talk rather a lot, except for Hanus, and Gragas seems to enjoy the talk and accepts the flattering things that are said about him as friendly gifts; too much, but friendly given and therefore friendly received. Sverri hugs the old man. Then we drive back up into the fells and our last view of the village is cut off by a snow flurry.

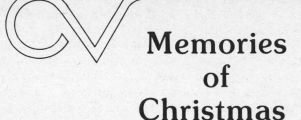

# Memories of Christmas

## Dylan Thomas

One Christmas was so much like another, in those years, around the sea-town corner now, and out of all sound except the distant speaking of the voices I sometimes hear a moment before sleep, that I can never remember whether it snowed for six days and six nights when I was twelve or whether it snowed for twelve days and twelve nights when I was six; or whether the ice broke and the skating grocer vanished like a snowman through a white trap-door on that same Christmas Day that the mince-pies finished Uncle Arnold and we tobogganed down the seaward hill, all the afternoon, on the best tea-tray, and Mrs. Griffiths complained, and we threw a snowball at her niece, and my hands burned so, with the heat and the cold, when I held them in front of the fire, that I cried for twenty minutes and then had some jelly.

All the Christmases roll down the hill towards the Welsh-speaking sea, like a snowball growing whiter and bigger and rounder, like a cold and headlong moon bundling down the sky that was our street; and they stop at the rim of the ice-edged, fish-freezing waves, and I plunge my hands in the snow and bring out whatever I can find; holly or robins or pudding, squabbles and carols and oranges and tin whistles, and the fire in the front room, and bang go the crackers, and holy, holy, holy, ring the bells, and the glass bells shaking on the tree, and Mother Goose, and Struwelpeter—oh! the baby-burning flames and the clacking scissor-man!—Billy Bunter and Black Beauty, Little Women and boys who have

Dylan Thomas, *Quite Early One Morning* (J.M. Dent, London edition). All rights reserved. Reprinted by permission of J.M. Dent & Sons Ltd., and the Trustees for the Copyrights of the late Dylan Thomas.

three helpings, Alice and Mrs Potter's badgers, penknives, teddy-bears—named after a Mr Theodore Bear, their inventor, or father, who died recently in the United States—mouth-organs, tin-soldiers, and blanc-mange, and Auntie Bessie playing 'Pop Goes the Weasel' and 'Nuts in May' and 'Oranges and Lemons' on the untuned piano in the parlour all through the thimble-hiding musical-chairing blind-man's-buffing party at the end of the never-to-be-forgotten day at the end of the unremembered year.

In goes my hand into that wool-white bell-tongued ball of holidays resting at the margin of the carol-singing sea, and out come Mrs Prothero and the firemen.

It was on the afternoon of the day of Christmas Eve, and I was in Mrs Prothero's garden, waiting for cats, with her son Jim. It was snowing. It was always snowing at Christmas; December, in my memory, is white as Lapland, though there were no reindeers. But there were cats. Patient, cold, and callous, our hands wrapped in socks, we waited to snowball the cats. Sleek and long as jaguars and terrible-whiskered, spitting and snarling they would slink and sidle over the white back-garden walls, and the lynx-eyed hunters, Jim and I, fur-capped and moccasined trappers from Hudson's Bay off Eversley Road, would hurl our deadly snowballs at the green of their eyes. The wise cats never appeared. We were so still, Eskimo-footed arctic marksmen in the muffling silence of the eternal snows—eternal, ever since Wednesday—that we never heard Mrs Prothero's first cry from her igloo at the bottom of the garden. Or, if we heard it at all, it was, to us, like the far-off challenge of our enemy and prey, the neighbour's Polar Cat. But soon the voice grew louder. 'Fire!' cried Mrs Prothero, and she beat the dinner-gong. And we ran down the garden, with the snowballs in our arms, towards the house, and smoke, indeed, was pouring out of the dining-room, and the gong was bombilating, and Mrs Prothero was announcing ruin like a town-crier in Pompeii. This was better than all the cats in Wales standing on the wall in a row. We bounded into the house, laden with snowballs, and stopped at the open door of the smoke-filled room. Something was burning all right; perhaps it was Mr Prothero, who always slept there after midday dinner with a newspaper over his face; but he was standing in the middle of the room, saying 'A fine Christmas!' and smacking at the smoke with a slipper.

'Call the fire-brigade,' cried Mrs Prothero as she beat the gong.

'They won't be there,' said Mr Prothero, 'it's Christmas.'

There was no fire to be seen, only clouds of smoke and Mr Prothero standing in the middle of them, waving his slipper as though he were conducting.

'Do something,' he said.

And we threw all our snowballs into the smoke—I think we missed Mr

Prothero—and ran out of the house to the telephone-box.

'Let's call the police as well,' Jim said.

'And the ambulance.'

'And Ernie Jenkins, he likes fires.'

But we only called the fire-brigade, and soon the fire-engine came and three tall men in helmets brought a hose into the ,iouse and Mr Prothero got out just in time before they turned it on. Nobody could have had a noisier Christmas Eve. And when the firemen turned off the hose and were standing in the wet and smoky room, Jim's aunt, Miss Prothero, came downstairs and peered in at them. Jim and I waited, very quietly, to hear what she would say to them. She said the right thing, always. She looked at the three tall firemen in their shining helmets, standing among the smoke and cinders and dissolving snowballs, and she said: 'Would you like something to read?'

Now out of that bright white snowball of Christmas gone comes the stocking, the stocking of stockings, that hung at the foot of the bed with the arm of a golliwog dangling over the top and small bells ringing in the toes. There was a company, gallant and scarlet but never nice to taste though I always tried when very young, of belted and busbied and musketed lead soldiers so soon to lose their heads and legs in the wars on the kitchen table after the tea-things, the mince-pies, and the cakes that I helped to make by stoning the raisins and eating them, had been cleared away; and a bag of moist and many-coloured jelly-babies and a folded flag and a false nose and a tram-conductor's cap and a machine that punched tickets and rang a bell; never a catapult; once, by a mistake that no one could explain, a little hatchet; and a rubber buffalo, or it may have been a horse, with a yellow head and haphazard legs; and a celluloid duck that made, when you pressed it, a most unducklike noise, a mewing moo that an ambitious cat might make who wishes to be a cow; and a painting-book in which I could make the grass, the trees, the sea, and the animals any colour I pleased; and still the dazzling sky-blue sheep are grazing in the red field under a flight of rainbow-beaked and pea-green birds.

Christmas morning was always over before you could say Jack Frost. And look! suddenly the pudding was burning! Bang the gong and call the fire-brigade and the book-loving firemen! Someone found the silver three-penny-bit with a currant on it; and the someone was always Uncle Arnold. The motto in my cracker read:

> Let's all have fun this Christmas Day,
> Let's play and sing and shout hooray!

and the grown-ups turned their eyes towards the ceiling, and Auntie Bessie, who had already been frightened, twice, by a clockwork mouse, whimpered at the sideboard and had some elderberry wine. And someone put a glass bowl full of nuts on the littered table, and my uncle said, as he said once every year: 'I've got a shoe-nut here. Fetch me a shoe-horn to open it, boy.'

And dinner was ended.

And I remember that on the afternoon of Christmas Day, when the others sat around the fire and told each other that this was nothing, no, nothing, to the great snowbound and turkey-proud yule-log-crackling holly-berry-bedizined and kissing-under-the-mistletoe Christmas when *they* were children, I would go out, school-capped and gloved and muf-flered, with my bright new boots squeaking, into the white world on to the seaward hill, to call on Jim and Dan and Jack and to walk with them through the silent snowscape of our town.

We went padding through the streets, leaving huge deep footprints in the snow, on the hidden pavements.

'I bet people'll think there's been hippoes.'

'What would you do if you saw a hippo coming down Terrace Road?'

'I'd go like this, bang! I'd throw him over the railings and roll him down the hill and then I'd tickle him under the ear and he'd wag his tail. . .'

'What would you do if you saw *two* hippoes. . .?'

Iron-flanked and bellowing he-hippoes clanked and blundered and bat-tered through the scudding snow towards us as we passed by Mr Daniel's house.

'Let's post Mr Daniel a snowball through his letterbox.'

'Let's write things in the snow.'

'Let's write "Mr Daniel looks like a spaniel" all over his lawn.'

'Look,' Jack said, 'I'm eating snow-pie.'

'What's it taste like?'

'Like snow-pie,' Jack said.

Or we walked on the white shore.

'Can the fishes see it's snowing?'

'They think it's the sky falling down.'

The silent one-clouded heavens drifted on to the sea.

'All the old dogs have gone.'

Dogs of a hundred mingled makes yapped in the summer at the sea-rim and yelped at the trespassing mountains of the waves.

'I bet St Bernards would like it now.'

And we were snowblind travellers lost on the north hills, and the great dewlapped dogs, with brandy-flasks round their necks, ambled and shambled up to us, baying 'Excelsior.'

We returned home through the desolate poor sea-facing streets where only a few children fumbled with bare red fingers in the thick wheel-rutted snow and cat-called after us, their voices fading away, as we trudged uphill, into the cries of the dock-birds and the hooters of ships out in the white and whirling bay.

Bring out the tall tales now that we told by the fire as we roasted chestnuts and the gaslight bubbled low. Ghosts with their heads under their arms trailed their chains and said 'whooo' like owls in the long nights when I dared not look over my shoulder; wild beasts lurked in the cubby-hole under the stairs where the gas-meter ticked. 'Once upon a time,' Jim said, 'there were three boys, just like us, who got lost in the dark in the snow, near Bethesda Chapel, and this is what happened to them. . . .' It was the most dreadful happening I had ever heard.

And I remember that we went singing carols once, a night or two before Christmas Eve, when there wasn't the shaving of a moon to light the secret, white-flying streets. At the end of a long road was a drive that led to a large house, and we stumbled up the darkness of the drive that night, each one of us afraid, each one holding a stone in his hand in case, and all of us too brave to say a word. The wind made through the drive trees noises as of old and unpleasant and maybe web-footed men wheezing in caves. We reached the black bulk of the house.

'What shall we give them?' Dan whispered.

'"Hark the Herald"? "Christmas comes but Once a Year"?'

'No,' Jack said: 'We'll sing "Good King Wenceslas." I'll count three.'

One, two, three, and we began to sing, our voices high and seemingly distant in the snow-felted darkness round the house that was occupied by nobody we knew. We stood close together, near the dark door.

> Good King Wenceslas looked out
> On the Feast of Stephen.

And then a small, dry voice, like the voice of someone who has not spoken for a long time, suddenly joined our singing: a small, dry voice from the other side of the door: a small, dry voice through the keyhole. And when we stopped running we were outside *our* house; the front room was lovely and bright; the gramophone was playing; we saw the red and white balloons hanging from the gas-bracket; uncles and aunts sat by the fire; I thought I smelt our supper being fried in the kitchen. Everything was good again, and Christmas shone through all the familiar town.

'Perhaps it was a ghost,' Jim said.

'Perhaps it was trolls,' Dan said, who was always reading.

'Let's go in and see if there's any jelly left,' Jack said. And we did that.

# A Thing Shared

## M.F.K. Fisher

(1918)

Now you can drive from Los Angeles to my Great-Aunt Maggie's ranch on the other side of the mountains in a couple of hours or so, but the first time I went there it took most of a day.

Now the roads are worthy of even the All-Year-Round Club's boasts, but twenty-five years ago, in the September before people thought peace had come again, you could hardly call them roads at all. Down near the city they were oiled, all right, but as you went farther into the hills toward the wild desert around Palmdale, they turned into rough dirt. Finally they were two wheel-marks skittering every which way through the Joshua trees.

It was very exciting: the first time my little round brown sister Anne and I had ever been away from home. Father drove us up from home with Mother in the Ford, so that she could help some cousins can fruit.

We carried beer for the parents (it exploded in the heat), and water for the car and Anne and me. We had four blowouts, but that was lucky, Father said as he patched the tires philosophically in the hot sun; he'd expected twice as many on such a long hard trip.

The ranch was wonderful, with wartime crews of old men and loud-voiced boys picking the peaches and early pears all day, and singing and rowing at night in the bunkhouses. We couldn't go near them or near the pen in the middle of a green alfalfa field where a new prize bull, black as thunder, pawed at the pale sand.

We spent most of our time in a stream under the cottonwoods, or with Old Mary the cook, watching her make butter in a great churn between her mountainous knees. She slapped it into pats, and put them

Reprinted with permission of Macmillan Publishing Company from *The Art of Eating* by M.F.K. Fisher. Copyright ©1943, renewed 1971, by M.F.K. Fisher.

down in the stream where it ran hurriedly through the darkness of the butter-house.

She put stone jars of cream there, too, and wire baskets of eggs and lettuces, and when she drew them up, like netted fish, she would shake the cold water onto us and laugh almost as much as we did.

Then Father had to go back to work. It was decided that Mother would stay at the ranch and help put up more fruit, and Anne and I would go home with him. That was as exciting as leaving it had been, to be alone with Father for the first time.

He says now that he was scared daft at the thought of it, even though our grandmother was at home as always to watch over us. He says he actually shook as he drove away from the ranch, with us like two sudden-ly strange small monsters on the hot seat beside him.

Probably he made small talk. I don't remember. And he didn't drink any beer, sensing that it would be improper before two unchaperoned young ladies.

We were out of the desert and into deep winding canyons before the sun went down. The road was a little smoother, following streambeds under the live-oaks that grow in all the gentle creases of the dry tawny hills of that part of California. We came to a shack where there was water for sale, and a table under the dark wide trees.

Father told me to take Anne down the dry streambed a little way. That made me feel delightfully grown-up. When we came back we held our hands under the water faucet and dried them on our panties, which Mother would never let us do.

Then we sat on a rough bench at the table, the three of us in the deep green twilight, and had one of the nicest suppers I have ever eaten.

The strange thing about it is that all three of us have told other peo-ple that same thing, without ever talking of it among ourselves until late-ly. Father says that all his nervousness went away, and he saw us for the first time as two little brown humans who were fun. Anne and I both felt a subtle excitement at being alone for the first time with the only man in the world we loved.

(We loved Mother too, completely, but we were finding out, as Father was too, that it is good for parents and for children to be alone now and then with one another...the man alone or the woman, to sound new notes in the mysterious music of parenthood and childhood.)

That night I not only saw my Father for the first time as a person. I saw the golden hills and the live-oaks as clearly as I have ever seen them since; and I saw the dimples in my little sister's fat hands in a way that still moves me because of that first time; and I saw food as something beautiful to be shared with people instead of as a thrice-daily necessity.

I forget what we ate, except for the end of the meal. It was a big round peach pie, still warm from Old Mary's oven and the ride over the desert. It was deep, with lots of juice, and bursting with ripe peaches picked that noon. Royal Albertas, Father said they were. The crust was the most perfect I have ever tasted, except perhaps once upstairs at Simpson's in London, on a hot plum tart.

And there was a quart Mason jar, the old-fashioned bluish kind like Mexican glass, full of cream. It was still cold, probably because we all knew the stream it had lain in, Old Mary's stream.

Father cut the pie in three pieces and put them on white soup plates in front of us, and then spooned out the thick cream. We ate with spoons too, blissful after the forks we were learning to use with Mother.

And we ate the whole pie, and all the cream...we can't remember if we gave any to the shadowy old man who sold water...and then drove on sleepily toward Los Angeles, and none of us said anything about it for many years, but it was one of the best meals we ever ate.

Perhaps that is because it was the first conscious one, for me at least; but the fact that we remember it with such queer clarity must mean that it had other reasons for being important. I suppose that happens at least once to every human. I hope so.

Now the hills are cut through with super-highways, and I can't say whether we sat that night in Mint Canyon or Bouquet, and the three of us are in some ways even more than twenty-five years older than we were then. And still the warm round peach pie and the cool yellow cream we ate together that August night live in our hearts' palates, succulent, secret delicious.

# Behind
# the
# Salmon

## Roderick Haig-Brown

When the salmon turn into the estuary of a small stream one has a right to expect that some big cutthroat trout will be near them. Often they are, but often, too, they can be quite hard to find. Then, particularly if it is late in the season, one is likely to get an uneasy feeling that they have all moved up into the creek and that fishing the estuary may be a waste of time.

I know much better than to go up into the lower reaches of Cedar Creek and try to fish them, even though there are several pools that hold both cutthroats and steelheads really well. These pools are long and slow, for the most part too deep to wade and with steep slippery clay banks that support tangled crab-apple thickets on one side and over-hanging alders on the other side. Any kind of a backcast is out of the question and even a roll or spey cast is grossly inhibited by the precarious stance and crowding brush; it must also find a way into the water between the overhanging limbs. Inevitably one accepts all this and makes a cast or two. Just as inevitably, all goes well at first, one falls into easy admiration of the accurate and tidy way in which the fly settles close under the hazards of the far bank, its cunning search of likely places, the precariously smooth roll that sets it out again to search again. Then, and it can happen in various ways, from a slip on the clay bottom that fills waders to a hang-up in a high branch that catches the peak of the roll, all the ease and smoothness goes out of things and one recalls the forsaken resolve to stay away from such places.

As recently as last fall I found things too slow in Cedar Creek estuary

From *Fisherman's Fall* by Roderick Haig-Brown, Wm. Collins Sons & Co. Canada Ltd. 1964.

and decided to take a quick look up the creek in the hope of finding a good fish or two to round out the day. It was well on in October and I knew that a strong run of humpback salmon had moved in, so it was reasonable to suppose the estuary cutthroats had all moved up behind them.

The head of the long pool is not too bad a place to get at. After a wild struggle with the crab apples I found myself in the water at the head of the pool, fairly securely placed and with a nice space between the alder limbs inviting my fly to a strongish run on the far side. The creek was flowing well with good fall water, dark but clear, and past experience suggested I should find the first fish twenty or thirty yards further downstream, probably near my own bank where the current spread. I had put up a Harger's Orange, one of several I had tied with claret-colored hair in the wing instead of orange a few years before and a fly I like particularly well for fall cutthroats as well as steelhead. It rolled out nicely, settled into the water and was immediately chased and taken by a fine cutthroat of about three pounds.

At this stage I wasn't really fishing—just getting my fly out. I did set the hook, but then I stood like a particularly dull-witted sheep while the fish ran off downstream. There was an impressive tangle of brush against my bank about forty yards downstream; before I came to and started to move, the line was well tangled in it and the fish was jumping below.

I had sense enough to forget him and work my way carefully downstream—after all, he could only break the leader and if he chose instead to lie quietly I might even be able to disentangle the line and tighten up on him again. The tangle was worse than I had expected, but I struggled with it in admirable calm, freed the worst of it with no more harm than my right arm wet to the armpit and saw my empty fly trailing in the current below. It was a mild disappointment, because it is always satisfying to free a mess of this sort and find that the fish has waited through one's patient efforts, but I knew very well I had earned nothing better—that recovering the fly was a good deal more than I deserved.

For a moment I considered working on down the pool from the brush pile, but that seemed wrong since I had made only one cast at the head of the pool, so I worked my way back up again to where I had started. I placed myself carefully, repeated my first cast exactly, watched my fly settle again neatly between the alder branches and began to think of the next cast and the next after that, when I might reasonably expect to find another fish. Then I saw the fish shouldering across behind the fly, an exact double of the one I had just lost. He took, I tightened; two minutes later my line was tangled in the same brush pile and I was floundering down, by no means calmly, to free it again. And again the fish was lost but the fly was there. In the end I did hook and kill a good fish far below the brush pile, almost at the tail of the pool, but I solemnly renewed all my resolutions about avoiding the crab apples and clay banks and other humiliations of Cedar Creek's most productive pools.

The next day I went about forty miles down along the coast of Vancouver Island to look at several small creeks and their estuaries, among them Sedge Creek. The sensible way to Sedge Creek estuary is to wade down the gravel bed of the creek itself from the highway bridge. It is clear and comfortable going, and one can make an occasional cast to where the creek deepens on a bend or under a root.

Just below the highway bridge the creek bed has been deepened by a bulldozer for several hundred yards to give the flood water an open, easy channel. To break the flow still more and prevent washing of the gravel there are heavy cross logs set into the high gravel banks at intervals of fifty or sixty yards. Behind these, long shallow pools of gently flowing water with a few deeper spots make good lying places for dog and coho salmon—and sometimes cutthroats.

On this particular day there was a school of some twenty or thirty dog salmon in the upper pool, big fish, moving a little, calm and lazy. There was every possible chance that a few cutthroats were lying somewhere amongst them, so I kept as well back from the water as I could and began to drop my Harger's Orange as nearly as I could behind individual members of the scattered, shifting school. Every so often a fish would move up under the swing of the fly and I would feel the fly or the leader scrape against him, but I slacked carefully at such times and for a while all went well. Then the inevitable happened. A fish moved up under the fly almost as it landed. For a moment of time Harger's Orange was swinging freely across the current, a moment later it had stopped, securely set in the dorsal fin of a fifteen-pound dog salmon.

At first neither I nor the fish was greatly concerned. I thought I should get my fly back without too much difficulty, he didn't think the slight restraint of the line was particularly significant. He began to swim slowly upstream. I left the line slack, hoping the fly would come free. Near the head of the pool he turned and began to swim, still quite slowly, downstream. I decided to tighten, again in the hope that the fly would come free. My fish resented this and swam a little harder, taking line nicely and stirring up the other fish in the pool. By the time he turned, just above the cross log at the tail, most of them were following him. By the time he had swum his majestic way back to the head of the pool they were tightly schooled around him, sympathetic or curious or both or neither.

The next trip down the pool was a lot faster and at the tail he broke with some violence, the school all about him still. He liked it down there and I had some difficulty in persuading him to come back up. In the end he came, the whole school still with him. And so it went on, up and down the pool, the school so closely together that it seemed I had hooked twenty fish at once on my single poor little fly. And my one fish felt like twenty. I had to accept that he was not tiring in the slightest and that my little eight foot rod was not going to bring him to beach or to hand within the foreseeable future. I tried my best, because I was really quite fond of that fly. I could direct him a little, turn him at the tail of the pool, even force him to break water, but that was about all. In the end I pointed the rod at him and broke.

Although I had kept fairly well back from the edge of the water throughout the performance, it seemed certain that the pool must be completely disturbed, so I climbed the high gravel bank on the left and started down it. I kept back in the shade of the timber, though, and watched curiously, because I wanted to see how the salmon settled down and how the fish behaved with my fly still in his dorsal fin. I found him easily, with the claret of hackle and wing in the fly showing up nicely, and he seemed just as calm as the others still schooled around him. They were already beginning to spread out through the pool and their movements were slow and lazy. As I turned my eyes from them to search the lower part of the pool I found the quiet, still shapes of two good cutthroats under the overhanging limbs of a small fir, some sixty feet up from the cross log.

These were the fish I had hoped to find among the salmon. They were flat on the bottom now, unmoving and apparently uninterested in anything about them. But it was not the sort of chance one passes up without a try of some sort. I drew farther back into the brush and circled carefully around to the tail of the pool.

My first guess was a good big floating fly. The larger fish of the two was lying a little farther out and a little downstream, so I put it over him, accurately and carefully, with a right-hand curve cast that kept the leader upstream of the drifting fly. Neither fish made the slightest move and though I repeated the cast a dozen times I could not detect even the quiver of a fin to give me encouragement.

My next thought was a nymph, but I discarded this in favor of an orange fly with a weighted body. I aimed for the same right-hand curve cast, but forgot to allow for the reduced air resistance and greater weight of the new fly. It overshot badly and whipped round into a left-hand curve that dropped it in midstream, at least eight feet over from where the fish was lying. He moved like a flash the second it touched the water and took perfectly. I tightened, held him for a second or two, then the fly came away. To my surprise he returned at once to his old position, though the second fish had disappeared.

It seemed a safe assumption that I had mistimed the strike in the surprise of seeing him come so far for the fly. To expect him to take again was totally unreasonable, but I threw the fly up anyway. It landed about six inches to his left and a foot upstream of him, and again he was on it the second it touched the water. This time I was certain of my strike. He was a strong, very fast fish of rather over two pounds, but I controlled him after two or three good runs and moved to a favorable spot to beach him, just above the cross log. As I brought him in there, the fly came away. This time I looked at the fly and found that the point and barb were broken off, no doubt by touching the rocks of the high gravel banks on a backcast.

The lesson is, I suppose, that if you are as careless a fisherman as I seem to be you should stay away from the upstream reaches of the small creeks. If you do not, they will certainly temper your pride, test your vocabulary and perhaps humiliate you in other unforeseen ways. But in the fall they hold some very good fish and the slightly larger ones like Cedar Creek and Sedge Creek may present some very pretty and interesting situations. Any resolve to stay away is only good for a few days. One can so easily make a counterresolve to be careful, respectful, farsighted and extremely skillful. Beside this the frustrations of entangling brush, slippery banks and limited casting room fade into insignificant memory. Pride is completely restored and all is ready for the next fall.

# Living Like Weasels

## Annie Dillard

A weasel is wild. Who knows what he thinks? He sleeps in his underground den, his tail draped over his nose. Sometimes he lives in his den for two days without leaving. Outside, he stalks rabbits, mice, muskrats, and birds, killing more bodies than he can eat warm, and often dragging the carcasses home. Obedient to instinct, he bites his prey at the neck, either splitting the jugular vein at the throat or crunching the brain at the base of the skull, and he does not let go. One naturalist refused to kill a weasel who was socketed into his hand deeply as a rattlesnake. The man could in no way pry the tiny weasel off, and he had to walk half a mile to water, the weasel dangling from his palm, and soak him off like a stubborn label.

And once, says Ernest Thompson Seton—once, a man shot an eagle out of the sky. He examined the eagle and found the dry skull of a weasel fixed by the jaws to his throat. The supposition is that the eagle had pounced on the weasel and the weasel swiveled and bit as instinct taught him, tooth to neck, and nearly won. I would like to have seen that eagle from the air a few weeks or months before he was shot: was the whole weasel still attached to his feathered throat, a fur pendant? Or did the eagle eat what he could reach, gutting the living weasel with his talons before his breast, bending his beak, cleaning the beautiful airborne bones?

I have been reading about weasels because I saw one last week. I startled a weasel who startled me, and we exchanged a long glance.

Twenty minutes from my house, through the woods by the quarry and across the highway, is Hollins Pond, a remarkable piece of shallow-

"Living Like Weasels" (pp. 11-16) from *Teaching a Stone to Talk* by Annie Dillard. Copyright 1982 by Annie Dillard. By permission of Harper & Row, Publishers, Inc.

ness, where I like to go at sunset and sit on a tree trunk. Hollins Pond is also called Murray's Pond; it covers two acres of bottomland near Tinker Creek with six inches of water and six thousand lily pads. In winter, brown-and-white steers stand in the middle of it, merely dampening their hooves; from the distant shore they look like miracle itself, complete with miracle's nonchalance. Now, in summer, the steers are gone. The water lilies have blossomed and spread to a green horizontal plane that is terra firma to plodding blackbirds, and tremulous ceiling to black leeches, crayfish, and carp.

This is, mind you, suburbia. It is a five-minute walk in three directions to rows of houses, though none is visible here. There's a 55 mph highway at one end of the pond, and a nesting pair of wood ducks at the other. Under every bush is a muskrat hole or a beer can. The far end is an alternating series of fields and woods, fields and woods, threaded everywhere with motorcycle tracks — in whose bare clay wild turtles lay eggs.

So. I had crossed the highway, stepped over two low barbed-wire fences, and traced the motorcycle path in all gratitude through the wild rose and poison ivy of the pond's shoreline up into high grassy fields. Then I cut down through the woods to the mossy fallen tree where I sit. This tree is excellent. It makes a dry, upholstered bench at the upper, marshy end of the pond, a plush jetty raised from the thorny shore between a shallow blue body of water and a deep blue body of sky.

The sun had just set. I was relaxed on the tree trunk, ensconced in the lap of lichen, watching the lily pads at my feet tremble and part dreamily over the thrusting path of a carp. A yellow bird appeared to my right and flew behind me. It caught my eye; I swiveled around — and the next instant, inexplicably, I was looking down at a weasel, who was looking up at me.

Weasel! I'd never seen one wild before. He was ten inches long, thin as a curve, a muscled ribbon, brown as fruitwood, soft-furred, alert. His face was fierce, small and pointed as a lizard's; he would have made a good arrowhead. There was just a dot of chin, maybe two brown hairs' worth, and then the pure white fur began that spread down his underside. He had two black eyes I didn't see, any more than you see a window.

The weasel was stunned into stillness as he was emerging from beneath an enormous shaggy wild rose bush four feet away. I was stunned into stillness twisted backward on the tree trunk. Our eyes locked, and someone threw away the key.

Our look was as if two lovers, or deadly enemies, met unexpectedly on an overgrown path when each had been thinking of something else: a clearing blow to the gut. It was also a bright blow to the brain, or a sudden beating of brains, with all the charge and intimate grate of rubbed balloons. It emptied our lungs. It felled the forest, moved the fields, and drained the pond; the world dismantled and tumbled into that black hole of eyes. If you and I looked at each other that way, our skulls would split and drop to our shoulders. But we don't. We keep our skulls. So.

He disappeared. This was only last week, and already I don't remember what shattered the enchantment. I think I blinked, I think I retrieved my brain from the weasel's brain, and tried to memorize what I was seeing, and the weasel felt the yank of separation, the careening splash-down into real life and the urgent current of instinct. He vanished under the wild rose. I waited motionless, my mind suddenly full of data and my spirit with pleadings, but he didn't return.

Please do not tell me about "approach-avoidance conflicts." I tell you I've been in that weasel's brain for sixty seconds, and he was in mine. Brains are private places, muttering through unique and secret tapes— but the weasel and I both plugged into another tape simultaneously, for a sweet and shocking time. Can I help it if it was a blank?

What goes on in his brain the rest of the time? What does a weasel think about? He won't say. His journal is tracks in clay, a spray of feathers, mouse blood and bone: uncollected, unconnected, loose-leaf, and blown.

I would like to learn, or remember, how to live. I come to Hollins Pond not so much to learn how to live as, frankly, to forget about it. That is, I don't think I can learn from a wild animal how to live in particular— shall I suck warm blood, hold my tail high, walk with my footprints precisely over the prints of my hands?—but I might learn something of mindlessness, something of the purity of living in the physical senses and the dignity of living without bias or motive. The weasel lives in necessity and we live in choice, hating necessity and dying at the last ignobly in its talons. I would like to live as I should, as the weasel lives as he should. And I suspect that for me the way is like the weasel's: open to time and death painlessly, noticing everything, remembering nothing, choosing the given with a fierce and pointed will.

I missed my chance. I should have gone for the throat. I should have lunged for that streak of white under the weasel's chin and held on, held on through mud and into the wild rose, held on for a dearer life. We could live under the wild rose wild as weasels, mute and uncomprehending. I could very calmly go wild. I could live two days in the den, curled, leaning on mouse fur, sniffing bird bones, blinking, licking, breathing musk, my hair tangled in the roots of grasses. Down is a good place to go, where the mind is single. Down is out, out of your ever-loving mind and back to your careless senses. I remember muteness as a prolonged and giddy fast, where every moment is a feast of utterance received. Time and events are merely poured, unremarked, and ingested directly, like blood pulsed into my gut through a jugular vein. Could two live that way? Could two live under the wild rose, and explore by the pond, so that the smooth mind of each is as everywhere present to the other, and as received and as unchallenged, as falling snow?

We could, you know. We can live any way we want. People take vows of poverty, chastity, and obedience—even of silence—by choice. The thing is to stalk your calling in a certain skilled and supple way, to locate the most tender and live spot and plug into that pulse. This is yielding, not fighting. A weasel doesn't "attack" anything; a weasel lives as he's meant to, yielding at every moment to the perfect freedom of single necessity.

I think it would be well, and proper, and obedient, and pure, to grasp your one necessity and not let it go, to dangle from it limp wherever it takes you. Then even death, where you're going no matter how you live, cannot you part. Seize it and let it seize you up aloft even, till your eyes burn out and drop; let your musky flesh fall off in shreds, and let your very bones unhinge and scatter, loosened over fields, over fields and woods, lightly, thoughtless, from any height at all, from as high as eagles.

# Intimations

## Bharati Mukherjee

My life, I now realize, falls into three disproportionate parts. Till the age of eight I lived in the typical joint family, indistinguishable from my twenty cousins, indistinguishable, in fact, from an eternity of Bengali Brahmin girls. From eight till twenty-one we lived as a single family, enjoying for a time wealth and confidence. And since twenty-one I have lived in the West. Each phase required a repudiation of all previous avatars; an almost total rebirth.

Prior to this year-long stay in India, I had seen myself as others saw me in Montreal, a brown woman in a white society, different, perhaps even special, but definitely not a part of the majority. I receive, occasionally, crazy letters from women students at McGill accusing me of being "mysterious," "cold," "hard to get to know," and the letter writers find this mysteriousness offensive. I am bothered by these letters, especially by the aggressive desire of students to "know" me. I explain it as a form of racism. The unfamiliar is frightening; therefore I have been converted into a "mystery." I can be invested with powers and intentions I do not possess.

In a life of many cultural moves, I had clung to my uniqueness as the source of confidence and stability. But in India I am not unique, not even extraordinary. During the year, I began to see how typical my life had actually been, and given the limited options of a woman from my class and from my city, how predictably I had acted in each crisis. And I see how, even in the West, I have acted predictably. My writing is a satellite of my marriage and profession; I have chosen, or fallen into, the role of bourgeois writer, limited to a month of writing in a year, or one year of writing for every seven of teaching. The American alternative, *Mama Doesn't Live Here Anymore*, remains unthinkable.

From *Days and Nights in Calcutta*. Copyright ©1977 by Clark Blaise and Bharati Mukherjee. Reprinted by permission of Russell & Volkening, Inc. as agents for the author.

Only the first eight years were spent in Ballygunge, in a flat crowded with relatives, and friends of relatives who needed a place for sleeping and eating while they went to college in the city, and hangers-on, whose connection with my family I did not have the curiosity to determine. I was not happy in that joint family. Perhaps some of my mother's frustration seeped down to me. People say that I look very much like her. Certainly I am, like her, a collector of resentments and insults, and am stubbornly unforgiving. I suspect that in those early years, it was more important to me to retain my position as my father's favorite daughter (he had written a poem about me, titled "Treasure of the Heart") than it was to imitate, in proper fashion, the personality of my mother. But I am sure that from her I learned only to feel relief when we could close the door of our bedroom and shut out the forty-odd relatives.

It was a small room after the corners and sides had been filled with the bulky furniture of my mother's dowry. Two beds—one was the bridal four-poster, the other was a simple *chowki*—were pushed together for the five of us, two adults and three daughters. I recall that because of shortage of space, my father used to store an untidy pile of scientific books and journals on the bridal bed itself and that we children had to be careful not to kick the books in our sleep. In a household where no one kept his opinions to himself, this room was our shrine of privacy.

Sometimes there were invasions by cousins or younger uncles. Once my mother, sisters, and I returned from our customary afternoon visit to Southern Avenue to find that my eldest sister's British-made painting book and paintbox, which she had won as a school prize, had been vandalized. Another time, the lock of the wooden cabinet in which my mother kept her jewelry and small cash savings had been forced open, and some money was missing. I was taught to think of these episodes as an assault on our desire to maintain slight separateness within the context of the joint family, rather than expressions of mischief by relatives.

Within the small perimeters of that room, it became clear to me that if I wished to remain sane I should not permit myself to squander my affections on too many people or possessions. With over-population of that sort, possessions and relationships could at best be fragile. I learned also to be always on my guard, and because I was small, shy, and the second youngest in the family, to stay in the background, out of danger's reach. During communal meals, when all the children sat on the floor of the corridor surrounding an inner courtyard, I did not demand the prized items—eyes and brain of carp—because I knew that if I set myself no goals, there could be no defeat. I had, I felt, an intimate knowledge and horror of madness. There was a mad aunt in the family, and during a long stay that she, her husband and four children inflicted on us (because there was some natural disaster, probably a flood, in the part of East Bengal where they lived), I had seen her chase her husband with an ugly piece of firewood. I cannot recall if I had actually seen her hit her husband on the head with the firewood before I was hustled off by my mother into the privacy of our bedroom, or if the aunt had only been standing, weapon poised, about to hit him. I did not think of the uncle, whom I disliked, as the victim. But I thought of madness as grotesque, and as shameful, for I had been told by my parents that if too many people came to know about the craziness in the family, it would be hard to marry us daughters off. I resolved immediately to fight in myself the slightest signs of insanity.

I was released from all that terrifying communal bonding by a single decisive act of my father's, shortly after my eighth birthday. Because of certain circumstances in the pharmaceutical company that he and his partner, a Jewish immigrant from the Middle East, had set up, circumstances that he did not explain to his daughters though he probably did to his wife, he brought home colorful brochures one day of an all-first-class boat on the Anchor Line, and within weeks we left the joint family, and Calcutta, in order to make a new start in London.

We were happy in Britain and Switzerland where my father worked on his research projects, and where we went to school and were remarkable for our good manners as well as our intelligence, and where my mother took night courses in flan baking and basket weaving. But my parents did not make for themselves a new life. The partner followed my father to London, for a while installed us in a company flat at the corner of Curzon and Half Moon streets, vacationed with us in Montreux, and was, I suspect, persuasive about his plan for the pharmaceutical company in Calcutta. And so, after almost three years abroad, we returned to Calcutta, not quite where we had left off, and certainly not to Ballygunge and the joint family.

That period abroad is the only time I have felt perfectly bilingual. It was a time of forgetting Bengali and acquiring English until I reached an absolute equilibrium. But that gradual erosion of the vernacular also contained an erosion of ideas I had taken for granted. It was the first time I was forced to see myself not reflected in people around me, to see myself as the curiosity that I must have seemed to the majority—a skinny brown child, in stiff school uniform and scarred knees, who could not do cartwheels. The sense that I had had of myself in Ballygunge, of being somehow superior to my cousins, was less destructive than this new sense of being a minority on account of my color. I felt I was a shadow person because I was not white. We were an extraordinarily close-knit family, but since I had been brought up to please, I felt I could not burden my parents with these anxieties. It would have made them unhappy, and I could not bear to do that. I could count only on myself for devising strategies of survival in London, our adopted city. I became less passive than I had been among relatives and friends in Ballygunge: I began to regard facility in

English as my chief weapon for bending my own personality and for making friends among the British.

In sacrificing a language, we sacrifice our roots. On returning to Calcutta, we found that our image of ourselves had changed radically. It was not at all a question of money. *Jethoo*, my father's oldest brother, owned rice mills and lumber mills in Assam, but he would not be comfortable outside of Ballygunge. But to us, the thought of re-entry into that closed, conspiratorial joint-family world was unbearable. So we sublet a flat in fashionable Chowringhee, the break from the joint family being facilitated by a quarrel between my mother and another relative. We changed schools too, from the Anglicized Bengali school on the edge of Ballygunge to the most renowned girls' school on Middleton Row, a school where, it was rumored, Indian children had for a long time been denied admission. And in our new school, the foreign nuns treasured us for our faintly British accents which had survived the long homeward journey.

From our return to Calcutta after the false start in Europe until the middle of 1959, we lived in the compound of the pharmaceutical factory which my father and his partner had set up in Cossipore, on the outskirts of the city. My parents now refer to that phase of our lives as "the good days." I thought of the compound walls as the boundaries of a small constitutional monarchy in which my sisters and I were princesses. We presided at factory functions, such as sports events, religious celebrations, variety shows for workers, and looked on that as our necessary duty.

The pharmaceutical company had bought out the garden house and estate of a refined Bengali gentleman after whom a street had been named in happier times, but whose fortunes had now declined completely. His botanical gardens—full of imported rarities—were cut down and cleared, the snakes scared away, the pools filled, the immense Victorian house converted into a production plant for capsules, syrups, and pills. I saw the conversion as a triumph of the new order over the old, and felt no remorse. Nothing would return me to the drabness and tedium of Ballygunge.

For me, being part of the new order meant walking under arches of bougainvillaea with my sisters and a golden spaniel we had acquired immediately after moving in, while neighbors gawked at us from their rooftops. We were inviolable and inaccessible within our walled compound. To our neighbors, we were objects of envy, and probably freaks. There were screening devices to protect us: gates, guards, internal telephones. We were at home to only those we wished to see; others could be sent away from the front gate. Having been deprived of privacy in early childhood, I carried my privacy to an extreme; I did not even learn the names of the streets around the factory.

Every day we shuttled between this fortressed factory compound and the school compound in an old gray Rover, once owned by a British executive who had decided independent India was no longer the best place for him. Our privacy was guaranteed on these trips by a bodyguard who looked like Oliver Hardy. The ride from Cossipore to Middleton Row and back is very long, and the cityscape unusually unpleasant. I learned very quickly, therefore, to look out of the window and see nothing. During those rides, my sisters and I talked endlessly about the kinds of men we wanted to marry, and memorized passages from Shakespeare or from the Gospels for the morning's quizzes. My older sister, who is four years older than I and currently is a childless, working wife in Detroit, was the most romantic among us. She said that she did not care about money, but that the groom would have to have excellent table manners and be perfect at ballroom dancing. My younger sister and I knew what she meant by that: She wanted a "Westernized" groom who had studied abroad, and who could command for her a "Westernized" life-style in a pretty flat on Park Street or Chowringhee. Like us, she did not want to lapse into the self-contained vernacular world of Ballygunge.

During this period we were once visited by some female relatives of Mr. D. Gupta, former owner of the garden house that we had converted into a factory. My father arranged for the visiting women to be taken on a guided tour of the plant and then to have tea with us. It was intended by my father to be, and therefore was, an amiable occasion. We sat on the Georgian and Jacobean imported furniture that my parents had extravagantly selected from auction houses on Park and Free School streets, and we listened to the niece of the former owner describe how pretty the chute of colored syrups and capsules had been. It was amiable because the old and new orders had treated each other courteously. Confrontations would come later, and my sisters and I would one day not long after that tea, on our return from school, have to walk through a crowd of striking employees who had blocked our car and who carried placards we were too well-brought-up to read. This tea among the women of the former and current owners was an acknowlegment of another sort: the vulnerability of individual heroes or families in the face of larger designs. Having a street named after oneself was no permanent guarantee of dignity or survival.

That is why, on this 1973 trip back to India, when a newer order has replaced us within the walls of that same compound, I chose not to visit the factory, nor to walk once more under the flowering arches where my sisters and I dreamed about our "Westernized" grooms and "Westernized" life-styles. On this latest trip, I was told that the neighborhood around the factory had become dangerous, and that during the recent Naxalite agitations, workers had been beaten up and that a chemist I recalled well had been knifed in the head a block and a half from the factory gates.

For me the walled factory compound, the guards at the gate office, the bodyguard inside our Rover, the neighbors staring at us from the rooftops, are now emblems. We were typical of a class in the city. There was surely nothing ignoble in our desire to better our condition. In a city that threatens to overwhelm the individual who is passive, there was nothing immoral in self-protection. But we had refused to merge with the city; we had cleared the snakes and shrubberies; we had preoccupied ourselves with single layers of existence—getting ahead, marrying well—and we had ignored the visionary whole. And now, years later, those of us who left and settled in far-off cities like Detroit and Montreal, as well as those of my school friends who stayed and who now live in flats on Park Street or own houses on Rawdon Street, are paying for having scared the snakes and gutted the shrubberies.

My parents moved out of Calcutta long ago. But the impulse to erect compound walls, to isolate and exclude, appears all around me in Calcutta in 1973. My friends live in mansions that the British had built in less volatile times to separate themselves from the bazaars and settlements of the natives. These mansions, even now, are fronted by spacious lawns, gravel driveways, enormous gates with wooden watch posts, and one or more uniformed guards. The guards are not always alert on the job. One rainy July morning as we swung into the driveway of the home of a managing director of a former British firm, we caught the guard urinating against the compound wall.

The cry these days is more for protection than for privacy, and this cry is more shrill than I have ever heard. The women who live in these mansions and whom I meet very regularly for lunch and charity work, study groups and cocktails on the lawn, tell me about the "troubled times" when everything was "topsy-turvy" because the Naxalite gangs took over. With manicured nails jabbing the air, they describe to me how the Naxals scared the guards, sometimes invaded the compounds, threw gravel against the bathroom windows, tore up the lawns by playing soccer. One elegant young woman wearing a delicate pink nylon sari and Japanese pearls (it is hard for me to adjust to this new image, for I had last seen her as a pig-tailed schoolgirl with socks that kept sliding into her shoes) wants me to know that "the troubled times" are not over yet, that what I am seeing is simply a lull before the coming class confrontation. I do not disbelieve her; it is a common conviction all over Calcutta. A woman I had met a week before is now hiding out with her family in the house of another friend in order to avoid what she calls "mischievous acts"—acid bombs? sieges? kidnapings? —by striking employees in her husband's firm?

Here in Calcutta, my friends go out into the city in groups, beautiful women in well-waxed cars, and they pack pills for lepers for Mother Teresa. They supervise sewing workshops for destitute women, even clean streets in front of photographers and journalists in order to save and beautify Calcutta. "CALCUTTA IS FOREVER" announces a billboard on Ballygunge Circular Road, paid for by the Beautification Committee. "KEEP YOUR CITY CLEAN AND DESCENT" mocks a less-professional effort near Free School Street. They have made their commitment to this decayed and turbulent city. In exchange, they want protection for themselves and their children.

To protect oneself is to be sensible, I am told. It is a city-wide obsession. Even the Scholar's Guest House where Clark and I stay and which is run by the Ramakrishna Mission, a religious Hindu order, is set apart from the street by high walls. Outside the walls are the accouterments of Ballygunge life: hawkers, beggars, loiterers, squatters, sleepers, cows and pariahs, cars, taxis, buses, mini-buses, cycles, rickshaws, bullock carts, and heedless pedestrians. Inside there is greenery, flowers, a studied calm. The *durwan* at the gate sits on a stool and separates the two worlds. He has a register and pencil to keep track of all visitors. But still the brutal world invades the mission, and brass gas rings disappear from the secondary kitchen, and dissatisfied employees demonstrate on the edge of the judiciously kept lawn.

We do not seem to have heeded the message of the anonymous sculptor from Deoghar. We have confined ourselves to single obsessions. We have protected our territory, and posted uniformed servants to keep out the confusions of the city. We have forgotten that the guard himself is in an ambiguous position and that his loyalties may be fragile. In a city like this, an elderly relative tells me as he chews an endless mouthful of betel nuts, *You just can't be too careful. If you relax for a second, someone will snatch your gold necklace or your purse.* He advises me against certain doctors—there have been stories about nearly any doctor that I mention. *That man is too black, That man is unmarried, Never go to a doctor alone.* But to be so wise, I would like to answer, is also to distort.

Out there beyond our walled vision is a reality that disgusts and confounds the intellect, and a populace that is too illiterate, too hungry, too brutish, to be gently manipulated. Or, just as confounding, a populace too gentle to be brutishly commanded. The odds against survival for an individual are enormous, and rewards, at best, are uncertain.

*Merge*, commands the Deoghar sculptor, *there are no insides and outsides, no serpents, no gods.*

But at this time, we who consider ourselves more intelligent, more politically conscious, more sophisticated, more charming than the ancient stoneworker, know that to merge, to throw in our lot with Calcutta, is also to invite self-destruction. If we take down the compound walls and remove the ceremonial guard who relieves himself in the street and picks his nose while opening the gates to visitors, what will happen to our children?

It is at this point that I separate myself from the chorus of my old school friends in Calcutta. My sons will return to Montreal at the end of the year, study very little, ski a little more, watch Saturday cartoons on TV, and inherit the promises of the New World.

For the children of my friends who have chosen to remain in Calcutta, the range of future possibilities is infinitely more frightening. Though we never discuss it, we all know that this city will yield its rewards only to the strongest, the smartest, or the most powerful.

### Bombay: May-June 1973

For me, 1973 was a year of luxurious nostalgia. This nostalgia could be triggered by the smallest objects, such as a Venetian liqueur glass bought at Staynor's auction house during the "good days" and transported with love during the reluctant move from Calcutta to Baroda and Bombay. Nostalgia could overtake me anywhere and transform the immediate surroundings until my parents' carelessly furnished Chembur living room become once more the room stocked with Jacobean sofas that I had lolled on as a teenager.

But for many Indians, 1973 was a year in which nostalgia gave way to bewilderment and anger. The papers and periodicals were full of stories of misunderstandings. I read that an eighteen-year-old pregnant woman who had been cooking supper on the platform of a clean, new railway station was kicked to death by an outraged railway official. And that a starving mother threw her four daughters and herself into a well but succeeded in killing only two.

Then there were the standard stories of rage and frustration, of men killing each other in movie house queues, of knifings among street sleepers because a child had cried too loud and too long or one man had made a pass at another man's wife. The time for good humor seemed about to disappear. There were endless complaints about endless shortages, and short fierce strikes all over India, but no one had yet taken radical, irrevocable measures.

In Chembur, where we spent the first month and a half seeing my family and preparing for the trip farther east to Calcutta, I learned that fear is not an affliction; it merely is a way of ordering a confused world. The wives I met in Bombay relied on fear to give meaning to lives that might otherwise have seemed, even to them, banal. Like my mother, these women lived in compounds of factories in which their husbands worked, in executives' quarters which were considered luxurious. The compounds had the usual paraphernalia of security: walls, sometimes topped with barbed wire and always with wicked shards of glass, check posts, emergency "hot lines" to the general manager, uniformed and ununiformed guards. These executives' wives thrilled to the lazy salute of the watchmen as they drove in and out of the main gate on their way to the bazaar: The salute was reassurance of status. These women were valuable while the millions outside the gates were not. The compound literally isolated them from the world of unassorted passions. The factory walls gave them their corporate identity, loyalty, and self-respect, created a calming communal village in a chaotic industrial zone. The women were grateful for the rigid security and for the group privacy, relieved to be cut off from the other Chembur in which degenerate or starving people burgled, murdered, cheated, used dirty words. They had intimations of danger each time they went to the bazaar in groups of two and three in private cars, or (because of gasoline prices) mostly in the factory's bus. More often than not the buses that bumped them along the narrow highways and city roads had windows covered with wire mesh to deflect any projectiles hurled by unhappy laborers.

Inside the compound, they lived in neatly kept houses, set in hierarchical rows, and separated from the noisy, smelly work site by trees or hill slopes or at least a bamboo grove. Their children watched television in the company's recreation room, and sometimes if there was a really good movie being run, the women joined the children for an hour or two, fighting mosquitoes that preyed on all the viewers. There was also a Ping-Pong table, and though none of the women played themselves, they took secretive, unacknowledged pride in the Ping-Pong skills of their husbands and sons. They did not worry that there were no telephones, except in the houses of perhaps the general manager and the managing director. Their husbands handled all their serious relationships with the outside world; all they needed was the factory intercom so that they could call each other to set up visits and call their husbands home for lunch.

The women I met in that preparatory period before Calcutta were friendly, anxious to let me know that they did not hold my eccentric marriage against me, though, when pressed, they admitted they did not want their daughters or younger sisters to marry outside their state and caste. Their friendliness took the form of solicitous advice to Clark and myself. They found us naive, helpless, untutored in strategies of self-defense. So they became our eager tutors.

"Don't let Bart and Bernie go off to the park with the servant. You never know what gets into servants' heads. They should post a guard there."

"Did you read about that murder? After six and a half years, a servant goes crazy and murders the lady when her husband is at work. I tell you, you simply can't trust anyone."

"Chembur is one of the worst areas, one of the very worst," agrees another.

"Chembur is nothing compared to Calcutta. I don't know why you want to go to Calcutta. It's so nice here."

"Never ride a taxi in Calcutta. Tell your old friends to send cars if they want to see you."

"Make sure Clark gets in first . . . ."

"Have you told them about that European who lost his passport? Don't ever leave your hotel room for a visitor downstairs—make him come up."

"During the troubles people would just walk up to you on the street in broad daylight and snatch your gold necklace. They would cut off your fingers to get your rings."

"Things are better now, I must say. Hats off to Siddhartha Shankar Ray. He's been good and tough."

"Maybe a little bit better for the local people, but Bharati and Clark won't be able to manage. They are too trusting. I see Clark and I say to myself he is so open, always laughing, what will he do in Calcutta? He'll take his big Nikon camera to New Market and the *goondas* will beat him up. You tell him to be careful."

They told more stories. A niece whose earrings had been torn from her ears, shredding the flesh. An old widow whose gold chain was clipped from her neck in plain view of fifty people on a tram. For her complaints, she'd been lectured to by fellow passengers for having provoked the attack by wearing gold.

"Bharati, you better not wear *two* gold chains like that in Calcutta. It looks very nice—you have a very nice throat and collarbone area for necklaces—but in Calcutta that's an open invitation to burglars."

"There are so many gold smugglers around and they'll do anything."

"I'll tell you a story that happened to relatives of a friend of mine."

"Is this the one about prostitute rings?"

"No, this one is much worse."

She began the story; Clark was nearby, reading. It was all in Bengali, with a cluster of executives' wives hanging on every word.

"These people were quite young and the husband had a good job. One day they went to New Market to shop. They had an infant daughter who also went to the market with them. She was fast asleep, so the parents—and this is fate—left the baby locked in the car while they went in for a second to buy something, I've forgotten what—"

"They have *very* nice petticoats in New Market," my mother said. "It was probably petticoats."

"Anyway, they went to the store, and when they came back, there was no sign of the baby."

"It is fate," suggested another neighbor.

"Car was locked you said?"

"Completely locked. So there is absolute pandemonium. They informed the police, interrogated those Muslim chaps who hang around New Market acting as porters and touts, but no trace."

"They are absolute *goondas*—Mex, you hear that?"

"So, anyway these people had some important connections, and a real serious search was made, but still nothing turned up."

"That is good. These days in our country unless you have connections nobody will care."

"Nobody cares, that is right. It is terrible."

"Never let Bart and Bernie out of your sight for a minute."

"Every day, they had to drive here and there and everywhere to look at babies, but it was always the wrong baby. It gives you an idea how many stolen babies there are. Meanwhile the poor mother was so upset that she was almost mad, unable to eat or sleep. Then they got a call from the police to come out to the airport where a suspicious-looking mother and child had been detained. The husband and wife rushed out there, and sure enough, the mother recognized her daughter, and threw herself on the kidnaper—"

"Oh, thank God!" the women exclaimed.

"No, no—here comes the worst part. It was their baby all right, but she was dead."

"No! *Baapré-ba!*" They touched their foreheads.

"*Yes.* The smugglers—they were Muslims trying to get back to Abu Dhabi to get more gold—had taken out the baby's intestines and stuffed the cavity with gold bars, then sewn the stomach flaps back. Go ahead, translate it for Clark." He raised his head at the mention of his name. "*That's right, Clark, Calcutta no good. Calcutta full of goondas and very bad behavior.*"

My mother likes to lock doors. Also windows, safes, cupboards, closets, trunks, valises. Her closest friend in Chembur has installed a padlock and chain around the door of her refrigerator. Foodstuffs such as sugar, gram flour, cloves, cardamom, and cigarettes that cannot be fitted with locks are poured into plastic canisters and placed in neat rows inside lockable cupboards. Keys to locked cupboards are stored in other locked cupboards. My mother carries only one key on her person; it is frail and black and hangs limply from a knot in her sari, just below her left shoulder. Heavier rings of keys, the ones that issue insolent challenges to potential burglars—for example, the ring of keys to get to the purse that contains the key to another cupboard and to another purse which holds the key to a steel cabinet with a safe fitted with a double lock where my mother has stowed my scratched German leather purse full of passports, health certificates, and the children's photographs—these remain out of sight.

Clark considers this paranoia. He tells me that since the gate office of the factory compound screens all those who try to enter, this elaborate security system is designed to discourage only the live-in servant and part-time maids who come to wash the dishes, do the laundry, and to clean floors and toilets. I know, of course, that Clark is wrong. He does not understand the apocalyptic vision of my mother. He is annoyed that he cannot get to his tape recorder without having the women unlock several cupboards, or that when he is ready and waiting in the car for the long drive downtown it takes my mother and me several extra minutes of co-ordinated effort to give him his traveler's checks and identification cards. I explain to him that if the servant wanted to burgle or murder, he could easily do so during the siesta hour. My mother, though heavy, is not at all strong. She is totally at the mercy of any sinister intruder. Locking is her way of integrating belief in karma and belief in individual resourcefulness. She is alert to the conditions of modern India; she assumes that disaster, which in her childhood had seemed to lie in some unrealizable future, is now about to occur in her lifetime. Perhaps she remembers those wooden cupboards back in the joint family, when the forcing of a door was an attack upon all her defenses. She will not set herself impossible goals about reversing her fate or the country's; she will simply use her common sense to minimize the personal effects of disaster.

We suffer an unacknowledged crisis over Bernie's electric train, which we bought in Geneva en route to India and which we cannot permit him to play with guiltlessly in Chembur because of the factory's policy of "voluntary" power restraint. Bernie, who is obsessed by trains and planes, lies on the cool floor of his room and pushes his locomotive with his finger. My mother would like us to store the train set in a locked wall cabinet whenever Bernie is not playing with it. Clark refuses to do that.

"But that *chokra*-boy will wreck it in no time," my mother objects (to me, never to Clark). "He's a very curious and careless boy."

"It's a toy, for God's sake," Clark explodes with undue passion.

He is correct; he wins the round. We leave the electric train set out, and in a matter of weeks, the monsoon deposits rust flowers on the tracks, stealthily adventurous fingers leave dents on the underpinnings of carriages (it is Rajan who encourages Bernie to pry the tops off the passenger cars; it would not surprise me if Rajan had expected miniature people inside, reading their German newspapers), and the locomotive seems clogged with fluff and hair balls. And so my mother and Bernie conspire to save the train from further damage. They wrap the broken set in an old cotton sari and place it on the top shelf of a cupboard; it is transformed from a toy that functions to a souvenir of a nearly perfect visit by the family of a favorite daughter. I try once more to explain the episode of the train to

Clark. I paint him a middle-aged woman with an overwhelming sense of doom. A middle-aged woman who no longer reads, sews, goes to parties, sees films or television, visits friends, and whose children now lead independent lives in far-off cities or continents. Locking out hazard, locking in happiness. To deprive her of that would be brutal.

My mother has raised precaution to a high art. She has not only experimented with locks of various sizes and brands—on trips abroad to visit me or my sister, she has spent meticulous half-days at the key and padlock counters—but she has also extended the range of items to be locked out. In Chembur she locks out sunlight, insects, bats, toads, pariah dogs, servants' chums, and cobras. She is full of cautionary tales about the cobra that had slithered into the neighbor's bathroom because a window had been left unlatched. All her windows are still covered over with the heavy black paper that had been given out to all residents of the compound to block out house lights during the Indo-Pakistan war. During the war, she had supervised the cutting and pasting, making sure the servant did not let a single sliver of light slip through. You could develop film in some of those rooms, even in tropical daytime. Now when she shuts her windows during the day— and she does that by nine o'clock to keep out industrial soot and smells, heat, undesirable creatures—the house is peaceful, dark, and cavernous. With doors and windows battened down, and with her hands on the panel of fan and light switches, she can control her universe. Manipulation of breezes and light, she construes as a triumph of will over chaos. Each time she bars a window, causing the papered-over panes to cut off the sun, she sees it as a stalling of a future disaster.

The wartime paper, as it turns out, is destined to go. Clark does not like the paper; he cannot work behind closed windows. He likes to work, and he is more self-reliant than anyone else in the compound. Also, he has allies in the servant and the chauffeur, whose full names he, rather than my parents, has been the first to find out. After three weeks of writing longhand in bed under a ceiling fan that scattered his writing materials without cooling him, he has the chauffeur drive him out to the bazaar, where, without engaging in acrimonious and exhaustive comparison shopping, he buys a metal desk and a metal chair, and installs them himself in front of windows in our bedroom. Then, with Rajan's help, he rips aside the company curtains, unlocks the windows, peels off the black paper, takes a long gulp of the outside air, and writes uninterruptedly for five hours.

My mother looks in now and then and says in the direction of the servant, "Don't interrupt, *Sahib* at work here."

But to me she says, "Are you sure he'll be all right? All that black stuff from the factory chimney will make his eyes sore. Ask him, does he need anything? Shall I bring him some mangoes or sweet lime? Or how about tea? He needs to eat more."

Over the next few days, the servant continues with the paper-removing work that Clark began. The curtains in all the bedrooms start to bleach in window-sized rectangles. Those of us who suffer from nervous sick headaches in the sun suffer them more than usual. Clark, whose desk looks out over the rise and the chimney, develops itchy eyes and has to return to his original writing position on the bed under the fan. The children suffer continuous hay fever. Dust from the open window covers his desk, typewriter, arms, hands, and papers; he can't erase without smearing the page. The servant mops a great deal more than he has before. A window has been opened and a foreign element permitted indoors. Clark does not yet understand an Indian's relationship to "nature"; he still suffers from the American myth of nature's benevolence.

When it is time for Clark and me to fly from Santa Cruz Airport to Calcutta, I am not afraid to leave Bart and Bernie with my mother. She will, of course, be even more overprotective when she is their sole guardian. My father will be at his office until the boys' supper hour; so she will see herself as their principal custodian, and love will make her more fearful than usual.

I hear her shout as I pack my bags, "Bertie, don't play in the puddle. Hookworms will get you." And five minutes later, "Barnie, come back here darling, big, big cobras outdoors." These, I know, are her ways, and perhaps her only ways, of expressing affection to her stranger-grandsons. To love is also to minimize the beloved's exposure to danger. And, having been brought up in monsoon country, I know that hookworms and snakes slither in and out of maladied, middle-aged imaginations. Bernie has already shown me, five yards from our front door, six dead baby vipers (he called them "fat worms, Mommy"), washed down the hillsides by the heavy seasonal rains. So I do not shout out counterinstructions to the boys to go out into the rain and find their own adventure, to be resourceful and independent and not bother the grown-ups. I do not whisper to my mother to disguise or restrain the force of her love. This will probably be the last time that the boys, my hardy North American boys, will experience familial affection and not consider it burdensome.

But for many Indians, the excellent balance between fear and love is part of nostalgia. Extravagant, unrestrained love can no longer be expressed and extravagant fear has come to replace it. Only partially hidden under the stiff Indian-English of newspaper journalism, I see the spurts and flares of private terror in this year of threatened famine and deteriorating nerves.

Mr. Suprio Das, in *The Statesman* of August 1, 1973, writes that while out on the V.I.P. Road for his customary evening constitutional stroll, he had stumbled upon a decomposing corpse bearing obvious knife wounds, and that though he had done his civic duty by calling the police, he had not been able to arrange for immediate corpse removal. Three days later the corpse had disappeared, thanks to the efforts (he believed) of neighborhood pariah dogs and vultures. And now, the writer wants to know of the editor of that respected newspaper, what should he do if during another evening stroll, he happens on another corpse full of knife wounds?

In Habibur area, in the district of Malda, sixty-five-year- old landlord (*jotedar*) wins posthumous notice by becoming North Bengal's first fatal casualty during the crop-cutting and harvesting season. He is rumored to have been shot full of arrows by a tribal group who did not want him harvesting in that area.

Hungry or simply immoral youths, in large gangs, attempt to hijack loaded trucks in the Siliguri area, by blockading the highway with boulders, then by throwing stones at the wind-shield of the stopped truck in order to injure the driver and his guard. This results in an organized protest by truck drivers who tie up traffic on Highway 31 and demand better protection. The protesters are finally persuaded to cease their demonstration in time for the motorcade of West Bengal's Chief Minister, Siddhartha Shankar Ray, who is making an official visit to Kalimpong.

In India, then, for some people at least, it is a year of eroding faith in inevitable destinies. The daily newspapers, still uncensored, publish scorching indictments of official pronouncements and heap abuse on ministerial fiats. The workers at Calico go out on strike. It is to last only a week, but it drags on and on, sharpening into a show of force. Six months later, after a death and several beatings, the workers will return, accepting the company offer. Force alone still carries the greatest respect.

# Once More to the Lake

## E.B. White

(August 1941)

One summer, along about 1904, my father rented a camp on a lake in Maine and took us all there for the month of August. We all got ringworm from some kittens and had to rub Pond's Extract on our arms and legs night and morning, and my father rolled over in a canoe with all his clothes on; but outside of that the vacation was a success and from then on none of us ever thought there was any place in the world like that lake in Maine. We returned summer after summer—always on August 1st for one month. I have since become a salt-water man, but sometimes in summer there are days when the restlessness of the tides and the fearful cold of the sea water and the incessant wind which blows across the afternoon and into the evening make me wish for the placidity of a lake in the woods. A few weeks ago this feeling got so strong I bought myself a couple of bass hooks and a spinner and returned to the lake where we used to go, for a week's fishing and to revisit old haunts.

I took along my son, who had never had any fresh water up his nose and who had seen lily pads only from train windows. On the journey over to the lake I began to wonder what it would be like. I wondered how time would have marred this unique, this holy spot—the coves and streams, the hills that the sun set behind, the camps and the paths behind the camps. I was sure that the tarred road would have found it out and I wondered in what other ways it would be desolated. It is strange how much you can remember about places like that once you allow your mind to return into the grooves which lead back. You remember one thing, and that suddenly

"Once More to the Lake" (pp. 246-253) from *One Man's Meat* by E. B. White. Copyright 1941 by E. B. White.

reminds you of another thing. I guess I remembered clearest of all the early mornings, when the lake was cool and motionless, remembered how the bedroom smelled of the lumber it was made of and of the wet woods whose scent entered through the screen. The partitions in the camp were thin and did not extend clear to the top of the rooms, and as I was always the first up I would dress softly so as not to wake the others, and sneak out into the sweet outdoors and start out in the canoe, keeping close along the shore in the long shadows of the pines. I remembered being very careful never to rub my paddle against the gunwale for fear of disturbing the stillness of the cathedral.

The lake had never been what you would call a wild lake. There were cottages sprinkled around the shores, and it was in farming country although the shores of the lake were quite heavily wooded. Some of the cottages were owned by nearby farmers and you would live at the shore and eat your meals at the farmhouse. That's what our family did. But although it wasn't wild, it was a fairly large and undisturbed lake and there were places in it which, to a child at least, seemed infinitely remote and primeval.

I was right about the tar: it led to within half a mile of the shore. But when I got back there, with my boy, and we settled into a camp near a farmhouse and into the kind of summertime I had known, I could tell that it was going to be pretty much the same as it had been before—I knew it, lying in bed the first morning, smelling the bedroom, and hearing the boy sneak quietly out and go off along the shore in a boat. I began to sustain the illusion that he was I, and therefore, by simple transposition, that I was my father. This sensation persisted, kept cropping up all the time we were there. It was not an entirely new feeling, but in this setting it grew much stronger. I seemed to be living a dual existence. I would be in the middle of some simple act, I would be picking up a bait box or laying down a table fork, or I would be saying something, and suddenly it would be not I but my father who was saying the words or making the gesture. It gave me a creepy sensation.

We went fishing the first morning. I felt the same damp moss covering the worms in the bait can, and saw the dragonfly alight on the tip of my rod as it hovered a few inches from the surface of the water. It was the arrival of this fly that convinced me beyond any doubt that everything was as it always had been, that the years were a mirage and there had been no years. The small waves were the same, chucking the rowboat under the chin as we fished at anchor, and the boat was the same boat, the same color green and the ribs broken in the same places, and under the floorboards the same fresh-water leavings and débris—the dead helgramite, the wisps of moss, the rusty discarded fishhook, the dried blood from yesterday's catch. We stared silently at the tips of our rods, at the dragonflies that came and went. I lowered the tip of mine into the water, tentatively, pen-sively dislodging the fly, which darted two feet away, poised, darted two feet back, and came to rest again a little farther up the rod. There had been no years between the ducking of this dragonfly and the other one—the one that was part of memory. I looked at the boy, who was silently watching his fly, and it was my hands that held his rod, my eyes watching. I felt dizzy and didn't know which rod I was at the end of.

We caught two bass, hauling them in briskly as though they were mackerel, pulling them over the side of the boat in a businesslike manner without any landing net, and stunning them with a blow on the back of the head. When we got back for a swim before lunch, the lake was exactly where we had left it, the same number of inches from the dock, and there was only the merest suggestion of a breeze. This seemed an utterly en-chanted sea, this lake you could leave to its own devices for a few hours and come back to, and find that it had not stirred, this constant and trustworthy body of water. In the shallows, the dark, water-soaked sticks and twigs, smooth and old, were undulating in clusters on the bottom against the clean ribbed sand, and the track of the mussel was plain. A school of minnows swam by, each minnow with its small individual shadow, doubling the attendance, so clear and sharp in the sunlight. Some of the other campers were in swimming, along the shore, one of them with a cake of soap, and the water felt thin and clear and unsubstantial. Over the years there had been this person with the cake of soap, this cultist, and here he was. There had been no years.

Up to the farmhouse to dinner through the teeming, dusty field, the road under our sneakers was only a two-track road. The middle track was missing, the one with the marks of the hooves and the splotches of dried, flaky manure. There had always been three tracks to choose from in choosing which track to walk in; now the choice was narrowed down to two. For a moment I missed terribly the middle alternative. But the way led past the tennis court, and something about the way it lay there in the sun reassured me; the tape had loosened along the backline, the alleys were green with plantains and other weeds, and the net (installed in June and removed in September) sagged in the dry noon, and the whole place steamed with midday heat and hunger and emptiness. There was a choice of pie for dessert, and one was blueberry and one was apple, and the waitresses were the same country girls, there having been no passage of time, only the illusion of it as in a dropped curtain—the waitresses were still fifteen; their hair had been washed, that was the only difference—they had been to the movies and seen the pretty girls with the clean hair.

Summertime, oh summertime, pattern of life indelible, the fadeproof lake, the woods unshatterable, the pasture with the sweetfern and the juniper forever and ever, summer without end; this was the background, and the life along the shore was the design, the cottages with their innocent and tranquil design, their tiny docks with the flagpole and the American flag floating against the white clouds in the blue sky, the little paths over the roots of the trees leading from camp to camp and the paths leading back to the outhouses and the can of lime for sprinkling, and at the souvenir counters at the store the miniature birch-bark canoes and the post cards that showed things looking a little better than they looked. This was the American family at play, escaping the city heat, wondering whether the newcomers in the camp at the head of the cove were "common" or "nice," wondering whether it was true that the people who drove up for Sunday dinner at the farmhouse were turned away because there wasn't enough chicken.

It seemed to me, as I kept remembering all this, that those times and those summers had been infinitely precious and worth saving. There had been jollity and peace and goodness. The arriving (at the beginning of August) had been so big a business in itself, at the railway station the farm wagon drawn up, the first smell of the pine-laden air, the first glimpse of the smiling farmer, and the great importance of the trunks and your father's enormous authority in such matters, and the feel of the wagon under you for the long ten-mile haul, and at the top of the last long hill catching the first view of the lake after eleven months of not seeing this cherished body of water. The shouts and cries of the other campers when they saw you, and the trunks to be unpacked, to give up their rich burden. (Arriving was less exciting nowadays, when you sneaked up in your car and parked it under a tree near the camp and took out the bags and in five minutes it was all over, no fuss, no loud wonderful fuss about trunks.)

Peace and goodness and jollity. The only thing that was wrong now, really, was the sound of the place, an unfamiliar nervous sound of the outboard motors. This was the note that jarred, the one thing that would sometimes break the illusion and set the years moving. In those other summertimes all motors were inboard; and when they were at a little distance, the noise they made was a sedative, an ingredient of summer sleep. They were one-cylinder and two-cylinder engines, and some were make-and-break and some were jump-spark, but they all made a sleepy sound across the lake. The one-lungers throbbed and fluttered, and the twin-cylinder ones purred and purred, and that was a quiet sound too. But now the campers all had outboards. In the daytime, in the hot mornings, these motors made a petulant, irritable sound; at night, in the still evening when the afterglow lit the water, they whined about one's ears like mosquitoes. My boy loved our rented outboard, and his great desire was to achieve single-handed mastery over it, and authority, and he soon learned the trick of choking it a little (but not too much), and the adjustment of the needle valve. Watching him I would remember the things you could do with the old one-cylinder engine with the heavy flywheel, how you could have it eating out of your hand if you got really close to it spiritually. Motor boats in those days didn't have clutches, and you would make a landing by shutting off the motor at the proper time and coasting in with a dead rudder. But there was a way of reversing them, if you learned the trick, by cutting the switch and putting it on again exactly on the final dying revolution of the flywheel, so that it would kick back against compression and begin reversing. Approaching a dock in a strong following breeze, it was difficult to slow up sufficiently by the ordinary coasting method, and if a boy felt he had complete mastery over his motor, he was tempted to keep it running beyond its time and then reverse it a few feet from the dock. It took a cool nerve, because if you threw the switch a twentieth of a second too soon you would catch the flywheel when it still had speed enough to go up past center, and the boat would leap ahead, charging bull-fashion at the dock.

We had a good week at the camp. The bass were biting well and the sun shone endlessly, day after day. We would be tired at night and lie down in the accumulated heat of the little bedrooms after the long hot day and the breeze would stir almost imperceptibly outside and the smell of the swamp drift in through the rusty screens. Sleep would come easily and in the morning the red squirrel would be on the roof, tapping out his gay routine. I kept remembering everything, lying in bed in the mornings—the small steamboat that had a long rounded stern like the lip of a Ubangi, and how quietly she ran on the moonlight sails, when the older boys played their mandolins and the girls sang and we ate doughnuts dipped in sugar, and how sweet the music was on the water in the shining night, and what it had felt like to think about girls then. After breakfast we would go up to the store and the things were in the same place—the minnows in a bottle, the plugs and spinners disarranged and pawed over by the youngsters from the boys' camp, the fig newtons and the Beeman's gum. Outside, the road was tarred and cars stood in front of the store. Inside, all was just as it had always been, except there was more Coca Cola and not so much Moxie and root beer and birch beer and sarsaparilla. We would walk out with a bottle of pop apiece and sometimes the pop would backfire up our noses and hurt. We explored the streams, quietly, where the turtles slid off the sunny logs and dug their way into the soft bottom; and we lay on the town wharf and fed worms to the tame bass. Everywhere we went I had trouble making out which was I, the one walking at my side, the one walking in my pants.

One afternoon while we were there at that lake a thunderstorm came up. It was like the revival of an old melodrama that I had seen long ago with childish awe. The second-act climax of the drama of the electrical disturbance over a lake in America had not changed in any important respect. This was the big scene, still the big scene. The whole thing was so familiar, the first feeling of oppression and heat and a general air around camp of not wanting to go very far away. In midafternoon (it was all the same) a curious darkening of the sky, and a lull in everything that had made life tick; and then the way the boats suddenly swung the other way at their moorings with the coming of a breeze out of the new quarter, and the premonitory rumble. Then the kettle drum, then the snare, then the bass drum and cymbals, then crackling light against the dark, and the gods grinning and licking their chops in the hills. Afterward the calm, the rain steadily rustling in the calm lake, the return of light and hope and spirits, and the campers running out in joy and relief to go swimming in the rain, their bright cries perpetuating the deathless joke about how they were getting simply drenched, and the children screaming with delight at the new sensation of bathing in the rain, and the joke about getting drenched linking the generations in a strong indestructible chain. And the comedian who waded in carrying an umbrella.

When the others went swimming my son said he was going in too. He pulled his dripping trunks from the line where they had hung all through the shower, and wrung them out. Languidly, and with no thought of going in, I watched him, his hard little body, skinny and bare, saw him wince slightly as he pulled up around his vitals the small, soggy, icy garment. As he buckled the swollen belt suddenly my groin felt the chill of death.

# My Wood

## E.M. Forster

A few years ago I wrote a book which dealt in part with the difficulties of the English in India. Feeling that they would have had no difficulties in India themselves, the Americans read the book freely. The more they read it the better it made them feel, and a cheque to the author was the result. I bought a wood with the cheque. It is not a large wood—it contains scarcely any trees, and it is intersected, blast it, by a public footpath. Still, it is the first property that I have owned, so it is right that other people should participate in my shame, and should ask themselves, in accents that will vary in horror, this very important question: What is the effect of property upon the character? Don't let's touch economics; the effect of private ownership upon the community as a whole is another question—a more important question, perhaps, but another one. Let's keep to psychology. If you own things, what's their effect on you? What's the effect on me of my wood?

In the first place, it makes me feel heavy. Property does have this effect. Property produces men of weight, and it was a man of weight who failed to get into the Kingdom of Heaven. He was not wicked, that unfortunate millionaire in the parable, he was only stout; he stuck out in front, not to mention behind, and as he wedged himself this way and that in the crystalline entrance and bruised his well-fed flanks, he saw beneath him a comparatively slim camel passing through the eye of a needle and being woven into the robe of God. The Gospels all through couple stoutness and slowness. They point out what is perfectly obvious, yet seldom realized: that if you have a lot of things you cannot move about a lot, that furniture requires dusting, dusters require servants, servants require insurance stamps, and the whole tangle of them makes you think twice before you accept an invitation to dinner or go for a bathe in the Jordan. Sometimes the Gospels proceed further and say with Tolstoy that property is sinful; they approach the difficult ground of asceticism here,

From E.M. Forster, *Abinger Harvest*, London: Edward Arnold (Publishers) Ltd. (1936).

where I cannot follow them. But as to the immediate effects of property on people, they just show straightforward logic. It produces men of weight. Men of weight cannot, by definition, move like the lightning from the East unto the West, and the ascent of a fourteen-stone bishop into a pulpit is thus the exact antithesis of the coming of the Son of Man. My wood makes me feel heavy.

In the second place, it makes me feel it ought to be larger.

The other day I heard a twig snap in it. I was annoyed at first, for I thought that someone was blackberrying, and depreciating the value of the undergrowth. On coming nearer, I saw it was not a man who had trodden on the twig and snapped it, but a bird, and I felt pleased. My bird. The bird was not equally pleased. Ignoring the relation between us, it took fright as soon as it saw the shape of my face, and flew straight over the boundary hedge into a field, the property of Mrs. Henessy, where it sat down with a loud squawk. It had become Mrs. Henessy's bird. Something seemed grossly amiss here, something that would not have occurred had the wood been larger. I could not afford to buy Mrs. Henessy out, I dared not murder her, and limitations of this sort beset me on every side. Ahab did not want that vineyard—he only needed it to round off his property, preparatory to plotting a new curve—and all the land around my wood has become necessary to me in order to round off the wood. A boundary protects. But—poor little thing—the boundary ought in its turn to be protected. Noises on the edge of it. Children throw stones. A little more, and then a little more, until we reach the sea. Happy Canute! Happier Alexander! And after all, why should even the world be the limit of possession? A rocket containing a Union Jack, will, it is hoped, be shortly fired at the moon. Mars. Sirius. Beyond which . . . But these immensities ended by saddening me. I could not suppose that my wood was the destined nucleus of universal dominion—it is so very small and contains no mineral wealth beyond the blackberries. Nor was I comforted when Mrs. Henessy's bird took alarm for the second time and flew clean away from us all, under the belief that it belonged to itself.

In the third place, property makes its owner feel that he ought to do something to it. Yet he isn't sure what. A restlessness comes over him, a vague sense that he has a personality to express—the same sense which, without any vagueness, leads the artist to an act of creation. Sometimes I think I will cut down such trees as remain in the wood, at other times I want to fill up the gaps between them with new trees. Both impulses are pretentious and empty. They are not honest movements towards money-making or beauty. They spring from a foolish desire to express myself and from an inability to enjoy what I have got. Creation, property, enjoyment form a sinister trinity in the human mind. Creation and enjoyment are both very very good, yet they are often unattainable without a material basis, and at such moments property pushes itself in as a substitute, saying, 'Accept me instead—I'm good enough for all three.' It is not enough. It is, as Shakespeare said of lust, 'The expense of spirit in a waste of shame': it is 'Before, a joy proposed; behind, a dream.' Yet we don't know how to shun it. It is forced on us by our economic system as the alternative to starvation. It is also forced on us by an internal defect in the soul, by the feeling that in property may lie the germs of self-development and of exquisite or heroic deeds. Our life on earth is, and ought to be, material and carnal. But we have not yet learned to manage our materialism and carnality properly; they are still entangled with the desire for ownership, where (in the words of Dante) 'Possession is one with loss.'

And this brings us to our fourth and final point: the blackberries.

Blackberries are not plentiful in this meagre grove, but they are easily seen from the public footpath which traverses it, and all too easily gathered. Foxgloves, too—people will pull up the foxgloves, and ladies of an educational tendency even grub for toadstools to show them on the Monday in class. Other ladies, less educated, roll down the bracken in the arms of their gentlemen friends. There is paper, there are tins. Pray, does my wood belong to me or doesn't it? And, if it does, should I not own it best by allowing no one else to walk there? There is a wood near Lyme Regis, also cursed by a public footpath, where the owner has not hesitated on this point. He has built high stone walls each side of the path, and has spanned it by bridges, so that the public circulate like termites while he gorges on the blackberries unseen. He really does own his wood, this able chap. Dives in Hell did pretty well, but the gulf dividing him from Lazarus could be traversed by vision, and nothing traverses it here. And perhaps I shall come to this in time. I shall wall in and fence out until I really taste the sweets of property. Enormously stout, endlessly avaricious, pseudo-creative, intensely selfish, I shall weave upon my forehead the quadruple crown of possession until those nasty Bolshies come and take it off again and thrust me aside into the outer darkness.

# The
# Street-Car
# Conductor

## Hugh MacLennan

The street-car rattling westward was almost empty, for it was the slack hour of the early afternoon. The conductor was half-sitting, half-standing in his cage at the back of the car. On his cuff were six tarnished service stripes. On his face was an expression of unfathomable calm.

A bell buzzed. A passenger rose, moved down the aisle to the rear of the car and stood by the conductor's cage. This citizen was short, square, elderly and decisive. He carried a worn brief-case in his left hand; the fingers of his right drummed firmly on the polished steel rail of the conductor's cage. His grey face was stern and his wide mouth had formed itself into the thin straight line of a man who has waited too long to buy a set of false teeth. He fixed the conductor with accusing eyes and spoke in a harsh, clear voice.

"*La situation internationale est terrible!* "
"*Ouais,*" the conductor said, not turning his head.
"*L'Angleterre est finie!* "
"*Ouais.*"
"*La France est manifestement finie!* "
"*Ouais.*"
"*La troisième guerre vient pour sûr!* "
"*Ouais.*"
"*Nous sommes donc tous finis!* "
"*Ouais.*"

From *Thirty and Three*. Copyright ©1954 by Hugh MacLennan, renewed 1982. Reprinted by permission of Russell & Volkening, Inc. as agents for the author.

The car stopped, the doors opened, the citizen stepped out, the doors closed, the car jerked forward, and as I looked at the conductor's quarter-profile from where I sat near the end of the long bench at the back of the car, I wondered why most of us take conductors for granted, seeing them but not seeing them, as though they were mechanical fixtures of their cars.

For thirty years, perhaps longer, this man had been half-sitting, half-standing in the sterns of street-cars in such a posture that he had always to watch the world recede from him as the car advanced. Summer and winter, fall and spring, millions of citizens had jostled him as his trams carried them to and from their work, to and from their sports and business *coups* and parties and love affairs. Girls with shining eyes had stared into the rapt faces of boys. Young married men with pay cheques in their pockets had stood cheerfully in the jam beside him thinking how happy they were going to make their wives that evening. Desperate men had plotted suicide and women in middle age had wondered how much longer they could stand it. The mothers of two generations had pushed children past him while they fumbled for tickets, and behind him old ladies had smiled when young men had risen to offer them seats. Billions of loves, hates, lusts, fears, hopes, boredoms and little private amusements had cavorted through the busy brains surrounding this man. And always *la situation internationale* had been *terrible*.

For thirty years, perhaps longer, this man had lived in the midst of it. In the headlines of newspapers tucked under arms or crunched before faces the epic of the twentieth century had been displayed in all editions and in both languages of the city. But because the papers were usually folded in the middle he had seen only half the headlines recording fires and floods, murders and rescues, rising and collapsing governments, and the land, sea and air battles of three wars. In the splintering anxieties of an apocalyptic epoch he had remained half-sitting, half-standing at his post in the stern of his car. On the morning in 1940 when France fell he was passing out his transfers. When the Third Reich dissolved in smoke and bomb-bursts he was calling out *Ghee—Guy—Côte des Neiges*. When the Chinese invaded Korea the world was still receding from him. Through all the tempests of his century he had ridden the street-cars of Montreal, half-sitting, half-standing, with an expression as mysterious, as remote, as profound as that of a Buddha in the jungle-infested ruins of Ankor Vat.

The car began to sway as it ran the straight passage of Sherbrooke Street past Westmount Park; it staggered a little as it took the curving slope towards Decarie; then it settled down for its run through Notre Dame de Grâce. Fifteen to twenty years ago this district had been loud and gay with the voices of children and adolescents, for it was the part of the city where young couples had moved to raise their families after the Old War. Now several thousands of those who had grown up in the nineteen-thirties had been killed in the Second War, and most of their brothers and sisters had married and moved away. The people on the sidewalks seemed to be in late middle age. For Notre Dame de Grâce *la situation internationale* had indeed been *terrible*. . .

We get into the habit of steeling ourselves for bad news, I thought, with the echo of the dour citizen's words still in my mind. The moment we stop worrying about something, we suspect we are losing our grip on reality. Troubles will arise—what would we do without them? but whatever evil we see in the near future can hardly rival the evils this conductor has been carrying about in the headlines of the papers his passengers have been reading over the past thirty years.

It was fashionable during the nineteen-thirties to talk of the death-wish that ruled the world. By feeding it with the incense of our fears we fattened it into a monster more frightening than Hitler's armies. Today we no longer consider it our master. Today we are tired of its company, and scorn ourselves for having invited it into our homes. But its strange and ghastly reign during the first forty years of the twentieth century will give historians of the future an opportunity to say some pretty nasty things about us.

When we first became aware, through Freud, of this thing in all of us which he called the death-wish—this thing which caused the dour citizen to assert with such relish *nous sommes tous finis*—it seemed romantic and exciting. In 1914 Rupert Brooke, most innocent of twentieth-century poets, sang of giving the world away and pouring out "the red, sweet wine of youth". The first of our wars gave many millions the opportunity of doing so. In the nineteen-twenties the face of the death-wish was painted with a false, bright gaiety, and young novelists like Ernest Hemingway began to glorify bullfights and hangovers, while older poets like T.S. Eliot chanted of the wasteland and hollow men with a loving eloquence which proclaimed that it was only in corruption and impotence that we could discover the seeds of beauty. The mask of the death-wish was weary and sophisticated in the first days of the depression when the blonde in Noel Coward's *Cavalcade* swung her pretty legs from the piano top and crooned "Twentieth Century Blues", asking what there was to strive for, love or keep alive for. By the late nineteen-thirties the death-wish had lost both its charm and its sophistication. Now it wore the mask of staring fear. It was distorted with fear on the day Chamberlain and Daladier flew back from Munich, when the populations of the two most civilized nations in the world cried out in rejoicing for the deal Hitler had made to destroy them.

The death-wish did more than make us act like cowards. It hypnotized us as though we were birds cowering before snakes. It sucked potency from our men and charm from our women. (Remember, those of you who can, the styles of the 1920's?) It made the old and rich ask only to be let alone. It persuaded the young and poor that every man in authority was their enemy. It made us pray for security instead of for courage. And when we discovered that we had courage nevertheless, we no longer talked about the death-wish, for by that time another generation had come along, and they took Freud for granted. But the old slogans glorifying security still had enough power to win elections. Worst of all, they persuaded Stalin, as they had persuaded Hitler, that we were ripe to be picked . . .

The tram began swaying again as it left Royal Avenue with the additional freight of three small boys who had been let out early at Lower Canada College. The conductor, half-sitting, half-standing, was concerned with his own cavernous thoughts as he watched the brick apartment buildings and small shops move away to his rear. From the folded front of my newspaper half of Winston Churchill's face stared upward. He looked older, but his expression was not much different from what it had been fifteen years ago when so many of us called him irresponsible merely because he was brave. The tendons in his neck were more prominent, but not much more than they had been in the days when he took the death-wish by the throat and choked it, and then turned and breathed some of his own courage into us as God breathed life into Adam.

"Were you working on this same route fifteen years ago?" I asked the conductor, wondering if he would know that my question was addressed to him.

"*Ouais.*"

Fifteen years ago Hemingway, our hero among the novelists of that time, had written that he was always embarrassed by words like "sacred", "glorious" and "sacrifice", for "the things that were glorious had no glory and the sacrifices were like the stockyards of Chicago if nothing was done with the meat except to bury it". Hemingway had written these words and we all knew that he himself was a brave man. We thought we knew everything in those days. We knew that Hitler and Mussolini had to be stopped and at the same time we knew that wars decide nothing. So we voted to stop Hitler and Mussolini and at the same time we voted to reduce the budget for armaments. *La situation internationale?* Today we shrug our shoulders and say, "But what do you expect?" Or merely, "*Ouais.*"

The tram and its impassive guardian continued to sway onward and I got up as I saw my stop a few blocks ahead. The acres of apartments on the old Benny Farm slid past and sunlight glinted on snow in open spaces. Again we were in a district filled with children.

In Red River suits they played in the snow or were drawn on sleds by their mothers (younger mothers these days than when we were married, young enough to enjoy their families vigorously and to remain young when their children grow up, so that in their early forties they will be free to make full use of what the world has taught them). The tram was nearing my stop and I reached up to press the bell. I stood beside the conductor and spoke to him again.

"Things aren't so bad these days."

"*Ouais*," he said.

The car stopped, the doors opened and I stepped out into the street. The doors closed, the car jerked forward and I stood watching the conductor, half-sitting, half-standing, his image blurred behind the glass, riding off into the west.

# The Creature from the Marsh

## Loren Eiseley

### I

The only thing strange about me is my profession. I happen to be one of those few persons who pursue the farther history of man on the planet earth, what Darwin once called "the great subject." But my business is not with the formal art of the history books. Take, for example, today.

Today I have been walking in the ruins of the city. The city still moves, it is true, the air drills ring against iron, and I am aware of laughter and of feet hurrying by at the noon hour. Nevertheless the city is in ruins. This is what the trained eye makes of it. It stands here in the morning sun while rust flakes the steel rails and the leaves of innumerable autumns blow mistily through the ribs of skyscrapers and over the fallen brick work lies a tangle of morning glories. I have seen this before in the dead cities of Mexico—the long centuries wavering past with the curious distortion of things seen through deep sea water. Even the black snake gliding down the steps of the cathedral seems a repetition, past and future being equally resolvable in the curious perspective of the archaeological eye.

But it was not for this that I hurried out to walk in the streets of the city. I wanted to find a symbol, something that would stand for us when the time came, something that might be proud after there was no stone upon another—some work of art, perhaps, or a gay conceit that the rains had not tarnished, something that would tell our story to whatever strange minds might come groping there.

I think I must have walked miles in those ruins. I studied a hundred

Reprinted with the permission of Charles Scribner's Sons from *The Night Country* by Loren Eiseley, copyright © 1971 Loren Eiseley.

shop windows. I weighed with a quarter century of digging experience the lasting qualities of metal, stone, and glass. I hesitated over the noble inscriptions upon public buildings, while the rain dissolved in the locked containers the files of treaties and the betrayal of all human trust. I passed by the signs of coruscating heat and the wilted metal of huge guns. I found the china head of a doll in the metal of a baby carriage that my mind took hold of and considered carefully, though later I realized I stood by a living nursemaid in the Park.

I looked at tools, and at flowers in the windows of tenements. (They will creep out and grow, I thought.) And I heard a dog howl in the waste streets for the comforting hand of man. I saw the vacant, ashy leaves of books blow by, but I did not pick them up. There were dead television screens and the curious detached loneliness of telephone receivers whose broken wires still thrummed in the winds over the Sierra.

It will never do, I thought; there was more to us than this—with all the evil, with all the cruelty. I remembered an inscribed gold ring in a pawnshop window. "From Tom to Mary," it had read, "for always." It is back there, I thought; that might be it—there was love in us, things we spoke to each other in the evening or on deathbeds, the eyes frank at last. It might be there. I turned and hurried back.

But the little shop was gone, and finally I came up short at a place where stones had tumbled in a peculiar way, half sheltering a fallen window. There were bones there, and at first this made no sense because bones in exposed places do not last well, and there are so many of them finally that the meaning escapes you.

There was a broken sign LED—Fi—Av—. And among the bits of glass, a little cluster of feathers, and under a shattered pane, the delicate bones of a woman's hand that, dying, had reached wistfully out, caught there, when the time came.

Why not? I mused. The human hand, the hand is the story. I touched one of the long, graceful bones. It had come the evolutionary way up from far eons and watery abysses only to perish here.

There was a little restless stirring beside me.

So it died after all that effort, I thought on. Five hundred million years expended in order that the shining thread of life could die reaching after a little creation of feathers in the window of a shop. And why not? Even my antique reptilian eye had a feel for something, a kind of beauty here.

The tugging at my sleeve continued. The slow, affectionate voice of my wife said to me, "Wait here. I want to go in."

"Of course," I said, and took and squeezed her slender hand as I returned from some far place. "It will look becoming," I said. "I will stand here and watch."

"The gloves to match it are of green lizard skin," she exulted.

"That will look just right," I ventured, and did not quite know what I meant. "I will stand here and watch."

A swinging light like a warning at a railroad crossing began flashing in the darkness below consciousness. A bell began jangling. Then it subsided. My wife was pointing, for the benefit of an attentive clerk, at a little cluster of feathers in the window. I came forward then and beckoned hastily. "But why—?" she said. "Another day," I said, wiping my forehead. It was just that—"Another time," I promised and urged her quickly away.

It is the nature, you see, of the profession—the terrible *déjà vu* of the archaeologist, the memory that scans before and after. For instance, take the case of the black skull, a retreat, some might say, in another direction.

## II

The skull was black when they brought it to me. It was black from the irons and acids and mineral replacements of ice-age gravels. It was polished and worn and gleaming from the alterations of unnumbered years. It had made strange journeys after the death of its occupant; it had moved with glacial slowness in the beds of rivers; it had been tumbled by floods and, becoming an object of grisly beauty, had been picked up and passed from hand to hand by men the individual had never seen in life.

Finally it was brought to me.

It was my duty to tell them about the skull.

It was my professional duty to clothe these bones once more with the faint essence of a personality, to speak of a man or a woman, young or old, as the bones might tell the story. It was my task to read the racial features in a forgotten face, stare deep into the hollow sockets through which had once passed in endless procession the days and seasons and the shed tears of long ago.

The woman had been young. I could tell them that. I could tell them she had once fallen or been struck and that after a long time the bone had mended and she had recovered—how, it was difficult to say, for it had been a dangerous and compound fracture. Today such a wound would mean months of immobilization in a hospital. This woman had survived without medical attention through the endless marchings and journeyings of the hunters' world. Even the broken orbit of the left eye had dropped by a quarter of an inch—a serious disfigurement. Nevertheless she had endured and lived on toward some doom that had come fast upon her but was not written in the bones. It was, in all likelihood, a death by violence. Her skull had not been drawn from a grave. It had come from beneath the restless waters of a giant river that is known to keep its secrets well.

They asked me for the time of the events, and again, obediently, I went down that frail ladder which stretches below us into the night of time. I went slowly, by groping deductions and the hesitant intuitions of long experience that only scholars know. I passed through ages where water was wearing away the shapes of river pebbles into crystalline sand and the only sound in the autumn thickets was the gathering of south-flying birds. Somewhere in the neighborhood of the five thousandth millennium—I could place it no closer than that—the ladder failed me. The river was still there but larger—an enormous rolling waste of water and marshes out of which rose a vast October moon.

They interrupted me then, querulously, asking if archaeologists could do no better than this, and was it not true that there were new and clever methods by which physicists could call the year in the century and mark the passage of time by the tick of atoms in the substance of things. And I said, yes, within limits it was true, but that the methods were not always usable, and that the subtle contaminations possible among radioactive objects sometimes defeated our attempts.

At this point they shook their heads unwillingly, for, as I quickly saw, they had the passion of modern men for the precision of machines and disliked vagueness of any sort. But the skull lay there on the table between us, and over it one man lingered, fascinated in spite of himself. I knew what he was thinking: Where am I going? When shall I become like this?

I heard this in his mind for just an instant while I stared across at him from among my boxes of teeth and flint arrowheads that had grown chalky and dull with the passage of long centuries in the ground.

"Thank you," the visitor said finally, moving after his party to the door. He was, I saw, unsure for what it was he thanked me.

"You are quite welcome," I said, still returning slowly from that waste of forgotten water over which the birds of another century cried dolefully, so that I could hear them keening in my head. Like the man who asks a medium to bring back some whimpering memoryless ghost and make it speak out of a living mouth for the amusement of a group of curiosity seekers, he may have felt remorse. At any rate, he nodded uncertainly and fled.

I was the instrument. I had made this journey a hundred times for students who scrawled their initials on my skulls, a hundred times for reporters who wanted sensational accounts of monkey-men, a hundred times for people who came up at the end of lectures and asked, "How much money are the bones worth, doctor? Are they easy to find?"

In spite of this I have continued to make these journeys. It is old habit now. I go back into the past alone. I would do so if I fled my job and sought safety in some obscure room. My sense of time is so heightened that I can feel the frost at work in stones, the first creeping advance of grass in a deserted street. I have stood by the carved sarcophagi of dead knights in a European cathedral, men seven hundred years away from us with their steel and their ladies, and from that point striven to hurl the mind still backward into the wilderness where man coughs bestially and vanishes into the shape of beasts.

I cannot say I am a student of the dates in the history books. My life is mostly occupied with caves filled up and drifted over with the leaves of ten thousand thousand autumns. My speciality is the time when man was changing into man. But, like a river that twists, evades, hesitates through slow miles, and then leaps violently down over a succession of cataracts, man can be called a crisis animal. Crisis is the most powerful element in his definition. Of his entire history, this he understands the least. Only man has continued to turn his own definition around upon his tongue until, in the end, he has looked outside of nature to something invisible to any eye but his own. Long ago, this emotion was well expressed in the Old Testament. "Oh Lord," exclaimed the prophet Jeremiah, "I know that the way of man is not in himself." Therefore, I would add, as a modern evolutionist, "the way" only lies through man and has to be sought beyond him. It was this that led to a very remarkable experience.

### III

"The greatest prize of all," once confessed the British plant explorer F. Kingdon Ward, "is the skull of primitive man." Ward forgot one thing: there are other clues to primitive men than those confined to skulls. The bones of fossil men are few because the earth tolerated them in scant numbers. We call them missing links on the road to ourselves. A little less tooth here, a little more brain there, and you can see them changing toward ourselves in that long historyless time when the great continental ice sheets ebbed and flowed across the northern continents. Like all the students of that age, I wanted to find a missing link in human history. That is what this record is about, for I stumbled on the track of one.

Some men would maintain that a vague thing called atmosphere accounts for such an episode as I am about to relate, that there are houses that demand a murder and wait patiently until the murderer and his victim arrive, that there are great cliffs that draw the potential suicide from afar or mountains of so austere a nature that they write their message on the face of a man who looks up at them. This all may be. I do not deny it. But when I encountered the footprint in the mud of that remote place I think the thing that terrified me most was the fact that I knew to whom it belonged and yet I did not want to know him. He was a stranger to me and remains so to this day. Because of a certain knowledge I had, however, he succeeded in impressing himself upon me in a most insidious manner. I have never been the same since the event took place and often at night I start up sweating and think uncannily that the creature is there with me in the dark. If the sense of his presence grows, I switch on the light, but I never look into the mirror. This is a matter of old habit with me.

First off, though, we must get straight what we mean by a missing link.

A missing link is a day in the life of a species that is changing its form and habits, just as, on a smaller scale, one's appearance and behavior at the age of five are a link in one's development to an adult man or woman. The individual person may have changed and grown but still the boy or girl of many years ago is linked to the present by a long series of steps. And if one is really alive and not already a living fossil, one will go on changing till the end of one's life and perhaps be the better for it. The term "missing link" was coined because some of the physical links in the history of man as a species are lost, and those people who, like myself, are curious about the past look for them.

My album is the earth, and the pictures in it are faded and badly torn and have to be pieced together by detective work. If one thinks of oneself at five years of age, one may get a thin wisp of disconnected memory pictures. By contrast, the past of a living species is without memory except as that past has written its physical record in vestigial organs like the appendix or a certain pattern on our molar teeth. To eke out what those physical stigmata tell us, we have to go grubbing about in caves and gravel for the bones of very ancient men. If one can conceive of the trouble an archaeologist might have in locating one's remains a half-million years from now, supposing they still existed, one will get an idea of the difficulties involved in finding traces of man before his bones were crowded together in cities and cemeteries.

I was wandering inland along a sunken shore when the thing happened—the thing I had dreamed of so long. In other words, I got a clue to man. The beaches on that coast I had come to visit are treacherous and sandy and the tides are always shifting things about among the mangrove roots. It is not a place to which I would willingly return and you will get no bearings from me. Anyway, what it was I found there could be discovered on any man's coast if he looked sharp for it. I had come to that place with other things in mind, and a notion of being alone. I was tired. I wanted to lie in the sun or clamber about like an animal in the swamps and the forest. To secure such rest from the turmoil of a modern city is the most difficult thing in the world to accomplish and I have only achieved it twice: once in one of the most absolute deserts in the world and again in this tropical marsh.

By day and night strange forms of life scuttled and gurgled underfoot or oozed wetly along outthrust branches; luminous tropical insects blundered by in the dark like the lamps of hesitant burglars. Overhead, on higher ground, another life shrieked distantly or was expectantly still in the treetops. Somehow, alone as I was, I got to listening as if all that world were listening, waiting for something to happen. The trees drooped a little lower listening, the tide lurked and hesitated on the beach, and even a tree snake dropped a loop and hung with his face behind a spider web, immobile in the still air.

A world like that is not really natural, or (the thought strikes one later) perhaps it really is, only more so. Parts of it are neither land nor sea and so everything is moving from one element to another, wearing uneasily the queer transitional bodies that life adopts in such places. Fish, some of them, come out and breathe air and sit about watching you. Plants take to eating insects, mammals go back to the water and grow elongate like fish, crabs climb trees. Nothing stays put where it began because everything is constantly climbing in, or climbing out, of its unstable environment.

Along drowned coasts of this variety you only see, in a sort of speeded-up way, what is true of the whole world and everything upon it: the Darwinian world of passage, of missing links, of beetles with soldered, flightless wings, of snakes with vestigial feet dragging slowly through the underbrush. Everything is marred and maimed and slightly out of focus— everything in the world. As for man, he is no different from the rest. His back aches, he ruptures easily, his women have difficulties in childbirth— all because he has struggled up upon his hind legs without having achieved a perfect adjustment to his new posture.

On this particular afternoon, I came upon a swamp full of huge waterlilies where I had once before ventured. The wind had begun to rise and rain was falling at intervals. As far as I could see, giant green leaves velvetly impervious to water were rolling and twisting in the wind. It was a species of lily in which part of the leaves projected on stalks for a short distance above the water, and as they rolled and tossed the whole swamp flashed and quivered from the innumerable water drops that were rolling around and around like quicksilver in the great cupped leaves. Everything seemed flickering and changing as if in some gigantic illusion, but so soft was the green light and so delicate the brushing of the leaves against each other that the whole effect was quite restful, as though one could be assured that nothing was actually tangible or real and no one in his senses would want it to be, as long as he could sway and nod and roll reflecting water drops about over the surface of his brain.

Just as I finally turned away to climb a little ridge I found the first footprint. It was in a patch of damp, exposed mud and was pointed away from the water as though the creature had emerged directly out of the swamp and was heading up the shore toward the interior. I had thought I was alone, and in that place it was wise to know one's neighbors. Worst of all, as I stood studying the footprint, and then another, still heading up the little rise, it struck me that though undoubtedly human the prints were different in some indefinable way. I will tell you once more that this happened on the coast of another country in a place where form itself is an illusion and no shape of man or beast is totally impossible. I crouched anxiously in the mud while all about the great leaves continued to rotate on their stems and to flash their endlessly rolling jewels.

But there were these footprints. They did not disappear. As I fixed the lowermost footprint with every iota of scientific attention I could muster, it became increasingly apparent that I was dealing with some transitional form of man. The arch, as revealed in the soft mud, was low and flat and implied to the skilled eye an inadequate adjustment to the upright posture. This, in its turn, suggested certain things about the spine and the nature of the skull. It was only then, I think, that the full import of my discovery came to me.

Good Lord, I thought consciously for the first time, the thing is alive. I had spent so many years analyzing the bones of past ages or brooding over lizard tracks turned to stone in remote epochs that I had never contemplated this possibility before. The thing was alive and it was human. I looked uneasily about before settling down into the mud once more. One could make out that the prints were big but what drew my fascinated eye from the first was the nature of the second toe. It was longer than the big toe, and as I crawled excitedly back and forth between the two wet prints in the open mud, I saw that there was a remaining hint of prehensile flexibility about them.

Most decidedly, as a means of ground locomotion this foot was transitional and imperfect. Its loose, splayed aspect suggested inadequate protection against sprains. That second toe was unnecessarily long for life on the ground, although the little toe was already approximating the rudimentary condition so characteristic of modern man. Could it be that I was dealing with an unreported living fossil, an archaic ancestral survival? What else could be walking the mangrove jungle with a foot that betrayed clearly the marks of ancient intimacy with the arboreal attic, an intimacy so long continued that now, after hundreds of thousands of years of ground life, the creature had squiggled his unnecessarily long toes about in the mud as though an opportunity to clutch at something had delighted his secret soul.

I crouched by the footprint and thought. I remembered that comparisons with the living fauna, whenever available, are good scientific procedure and a great aid to precise taxonomy. I sat down and took off my shoes.

I had never had much occasion to look critically at my own feet before. In modern man they are generally encased in shoes—something that still suggests a slight imperfection in our adaptations. After all, we don't normally find it necessary to go about with our hands constantly enclosed in gloves. As I sat contemplating and comparing my feet with the footprints, a faintly disturbing memory floated hazily across my mind. It had involved a swimming party many years before at the home of one of the most distinguished comparative anatomists in the world. As we had sat on the bench alongside his pool, I had glanced up suddenly and caught him staring with what had seemed unnecessary fascination at my feet. I remembered now that he had blushed a deep pink under his white hair and had diverted my inquiring glance deftly to the scenery about us.

Why I should have remembered the incident at all was unclear to me. I thought of the possibility of getting plaster casts of a footprint and I also debated whether I should attempt to trail the creature farther up the slope toward which he appeared to have been headed. It was no moment for hesitation. Still, I did hesitate. The uneasy memory grew stronger, and a thought finally struck me. A little sheepishly and with a glance around to see that I was not observed, I lowered my own muddy foot into the footprint. It fitted.

I stood there contemplatively clutching, but this time consciously, the mud in my naked toes. I was the dark being on that island shore whose body carried the marks of its strange passage. I was my own dogging Man Friday, the beast from the past who had come with weapons through the marsh. The wind had died and the great green leaves with their rolling jewels were still. The mistake I had made was the mistake of all of us.

The story of man was not all there behind us in the caves of remote epochs. Even our physical bodies gave evidence that the change was not completed. As for our minds, they were still odd compounds of beast and saint. But it was not by turning back toward the marsh out of which we had come that the truly human kingdom was to be possessed and entered—that kingdom dreamed of in many religions and spoken of in many barbarous tongues. A philosopher once said in my presence, "The universe is a series of leaping sparks—everything else is interpretation." But what, I hesitated, was man's interpretation to be?

I drew a foot out of the little steaming swamp that sucked at it. The air hung heavily about me. I listened as the first beast might have listened who came from the water up the shore and did not return again to his old element. Everything about me listened in turn and seemed to be waiting for some decision on my part. I swayed a moment on my unstable footing.

Then, warily, I stepped higher up the shore and let the water and the silt fill in that footprint to make it, a hundred million years away, a fossil sign of an unknown creature slipping from the shadows of a marsh toward something else that awaited him. I had found the missing link. He walked on misshapen feet. The stones hurt him and his belly sagged. There were dreams like Christmas ornaments in his head, intermingled with an ancient malevolent viciousness. I knew because I was the missing link, but for the first time I sensed where I was going.

I have said I never look into the mirror. It is a matter of old habit now. If that other presence grows too oppressive I light the light and read.

# Terms and Topics

## TERMS

1. **Vocabulary, Section I:** acrimonious, apocalyptic, asceticism, avaricious, balking, carnality, coruscating, destitute, dolefully, ensconced, giddy, grisly, grossly, hierarchical, ignoble, impassive, impervious, incessant, indelible, insidious, irrevocable, languidly, malevolent, meagre, meticulous, paranoia, paraphernalia, pensively, petulant, placidity, premonitory, pretentious, primeval, querulously, rudimentary, solicitous, squander, succulent, supple, tangible, taxonomy, teeming, tranquil, turmoil, vernacular, vestigial.

2. **Formal, informal, colloquial, slang** Think of these so-called "levels" of diction or style as occurring on a spectrum. One point on the spectrum is not intrinsically better (or worse) than another; rather each is right, or appropriate, for a given subject, audience, and purpose. Sharpen your sense of the distinctions between them as you read and write. Most writing today uses a relatively informal style. But for what kind of occasion would a relatively formal style be most appropriate? or a colloquial style? Can you think of an occasion for which you would want to mix formal diction and slang? Can you find any instances of such a mixture in the essays in this book?

3. **Synecdoche** A figurative use of language in which a part is made to stand for a whole, or sometimes a whole for a part. For example we speak of workers as "hands" or, slangily, of a car as "wheels"; the word "Ottawa" often means "the government" which is located there. Synecdoche is essentially a form of **metonymy**, in which one of a thing's attributes, or a cause or effect of it, or something associated with it, in fact or in fancy, is made to stand for it, as when we say

84

"crown" when referring to the Queen or her government. When White says he has become a "salt-water man" he is not identifying himself with the sea metaphorically; rather he is declaring his literal association with it and for the moment letting that connection stand metonymically for his whole self. And when he refers to "the road under our sneakers," the word *sneakers*, though literally apt, also stands in place of "feet" or even "us," the whole bodies above the feet. When MacLennan writes that the new generation "took Freud for granted," the name *Freud* refers not so much to the man as to his works, his theories, his influence. Dillard gets a little metonymic twist by referring to Hollins Pond as "a remarkable piece of shallowness." Much descriptive writing is essentially metonymic, in that an author selects certain details from the great number available and uses them to stand for, suggest, or evoke the total reality of which they are a part, as when Mukherjee writes of "the walls" and "the accouterments of Ballygunge life" outside them: "hawkers, beggars, loiterers, squatters, sleepers, cows and pariahs, cars, taxis, buses, mini-buses, cycles, rickshaws, bullock carts, and heedless pedestrians. Inside," she adds, "there is greenery, flowers, a studied calm." Metonymy is often considered a form of metaphorical language, but it is better understood as fundamentally different, for whereas the effect of metaphor depends partly on the difference, the distance, between two things that are nonetheless being equated with each other (the ship and the plough, the weasel's teeth and the plug), metonymy depends on their contiguity, their sameness, their close association with each other: "shallowness" is an actual feature of the pond; "walls" are a prominent physical part of the scene.

4. *Personification*   A form of metaphorical language in which human attributes are ascribed to something nonhuman—usually something inanimate or abstract. White assumes, about the camp as he remembers it, "that the tarred road would have found it out," as if the road could think and seek out its victim. He provides the rowboat with a "chin" under which it can be chuck[ed]" by the waves, themselves thus personified. Forster refers to the boundary of his wood as a "poor little thing" that needs protection, as if it were a helpless child. Haig Brown's fly conducts a "cunning search of likely places" to find a fish. In a more complicated metaphor, but one depending basically on personification, Eiseley writes of "mountains of so austere a nature that they write their message on the face of a man who looks up at them." Dylan Thomas refers to "the carol-singing sea." (Since Thomas was also a major poet, it isn't surprising to find his prose filled with metaphors of various kinds.) Animate creatures can, in effect, also be personified, as when Forster describes the bird as having "the belief that it belonged to itself." And the conclusion of Fisher's reminis-

cence includes a kind of personification when she speaks of "our hearts' palates"—even though the hearts are, strictly speaking, parts of human beings.

5. **Paradox**  A statement that is seemingly illogical, self-contradictory, or otherwise absurd, but that is somehow actually or at least possibly true. Many proverbs, for example, express paradoxes: slow but sure wins the race; the shortest way round is the longest way home; he who cannot obey cannot command. Shakespeare's "Sweet are the uses of adversity" (*As You Like It*) is another. It is paradoxical, yet true, that the best person for a particular job might be the one who knows least about it, or that a difficult task often makes one do better work than if the task were easy.

6. **Rhetorical question**  A question that does not expect an answer, because the answer is implicit in the question or in the context. Such a question is thus for rhetorical effect only.

7. **Subject, thesis**  A *subject*, or a *topic* (a term often used to designate a narrowed-down subject area), is what is being written about; a *thesis* is a proposition about a subject which governs what a writer says about it. For example, a subject such as "modern travel" could have any number of theses: "Travel by ship is more romantic than travel by air," "Travel is safer today than it used to be," "Sometimes planning a trip is more fun than the actual travelling," and so on. But a thesis need not be so explicitly argumentative—for example, "Travel is broadening." Good writers almost always state their theses in some way, usually near either the beginning or the end of an essay—and often in both places. A thesis may, however, be partly or even entirely implicit. Look for the thesis in each of these essays. Make up several subjects of your own and then construct several possible theses for each.

8. **Subjective, objective**  These adjectives, as they apply here, designate opposite qualities of a piece of writing or of a writer's attitude. *Objective* means independent of the mind, free of any influence by the attitudes, emotions, or special interests of the writer; *subjective* means just the opposite. An objective writer could be said to be writing from a detached point of view. Subjectivity or objectivity is almost always a matter of degree: one is relatively subjective or objective at any given time. Even a camera can lie.

9. **Parallellism**  Parallel or repeated structure or phrasing, within a sentence or in successive sentences or paragraphs, to strengthen coherence and to create rhetorical effects, for example through emphasis. Parallelism obviously also affects rhythm.

# TOPICS: On Individual Essays

### JOHN UPDIKE   "Central Park"

1. Most of the details Updike lists are basically simple. Which ones would you call relatively complex? What makes them so?

2. Point out all the metaphors in this piece. Are there many? How do they work? What effects does each produce? Is the final item metaphorical? Who is Giuseppi Mazzini? Is treating his statue as if it were alive an instance of personification? Could the whole piece be considered an example of metonymy, depending for much of its effect on the process of association that goes on in a reader's mind? Could it be thought of along with those in section II, "Writing to Reveal"? What does it reveal about the place described? about the describer?

3. In 1956 the word "colored" was standard. When and why did it change? Is it still considered acceptable? What term would you use?

4. Updike's piece is proof that, to the observant eye, there are things all around us interesting enough to think about and write about. Try using his technique. Go for a walk. Make a descriptive list of the things you see. Or describe one of the following by assembling observed details: a shopping mall, a fast-food restaurant, a public beach, the view from a bridge, a post office, a downtown bus-stop during rush hour. Will you use every detail you record, or will you select from them? What principle of selection might you use? Will you let them stand in the order in which they came to you, or will you try to make some kind of pattern out of the sights you see? Use some metaphors, perhaps even personification.

### GEORGE JOHNSTON   "The Site at Kvivik"

1. Is Johnston trying to convey anything more than his immediate impressions? Do his descriptions enable you to visualize what he's describing, or do you wish there were accompanying photographs? Is his interest that of an archaeologist exploring a site? Is there a focus, or does it all seem random and arbitrary? Although at first this may seem to be an extract from an objective journal, written virtually on the spot, think about what Johnston manages to evoke: Think of the contrast between past and present, between the heroic age of the Vikings, with their ceremony, ritual, and tradition, and the modern age, with its cars, its vacuum cleaners, and its NATO bases. And think of old Gragas, who seems somehow to be and behave like a relic of the past living on into the present, like a living counterpart of the derelict and ruined buildings. What does it all suggest about the meaning or importance of time and age?

2. Why does Johnston not tell us Gragas's name until some time after introducing him? What is the effect of Johnston's shifting back and forth between past and present tense? Try using that technique yourself.

3. Johnston is a poet. How then do you account for there being so little metaphor in this piece? Are there other kinds of evidence of the poet's way of looking at things? Do the references to the weather work in a way analogous to metaphor?

4. The next time you travel to an unfamiliar place and meet new people—even if it's just a neighbourhood that's new to you—record your impressions in some sort of journal. Feel free to use minor or fragmentary sentences, as both Johnston and Updike do; but develop your material beyond a mere list, like Updike's, into a more coherent discourse, like Johnston's.

### DYLAN THOMAS   "Memories of Christmas"

1. Is *bombilating* a good word for the context? What is a *golliwog*? What is the point of the allusion to Pompeii? What are *trolls*? Is Thomas right about teddy-bears?

2. How does Thomas achieve the tone or outlook of a child without sounding childish? Consider for example his sentence structures.

3. Analyze the unusual metaphors at the beginning of the second paragraph. How do they work? Point out some metaphors elsewhere in the essay. Make up some metaphors imitating Thomas's.

4. What is the effect of the word *those* near the beginning of the first sentence (or paragraph)? What attitudes toward the writer and his subject does it virtually force a reader to adopt?

5. Does Thomas's essay have any "meaning" beyond evoking the past in a pleasant way? If so, how does he bring it out? Is the tone nostalgic? Does he avoid sentimentality?

6. To what extent does Thomas develop the other characters he mentions? Can you visualize them? Is it important?

7. Thomas was fond of compound adjectives. Examine some of them to see how much he achieved with how few words. Does he anywhere seem to you to overdo it? Does the style anywhere call too much attention to itself? Or do even the more striking turns of phrase contribute to the effect in justifiable ways?

8. Recall some recurring occasion of childhood—Christmas, birthdays, family reunions, camping holidays…— and describe those features that you have found particularly memorable.

9. Describe some setting that you remember from your childhood. Use as much metaphor and conscious rhythm as you feel the prose will

bear; maybe even try a string of compound adjectives. Use as much narration as you wish, and put as many people into your scene as you need to create the effect you want. Does your piece have a thesis, even if only an implicit one?

### M.F.K. FISHER  "A Thing Shared"

1. Fisher is writing in 1943 about 1918. What is the point of her reference to "the September before people thought peace had come again"?
2. To what extent does this reminiscence constitute a comparison or contrast of *then* and *now*?
3. Write a brief memory-piece about a moment of discovery or happiness you shared with someone when you were five or six. Don't get caught up in sentimental nostalgia. Try to recapture some of your experiences and sensations and thoughts as a child, perhaps even focussing on a "first time" for one or more of them. What is the first meal you consciously remember eating? Why do you remember it?
4. Choose an event in your life that had unexpected significance for you, and try to recreate the experience and its impact on you at the time.

### RODERICK HAIG-BROWN  "Behind the Salmon"

1. For the uninitiated, are terms like "Harger's Orange," "backcast," "spey cast," "set the hook," "shouldering," and "leader" unnecessarily confusing, or do they add authenticity? For a reader who doesn't fish, what is there to hold the attention? Is the essay more likely to appeal to someone who does fish?
2. What is the purpose of this essay? What is your interest focussed on? At what point or points does Haig-Brown state his thesis? What is the tone of the essay? Point out some of the stylistic features that create the tone.
3. Note how Haig-Brown moves from the pronoun *one* at the beginning, to *I*, and finally to *you* in the last paragraph, along with one final *one*. Does this indicate a careless inconsistency in his handling of point of view, or do you think it is intentional? Does he make it work?
4. The final sentence includes an allusive pun (see Terms, section VI). Look back through the essay for earlier occurrences of the word *fall*, and remember that this essay is from the book *Fisherman's Fall*. Is a pun a cheap trick? How does this one function thematically?
5. Analyze Haig-Brown's descriptive technique. Note for example how paragraph 9 moves from general fact through increasingly specific

details to the final focus on the possible fish. Do other paragraphs follow a similar pattern?

6. At the end of paragraph 10 and in the second sentence of paragraph 11, Haig-Brown uses a comma to join pairs of independent clauses. Technically these are comma splices, a serious writing error; but can his practice here be defended?

7. Write an essay about your engagement in some pursuit, unusual hobby or sport or pastime, that you believe is not an interest shared by many. Try to convey your enthusiasm to your audience.

### ANNIE DILLARD   "Living Like Weasels"

1. Who is Ernest Thompson Seton?

2. Analyze some of Dillard's metaphors, similes, and analogies. Does she ever seem to push too hard for an effective image? Comment on other details of her style. Does she pick up the metaphor of "socketed" (paragraph 1) elsewhere in the essay? What is the effect of the several questions scattered through the essay? Are they rhetorical questions? Why does she twice use the one word *So* as a sentence—once to begin a paragraph and once to end one?

3. Is Dillard's essay finally about "how to live," about living as we are meant to, by instinct rather than by choice? What is her thesis, either explicit or implicit? How effective is the ending? Is her advice "to grasp your one necessity" also implicit in Gould's essay (section IV)? Is it comparable to what Brink (section III) quotes: "We must grasp what grips us?" Explain the paradox of "the perfect freedom of single necessity."

4. Notice how Dillard revivifies clichés. Comment for example on "held on for a dearer life" and "down is out." Are there any other clichés? Try playing in a similar way with several clichés; through context or variation, make them fresh and meaningful again.

5. Identify the various internal strategies or methods of development Dillard uses in this short essay: narration and description of course, and analogy. Does she use cause-and-effect? definition? contrast?

6. Write a short essay developing an analogy between human beings and some creature you know or know about.

7. Write a paragraph that starts with a description of something natural and moves from concrete to abstract by way of analogy or metaphor.

### BHARATI MUKHERJEE   "Intimations"

1. What are *avatars* (paragraph 1)? Explain the italicized allusion at the end of the third paragraph. What did Oliver Hardy look like (paragraph 15)? Explain the title, "Intimations."

2. How can "the aggressive desire of students to 'know' her" (paragraph 2) be explained "as a form of racism"?

3. In the chapter before the one reprinted here Mukherjee writes: "In Deoghar several time sequences coexist in what appears to be a single frieze." In this one she writes: "We do not seem to have heeded the message of the anonymous sculptor from Deoghar." What is the relation between this allusion and the way she handles time? Is time rendered in a simple narrative or historic line? through retrospect and prospect? Are there several "layers" of time? If so, is one more important than the others? Is time itself in any way a subject of her essay?

4. Nostalgia, along with associated feelings, is both explicit and implicit in this piece, but it is far from the simple nostalgia we commonly indulge in. Point out some instances where nostalgia is qualified and complicated in various ways.

5. To what degree is this piece "travel writing"? The focus is on Calcutta, but how does she illuminate it by contrasting it with other places?

6. Compare where you and your family live with modern Calcutta as Mukherjee describes it. How important is "protection" in your life? Can "privacy" itself be a kind of protection?

7. How does Mukherjee force us to see various things through eyes other than hers? What is the point of view? Does she succeed in juggling subjectivity and objectivity so as to make you see things through your own eyes? Note how she shifts from commenting on the ordinary to reflecting on the extraordinary, the unusual, the insane. How does she use anecdote to alter a reader's perception of what constitutes ordinariness? How does ordinariness relate to political, cultural, economic, or philosophical matters?

8. Write a brief narrative and descriptive essay about some event or condition that requires a similar adjustment of more than one point of view for full understanding.

### E.B. WHITE  "Once More to the Lake"

1. Consult one or more good dictionaries of quotations; then try to make a case for the title's including a literary allusion, possibly a multiple one.

2. The penultimate paragraph is almost pure description. What is its function in the essay? Why does White liken the scene to a "melodrama"? What are the characteristic qualities or features of melodrama? Is White being melodramatic?

3. Try to decide how much of this essay is description and how much narration. Is it impossible to call some parts either one or the other?

Is the overall purpose primarily narrative? descriptive? neither? Find or supply a thesis for it.

4. White's diction and syntax are basically simple; when he departs from that level he does so for a purpose. Find places where the level of diction or sentence structure shifts, and discuss the reason for the shifts.

5. What is the function of the last word of the second paragraph? What does White mean by "the grooves which lead back" (paragraph 2)?

6. Why does White repeatedly refer to time? In what different ways does he introduce the idea of time? How appropriate is the colloquial and cliché metaphor in "everything that had made life tick" (penultimate paragraph)?

7. Analyze the fourth sentence. Comment on its style and on its function in the opening and in the essay as a whole. What connection has it with the passage (paragraph 6) in which he says "the lake was exactly where we left it"? What saying or proverb is implicitly alluded to in these spots and elsewhere?

8. Describe a return (real or imagined) to a place you've not visited for several years, and explain the differences you perceive, either in the place or in yourself.

9. Write a narrative of personal experience focussing on the effects of time on someone or something. Try to avoid merely stating or asserting your point; let your thesis remain implicit. But use as much description as necessary to make your meaning clear.

**E.M. FORSTER   "My Wood"**

1. Forster's first paragraph is a good example of the kind of introductory paragraph that begins broadly and gradually narrows down to a particular thesis—here partly by a process of elimination and partly by moving from general to increasingly specific. Practise writing this handy kind of opening paragraph, perhaps sometimes ending one, as Forster does here, with a thesis *question* rather than a thesis statement.

2. Is there any point to Forster's reference to his last novel, *A Passage to India*, or is it just a convenient anecdotal opening? Consider what he says about the novel's subject matter.

3. Does the short sentence "My bird," in paragraph 4, seem to you a deliberate echo of the essay's title? If so, what is the point of the similarity?

4. Using whatever reference books you need, analyze the complicated metaphor and allusion in the fourth sentence of the second paragraph. Find the other Biblical allusions and the literary and historical ones as well. Explain the function of each.

5. How would you characterize the tone of this essay? Is it consistent, or are there shifts? If there are shifts, do they jar, or is there a pattern and purpose to them?

6. In paragraph 2 Forster plays with words, punning on the word *weight*. Explain the pun. Is it fruitful? Does it fit the tone of the paragraph? Is there wordplay elsewhere in the essay? Forster has made the structure of his essay unusually obvious. How has he done this, and why do you think he did it? Does it work, or do you find it obtrusive?

7. Forster's essay could also be classified as writing to reveal. Write an essay that reveals how some attitude (hatred of or affection for something or someone?) or possession (a car? a dress? a computer? a collection of something? a swimming pool?) affects you. Model the structure of your essay as closely as possible on that of Forster's, and be just as obvious about it as he is.

### HUGH MacLENNAN  "The Street-Car Conductor"

1. Do you think MacLennan means to blame Freud for the ills of the twentieth century? How valid was Freud's theory of the death instinct? Compare MacLennan's attitude with what Tuchman says (section III) about Freud and the influence of his ideas on the twentieth century, and with what is implicit in Szasz's essay (section III).

2. How much does the development of MacLennan's thesis depend on comparison and contrast of past and present? on cause and effect? Is it also in part a process analysis?

3. What is the effect of the parenthesis in the paragraph beginning "In Red River suits"? What are Red River suits?

4. Analyze the paragraph beginning "It was fashionable" for rhythm, sentence length and structure, coherence, parallelism, diction, metaphor, and any other stylistic feature you think worth mentioning. Discover all you can about the way the paragraph works. Does it use any internal strategy other than that of cause and effect? To what degree is it a substantive paragraph as well as a transitional one? What "nasty things" have historians said about the first forty years of this century?

5. What is the point of the final exchange, "Things aren't so bad these days" followed by the customary "*Ouais*"? Is this the beginning of the ending? How has MacLennan prepared for it, led up to it? Note for example the refrain of *la situation internationale* and *terrible*.

6. Analyze the essay's final sentence for everything you can find out about it and how it works.

7. Are you less likely in future to take for granted such an individual as this conductor? Has MacLennan made you "see" him? Or is he not the real subject of the essay? If not, what is?

8. Write an essay that focusses on some "little person" of your experience — perhaps a friend, a neighbour, or a relative — that is only nominally about that person, but instead uses him or her as a peg on which to hang other matter.

LOREN EISELEY   **"The Creature from the Marsh"**

1. How precisely can you define *eons*? What is a *déjà vu* experience? Have you ever had one? What is *keening*?

2. Do you know anyone you could describe as a "living fossil"?

3. Would you describe the way Eiseley begins his essay as strange, even bizarre? Why has he chosen to begin that way? He doesn't clearly announce his subject until part III (though it's suggested near the beginning). Can you justify so long a delayed beginning? What is the function of part I? of part II? Does the mystery-story technique seem appropriate to the essay's subject and purpose?

4. If you haven't already done so, re-read the essay. Do things that were puzzling the first time become clearer? Do you think Eiseley intended the essay to need two readings, or can a reader, with sufficient care, understand all the points the first time through? Is it imposing on readers to expect them to read something more than once? Does a third reading help still more?

5. In the paragraph beginning "On this particular afternoon" (part III), what is the proportion of monosyllabic words? Write a long descriptive paragraph using at least as high a proportion of monosyllables.

6. Note how, toward the end, Eiseley turns explicitly to *comparison* as a thematic technique — comparison of the footprint with his own foot. What other internal strategies does he use? Examine also his metaphors and his use of sound patterns and rhythm. Write sentences imitating the forms of some of his that you find particularly striking.

7. Write a short essay that doesn't fully reveal its subject until about halfway through and that doesn't state its thesis until the end. But don't be too obviously mysterious, and be sure that your readers, though somewhat in the dark, will be interested enough to read on.

## TOPICS: General and Comparative

1. The writers in this section all make excellent use of concrete *details*. Updike's list, for example, necessarily consists of concrete details. Is Johnston's journal entry much the same? How firmly is Fisher's memoir anchored in concrete? How does Haig-Brown's knowledge of the specifics of fly-fishing add visually or descriptively to his essay? What kinds of details does Mukherjee amass to support her evocations of

feelings and attitudes? What is the force of the opening paragraph of White's essay, or almost any other paragraph, for example the third from the end? When you write descriptively and narratively, be especially alert to the need for details; it's difficult to overdo them.

2. *Rhythm* can derive from repetition (see MacLennan's essay), from the use of voice patterns (see Thomas's essay), and from paragraph length (see Forster's essay). What else determines rhythm? How for example do punctuation and sentence length affect rhythm? Point out some examples in Dillard's essay and elsewhere. How does a writer's choice of monosyllabic words affect rhythm? Find some examples of metrical patterns in Thomas's essay. Try scanning Mukherjee's final sentence. Look for effective uses of sound patterns—especially alliteration—in these essays (see A Note to the Reader). Do you find more in Thomas than elsewhere, as you might expect? How do such patterns affect rhythm? Analyze the rhythms and sound patterns in the short fourteenth paragraph of Haig-Brown's essay; could any of its rhythms be called metrical? How do rhythm and sentence length affect tone, for example in Thomas's and Forster's essays? How does rhythm affect meaning—for example through emphasis?

3. Consider the effectiveness of the *structure* of the essays in this section.
   (a) Has Updike arranged his details so as to make his piece more than a mere list of things observed?
   (b) Is the order of Johnston's piece—as you might expect from a journal—simply chronological?
   (c) See if you can discover any principle of form or structure in Thomas's essay. Why are things related in the order they are? Is it simply chronological? Or is it haphazard, a grab-bag, as Thomas implies?
   (d) Haig-Brown's essay is straightforwardly chronological. Would any other scheme have worked as well or better? Where is its climax?
   (e) Note how White relies on a shift in tone. Does the last paragraph look back to any earlier parts? How does it alter the tone and the effect of the essay?
   (f) The structure of Forster's essay is aggressively obvious. What is the rationale for the order of the four parts? Is there a progression of any kind? Point out how Forster controls emphasis through tone, proportion, and position. As he controls and alters the image of the wood, does he succeed in elevating it into a symbol?
   (g) Would you call MacLennan's essay "plotted"? Explain its organization and movement.
   (h) Note how Eiseley suspends the identification of his "discovery." What does this add to his inquiry? Suspense? Why is point of view important in this essay? And in White's?

4. Does history impose its own order on essays about historical sub-jects? Write an essay about some historical event, such as a battle, a journey of exploration and discovery, or an election. How does the chronology of the event affect the structure of your essay? Did you try using a flashback—for example as a way of beginning?

5. How does a knowledge of history benefit a reader of MacLennan and Mukherjee? Do you need it for Forster and Fisher? What historical allusions does MacLennan use? Compare the ways MacLennan and Mukherjee make thematic use of the ideas of *fear* and *security*.

6. Near the end of "My Wood" Forster refers to walls around a piece of property. Are Mukherjee's frequent references to walls at all similar? Analyze her short paragraph beginning "Out there beyond our walled vision." What does she mean by "walled vision"? Is it a simple meta-phor? Is it akin to the gulf-traversing "vision" referred to by Forster? How important is seeing, or the way we see, in other essays? Dillard for example writes about observing nature. What does she see in it? Compare the way it functions in her essay with the way it works in others, for example those by Haig-Brown, White, and Eiseley.

7. Compare Fisher's treatment of memory and the past with that of others who write about their childhood—Dylan Thomas, White, Mukherjee, and Sheehan (section II). How importantly, for example, do parents figure in these essays? How do the writers use details and terms of another day to help evoke the past? What levels of diction and style do they use?

8. Consider the effects writers can achieve by using descriptive adjec-tives carefully. Do they ever overuse adjectives? Examine Eiseley's paragraph beginning "By day and night" (part III). On what words does the force, the vividness, of the description depend? What pro-portion of them are adjectives (excluding verbal adjectives)? The first half of Thomas's fourth paragraph has many adjectives, the last half few. Why the difference? What is the effect? Are there occasions when precise nouns and verbs are preferable to adjectives and adverbs? Examine your own style in light of this distinction. Try writing a de-scription with few or no adjectives.

9. Take a representative passage from each of the essays and list and classify its verbs (as we do with the passage from Schreiner in the preface to this section). Try to justify what you find out about these verbs in terms of the purposes of the different essays.

10. Compare and discuss two or more of the essays in terms of some of the following features: sentence length, sentence structure, level of diction, frequency and length and kind of metaphor, proportion of concrete detail, handling of chronology. You can probably think of still other ways to make useful comparisons.

11. If you should see a traffic accident, would you make a good witness? Try to record exactly a sequence of events that you observed or a conversation you overheard this morning, or to describe exactly a person you saw several hours ago. What was your sister, brother, or roommate wearing yesterday?

12. Taking one of the writers in this section as your stylistic model, write a paragraph or two of personal narrative. Think about your subject first. What incident do you want to focus on? Why? What purpose or purposes do you want the incident to serve? Why do you want to share this particular incident with a reader? Which reader? How will you engage the reader? With detail? a certain tone? an anecdote? metaphoric language? transcribed conversation?

13. Try writing a few sentences to describe exactly some of the following items or circumstances:

> a red frisbee, a screen door, the sound of moving water, warts, ice, a clear glass window, dirt, safety pins, escalator steps, sore feet, hair, a running-shoe, wheat, porridge, dogs' noses, a car tire, a glove compartment, fish scales, a soccer ball, a dime, night, oil, lemons, linen, a cup of tea, bees, dancing, moustaches, the income tax department, a line-up in a bank, a row of houses, lipstick, the 42nd floor, spaghetti sauce, gargling, blue, happiness, a butcher shop, a chess piece, an orange, anger, a blade of grass, bare feet, a hamburger, a tightrope walker.

What are the difficulties in each case? Finding the words to convey the appropriate sense impression? Making an abstract notion concrete? Avoiding clichés? What else? Where does the force of your description lie? In the verbs? adjectives? nouns? sentence rhythms? In some combination of these? Have you in each instance focussed on a *dominant impression* that you want to convey?

Now try writing advertising copy for some of these same items. How does your language differ?

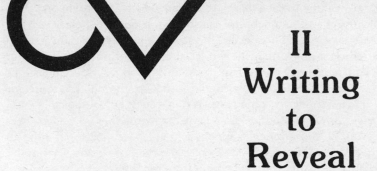

# II
# Writing
# to
# Reveal

On bookstore shelves a few years ago, there appeared a work with an entire conversation for a title: *Where Did You Go? Out. What Did You Do? Nothing.* On the surface this brief exchange between parent and child does not appear to say much; the questions are pointedly clear, but the answers are evasive and unspecific. Indirectly, however, the conversation says a good deal more than the words alone declare. It *implies* rather than declares; it *reveals* more than it explains. Even the direct questions reveal the parent's concern; the answers suggest the child's desire for privacy. "I'm busy now—ask me later" is one way of psychologically interpreting these answers. Another is to hear the words that go unspoken— "Nothing *out of the ordinary* happened: don't be concerned"—and to realize that the covert message is essentially a reassuring one, even if the surface words appear to frustrate communication entirely.

Dialogues of all kinds depend on such indirect revelations, often as much as they depend on clear explanation and argument. For example, lawyers in cross-questioning witnesses sometimes strive to catch people in self-revelatory (and perhaps self-condemning) inconsistencies. Interviewers often seek to induce interviewees to reveal more of themselves than they might ordinarily put on public display. Gossips hint at dark secrets, and wait to see what seems embarrassing and might therefore be confirmed. Sophisticated listeners respond to body language as well as to verbal utterances, and the fact that television has made body language a manipulative art of communication in its own right has turned people into sophisticated watchers as well. It is the very sense of something hidden (and the accompanying promise of candidness, of the exposure of some behind-the-scenes truth) that constitutes the fascination of revelatory forms of address. But such forms are not simply accidents of conversation; they are open to shaping, and the results can be triumphs of psychological and political commentary.

Consider, for example, Robert Browning's 1842 poem "My Last Duchess." It is a *dramatic monologue*, a poem in which only one speaker is heard, one whose speech is an extraordinary act of unwitting self-revelation. It not only reveals the context of the conversation, but also (as with many a journal and diary) reveals far more of the speaker than he is himself aware of. In this particular poem the speaker is the Duke of Ferrara, and we know from context that he is speaking to an emissary from a prospective father-in-law:

### FERRARA

> That's my last Duchess painted on the wall,
> Looking as if she were alive. I call
> That piece a wonder, now: Frà Pandolf's hands
> Worked busily a day, and there she stands.

Will't please you sit and look at her? I said
"Frà Pandolf" by design, for never read
Strangers like you that pictured countenance,
The depth and passion of its earnest glance,
But to myself they turned (since none puts by
The curtain I have drawn for you, but I)
And seemed as they would ask me, if they durst,
How such a glance came there; so, not the first
Are you to turn and ask thus. Sir, 'twas not
Her husband's presence only, called that spot
Of joy into the Duchess' cheek: perhaps
Frà Pandolf chanced to say, "Her mantle laps
Over my lady's wrist too much," or "Paint
Must never hope to reproduce the faint
Half-flush that dies along her throat": such stuff
Was courtesy, she thought, and cause enough
For calling up that spot of joy. She had
A heart—how shall I say?—too soon made glad,
Too easily impressed; she liked whate'er
She looked on, and her looks went everywhere.
Sir, 'twas all one! My favour at her breast,
The dropping of the daylight in the West,
The bough of cherries some officious fool
Broke in the orchard for her, the white mule
She rode with round the terrace—all and each
Would draw from her alike the approving speech,
Or blush, at least. She thanked men,—good!
   but thanked
Somehow—I know not how—as if she ranked
My gift of a nine-hundred-years-old name
With anybody's gift. Who'd stoop to blame
This sort of trifling? Even had you skill
In speech—(which I have not)—to make your will
Quite clear to such an one, and say, "Just this
Or that in you disgusts me; here you miss,
Or there exceed the mark"—and if she let
Herself be lessoned so, nor plainly set
Her wits to yours, forsooth, and made excuse,
—E'en then would be some stooping; and I choose
Never to stoop. Oh sir, she smiled, no doubt,
Whene'er I passed her; but who passed without
Much the same smile? This grew; I gave commands;
Then all smiles stopped together. There she stands
As if alive. Will't please you rise? We'll meet
The company below, then. I repeat,
The Count your master's known munificence
Is ample warrant that no just pretence

Of mine for dowry will be disallowed;
Though his fair daughter's self, as I avowed
At starting, is my object. Nay, we'll go
Together down, sir! Notice Neptune, though,
Taming a sea-horse, thought a rarity,
Which Claus of Innsbruck cast in bronze for me!

Listening between the lines, readers can interpret what the Duke is saying and come quickly to understand him better than he might wish. We glimpse an egocentric and powerful man for whom people and art matter only as personal possessions. Power and his public position matter more. He needs to be admired. He thinks himself grand and needs to feel that others think so too. So he boasts, seeks praise, ensures that his power is known about, and yet pretends to be elegant, civilized, fastidious, perhaps even humane. But how does Browning make sure that his readers know better? And does the listener in the poem know the Duke as well as we do?

Occasional interviews and recorded everyday conversations are scarcely as compact and as finely organized as this poem is, but many essays nonetheless consciously adapt the techniques of revelation to similarly deliberate ends. Lane and Davenport, for example, seem to provide neutral accounts of the lives of Potter and Wittgenstein, yet they also offer their readers opportunities to draw other-than-neutral conclusions. McClung, not so neutrally, makes some direct and evaluative statements, but in reproducing parts of her conversations with the Premier, she not only lets him reveal the weaknesses of his attitudes and assumptions, but also indicates her own strength and determination. Lane addresses the very problem that an interviewee's masks can become for an interviewer; yet in recording interviews that have gone awry she still manages to reveal features of her subject's personality. And also her own? Rooney, drawing up rules for others' lives, quite consciously puts much of his own personality on display. Sheehan, ostensibly writing about baseball, obliquely outlines a whole code of behaviour; baseball is simply the surface subject, behind which lies a message of another order entirely. Doesn't it?

The other essays in this section—by Ludwig, Huxley, and Orwell—all in one way or another record the voices of people whom the authors have interviewed, listened to, observed, and overheard. But these voices then combine creatively with their own. The effects are subtly varied. Each writer, using a form something like that of a personal journal, notes down observed details and fragments of conversation; each then sets about to connect, weigh, and interpret them. But in so doing, each writer filters the revelations he perceives through his own social consciousness, making them part of a process of self-revelation as well. In none of the three essays is the covert message neutral; it is passionate, and it is political.

The writers are *aware* of what they are doing. And it is a mark of their verbal craftsmanship that what sets out to be—or to appear to be—a personal and private record can turn so compellingly into an act of public persuasion.

# Interview with Robertson Davies:
## The Bizarre and Passionate Life of the Canadian People

### Silver Donald Cameron

*Walking into the porter's lodge of Massey College in the University of Toronto, I was frightened. Robertson Davies, the Master of Massey College, is not only a sensitive and urbane novelist, but also an accomplished playwright, an exceptional journalist, a penetrating critic, a professional actor, a scholar, and an astringent wit. "Mr. Davies," A.J.M. Smith once wrote, "brings the virtues of urbanity, sophistication, good humour, and a certain consciousness of superiority to bear on books, food, wine and social behaviour." I greatly admired Davies' 1957 essay on Stephen Leacock, but I felt his Leacock anthology,* Feast of Stephen, *was a waste of time; Davies in turn considered my* Faces of Leacock *altogether too earnestly academic; and both of us had published these opinions. I knew, too, that Davies was at the top of his powers: at fifty-eight, he had just published* Fifth Business, *by any standard the best novel he had ever written. I expected an ironic and uncomfortable afternoon.*

*Inside Davies' study—a room so elegantly comfortable can hardly be called an office—I encountered someone considerably more rumpled, more round, and more quiet than the tall, suave, saturnine figure I had prepared for. I began asking questions suited to the man I thought he was, and got disconcerting answers. Was he a connoisseur of wine and cheese? No, he didn't know much about wine and didn't greatly enjoy cheese. Didn't the Salterton novels assume the reader and author agreed on the*

Excerpt from *Conversations with Canadian Novelists* by Silver Donald Cameron. Copyright © 1973 by Donald Cameron. Reprinted by permission of the Colbert Agency, Inc.

*primary importance of social reality? No: consider the use of sermons, music, fantasy.*

*Confused, I resorted to the basic principle of good interviewing: when in doubt, shut your mouth and really listen. I heard Davies saying that he was very different from his public image, and as I reshaped my view of him I found myself experiencing a deeply personal, almost confessional conversation.*

*Cameron:* As I read them, the Salterton novels show a very strong feeling for the Western cultural tradition, and specifically the English tradition.

*Davies:* Well, I am interested in a lot of cultural traditions, as many as I can experience, really, but what is apparent in the Salterton novels is a Canadian cultural tradition which I don't think gets the kind of attention in Canadian fiction that it might expect: a sort of delayed cultural tradition. About the period that I was working on the Salterton novels, just after the 1945 war, there were still people living in places like Salterton whose tradition was directly Edwardian, and who saw nothing wrong with that. They weren't even conscious that their ideas were not contemporary. I remember driving with my wife from Peterborough to Cobourg to see a production of Chekhov's *The Cherry Orchard*, and in that very beautiful little theatre was an audience which contained a considerable number of people in evening dress, which I thought was very curious. They had come from that district, and they felt that that was the way that they ought to dress for a theatrical production. After the first act I wandered around in the corridors listening to the people talk, and they were talking about the play as if it were a brand new play—because it *was* a brand-new play to most of them, and yet they were people of some education, of a very considerable amount of tradition; they had the kind of dress clothes that suggested that they were well accustomed to wearing them and had indeed been wearing them for a very long time. Suddenly it broke in upon me: these people don't know that the play is about *them*—and yet there it was. I knew who some of them were: they were descendants of people who'd come to this country in the middle of the nineteenth century or earlier; they had homes in which they used silver which their families had brought with them, they had pictures of Great-grandfather in his Bengal uniform, they had connections with England, cousins that they wrote to, and they still hadn't grasped the fact that an entirely new Canada had come into being, and that their sort of person was really almost dinosaur-like in its failure to fit into the modern scene. You could see what happened in *The Cherry Orchard* happening around there, because all kinds of places were having to be bought up, and people didn't quite know why, but somehow the money had run out. Canada is full of these people, and very rarely do they get written about, but I write about them, and they're *real*. I could lead you out on a walk within a mile of where we sit which would uncover a great many of them. This is something in Canada which people on the whole don't recognize: we've got a fantastic sort of fossilized past here. We always talk about ourselves as a country with a great future, but we never talk about ourselves as a country with a sort of living past.

*Cameron*: Don't those novels show a fairly strong current of sympathy for some aspects of that tradition?

*Davies:* It is sympathy for the people—not, I think, the tradition—because they *are* people. They're not caricatures, they're not oddities, they're not cardboard. They bleed when you stick them and they weep when they are miserable, and their sorrows and their distresses are made sometimes more poignant by the fact that they don't know why things are happening to them.

*Cameron*: The shape of the novels themselves is rather in the tradition of English domestic comedy, like Jane Austen or Henry James, in a way.

*Davies*: No. No, I've never read a novel by Henry James in my life, and I don't like Jane Austen. I agree with Max Beerbohm that the novels of Jane Austen are a marionette opera. I have no use for them whatever.

*Cameron*: I'm becoming convinced I've misread you—but I thought there was an assumption in the Salterton novels of a kind of accepted social reality.

*Davies*: The people in the novels agree that there is a certain kind of reality; I don't think that should be taken as the *author's* opinion. In *A Mixture of Frailties* there are things which a lot of people who'd liked the previous two novels disliked very much indeed, because it suggested that I and they had not agreed upon a kind of little provincial city which they could be cozy about it. *They* may have reached some such idea—but *I* never did.

*Cameron*: You must have surprised them even more with *Fifth Business*.

*Davies*: Yes, and I hope to go on surprising them.

*Cameron*: Are you working on a novel now?

*Davies*: Yes, and a great many people, I think, will find it uncongenial. Some people wrote to me and said that they liked *Fifth Business*, but it wasn't as funny as the other books. I'm grateful that they found the other books funny, but I am a little dismayed that they thought that funny was *all* they were. I think it is the writer's duty to be as amusing as he can manage, but not to sacrifice everything to that. That was what happened to Leacock: he eventually got so that he'd rather be funny than honest or sensible or intelligent, and that's bad.

*Cameron*: Isn't it true that the comedy of the Salterton novels is a rather anguished comedy, too? That the reader is invited to feel for the character who is the butt of the comedy, as well as laughing at him?

*Davies:* Yes, he is the victim as well as the sort of originator. One of the things I was interested in doing when I wrote those novels was to try and find out whether such novels about Canada were possible, because I don't know of any others that deal with Canadian situations in quite that way—and yet they *are* Canadian. Many people said, Oh, I was trying to write as if Canada were England or as if I were an Englishman—but I'm *not* an Englishman, and Canada is *not* England, and English people found the books quite peculiar.

*Cameron:* The play you mentioned in Cobourg was Russian. I've talked to novelists who've said that if some things that go on in Canada were written about accurately, the only parallel would be in Russian literature.

*Davies:* Exactly; I agree a hundred per cent. In fact sometimes I get irritated with people who complain that Canada has no drama. The two great Canadian dramatists are Chekhov and Ibsen. The Ibsen and Chekhov situations can be paralleled in Canada twenty times over—the same sort of rather uncomprehending clinging to the past on the part of a certain group of people, and the same sort of self-satisfied littleness of mind that you get savagely dealt with in so many of the Ibsen plays. What do the trolls tell Peer Gynt is their philosophy? Troll, to thyself be self-sufficient: now that's *Canadian*. We make modest faces sometimes to the rest of the world, but the hopeless self-satisfaction of a large number of Canadians is a marvel to behold.

*Cameron:* I sense a good deal of Freudianism in your thinking. Is Freud someone you've read seriously and thought about a lot?

*Davies:* Yes, I have, as a matter of fact. I am, I guess, one of the very few people I know who has read Freud's collected works from end to end. Freud was an enormous enthusiasm of mine before I was forty; after forty I came to examine the works of his great colleague Carl Gustav Jung, and I have been, over many years, reading and re-reading and reading again the collected works of C.G. Jung.

*Cameron:* What gave you that serious an interest in psychoanalytic thought in the first place?

*Davies:* Well, I had been interested in the notion that this line of thought existed even when I was a schoolboy; when I went to Queen's University there was a remarkable professor of psychology there, Dr. George Humphrey, a notable man who later on became Professor of Psychology at Oxford and wrote a great book on the theory of learning. Humphrey talked a great deal about Freud, about whom he knew a lot, and so I was led to read some Freud. One of the things that enchanted me was that Freud was saying explicitly things which I had vaguely apprehended as possibilities. This whetted my appetite enormously, so on I went. Later on I discovered the same thing in Jung: he had the intellect and the ability to go into very deeply, and to talk about superbly, things which I had dimly apprehended, and so I was eager to follow.

*Cameron:* Was there something that you became unsatisfied with in Freud?

*Davies:* Yes, there was. It was Freud's reductive train of thought, which is very welcome to the young mind but becomes, I find, less welcome to the older mind. Freud didn't indulge in this kind of thing, but a great many of his disciples do: you're afraid of thunder because when you were little you heard your father fart and then he spanked you, or something of that sort. Well, this seems to me unworthy of the human race. It's not the kind of cheap wares in which Freud dealt, but it's a thing that people have rather developed from his line of thinking, and much of his thought *is* violently reductive—the tendency to feel that the sexual etiology of neurosis explains everything, and that sort of thing. As Jung pointed out, a surprising number of people seemed to turn up in Jung's consulting room with manifest neuroses which were not primarily related to any sort of sexual hangup. As Jung also pointed out, Freud was an extraordinarily brilliant and very, very successful young man—the darling of his doting mother—who had always lived a city life. Jung had led much more the kind of childhood I myself had had—going to country schools, living with country children, knowing country things, being quite accustomed to animals and the sort of rough and rather sexually oriented—but in an ordinary, daily way—life of the country person.

*Cameron:* Robert Kroetsch, who lives in the States, feels that Freudianism had great success there because it really appeals to something in American experience, in American ideology: the stress between the good guy and the bad guy, the id and the ego, a kind of Manichean view of the psyche.

*Davies:* That's extremely interesting.

*Cameron:* And he felt that Canada was a much more Jungian society.

*Davies:* Ooooh, this is music to my soul! I think we're a much softer-focussed country. In the intellectual life of the United States, there seems to be such a very, very strong Jewish strain—I would not for an instant suggest that that was a bad thing, but it is an intensely *conditioning* thing. This intellectual ferocity and sort of black/white quality is very strong there. We're fuzzier, but I think we're more humane, and that's what I think about Jung, too.

*Cameron:* Kroetsch thinks that instead of seeing polar oppositions all the time, we tend to see two sides of a conflict as aspects of the same thing.

*Davies:* Yes, and tending to run into one another. You know, we had a very extraordinary evidence of that, in something which I think of as enormously important and significant about Canada: in the character of Mackenzie King, who was our Prime Minister for longer than any other man in any British country in the world. Mackenzie King seemed to be the quintessence of dullness. When you read in his diary that when he met Barbara Ann Scott, the skater, it seemed that he was expected to kiss her, and he "acquiesced"—a duller, more pedantic, dreary man you could scarcely think to find. But what was he in reality? A man who communed with the portrait of his dead mother to get political advice; a man who never set the date of a general election without consulting Nan Skinner, the Kingston fortune-teller; a man who could—and I know this from my father, who knew Mr. King quite well—burst into the most highly coloured and inflammatory kind of blasphemous, evil language when he was discussing certain topics; a man who wooed and sort of managed to keep peace with Québec, but who could talk about French Canadians in a way that would take the paint off a barn door—this was Mackenzie King, this was the opposites running into one another, and this is very Canadian. We now blackmouth him and pretend that we knew about him all the time, but he got elected over and over again; he knew this country marvellously, because he was essentially one of us. We're great withholders, Canadians. This is the sort of thing that my Australian-born wife has pointed out to me. Accept the bland, quiet, rather dull Canadian for what he seems to be: it's just like putting your hand into a circular saw, he'll have the hand before you know what's happened. I think this is very characteristic of our country, and when we really come to ourselves, we're going to be a very formidable people. We're going to be as formidable, I would say, as the Norwegians, or the Swedes, who are very formidable nations indeed; perhaps as formidable as the Russians. I was asked in connection with *Fifth Business* to say what I was trying to do, and I said that I was trying to record the bizarre and passionate life of the Canadian people. Well, I was dropped on by some Canadian critics who said, There I was again, trying to make an effect and talking silly so that people would look at me and think what a fancy fellow I was. *They* were the ones who didn't see what it was. I was speaking the exact truth, but they didn't see it. They *will* not see it.

*Cameron:* As you spoke, I thought, This is the theme of *Fifth Business*, the contrast between—

*Davies:* —the appearance and the reality, the grey schoolmaster and the man who was burning like an oil gusher inside.

*Cameron:* Yes, and at a place much like Upper Canada College, which many people consider the epitome of all that is dull and Edwardian.

*Davies:* You see, they don't know anything about it. I went to Upper Canada College, and I know what a tempest of passion can go on in there. I'm not saying it's individual to that college; it would be so in any school in Canada, I would think, if you just look. Some very rum things indeed go on in them. Every once in a while a teacher commits suicide, and everyone says, "Poor old Joe, you wouldn't have thought it of him, would you? He seemed to be the most level-headed fellow there ever was." But if you knew old Joe, you knew old Joe had been nutty as a fruit cake for years. I went to a collegiate institute for a while where there was a mathematics teacher who used to break down in the class sometimes; he would burst into tears and say, "Children, I don't want to die of cancer, I don't want to die of cancer." He eventually did—he wasn't doing it at that moment—but we just thought, well, that's the way old Scotty is. The goddamndest things go on in schools.

*Cameron:* How on earth did you get that astonishing report of the experience of a foot soldier in the First World War? You were all of one year old when the war broke out.

*Davies:* I wish I could give you some helpful and illuminating answer, but I can't. I just remember when I was a very little boy what some men who were in the war had said. They weren't very eloquent, but it was like that. But I will tell you something which is not dissimilar. In *Fifth Business* I mentioned that the Bollandists, and particularly Padre Blazon, wrote in purple ink. Well, I've never seen a Bollandist, and I think I've only met one Jesuit, and I've never visited the Bollandist Institute in Brussels, or anything of that sort, but I did meet a man in New York called Israel Shenker, who knows the Bollandists very well and is, as far as a layman and a visitor can be, a familiar there. And he said, How on earth did you know that they wrote in purple ink? I said, Well, I divined it—and he nearly fell out of his chair with indignation, because this was a bad answer. But it seemed to me very probable that they would write in purple ink, and apparently they do.

*Cameron:* But you didn't check.

*Davies:* How would you check? Would you write to them and say, Please, do you write in purple ink? It isn't a matter of importance, really. I could have just said that they wrote in ink. But it seemed to me—wellllllll, *purple* ink. And they do.

*Cameron:* That's quite a chance to take. Certain kinds of reviewers would be very indignant if they were to find out that in fact it was green ink.

*Davies:* Yes, they would. They'd be very cross.

*Cameron:* The religious theme that emerged so strongly in *Fifth Business* had been seen primarily in social terms, I would have thought, in the Salterton novels.

*Davies:* Yes, but not entirely in social terms. In *Leaven of Malice*, the Dean makes it pretty clear what his view is about what has been going on, and puts in his ten cents' worth in a way I hoped was of some significance. Only a very few people have ever commented on the Dean's sermon at the very end of *A Mixture of Frailties*, which is going on contrapuntally to what the girl Monica is thinking when she's trying to make up her mind whether she'll marry Domdaniel or not. The Dean is preaching a sermon on the revelation of God to man in three forms: a revolution of nature for the shepherd, a penetration by wisdom for the wise man, and a sort of natural grace to Simeon. I think most people look at the italics and say, Oh yes, this is the sermon, and hop to where it gets to be roman type next, to see whether the girl's going to marry the old man or not. But it's there, and it's vital to the book.

*Cameron:* Has religion something to do with your interest in Freud and Jung?

*Davies:* Yes. One reason I was drawn to the study of Freud and of Jung was my religious interest, because I very quickly found that for my taste, investigation of religion by orthodox theological means was unrewarding. You never got down to brass tacks, or at least nothing that I ever read did so. You started off by assuming that certain things were true, and then you developed all kinds of splendid things on top of that. I wanted to see about the basic things, so I thought that I would have a look at people who had had a wrestle with these very, very basic things, and Freud was one of them. Freud decided that religion is essentially an illusion: well, I read that, I studied it and chewed on it and mulled it over for quite a long time, but it never fully satisfied me, because it seemed to me that brilliant as Sigmund Freud was, there have been men of comparable brilliance or even greater brilliance who had been enormously attached to this concept which seemed to him to be nothing better than an illusion. One of the figures which bulked very large in my ideas was St. Augustine. I was very interested as a very young boy to discover that I was born on the day of St. Augustine, the 28th of August, and also on the birthday of Tolstoy and Goethe; and I thought, Oh, that's great stuff, splendid! This is an omen. But St. Augustine was a man of the most towering intellectual powers, and if he was willing to devote his life to the exposition of this thing which Freud called an illusion, I felt that the betting couldn't all be on Saint Sigmund; some of it conceivably ought to be on St. Augustine. And there were other figures whom I thought intensely significant. I thought a great deal about it, and then I gradually began to look into the works of Jung and found a much more—to me—satisfying attitude towards religion, but it was not an orthodox Christian one. Orthodox Christianity has always had for me the difficulty that it really won't come, in what is for me a satisfactory way, to grips with the problem of evil. It knows an enormous amount about evil, it discusses evil in fascinating terms, but evil is always the other thing: it is something which is apart from perfection, and man's duty is to strive for perfection. I could not reconcile that with such experience of life as I had, and the Jungian feeling that things tend to run into one another, that what looks good can be pushed to the point where it becomes evil, and that evil very frequently bears what can only be regarded as good fruit—this was the first time I'd ever seen that sort of thing given reasonable consideration, and it made enormous sense to me. I feel now that I am a person of strongly religious temperament, but when I say "religious" I mean immensely conscious of powers of which I can have only the dimmest apprehension, which operate by means that I cannot fathom, in directions which I would be a fool to call either good or bad. Now that seems hideously funny, but it isn't really; it is, I think, a recognition of one's position in an inexplicable universe, in which it is not wholly impossible for you to ally yourself with, let us say, positive rather than negative forces, but in which anything that you do in that direction must be done with a strong recognition that you may be very, very gravely mistaken. This is something which would never satisfy the humblest parish priest, but I live in a world in which forces are going on which I am unable to tab and identify so that the tickets will stick. I just have to get on as well as I can. Various kind people in writing about my books have called me an existentialist, and they won't believe me when I tell them I don't know what an existentialist is. I've had it explained to me many times, but the explanation never really makes enough sense to me to cling. But I have tried to state for you what my position is, and I fear that I've done so clumsily and muddily—but if it comes in clumsy and muddy, it's just got to be that way. Better that than slick and crooked.

*Cameron:* Perhaps people find it difficult to believe that you don't know what an existentialist is because of your public *persona*, your image, to use the ad-man's word, which—

*Davies:* —my image, if I've got an image—I suppose I have—has been made for me by other people. Nobody wants to listen to what I want to say. They want to tell me what I think.

*Cameron:* Well, the image presents you as a man of formidable learning, formidable intellect, and fearsome wit, a man who *would* know about things like existentialism.

*Davies:* I am not of formidable learning; I am a very scrappily educated person, and I am not of formidable intellect; I really am not a very good thinker. In Jungian terms I am a feeling person with strong intuition. I *can* think, I've *had* to think, and I *do* think, but thinking isn't the first way I approach any problem. It's always, What does this say to me?

And I get it through my fingertips, not through my brain. *Then* I have to think about it, but the thinking is a kind of consciously undertaken thing rather than a primary means of apprehension. Also intuition is very strong in me; I sort of smell things. As for this wit business, it's primarily defence, you know. Witty people are concealing something.

*Cameron:* What are you concealing?

*Davies:* I suppose I'm concealing—hmmm. Well, you see, if it were easy for me to tell you, I wouldn't be concealing. I think I am concealing a painful sensitivity, because I am very easily hurt and very easily rebuffed and very easily set down; and very early in life I found out that to be pretty ready with your tongue was a way of coping with that. You know that is a thing which is attributed to Dunstan Ramsay in *Fifth Business*. He was always "getting off a good one". If you can get off a good one once or twice a day, people don't rasp you as much as they otherwise might. They'll do it enough, however defensive you are.

*Cameron:* Humour does fend people off.

*Davies:* It's defensive and it's diverting. You know, you suddenly send the dogs off in that direction, instead of straight ahead.

*Cameron:* One can't talk about these things as a dispassionate interviewer, you know. I've been known in some circles as a person of fairly savage humour myself, and I've always felt that in my case it had to do with profound feelings of insecurity and inadequacy, the sense that I was surrounded by people who knew their way around the world and were at home in it in a way that I wasn't.

*Davies:* Yes, there's that, and there's also a thing which I expect you have experienced, and which certainly I've experienced: the narrow outlook, and limited sympathies, and want of charity, and general two-bit character of what is going on under your very eyes, which drives you to the point of great extravagance. It comes out in terms of savage, bitter humour, just because you don't quite want to go to savage denunciation, but you want to blast them like an Old Testament prophet. Instead you just swat them around with the jester's bladder. But the impulse is the same.

*Cameron:* Isn't the effect actually more powerful through humour, and isn't that something else one easily learns?

*Davies:* Yes, but you haven't learned enough. If you blasted them like a prophet, they might forgive you; if you mock them like a jester, they'll *never* forgive you.

*Cameron:* That's true, but it's because making a joke of them is a more powerful thing to do.

*Davies:* Yes, I guess it is, in a way. Oh, it hurts, it stings, and they never forgive it. Now this is interesting: you have made a confession and I've made one. That's why one makes jokes, very often.

*Cameron:* To make confessions—?

*Davies:* No, to keep things at bay. It's a sort of distancing thing very often. Not always: I mean, sometimes you do it out of sheer lark.

*Cameron:* There's a very interesting interplay in your work between theatre and fiction. I suspect that for you theatre is a metaphor of some dimensions.

*Davies:* It's the element of illusion in life, the difference between appearance and reality. In the theatre you can be in the know about what makes the difference, and it is fascinating that you can know what creates the illusion, know everything about it, be part of it, and yet not despise the people who want the illusion, who cannot live without it. That's important, you know. So frequently it is assumed that if you know how something's done you despise the people who don't. You don't do that in the theatre. You respect them; you know that they know a good thing when they see it.

*Cameron:* You were with the Old Vic at one point, weren't you?

*Davies:* Yes, not for very long. For three years, until the war broke out and there was nothing further to be done there or anywhere else in England, so I came back to Canada.

*Cameron:* You are very strongly Canadian, aren't you, in that you have a very clear sense of who you are and which national community is yours.

*Davies:* Yes, indeed, and this became very very clear to me within the last two or three years. I've always felt strongly Canadian, which doesn't mean complacently or gleefully Canadian, but Canadian; and my father, who was a Welshman, had always, during the latter part of his life, spent all his summers in his native country, in Wales. My mother was Canadian and her family had been here for a very long time—since 1785 as a matter of fact—but my father always had this extraordinary pull back to his home country. Living in this college, I live in a house which is attached to the college, which is not mine, and when I retire I will not, of course, continue to live there. So my wife and I thought the time had come when we ought to have some place where we'll be able to go when we retire. Distant though that time may be, now is the time to get on with doing it, because when you're retired you don't want to plunge right into the business of finding a dwelling or building one. So we thought, what'll we do? Will we acquire some place in England and retire there? Now this would have been comprehensible because there was this very strong pull of my father's towards the old land, and my wife's family, who were Australians, were always drawn back to England as the great, good place in which all important things happened. We talked it over and decided that my wife had been a Canadian far longer than she'd been an Australian, and that I was really a Canadian, and that to leave this country would be like cutting off my feet. So we built a house in the country in Canada. That was a decision which went far beyond a matter of bricks and mortar. It would be impossible now to leave with the feeling that you'd left for good. We like to travel, we like to get around to see what's doing, we're both terribly interested in the theatre, which means we like to get over to England where the theatre is most lively, and to the continent. But to live, to have your being, to feel that this is where you're going to get old and die, that's another thing—and that's *here.*

*Cameron:* That doesn't surprise me now, but it might have before I met you.

*Davies:* Well, as we've said, the popular notion of what I am and why I do things is very wide of the mark. The mainstream of what I do is this sense which I can only call a religious sense, but which is not religious in a sectarian, or aggressive, or evangelistic sense. And also, you know, I really think I've now got to the age where I have to consider what I am and how I function, and I can only call myself an artist. Now people hesitate very much in Canada to call themselves artists. An extraordinary number of authors shrink from that word, because it suggests to them a kind of fancy attitude, which might bring laughter or might seem overstrained—but if you really put your best energies into acts of creation, I don't know what else you can call yourself. You'd better face it and get used to it, and take on the things that are implied by it.

*Cameron:* What sorts of things are implied?

*Davies:* A duty to be true to your abilities in so far as you can and as deeply as you can. I think this is where Leacock didn't trust himself, didn't trust his talent. He never thought of himself as an artist, which he started out, I'm sure, to be; his early work has a lot of that quality about it. He decided he was going to be a moneymaker instead, so he didn't become the writer he might have been, and I think that's what you've got to do if you have a chance. I couldn't have said this until fairly recently—you know, you step out in front of the public and say, I am an artist, and they shout, Yeah? Look who's talking, and throw eggs. If you step out in front of them and say, I am a humorist, they say, All right, make us laugh. You can do that fairly easily, but if you say, I can make you feel; I can maybe even make you cry, that's claiming a lot.

*Cameron:* And do they want you to do it?

*Davies:* They really do, but they want to be sure that they're in safe hands before they let you do it, because you might be kidding them: you might make them cry and then say, Yah, yah, look who's crying; I did that as a trick—and that's what would hurt them. They're sensitive too. It's an awareness of approaching and retreating sensibilities that is not very easy to acquire.

*Cameron:* W. O. Mitchell refers to the reader as a "creative partner".

*Davies: Yes!* Exactly! And you've got to find the way to make it possible for him to create without being ashamed of himself afterwards. Only an artist can do that.

November 9, 1971

# A Gentleman of the Old School

## Nellie McClung

The big city gathered us in when the pleasant summer at the beach was over. Mark, our youngest child, was born in October of that year, and quickly became the idol of the family, with his blonde curls, blue eyes and quaint wisdom. The other children were all at school and Jack had started at Wesley College. Every day was full of interest. I enjoyed my association with the Canadian Women's Press Club, when we met once a week for tea in our own comfortable quarters. There great problems were discussed and the seed germ of the suffrage association was planted. It was not enough for us to meet and talk and eat chicken sandwiches and olives. We felt we should organize and create a public sentiment in favor of women's suffrage.

The visit of Mrs. Emmeline Pankhurst and of Miss Barbara Wiley, also one of the British Militant Suffragettes, created a profound impression. The immediate cause of our desire to organize was the plight of women workers in small factories. Some of our members had visited these and we were greatly stirred over the question of long hours, small wages and distressing working conditions.

Mrs. Claude Nash spoke one day on this subject at a Local Council meeting, and as a result of this meeting she and I were deputed to bring pressure to bear on the government for the appointment of a woman factory inspector. We decided to go to see Sir Rodmond Roblin, the Premier, and if possible, get him to come with us to see some of the factories. She knew him quite well and I had often listened to him in the Legislative Assembly from the visitors' gallery. He was a florid, rather good-looking man in his early sixties, somewhat pompous in manner but very popular with his party and firmly seated on the political throne by what was known as the "Machine". He believed in the patronage system

From Nellie McClung, *A Stream Runs Fast: My Own Story* (Markham, Ont.: Thomas Allen and Son, 1945).

and distributed governmental favors to the faithful in each riding. However, even in all the exposures which followed his defeat in 1914, there was no proof that he had ever enriched himself at the country's expense.

Mrs. Nash must have had some political standing, for I certainly had not, and we got an interview. We found Sir Rodmond in a very genial mood, and he expressed his delight at our coming. Mrs. Nash was a very handsome young woman, dressed that day in a grey lamb coat and crimson velvet hat. I wasn't looking so poorly myself for I, too, had youth on my side, and we could see that the old man was impressed favorably. I told him I had just come to live in the City from Manitou and I mentioned the name of W. H. Sharpe (afterwards Senator Sharpe) and I think that Sir Rodmond took it for granted that I, too, was a good Conservative, or, as he expressed it, was of the "household of faith." Sir Rodmond had once been a lay preacher in the Methodist Church, and scriptural references came natural to him. He balked a bit when we asked him if he would come with us to see some of the factories and tried to get us to be satisfied with one of his deputies, but Mrs. Nash and I held firm, and much to our surprise, he consented. He called his car and we set out. He looked very well in his beaver coat, and his car was the most pretentious I had ever ridden in. The cut glass vase filled with real carnations impressed my country eyes.

On the way to the first factory, the Premier, who sat between us, with his plump hands resting on a gold-headed cane, gave us his views on women working in factories. He believed in work, especially for young women. There was too much idleness now, with electricity and short cuts in labor. As a boy he had worked from sunrise, and before, until the shadows of evening fell, and enjoyed it. Happiest days of his life...running barefoot under the apple trees. Perhaps we were over-sentimental about factory conditions....Women's hearts were often too kind...but he liked kind women—and hoped they would never change. And these young girls in the factories whom we thought were underpaid, no doubt they lived at home, and really worked because they wanted pin-money. Anyway, working wouldn't hurt them, it would keep them off the streets...

Knowing what we did, we let the monologue go on. He advised us not to allow our kind hearts to run away with us. Most of the women in the factories, he understood, were from foreign countries, where life was strenuous (that word was in the first flush of its popularity then). They did not expect to be carried to the skies on a flowery bed of ease! It doesn't do women any harm to learn how money comes....Extravagant women are the curse of this age.

We conducted the Premier down dark, slippery stairs to an airless basement where light in mid-day came from gaunt light bulbs, hanging from smoky ceilings. The floor was littered with refuse of apple peelings and discarded clothing. There was no ventilation and no heat. The room

was full of untidy women operating sewing machines and equally un-
attractive men cutting out garments on long tables. We urged Sir Rodmond
to speak to some of the workers, but he was willing to call it a day at the
first glance. He was shocked at the filth of the place, and asked one of
the women if anybody ever swept the floor? He had to shout to drown
the sound of the machines. The woman shook her head and kept on
working. Then we reminded him that all these people were on piece work.

We led the Premier through a side door into the foul passage where
a queue had formed before a door marked "Toilet". We could see that
Sir Rodmond was deeply shocked that we should know about such things
but Mrs. Nash led the way, and I pushed him along from behind. We drew
his attention to the fact that there was no separate accommodation for
the women, and we did not need to mention that the plumbing had evidently gone wrong. We knew that he was soon going to bolt away from
us, so we didn't spare him anything.

"For God's sake, let me out of here," he cried at last. "I'm choking! I
never knew such hell holes existed!"

"These people work from 8:30 to 6:00, Sir Rodmond. Six days a
week," Mrs. Nash told him sweetly. "But no doubt they get used to it." I
am afraid her sarcasm was lost on Sir Rodmond.

When we got him up on the street again, he remembered an important interview he had promised, but we coaxed him to come to one more
factory where men's shirts were being made, and all the workers were
young women, and by promising him that this would be the last one, he
came with us. This workroom was in rather a better building and some
daylight came in from the windows. We wanted him particularly to see
these young girls who were being "kept off the streets". At one machine a
girl worked with a bandaged hand, a badly hurt hand and a very dirty
bandage. At another one a girl coughed almost continuously. I asked
her how long she had had her cold and she said she had no cold, it was
just a bit of bronchitis she had every winter, but she daren't stop work for
there were plenty more to take her place, and someone had to earn some
money in their family, as their father was out of work. She said she had
been lucky to get the job. The manager came over to speak to us, anxious
to show us the fine product they were turning out. Mrs. Nash asked him
how often the factory inspector came around, but he didn't seem to know
anything about factory inspectors. "In fact," he said, "we hardly need
one. All the girls are glad of the work. I have no trouble with them."

"How about the girl who coughs so much?" I asked. "Couldn't she be
given a few days off with pay to get built up a bit?"

The manager regarded me sternly.

"The company is not a charitable institution," he said, "and makes
no provision for anything like that. If the girl is sick, she can always quit!"
He threw out his hands expressively in a fine gesture of freedom.

Sir Rodmond was moving towards the door, and we followed. When we got back into the car we could see that the fine old gentleman of the old school was really shocked at what he had seen.

"Now, Sir Rodmond," we said, "do you still think that these women are pleasurably employed in this rich land of wide spaces and great opportunities?"

Sir Rodmond let down one of the windows of the car and said:

"I still can't see why two women like you should ferret out such utterly disgusting things."

"Your factory inspector knows about these places," we told him. "We mailed him a list of them and described them, but he has done nothing. He takes your attitude: Why should women interfere with what does not concern them? But we are not discouraged and have no intention of allowing these conditions to continue. We would like you to appoint a woman factory inspector, a real, trained social worker."

Sir Rodmond grew impatient at that. "I tell you it's no job for a woman. I have too much respect for women to give any of them a job like this....But I don't mind admitting that I'm greatly disturbed over all this, greatly disturbed," he repeated. "I'll admit I didn't know that such places existed and I promise you that I will speak to Fletcher about it."

With this understanding we parted, thanking Sir Rodmond for giving us so much of his time.

Our investigations went on. We were only amateurs but we did find out a few things about how the "other half" lived. We made some other discoveries too. We found out that the Local Council of Women could not be our medium. There were too many women in it who were afraid to be associated with any controversial subject. Their husbands would not let them "go active". It might imperil their jobs. The long tentacles of the political octopus reached far. So one night at Jane Hample's house on Wolsley Avenue we organized the Political Equality League, with a membership of about fifteen. We believed that fifteen good women who were not afraid to challenge public opinion could lay the foundations better than a thousand. Some good work had been already done by the Icelandic women of the city, who had organized the first suffrage society many years before, and the W.C.T.U. women could always be counted on and the same was true of the Labor women.

We wanted to get first-hand information on the status of women in Manitoba, and, of course, the whole Dominion. Then it was our purpose to train public speakers and proceed to arouse public sentiment. We would be ready for the next election and hoped to make our influence felt. We had all the courage of youth and inexperience with a fine underpinning of simplicity that bordered on ignorance, but anything we lacked in knowledge we made up in enthusiasm.

On a sudden impulse one day I phoned to the Premier's office when the House was in session and asked for an interview with Sir Rodmond Roblin, and to my surprise I found myself speaking to the gentleman himself, who in his most gracious manner assured me he would be pleased to see me and I could come at once, which I did. There in his private office with its red plush hangings and heavy leather furniture, I told the head of the government what we were doing and what we hoped to do. He listened with amused tolerance, but I was grateful to him for listening.

"Sir Rodmond," I said, "the women of Manitoba are going to be given the vote, either by you or someone else, and as you are the present Premier, it can be your proud privilege to have this piece of progressive legislation to your credit. I know what you're thinking; you're not impressed with the importance of this matter but that's because you never thought of it and you really should begin to think about it. You can no longer afford to take this attitude of indifference, and that's why I came to see you."

He looked up at me then and said:

"What in the world do women want to vote for? Why do women want to mix in the hurly-burly of politics? My mother was the best woman in the world, and she certainly never wanted to vote! I respect women," he went on, "I honor and reverence women, I lift my hat when I meet a woman."

"That's all very nice to hear," I said, "but unfortunately that's not enough. The women of Manitoba believe that the time has come to make an effort to obtain political equality. The laws are very unfair to women. I would like to tell you about some of them, for I don't believe you know, and what I would really like to do this afternoon is to have a chance to talk to you and your cabinet. It wouldn't take me long; I think fifteen minutes would be enough, and if you and the cabinet could be convinced that it is the right thing to do, it would certainly be easier, more dignified and less disturbing than if we are compelled to make a fight for it. But that is what we are prepared to do, if that is the way you want it. I wish you would call them in, Sir Rodmond, there's plenty of room here in your office."

Sir Rodmond removed the dead cigar from his mouth and his eyes hardened.

"The cabinet wouldn't listen to you," he said.

"You'd be surprised," I answered. "I'm really not hard to listen to, and I don't believe the cabinet would mind at all. In fact," I said brazenly, "I think they'd like it. It would be a welcome change in the middle of a dull day."

He could scarcely find words to express his astonishment and disapproval.

"You surprise me," he said slowly. "Now who do you think you are?"

"At this moment," I said, "I'm one of the best advisers you ever had in all your life. I'm not asking you for a favor, I'm really offering you help."

"What if I tell you that I don't need your help?" he said severely. "And that I think you're rather a conceited young woman, who has perhaps had some success at Friday afternoon entertainments at country school houses, and so are laboring under the delusion that you have the gift of oratory. What would you say to that?"

"I wouldn't mind," I answered. "I wouldn't even resent it. But I wish to tell you again, Sir Rodmond, as clearly as I can make it, that we are going to create public sentiment in this province, which will work against you at the next election. Did you ever hear that quotation about there being a tide in the affairs of men, which taken at the flood leads on to fortune?"

We looked at each other across the wide space of his mahogany desk and the silence was eloquent. Then Sir Rodmond's mood changed. His self-confidence came back; for a moment a doubt had assailed him. But the absurdity of the situation gave him courage. After all, what had he to be afraid of? His party was firmly entrenched, having 29 of the 42 members. He grew jocular.

"It would never do to let you speak to the cabinet," he said in the tone that one uses to a naughty child. "Even if they listened to you, which I doubt, you would only upset them, and I don't want that to happen. They are good fellows—they do what they are told to do, now. Every government has to have a head, and I'm the head of this one; and I don't want dissension and arguments. I believe in leaving well enough alone. Take the Indians, for example, they were far happier eating muskrats and the bark of trees before the white man came with education and disturbing ideas. Now they've lost all their good old-fashioned ways. No, you can't come in here and make trouble with my boys, just when I have them trotting easy and eating out of my hand. Now you forget all this nonsense about women voting," he went on in his suavest tones. "You're a fine, smart young woman, I can see that. And take it from me, nice women don't want the vote."

His voice dripped fatness.

"By nice women," I said, "you probably mean selfish women who have no more thought for the underpaid, overworked women than a pussycat in a sunny window has for the starving kitten on the street. Now in that sense I am not a nice woman, for I do care. I care about those factory women, working in ill-smelling holes, and we intend to do something about it, and when I say 'we' I'm talking for a great many women, of whom you will hear more as the days go on."

I stood to go. Then he smiled good-humoredly at me and said:

"Now don't go away mad. You know you amuse me. Come any time,

I'll always be glad to see you." My smile was just as good-natured as his when I said:

"I'll not be back, Sir Rodmond; not in your time. I hadn't much hope of doing any good by coming, but I thought it only fair to give you the chance. I'll not be back, but it's just possible that you will hear from me, not directly, but still you'll hear; and you may not like what you hear, either."

"Is this a threat?" he laughed.

"No," I said. "It's a prophecy."

# The Ghost of Beatrix Potter

## Margaret Lane

Most of the hallowed books of childhood lose something of their magic as we grow older. Beatrix Potter's never. She even, to the mature eye, reveals felicities and depths of irony which pass the childish reader by; the dewy freshness of her landscape recalls Constable; her animals, for all the anthropomorphism of their dress and behaviour, show an imaginative fidelity to nature, a microscopic truth that one finds in the hedgerow woodcuts of Thomas Bewick.

It would be unwise to say any of this if she were still alive. She died in 1943, her brief creative period (thirteen years in all) having come to a close some thirty years before, since when she had evolved into a rather crusty and intimidating person, interested mainly in acquiring land and breeding Herdwick sheep, and whom nothing annoyed more than to have her books appraised on a critical level.

Graham Greene was sharply rebuked when he wrote an essay (a more or less serious one, though Miss Potter took umbrage at what she interpreted as mockery) in which he discussed the period of the 'great comedies'—*Tom Kitten*, *The Pie and the Patty-Pan*, *Tiggy-Winkle*—and the subsequent 'dark period' of *The Roly-Poly Pudding* and *Mr. Tod*, the 'near-tragedies', using the tone of a sober scholar discussing Shakespeare. 'At some time between 1907 and 1909,' he wrote, 'Miss Potter must have passed through an emotional ordeal which changed the character of her genius. It would be impertinent to inquire into the nature of the ordeal. Her case is curiously similar to that of Henry James. Something happened which shook their faith in appearances.'

From Margaret Lane, *Purely for Pleasure*, London: Hamish Hamilton Limited (1966).

Miss Potter was affronted. Nothing, she told him in a 'somewhat acid letter', had disturbed her at the time of writing *Mr. Tod* save the after-effects of 'flu, which had not altered her so-called genius in any way. She sharply deprecated any examination of her work by the 'Freudian school' of criticism. Yet the essay, despite its Gioconda smile, was a flattering one, and anybody but the author of *Peter Rabbit* would have been pleased. She had become, indeed, curiously ambivalent about the whole of her *œuvre*. On the one hand, though she enjoyed the matter-of-fact acceptance of children, she was irritated to fury by any considered appraisal of her work; yet at the same time she could not have enough of the adulation which came to her in her latter years from America. Though she would see no others she would welcome reverent strangers from America, and the two or three poor-quality children's books of her late middle age all went to American publishers and were not in her lifetime allowed to be printed in this country. The reason for this, I believe, was that she was privately aware that they showed a sad falling-off, and while she was fairly confident of praise from the professional priestesses of 'kid lit.' in America she was unwilling to expose herself at home. Though she was impatient of serious attention from her compatriots, any hint of criticism exasperated her still more.

Miss Janet Adam Smith fell into this thorny trap in 1942 with an article in *The Listener*. 'Great rubbish, absolute bosh!' Beatrix Potter wrote to her publishers, who had thoughtfully sent her a copy, thinking she would be pleased to see herself placed, within her limits, in the 'same company as... Palmer, Calvert, Bewick and a host of earlier English artists'. To Miss Adam Smith she also wrote that she had read the article with 'stupefaction'. Her wrath was increased by a humourless misconception, since she plainly thought she was being accused of copying these artists. Much taken aback, Miss Adam Smith hastened to reassure her, explaining that 'your illustrations often give the reader the same kind of pleasure as the pictures of these earlier artists', and quoting a relevant passage from one of Constable's letters. Worse and worse. Miss Potter (or Mrs Heelis as she was in private life) now thought she was accused of copying Constable, and replied with a long expostulatory letter, ending with the tart postscript, 'When a person has been nearly thirty years married it is not ingratiating to get an envelope addressed to "Miss".' (An observation which would pass without comment in any of the several books about Tabitha Twitchet.)

I could, if asked, have warned anybody that it was unwise to meddle at all with Beatrix Potter, having nearly done so myself in 1939, when I was very sharply sent about my business. Like most people who have been wholly entranced by her little books in infancy, I had long believed that Beatrix Potter was dead. The occasional new production that one came across in bookshops (*A Fierce Bad Rabbit*, for example) was so egregiously bad compared with the early masterpieces as to strengthen the suspicion that they were written by somebody else. The bookshops denied this, and were not believed. It was no good asking questions about Beatrix Potter, because at that time nobody knew anything about her.

It was in the early days of the war that I first discovered that she was still alive, and living in the Lake District. My step-daughter was at school near Windermere, and brought home tempting scraps of some local legends that were current about her. She was very old. She was very rich. She was a recluse. She was a little mad. She drove round the lake on Sundays in an open carriage, wearing black lace and sitting very stiffly behind the coachman. (This, it turned out, was a memory of her mother, Mrs Rupert Potter, who had done exactly that.) Or alternatively, and this was the most popular legend of all, she did labourer's work in the fields, wearing sacks and rags.

It was very puzzling, but at least it seemed undeniable that she was still alive, and I fell, like Graham Greene and Miss Adam Smith soon after, into the innocent folly of wishing to write about her. Clearly, if she were as reclusive as people said, one must approach with care, and since it seemed desirable to go to the fountain-head as a precaution against inaccuracy or offence, I decided to write to her.

The sensible approach, indeed the only one, since I did not know where she lived, was through her publishers, and I wrote to Frederick Warne and Co. for her address. They replied with ill-concealed horror that on no account, in no possible circumstances, could her address be given. She lived in close retirement, she never saw anybody, they had her express instructions that nobody must ever be allowed to write her a letter.

This could have been final, but it was also rather a challenge to ingenuity, and since my intentions were of the most serious and respectful description I could not see why they should refuse to forward a letter. They did not refuse, though they clearly shrank from the impertinence, and in due course an extremely polite missive was forwarded to Sawrey. I told her of my lifelong pleasure in her books (addressing her, I am thankful to remember, as Mrs Heelis), expressed my admiration and my wish to write an essay on her work, and asked if I might one day call on her to check some facts and submit what I should write for her approval.

Back came, in a few days, the rudest letter I have ever received in my life. Certainly not, she said; nothing would induce her to see me. 'My books have always sold without advertisement, and I do not propose to go in for that sort of thing now.' Her reply could hardly have been more offensively worded if I had asked her to sponsor a deodorant advertisement.

Well, that was that, I thought. It would be impossible to write anything in the face of such hostility, a snub so out of proportion to the occasion. I tore up the letter in indignation, not knowing that I was only one of innumerable people who had had the breath knocked out of them by her acerbity.

And then, in 1943, she died; and Raymond Mortimer, at that time literary editor of *The New Statesman*, asked if I could write him an article on Beatrix Potter. I did my best but it was a poor best, for nobody seemed to know anything about her and the crumbs of fact I could gather were contemptible. I knew only that she had lived and farmed for years in the Lake District and was the wife of a country solicitor. I had to confine myself to an appreciation of her work, and even this contained some sad inaccuracies.

It soon became apparent, from the meagre obituary notices which followed, that I was not the only one who had failed to find out anything. The tone, everywhere, was one of surprise that she had been so recently alive, and it was suddenly borne in on me that what I wanted to do was to write her biography. Alas for such optimism! Here was a life so innocent, so uneventful that one would have supposed the only difficulty would be in finding something to say. Yet, when I approached her widower, the gentlest of men, who received me with a trembling blend of terror and courtesy, it appeared that he considered himself under oath to conceal the very few facts that he had in his possession. He knew remarkably little about her life before their marriage, which had taken place when she was approaching fifty, and what he did know he was unwilling to divulge. He impressed me as a man who for thirty years had lived under the rule of a fairly dominant feminine authority, and whenever, reluctantly, he imparted a scrap of information or a date, he would glance apprehensively over his shoulder, as though every moment expecting the door to open.

The house was indeed palpably haunted by her. She had not long been dead, and the imprint of her personality, clearly the more dynamic one in that marriage, was on every chair and table. Her clothes still hung behind the door, her geraniums trailed and bloomed along the window-sill, her muddles lay unsorted at one end of the table while he took his meals at the other, even a half-eaten bar of chocolate with her teeth-marks in it lay whitened and stale among the litter of letters on her writing-table.

Yet he had expressed himself willing, after much patient argument, that a biography should be written, and as a man of honour truly believed that he was doing his best. He had been, it is true, quite implacable at first, and had been at pains to explain, with the most considerate politeness, why such a project was impossible. She would not have wished it, he said; what was more, she would never have allowed it; and here he looked over his shoulder again and blew his nose in a large and dubious handkerchief. The argument which finally convinced him, in spite of his obvious misgiving that agreement was treachery, was that sooner or later, either in England or America, a biography would be written, and it was perhaps better to have it written while he was still alive and could presumably exercise some control over the biographer. He seemed relieved to think that by this means he might escape the attentions of some frantic American, but I had to promise that every word of every line should be subject to his inspection, and left the cottage after that first interview with my point gained, in the deepest possible dejection.

I knew exactly what he had in mind; the sort of biography he had at last brought himself, after the most scrupulous searching of conscience, to consider. It would be about a quarter of an inch thick, bound in navy blue boards with gilt lettering, and would be called *A Memoir of the late Mrs William Heelis*. We did not discuss the point, but I am sure he took it for granted that it would be for private circulation.

Then began a series of evenings which we spent together and which I look back on with misery. Every question, however innocuous, was met with the frightened response, 'Oh, you can't mention *that!*' Any detail of her parents, the date of her birth, even the fact of her marriage to himself fell under this extraordinary prohibition. Night after night I stretched my tact and ingenuity to breaking-point, feverishly changing from subject to subject, retreating at once when I saw his poor eyes watering in alarm, creeping back each night to my cold bedroom at the Sawrey inn to sleepless hours of knowing the whole thing to be impossible.

And then, after many evenings and by the merest accident, I changed my tune. Some tremulous negative, some futile protest over a harmless question, produced that sudden trembling which I have experienced only two or three times in my life and associate with the crisis known as losing one's temper. I found myself banging the table with clenched fist and crying 'Mr Heelis, you *must not obstruct me in this way!* ' The moment it had happened, in the petrified silence, I was overcome with embarrassment. But the effect was magical. He jumped, looked over his shoulder again as towards a voice he knew, pulled himself together, blew his nose, apologized, and suddenly seemed to feel remarkably better. I had never meant to do it, but the inference was plain. Tact, compliance, the yielding deviousness that had cost me so much effort, were things he was unaccustomed to and could not deal with. With decision, with firm opinion, he felt at home, and responded in the most eager and obliging manner. Pleased at last to be able to express his pride in his wife's fame he brought out his boxes of letters, rummaged in the bottoms of wardrobes and at the backs of drawers for photographs, produced such addresses and names as from time to time crossed his uncertain memory. The thing was started; I breathed a sigh of relief; though not without foreboding that my difficulties were only begun.

They were indeed, for over his eager compliance, which even extended to giving me two of her water-colours, hung the cloud of that final inspection of the manuscript which I knew would mar all. Left to himself, with typescript before him, I knew how his trembling hand would score it through, how little, how very little would come back unscathed, how in despair I would fling that little into the wastepaper basket.

Outside the precincts of Castle Cottage there was no such reticence; there were many people living who had known her well, Potter cousins, the niece of her last governess, Miss Hammond, innumerable farm and cottage neighbours who thought of her only as the eccentric little figure that the Lake District remembers—the odd bundle of country clothing, clad in innumerable petticoats, full of good humour, of authority, of sudden acerbities which could flash out quite brutally and inflict hurts where she probably never intended them. 'I began to assert myself at seventy', she wrote to one of her cousins a few months before she died, but this was an understatement. She had been asserting herself for thirty years, and the Lake District had come to respect her as a person it was dangerous to oppose, but very safe to love.

Those who spoke of her with the most feeling were the shepherds and farmers with whom she was most akin in temperament, and to the poetry of whose lives she had always responded, almost with the nostalgia of an exile. On her deathbed she had scribbled a note of indecipherable farewell to her old Scottish shepherd, the 'lambing-time man' who had come to her every spring for nearly twenty years, and with whom she had kept up a long and affectionate correspondence. He had preserved all her letters, dated and wrapped up in little parcels in the recesses of his cottage, and he sent them to me as an act of piety, for love of her memory.

I took innumerable journeys, sometimes with Mr Heelis, more often (and more fruitfully) alone, over the fells and along the valleys, to cottages and farmhouses that she owned, talking to the people who had known her. She had been a workmanlike landlord, most practically interested in fences and gates, the felling and planting of timber, the repairing of walls. As a sheep-breeder she was knowledgeable and shrewd, and the farmers round about thought of her principally as a dangerous rival at sheep fairs and ram shows, an enigmatic and authoritative presence in the Keswick tavern where the Herdwick Sheep Breeders' Association held its meetings.

At the same time I embarked on a sea of correspondence, which ebbed and flowed for more than a year. Beatrix Potter, for all the crowded busyness of her later years, when she was managing a number of farms and doing important work for the National Trust in the Lake District, possessed that last-century sense of leisure which permitted her to write long and frequent letters to a great many people—sometimes even to people she had never met, but whose personalities, when they wrote to her, had taken her fancy. Now, these letters began to flow into my hands, not only from English senders, but from places as far afield as America and New

Zealand; and the task of deciphering and sifting them for their shreds of biographical interest was for a time quite heavy.

To me, the series of letters which Warne's, her publishers for more than forty years, had kept without a gap since the day when they first accepted *Peter Rabbit*, was the most interesting of all, for they reflected her slow and painstaking development as an artist, her emotional growth from girl to woman, her emergence from unhappy and respectable nonentity into the kind of personality about whom biographies are written. The Warne family had played an important, and more than professional, part in her life, and without their help and confidence the book could never have been written.

But however much help I had from her publishers, relations and other friends, there was still to be faced the final confrontation with Mr Heelis, when, as I privately guessed, he would bring up reinforcements of prohibition and his mandate would fall on everything I had written.

I remember that on my last evening in Sawrey, returning from a walk with which I had tried in vain to recruit my spirits, I found a penny lying at the foot of a stile and decided to toss for it; whether I should give it up there and then or write the book as I saw it and be prepared to forget it for years in a locked drawer. The penny said heads, and I put it in my pocket as a charm. The drawer was the thing. I did not know how old Mr Heelis was, nor how I should explain my curious delay; but I was resolved I would not expose myself, or him, to the long-drawn agony of his excisions.

As it turned out, the penny proved a true oracle, for the poor widower, left alone and at a loss without the mainstay on which his thoughts and decisions had so long depended, died a few months after, before the book was finished, and I never paid that final visit to Sawrey. I do not believe he turns in his grave, honest man, nor that the stout little ghost which haunts the place would still, after all this time, find it necessary to be angry.

# Wittgenstein

## Guy Davenport

Like the gentle Anton Bruckner, who counted leaves on trees to while away a Sunday afternoon, Ludwig Wittgenstein in odd moments calculated the height of trees by pacing off from the trunk the base of a right triangle, wheeling around and sighting along his walking stick (up the hypotenuse) to the tree's top, invoking then the majestic theorem of Pythagoras. Together with inventing a sewing machine (in his teens), designing a house in Vienna (still standing) that elicited the admiration of Frank Lloyd Wright, and following assiduously the films of the Misses Betty Hutton and Carmen Miranda, this is one of the few acts of the philosopher that was at all transparent. No mystery, however, surrounds either his life or his thought. If he was not the greatest philosopher of our age, he was the most significant. He founded (inadvertently) and disowned two major philosophies. He was "getting at something" when he died, just what we shall never know. At the end of his first book, the *Tractatus Logico-Philosophicus* (completed in a concentration camp during the First World War) he wrote: "My propositions serve as elucidations in the following way: anyone who understands me eventually recognizes them as nonsensical, when he has used them as steps to climb up beyond them." At the beginning of his other book, the *Philosophical Investigations*, he wrote: "It is not impossible that it should fall to the lot of this work, in its poverty and in the darkness of this time, to bring light into one brain or another—but, of course, it is not likely." Once, when a student posed a question during one of his classes at Cambridge, Wittgenstein said: "I might as well be lecturing to the stove." A box of slips of paper— *Zettel*—was found among Wittgenstein's effects. On each slip is written a thought. The order of the slips, if any, is of course unascertainable. To

Reprinted from *The Geography of the Imagination: Forty Essays by Guy Davenport*, copyright ©1981 by Guy Davenport. Published by North Point Press and reprinted by permission. ALL RIGHTS RESERVED.

come to some understanding of them is not, as Sir Thomas Browne would cheer us on, beyond all conjecture, but we must go about it with the ghost of Wittgenstein whispering: "But, of course, it is not likely."

Wittgenstein before he came to philosophy was a mathematician, a musician, an architect, a sculptor, a mechanical engineer, a grade-school teacher, a soldier, and an aviator. He could have followed any of these careers doubtless with brilliant success; just before he came to Cambridge (they gave him a doctorate at the door) he was strongly inclined to "be an aeronaut." Every account of his strange life indicates that he *tried* to teach. He did not dine with the faculty, as the faculty in its grandeur always dines in academic gowns, black shoes, and neck tie. Wittgenstein was forever tieless and wore a suede jacket that opened and closed with that marvellous invention the zipper; and his shoes were brown. He held his lectures in his rooms, in the continental manner. As there was no furniture except an army cot, a folding chair, a safe (for the *Zettel*), and a card table, the students brought their own chairs. Philosophy classrooms in our century have frequently been as dramatic as stages: Santayana, Samuel Alexander, Bergson—men of passionate articulateness whose lectures fell on their students like wind and rain. But Wittgenstein, huddled in silence on his chair, stammered quietly from time to time. He was committed to absolute honesty. Nothing — nothing at all—was to be allowed to escape analysis. He had nothing up his sleeve; he had nothing to teach. The world was to him an absolute puzzle, a great lump of opaque pig iron. Can we think about the lump? What is thought? What is the meaning of *can*, of *can we*, of *can we think*? What is the meaning of *we*? What does it mean to ask what is the meaning of *we*? If we answer these questions on Monday, are the answers valid on Tuesday? If I answer them at all, do I think the answer, believe the answer, know the answer, or imagine the answer?

It was apparently not of the least interest to Wittgenstein that Plato had answered certain questions that philosophers need to ask, or that Kant or Mencius had answered them. He sometimes liked other philosophers' questions; he seems never to have paid any attention to their answers. Truth was stubborn; Wittgenstein was stubborn; and neither faced the other down. We have to look back to the stoic Musonius to find another man so nakedly himself, so pig-headedly single-minded. He actually taught for very little of his life. He was forever going off into the Norwegian forests, to Russia, to the west of Ireland where—and this is all we know of these solitudes—he taught the Connemara birds to come and sit in his hands. He mastered no convention other than speech, wearing clothes, and — grudgingly and with complaint—the symbols of mathematics. The daily chores of our civilization were wonders to him, and when he participated in them they became as strange as housekeeping among the Bantu. He liked washing dishes after a meal. He put the dishes and silverware in the bathtub, studied carefully the detergent, the temperature of the water, and spent hours at his task, and hours more in the rinsing and drying. If he was a guest for several days, all the meals had to be identical with the first, whether breakfast, lunch, or dinner. What he ate was of no matter, just so it was always the same. He listened carefully to human speech, and took it to pieces before one's eyes. Language, he decided, was a game men had learned to play, and he was always, like an anthropologist from Mars, trying to find out the rules. When he lay dying of cancer at his doctor's house, the doctor's kind wife remembered his birthday and baked him a cake. Moreover, she wrote on it with icing, "Many Happy Returns." When Wittgenstein asked her if she had examined the implications of that sentiment, she burst into tears and dropped the cake. "You see," Wittgenstein said to the doctor when he arrived on the scene, "I have neither the cake nor an answer to my question." Some days before, the doctor's wife, patient martyr in the history of philosophy, had shown Wittgenstein her new coat that she was to wear to a party that very evening. Silently he fetched the scissors, silently he snipped the buttons from the coat, silently he replaced the scissors. The sainted wife remarked that, yes indeed, come to think of it, the coat did look better without its buttons, but only when the seals are opened at Doom will the philosopher's skill with the scissors declare its meaning.

Except for the mathematician David Pinsent, to whom the *Tractatus* is dedicated and who was killed in the First World War, he was luckless in friends; he seems to have noticed women in order to know where to flee. The idea of a female philosopher made him close his eyes in despair. Insanity and suicide ran in his family. He pleaded with his students to take menial jobs (as he did from time to time, as a country schoolteacher and mechanic). Life was perhaps a strange disease which one suffered with heroism; thought was certainly a disease which philosophy, perhaps, could cure. Like Henry Adams he felt that a healthy intellect would be unaware of itself, and would get on with life's business, making beautiful machines, music, and poetry, without reflection. Whatever the truth of the world, it was simple in the sense that one can say, for instance, that death is not a part of life (one of the perceptions in the *Tractatus*) and that the world is independent of my will (another); and it was complex in the sense that all that happens is the result of many causes not all of which can ever be known.

It is only Wittgenstein's writing in the middle of his career that gives one fits—the part that gave birth (to his regret) to linguistic analysis, philosophy's darkest night. The early work—the *Tractatus*—is lucid and powerful. The newly discovered *Zettel* can only be compared to the fragments of Heraclitus. Indeed, Wittgenstein admired all his life the epigrams of the acid-tongued Lichtenberg, and felt that thought was basically perception. What the philosopher says about the world is not too different from the proverb, the old saw, the infinitely repeatable line of poetry. It is clear that the *Zettel* are a return to the manner of the *Tractatus*, back to the archaic period of philosophy, back before the talkative charm of Socrates. The philosopher, as Wyndham Lewis said of the artist, goes back to the fish. Physics in Wittgenstein's lifetime was going back to Heraclitus (a clue to cracking the atom was found in Lucretius by Niels Bohr); so was art; so was architecture. What could be more nakedly Pythagorean than the geodesic structures of Buckminster Fuller, what more household caveman than the paintings of Paul Klee? One definition of *modern* is a renaissance of the archaic (as *the* Renaissance was a reaching back to Hellenism, to Rome, to a ripened civilization rather than to the green springtime of that same civilization).

"The limits of any language are the limits of my world." "The most beautiful order of the world is still a random gathering of things insignificant in themselves." Which is Heraclitus, which Wittgenstein? "The philosopher," says one of the *Zettel*, "is not a citizen of any community of ideas. That is what makes him a philosopher." And: "What about the sentence—*Wie ist es mit dem Satz*—'One cannot step into the same river twice'?" That Heraclitean perception has always been admired for its hidden second meaning. *One* cannot step...; it is not only the flux of the river that makes the statement true. But is it true? No, Wittgenstein would smile (or glare), but it is wise and interesting. It can be examined. It is harmonious and poetic.

The more we read Wittgenstein the more we feel that he is *before* Heraclitus, that he deliberately began an infinite recession (in order, of course, to go forward when he found a footing). He bowed out of the tradition whereby all philosophers digest all other philosophers, refuting and enriching, forming allegiances and enmities, and emitting their version of what they have learned from a conquered vantage which must be defended night and day. Wittgenstein declined to inspect the history of philosophy. It is questionable if when he died he had ever come to any understanding of the number 2. Two *what*? Two things would have to be identical, which is absurd if identify has any meaning. One of the *Zettel* wonders what the phrase "friendly hand" could mean. Another, if the absence of feeling is a feeling. Another, if his stove has an imagination and what it means to assume that the stove does not have an imagination.

Wittgenstein did not argue; he merely thought himself into subtler and deeper problems. The record which three of his students have made of his lectures and conversations at Cambridge discloses a man tragically honest and wonderfully, astoundingly absurd. In every memoir of him we meet a man we are hungry to know more about, for even if his every sentence remains opaque to us, it is clear that the archaic transparency of his thought is like nothing that philosophy has seen for thousands of years. It is also clear that he was trying to be wise and to make others wise. He lived in the world, and for the world. He came to believe that a normal, honest human being could not be a professor. It is the academy that gave him his reputation of impenetrable abstruseness; never has a man deserved a reputation less. Disciples who came to him expecting to find a man of incredibly deep learning, found a man who saw mankind held together by suffering alone, and he invariably advised them to be as kind as possible to others. He read, like all inquisitive men, to multiply his experience. He read Tolstoy (always getting bogged down) and the Gospels and bales of detective stories. He shook his head over Freud. When he died he was reading *Black Beauty*. His last words were: "Tell them I've had a wonderful life."

# The Calgary Stampede

## Jack Ludwig

Start with its end, a July Saturday night, the Stampede cowboys pack-rolled, moving on, the rodeo pens and chutes empty, the chuckwagon races over. No race horses parade the track, people in the grandstand want broad-spectrum entertainment, "good fun," "real enjoyment." By 9 P.M. the Calgary Stampede has changed utterly. Now it's all tent show and provincial fair. Western sunset opens its sensational act, turning the uppermost third of the Ferris wheel into a burnished bridge, blinding the roller-coaster cowboys as, whooping up, they slingshot out of the shadowy lower depths. Gears mesh, lock, unlock, release, ratchet a coaster car slowly upward with the sound of a wooden stick rippling a picket fence, electronically augmented, a hundred times magnified, exploding then in a rush of screams and ooh's as subterfuge and centrifuge counterpoint the cry of "Come in, have your pitchur taken—hey, lady, take his pitchur so when he gets older he can see how much fun he had today."

But the barkers are bored, and the shills. That's the way it is at the fag end of any carnie stand. In these closing hours even the suckers may get an even break. A child losing at ringtoss is thrown a huge chartreuse hound dog with cerise tongue and pasted paper goo-goo eyes. A local hardball star has triumphed over the weighted milk bottles, and he and his woman friend walk off swathed in fuzzy Sicilian-tinted snakes and turtles luminous with purples, pinks, greens neither nature nor man ever expected or intended. Five bucks' worth of gaming has pecked out two bits' worth of kewpie dolls for the passing pigeons. Yet they come. Lines

©Jack Ludwig 1976. This article was first published in *Maclean's*.

everywhere, ten, twelve deep for every blackjack seat at the Frontier Casino, as many or more waiting for a "color" of chips at the roulette tables. Those who never play from anything but "the farthest seat on the dealer's right" in blackjack will take any available place now; and those who never play any color but "blue" or "green" at roulette find all chips grey in the gathering dark. In only a matter of hours the Stampede will close, and who has the patience to wait till next year to lose a winter's stash of coins and bills?

Under canopies, in the few places one may sit and nurse a soft drink or beer without ransoming away an arm and a leg, the older folk stake claims to a seat, sip slowly, sagged and wilted. Arm in arm, leather-jacketed and blue-jeaned couples, parties, gangs, sweep through the crowd, in a great hurry to do it all before the chuckwagon horses change back to mice. Anyone dreaming of "one big break" must make his hit in the next few hours. So it's *hurry hurry*, *hurry scurry*, the rhythm on the midway, *click shuffle*, *scrape curse* in the casino, while in easy contrast, the young people space themselves out in front of the Sun Tree, make one joint service a dozen unhurried smokers while tired rock music ekes out its wobbly decibels. From time to time a pot-fogged dreamer floats off in the direction of food and finds lines—lines and lines here as elsewhere, sullen lines, giggly lines, crying lines (where the children wait for their last Stampede ride). The masses mass to pay out what was saved from bread to spend on circuses. In the Stampede's waning moments there are no good rides and bad rides, only short-line rides. If standards existed for what one eats, they're gone too. Soggy corn-on-the-cob turned sodden being served is sloshed over with watery butter, then devoured as if it were the manna. Cotton candy shows bald spots, iced drinks are warm, hot dogs clammy cool, ice cream runny, candy apples adhesive—the standard ingredients of "enjoyment." A massive burned onion cloud hangs over the spielway, memorializing every singed hamburger of Calgary's ten-day blow.

Calgary's a city on the tilt, sloping up from foothills to the Rockies, cowboy country, half cowboytown, and, eastward, flat as Saskatchewan, farmer country, half farmertown. Farmers and cowboys—even without the oil people—were never that easy to tell apart. Now, of course, the Western craze shrouds woman, man and child in blue denim. Farmboys regularly spruce up in boots, cowboy hats, string ties. To resemble their fathers, they part slicked-down hair just over the ear, then lay what's gained right across the forehead to look as up-to-date as dad's wig. Cowboys, farmers, oilmen still hang tight with Elvis sideburns. Women, to save the Stampede from going snooty, wear a metal clip on side curls, but, to prove the Stampede's a night out, forgo plastic rollers and curlers. The inevitable bikers loom up, black leather and studs, studded wristbands, silver zippers, black sunglasses, buckle boots, wartime/peacetime issue, worn by all male members of the enlarged nuclear family, the women in black leather, and democratically studded, everything but the receiving blankets a few have wrapped around infants.

These are the night people. In the morning and afternoon crowds summer was the dominant theme—short shorts, tank tops, cotton dresses, wash-and-wear dude shirts. What's ominous at night—the anachronistic freak show on the midway—in bright sunlight is only absurd. The flack for the Royal American Shows says that complaints "about bad taste from local patrons" persuaded the firm to cut out its "two-headed baby act," stout fellow! *And* its "chamber of horrors." Still, it offers midwayniks a Palace of Illusions featuring such nonbad taste items as Madam Twisto, whose thing is "revolving...alive," and another woman called "The Long Neck...alive," still another called "The Girl Without a Middle...alive," and several other "alives" who, it seems, survived electrocution, hanging, though presumably the biblical fates of stoning and beheading weren't considered worthy of midway display. Lined up to go into one of the Palace's "Main Entrances" is a man seemingly unaware he will soon be under contract—tiny of head, pigeon in the chest, and ballooned-out extravagantly in the middle. Madam Twisto will probably spin seeing him. He is not alone. That guy in glasses you always see coming out of peepshows and bumshows is with him—and several hundred others with forefinger upraised to catch the freaks on an Instamatic, "all alive"!

During its first days I came out to the Stampede when rain washed attendance away. The grandstand was new, all sorts of shifts and changes had been made since 1973's show. The result was little parking, a fair amount of inconvenience. Till more than 140,000 people turned up on closing day the Stampede seemed to be in deep trouble (as it was, attendance in 1974 was only 20,000 shy of the 1973 record—993,777). The new setup, good for horseracing, was, I found, far less suited to the rodeo events. Not till Paul Matte of the Stampede office sneaked me across the racetrack and I climbed into a TV tower just above the chutes was I able to see *the* Stampede. Behind those chutes sat the families, the friends of contestants, the rodeo aficionados as oblivious of the midway as the midway is of the rodeo.

These Calgarians and visitors know rodeo champions the way *Hockey Night in Canada* watchers have a legend on Bobby Orr, or Ken Dryden, or the guys in the "other league," Gordie Howe and Bobby Hull. Aficionados take it personally when the world champion bull rider, Bobby Steiner, doesn't compete in the 1974 Stampede. They want to know if it's because Bobby's hurt or because some other rodeo dares to compete on these dates with the Stampede. If it's the latter, they want to know if Steiner's absence doesn't downgrade the competing this year.

When they check down the program they look for the other "world" (*i.e.*, North American) champions, and, happily, find the champion of champions, Larry Mahan, of Dallas, Texas, on the premises. Mahan has been the All-Around champion five years in a row (six times in all), has won more money in a single year than any other competitor, and has won more money in total than any other competitor. Larry Mahan's presence more than makes up for Bobby Steiner's absence. The rodeo pushers call him, alas, "Mr. Supersaddle," and with a touch of Grand Old Opry refer to him as "the world's most winningest cowboy," but Larry Mahan doesn't need that breed of bull. At the 1974 Stampede he won the All-Around by winning the Bareback bronc championship and placing second in the bull-riding (won by a Saskatoon rider, Brian Claypool, ranked fifth in the "world" behind Bobby Steiner).

There's a great deal of controversy about rodeos. The rodeo people have set up their own "humane" society to take the heat off the charges made by various local, national and international branches of the Society for the Prevention of Cruelty to Animals. Watching the bareback bronc and bull-riding events, I wondered if anybody thought to include man among those animals. There is no way for someone to sit a horse or a bull for eight seconds (or ten, when that's called for) without taking a lot of cruel and unusual punishment. Every rider—successful or instantly thrown—suffers disorientation on touching ground. A sine wave passes through a man's body, not smoothly but powerfully; whiplashing both ends against the humped-up, bucked and belted middle. That kind of violence sends shocks against the brain pan as severe, it seems to me, as a succession of uppercuts on the chin of a boxer. A rider goes against an animal who may be familiar to him, or strange. If strange, regardless of what other riders have told him about the animal's rhythm, he must key on that rhythm in about a second, and then, instantly programmed, adapt what he has learned to the variations in the animal's tricks. Think of the difficulty one has trying to figure an electric maze of complexity and trickiness: a bucking surging bronc or wildly spinning bull of the championship class is far more difficult to figure than a maze, and eight seconds, which, as punishment, may seem a century, is, as time allowed for problem-solving, incredibly short.

Larry Mahan's formula for bull-riding is pure Plato:

"I try," he says, "to picture a ride in my mind before I get on the bull. Then I try to do it by the picture."

Professional cowboys have among their rodeo icons not only the great cowboys but the great animals of circuit history, the most famous of which, a Canadian horse named Midnight, is mentioned whenever the serious challenges of the sport come up. Midnight is buried in the grounds of the Cowboy Hall of Fame in Oklahoma City, Oklahoma, his grave marked by a plaque, "1910-1936," and Angus Cameron, perhaps the most famous of horse book editors and a frequent visitor to the Hall of Fame, tells me the greatest attraction there is Midnight's grave. Cowboys talk about Midnight and such famous bulls as Tornado as "athletes:" they characterize the animals as "honest," by which they mean nothing is held back, and boast of the bronc nobody could ride with almost the same enthusiasm they talk of those great animals someone eventually did stay on.

Transport, the horse Larry Mahan rode to win his bareback bronc riding championship was such an "athlete." To ride him, Mahan lay back like a swimmer trying to float a whipping, powerful, spine-snapping wave. From fifty feet away I could hear the cracking and lashing sounds of Mahan's body as Transport strained and humped to shoot him off—this above the crowd shouts and the announcer's amplifiers. At the eight-second signal two pickup men charged toward Transport and swept Mahan off the still-bucking back, dropped him, stumbling, dazed, rocking on his feet, while they chased and steered the bronc out of the arena into a narrow runway.

Events in a rodeo follow upon one another with the speed and smoothness of a well-managed three-ring circus. At the Stampede I was as impressed by those who make a rodeo work as I was by the contestants. These were the professionals who keep the stock moving into the pens and chutes, who do the saddling, who measure the lengths of braided manila rope needed in bull-riding and saddle bronc-riding, who raise and lower the pen gates, who time an animal's release, who, on a Stampede after-noon when horseracing punctuates the rodeo events, use the putting up of the swinging gates as a rhythmic pause in the largely uninterrupted con-tests they must manage. The mounted pickup men in the bronc-riding and the rodeo clowns in the bull-riding were other pros absolutely essential to the continuity and safety of the bronc- and bull-riding events. By either ac-cident or intent a bull could gore or trample a bucked-off rider, which means, of course, that the "clowns" in their 100-pound rubber barrels or running on cleated football shoes to divert the charging bulls are engaged in a serious and dangerous business. If, say, pickup men on horses tried to scoop up a fallen bull rider the horse would become a most vulnerable target. Therefore the clown operates on foot, always risking a stumble and a fall, and the almost certain injury that would follow. For this reason three clowns usually stand by for the bull-riding events. In the circus, clowns not only amuse but act as a diverting bridge between acts; in the rodeo the clown is an actor and participant. There could be no bronc- or bull-riding events without the pickup men and these clowns.

The rodeo, like a one-ring circus, aims at an illusion: that all contests dovetail, making the rodeo one continuous event, from the opening "Grand Parade" to the climactic bull-riding contest. The rodeo, like any other spectacle, structures its program, starts with "crowd-pleasers," leads into the main events—steer-wrestling, calf-roping, bareback and saddle bronc-riding, bull-riding—careful to intersperse "novice" and "boys" among the professional contests.

At the Stampede finale the Buffalo Ride, featuring young Canadian Indians, or pseudo-Indians mostly, served as "warm-up," "prelim," free-for-all show biz calculated to make an audience not only laugh but pay attention. In the insane confusion of buffalo charging, riders slipping and falling into the dirt, the crowd howled, egged on by the chortle and shout of the announcer. The Buffalo Ride and the Wild Cow Milking contest that followed, though connected to the rodeo, could as easily have been part of the midway hoke outside. The Buffalo Ride particularly, in which almost every contestant was tumbled, bumped, or fell staggering—running off, reeling, or limping—was something Nero's Roman compatriots might have enjoyed as a rather tame prelim for the bigger and better lion games that followed.

With the spectators still yowling and hooting like a studio audience at a TV participation show, the Buffalo Ride gave way to the Wild Cow Milking "fun," with the announcer's shouts even louder now, to encourage the aspiring hysterical. Only then, with the spectators ostensibly "delivered," did the rodeo proper begin, featuring "real" cowboys in a *real* contest directed to the *real* spectators in the rodeo seats behind *real* animals in their pens and chutes. Laughter stopped. Show biz disappeared. Everything, now, was between man and animal. Frequently a child's voice cut through, imploring a father or brother to be careful, or to "give 'im hell, Dad." During the boys' or novices' events women could be heard shouting, for the most part, *stay-on, stick-with-it, hang-in* encouragement. Nationalism touched the Stampede as it does most things Canadian: though the spectators wanted the big-time American rodeo contestants at the Stampede, they also wanted their Canadian heroes to knock them off.

In the first real rodeo event, bareback bronc-riding, the competition, curiously, fell into two groups—Canadian novices who hadn't scored *higher* than 138 in two previous short go-rounds (or heats), competitors who hadn't scored *lower* than 140. Yet even here, with little chance to beat the eventual winner, Mahan, Mel Hyland of Alberta cowboytown, Ponoka, the 1972 "world" saddle bronc champion, made a great try, actually outscoring Mahan on the short-go, 76-75. Every year, people in the stands told me, they look for signs that more Canadians are arriving as rodeo champions. If 1974 wasn't a good year for the bareback, it was an excellent year for the saddle bronc- and bull-riding events.

What Calgary saw were two young Saskatchewan competitors, eighteen-year-old Melvin Coleman, of Pierceland, and twenty-year-old Brian Claypool, of Saskatoon, win the saddle bronc- and bull-riding championships respectively. It was only Mel Coleman's first year as a non-novice competitor. A few old grizzled American cowboys grumbled that the judging seemed to favor Canadians but, for the most part, the results were conceived as fair. Brian Claypool, as I've already indicated, stood high among bull-riding competitors on the continent, so his victory wasn't all that surprising, though Coleman's, won in competition against such stars as Dennis Reiners and Marty Wood, was. Not only was Coleman young; this was his first try at a Stampede "North American" championship; in 1973 he was second in the *novice* competition.

"Hey," I hollered down from my tower platform at a cowboy who didn't look too happy when Coleman's high short-go score of 82 was announced, "what do you think of that?"

"He-e-ll," the man said in an accent I took for Texan, "they musta give him a little somethin' extra for wearing' that checker shirt."

A third Saskatchewan competitor, Richard Todd of Wood Mountain, had a superb short-go time of 4.2 in his last steer-wrestling try, actually beating the eventual champion, Tom Ferguson, the present "world" All-Around champ, by half a second, but in the aggregate and average lagged far behind Ferguson and another circuit star, Darryl Sewell.

Event followed event, each one settling a championship, each one meaning money. As usual, Larry Mahan's winnings put him in front of everybody else; but when one thinks of the punishment someone like Mahan has to absorb in order to win a total of, in Calgary, $7,468, it shivers the sports perspective. A successful rodeo rider will earn in a year what Johnny Miller or Jack Nicklaus walks off with winning a big stop on the golf tour—$50,000. Only a few top rodeo figures will earn in a year two-thirds of what Miller or Nicklaus get for coming out on top *twice*. No cowboy could hope to earn, in three or four years, the more than $300,000 Nicklaus and Miller have each won in their best tour years.

"We know it don't make sense," says Freckles Brown, a more or less retired rodeo cowboy, "get on another head o' stock, land on your shoulder, land on your head, pick yourself up, get on a rig, go another 900 miles, and get on another head o'stock..."

In the novice saddle bronc ride, a young Alberta rider, Tom Crowe, thrown from his mount before he knew he was on a "head o' stock," crashed to the ground, then crawled through the sunwarmed dirt to curl up like some hurt creature in the shade of the cement dugout under the grandstand stage. Stunned and huddled into himself, obviously hurting, Crowe spurned the stretcher bearers who raced out to help him. Cowboy *macho*. The code: *Walk off under your own legs, even if they is broke. Don't give no head o' stock the satisfaction o' knowin' he hurt you.* Shaky, doubled up, hobbling, Crowe made it out of the arena to much code applause, the spurned stretcher-bearers jogging beside him.

In the boys' steer-riding championship, though, the rodeo clown closest to the youngest, smallest contestant, Cam Bruce, snatched him off the steer's back at the horn, rather than risk the small boy being thrown that long fall from the animal roof. In the second half of the steer-riding, Daryl Schacher shot out of the chute, clinging two-handed (by the rules) as his steer bolted, smashing into the fence with Daryl still holding on tight, and everyone in the stands shouting. The clowns rushed in to pull Daryl free while other clowns chased the steer back through the runway. The result of it all? Daryl was given an official re-ride!

Sometimes the novices, disappointed, reacted like much younger boys. In the saddle bronc competition one competitor came in far ahead of everyone else but was penalized for a rule infraction on his final short-go, and assigned a zero. In a second the certain winner was turned into a loser. In disappointment and anger he began to cry, while his friends and fellow-competitors gathered to console him.

Only once—after the Buffalo Ride and the Wild Cow Milking show biz act—was anything in the arena arranged for Nero and his Romans, the Wild Horse Race. The rules called for several competing three men-with-a-wild-horse teams, each made up of:

1. a wild horse
2. an "ear man" who was supposed to bite the wild horse's ear in a Spockian touch intended to "distract and calm the animal"
3. the "shank man" who clings to the horse's shank while
4. the rider, or, one assumes, "ass man," tries to vault himself up into a saddle he himself has attached to the horse.

At the signal to begin, all aspiring riders try to saddle, mount, and then ride over a short designated "track," the first horse and rider to cross a white washed line being the winner.

While the announcer chuckled and confounded, while the tucked-up-in-the-stands spectators screamed and laughed, terror dominated the arena below. I saw it in the ear man's face, the shank man's spine, the aspiring rider's eyes—because his face tried hard to show *macho*, arrogance, pugnaciousness. Knee-bent the ear man cringed. Terror showed in the team ducked beneath a rearing horse's flailing hooves in fear that the wild horse, and animal retribution, would come crashing down. And greater terror, of being trampled by frightened, swerving animals bolted free of aspiring saddlers. Ear men and shank men hanging on as horse body slammed up against horse body, dragging neverseated riders through the dust spitting dirt and clutching at empty saddles. A few horses charged about aimlessly, saddles slung below their bellies like mailman's pouches. Heels dug in the dirt, captive heroes skidded by like water skiers, or startled farmboys trying to hang onto a plow behind Secretariat.

Loosed, horses struggled into an animal circle, a willed roundup full of nightmare Picasso images—teeth bared, streaming manes, frightened eyes, distended nostrils, taut vein-swollen necks, bodies shiny with sweat.

And what was it all for? The Emperor Nero, and many others in the stands, told the horses wouldn't kill anybody during their act, decided this was as good a time as any to go out for a hot dog and/or the men's room, and so missed the whole shebang. And those who run the midway "freak" show, interested in nothing *but* the Wild Horse Race, could now go back to their own exhibitionism, satisfied they had seen everything the rodeo had to offer.

Steer-wrestling and bull-riding slowly brought the rodeo back to the Stampede, and when those contests were over, so was the cowboy's Stampede—all but the chuckwagon races. But to see the chuckwagon races one had to leave the grandstand, wander the midway or casino areas for about three hours, spending, drinking, eating, and then, in order to watch the chuckwagons, pay another ticket's worth. The younger people around the Sun Tree wanted to see the chuckwagon races, they told me, but couldn't afford the price of another ticket. Some had already put out seven or eight dollars on little or nothing—without seeing any of the rodeo events they said they were most interested in seeing.

"It's all rip-off," an Edmonton girl told me. "This is supposed to be fun and we can't even make it into that grandstand. Why couldn't they have the rodeo and the chuckwagons all at once? Rip-off—just rip-off. Even this, that's free," she said, waving her hand at the Sun Tree, "this is supposed to be what young people want. It's insulting. It's the worst rip-off of all."

I left the Stampede grounds after the rodeo events, took a cab to a restaurant next to the Calgary Inn where a long line waited neatly to get in. Dates, twos, couples, all neat, all dressed up. I asked a couple what the line was all about.

"Cabaret," a young man said, beaming, "live entertainment."

He sounded as if he had just recently experienced the very opposite of live entertainment. Or, to put it another way, the Stampede midway.

When I got back to the Stampede the urgency of do-it-all-before-midnight-tolls had taken over. People were turning up for sweepstake draws, pots o' gold—that sort of thing. And the chuckwagon races.

From the very top of the grandstand I could see the racetrack, the stock pens, the stable area for racing horses, the river, everything now, in reddened sun tones, cast in the segment of the color spectrum that excludes anything blue. In the two symmetrical rodeo pens—one for horses, one for steers and calves—animal and earth and corral fence were all tinted brown, golden, orange. Everything was peaceful, serene—no hoke, no hype, no spiel, no violence, no show biz. The track, on which the chuckwagon race would begin, was in evening shade, but behind the pens the track lay in bright sunshine. Even as a recreation of something that might never have been, the chuckwagon race made it—the rig, the four horses, the hunched-forward driver, the tense outriders in helmets, cowboy hats or jockey caps getting ready to stow the stove and tent poles, mount, and race. Four wagons, everybody frozen except for the horses swishing tails at un-race-conscious flies.

All four teams broke at the start, inscribed their beautiful figure eights, then galloped onto the track, tails streaming, the drivers up and hollering, the outriders on their horses and out on the track in their race within the race. It took less than half an hour to run the four last heats of the chuckwagon finale and out of it emerged another young Canadian champion, Kelly Sutherland, 22, not only the grand winner but also the winner of the third spot, and a total of almost $11,500 out of a possible $67,000.

When the chuckwagon races ended, so, for many, did the Stampede. The midway was still open, the casino thrived, the rides went their appointed round, but the rodeo was gone. The year's peak flattened, the end of the circus that made the struggle for bread mean something special. At midnight the coach and horses were only pumpkin and mice—till summer '75.

# A Penny Saved Is a Waste of Time

## Andrew A. Rooney

What follows is some advice I forgot to give our kids before they left home:

—There is a Santa Claus but he doesn't always come.

—Being well dressed is like being six feet tall. You either are or you aren't and there isn't much you can do about it.

—Learn to drink coffee without sugar.

—Throw away the can of paint after you've finished painting something, no matter how much there is left in the can.

—Don't keep your watch five minutes fast.

—Go to bed. Whatever you're staying up late for isn't worth it.

—Don't expect too much from the company you work for even if it's a good company.

—You're almost always better off keeping your mouth shut, but don't let that stop you from popping off.

—There are few satisfactions in life better than holding a grudge. Pick them carefully but hold them.

—Don't fuss a whole lot with your hair.

—You're better off missing a bus or an airplane once in a while than you are getting there too early all the time.

—Don't save string. If you need string, buy it.

—Don't save pennies, either. They don't add up to anything.

—If you can't find comfortable shoes that are good-looking, buy comfortable shoes that aren't, but don't buy good-looking shoes that are uncomfortable.

—Don't call in sick except when you're sick.

Andy Rooney, "A Penny Saved is a Waste of Time" from *Pieces of My Mind*. Copyright © 1984 Essay Productions, Inc. Reprinted with the permission of Atheneum Publishers, Inc.

—You aren't the only one who doesn't understand the situation in the Middle East.

—Nothing important is ever said in a conversation that lasts more than three minutes.

—Very few things you buy will be the answer to the problem you bought them to solve.

—There's seldom any good reason for blowing the horn on your car.

—If you work moderately hard you'll find a lot of people aren't working as hard as you are.

—It is unlikely that you'll have any success gluing a broken chair together.

—If you buy a book and feel like making marks in it with a pen or pencil, make them. It's your book and it doesn't ruin it for anyone else anyway.

—Be careful but don't be too careful.

—In a conversation, keep in mind that you're more interested in what you have to say than anyone else is.

—If nothing else works, take a hot shower.

—Don't keep saying, "I don't know where the time goes." It goes the same place it's always gone and no one has ever known where that is.

—If you own something useless which you like, don't throw it away just because someone keeps asking what you're keeping it for.

—The fewer, the merrier.

—Don't believe everything you read in the newspaper but keep in mind almost all of it is true.

—Keep the volume down on everything. It's like salt. You can get used to less of it.

—Money shouldn't be saved for a rainy day. It should be saved and spent for a beautiful day.

—Language is more important than numbers.

—Don't make a date for anything more than a month in advance.

—It's *i* before *e* except in the following words: "Neither leisure foreigner seized the weird height."

—Travel just for the sake of going somewhere is usually a disappointment.

—Use profanity sparingly and don't use any obscenities at all.

—If you can't afford the expensive one, don't buy it.

—Try to be aware of how you're being.

—You'll be better off in the long run making decisions quickly even if a lot of them are wrong. They probably won't be wrong any more often than if you took a lot of time making them.

—When you cross a street, look both ways... even on a one-way street.

# How to Play Second Base

## Laurence Sheehan

Second base is the most important position in baseball. Nobody realizes. A lot of coaches don't even bother to tell their second basemen the first thing about the job. They don't think second base is worth the effort.

The unfortunate name of second base is partly to blame. It just sounds like a hand-me-down. I think the ill-fated manager Joe McCarthy of the Boston Red Sox also once said something like second base is neither first nor third. That was the situation when I was playing for Centerville School, and I doubt if it's improved much since then, not at Centerville or in the majors.

Why is second base so important? Because when an easy grounder or a high pop-up is hit to that position, and you kick it away, or misjudge it and let it bounce on your head, the whole team gets demoralized. The shortstop comes over and says, Too bad the school bus didn't clip you this morning. The first baseman slaps his leg and laughs. The pitcher gives you the finger in front of everybody. Of course there may not be that many people at the game, so the public humiliation won't count for much. Centerville hardly ever drew a crowd because it was always in last place in its division, thanks in part to slight miscalculations by the second baseman.

I got my little sister Evie to come a lot when games were played at Legion Field in our neighborhood. But she didn't understand baseball. She would see me strike out on three consecutive pitches, or get run through by a steaming grounder. But she wouldn't find such happenings interesting enough to report to our parents. I'd have to tell them myself at supper.

Laurence Sheehan, "How to Play Second Base." *The Atlantic Monthly* (September, 1974). Reprinted by permission of the author.

You might say that for Evie my baseball failings went in one eye and out the other. She was a lousy fan. I sometimes wondered why I had her come to the games at all, which I did starting when I made the team in sixth grade and got my uniform. I don't think she even knew what number I wore (9—The Thumper's own!). Anyway, if it weren't for the bubble gum my black pal Herman kept giving her, she probably would have stopped coming long before she finally did. Herman played third. She would chew gum or eat an apple or orange from home, and watch out that no one stole our gloves when we were at bat, but basically Evie paid no attention to what was going on. She usually sat on the opposing team's bench, to my great embarrassment. It was closer to the water fountain.

Back to second base now. There are tips that can make anybody play this position better and I'd like to pass them along.

By the way, I didn't mean to imply I minded my teammates groaning and hooting at my errors. I mean I minded, but I understood. And basically we had a close-knit infield. It wasn't any dream infield, such as the Bosox built around the great Bobby Doerr and Johnny Pesky in the same years I was at Centerville, but we had a pretty good team feeling. Erwin, our regular pitcher, would put up with four or five errors in one inning before going to the finger. Lover Boy, the first baseman, would laugh at errors and kid a lot, but actually he didn't care where the ball went or even who won. His mind was always on his girlfriends who were waiting for him up in the nearly empty stands. Bert, our team captain at short, would come over after I'd let one go through my legs, and say, "All right, let's get back in this game now." And of course Herman, who never made an error himself over at third, would not get upset by anything I did. Or anybody did. He was the coolest cucumber on the squad.

Not even State Street's Butch Mendoza, the division's Home Run King and number-one razzer, could get through to Herman. We had no regular coaches on the bases. Older players on each team did the job. Mendoza liked to do it for State Street. He'd coach first base and rib Lover Boy about his shaggy hair and his white cleats, and Lover Boy would nod and smile, probably not even hearing Butch's taunts, too busy dreaming about those girls of his up in the stands and about his plans for them all after the game. When Butch coached third he liked to rib Herman about his color. "Hey, boy, where's your watermelon today?" he'd say, or "How come you're not picking cotton this week?" At that time blacks were few and far between in our town, no matter what grammar school you went to, and Butch probably thought of Herman as a foreigner. The important thing is, Herman paid no attention to Butch and never did make an error before his eyes.

I'll spare the outfielders on Centerville. Like most outfielders they were hotshots, and I suppose because they managed to get more hits and runs than anyone else, they had a right to parade around out there and editorialize on every move the infielders made.

Now, then, the hardest play to handle is the infield fly. I say anytime a ball goes higher than it goes farther, it is going to be a son of a gun to catch. In my playing days, half the time I wouldn't even know when one of those high pops was entering my territory. I'd need to hear Lover Boy call over, "Hey, little man, here comes trouble!"

Anyway, you've got to get set. A good thing is to get your feet in motion. And bend your neck back far enough so your eyes see more than the brim of the baseball cap. Everything about school uniforms is fine except the brims on the caps. They are made for adult heads, and if you stand 4 feet 3 and weigh 75 pounds, the hat will be like an awning on your forehead. The only thing you'll be able to see without any strain is your feet, which as I said should be in motion anyway—as you commence dancing into position to make a stab at the catch.

Of course, once you get your head tilted back far enough so you can see past the brim of your cap, you risk being temporarily blinded by the sun. Even on cloudy days it is possible for the sun to come out just at the crucial instant and make you lose sight of the damn ball, assuming you ever saw it in the first place.

Another bad thing about the high fly is that it gives you too much time to think. Like the drowning man, a ten-year-old tends to experience all the important moments in his life while waiting for a baseball to drop. Moments such as when you saw your name on the Centerville School baseball roster for the first time.

To tell the truth, the reason I got to play second base for Centerville for three years in a row is that my growth was stunted at the time, and provided I didn't swing at the ball when I was up to bat, opposing pitchers tended to walk me. My strike zone was about the size of a civics workbook. If I waited out the pitchers, I could count on getting on base almost every time.

Not that I wouldn't go for the hit once in a while. I would pretend to miss the signal telling me to wait for the walk that would invariably come from the third-base coach when I was up. The signal was always the same: doff cap, scratch left knee, blow nose in hanky, in that order. By the end of the season every team in the division knew all our coaching signals, but it was too confusing to try to change them.

Anyway, sometimes I would just ignore the signal and go for the hit. Each time I missed the ball, of course, the third-base coach would slam his cap on the ground or throw his hanky down, mad as can be. The opposing team's catcher would grin and hold the ball up in front of my eyes for my inspection before tossing it back to the mound. I would ignore all this and just dig in deeper with my cleats and take a couple of fierce practice swings. Digging in was itself a problem because the batter's box was furrowed over from other stances. Following the example of The Thumper and Vern Stephens and other Beantown sluggers, the boys in our division liked to get a really firm hold on the planet when at bat. They would dig and kick with their cleats like dogs tearing up the ground after peeing, and the result would be a set of gullies in the batter's box among which I was supposed to find a place to stand. I had the narrow stance that comes with a 4-foot, 3-inch frame, and sometimes I had one foot on a hillside and the other in a gully. No wonder my average was low.

That's really part of the story of how Herman and I got to be friends — we were built the same. We were the only two to make the team in sixth grade. Herman made it on his talent in spite of his size and I made it on my size in spite of my talent. In a way we came up together from the minors. Also we tended to sit right near each other in classrooms because our last names started with the same initial and in those days everything was done alphabetically, from choking on cod-liver-oil pills to taking cover in the lavatory during practice A-bomb attacks.

Now about the high fly. Your own thoughts are not the only distractions when you're looking for a ball somewhere up there in the blinding blue infinity of outer space. People are chattering all around you. Once I heard my sister call to me, "Hey, I'm going to play on the swings now, OK?" Another time, when we were playing State Street, Butch Mendoza hit a real rainmaker somewhere in my neighborhood. Running down the line to first, Butch had plenty of time on his hands, so he hollered, "Hey, kid, you're gonna miss it, you're gonna miss it!" Of course I was; nobody had to broadcast it.

State Street always won the division and usually went on to win the town title by beating the leader of the other division. They were tough boys at State Street. If they didn't beat you in the game, they'd beat you up afterwards. A lot of the State Street players had stayed back in grades a couple of times, which gave them the edge of experience over the boys at Centerville. I don't know how old Butch was. I did hear once that when he finally graduated from State Street he was eligible for the draft. That may have been an exaggeration, but no question, he was big. He would pole tremendous flies that our outfielders wouldn't even bother running for. There was no proper fence at Legion Field such as they have at Fenway Park, and after a certain point, say 250 feet out, the field slanted sharply into an old cemetery and it was the devil finding the ball if it got that far.

Butch and one other boy in our division were the only ones who could reach the cemetery, so it really wasn't a problem. The other boy played for Mount Carmel but I don't remember his name. He missed a lot of the games, anyway, because he often had to work on his family's farm after school. Mount Carmel was in the town's last rural section and boasted a number of hayseeds on its squad, boys with eyebrows that grew together and hard bones.

The only other good team in our division was Spring Glen. It always amazed me how the rich families who lived in the Spring Glen section of town could produce so many ballplayers. As far as I could tell, Ted Williams, Dom DiMaggio, Walt Dropo, Birdie Tebbetts, Billy Goodman, and the rest all came from humble backgrounds. On that basis I used to think there was some connection between rough childhoods and good batting averages, which is why I sometimes wished my own house would burn down, to give me an edge.

My final advice on high pops is to play them on the first bounce. Just let the ball drop and say you thought the infield fly rule was in effect. Of course the infield fly rule is in effect only when two or more players are on base, and then the batter is automatically out. Actually, though, high infield flies are never hit to the second baseman when the rule happens to apply. That is one of the unfair parts a second baseman learns to live with.

I could go into what kind of glove to buy and how to keep it oiled and such, but you probably know all that. Anyway the glove doesn't make the ballplayer. When I was named to the team in sixth grade, I talked my folks into buying me a nice new glove with a big web and all, in honor of the miracle. But the only thing I ever caught in it was a cold—that's what Lover Boy always said. In comparison, Herman's glove looked like it had come off the world's last buffalo. It had no padding and hardly any webbing and one of the fingers was always coming unstitched. But Herman nabbed everything that came anywhere near third base.

I guess Evie knew Herman's glove was magical even though she hardly watched the action, because she would hold it in her lap for him between innings. Mine she just kept handy. Herman would pay her off in bubble gum for the service.

Now for grounders. I used to practice fielding grounders all winter by flinging a ball against the concrete wall in our basement. It drove my parents batty and scarred the patio furniture in storage and worst of all it taught me how to catch only one kind of grounder—the grounder that comes directly at you and bounces into your glove at knee level. In three years of play in our division, this particular type of ground ball was never once hit to my position.

The key thought at second is not to catch the grounder, anyway, but to stop it. That keeps the right fielder off your back and if you manage to find the ball after it's bounced off your knee or chest, you still might be able to get it to first in time for the out. A danger here is to get so excited about actually getting the ball in your bare hand that you send it sailing over the first baseman's head and over by the swings. So concentrate on the throw to first during infield warm-up at the start of every inning. This is when the first baseman throws a few grounders to the other infielders to loosen them up. Lover Boy was always careful to give me a grounder underhanded, so I would be more likely to catch it and not have to trot out into shallow center to get the ball back again.

Maybe even more important than handling pops and stopping ground balls with your chin if necessary is the second baseman's role in boosting team spirit. A lot of boosting comes in the form of infield chatter in support of the pitcher. "Come on you kid, come on you babe," is a proven morale-booster. So are "No hitter no hitter up there" and "Chuck it in there, baby."

I was practically the psychological cornerstone of the Centerville infield because Erwin, our regular pitcher, was lefthanded. In the course of winding up, especially when there were men on base—as there usually were—Erwin would always pause briefly and be forced to look in my direction, as a southpaw, before collecting his energies for the assault on the strike zone. Sometimes he had a faintly disgusted look which seemed to say, "Well, I suppose you're getting ready to make another error." But I knew the importance of giving him confidence and I would stare right back and say, "Come on you kid come on you babe no hitter no hitter."

Erwin sucked on Life Savers during a game, which I don't approve of for a second baseman. If the second baseman gets knocked down by a runner, or happens to trip of his own accord, with a Life Saver in his mouth, it is quite possible he will get the candy jammed in his throat. I chewed gum and recommend the same. Chewing gum keeps your mouth from getting dry as a resin bag on those hot, dusty days when baseball was meant to be played, and it relaxes your jaw muscles, which are the first to freeze up under tension.

Covering the bag properly is another important duty. I never had much practice taking throws from the catcher, to put out base stealers, because in such cases the Centerville catchers either threw the ball way into the outfield or hit poor Erwin with it as he tried to get out of the way. I did handle throws from the outfield a lot. Naturally our outfielders had to show off their powerful throwing arms so, on an attempted double, say, I would face two means of extinction: (1) breaking my hand on the hard throw from the field, or (2) getting run over from behind by the base runner.

Actually I never got spiked or knocked down by runners, but there were many close calls. By far the most dangerous man on base in the division was Butch Mendoza, as you might have guessed by what I've mentioned about him already. Once Butch knocked Herman on his ass coming into third. Right away we had to bring in a young kid at Herman's position who was about as bad as I was out there. I remember Lover Boy saying, "My, my, we are now fielding a hole at second and a sieve at third!"

Herman was nowhere near the base and Butch should have been called out for running outside his normal course. He deliberately picked Herman off because of Herman's color and maybe even more because of Herman's indifference to Butch's many taunts. He should have been called out, but even the umpires were afraid of Butch Mendoza in those days. He was three times Herman's height and twice his weight, I'd guess. So Herman got carted off by Bert and Erwin and me, wind knocked out of him, and as it turned out, one arm busted.

In the meantime, I remember, Evie got up from the State Street bench, where she was sitting, naturally, and hit Butch with what was left of the apple she'd been chomping on. Got him in the face with her apple core after he'd crossed home plate. She turned and ran toward home and Butch was too surprised and out of breath anyway to do much about it. He just looked confused. I felt like catching up with Evie and buying her a Popsicle for trying to avenge Herman as she had done. I guess I knew, even as I helped cart off Herman, who was chewing his bubble gum like crazy at the time, to keep from crying probably—I guess I knew Butch had done something he would be ashamed of in later years, provided he ever stopped to think about it. And little Evie had done something she'd never stop to think about, because she was at that age when you can deal with villains cleanly.

In any case I couldn't have walked out on Centerville even though we were losing by about 12 to 3 at the time. We got Herman settled down and took the field again and finished the last two or three innings. I think State Street got a couple more runs off us, to rub it in. We never got on base again, but that didn't make any difference—we stuck it out. That's really about the last thing I wanted to pass along about the job of playing second base, whether you're winning or losing, or making five errors per game, or seeing one of your teammates get a bad break, or losing your only fan. Stick it out. That's what second base is all about.

# Usually
# Destroyed

## Aldous Huxley

Our guide through the labyrinthine streets of Jerusalem was a young Christian refugee from the other side of the wall, which now divides the ancient city from the new, the non-viable state of Jordan from the non-viable state of Israel. He was a sad, embittered young man—and well he might be. His prospects had been blighted, his family reduced from comparative wealth to the most abject penury, their house and land taken away from them, their bank account frozen and devaluated. In the circumstances, the surprising thing was not his bitterness, but the melancholy resignation with which it was tempered.

He was a good guide—almost too good, indeed; for he was quite remorseless in his determination to make us visit all those deplorable churches which were built, during the nineteenth century, on the ruins of earlier places of pilgrimage. There are tourists whose greatest pleasure is a trip through historical associations and their own fancy. I am not one of them. When I travel, I like to move among intrinsically significant objects, not through an absence peopled only by literary references, Victorian monuments and the surmises of archaeologists. Jerusalem, of course, contains much more than ghosts and architectural monstrosities. Besides being one of the most profoundly depressing of the earth's cities, it is one of the strangest and, in its own way, one of the most beautiful. Unfortunately our guide was far too conscientious to spare us the horrors and the unembodied, or ill-embodied, historical associations. We had to see everything—not merely St Anne's and St James's and the Dome of the Rock, but the hypothetical site of Caiaphas's house and what the Anglicans had built in the 'seventies, what the Tsar and the German

"Usually Destroyed" from *Adonis and the Alphabet* by Aldous Huxley, London (1956). Reprinted by permission of Chatto and Windus Ltd., and Mrs. Laura Huxley.

Emperor had countered with in the 'eighties, what had been considered beautiful in the early 'nineties by the Copts or the French Franciscans. But, luckily, even at the dreariest moments of our pilgrimage there were compensations. Our sad young man spoke English well and fluently, but spoke it as eighteenth-century virtuosi played music—with the addition of *fioriture* and even whole cadenzas of his own invention. His most significant contribution to colloquial English (and, at the same time, to the science and art of history) was the insertion into almost every sentence of the word 'usually.' What did he mean by it? The answer is, Nothing at all. What sounded like an adverb was in fact no more than one of those vocalized tics to which nervous persons are sometimes subject. I used to know a professor whose lectures and conversation were punctuated, every few seconds, by the phrase, "With a thing with a thing." "With a thing with a thing" is manifestly gibberish. But our young friend's no less compulsive 'usually' had a fascinating way of making a kind of sense—much more sense, very often, than the speaker had intended. "This area," he would say as he showed us one of the Victorian monstrosities, "this area" (it was one of his favourite words) "is very rich in antiquity. St Helena built here a very vast church, but the area was usually destroyed by the Samaritans in the year 529 after Our Lord Jesus Christ. Then the Crusaders came to the area, and built a new church still more vast. Here were mosaics the most beautiful in the world. In the seventeenth century after Our Lord Jesus Christ the Turks usually removed the lead from the roof to make ammunition; consequently rain entered the area and the church was thrown down. The present area was erected by the Prussian Government in the year 1879 after Our Lord Jesus Christ and all these broken-down houses you see over there were usually destroyed during the war with the Jews in 1948."

Usually destroyed and then usually rebuilt, in order, of course, to be destroyed again and then rebuilt, *da capo ad infinitum*. That vocalized tic had compressed all history into a four-syllabled word. Listening to our young friend, as we wandered through the brown, dry squalor of the Holy City, I felt myself overwhelmed, not by the mere thought of man's enduring misery, but by an obscure, immediate sense of it, an organic realization. These pullulations among ruins and in the dark of what once were sepulchres; these hordes of sickly children; these galled asses and the human beasts of burden bent under enormous loads; these mortal enemies beyond the dividing wall; these priest-conducted groups of pilgrims befuddling themselves with the vain repetitions, against which the founder of their religion had gone out of his way to warn them—they were dateless, without an epoch. In this costume or that, under one master or another, praying to whichever God was temporarily in charge, they had been here from the beginning. Had been here with the Egyptians, been here with Joshua, been here when Solomon in all his glory ordered his slaves in all their misery to build the temple, which Nebuchadnezzar had usually demolished and Zedekiah, just as usually, had put together again. Had been here during the long pointless wars between the two kingdoms, and at the next destruction under Ptolemy, the next but one under Antiochus and the next rebuilding under Herod and the biggest, best destruction of all by Titus. Had been here when Hadrian abolished Jerusalem and built a brand-new Roman city, complete with baths and a theatre, with a temple of Jupiter, and a temple of Venus, to take its place. Had been here when the insurrection of Barcochebas was drowned in blood. Had been here while the Roman Empire declined and turned Christian, when Chosroes the Second destroyed the churches and when the Caliph Omar brought Islam and, most unusually, destroyed nothing. Had been here to meet the Crusaders and then to wave them goodbye, to welcome the Turks and then to watch them retreat before Allenby. Had been here under the Mandate and through the troubles of 'forty-eight, and was here now and would be here, no doubt, in the same brown squalor, alternately building and destroying, killing and being killed, indefinitely.

"I do not think," Lord Russell has recently written, "that the sum of human misery has ever in the past been so great as it has been in the last twenty-five years." One is inclined to agree. Or are we, on second thoughts, merely flattering ourselves? At most periods of history moralists have liked to boast that theirs was the most iniquitous generation since the time of Cain—the most iniquitous and therefore, since God is just, the most grievously afflicted. Today, for example, we think of the thirteenth century as one of the supremely creative periods of human history. But the men who were actually contemporary with the cathedrals and Scholastic Philosophy regarded their age as hopelessly degenerate, uniquely bad and condignly punished. Were they right, or are we? The answer, I suspect is: Both. Too much evil and too much suffering can make it impossible for men to be creative; but within very wide limits greatness is perfectly compatible with organized insanity, sanctioned crime and intense, chronic unhappiness for the majority. Every one of the great religions preaches a mixture of profound pessimism and the most extravagant optimism. "I show you sorrow," says the Buddha, pointing to man in his ordinary unregenerate condition. And in the same context Christian theologians speak of the Fall, of Original Sin, of the Vale of Tears, while Hindus refer to the workings of man's home-made destiny, his evil karma. But over against the sorrow, the tears, the self-generated, self-inflicted disasters, what superhuman prospects! If he so wishes, the Hindu affirms, a man can realize his identity with Brahman, the Ground of all being; if he so wishes, says the Christian, he can be filled with God; if he so wishes, says the Buddhist, he can live in a transfigured world where Nirvana and Samsara, the eternal and the temporal, are one. But, alas—and from optimism based on the experience of the few, the saints and sages return to the pessimism forced upon them by their observation of the many—the gate is narrow, the threshold high, few are chosen because few choose to be chosen. In practice man usually destroys himself—but has done so up till now a little less thoroughly than he has built himself up. In spite of everything, we are still here. The spirit of destruction has been willing enough, but for most of historical time its technological flesh has been weak. The Mongols had only horses as transport, only bows and spears and butchers' knives for weapons; if they had possessed our machinery, they could have depopulated the planet. As it was, they had to be content with small triumphs—the slaughter of only a few millions, the stamping out of civilization only in Western Asia.

In this universe of ours nobody has ever succeeded in getting anything for nothing. In certain fields, progress in the applied sciences and the arts of organization has certainly lessened human misery; but it has done so at the cost of increasing it in others. The worst enemy of life, freedom and the common decencies is total anarchy; their second worst enemy is total efficiency. Human interests are best served when society is tolerably well organized and industry moderately advanced. Chaos and ineptitude are anti-human; but so too is a superlatively efficient government, equipped with all the products of a highly developed technology. When such a government goes in for usually destroying, the whole race is in danger.

The Mongols were the aesthetes of militarism; they believed in gratuitous massacre, in destruction for destruction's sake. Our malice is less pure and spontaneous; but, to make up for this deficiency, we have ideals. The end proposed, on either side of the Iron Curtain, is nothing less than the Good of Humanity and its conversion to the Truth. Crusades can go on for centuries, and wars in the name of God or Humanity are generally diabolic in their ferocity. The unprecedented depth of human misery in our time is proportionate to the unprecedented height of the social ideals entertained by the Totalitarians on the one side, the Christians and the secularist democrats on the other.

And then there is the question of simple arithmetic. There are far more people on the earth today than there were in any earlier century. The miseries, which have been the usual consequence of the usual course of nature and the usual behaviour of human beings, are the lot today, not of the three hundred millions of men, women and children who were contemporary with Christ, but of more than two and a half billions. Obviously, then, the sum of our present misery cannot fail to be greater than the sum of misery in the past. Every individual is the centre of a world, which it takes very little to transform into a world of unadulterated suffering. The catastrophes and crimes of the twentieth century can transform almost ten times as many human universes into private hells as did the catastrophes and crimes of two thousand years ago. Moreover, thanks to improvements in technology, it is possible for fewer people to do more harm to greater numbers than ever before.

After the capture of Jerusalem by Nebuchadnezzar, how many Jews were carried off to Babylon? Jeremiah puts the figure at four thousand six hundred, the compiler of the Second Book of Kings at ten thousand. Compared with the forced migrations of our time, the Exile was the most trivial affair. How many millions were uprooted by Hitler and the Communists? How many more millions were driven out of Pakistan into India, out of India into Pakistan? How many hundreds of thousands had to flee, with our young guide, from their homes in Israel? By the waters of Babylon ten thousand at the most sat down and wept. In the single refugee camp at Bethlehem there are more exiles than that. And Bethlehem's is only one of dozens of such camps scattered far and wide over the Near East.

So it looks, all things considered, as though Lord Russell were right—that the sum of misery is indeed greater today than at any time in the past. And what of the future? Germ warfare and the H-bomb get all the headlines and, for that very reason, may never be resorted to. Those who talk a great deal about suicide rarely commit it. The greatest threat to happiness is biological. There were about twelve hundred million people on the planet when I was born, six years before the turn of the century. Today there are two thousand seven hundred millions; thirty years from now there will probably be four thousand millions. At present about sixteen hundred million people are underfed. In the nineteen-eighties the total may well have risen to twenty-five hundred millions, of whom a considerable number may actually be starving. In many parts of the world famine may come even sooner. In his Report on the Census of 1951 the Registrar General of India has summed up the biological problem as it confronts the second most populous country of the world. There are now three hundred and seventy-five million people living within the borders of India, and their numbers increase by five millions annually. The current production of basic foods is seventy million tons a year, and the highest production that can be achieved in the foreseeable future is ninety-four million tons. Ninety-four million tons will support four hundred and fifty million people at the present sub-standard level, and the population of In dia will pass the four hundred and fifty million mark in 1969. After that, there will be a condition of what the Registrar General calls 'catastrophe.'

In the index at the end of the sixth volume of Dr Toynbee's *A Study of History*, Popilius Laena gets five mentions and Porphyry of Batamaea two; but the word you would expect to find between these names, *Population*, is conspicuous by its absence. In his second volume, Mr Toynbee has written at length on 'the stimulus of pressures'—but without ever mentioning the most important pressure of them all, the pressure of population on available resources. And here is a note in which the author describes his impressions of the Roman Campagna after twenty years of absence. "In 1911 the student who made the pilgrimage of the Via Appia Antica found himself walking through a wilderness almost from the moment when he passed beyond the City Walls.... When he repeated the pilgrimage in 1931, he found that, in the interval, Man had been busily reasserting his mastery over the whole stretch of country that lies between Rome and the Castelli Romani.... The tension of human energy on the Roman Campagna is now beginning to rise again for the first time since the end of the third century B.C." And there the matter is left, without any reference to the compelling reason for this 'rise of tension.' Between 1911 and 1931 the population of Italy had increased by the best part of eight millions. Some of these eight millions went to live in the Roman Campagna. And they did so, not because Man with a large M had in some mystical way increased the tension of human energy, but for the sufficiently obvious reason that there was nowhere else for them to go. In terms of a history that takes no cognizance of demographical facts, the past can never be fully understood, the present is quite incomprehensible and the future entirely beyond prediction.

Thinking, for a change, in demographic as well as in merely cultural, political and religious terms, what kind of reasonable guesses can we make about the sum of human misery in the years to come? First, it seems pretty certain that more people will be hungrier and that, in many parts of the world, malnutrition will modulate into periodical or chronic famine. (One would like to know something about the Famines of earlier ages, but the nearest one gets to them in Mr Toynbee's index is a blank space between Muhammad Falak-al-Din and Gaius Fannius.) Second, it seems pretty certain that, though they may help in the long run, remedial measures, aimed at reducing the birth-rate will be powerless to avert the miseries lying in wait for the next generation. Third, it seems pretty certain that improvements in Agriculture (not referred to in Mr Toynbee's index, though Agrigentum gets two mentions and Agis IV, King of Sparta, no less than forty-seven) will be unable to catch up with current and foreseeable increases in population. If the standard of living in industrially backward countries is to be improved, agricultural production will have to go up every single year by at least two and a half per cent, and preferably by three and a half per cent. Instead of which, according to the FAO, Far Eastern food production per head of population will be ten per cent less in 1956 (and this assumes that the current Five-Year Plans will be fully realized) than it was in 1938.

Fourth, it seems pretty certain that, as a larger and hungrier population 'mines the soil' in a desperate search for food, the destructive processes of erosion and deforestation will be speeded up. Fertility will therefore tend to go down as human numbers go up. (One looks up *Erosion* in Mr Toynbee's index but finds only Esarhaddon Esotericism and Esperanto; one hunts for *Forests*, but has to be content, alas, with Formosus of Porto.)

Fifth, it seems pretty certain that the increasing pressure of population upon resources will result in increasing political and social unrest, and that this unrest will culminate in wars, revolutions and counter-revolutions.

Sixth, it seems pretty certain that, whatever the avowed political principles and whatever the professed religion of the societies concerned, increasing pressure of population upon resources will tend to increase the power of the central government and to diminish the liberties of individual citizens. For, obviously, where more people are competing for less food, each individual will have to work harder and longer for his ration, and the central government will find it necessary to intervene more and more frequently in order to save the rickety economic machine from total breakdown, and at the same time to repress the popular discontent begotten by deepening poverty.

If Lord Russell lives to a hundred and twenty (and, for all our sakes, I hope most fervently that he will), he may find himself remembering these middle decades of the twentieth century as an almost Golden Age. In 1954, it is true, he decided that the sum of human misery had never been so great as it had been in the preceding quarter century. On the other hand, 'you ain't seen nuthin' yet.' Compared with the sum of four billion people's misery in the 'eighties, the sum of two billion miseries just before, during and after the Second World War may look like the Earthly Paradise.

But meanwhile here we were in Jerusalem, looking at the usually destroyed antiquities and rubbing shoulders with the usually poverty-stricken inhabitants, the usually superstitious pilgrims. Here was the Wailing Wall, with nobody to wail at it; for Israel is on the other side of a barrier, across which there is no communication except by occasional bursts of rifle fire, occasional exchanges of hand grenades. Here, propped up with steel scaffolding, was the Church of the Holy Sepulchre—that empty tomb to which, for three centuries, the early Christians paid no attention whatsoever, but which came, after the time of Constantine, to be regarded, throughout Europe, as the most important thing in the entire universe. And here was Siloam, here St Anne's, here the Dome of the Rock and the site of the Temple, here, more ruinous than Pompeii, the Jewish quarter, levelled, usually, in 1948 and not yet usually reconstructed. Here, finally, was St James's, of the Armenians, gay with innumerable rather bad but charming paintings, and a wealth of gaudily coloured tiles. The great church glowed like a dim religious merry-go-round. In all Jerusalem it was the only oasis of cheerfulness. And not alone of cheerfulness. As we came out into the courtyard, through which the visitor must approach the church's main entrance, we heard a strange and wonderful sound. High up, in one of the houses surrounding the court, somebody was playing the opening Fantasia of Bach's Partita in A minor—playing it, what was more, remarkably well. From out of the open window, up there on the third floor, the ordered torrent of bright pure notes went streaming out over the city's immemorial squalor. Art and religion, philosophy and science, morals and politics—these are the instruments by means of which men have tried to discover a coherence in the flux of events, to impose an order on the chaos of experience. The most intractable of our experiences is the experience of Time—the intuition of duration, combined with the thought of perpetual perishing. Music is a device for working directly upon the experience of Time. The composer takes a piece of raw, undifferentiated duration and extracts from it, as the sculptor extracts the statue from his marble, a complex pattern of tones and silences, of harmonic sequences and contrapuntal interweavings. For the number of minutes it takes to play or listen to his composition, duration is transformed into something intrinsically significant, something held together by the internal logics of style and temperament, of personal feelings interacting with an artistic tradition, of creative insights expressing themselves within and beyond some given technical convention. This Fantasia, for example—with what a tireless persistence it drills its way through time! How effectively—and yet with no fuss, no self-conscious heroics—it transfigures the mortal lapse through time into the symbol, into the very fact, of a more than human life! A tunnel of joy and understanding had been driven through chaos and was demonstrating, for all to hear, that perpetual perishing is also perpetual creation. Which was precisely what our young friend had been telling us, in his own inimitable way, all the time. Usually destroyed—but also, and just as often, usually rebuilt. Like the rain, like sunshine, like the grace of God and the devastations of Nature, his verbalized tic was perfectly impartial. We walked out of the courtyard and down the narrow street. Bach faded, a donkey brayed, there was a smell of undisposed sewage. "In the year of Our Lord 1916," our guide informed us, "the Turkish Government usually massacred approximately seven hundred and fifty thousand Armenians."

# How the Poor Die

## George Orwell

In the year 1929 I spent several weeks in the Hôpital X, in the fifteenth arrondissement of Paris. The clerks put me through the usual third degree at the reception desk, and indeed I was kept answering questions for some twenty minutes before they would let me in. If you have ever had to fill up forms in a Latin country you will know the kind of questions I mean. For some days past I had been unequal to translating Reaumur into Fahrenheit, but I know that my temperature was round about 103, and by the end of the interview I had some difficulty in standing on my feet. At my back a resigned little knot of patients, carrying bundles done up in colored handkerchiefs, waited their turn to be questioned.

After the questioning came the bath—a compulsory routine for all newcomers, apparently, just as in prison or the workhouse. My clothes were taken away from me, and after I had sat shivering for some minutes in five inches of warm water I was given a linen nightshirt and a short blue flannel dressing gown—no slippers, they had none big enough for me, they said—and led out into the open air. This was a night in February and I was suffering from pneumonia. The ward we were going to was two hundred yards away and it seemed that to get to it you had to cross the hospital grounds. Someone stumbled in front of me with a lantern. The gravel path was frosty underfoot, and the wind whipped the nightshirt round my bare calves. When we got into the ward I was aware of a strange feeling of familiarity whose origin I did not succeed in pinning down till later in the night. It was a long, rather low, ill-lit room, full of murmuring

From *Shooting an Elephant and Other Essays* by George Orwell, copyright, 1945, 1946, 1949, 1950, by Sonia Brownell Orwell; renewed, 1973, 1974, 1977 by Sonia Orwell; renewed 1978 by Sonia Pitt-Rivers. Reprinted by permission of Mrs. Sonia Brownell Orwell.

voices and with three rows of beds surprisingly close together. There was a foul smell, fecal and yet sweetish. As I lay down I saw on a bed nearly opposite me a small, round-shouldered, sandy-haired man sitting half naked while a doctor and a student performed some strange operation on him. First the doctor produced from his black bag a dozen small glasses like wine glasses, then the student burned a match inside each glass to exhaust the air, then the glass was popped on to the man's back or chest and the vacuum drew up a huge yellow blister. Only after some moments did I realize what they were doing to him. It was something called cupping, a treatment which you can read about in old medical textbooks but which till then I had vaguely thought of as one of those things they do to horses.

The cold air outside had probably lowered my temperature, and I watched this barbarous remedy with detachment and even a certain amount of amusement. The next moment, however, the doctor and the student came across to my bed, hoisted me upright, and without a word began applying the same set of glasses, which had not been sterilized in any way. A few feeble protests that I uttered got no more response than if I had been an animal. I was very much impressed by the impersonal way in which the two men started on me. I had never been in the public ward of a hospital before, and it was my first experience of doctors who handle you without speaking to you or, in a human sense, taking any notice of you. They only put on six glasses in my case, but after doing so they scarified the blisters and applied the glasses again. Each glass now drew out about a dessert-spoonful of dark-colored blood. As I lay down again, humiliated, disgusted, and frightened by the thing that had been done to me, I reflected that now at least they would leave me alone. But no, not a bit of it. There was another treatment coming, the mustard poultice, seemingly a matter of routine like the hot bath. Two slatternly nurses had already got the poultice ready, and they lashed it round my chest as tight as a strait-jacket while some men who were wandering about the ward in shirt and trousers began to collect round my bed with half-sympathetic grins. I learned later that watching a patient have a mustard poultice was a favorite pastime in the ward. These things are normally applied for a quarter of an hour and certainly they are funny enough if you don't happen to be the person inside. For the first five minutes the pain is severe, but you believe you can bear it. During the second five minutes this belief evaporates, but the poultice is buckled at the back and you can't get it off. This is the period the onlookers enjoy most. During the last five minutes, I noted, a sort of numbness supervenes. After the poultice had been removed a waterproof pillow packed with ice was thrust beneath my head and I was left alone. I did not sleep, and to the best of my knowledge this was the only night of my life—I mean the only night spent in bed—in which I have not slept at all, not even a minute.

During my first hour in the Hôpital X I had had a whole series of different and contradictory treatments, but this was misleading, for in general you got very little treatment at all, either good or bad, unless you were ill in some interesting and instructive way. At five in the morning the nurses came round, woke the patients, and took their temperatures, but did not wash them. If you were well enough you washed yourself, otherwise you depended on the kindness of some walking patient. It was generally patients, too, who carried the bedbottles and the grim bedpan, nicknamed *la casserole*. At eight breakfast arrived, called army-fashion *la soupe*. It was soup, too, a thin vegetable soup with slimy hunks of bread floating about in it. Later in the day the tall, solemn, black-bearded doctor made his rounds, with an interne and a troop of students following at his heels, but there were about sixty of us in the ward and it was evident that he had other wards to attend to as well. There were many beds past which he walked day after day, sometimes followed by imploring cries. On the other hand if you had some disease with which the students wanted to familiarize themselves you got plenty of attention of a kind. I myself, with an exceptionally fine specimen of a bronchial rattle, sometimes had as many as a dozen students queuing up to listen to my chest. It was a very queer feeling—queer, I mean, because of their intense interest in learning their job, together with a seeming lack of any perception that the patients were human beings. It is strange to relate, but sometimes as some young student stepped forward to take his turn at manipulating you, he would be actually tremulous with excitement, like a boy who has at last got his hands on some expensive piece of machinery. And then ear after ear—ears of young men, of girls, of Negroes—pressed against your back, relays of fingers solemnly but clumsily tapping, and not from any one of them did you get a word of conversation or a look direct in your face. As a nonpaying patient, in the uniform nightshirt, you were primarily *a specimen*, a thing I did not resent but could never quite get used to.

After some days I grew well enough to sit up and study the surrounding patients. The stuffy room, with its narrow beds so close together that you could easily touch your neighbor's hand, had every sort of disease in it except, I suppose, acutely infectious cases. My right-hand neighbor was a little red-haired cobbler with one leg shorter than the other, who used to announce the death of any other patient (this happened a number of times, and my neighbor was always the first to hear of it) by whistling to me, exclaiming "Numero 43!" (or whatever it was) and flinging his arms above his head. This man had not much wrong with him, but in most of the other beds within my angle of vision some squalid tragedy or some plain horror was being enacted. In the bed that was foot to foot with mine there lay, until he died (I didn't see him die—they moved him to another bed), a little weazened man who was suffering from I do not know what disease, but

something that made his whole body so intensely sensitive that any movement from side to side, sometimes even the weight of the bedclothes,
would make him shout out with pain. His worst suffering was when he
urinated, which he did with the greatest difficulty. A nurse would bring him
the bedbottle and then for a long time stand beside his bed, whistling, as
grooms are said to do with horses, until at last with an agonized shriek of
*"Je pisse!"* he would get started. In the bed next to him the sandy-haired
man whom I had seen being cupped used to cough up blood-streaked
mucus at all hours. My left-hand neighbor was a tall, flaccid-looking young
man who used periodically to have a tube inserted into his back and
astonishing quantities of frothy liquid drawn off from some part of his
body. In the bed beyond that a veteran of the war of 1870 was dying, a
handsome old man with a white imperial, round whose bed, at all hours
when visiting was allowed, four elderly female relatives dressed all in black
sat exactly like crows, obviously scheming for some pitiful legacy. In the
bed opposite me in the further row was an old bald-headed man with
drooping moustaches and greatly swollen face and body, who was suffering from some disease that made him urinate almost incessantly. A huge
glass receptacle stood always beside his bed. One day his wife and
daughter came to visit him. At sight of them the old man's bloated face lit
up with a smile of surprising sweetness, and as his daughter, a pretty girl of
about twenty, approached the bed I saw that his hand was slowly working
its way from under the bedclothes. I seemed to see in advance the gesture
that was coming—the girl kneeling beside the bed, the old man's hand laid
on her head in his dying blessing. But no, he merely handed her the bedbottle, which she promptly took from him and emptied into the receptacle.

About a dozen beds away from me was Numero 57—I think that was
his number—a cirrhosis of the liver case. Everyone in the ward knew him
by sight because he was sometimes the subject of a medical lecture. On
two afternoons a week the tall, grave doctor would lecture in the ward to a
party of students, and on more than one occasion old Numero 57 was
wheeled in on a sort of trolley into the middle of the ward, where the doctor would roll back his nightshirt, dilate with his fingers a huge flabby pro-
tuberance on the man's belly—the diseased liver, I suppose—and explain
solemnly that this was a disease attributable to alcoholism, commoner in
the wine-drinking countries. As usual he neither spoke to his patient nor
gave him a smile, a nod or any kind of recognition. While he talked, very
grave and upright, he would hold the wasted body beneath his two hands,
sometimes giving it a gentle roll to and fro, in just the attitude of a woman
handling a rolling-pin. Not that Numero 57 minded this kind of thing. Obviously he was an old hospital inmate, a regular exhibit at lectures, his liver
long since marked down for a bottle in some pathological museum. Utterly

uninterested in what was said about him, he would lie with his colorless eyes gazing at nothing, while the doctor showed him off like a piece of antique china. He was a man of about sixty, astonishingly shrunken. His face, pale as vellum, had shrunken away till it seemed no bigger than a doll's.

One morning my cobbler neighbor woke me up plucking at my pillow before the nurses arrived. "Numero 57!"—he flung his arms above his head. There was a light in the ward, enough to see by. I could see old Numero 57 lying crumpled up on his side, his face sticking out over the side of the bed, and toward me. He had died some time during the night, nobody knew when. When the nurses came they received the news of his death indifferently and went about their work. After a long time, an hour or more, two other nurses marched in abreast like soldiers, with a great clumping of sabots, and knotted the corpse up in the sheets, but it was not removed till some time later. Meanwhile, in the better light, I had had time for a good look at Numero 57. Indeed I lay on my side to look at him. Curiously enough he was the first dead European I had seen. I had seen dead men before, but always Asiatics and usually people who had died violent deaths. Numero 57's eyes were still open, his mouth also open, his small face contorted into an expression of agony. What most impressed me, however, was the whiteness of his face. It had been pale before, but now it was little darker than the sheets. As I gazed at the tiny, screwed-up face it struck me that this disgusting piece of refuse, waiting to be carted away and dumped on a slab in the dissecting room, was an example of "natural" death, one of the things you pray for in the Litany. There you are, then, I thought, that's what is waiting for you, twenty, thirty, forty years hence: that is how the lucky ones die, the one who lives to be old. One wants to live, of course, indeed one only stays alive by virtue of the fear of death, but I think now, as I thought then, that it's better to die violently and not too old. People talk about the horrors of war, but what weapon has man invented that even approaches in cruelty some of the commoner diseases? "Natural" death, almost by definition, means something slow, smelly, and painful. Even at that, it makes a difference if you can achieve it in your own home and not in a public institution. This poor old wretch who had just flickered out like a candle end was not even important enough to have anyone watching by his deathbed. He was merely a number, then a "subject" for the students' scalpels. And the sordid publicity of dying in such a place! In the Hôpital X the beds were very close together and there were no screens. Fancy, for instance, dying like the little man whose bed was for a while foot to foot with mine, the one who cried out when the bedclothes touched him! I dare say *"Je pisse!"* were his last recorded words. Perhaps the dying don't bother about such things—that at least would be the standard answer: nevertheless dying people are often more or less normal in their minds till within a day or so of the end.

In the public wards of a hospital you see horrors that you don't seem to meet with among people who manage to die in their own homes, as though certain diseases only attacked people at the lower income levels. But it is a fact that you would not in any English hospitals see some of the things I saw in the Hôpital X. This business of people just dying like animals, for instance, with nobody standing by, nobody interested, the death not even noticed till the morning—this happened more than once. You certainly would not see that in England, and still less would you see a corpse left exposed to the view of the other patients. I remember that once in a cottage hospital in England a man died while we were at tea, and though there were only six of us in the ward the nurses managed things so adroitly that the man was dead and his body removed without our even hearing about it till tea was over. A thing we perhaps underrate in England is the advantage we enjoy in having large numbers of well-trained and rigidly disciplined nurses. No doubt English nurses are dumb enough, they may tell fortunes with tea leaves, wear Union Jack badges, and keep photographs of the Queen on the mantelpieces, but at least they don't let you lie unwashed and constipated on an unmade bed, out of sheer laziness. The nurses at the Hôpital X still had a tinge of Mrs. Gamp about them, and later, in the military hospitals of Republican Spain, I was to see nurses almost too ignorant to take a temperature. You wouldn't, either, see in England such dirt as existed in the Hôpital X. Later on, when I was well enough to wash myself in the bathroom, I found that there was kept there a huge packing case into which the scraps of food and dirty dressings from the ward were flung, and the wainscotings were infested by crickets.

When I had got back my clothes and grown strong on my legs I fled from the Hôpital X, before my time was up and without waiting for a medical discharge. It was not the only hospital I have fled from, but its gloom and bareness, its sickly smell and, above all, something in its mental atmosphere stand out in my memory as exceptional. I had been taken there because it was the hospital belonging to my arrondissement, and I did not learn till after I was in it that it bore a bad reputation. A year or two later the celebrated swindler, Madame Hanaud, who was ill while on re-mand, was taken to the Hôpital X, and after a few days of it she managed to elude her guards, took a taxi, and drove back to the prison, explaining that she was more comfortable there. I have no doubt that the Hôpital X was quite untypical of French hospitals even at that date. But the patients, nearly all of them working men, were surprisingly resigned. Some of them seemed to find the conditions almost comfortable, for at least two were destitute malingerers who found this a good way of getting through the winter. The nurses connived because the malingerers made themselves useful by doing odd jobs. But the attitude of the majority was: of course this is a lousy place, but what else do you expect? It did not seem strange to them that you should be woken at five and then wait three hours before starting the day on watery soup, or that people should die with no one at their bedside, or even that your chance of getting medical attention should depend on catching the doctor's eye as he went past. According to their traditions that was what hospitals were like. If you are seriously ill, and if you are too poor to be treated in your own home, then you must go into hospital, and once there you must put up with harshness and discomfort, just as you would in the army. But on top of this I was interested to find a lingering belief in the old stories that have now almost faded from memory in England—stories, for instance, about doctors cutting you open out of sheer curiosity or thinking it funny to start operating before you were properly "under." There were dark tales about a little operating room said to be situated just beyond the bathroom. Dreadful screams were said to issue from this room. I saw nothing to confirm these stories and no doubt they were all nonsense, though I did see two students kill a sixteen-year-old boy, or nearly kill him (he appeared to be dying when I left the hospital, but he may have recovered later) by a mischievous experiment which they probably could not have tried on a paying patient. Well within living memory it used to be believed in London that in some of the big hospitals patients were killed off to get dissection subjects. I didn't hear this tale repeated at the Hôpital X, but I should think some of the men there would have found it credible. For it was a hospital in which not the methods, perhaps, but something of the atmosphere of the nineteenth century had managed to survive, and therein lay its peculiar interest.

During the past fifty years or so there has been a great change in the relationship between doctor and patient. If you look at almost any literature before the later part of the nineteenth century, you find that a hospital is popularly regarded as much the same thing as a prison, and an old-fashioned, dungeon-like prison at that. A hospital is a place of filth, torture, and death, a sort of ante-chamber to the tomb. No one who was not more or less destitute would have thought of going into such a place for treatment. And especially in the early part of the last century, when medical science had grown bolder than before without being any more successful, the whole business of doctoring was looked on with horror and dread by ordinary people. Surgery, in particular, was believed to be no more than a peculiarly gruesome form of sadism, and dissection, possible only with the aid of body-snatchers, was even confused with necromancy. From the nineteenth century you could collect a large horror-literature connected with doctors and hospitals. Think of poor old George III, in his dotage, shrieking for mercy as he sees his surgeons approaching to "bleed him till he faints"! Think of the conversations of Bob Sawyer and Benjamin Allen, which no doubt are hardly parodies, or the field hospitals in *La Débâcle* and *War and Peace*, or that shocking description of an amputation in Melville's *Whitejacket!* Even the names given to doctors in nineteenth-century English fiction, Slasher, Carver, Sawyer, Fillgrave, and so on, and the generic nickname "sawbones," are about as grim as they are comic. The anti-surgery tradition is perhaps best expressed in Tennyson's poem, *The Children's Hospital*, which is essentially a pre-chloroform document though it seems to have been written as late as 1880. Moreover, the outlook which Tennyson records in this poem had a lot to be said for it. When you consider what an operation without anaesthetics must have been like, what it notoriously *was* like, it is difficult not to suspect the motives of people who would undertake such things. For these bloody horrors which the students so eagerly looked forward to ("A magnificent sight if Slasher does it!") were admittedly more or less useless: the patient who did not die of shock usually died of gangrene, a result which was taken for granted. Even now doctors can be found whose motives are questionable. Anyone who has had much illness, or who has listened to medical students talking, will know what I mean. But anaesthetics were a turning point, and disinfectants were another. Nowhere in the world, probably, would you now see the kind of scene described by Axel Munthe in *The Story of San Michele*, when the sinister surgeon in top-hat and frock-coat, his starched shirtfront spattered with blood and pus, carves up patient after patient with the same knife and flings the severed limbs into a pile beside the table. Moreover, national health insurance has partly done away with the idea that a working-class patient is a pauper who deserves little consideration. Well into this century it was usual for "free" patients at the big hospitals to have their teeth extracted with no anaesthetic. They didn't pay, so why should they have an anaesthetic—that was the attitude. That too has changed.

And yet every institution will always bear upon it some lingering memory of its past. A barrack-room is still haunted by the ghost of Kipling, and it is difficult to enter a workhouse without being reminded of *Oliver Twist*. Hospitals began as a kind of casual ward for lepers and the like to die in, and they continued as places where medical students learned their art on the bodies of the poor. You can still catch a faint suggestion of their history in their characteristically gloomy architecture. I would be far from complaining about the treatment I have received in any English hospital, but I do know that it is a sound instinct that warns people to keep out of hospitals if possible, and especially out of the public wards. Whatever the legal position may be, it is unquestionable that you have far less control over your own treatment, far less certainty that frivolous experiments will not be tried on you, when it is a case of "accept the discipline or get out."

And it is a great thing to die in your own bed, though it is better still to die in your boots. However great the kindness and the efficiency, in every hospital death there will be some cruel, squalid detail, something perhaps too small to be told but leaving terribly painful memories behind, arising out of the haste, the crowding, the impersonality of a place where every day people are dying among strangers.

The dread of hospitals probably still survives among the very poor, and in all of us it has only recently disappeared. It is a dark patch not far beneath the surface of our minds. I have said earlier that when I entered the ward at the Hôpital X I was conscious of a strange feeling of familiarity. What the scene reminded me of, of course, was the reeking, pain-filled hospitals of the nineteenth century, which I had never seen but of which I had a traditional knowledge. And something, perhaps the black-clad doctor with his frowsy black bag, or perhaps only the sickly smell, played the queer trick of unearthing from my memory that poem of Tennyson's, *The Children's Hospital*, which I had not thought of for twenty years. It happened that as a child I had had it read aloud to me by a sick-nurse whose own working life might have stretched back to the time when Tennyson wrote the poem. The horrors and sufferings of the old-style hospitals were a vivid memory to her. We had shuddered over the poem together, and then seemingly I had forgotten it. Even its name would probably have recalled nothing to me. But the first glimpse of the ill-lit murmurous room, with the beds so close together, suddenly roused the train of thought to which it belonged, and in the night that followed I found myself remembering the whole story and atmosphere of the poem, with many of its lines complete.

# Terms and Topics

## TERMS

1. ***Vocabulary, Section II:*** abstruseness, acerbity, adroitly, adulation, aesthetes, affronted, ambivalent, anachronistic, anthropomorphism, assiduously, astringent, blighted, brazenly, chortle, chronic, complacently, compliance, connived, counterpoint, demoralized, deprecated, dispassionate, dissension, diverting, divined, dotage, egregiously, elicited, elucidations, enigmatic, epitome, expostulatory, felicitous, forgo, gratuitous, hallowed, icons, implacable, ineptitude, iniquitous, innocuous, orthodox, ostensibly, palpably, pathological, penury, piety, poignant, pugnacious, recluse, reticence, sadism, saturnine, squalor, stupefaction, subterfuge, supervenes, surmise, tremulous, umbrage, urbane.

2. What does the word ***interview*** mean? Does knowing its origins—its ***etymology***—help you understand its full meaning?

3. ***Irony*** Verbal irony consists in saying one thing and meaning another, usually with at least some humorous intent. If it is raining cats and dogs, and someone looks out the window and says, "It's a great day for a picnic!" everyone understands the intended meaning. Verbal irony that is lacking in wit or cleverness, that is particularly crude and obvious, or that is especially biting or brutal, is usually called ***sarcasm***. There are other kinds of irony; for example ***dramatic irony***, common in literature, is present when a character knows less about his or her circumstances than the audience does, or when expectations are aroused but not fulfilled. Irony always involves contrast.

4. ***Mask*** Another kind of irony is ***Socratic irony***, so called because in Plato's dialogues Socrates characteristically pretends to be naive or ignorant in order to trap an opponent during an argument. In other words, figuratively speaking he wears a *mask* of innocence, though

172

beneath it he is very wise indeed. Writers often put on such a mask, present a particular kind of image of themselves, adopt a **persona** or character other than their true or everyday one, in order to achieve certain rhetorical effects. An extreme and obvious example: In Browning's poem it is of course not Browning himself speaking but the Duke of Ferrara, the persona that Browning has assumed for the occasion of the poem. Interestingly, even the character the Duke presents could be considered a mask covering his true self. Could such a mask be useful for an interviewer as well as an interviewee?

5. *Caricature*   Exaggeration, whether in a picture or in words, of certain prominent features of the subject. If the features exaggerated are outstanding defects, caricature can be used to ridicule a subject.

## TOPICS: On Individual Essays

SILVER DONALD CAMERON   **"Interview with Robertson Davies: The Bizarre and Passionate Life of the Canadian People"**

1. Davies is obviously highly sophisticated, but his style as recorded here contains a good deal of informality, of colloquialism and even slang, as well as words like *etiology*. List some of the words and phrases that contribute to the conversational flavour. Does that level of style suit the occasion? Read some of Davies's nonfictional writing and compare its style with what appears here.

2. Cameron says that the Davies he talked to was not the Davies he had expected. Judging from his conversation, what kind of man do *you* think he is? Try writing a brief character sketch of him. Does he reveal any traits involuntarily rather than directly? Do you agree that the conversation is "almost confessional"? Davies says Cameron, too, has "made a confession." What has he confessed? Does Cameron reveal anything further about himself, either directly or indirectly? What for example might you say about *his* style?

3. Explain in your own terms what you think Davies means when he says he is "religious" and when he says he is an "artist." When he defines "religious," why does he think that "that seems hideously funny"? How would *you* define "religious"?

4. What is an existentialist? Do you believe Davies when he says he doesn't know?

5. If you've read Davies's Salterton novels (*Leaven of Malice, Tempest-Tost, A Mixture of Frailties*), do his remarks about them change your view of them in any way? Is there a "fossilized past" in your neighbourhood analogous to what Davies finds around Peterborough? Does his characterization of Canada and Canadians jibe with your own?

### NELLIE L. McCLUNG  "A Gentleman of the Old School"

1. What does *suffrage* mean? What is its etymology? What is McClung quoting when she refers to "a tide in the affairs of men, which taken at the flood leads on to fortune"?

2. Were you surprised that the feminist movement and concerns about "the status of women" were so strong so long ago? Investigate the history of women's rights in Canadian society—perhaps write a research report. How successful were McClung and the women's suffrage movement? When did women get the vote in Canada? in England? in the United States? The quotation from Charles Tilley in Jenkins's essay (section III) refers to suffragettes. Did anything like what he describes occur in Canada?

3. Is there today, eighty years or so after what McClung describes, still an "other half"? How does it live?

4. What is McClung's attitude toward the Premier? What effect does she have on him? McClung uses direct statement, but the dialogues and monologues are more dramatically revealing. What attitudes toward women do the Premier's words convey—for example his use of the verb "ferret out"? Show how McClung uses the record of conversation to reveal the character and attitudes and expectations of the speakers.

5. Point out some of the occurrences of irony in this chapter. How is the title ironic?

6. Write an account of someone you know or have had dealings with. Reveal character indirectly—for example through conversation and through seemingly objective, straightforward description that implies more than is said.

### MARGARET LANE  "The Ghost of Beatrix Potter"

1. What are the predilections of the "Freudian School" of criticism? What is a "Gioconda smile"? Are Beatrix Potter's illustrations anything like Constable's paintings?

2. Read, or re-read, some of Beatrix Potter's better early works and try to reconcile their author's personality, insofar as you can infer it, with the character of Mrs. Heelis that peers out of Lane's memoir about not meeting her.

3. How would you characterize the tone of Lane's piece? On what grounds?

4. Are the details Lane mentions or quotes sufficient to support her statement that Mrs. Heelis's reply to her letter was "the rudest letter I have ever received"? Do the details Lane provides make it believable

that Mr. Heelis could have undergone so sudden and complete a turnabout in his attitude toward her and her inquiries? If not, does it matter—that is, can we simply take her word for it?

5. Where does Lane reveal things about herself? Are any of these revelations implicit, indirect?

6. Try psychoanalyzing the author of some piece of children's literature you know well.

7. Compose a brief essay about not meeting someone.

8. Write a character sketch of someone you know only by hearsay, such as a grandparent who died before you were born. In order to gather data, you may need to interview some people who did know your subject.

### GUY DAVENPORT   "Wittgenstein"

1. Do some research on Klee, Bohr, Fuller, and the rest in order to get a sense of the significance of Davenport's many allusions. Is he name-dropping? How do Betty Hutton and Carmen Miranda fit into the company of Pythagoras, Wright, Kant, Mencius, and the rest?

2. In the first paragraph Davenport calls Wittgenstein "the most significant" "philosopher of our time." But then he refers to "his strange life," his dish-washing routine, his odd behaviour as a guest, his saying that his propositions will be recognized as "nonsensical," and his being "stubborn," "pig-headedly single-minded," "absurd," and so on. How can one possibly reconcile these and other points? Look up Wittgenstein in some standard encyclopedia or other reference work. Does Davenport seem to reveal a different man than the one you find discussed there? Which seems the more real, the more human, the more interesting? As a result of reading Davenport's essay, are you "hungry to know more" about Wittgenstein? Would you like to have met Wittgenstein? Why, or why not? What does the essay *tell* of the man, and what does it imply and reveal?

3. Try to answer, in writing, some of the questions posed at the end of the second paragraph and elsewhere in the essay. Is the absence of feeling a feeling?

4. Evaluate the force of the ending. Where does the ending begin?

5. Write a short impressionistic profile or sketch of some notable person you've learned about from reading. Don't necessarily play down the learned or serious side, the reputation for great achievements, but select and arrange your details so as to bring out your subject's more human character.

## JACK LUDWIG "The Calgary Stampede"

1. Analyze Ludwig's third paragraph in order to determine the techniques that make it effective. Note everything that contributes to the effect, for example the diction (including slang and neologisms), the puns and other wordplay, the metaphors, the rhythm, the descriptive details, the length and movement of the whole paragraph. Note too the allusions—to the Bible, ancient Rome, and fairy tale—two of which Ludwig echoes at the end of the essay. Would you call this paragraph strongly subjective? How and what does it *reveal*?

2. Does Ludwig's overall attitude toward the Stampede seem to you to be favourable, unfavourable, or simply neutral?

3. Write an essay in which you use a basic, overall contrast to support your point, as Ludwig uses the contrast with "the midway hoke outside" to point up the qualities of *"the* Stampede," "the rodeo proper." Make the contrast *reveal* qualities of the subject you're focussing on. Is Ludwig's essay really about the competition and heroism of the rodeo? What proportion of attention does he devote to the two aspects?

4. Conduct several interviews with people engaged in some activity or event (a sporting event, such as a race or a golf tournament; a church bazaar or some other fund-raising enterprise; a reunion or some other kind of party). From whatever notes or tapes you collect, write up the event and its atmosphere, trying to portray it as seen through the eyes of the participants, but avoiding long stretches of quotation.

## ANDREW A. ROONEY "A Penny Saved Is a Waste of Time"

1. Is the order of the items in this list random, or is it carefully controlled? Are the pieces of advice of similar importance or seriousness? If not, why do you think Rooney includes them all? Is he trying to be funny? Is he trying to provoke thought? argument? Are any items too vague, general, or abstract to seem meaningful? Are any just plain confusing? If so, why are they there?

2. What does this list reveal about the character of its author? Do you like the Andy Rooney who comes through, or do you dislike him? Why? Write a character sketch showing what you think he must be like, based on the kind of advice he *forgot* to give. What advice do you think he *gave*?

3. Choose one of these pieces of advice and use it as a thesis statement for a brief explanatory essay (perhaps partly argumentative). For example, what are the implications of the final item? Does it make a good note to end on? Or choose one piece of advice with which you instinctively disagree and compose a brief argument countering it. What proverb is Rooney twisting in the title? Is he right to disagree with it?

4.  Devise a list of your own for someone you care for: advice you'd give if you had something to do all over again, or advice you weren't given and wish you had been. What does your list reveal about you?

LAURENCE SHEEHAN  **"How to Play Second Base"**

1.  Sheehan purports to be writing an instructional essay about "How to Play Second Base," but he wanders from that topic a great deal. Why does he keep digressing—apparently? How has he controlled the wandering? What *persona* and tone does he establish, and by what means? How important is humour in this essay? How would you characterize the humour? What level of diction or style is he operating on? Are there any allusions (besides perhaps that to Ted Williams as "The Thumper")?

2.  What is the essay about? It consists mainly of a long series of anecdotes—but are they about baseball, or something else? What is the point of the many details that have nothing to do with baseball? What does the essay *reveal* about life, courage, shame, or the refusal to be humiliated? Does the moral stated in the final few sentences seem to you a satisfactory conclusion? Does it manage somehow to pull all the seemingly disparate elements together?

3.  Write an autobiographical essay ostensibly about participating in some sport or other activity, but handle your material so that the true purpose is to reveal one or more things about yourself, your friends, your community, or even life itself.

ALDOUS HUXLEY  **"Usually Destroyed"**

1.  Are you likely to use the words *pullulations* and *condignly*? What do they mean? Is such diction appropriate in the context of Huxley's essay? Is his tone overtly formal, or is he just learned? Do any other words he uses seem unlikely candidates for your vocabulary? Might you surprise yourself and use them?

2.  Look up any of the historical references you don't already know about, if only to get a feeling for the wide-ranging quality of Huxley's mind. Identify the allusions in "By the waters of Babylon" and "you ain't seen nuthin' yet." Do they sit comfortably together in the same essay?

3.  It has now been well over a generation since Huxley wrote this essay. Consult some current sources of information in order to assess the accuracy of his predictions and of the others he mentions.

4.  Is Huxley's principal concern what we now call *ecology*? What does the word mean, and when did it become current?

5.  Examine the structure of Huxley's essay. Obviously the title and the beginning and ending point up a principal theme, but much other matter comes in between. How is it ordered? What is the relevance of each part to the whole?

6. Write a short essay in which you make use of some recurrent or choric phrase in the way Huxley does, repeating it throughout, sometimes with different effects, but building cumulatively to the end. The phrase might be a friend's comment that you can apply more broadly, or a slogan from advertising or politics, or any other phrase that— with a little thought—will yield greater significance and resonances than at first appear.

**GEORGE ORWELL "How the Poor Die"**

1. Orwell is known for his use of a simple, straightforward style. Is this essay written in such a style? Did you have to look up any words? Characterize and explain the tone of the essay. What creates it? Consider sentence structure, rhythm, and diction, as well as the content of Orwell's statements. For example, how much do such words as *barbarous, slatternly, squalid, weazened, flaccid, contorted, sordid, reeking, frowsy,* and *murmurous* have to do with establishing the tone? Find other words that contribute in a similar way. Are the style and tone appropriate to the subject matter? What do allusions add? Who for example is Mrs. Gamp?

2. Study the way Orwell's essay moves from the particular to the general, and then back and forth between them. How effective is this technique? What is the overall proportion of generalizations to particular, concrete detail?

3. Orwell obviously expects his readers either to know Tennyson's poem or to consult it. Read it (the full title is "In the Children's Hospital") and comment on the appropriateness and effectiveness of Orwell's closing references to it (and note that in this ending he picks up the premonitory hint from the second paragraph).

4. How does Orwell's essay reveal a whole society's inner structure?

5. In a short essay, describe in a revealing way the dehumanizing effects of some particular place—a doctor's or dentist's office, the lobby of a building, a government office, a supermarket, a locker room, an elevator, or some other such place you know from personal experience.

## TOPICS: General and Comparative

1. Cameron says that the basic principle of good interviewing is to *listen*. Do you agree? Is the reader of an interview turned into a listener? What other successful interviewing techniques can you think of?

2. Consider the way some of the essays in this section begin.
   (a) Is Lane's second sentence—a fragmentary or minor sentence— effective as such? Can you improve the opening by revising what

some would call an awkward and egregious error? In her third sentence Lane refers to irony. How ironic is her essay?

(b) Do Davenport's style and his reference in the opening paragraph to the fact that the "order" of Wittgenstein's slips of paper is "unascertainable" suggest something about both his treatment of his subject and the subject himself—something about fragments as opposed to sustained coherence, randomness as opposed to order?

(c) Note how much the vivid and unusual verbs and adjectives contribute to the description in Ludwig's opening paragraph. Try your hand at writing a descriptive paragraph, first with no adjectives at all and with only quiet verbs, then with imaginative verbs and adjectives like those Ludwig uses.

(d) How effective is Sheehan's beginning? Is he being purposely misleading?

(e) Huxley uses the word *labyrinthine* in his first sentence. How does this establish an idea that the essay as a whole will embroider? How does it relate to his comments on the relation between music and time?

3. Compare the techniques used by Cameron, McClung, Lane, and Davenport to reveal aspects of their biographical subjects. What about Frayn (section VI)? How do biographical and autobiographical forms differ? Compare for example the essays by Lane and Davenport with those by Fisher, Haig-Brown, Mukherjee, and White (section I), Sheehan and Orwell (section II), Dryden and Atwood (section IV), and MacEwen (section VI). Is all autobiographical writing automatically revealing?

4. Is Huxley saying that we customarily go about looking at the history of mankind in the wrong way? Consider his criticism of Toynbee: how just is it? What do some of the other essays in this book have to say about history and the way we view it? Start with Tuchman's essay in section III. (Interestingly, in another essay, called "In Search of History," Tuchman disparages "the genus Toynbee" as "systematizers." Would she agree with Huxley's criticisms?) Look also at least at Mukherjee and MacLennan (section I), and Jenkins, Brink, and Broad and Wade (section III).

5. Note that much of the force of Orwell's point depends on contrast — both explicit and implicit—between French medical systems and others. He also draws a contrast between past and present medical practices. Does what he says contradict what Huxley says about "improvements in technology"? Compare their attitudes in this regard with that of Lewis Thomas (section IV). Compare what Orwell and Szasz (section III) say about the treatment of the rich and the poor in our society; and note that Roueché (section IV) remarks that the poor are

more likely to produce premature babies. Write an essay about some other instance of an implicit but strong distinction between how things go for the rich and how things go for the poor—or do you believe that in our society it isn't true that there is, in effect, one law for the rich and another for the poor? And what about those in between— the ever-present middle class?

6. To what degree do you think some of the writers in this section are wearing masks, adopting *personae* for the occasion?

7. Record a conversation verbatim. Does it sound natural and convincing as you have it written down? How do writers create the illusion of ordinary speech?

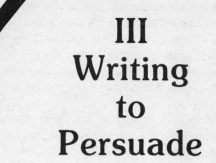

# III
# Writing
# to
# Persuade

By way of a preface: 1. This is the longest section in the book, so it's probably the best, and besides, we put a lot of work into it. 2. The undeniable quality of this section is clearly a result of the fact that one of us was given a lucky rabbit's foot just before we started working on it. 3. Intelligent readers will immediately recognize the importance and value of this section. 4. Previous readers of this section—sincere and professional people, some of them ministers and doctors, with a European education—all endorsed it strongly. 5. So if you don't like this section, you must have anchovy paste in your head instead of a brain, and you're probably a subversive too.

Our thesis in this section is quite straightforward. It is easy to write argumentatively. It is also easy to write logically, but logic and successful persuasion do not always go hand in hand. Even saying this is easy. But how can we prove it? That's the function of argumentative prose: to set out a thesis or proposition and prove it, or at least to persuade a reader or listener of the value or validity of a point of view or of a body of information. More than for any other kind of writing, therefore, argument depends upon engaging an audience.

Of course, preaching to the party faithful is easy, because there's little need for persuasion, logical or otherwise; all that's necessary is to trot out the slogans and the buzzwords that will confirm listeners in their existing belief. People say logic is persuasive. But logic will have little effect if listeners are already converted, so to speak—nor will it be of much use on an audience so committed to a contrary point of view that not even an earthquake would shake their commitment or their faith. And though logic should give a speaker some advantage, it is also true that illogical and emotional appeals are often successful. Sometimes, on these occasions, strict logic dissipates in a cloud of passion. If people are persuaded under such circumstances, one might well ask the question: Why?

The simple fact is that people make up and change their minds for countless reasons, some of them open, some covert, some rationally argued, some subliminally suggested. Such things, moreover, as fear, shame, moral outrage, nationalism, and emotional upheaval are among the most potent weapons a would-be influencer can use. Consider the five sample sentences at the beginning of this section. Are any of them convincing? Are any contentious? Do any seem "reasonable"? All are in some way emotional. And none of them is logical. Separately, therefore, they might or might not (a little equivocation here) be effective openings to an essay. Together, they illustrate some of the common ways that illogicalities creep into persuasive prose. The wary reader will be on the watch for these fallacies, whatever their guise. The conscious persuader uses them all the time. They have names, which may be useful as a guide to recognizing them:

1. Sentence 1 is an example both of the **non sequitur** (meaning "does not follow": size is not necessarily an indication of quality)

and of **special pleading** (why should it matter how much time we spent?). Watch for any flaw in a writer's reasoning; every time you see terms like *so, therefore, must be, obviously, clearly, of course,* and *because*—those tools-of-the-trade of the persuasive writer—check that the logical connections they imply in fact make sense in context.

2. Sentence 2 begins by **begging the question**, assuming as given, or proved, what in fact needs to be proved ("undeniable quality"). And it demonstrates a process called **post hoc ergo propter hoc** ("after this therefore because of this"), which assumes a cause-effect relationship based on mere sequence. Superstitions, such as wearing good-luck charms because they supposedly make good things happen, are examples of **post hoc** thinking. We could also have claimed that because section II is so good, section III is bound to be better. It is true that persuasive writing often organizes details in climactic order (strong first, weakest next, then on to strongest last); but things don't necessarily get better (or worse) because they're older, younger, nearer, bigger, or next.

3. Sentence 3 involves **argumentum ad populum** ("argument directed at the people"), or an appeal to the reader to identify with some approved quality of character (here, intelligence). Such arguments appeal to people's emotions, their prejudices and fears.

4. Sentence 4 also uses a kind of *argumentum ad populum,* the invitation to get on a **bandwagon**. As with the word "intelligent" in sentence 3, the implied message is "don't be left out." (Why do advertisers so often rely on this message? Why do consumers respond?) Sentence 4 also employs a covert **appeal to authority**. Appeals to authority frequently rely on precedent, and they depend upon people's faith in some model. (Perhaps covertly, they also imply people's lack of faith in themselves.) The "authority" can be the Bible, Aristotle, scientists, tradition, pop stars, the mayor, your Grade One teacher, a European education, or a variety of other persons and things. But ask: is it relevant to the case at hand? Is it truly authoritative? And is the language of the appeal **slanted** in any way: is it culturally biased, sexually biased, emotionally loaded? Check to see if an argument adequately takes contrary possibilities or points of view into account. A barrage of **statistics** often appears as a "proof," too, when 95% of the time (are you sure?) the questions that lead to the statistics are loaded or misleading, the statistical sample is too small to be valid, or the results are interpreted one-sidedly. Don't be bamboozled into belief.

5. Sentence 5 illustrates a combination of a false **either-or** option with **argumentum ad hominem** ("argument against the man"),

which tries to divert attention from the question being discussed to the character of some person. **Name-calling, mudslinging, innuendo**: these are the techniques of gutter journalism and sleazy political contests. Anything else? Be wary of insults, stated or implied. Also be wary when offered only two options: "If you're not for us, you're against us," "If you're not *one of us*, you're *one of them*," "If you don't agree, you must be..." (Fill in the blank: *a Communist, a fascist, a radical, anti-American, from Toronto*). Ask yourself if there isn't another alternative. Beware the *false dilemma*.

Such fallacies are not always as clear as they are here. Those masters of persuasive rhetoric—politicians, lawyers, advertisers, salespeople, editorial writers, cult leaders, fashion designers, publicists, and con men—are frequently artists with verbal illusion. They can also of course be artists with logic. But given the contexts of their arguments, the wary reader will ask: What purpose does their logic serve?

Writing logically, a person can present a range of examples and invite readers to come to general conclusions *inductively*. By an alternative procedure, a writer can present a generalization or a series of generalizations and ask readers to come *deductively* to conclusions about particular examples. A typical form of deductive reasoning is called the *syllogism*, or syllogistic argument. Using this pattern, a writer will draw conclusions from the apparent connections between two *premises*, or "axiomatic" presumptions. Baldly stated, the form looks like this:

1. All bananas grow on trees.
2. This is a banana.
3. Therefore it grew on a tree.

Obviously such a pattern is open to distortion. Look what happens if the first premise is faulty or if the second premise doesn't connect appropriately with the first:

1. All human beings have brown eyes.
2. My brother has blue eyes.
3. Therefore my brother isn't human.

1. All dogs have legs.
2. My canary has legs.
3. Therefore my canary is a dog.

The false reasoning here is easy to see and therefore easy to dismiss, or avoid. Fallacies that are less easy to recognize are often found in expressions of people's prejudices and fears; the conclusions derive from faulty—but concealed—syllogisms, as in the following:

1. Americans hate communists.
2. X is spreading socialist ideas.
3. Therefore X is anti-American.

or:

1. Businessmen approve of politically rightwing economic measures.
2. X is a businessman.
3. Therefore X is a fascist at heart.

or, multiplying the premises somewhat:

1. We are nice people.
2. We speak English.
3. Our neighbours speak another language.
4. Therefore they are (a) not nice people, (b) not worth knowing, (c) responsible for our problems—the garbage in the lane, violence in the streets, crowding in the stores, the loss of our jobs, etc.

This last example illustrates the process of faulty reasoning that leads to the making of **scapegoats**—a way of blaming others for a problem, and victimizing them for it, instead of looking for a reasonable solution. In such circumstances, the premises are sometimes not even expressed; instead they have been consciously or unconsciously suppressed, so that just the conclusions appear—making the conclusions look like axioms when in fact they are just the invalid results of faulty reasoning. It is easy to see why polemical writers would try to stir up emotionally based animosities. And why they would try, even while doing so, to appeal to people's sense of the logic of it all. People like to think that they think about what they believe and what they do. But sometimes they don't. And people who never stop to think about the process of persuasion are the most susceptible to being manipulated.

Yet it does not follow that people who are passionate about ideas are necessarily irrational, or that people who reason their way to conclusions are necessarily cold. The essays in this section—examples of reviewing, polemical letter-writing, political statement, feature journalism, formal lecture, editorial comment, and "scientific" organization of evidence — all take contentious stances, sometimes for emotional reasons, sometimes out of a deep-seated intellectual commitment, sometimes for debate. They vary in tone. Some are solemn; some are witty; some are passionate; some are acid. None is neutral. And none is grey. Their styles are as individual as the styles of personal narratives: argument does not imply an absence of personality. Indeed, the overt presence of an authorial perspective often greatly aids a writer or speaker in reaching and holding—and hence influencing—the members of an audience.

Thurber, for example, brings his sense of humour to bear on a serious subject without trivializing it (does Kael's caustic wit interfere with her judgment of sentimentality?). Morgan, Meigs, and Schlesinger all analyze forms of sexual politics (how do they differ from each other in tone and perspective as well as in particular subject?). Fulford and Brink both write of racism (how do their different national and political backgrounds affect their methods of argument?). The essays on psychiatry and scientific logic probe the limits of science (are they therefore dismissive, or are they arguing for greater thoughtfulness, greater attention to detail?). In each case, who is the writer's chosen audience? Are you? And are you persuaded? (you don't have to be; but if you disagree with what these writers say, how reasoned, how valid—and how emotional—are your objections?).

A final word is necessary. Lest the foregoing points imply that reason explains everything, that passion proves nothing, and that all discoveries and judgments ought to be based on rigorous processes of logical thought, let us point to what Broad and Wade in their essay say about the way science proceeds. And let us remind you of the *Eureka!* principle. When Archimedes leaped from his bath with a mathematical solution to the problem of displaced water, he undoubtedly had at least a glimmer of logical proof at the back of his mind. But sometimes reason is a servant rather than a leader. Sometimes the glimmer is a magnificent, unbidden leap of imaginative insight. Reason, then, can only trudge along after.

# The Sound of . . .

## The Sound of Music and The Singing Nun

## Pauline Kael

*The Singing Nun* will make you realize how good Fred Zinnemann's *The Nun's Story* was. Although the theme, the conflict and even the story line are similar, *The Singing Nun* reduces them to smiles, twinkles, banalities and falseness. It is almost a parody of *The Nun's Story* and, of course, without the courage of the conclusion of that earlier thoughtful, subtle film. Though *The Singing Nun* draws its ideas from *The Nun's Story*, its inspiration is obviously that movie phenomenon the trade press now refers to (very respectfully) as *The Sound of Money*. And perhaps to get at what goes on in a movie like *The Singing Nun*, we need to look at that phenomenon, which is so often called "wholesome" but which is probably going to be the single most repressive influence on artistic freedom in movies for the next few years.

The success of a movie like *The Sound of Music* makes it even more difficult for anyone to try to do anything worth doing, anything relevant to the modern world, anything inventive or expressive. The banks, the studios, the producers will want to give the public what it seems to crave. The more money these "wholesome" movies make, the less wholesome will the state of American movies be. "The opium of the audience," Luis Bunuel, the Spanish director, once said, "is conformity." And nothing is more degrading and ultimately destructive to artists than supplying the narcotic.

What is it that makes millions of people buy and like *The Sound of Music*—a tribute to "freshness" that is so mechanically engineered, so

*From Kiss Kiss, Bang Bang* by Pauline Kael. Copyright © 1968 by Pauline Kael. By permission of Little, Brown and Company in association with The Atlantic Monthly Press.

shrewdly calculated that the background music rises, the already soft focus blurs and melts, and, upon the instant, you can hear all those noses blowing in the theatre? Of course, it's well done for what it is: that is to say, those who made it are experts at manipulating responses. They're the Pavlovs of movie-making: they turn us into dogs that salivate on signal. When the cruel father sees the light and says, "You've brought music back into the house," who can resist the pull at the emotions? It's that same tug at the heartstrings we feel when Lassie comes home or when the blind heroine sees for the first time; it is a simple variant of that surge of warmth we feel when a child is reunited with his parents. It's basic, and there are probably few of us who don't respond. But it is the easiest and perhaps the most primitive kind of emotion that we are made to feel. The worst despots in history, the most cynical purveyors of mass culture respond at *this* level and may feel pleased at how tenderhearted they *really* are because they do. This kind of response has as little to do with generosity of feeling as being stirred when you hear a band has to do with patriotism.

I think it is not going too far to say that when an expensive product of modern technology like *The Sound of Music* uses this sort of "universal" appeal, it is because nothing could be safer, nothing could be surer. Whom could it offend? Only those of us who, *despite the fact that we may respond*, loathe being manipulated in this way and are aware of how self-indulgent and cheap and ready-made are the responses we are made to feel. And we may become even more aware of the way we have been *used* and turned into emotional and aesthetic imbeciles when we hear ourselves humming those sickly, goody-goody songs. The audience for a movie of this kind becomes the lowest common denominator of feeling: a sponge. The heroine leaves the nuns at the fence as she enters the cathedral to be married. Squeezed again, and the moisture comes out of thousands— millions—of eyes and noses.

And the phenomenon at the center of the monetary phenomenon? Julie Andrews, with the clean, scrubbed look and the unyieldingly high spirits; the good sport who makes the best of everything; the girl who's so unquestionably good that she carries this one dimension like a shield. The perfect, perky schoolgirl, the adorable tomboy, the gawky colt. Sexless, inhumanly happy, the sparkling maid, a mind as clean and well brushed as her teeth. What is she? Merely the ideal heroine for the best of all possible worlds. And that's what *The Sound of Music* pretends we live in.

Audiences are transported into a world of operetta cheerfulness and calendar art. You begin to feel as if you've never got out of school. Up there on the screen, they're all in their places with bright, shining faces. Wasn't there perhaps one little Von Trapp who didn't want to sing his head off, or who screamed that he wouldn't act out little glockenspiel routines for Papa's party guests, or who got nervous and threw up if he had to get on a stage? No, nothing mars this celebration of togetherness. Not only does this family sing together, they play ball together. This is the world teachers used to pretend (and maybe still pretend?) was the real world. It's the world in which the governess conquers all. It's the big lie, the sugarcoated lie that people seem to want to eat. They even seem to think they should feed it to their kids, that it's healthy, wonderful "family entertainment."

And this is the sort of attitude that makes a critic feel that maybe it's all hopeless. Why not just send the director, Robert Wise, a wire: "You win, I give up," or, rather, "We both lose, we all lose."

Yet there was a spider on the valentine: the sinister, unpleasant, archly decadent performance Christopher Plummer gives as the baron, he of the thin, twisted smile—my candidate for the man least likely to be accepted as a hero. Even the monstrously ingenious technicians who made this movie couldn't put together a convincing mate for Super Goody Two-Shoes. The dauntless heroine surmounts this obstacle: in the romantic scenes, she makes love to herself. And why not? We never believed for a moment that love or marriage would affect her or change her. She was already perfection.

Debbie Reynolds, as the character based on Soeur Sourire in *The Singing Nun*, is less than perfection. Her eyes are not so clear and bright, indeed they're rather anxious and, yes, almost bleary; and her singing isn't pure and pretty, it's sort of tacky and ordinary. So is the whole production. Henry Koster doesn't succeed even in making it very convincingly "wholesome." The religion is a familiar kind of Hollywood Christianity. The nuns are even more smiley and giggly—like a mush-headed schoolteacher's dream of ideally happy schoolchildren; Ricardo Montalban is a simperingly simple priest; and though Agnes Moorehead plays a nun like a witch, she is more than balanced by Greer Garson as the Mother Prioress. With her false eyelashes and her richly condescending manner, Greer Garson can turn any line of dialogue into incomparable cant. It's a gift, of a kind.

The people in *The Singing Nun* behave like the animals in a Disney movie: they are so cute and so full of little tricks. There are chintzy little pedagogical songs that are supposed to be full of *joy*, and there is Debbie's excruciating humility. "I have a lot to learn," she tells us; but we didn't need to be told. She gives up her singing career—which was giving her too much attention and adoration—in order to find her simple faith again. And so, at the end, we see her working as a nurse in Africa, posed like a madonna holding a Negro baby, surrounded by attentive, adoring Africans.... But then, of course, this movie is the kind of spiritual exercise in which the nuns say a little prayer for Ed Sullivan every day.

Why am I so angry about these movies? Because the shoddy falseness of *The Singing Nun* and the luxuriant falseness of *The Sound of Music* are part of the sentimental American tone that makes honest work almost impossible. It is not only that people who accept this kind of movie tend to resent work which says that this is not the best of all possible worlds, but that people who are gifted give up the effort to say anything. They attune themselves to *The Sound of Money*.

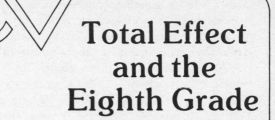

# Total Effect and the Eighth Grade

Flannery O'Connor

In two recent instances in Georgia, parents have objected to their eighth- and ninth-grade children's reading assignments in modern fiction. This seems to happen with some regularity in cases throughout the country. The unwitting parent picks up his child's book, glances through it, comes upon passages of erotic detail or profanity, and takes off at once to complain to the school board. Sometimes, as in one of the Georgia cases, the teacher is dismissed and hackles rise in liberal circles everywhere.

The two cases in Georgia, which involved Steinbeck's *East of Eden* and John Hersey's *A Bell for Adano*, provoked considerable newspaper comment. One columnist, in commending the enterprise of the teachers, announced that students do not like to read the fusty works of the nineteenth century, that their attention can best be held by novels dealing with the realities of our own time, and that the Bible, too, is full of racy stories.

Mr. Hersey himself addressed a letter to the State School Superintendent in behalf of the teacher who had been dismissed. He pointed out that his book is not scandalous, that it attempts to convey an earnest message about the nature of democracy, and that it falls well within the limits of the principle of "total effect," that principle followed in legal cases by which a book is judged not for isolated parts but by the final effect of the whole book upon the general reader.

I do not want to comment on the merits of these particular cases.

Reprinted with the permission of Farrar, Straus & Giroux, Inc. from *Mystery and Manners* by Flannery O'Connor, selected and edited by Sally and Robert Fitzgerald. Copyright © 1957, 1961, 1963, 1964, 1966, 1969 by the Estate of Mary Flannery O'Connor. Copyright © 1962 by Flannery O'Connor. Copyright © 1961 by Farrar, Straus & Cudahy (now Farrar, Straus & Giroux, Inc.)

What concerns me is what novels ought to be assigned in the eighth and ninth grades as a matter of course, for if these cases indicate anything, they indicate the haphazard way in which fiction is approached in our high schools. Presumably there is a state reading list which contains "safe" books for teachers to assign; after that it is up to the teacher.

English teachers come in Good, Bad, and Indifferent, but too frequently in high schools anyone who can speak English is allowed to teach it. Since several novels can't easily be gathered into one textbook, the fiction that students are assigned depends upon their teacher's knowledge, ability, and taste: variable factors at best. More often than not, the teacher assigns what he thinks will hold the attention and interest of the students. Modern fiction will certainly hold it.

Ours is the first age in history which has asked the child what he would tolerate learning, but that is a part of the problem with which I am not equipped to deal. The devil of Educationism that possesses us is the kind that can be "cast out only by prayer and fasting." No one has yet come along strong enough to do it. In other ages the attention of children was held by Homer and Virgil, among others, but, by the reverse evolutionary process, that is no longer possible; our children are too stupid now to enter the past imaginatively. No one asks the student if algebra pleases him or if he finds it satisfactory that some French verbs are irregular, but if he prefers Hersey to Hawthorne, his taste must prevail.

I would like to put forward the proposition, repugnant to most English teachers, that fiction, if it is going to be taught in the high schools, should be taught as a subject and as a subject with a history. The total effect of a novel depends not only on its innate impact, but upon the experience, literary and otherwise, with which it is approached. No child needs to be assigned Hersey or Steinbeck until he is familiar with a certain amount of the best works of Cooper, Hawthorne, Melville, the early James, and Crane, and he does not need to be assigned these until he has been introduced to some of the better English novelists of the eighteenth and nineteenth centuries.

The fact that these works do not present him with the realities of his own time is all to the good. He is surrounded by the realities of his own time, and he has no perspective whatever from which to view them. Like the college student who wrote in her paper on Lincoln that he went to the movies and got shot, many students go to college unaware that the world was not made yesterday; their studies began with the present and dipped backward occasionally when it seemed necessary or unavoidable.

There is much to be enjoyed in the great British novels of the nineteenth century, much that a good teacher can open up in them for the young student. There is no reason why these novels should be either too simple or too difficult for the eighth grade. For the simple, they offer simple pleasures; for the more precocious, they can be made to yield subtler ones if the teacher is up to it. Let the student discover, after reading the nineteenth-century British novel, that the nineteenth-century American novel is quite different as to its literary characteristics, and he will thereby learn something not only about these individual works but about the sea-change which a new historical situation can effect in a literary form. Let him come to modern fiction with this experience behind him, and he will be better able to see and to deal with the more complicated demands of the best twentieth-century fiction.

Modern fiction often looks simpler than the fiction that preceded it, but in reality it is more complex. A natural evolution has taken place. The author has for the most part absented himself from direct participation in the work and has left the reader to make his own way amid experiences dramatically rendered and symbolically ordered. The modern novelist merges the reader in the experience; he tends to raise the passions he touches upon. If he is a good novelist, he raises them to effect by their order and clarity a new experience—the total effect—which is not in itself sensuous or simply of the moment. Unless the child has had some literary experience before, he is not going to be able to resolve the immediate passions the book arouses into any true, total picture.

It is here the moral problem will arise. It is one thing for a child to read about adultery in the Bible or in *Anna Karenina*, and quite another for him to read about it in most modern fiction. This is not only because in both the former instances adultery is considered a sin, and in the latter, at most, an inconvenience, but because modern writing involves the reader in the action with a new degree of intensity, and literary mores now permit him to be involved in any action a human being can perform.

In our fractured culture, we cannot agree on morals; we cannot even agree that moral matters should come before literary ones when there is a conflict between them. All this is another reason why the high schools would do well to return to their proper business of preparing foundations. Whether in the senior year students should be assigned modern novelists should depend both on their parents' consent and on what they have already read and understood.

The high-school English teacher will be fulfilling his responsibility if he furnishes the student a guided opportunity, through the best writing of the past, to come, in time, to an understanding of the best writing of the present. He will teach literature, not social studies or little lessons in democracy or the customs of many lands.

And if the student finds that this is not to his taste? Well, that is regrettable. Most regrettable. His taste should not be consulted; it is being formed.

# Middlebrow

### Virginia Woolf

**TO THE EDITOR OF THE "NEW STATESMAN"**

Sir,

Will you allow me to draw your attention to the fact that in a review of a book by me (October) your reviewer omitted to use the word Highbrow? The review, save for that omission, gave me so much pleasure that I am driven to ask you, at the risk of appearing unduly egotistical, whether your reviewer, a man of obvious intelligence, intended to deny my claim to that title? I say "claim," for surely I may claim that title when a great critic, who is also a great novelist, a rare and enviable combination, always calls me a highbrow when he condescends to notice my work in a great newspaper; and, further, always finds space to inform not only myself, who know it already, but the whole British Empire, who hang on his words, that I live in Bloomsbury? Is your critic unaware of that fact too? Or does he, for all his intelligence, maintain that it is unnecessary in reviewing a book to add the postal address of the writer?

His answer to these questions, though of real value to me, is of no possible interest to the public at large. Of that I am well aware. But since larger issues are involved, since the Battle of the Brows troubles, I am told, the evening air, since the finest minds of our age have lately been engaged in debating, not without that passion which befits a noble cause, what a highbrow is and what a lowbrow, which is better and which is worse, may I take this opportunity to express my opinion and at the same time draw attention to certain aspects of the question which seem to me to have been unfortunately overlooked?

Now there can be no two opinions as to what a highbrow is. He is the man or woman of thoroughbred intelligence who rides his mind at a gallop

From *The Death of the Moth and Other Essays* by Virginia Woolf. Reprinted by permission of the Author's Literary Estate and The Hogarth Press Ltd.

across country in pursuit of an idea. That is why I have always been so proud to be called highbrow. That is why, if I could be more of a highbrow I would. I honour and respect highbrows. Some of my relations have been highbrows; and some, but by no means all, of my friends. To be a highbrow, a complete and representative highbrow, a highbrow like Shakespeare, Dickens, Byron, Shelley, Keats, Charlotte Brontë, Scott, Jane Austen, Flaubert, Hardy or Henry James—to name a few highbrows from the same profession chosen at random—is of course beyond the wildest dreams of my imagination. And, though I would cheerfully lay myself down in the dust and kiss the print of their feet, no person of sense will deny that this passionate preoccupation of theirs—riding across country in pursuit of ideas—often leads to disaster. Undoubtedly, they come fearful croppers. Take Shelley—what a mess he made of his life! And Byron, getting into bed with first one woman and then with another and dying in the mud at Missolonghi. Look at Keats, loving poetry and Fanny Brawne so intemperately that he pined and died of consumption at the age of twenty-six. Charlotte Brontë again—I have been assured on good authority that Charlotte Brontë was, with the possible exception of Emily, the worst governess in the British Isles. Then there was Scott—he went bankrupt, and left, together with a few magnificent novels, one house, Abbotsford, which is perhaps the ugliest in the whole Empire. But surely these instances are enough—I need not further labour the point that highbrows, for some reason or another, are wholly incapable of dealing successfully with what is called real life. That is why, and here I come to a point that is often surprisingly ignored, they honour so wholeheartedly and depend so completely upon those who are called lowbrows. By a lowbrow is meant of course a man or a woman of thoroughbred vitality who rides his body in pursuit of a living at a gallop across life. That is why I honour and respect lowbrows—and I have never known a highbrow who did not. In so far as I am a highbrow (and my imperfections in that line are well known to me) I love lowbrows; I study them; I always sit next the conductor in an omnibus and try to get him to tell me what it is like—being a conductor. In whatever company I am I always try to know what it is like—being a conductor, being a woman with ten children and thirty-five shillings a week, being a stockbroker, being an admiral, being a bank clerk, being a dressmaker, being a duchess, being a miner, being a cook, being a prostitute. All that lowbrows do is of surpassing interest and wonder to me, because, in so far as I am a highbrow, I cannot do things myself.

This brings me to another point which is also surprisingly overlooked. Lowbrows need highbrows and honour them just as much as highbrows need lowbrows and honour them. This too is not a matter that requires much demonstration. You have only to stroll along the Strand on a wet winter's night and watch the crowds lining up to get into the movies. These lowbrows are waiting, after the day's work, in the rain, sometimes for hours, to get into the cheap seats and sit in hot theatres in order to see what their lives look like. Since they are lowbrows, engaged magnificently and adventurously in riding full tilt from one end of life to the other in pursuit of a living, they cannot see themselves doing it. Yet nothing interests them more. Nothing matters to them more. It is one of the prime necessities of life to them—to be shown what life looks like. And the highbrows, of course, are the only people who can show them. Since they are the only people who do not do things, they are the only people who can see things being done. This is so—and so it is I am certain; nevertheless we are told—the air buzzes with it by night, the Press booms with it by day, the very donkeys in the fields do nothing but bray it, the very curs in the street do nothing but bark it—"Highbrows hate lowbrows! Lowbrows hate highbrows!"—when highbrows need lowbrows, when lowbrows need highbrows, when they cannot exist apart, when one is the complement and other side of the other! How has such a lie come into existence? Who has set this malicious gossip afloat?

There can be no doubt about that either. It is the doing of the middlebrows. They are the people, I confess, that I seldom regard with entire cordiality. They are the go-betweens; they are the busybodies who run from one to the other with their tittle tattle and make all the mischief—the middlebrows, I repeat. But what, you may ask, is a middlebrow? And that, to tell the truth, is no easy question to answer. They are neither one thing nor the other. They are not highbrows, whose brows are high; nor lowbrows, whose brows are low. Their brows are betwixt and between. They do not live in Bloomsbury which is on high ground; nor in Chelsea, which is on low ground. Since they must live somewhere presumably, they live perhaps in South Kensington, which is betwixt and between. The middlebrow is the man, or woman, of middlebred intelligence who ambles and saunters now on this side of the hedge, now on that, in pursuit of no single object, neither art itself nor life itself, but both mixed indistinguishably, and rather nastily, with money, fame, power, or prestige. The middlebrow curries favour with both sides equally. He goes to the lowbrows and tells them that while he is not quite one of them, he is almost their friend. Next moment he rings up the highbrows and asks them with equal geniality whether he may not come to tea. Now there are highbrows—I myself have known duchesses who were highbrows, also charwomen, and they have both told me with that vigour of language which so often unites the aristocracy with the working classes, that they would rather sit in the coal cellar, together, than in the drawing-room with middlebrows and pour out tea. I have myself been asked—but may I, for the sake of brevity, cast this scene which is only partly fictitious, into the form of fiction?—I myself, then, have been asked to come and "see" them—how strange a passion theirs is for being "seen"! They ring me up, therefore, at about eleven in the morning, and ask me to come to tea. I go to my wardrobe and consider, rather lugubriously, what is the right thing to wear? We highbrows may be smart, or we may be shabby; but we never have the right thing to wear. I proceed to ask next: What is the right thing to say? Which is the right knife to use? What is the right book to praise? All these are things I do not know for myself. We highbrows read what we like and do what we like and praise what we like. We also know what we dislike—for example, thin bread and butter tea. The difficulty of eating thin bread and butter in white kid gloves has always seemed to me one of life's more insuperable problems. Then I dislike bound volumes of the classics behind plate glass. Then I distrust people who call both Shakespeare and Wordsworth equally "Bill"—it is a habit moreover that leads to confusion. And in the matter of clothes, I like people either to dress very well; or to dress very badly; I dislike the correct thing in clothes. Then there is the question of games. Being a highbrow I do not play them. But I love watching people play who have a passion for games. These middlebrows pat balls about; they poke their bats and muff their catches at cricket. And when poor Middlebrow mounts on horseback and that animal breaks into a canter, to me there is no sadder sight in all Rotten Row. To put it in a nutshell (in order to get on with the story) that tea party was not wholly a success, nor altogether a failure; for Middlebrow, who writes, following me to the door, clapped me briskly on the back, and said "I'm sending you my book!" (Or did he call it "stuff?") And his book comes—sure enough, though called, so symbolically, *Keepaway*, it comes. And I read a page here, and I read a page there (I am breakfasting, as usual, in bed). And it is not well written; nor is it badly written. It is not proper, nor is it improper; in short it is betwixt and between. Now if there is any sort of book for which I have, perhaps, an imperfect sympathy, it is the betwixt and between. And so, though I suffer from the gout of a morning—but if one's ancestors for two or three centuries have tumbled into bed dead drunk one has deserved a touch of that malady—I rise. I dress. I proceed weakly to the window. I take that book in my swollen right hand and toss it gently over the hedge into the field. The hungry sheep—did I remember to say that this part of the story takes place in the country?—the hungry sheep look up but are not fed.

But to have done with fiction and its tendency to lapse into poetry—I will now report a perfectly prosaic conversation in words of one syllable. I often ask my friends the lowbrows, over our muffins and honey, why it is that while we, the highbrows, never buy a middlebrow book, or go to a middlebrow lecture, or read, unless we are paid for doing so, a middlebrow review, they, on the contrary, take these middlebrow activities so seriously? Why, I ask (not of course on the wireless), are you so damnably modest? Do you think that a description of your lives, as they are, is too

sordid and too mean to be beautiful? Is that why you prefer the middlebrow version of what they have the impudence to call real humanity?—this mixture of geniality and sentiment stuck together with a sticky
slime of calves-foot jelly? The truth, if you would only believe it, is much
more beautiful than any lie. Then again, I continue, how can you let the
middlebrows teach *you* how to write?—you, who write so beautifully when
you write naturally, that I would give both my hands to write as you
do—for which reason I never attempt it, but do my best to learn the art of
writing as a highbrow should. And again, I press on, brandishing a muffin
on the point of a tea spoon, how dare the middlebrows teach *you* how to
read—Shakespeare for instance? All you have to do is to read him. The
Cambridge edition is both good and cheap. If you find *Hamlet* difficult, ask
him to tea. He is a highbrow. Ask Ophelia to meet him. She is a lowbrow.
Talk to them, as you talk to me, and you will know more about
Shakespeare than all the middlebrows in the world can teach you—I do
not think, by the way, from certain phrases that Shakespeare liked middlebrows, or Pope either.

    To all this the lowbrows reply—but I cannot imitate their style of talk-
ing—that they consider themselves to be common people without education. It is very kind of the middlebrows to try to teach them culture. And
after all, the lowbrows continue, middlebrows, like other people, have to
make money. There must be money in teaching and in writing books
about Shakespeare. We all have to earn our livings nowadays, my friends
the lowbrows remind me. I quite agree. Even those of us whose Aunts
came a cropper riding in India and left them an annual income of four hundred and fifty pounds, now reduced, thanks to the war and other luxuries,
to little more than two hundred odd, even we have to do that. And we do
it, too, by writing about anybody who seems amusing—enough has been
written about Shakespeare—Shakespeare hardly pays. We highbrows, I
agree, have to earn our livings; but when we have earned enough to live
on, then we live. When the middlebrows, on the contrary, have earned
enough to live on, they go on earning enough to buy—what are the things
that middlebrows always buy? Queen Anne furniture (faked, but none the
less expensive); first editions of dead writers—always the worst; pictures,
or reproductions from pictures, by dead painters, houses in what is called
"the Georgian style"—but never anything new, never a picture by a living
painter, or a chair by a living carpenter, or books by living writers, for to
buy living art requires living taste. And, as that kind of art and that kind of
taste are what middlebrows call "highbrow," "Bloomsbury," poor middlebrow spends vast sums on sham antiques, and has to keep at it scribbling away, year in, year out, while we highbrows ring each other up, and
are off for a day's jaunt into the country. That is the worst of course of living in a set—one likes being with one's friends.

Have I then made my point clear, sir, that the true battle in my opinion lies not between highbrow and lowbrow, but between highbrows and lowbrows joined together in blood brotherhood against the bloodless and pernicious pest who comes between? If the B.B.C. stood for anything but the Betwixt and Between Company they would use their control of the air not to stir strife between brothers, but to broadcast the fact that highbrows and lowbrows must band together to exterminate a pest which is the bane of all thinking and living. It may be, to quote from your advertisement columns, that "terrifically sensitive" lady novelists overestimate the dampness and dinginess of this fungoid growth. But all I can say is that when, lapsing into that stream which people call, so oddly, consciousness, and gathering wool from the sheep that have been mentioned above, I ramble round my garden in the suburbs, middlebrow seems to me to be everywhere. "What's that?" I cry. "Middlebrow on the cabbages? Middlebrow infecting that poor old sheep? And what about the moon?" I look up and, beyond, the moon is under eclipse. "Middlebrow at it again!" I exclaim. "Middlebrow obscuring, dulling, tarnishing and coarsening even the silver edge of Heaven's own scythe." (I "draw near to poetry," see advt.) And then my thoughts, as Freud assures us thoughts will do, rush (Middlebrow's saunter and simper, out of respect for the Censor) to sex, and I ask of the sea-gulls who are crying on desolate sea sands and of the farm hands who are coming home rather drunk to their wives, what will become of us, men and women, if Middlebrow has his way with us, and there is only a middle sex but no husbands or wives? The next remark I address with the utmost humility to the Prime Minister. "What, sir," I demand, "will be the fate of the British Empire and of our Dominions Across the Seas if Middlebrows prevail? Will you not, sir, read a pronouncement of an authoritative nature from Broadcasting House?"

Such are the thoughts, such are the fancies that visit "cultured invalidish ladies with private means" (see advt.) when they stroll in their suburban gardens and look at the cabbages and at the red brick villas that have been built by middlebrows so that middlebrows may look at the view. Such are the thoughts "at once gay and tragic and deeply feminine" (see advt.) of one who has not yet "been driven out of Bloomsbury" (advt. again), a place where lowbrows and highbrows live happily together on equal terms and priests are not, nor priestesses, and, to be quite frank, the adjective "priestly" is neither often heard nor held in high esteem. Such are the thoughts of one who will stay in Bloomsbury until the Duke of Bedford, rightly concerned for the respectability of his squares, raises the rent so high that Bloomsbury is safe for middlebrows to live in. Then she will leave.

May I conclude, as I began, by thanking your reviewer for his very courteous and interesting review, but may I tell him that though he did not, for reasons best known to himself, call me a highbrow, there is no name in the world that I prefer? I ask nothing better than that all reviewers, for ever, and everywhere, should call me a highbrow. I will do my best to oblige them. If they like to add Bloomsbury, W.C.1, that is the correct postal address, and my telephone number is in the Directory. But if your reviewer, or any other reviewer, dares hint that I live in South Kensington, I will sue him for libel. If any human being, man, woman, dog, cat or half-crushed worm dares call me "middlebrow" I will take my pen and stab him, dead.

Yours etc.,

VIRGINIA WOOLF.

# Nobody Here but Us Dead Sheep

## William Zinsser

Nerve gas in Okinawa. Nuclear explosions in Nevada. Chemical Mace in the eyes. Every day it's something else in American life which strikes me as outlandish, but which evidently began in logic. I can no longer tell where we cross over from the normal to the insane.

I remember back in May seeing a picture of a tank and some infantrymen on the front page of the morning paper. I didn't bother to read the caption because it was the same combat picture of Vietnam that I've seen every other morning. But, it wasn't Vietnam—it was a college in North Carolina. A few days later I saw a photograph of several hundred soldiers standing guard in gas masks. They were in gas masks because a helicopter was poised overhead to spray chemicals. It was the University of California at Berkeley. In 1969 the incongruous becomes routine almost overnight.

I never knew, for instance, that the American Army has been storing nerve gas at its bases in other countries. The only way the Army lets us know about its nerve gas is to leak a little by mistake, as it did last month in Okinawa, briefly hospitalizing 24 men. Just routine deployment of deterrent power, the Pentagon said, explaining its policy on chemical weapons — nobody should be surprised.

Well, *I* was surprised. More surprised, actually, than the Okinawans, who suspected something last summer when 200 Okinawan children suffered skin burns while swimming at a beach 12 miles south of our 137th Ordnance Company's camp. The unusual still strikes them as unusual.

Not us. In the spring of 1968, 6,400 sheep dropped dead one week in

*Life* 67, No. 8 (August 22, 1969).

Utah—a mortality rate not common in sheep-raising—fairly near the Army's chemical warfare testing center. Queried about this coincidence, the Army said it couldn't imagine what could have possibly happened to those sheep. Luckily, a few people felt that the sudden death of 6,400 sheep taunted the laws of zoology, and they kept bringing the matter up, clinging to reason amid denials that persisted for 14 months, until finally the official lies were turned into official truths—as happened when the Pentagon admitted that it knew exactly what happened to those sheep. A valve malfunctioned. The wind changed. So sorry.

Should we laugh or cry? We teeter every day on the edge of absurdity and think it is solid ground. Recently the Army decided to get rid of 27,000 tons of obsolete chemical and bacteriological weapons stockpiled at a base in the Rockies—including 2,660 tons of rockets and 12,322 tons of bomb clusters, all filled with nerve gas—by hauling the whole load across the country in railroad cars and dumping it in the ocean off New Jersey. A routine operation, perfectly safe.

The Army didn't think anything could happen to those weapons as they moved secretly across the country by train, bouncing 1,500 miles through American cities and towns where the populace lay sleeping, snug in the belief that it was only the night mail. But actually the Army doesn't even have responsibility while its cargo is on a train. That belongs to the railroad—and anything *can* happen. Just a few weeks ago a cargo of Army "ammunition propellant" exploded on a freight train as it passed through Noel, Mo., killing one resident, injuring 100, and damaging all the businesses and most of the homes in town.

Maybe this is what finally nudged the Senate into realizing that the Army could use some supervision, and, with any luck, the measure approved last week—to restrict the storage, transportation and use of chemical weapons—will provide it. We'll need the luck because we obviously can't count on logic. Remember the grotesque shipment of nerve gas across the country? Apparently only one person heard about it and found it grotesque—Representative Richard D. McCarthy, Democrat of New York, who said there must be a safer way to get rid of the stuff. There was. The Pentagon gave it a second thought and decided that it could neutralize the gases without moving them anywhere at all.

Then there's the funny story about the atomic tests in Nevada. Somehow it never occurred to me that a hydrogen bomb explosion would be a spectacle that tourists would want to see, like Cypress Gardens or Colonial Williamsburg. But then I came upon an article in the travel and resort section of the New York *Times*—nestled among the Caribbean cruises and Riviera nights—which said that the Atomic Energy Commission has decided to let sightseers observe large-scale atomic tests at its new test site 200 miles north of Las Vegas.

I was surprised to see this announcement made in the travel section. I could only take it to mean that our nuclear arsenal has somehow crossed over from the realm of American defense to the realm of American leisure: a fun facility for Dad, Mom and the kids. Undecided about your vacation? Already done Disneyland? Why not go to Nevada for the blasts?

Unfortunately, "Observers will not experience the blinding flashes, awesome fireballs and deafening roars of the early aboveground tests," the *Times* article explained. "But even at a distance of 12 miles an underground megaton shot produces an artificial earthquake that makes the ground shudder and seemingly heave a couple of feet, a shock that can knock a man off his feet. A spectacular curtain of dust, miles wide, is sent up from the desert floor. There is always a possibility that the huge caverns blasted underground may cause a spectacular surface cave-in. The principal unexpected thing that can happen is a venting of radioactive gas through unpredictable fissures in the ground."

Well, I've got to admit that as a tourist attraction it goes far beyond your average gator farm or monkey jungle. There's the whole new element of surprise. I mean, we all know that Old Faithful is going to erupt every 65 minutes. So what else is new? And at Disneyland everything is so clean—you simply don't have the possibility of a surface cave-in or a curtain of dust.

I assume the AEC will build a luxury motel out at the site. It should have a name that will look folksy on billboards—Atomland, or Nuclear Village—and convey the idea of a resort where the whole family can come and have a good time between explosions. It would be a shame, after all, to arrive on a Monday and catch an ordinary megaton shot with just a medium earthquake. By waiting around for another test, the family might see a really decent cave-in and get some funny pictures for the photo album ("Me and Mom in front of atom bomb hole—that's Dad on the ground"). It might even open some unpredictable fissures that would vent enough radioactive gas to show up on Bobby's toy Geiger counter, the one he bought at the New Hiroshima Boutique & Coffee Shoppe where he got those wonderful blastburgers.

Got time for one more joke? Let's look at the droll story of Chemical Mace. Several congressional committees recently learned that Mace, used by more than 4,000 police departments, can cause permanent injury.

Now comes the funny part. Sixteen months ago—in April, 1968— the Army made a "biological assessment" of Chemical Mace Mark IV on rabbits, monkeys and dogs and found that it "could cause scarring of the corneal surface and scarring of the skin." Surgeon General William Stewart therefore advised all state, county and city health officers that Mace could cause "more than transient effects to the exposed individual unless treatment is prompt."

Now anyone might think that all those public health officers would try to get a substance banned which can scar the corneas of the public whose health they are officering. But evidently they all thought it was somebody else's business, and it was not until this spring—a year later—that the matter came up before the Senate Subcommittee on Executive Reorganization. (Where have *they* been all these years?)

Why, Surgeon General Stewart was asked by a reporter, did he not recommend discontinuing the use of Mace?

"I think there was a misunderstanding," he replied, "that we have some authority to ban Mace." Translation: "Don't look at me, I'm only the Surgeon General." Besides, he said, he wasn't asked to evaluate Mace. He was only asked "what were the health effects and what do you do with people who are Maced?" He pointed out that the Public Health Service has no control over Mace as a weapon used by police departments, partly because it does not fit the definition of a drug.

This was disputed by former Food and Drug Commissioner James Goddard, who told the Senate subcommittee that Mace does indeed fit the definition of a drug "as altering in some way the structure or function of the human body." He cited reports of corneal scars, chemical burns and sharp rises in blood pressure—up to 100 points within seconds. I would have to say that it is a dangerous substance and it does have potential for causing blindness, according to the reports I have read, and to cause death.

"To the best of my knowledge, Mr. Chairman," Goddard added, "no police officer has sprayed Mace at a citizen and then immediately flushed the victim's eyes with cool water and rinsed his clothing."

Meanwhile the head of the Federal Trade Commission, Paul Rand Dixon, said that his agency is trying to halt the "deceptive advertising of chemical sprays being sold to the general public," but that the job requires some cooperation. "The commission deplores the fact that all interested government agencies were not informed of the results of the Army's tests. Without the free and complete exchange of such information, the enforcement of our laws in the protection of the public interests is virtually an impossible task."

Again, I don't know whether to laugh or cry at an executive organization so hopelessly in need of reorganizing. I'm too old to cry, but it hurts too much to laugh—mainly around the cornea.

# The Psychosemanticist Will See You Now, Mr. Thurber

## James Thurber

I believe there are no scientific investigators that actually call themselves psychosemanticists, but it is surely time for these highly specialized therapeuticians to set up offices. They must not be carelessly confused with psychosomaticists, who study the effects of mental weather upon the ramparts of the body. The psychosemanticists will specialize in the havoc wrought by verbal artillery upon the fortress of reason. Their job will be to cope with the psychic trauma caused by linguistic meaninglessness, to prevent the language from degenerating into gibberish, and to save the sanity of persons threatened by the onset of polysyllabic monstrosititis.

We have always been a nation of categorizationists, but what was once merely a national characteristic is showing signs of malignancy. I shall not attempt to discover the incipient primary lesion, for I am not a qualified research scholar in this field. Indeed, for having had the impudence to trespass thus far I shall no doubt be denounced by the classificationists as a fractional impactionist (one who hits subjects a glancing blow), an unauthorized incursionist, a unilateral conclusionist, and a presumptuous deductionist. Our national predilection for ponderous phraseology has been traced by one authority as far back as the awkward expression "taxation without representation" (unjust impost). It is interesting to note that the irate American colonists of that period in our history would be categorized today as "anti-taxation-without–representationists."

Not long ago, for the most recent instance in my collection, Senator Lyndon Johnson was described by a Washington newspaperman as a pragmatic functionalist, a term that was used in a laudatory sense. It isn't

Copyright ©1957 James Thurber. From *Alarms and Diversions*, published by Harper & Row.

always easy nowadays to tell the laudatory from the derogatory at first glance, but we should be glad that this Democratic leader is not a dogmatic divisionary or an occlusive impedimentarian. The most alarming incidence of verbal premalignancy occurs, of course, in this very area of politics, but let us skip over such worn and familiar double-jointedisms as creeping Socialists, disgruntled ex-employees, ritualistic liberals, massive retaliationists, agonized reappraisalists, unorthodox thinkers, unwitting handmaidens (male), to name only a few out of hundreds, and take a look at excessive prewar anti-Fascism, a colossal (I use the adjective as a noun, in the manner of television's "spectacular") that was disgorged a few years ago. Here the classificatory degradationists brought a time element into what might be called the post-evaluation of political morality. The operation of this kind of judgment during and after the Civil War would have thrown indelible suspicion upon all the Northern patriots, including Abraham Lincoln, who wanted Robert E. Lee to take command of the Federal Armies in the field. They would be known today as "overenthusiastic pre-Manassas pro-Leeists."

The carcinomenclature of our time is, to be sure, an agglomerative phenomenon of accumulated concretions, to which a dozen different types of elaborative descriptivists have contributed—eminently the old Communist intellectuals, with their "dialectical materialists," "factional deviationists," "unimplemented obscurantists," and so on, and so on. Once the political terminologists of all parties began to cross-infect our moribund vocabulary, the rate of degeneration became appalling. Elephantiasis of cliché set in, synonym atrophied, the pulse of inventiveness slowed alarmingly, and paraphrase died of impaction. Multiple sclerosis was apparent in the dragging rhythms of speech, and the complexion of writing and of conversation began to take on the tight, dry parchment look of death. We have become satisfied with gangrenous repetitions of threadbarisms, like an old man cackling in a chimney corner, and the onset of utter meaninglessness is imminent.

The symptoms of this ominous condition show up most clearly in the tertiary stage of "controversial figure." The most complicated specimen of this type of modern American is the man of unquestionable loyalty, distinguished public service, and outstanding ability and experience who has nonetheless "lost his usefulness." Actually, this victim of verbositosis has not lost his usefulness, his nation has lost it. It doesn't do the national psyche any good to realize that a man may be cut off in the full flower of his usefulness, on the ground that that is not what it is. I trust I have made the urgent need for psychosemanticists apparent, even though I have admittedly become contaminated in the process, and I doubt whether my own psychosemanticist, after treating me, will ever be able to turn to my wife and say cheerfully, "Madam, your husband will write clearly again."

Before visiting my hypothetical psychosemanticist for a brief imaginary interview, I feel that I should get something reassuring into this survey of depressing ailments of the tongue. We have, then, cured, or at least survived, various incipient mouth maladies in the past. There was a moment when "globaloneyism," growing out of the Timethod of wordoggle, seemed likely to become epidemic, but it fortunately turned out to be no worse than a touch of pig Latin or a slight case of Knock, Knock, Who's There? Congress was not prepared to adopt the telescoping of words, which takes both time and ingenuity, and unless an expression becomes absorbed by Congressionalese, it has little chance of general survival. This brings me to what may easily be the direct cause of my being bundled off to the psychosemanticist's before long: the beating the word "security" is taking in this great, scared land of ours. It is becoming paralyzed. This is bound to occur to any forceful word when it loses its quality of affirmation and is employed exclusively in a connotation of fear, uncertainty, and suspicion. The most frequent use of "security" (I hate to add to its shakiness with quotation marks, which have taken on a tone of mockery in our day) is in "security risk," "weakest link in our chain of security," and "lulled into a false sense of security." Precision of speech and meaning takes a small tossing around in the last of those three phrases. "Lulled" is actually what happens to a nation after it has been argued, tricked, maneuvered, reasoned, coaxed, cajoled, or jockeyed into a false sense of security, but the inflexibility that has descended upon us has ruled out the once noble search for the perfect word and the exact expression. What Eric Partridge calls "a poverty of linguistic resource" is exemplified by the practically exclusive use of two verbs in any public-forum discussion of national security. It is threatened or it is bolstered; I never heard of its being supported, reinforced, fortified, buttressed, or shored up, and only very rarely is it menaced, endangered, or in jeopardy.

The word "insecurity," by the way, seems to have been taken over by the psychiatrists as their personal property. In politics, as in penology, "security" itself has come to mean "insecurity." Take, for example, this sentence: "He was considered a 'maximum security' prisoner because of his police record and was never allowed out of his cell block." Similarly, "security data" means data of the kind calculated to scare the living daylights out of you, if not, indeed, your pants off. I could prove that "maximum," in the case of the prisoner mentioned above, really means "minimum," but I don't want to get us in so deep that we can't get out. The present confused usage of "security" may have originated with the ancient Romans. Anyway, here is what Cassell's Latin Dictionary has to say about *securitas*: "I. *freedom from care*. A. In a good sense, *peace of mind, quiet*, Cic. B. In a bad sense, *carelessness, indifference*, Tac. II. Transf., *freedom from danger, security*, Tac."

A vital and restless breed of men, given to tapping our toes and drumming with our fingers, infatuated with every new crazy rhythm that rears its ugly beat, we have never truly loved harmony, the graceful structure of shapes and tones, and for this blindness and deafness we pay the awful price of continuous cacophony. It gets into language as well as music; we mug melody for the sake of sound effects, and the louder and more dissonant they are, the better we seem to like them. Our national veins have taken in the singing blood of Italy, Wales, Ireland, and Germany, but the transfusion has had no beneficial effect. Great big blocky words and phrases bumble off our tongues and presses every day. In four weeks of purposeful listening to the radio and reading the newspapers I have come up with a staggering list, full of sound and fury, dignifying nothing: "automation," "roadability," "humature," "motivational cognition" (this baby turned up in a series of travel lectures and was never defined), "fractionalization," "varietism," "redesegregation," "additive," "concertization" (this means giving a concert in a hall, and is not to be confused with cinematization or televisionization). The colloquial deformity "knowledgeable," which should have been clubbed to death years ago, when it first began crawling about like the late Lon Chaney, has gained new life in recent months. It is a dented derby of a word, often found in the scrawny company of such battered straw hats as "do-gooder," "know-how," "update," "uptake" (I recently uptook the iodine uptake test for thyroidism), and others so ugly and strange I can't decipher them in my notes. One of them looks like "de-egghead," which would mean to disintellectualize or mentally emasculate—a crippling operation approved of by an alarming number of squash-heads, in Washington and elsewhere.

During my month of vigil and research, I heard an able physiologist who has a radio program say, quite simply, "We do not use up all the food we take in." He wasn't allowed to get away with that piece of clarity, however. "Ah," cut in his announcer, for the benefit of those no longer able to understand simplicity, "the utilization factor!" I turned from this station to a droning psychologist, just in time to hear him say, "The female is sometimes the sexual aggressor." Here a familiar noun of mental illness and military invasion was clumsily at work beating in the skull of love with a verbal bung-starter. The sweetheart now often wears the fustian of the sick man and the Caesar. In the evening, I tuned in on one of the space-patrol programs that gleefully exude the great big blockyisms. "Your astrogation bank will tell you!" cried the captain of a space ship to another interplanetary pilot, meaning his navigational instruments. In a fairy tale, an astrogation bank would be a "star panel," but the quality of fairy tale is nowhere to be found in these dime novels of the constellations.

One Sunday morning, my head aching with "kiss-close" and "swivel-chair-it," meaning, I guess, "at kissing distance" and "maul it over in your executive brain," respectively, I stumbled upon a small radio station that had been captured by a man of God, ominous and squealful, who was begging his listeners to live on their knees, not as slaves but as supplicants. This particular fundamentalist, or maybe it is fundamentalitarian, had probably never heard of the great protest "I would rather die on my feet than live on my knees." But these yammering eschatologists, and many of their followers, have even less respect for the glory and grace of English than the unsaved politicians. "Let us cease to sugar-coat, let us cease to whitewash, let us cease to bargain-counter the Bible!" the speaker implored us. He finished second in vulgarity, I regret to say, to a reverend I had heard earlier in the year, who shouted, "I didn't cook up this dish, God cooked it up. I'm just dishing it out to ye!" The line between holiness and blasphemy becomes even thinner when some of the lay testimonialists begin ranting. "I own a shoe store in New Jersey," one of them confessed, "but Jesus Christ is my senior partner."

A recent investigation of the worries and concerns of five thousand selected Americans revealed that we are preoccupied almost wholly with the personal and private, and are troubled only mildly by political anxieties, including the danger of war, the state of civil liberties, and the internal Communist threat. This does not come as a surprise to me, since the nature of our national concern about Communism is proved to be personal by such expressions as "anti-anti-Communists" and "anti-anti-anti-Communists." The first actually means men who are against men who are against Communists, and the second, when you unravel it, means men who are against men who are against men who are against Communists. In these wonderful examples of our love of formidable elaborationisms, concept and doctrine are put aside, and personalities take their place. What we have left is pure personalism—a specific reactionary who is against a specific liberal who is against Senator Malone, let us say. The multiplicity of prefixes, another sign of linguistic poverty, was touched with a fine and healthful irony in Quincy Howe's invention of the phrase "ex-ex-Communist." (Many will claim that for their own, but Mr. Howe got to it first.) One would think that Americans would be worried, or at least concerned, by a man who may have ceased to be a man who may have ceased to be a Communist, but the Worry Research I have mentioned showed that this isn't so. We are worried about health, family matters and money, and we have no time for a man who may be lying about lying. Incidentally, a fairly new advertising slogan, "The portable portable," fits neatly into modern jargon: the typewriter that you can carry that you can carry.

While I was exploring the decline of expression in America, I spent a week in a hospital. Medical science has done much for humanity, but not in the area of verbal communication. It should undergo a prefectomy, and have some of its prefixes taken out. I should like to see the "semi" removed from "semi-private," a dispiriting word that originated in hospitals; there must be a less depressing way of describing a room with two or more beds. I am also for taking the "sub" out of "subclinical," and starting all over again with the idea in mind of making the word mean something. Incidentally, I discovered at the hospital the difference between "to be hospitalized" and "to become hospitalized." The first means to be placed in a hospital, and the second has two meanings: to get so that you can't stand it in the hospital any longer, and to like it so much there that you don't want to leave.

Lying in bed brooding over these matters, I turned on the radio and heard an American describe another American as "an old-time A.D.A. type of anti-Jeffersonian radical"—a beautiful specimen of bumblery. Sir Winston Churchill, in the exhilarating years of his public life, turned out many phrases as sharp as stilettos—for one example, "squalid gamin." But you can count on your fingers the Americans, since the Thomas Paine of "the summer soldier and the sunshine patriot," who have added bright, clear phrases to our language. If you can bumble an opponent to death why stab him seems to be the general feeling among our politicians, some of whom have got through the twelve years since the war ended with only five adjectives of derogation: naïve, hostile, unrealistic, complacent, and irresponsible. All these slither easily, if boggily, into bumblery, and the bumbler is spared the tedious exercising of his mental faculties.

The day I got dressed and was about to leave the hospital, I heard a nurse and an interne discussing a patient who had got something in his eye. "It's a bad city to get something in your eye in," the nurse said. "Yes," the interne agreed, "but there isn't a better place to get something in your eye out in." I rushed past them with my hair in my wild eyes, and left the hospital. It was high time, too.

When and if I find a reputable psychosemanticist, I want to take up with him something that happened to me one night more than two years ago. It may be the basis of my etymological or philological problems, if that's what they are—words, especially big ones, are beginning to lose their meaning for me. Anyway, I woke up one summer night, from a deep dream of peacelessness, only to realize that I had been startled by nothing whatever into a false sense of insecurity. I had a desperate feeling that I was being closed in on, that there was a menace in the woods behind my house or on the road in front of it, watchful, waiting, biding its time. A few weeks later I bought a .38-calibre Smith & Wesson police revolver, which startled my wife into a genuine sense of insecurity. She hid the gun somewhere, and the cartridges somewhere else, and I still don't know where they are. I have often thought of telling my psychosemanticist about it, and I sometimes have the feeling that I did call on him and that the interview went like this:

"Doesn't your wife's hiding the gun worry you?" he asked.

"No," I said.

"It would me," he confessed.

"It would *what* you?" I demanded.

It seemed to disturb him. "*What* would what me?" he asked cautiously.

I suddenly couldn't think of a thing. I didn't even know what what was, but I had to say something, so I said something: "Ill fares the land, to galloping fears a prey, where gobbledygook accumulates, and words decay."

About two years ago a wistful attempt was made by some Washington bureau to straighten out the governmentalization of English. Directives were sent to the various departments demanding, among other things, the elimination of "finalize." It was as hopeless as asking a tiny child to drop its popsicle and bathe the St. Bernard. Izationism is here to stay. It appeals to bureaucrats and congressmen because of its portentous polysyllabification. Politicians love it the way they love such expressions as "legislativewise." Lord Conesford, stout defender of the Queen's English, recently paraphrased Churchill's "Give us the tools and we will finish the job" by Washingtonizing it like this: "Supply us with the implements and we will finalize the solution of the matter."

Webster's Unabridged, to my sorrow, recognizes such mastadonisms as "psychologize" and "physiologize" and, a prime favorite of congressmen, "analogize." It was, however, the physiologist I have already mentioned who classified those of us who are still up and about as "the non-institutionalized." This is a piece of bungalorum calculated to give even the healthiest men a sense of monolithic insecurity. "Non" has an insidious way of creeping into izationisms. A piece of journalism was described on the air not long ago as "absolutely non-fictionalized." This negationization of what once could be described as verbal communication caused a Scot of my acquaintance to ask me, "Have you nothing that is positively American? It seems to me that everything one hears about in America is un-American." This abused and imprecise arrangement of letters seems bound to lose its proud A before long and to end up as "Un-american." President Eisenhower might well add to his imperatives the necessity to speak and write in such a way that we can be understood by the English-speaking peoples as well as the other races of a world that stands in grave need of clarity, accuracy, and sense.

The conspiracy of yammer and merchandising against literate speech reached a notorious height in 1956 with a singing commercial for a certain cigarette which we were told "tastes good like a cigarette should." I have one or two suggestions for the Madison Avenue illiterates in the gray flannel suits. The first is a slogan for a brewery: "We still brew good like we used to could." The second is an ad for some maker of tranquilizing drugs:

"Does he seldomly praise you any more? Those kind of husbands can be cured of the grumps with Hush-Up. So give you and he a break. Put Hush-Up in his food. It don't have no taste."

And now, for God's sake, let's go out and get a breath of fresh air.

# The Man-Made Myth

### Elaine Morgan

According to the Book of Genesis, God first created man. Woman was not only an afterthought, but an amenity. For close on two thousand years this holy scripture was believed to justify her subordination and explain her inferiority; for even as a copy she was not a very good copy. There were differences. She was not one of His best efforts.

There is a line in an old folk song that runs: "I called my donkey a horse gone wonky." Throughout most of the literature dealing with the differences between the sexes there runs a subtle underlying assumption that woman is a man gone wonky; that woman is a distorted version of the original blueprint; that they are the norm, and we are the deviation.

It might have been expected that when Darwin came along and wrote an entirely different account of *The Descent of Man*, this assumption would have been eradicated, for Darwin didn't believe she was an afterthought: he believed her origin was at least contemporaneous with man's. It should have led to some kind of breakthrough in the relationship between the sexes. But it didn't.

Almost at once men set about the congenial and fascinating task of working out an entirely new set of reasons why woman was manifestly inferior and irreversibly subordinate, and they have been happily engaged on this ever since. Instead of theology they use biology, and ethology, and primatology, but they use them to reach the same conclusions.

They are now prepared to debate the most complex problems of economic reform not in terms of the will of God, but in terms of the sexual

From *The Descent of Woman* by Elaine Morgan. Reprinted by permission of Souvenir Press Ltd., London, England.

behavior patterns of the cichlid fish; so that if a woman claims equal pay or the right to promotion there is usually an authoritative male thinker around to deliver a brief homily on hormones, and point out that what she secretly intends by this, and what will inevitably result, is the "psychological castration" of the men in her life.

Now, that may look to us like a stock piece of emotional blackmail—like the woman who whimpers that if Sonny doesn't do as she wants him to do, then Mother's going to have one of her nasty turns. It is not really surprising that most women who are concerned to win themselves a new and better status in society tend to sheer away from the whole subject of biology and origins, and hope that we can ignore all that and concentrate on ensuring that in the future things will be different.

I believe this is a mistake. The legend of the jungle heritage and the evolution of man as a hunting carnivore has taken root in man's mind as firmly as Genesis ever did. He may even genuinely believe that equal pay will do something terrible to his gonads. He has built a beautiful theoretical construction, with himself on the top of it, buttressed with a formidable array of scientifically authenticated facts. We cannot dispute the facts. We should not attempt to ignore the facts. What I think we can do is to suggest that the currently accepted interpretation of the facts is not the only possible one.

I have considerable admiration for scientists in general, and evolutionists and ethologists in particular, and though I think they have sometimes gone astray, it has not been purely through prejudice. Partly it is due to sheer semantic accident—the fact that "man" is an ambiguous term. It means the species; it also means the male of the species. If you begin to write a book about man or conceive a theory about man you cannot avoid using this word. You cannot avoid using a pronoun as a substitute for the word, and you will use the pronoun "he" as a simple matter of linguistic convenience. But before you are halfway through the first chapter a mental image of this evolving creature begins to form in your mind. It will be a male image, and he will be the hero of the story: everything and everyone else in the story will relate to him.

All this may sound like a mere linguistic quibble or a piece of feminist petulance. If you stay with me, I hope to convince you it's neither. I believe the deeply rooted semantic confusion between "man" as a male and "man" as a species has been fed back into and vitiated a great deal of the speculation that goes on about the origins, development, and nature of the human race.

A very high proportion of the thinking on these topics is androcentric (male-centered) in the same way as pre-Copernican thinking was geocentric. It's just as hard for man to break the habit of thinking of himself as central to the species as it was to break the habit of thinking of himself as central to the universe. He sees himself quite unconsciously as the main line of evolution, with a female satellite revolving around him as the moon revolves around the earth. This not only causes him to overlook valuable clues to our ancestry, but sometimes leads him into making statements that are arrant and demonstrable nonsense.

The longer I went on reading his own books about himself, the more I longed to find a volume that would begin: "When the first ancestor of the human race descended from the trees, she had not yet developed the mighty brain that was to distinguish her so sharply from all other species...."

Of course, she was no more the first ancestor than he was—but she was no *less* the first ancestor, either. She was there all along, contributing half the genes to each succeeding generation. Most of the books forget about her for most of the time. They drag her onstage rather suddenly for the obligatory chapter on Sex and Reproduction, and then say: "All right, love, you can go now," while they get on with the real meaty stuff about the Mighty Hunter with his lovely new weapons and his lovely new straight legs racing across the Pleistocene plains. Any modifications in her morphology are taken to be imitations of the Hunter's evolution, or else designed solely for his delectation.

Evolutionary thinking has been making great strides lately. Archeologists, ethologists, paleontologists, geologists, chemists, biologists, and physicists are closing in from all points of the compass on the central area of mystery that remains. For despite the frequent triumph dances of researchers coming up with another jawbone or another statistic, some part of the miracle is still unaccounted for. Most of their books include some such phrase as: "...the early stages of man's evolutionary progress remain a total mystery." "Man is an accident, the culmination of a series of highly improbable coincidences...." "Man is a product of circumstances special to the point of disbelief." They feel there is still something missing, and they don't know what.

The trouble with specialists is that they tend to think in grooves. From time to time something happens to shake them out of that groove. Robert Ardrey tells how such enlightenment came to Dr. Kenneth Oakley when the first Australopithecus remains had been unearthed in Africa: "The answer flashed without warning in his own large-domed head: 'Of course we believed that the big brain came first! We assumed that the first man was an Englishman!'" Neither he, nor Ardrey in relating the incident, noticed that he was still making an equally unconscious, equally unwarrantable assumption. One of these days an evolutionist is going to strike a palm against his large-domed head and cry: "Of course! We assumed the first human being was a man!"

First, let's have a swift recap of the story as currently related, for despite all the new evidence recently brought to light, the generally accepted picture of human evolution has changed very little.

Smack in the center of it remains the Tarzanlike figure of the prehominid male who came down from the trees, saw a grassland teeming with game, picked up a weapon, and became a Mighty Hunter.

Almost everything about us is held to have derived from this. If we walk erect it was because the Mighty Hunter had to stand tall to scan the distance for his prey. If we lived in caves it was because hunters need a base to come home to. If we learned to speak it was because hunters need to plan the next safari and boast about the last. Desmond Morris, pondering on the shape of a woman's breasts, instantly deduces that they evolved because her mate became a Mighty Hunter, and defends this preposterous proposition with the greatest ingenuity. There's something about the Tarzan figure which has them all mesmerized.

I find the whole yarn pretty incredible. It is riddled with mysteries, and inconsistencies, and unanswered questions. Even more damning than the unanswered questions are the questions that are never even asked, because, as Professor Peter Medawar has pointed out, "scientists tend not to ask themselves questions until they can see the rudiments of an answer in their minds." I shall devote this chapter to pointing out some of these problems before outlining a new version of the Naked Ape story which will suggest at least possible answers to every one of them, and fifteen or twenty others besides.

The first mystery is, "What happened during the Pliocene?"

There is a wide acceptance now of the theory that the human story began in Africa. Twenty million years ago in Kenya, there existed a flourishing population of apes of generalized body structure and of a profusion of types from the size of a small gibbon up to that of a large gorilla. Dr. L.S.B. Leakey has dug up their bones by the hundred in the region of Lake Victoria, and they were clearly doing very well there at the time. It was a period known as the Miocene. The weather was mild, the rainfall was heavier than today, and the forests were flourishing. So far, so good.

Then came the Pliocene drought. Robert Ardrey writes of it: "No mind can apprehend in terms of any possible human experience the duration of the Pliocene. Ten desiccated years were enough, a quarter of a century ago, to produce in the American Southwest that maelstrom of misery, the dust bowl. To the inhabitant of the region the ten years must have seemed endless. But the African Pliocene lasted twelve million."

On the entire African continent no Pliocene fossil bed has ever been found. During this period many promising Miocene ape species were, not surprisingly, wiped out altogether. A few were trapped in dwindling pockets of forest and when the Pliocene ended they reappeared as brachiating apes—specialized for swinging by their arms.

Something astonishing also reappeared—the Australopithecines, first discovered by Professor Raymond Dart in 1925 and since unearthed in considerable numbers by Dr. Leakey and others.

Australopithecus emerged from his horrifying twelve-million year ordeal much refreshed and improved. The occipital condyles of his skull suggest a bodily posture approaching that of modern man, and the orbital region, according to Sir Wilfred le Gros Clark, has "a remarkably human appearance." He was clever, too. His remains have been found in the Olduvai Gorge in association with crude pebble tools that have been hailed as the earliest beginning of human culture. Robert Ardrey says: "We entered the Pliocene crucible a generalized creature bearing only the human potential. We emerged a being lacking only a proper brain and a chin. What happened to us along the way?" The sixty-four-thousand-dollar question: "What happened to them? Where did they go?"

Second question: "Why did they stand upright?" The popular versions skim very lightly over this patch of thin ice. Desmond Morris says simply: "With strong pressure on them to increase their prey-killing prowess, they became more upright—fast, better runners." Robert Ardrey says equally simply: "We learned to stand erect in the first place as a necessity of the hunting life."

But wait a minute. We were quadrupeds. These statements imply that a quadruped suddenly discovered that he could move faster on two legs than on four. Try to imagine any other quadruped discovering that— a cat? a dog? a horse?—and you'll see that it's totally nonsensical. Other things being equal, four legs are bound to run faster than two. The bipedal development was violently unnatural.

Stoats, gophers, rabbits, chimpanzees, will sit or stand bipedally to gaze into the distance, but when they want speed they have sense enough to use all the legs they've got. The only quadrupeds I can think of that can move faster on two legs than four are things like kangaroos—and a small lizard called the Texas boomer, and he doesn't keep it up for long. The secret in these cases is a long heavy counterbalancing tail which we certainly never had. You may say it was a natural development for a primate because primates sit erect in trees—but *was* it natural? Baboons and macaques have been largely terrestrial for millions of years without any sign of becoming bipedal.

George A. Bartholomew and Joseph B. Birdsell point out: ". . .the extreme rarity of bipedalism among animals suggests that it is inefficient except under very special circumstances. Even modern man's unique vertical locomotion when compared to that of quadrupedal mammals, is relatively ineffective. . .A significant nonlocomotor advantage must have resulted."

What was this advantage? The Tarzanists suggest that bipedalism enabled this ape to race after game while carrying weapons—in the first instance, presumably pebbles. But a chimp running off with a banana (or a pebble), if he can't put it in his mouth, will carry it in one hand and gallop along on the others, because even *three* legs are faster than two. So what was our ancestor supposed to be doing? Shambling along with a rock in each hand? Throwing boulders that took two hands to lift?

No. There must have been a pretty powerful reason why we were constrained over a long period of time to walk about on our hind legs *even though it was slower*. We need to find that reason.

Third question: How did the ape come to be using these weapons, anyway? Again Desmond Morris clears this one lightly, at a bound: "With strong pressure on them to increase their prey-killing prowess. . . their hands became strong efficient weapon-holders." Compared to Morris, Robert Ardrey is obsessed with weapons, which he calls "mankind's most significant cultural endowment." Yet his explanation of how it all started is as cursory as anyone else's: "In the first evolutionary hour of the human emergence we became sufficiently skilled in the use of weapons to render redundant our natural primate daggers" (i.e., the large prehominid canine teeth).

But wait a minute—how? and why? Why did one, and only one, species of those Miocene apes start using weapons? A cornered baboon will fight a leopard; a hungry baboon will kill and eat a chicken. He could theoretically pick up a chunk of flint and forget about his "natural primate daggers," and become a Mighty Hunter. He doesn't do it, though. Why did we? Sarel Eimerl and Irven de Vore point out in their book *The Primates*:

"Actually, it takes quite a lot of explaining. For example, if an animal's normal mode of defense is to flee from a predator, it flees. If its normal method of defense is to fight with its teeth, it fights with its teeth. It does not suddenly adopt a totally new course of action, such as picking up a stick or a rock and throwing it. The idea would simply not occur to it, and even if it did, the animal would have no reason to suppose that it would work."

Now primates do acquire useful tool-deploying habits. A chimpanzee will use a stick to extract insects from their nests, and a crumpled leaf to sop up water. Wolfgang Köhler's apes used sticks to draw fruit toward the bars of their cage, and so on.

But this type of learning depends on three things. There must be leisure for trial-and-error experiment. The tools must be either in unlimited supply (a forest is full of sticks and leaves) or else in *exactly the right place*. (Even Köhler's brilliant Sultan could be stumped if the fruit was in front of him and a new potential tool was behind him—he needed them both in view at the same time.) Thirdly, for the habit to stick, the same effect must result from the same action every time.

Now look at that ape. The timing is wrong—when he's faced with a bristling rival or a charging cat or even an escaping prey, he won't fool around inventing fancy methods. A chimp sometimes brandishes a stick to convey menace to an adversary, but if his enemy keeps coming, he drops the stick and fights with hands and teeth. Even if we postulate a mutant ape cool enough to think, with the adrenalin surging through his veins, "There must be a better way than teeth," he still has to be lucky to notice that right in the middle of the primeval grassland there happens to be a stone of convenient size, precisely between him and his enemy. And when he throws it, he has to score a bull's-eye, first time and every time. Because if he failed to hit a leopard he wouldn't be there to tell his progeny that the trick only needed polishing up a bit; and if he failed to hit a springbok he'd think: "Ah well, that obviously doesn't work. Back to the old drawing board."

No. If it had taken all that much luck to turn man into a killer, we'd all be still living on nut cutlets.

A lot of Tarzanists privately realize that their explanations of bipedalism and weapon-wielding won't hold water. They have invented the doctrine of "feedback," which states that though these two theories are separately and individually nonsense, together they will just get by. It is alleged that the ape's bipedal gait, however unsteady, made him a better rock thrower (why?) and his rock throwing, however inaccurate, made him a better biped. (Why?) Eimerl and de Vore again put the awkward question: Since chimps can both walk erect and manipulate simple tools, "why was it only the hominids who benefited from the feed-back?" You may well ask.

Next question: Why did the naked ape become naked?

Desmond Morris claims that, unlike more specialized carnivores such as lions and jackals, the ex-vegetarian ape was not physically equipped to "make lightning dashes after his prey." He would "experience considerable overheating during the hunt, and the loss of body hair would be of great value for the supreme moments of the chase."

This is a perfect example of androcentric thinking. There were two sexes around at the time, and I don't believe it's ever been all that easy to part a woman from a fur coat, just to save the old man from getting into a muck-sweat during his supreme moments. What was supposed to be happening to the female during this period of denudation?

Dr. Morris says: "This system would not work, of course, if the climate was too intensely hot, because of damage to the exposed skin." So he is obviously dating the loss of hair later than the Pliocene "inferno." But the next period was the turbulent Pleistocene, punctuated by mammoth African "pluvials," corresponding to the Ice Ages of the north. A pluvial was century after century of torrential rainfall; so we have to picture our maternal ancestor sitting naked in the middle of the plain while the heavens emptied, needing both hands to keep her muddy grip on a slippery, squirming, equally naked infant. This is ludicrous. It's no advantage to the species for the Mighty Hunter to return home safe and cool if he finds his son's been dropped on his head and his wife is dead of hypothermia.

This problem could have been solved by dimorphism—the loss of hair could have gone further in one sex than the other. So it did, of course. But unfortunately for the Tarzanists it was the stay-at-home female who became nakedest, and the overheated hunter who kept the hair on his chest.

Next question: Why has our sex life become so involved and confusing?

The given answer, I need hardly say, is that it all began when man became a hunter. He had to travel long distances after his prey and he began worrying about what the little woman might be up to. He was also anxious about other members of the hunting pack, because, Desmond Morris explains, "if the weaker males were going to be expected to cooperate on the hunt, they had to be given more sexual rights. The females would have to be more shared out."

Thus it became necessary, so the story goes, to establish a system of "pair bonding" to ensure that couples remained faithful for life. I quote: "The simplest and most direct method of doing this was to make the shared activities of the pair more complicated and more rewarding. In other words, to make sex sexier."

To this end, the Naked Apes sprouted ear lobes, fleshy nostrils, and everted lips, all allegedly designed to stimulate one another to a frenzy. Mrs. A.'s nipples became highly erogenous, she invented and patented the female orgasm, and she learned to be sexually responsive at all times, even during pregnancy, "because with a one-male—one-female system, it would be dangerous to frustrate the male for too long a period. It might endanger the pair bond." He might go off in a huff, or look for another woman. Or even refuse to cooperate on the hunt.

In addition, they decided to change over to face-to-face sex, instead of the male mounting from behind as previously, because this new method led to "personalized sex." The frontal approach means that "the incoming sexual signals and rewards are kept tightly linked with the identity signals from the partner." In simpler words, you know who you're doing it with.

This landed Mrs. Naked Ape in something of a quandary. Up till then, the fashionable thing to flaunt in sexual approaches had been " a pair of fleshy, hemispherical buttocks." Now all of a sudden they were getting her nowhere. She would come up to her mate making full-frontal identity signals like mad with her nice new earlobes and nostrils, but somehow he just didn't want to know. He missed the fleshy hemispheres, you see. The position was parlous, Dr. Morris urges. "'If the female of our species was going to successfully shift the interest of the male round to the front, evolution would have to do something to make the frontal region more stimulating." Guess what? Right the first time: she invested in a pair of fleshy hemispheres in the thoracic region and we were once more saved by the skin of our teeth.

All this is good stirring stuff, but hard to take seriously. Wolf packs manage to cooperate without all this erotic paraphernalia. Our near relatives the gibbons remain faithful for life without "personalized" frontal sex, without elaborate erogenous zones, without perennial female availability. Why couldn't we?

Above all, since when has increased sexiness been a guarantee of increased fidelity? If the naked ape could see all this added sexual potential in his own mate, how could he fail to see the same thing happening to all the other females around him? What effect was that supposed to have on him, especially in later life when he noticed Mrs. A.'s four hemispheres becoming a little less fleshy than they used to be?

We haven't yet begun on the unasked questions. Before ending this chapter I will mention just two out of many.

First: If female orgasm was evolved in our species for the first time to provide the woman with a "behavioral reward" for increased sexual activity, why in the name of Darwin has the job been so badly bungled that there have been whole tribes and whole generations of women hardly aware of its existence? Even in the sex-conscious U.S.A., according to Dr. Kinsey, it rarely gets into proper working order before the age of about thirty. How could natural selection ever have operated on such a rickety, unreliable, late-developing endowment when in the harsh conditions of prehistory a woman would be lucky to survive more than twenty-nine years, anyway?

Second: Why in our species has sex become so closely linked with aggression? In most of the higher primates sexual activity is the one thing in life which is totally incompatible with hostility. A female primate can immediately deflect male wrath by presenting her backside and offering sex. Even a male monkey can calm and appease a furious aggressor by imitating the gesture. Nor is the mechanism confined to mammals. Lorenz tells of an irate lizard charging down upon a female painted with male markings to deceive him. When he got close enough to realize his mistake, the taboo was so immediate and so absolute that his aggression went out like a light, and being too late to stop himself he shot straight up into the air and turned a back somersault.

Female primates admittedly are not among the species that can count on this absolute chivalry at all times. A female monkey may be physically chastised for obstreperous behavior; or a male may (on rare occasions) direct hostility against her when another male is copulating with her; but between the male and female engaged in it, sex is always the friendliest of interactions. There is no more hostility associated with it than with a session of mutual grooming.

How then have sex and aggression, the two irreconcilables of the animal kingdom, become in our species alone so closely interlinked that the words for sexual activity are spat out as insults and expletives? In what evolutionary terms are we to explain the Marquis de Sade, and the subterranean echoes that his name evokes in so many human minds?

Not, I think, in terms of Tarzan. It is time to approach the whole thing again right from the beginning: this time from the distaff side, and along a totally different route.

# Pandora
# was a
# Feminist

Mary Meigs

Secrets. The origin of secrets—a great puzzle that I'm trying to solve, for it seems to me that there is an urgent need to decide which, if any, are necessary and which spring from the ego's need to protect its truths and its lies, hence, the idea that every self is a sacred place and that all secrets have the same sacred character. Other people's secrets, as we know, beg to be told, make up the fabric of gossip and innuendo even if severe penalties are attached to telling them. As for our own, they are raided, so to speak, by others with their conjectures, their analyses that we so fiercely reject (like ours of them). One's secret self is guarded as closely as spies guard secrets in wartime, not because of a real penalty for telling (unlike the spies), but an imaginary one, because of the feeling that it belongs to oneself, like one's brain, one's heart, and the illusion that it is invisible to others. But, in fact, those others are nibbling away, like fishes around bait, so that it might be better to give them an authentic whole to nibble on. Better still, perhaps, to sit in one of those cages in which one is completely visible but protected from over-eager sharks, the cage of indifference to what other people think. I often wonder if the secret of oneself is worth keeping, if it shouldn't be released like the contents of Pandora's box. That story is a wonderful example of patriarchal ingenuity, which has invented yet another mythical explanation for the woes of *man*kind, i.e. the unbridled curiosity of woman*kind*. Personally, I think of Pandora not as irresponsible and foolish but as a radical feminist, sister of Eve and Bluebeard's wives, of all women who *want to know*. We are all Pandoras,

From *Women and Words: the Anthology*, eds. Women and Words Committee (Madeira Park, B.C.: Harbour Publishing Company Ltd., 1984).

each with her box complete with instructions not to open it, the box of the secret self.

Pandora, according to Zimmerman's *Dictionary of Classical Mythology*, was made with clay by Hephaestus at the request of Zeus, who desired to punish Prometheus for stealing fire from heaven by giving him a wife. "All the gods and goddesses of Olympus vied in giving her gifts:" beauty, eloquence, the art of singing, beautiful clothes, a gold crown, etc., not to mention the famous box, a gift from Zeus himself. But Prometheus saw through Zeus, and Pandora ended by marrying his brother Epimetheus (which means Afterthought). "Don't open the box," said Zeus. Naturally, Pandora opened it. So do I open things: Christmas presents before Christmas, the last page of a book to see how it's going to end (I have to know whether it will have a happy ending, or whether so-and-so will still be alive at the end. I hate suspense, cannot read detective stories, cannot look at movies full of suspense without intolerable anxiety.) But to get back to Pandora. "When the box was opened, a host of plagues escaped to harass hapless man; only Hope remained in the box." Why? It seems to me it would have been much better to let Hope out, too. "Women's curiosity is always punished," I remarked to Paul, a male friend. "Pandora's, Eve's, Bluebeard's wives." "Of course," he says. "Evil is woman's fault. That's part of history." He's making fun of me, of course. I say I think people should be less possessive of their secrets, that Pandora was right to open the box. And then he tells me a fascinating story about himself. He used to dream, he says, to remember his dreams and write them down, until one day a dream told him something about himself that he didn't want to know. So he pushed it back into his subconscious. "And I never remembered another dream!" Pandora couldn't possibly have been more curious about the contents of her box than I am about this dream-truth that he doesn't want to think about. I say to him that nothing in my dreams makes me want to censure them, that there is nothing they tell me that I don't want to think about, that they have helped me to think about the things I don't want to think about. And far from wanting to turn them off, I want to stimulate them, I want them to tell me the worst!

Curiosity, how it can be thought of as either a virtue or a vice, how it is a virtue for men in men's eyes and a vice for women which must be punished, and how the punishment becomes dogma until women, too, feel impatient with Eve, Pandora and Bluebeard's wives for being so foolish, for wanting to know. God or Zeus or Bluebeard loves to tempt them by inventing rules that as high-spirited women, they are bound to break. Don't eat of the fruit of the tree! Don't open that box! Don't look in the closet! Sometimes God, just for good measure, tests a man. Don't ask me *why*, he says to Job. But much more often, men's curiosity is rewarded and women's is punished. And yet when it comes to opening the Pandora's box which is in each of us, men and women are alike. Paul's self-censorship—the Pandora's box of his dreams—he seemed to think it was wrong to know *too much* about himself and called on the Zeus in himself to close the box forever. I wondered how often he had told this story, whether each telling wasn't to reinforce the lock, whether the *thing* he wanted to shut away didn't manage to reach out a paw under the lid like an angry kitten in a basket. He told it smiling, with a kind of excitement, triumph, ha! *it* almost got out! It seemed to me that *it* was amazingly discreet; it could be talked about without betraying what it was even to Paul. Perhaps it had become so tame that it was ready to be let out of the box; perhaps he told it as a way of taming it?

I think about *it*, the beast, silenced but still there in the dreams that are not allowed over the threshold of consciousness, and want to say, "Let it out. It won't hurt you," want to say that secrets, once released, often sheath their claws, stretch, rub against other people's ankles and finally curl up in a comfortable chair and go to sleep. Interestingly, Pandora was not punished (note that the plagues "escaped to harass hapless *man*"). Long after the affair of the box, Zeus sent a deluge to destroy *man*kind and Pandora's daughter, Pyrrha, and her husband, Deucalion (Prometheus' son), were the only survivors. They had the foresight to replace "the loss of mankind by throwing stones behind their backs; those Deucalion threw became men; those Pyrrha threw became women." So the sexes, each reproduced by a kind of parthenogenesis (another case of patriarchal wish-fulfillment),were equal for a while, and Pandora was the grandmother of all the women in the world. True, the "host of plagues" was still at large, but Zeus himself had invented them and put them in the box, a cover-up, so to speak, and Pandora had the courage to show everybody what Zeus was up to. It was a tremendous victory over Zeus, just as Eve had won a victory over God by disobeying his senseless edict about eating the fruit of the tree. Confronted by boxes that are not supposed to be opened, we contemporary Pandoras say to ourselves, "Where did this rule come from? Was it Zeus who told me not open the box, and is he impersonating me so skillfully that I think his commands come from myself?"

# The Crisis of American Masculinity

## Arthur M. Schlesinger, Jr.

(1958)

What has happened to the American male? For a long time, he seemed utterly confident in his manhood, sure of his masculine role in society, easy and definite in his sense of sexual identity. The frontiersmen of James Fenimore Cooper, for example, never had any concern about masculinity; they were men, and it did not occur to them to think twice about it. Even well into the 20th century, the heroes of Dreiser, of Fitzgerald, of Hemingway remain men. But one begins to detect a new theme emerging in some of these authors, especially in Hemingway: the theme of the male hero increasingly preoccupied with proving his virility to himself. And by mid-century, the male role had plainly lost its rugged clarity of outline. Today men are more and more conscious of maleness not as a fact but as a problem. The ways by which American men affirm their masculinity are uncertain and obscure. There are multiplying signs, indeed, that something has gone badly wrong with the American male's conception of himself.

On the most superficial level, the roles of male and female are increasingly merged in the American household. The American man is found as never before as a substitute for wife and mother—changing diapers, washing dishes, cooking meals, and performing a whole series of what once were considered female duties. The American woman meanwhile takes over more and more of the big decisions, controlling them indirectly when she cannot do so directly. Outside the home, one sees a similar blurring of function. While men design dresses and brew up cos-

"The Crisis of American Masculinity" from *The Politics of Hope* by Arthur M. Schlesinger, Jr. Copyright ©1962 by Arthur M. Schlesinger. Reprinted by permission of Houghton Mifflin Company.

metics, women become doctors, lawyers, bank cashiers, and executives. "Women now fill many 'masculine' roles," writes the psychologist Dr. Bruno Bettelheim, "and expect their husbands to assume many of the tasks once reserved for their own sex." Women seem an expanding, aggressive force, seizing new domains like a conquering army, while men, more and more on the defensive, are hardly able to hold their own and gratefully accept assignments from their new rulers. A recent book bears the stark and melancholy title *The Decline of the American Male.*

Some of this evidence, it should be quickly said, has been pushed too far. The willingness of a man to help his wife around the house may as well be evidence of confidence in masculinity as the opposite; such a man obviously does not have to cling to masculine symbols in order to keep demonstrating his maleness to himself. But there is more impressive evidence than the helpful husband that this is an age of sexual ambiguity. It appears no accident, for example, that the changing of sex—the Christine Jorgensen phenomenon—so fascinates our newspaper editors and readers; or that homosexuality, that incarnation of sexual ambiguity, should be enjoying a cultural boom new in our history. Such developments surely express a deeper tension about the problem of sexual identity.

Consider the theater, that faithful mirror of a society's preoccupations. There have been, of course, popular overt inquiries into sexual ambiguities, like *Compulsion* or *Tea and Sympathy.* But in a sense these plays prove the case too easily. Let us take rather two uncommonly successful plays by the most discussed young playwrights of the United States and Great Britain—Tennessee Williams' *Cat on a Hot Tin Roof* and John Osborne's *Look Back in Anger.* Both deal with the young male in a singular state of confusion and desperation. In *Cat on a Hot Tin Roof,* Brick Pollitt, the professional football player, refuses to sleep with his wife because of guilty memories of his relations with a dead teammate. In *Look Back in Anger,* Jimmy Porter, the embittered young intellectual who can sustain a relationship with his wife only by pretending they are furry animals together, explodes with hatred of women and finds his moments of happiness roughhousing around the stage with a male pal.

Brick Pollitt and Jimmy Porter are all too characteristic modern heroes. They are, in a sense, castrated; one is stymied by fear of homosexuality, the other is an unconscious homosexual. Neither is capable of dealing with the woman in his life: Brick surrenders to a strong woman, Jimmy destroys a weak one. Both reject the normal female desire for full and reciprocal love as an unconscionable demand and an intolerable burden. Now not many American males have been reduced to quite the Pollitt-Porter condition. Still the intentness with which audiences have watched these plays suggests that exposed nerves are being plucked—that the Pollitt-Porter dilemma expresses in vivid and heightened form something that many spectators themselves feel or fear.

Or consider the movies. In some ways, the most brilliant and influential American film since the war is *High Noon*. That remarkable movie, which invested the Western with the classic economy of myth, can be viewed in several ways: as an existentialist drama, for example, or as a parable of McCarthyism. It can also be viewed as a mordant comment on the effort of the American woman to emasculate the American man. The sheriff plainly did not suffer from Brick Pollitt's disease. But a large part of the story dealt with the attempt of his girl to persuade him not to use force—to deny him the use of his pistol. The pistol is an obvious masculine symbol, and, in the end, it was the girl herself, in the modern American manner, who used the pistol and killed the villain. (In this connection, one can pause and note why the Gary Coopers, Cary Grants, Clark Gables, and Spencer Tracys continue to play romantic leads opposite girls young enough to be their daughters; it is obviously because so few of the younger male stars can project a convincing sense of masculinity.)

Psychoanalysis backs up the theater and the movies in emphasizing the obsession of the American male with his manhood. "Every psychoanalyst knows," writes one of them, "how many emotional difficulties are due to those fears and insecurities of neurotic men who are unconsciously doubting their masculinity." "In our civilization," Dr. Theodor Reik says, "men are afraid that they will not be men enough." Reik adds significantly: "And women are afraid that they might be considered only women." Why is it that women worry, not over whether they can fill the feminine role, but whether filling that role is enough, while men worry whether they can fill the masculine role at all? How to account for this rising tide of male anxiety? What has unmanned the American man?

There is currently a fashionable answer to this question. Male anxiety, many observers have declared, is simply the result of female aggression: what has unmanned the American man is the American woman. The present male confusion and desperation, it is contended, are the inevitable consequence of the threatened feminization of American society. The victory of women is the culmination of a long process of masculine retreat, beginning when Puritanism made men feel guilty about sex and the frontier gave women the added value of scarcity. Fleeing from the reality of femininity, the American man, while denying the American woman juridical equality, transformed her into an ideal of remote and transcendent purity with overriding authority over the family, the home, the school, and culture. This habit of obeisance left the male psychologically disarmed and vulnerable when the goddess stepped off the pedestal and demanded in addition equal economic, political, and legal rights. In the last part of the 19th century, women won their battle for equality. They gained the right of entry into one occupation after another previously reserved for males. Today they hold the key positions of personal power in our society and use this power relentlessly to consolidate their mastery. As mothers, they undermine masculinity through the use of love as a technique of reward and punishment. As teachers, they prepare male children for their role of submission in an increasingly feminine world. As wives, they complete the work of subjugation. Their strategy of conquest is deliberately to emasculate men—to turn them into Brick Pollitts and Jimmy Porters.

Or so a standard indictment runs; and no doubt there is something in it. American women have unquestionably gained through the years a place in our society which American men have not been psychologically prepared to accept. Whether because of Puritanism or the frontier, there has been something immature in the traditional American male attitude toward women—a sense of alarm at times amounting to panic. Almost none of the classic American novels, for example, presents the theme of mature and passionate love. Our 19th-century novelists saw women either as unassailable virgins or abandoned temptresses—never simply as women. One looks in vain through *Moby Dick* and *The Adventures of Huckleberry Finn*, through Cooper and Poe and Whitman, for an adult portrayal of relations between men and women. "Where," Leslie Fiedler has asked, "is the American *Madame Bovary, Anna Karenina, Wuthering Heights*, or *Vanity Fair?*"

Yet the implication of the argument that the American man has been unmanned by the emancipation of the American woman is that the American man was incapable of growing up. For the 19th-century sense of masculinity was based on the psychological idealization and the legal subjection of women; masculinity so spuriously derived could never—and should never—have endured. The male had to learn to live at some point with the free and equal female. Current attempts to blame "the decline of the American male" on the aggressiveness of the American female amount to a confession that, under conditions of free competition, the female was bound to win. Simple observation refutes this supposition. In a world of equal rights, some women rise; so too do some men; and no pat generalization is possible about the sexual future of society. Women have gained power in certain ways; in others, they have made little progress. It is safe to predict, for example, that we will have a Roman Catholic, perhaps even a Jew, for President before we have a woman. Those amiable prophets of an impending American matriarchy (all men, by the way) are too pessimistic.

Something more fundamental is involved in the unmanning of American men than simply the onward rush of American women. Why is the American man so unsure today about his masculine identity? The basic answer to this is plainly because he is so unsure about his identity in general. Nothing is harder in the whole human condition than to achieve a full sense of identity—than to know who you are, where you are going, and what you mean to live and die for. From the most primitive myths to the most contemporary novels—from Oedipus making the horrified discovery that he had married his mother, to Leopold Bloom and Stephen Dedalus searching their souls in Joyce's Dublin and the haunted characters of Kafka trying to make desperate sense out of an incomprehensible universe—the search for identity has been the most compelling human problem. That search has always been ridden with trouble and terror. And it can be plausibly argued that the conditions of modern life make the quest for identity more difficult than it has ever been before.

The pre-democratic world was characteristically a world of status in which people were provided with ready-made identities. But modern Western society—free, equalitarian, democratic—has swept away all the old niches in which people for so many centuries found safe refuge. Only a few people at any time in human history have enjoyed the challenge of "making" themselves; most have fled from the unendurable burden of freedom into the womblike security of the group. The new age of social mobility may be fine for those strong enough to discover and develop their own roles. But for the timid and the frightened, who constitute the majority in any age, the great vacant spaces of equalitarian society can become a nightmare filled with nameless horrors. Thus mass democracy, in the very act of offering the individual new freedom and opportunity, offers new moral authority to the group and thereby sets off a new assault on individual identity. Over a century ago Alexis de Tocqueville, the perceptive Frenchman who ruminated on the contradictions of equality as he toured the United States in the 1830's, pointed to the "tyranny of the majority" as a central problem of democracy. John Stuart Mill, lamenting the decline of individualism in Great Britain, wrote: "That so few now dare to be eccentric marks the chief danger of the time." How much greater that danger seems a century later!

For our own time has aggravated the assault on identity by adding economic and technological pressures to the political and social pressures of the 19th century. Modern science has brought about the growing centralization of the economy. We work and think and live and even dream in larger and larger units. William H. Whyte, Jr., has described the rise of "the organization man," working by day in immense business concerns, sleeping by night in immense suburban developments, deriving his fantasy life from mass-produced entertainments, spending his existence not as an individual but as a member of a group and coming in the end to feel guilty and lost when he deviates from his fellows. Adjustment rather than achievement becomes the social ideal. Men no longer fulfill an inner sense of what they *must* be; indeed, with the cult of the group, that inner sense itself begins to evaporate. Identity consists not of self-realization but of smooth absorption into the group. Nor is this just a matter of passive acquiescence. The group is aggressive, imperialistic, even vengeful, forever developing new weapons with which to overwhelm and crush the recalcitrant individual. Not content with disciplining the conscious mind, the group today is even experimenting with means of violating the subconscious. The subliminal invasion represents the climax of the assault on individual identity.

It may seem a long way from the loss of the sense of self to the question of masculinity. But if people do not know *who* they are, it is hardly surprising that they are no longer sure what sex they are. Nigel Dennis' exuberant novel *Cards of Identity* consists of a series of brilliant variations on the quest for identity in contemporary life. It reaches one of its climaxes in the tale of a person who was brought up by enlightened parents to believe that there was no such thing as pure male or female — everyone had elements of both—and who accepted this proposition so rigorously that he (she) could not decide what his (her) own sex was. "In what identity do you intend to face the future?" someone asks. "It seems that nowadays," comes the plaintive reply, "one must choose between being a woman who behaves like a man, and a man who behaves like a woman. In short, I must choose to be one in order to behave like the other." If most of us have not yet quite reached that condition of sexual chaos, yet the loss of a sense of identity is obviously a fundamental step in the decay of masculinity. And the gratification with which some American males contemplate their own decline should not obscure the fact that women, for all their recent legal and economic triumphs, are suffering from a loss of identity too. It is not accidental that the authors of one recent book described modern woman as the "lost sex."

If this is true, then the key to the recovery of masculinity does not lie in any wistful hope of humiliating the aggressive female and restoring the old masculine supremacy. Masculine supremacy, like white supremacy, was the neurosis of an immature society. It is good for men as well as for women that women have been set free. In any case, the process is irreversible; that particular genie can never be put back into the bottle. The key to the recovery of masculinity lies rather in the problem of identity. When a person begins to find out *who* he is, he is likely to find out rather soon what sex he is.

For men to become men again, in short, their first task is to recover a sense of individual spontaneity. And to do this a man must visualize himself as an individual apart from the group, whatever it is, which defines his values and commands his loyalty. There is no reason to suppose that the group is always wrong: to oppose the group automatically is nearly as conformist as to surrender to it automatically. But there is every necessity to recognize that the group is one thing and the individual—oneself—is another. One of the most sinister of present-day doctrines is that of *togetherness*. The recovery of identity means, first of all, a new belief in apartness. It means a determination to resist the overpowering conspiracy of blandness, which seeks to conceal all tension and conflict in American life under a blanket of locker-room affability. And the rebirth of spontaneity depends, at bottom, on changes of attitude *within* people—changes which can perhaps be described, without undue solemnity, as moral changes. These changes will no doubt come about in as many ways as there are individuals involved. But there are some general suggestions that can be made about the techniques of liberation. I should like to mention three such techniques: satire, art, and politics.

Satire means essentially the belief that nothing is sacred—that there is no person or institution or idea which cannot but benefit from the exposure of comedy. Our nation in the past has reveled in satire; it is, after all, the nation of Abraham Lincoln, of Mark Twain, of Finley Peter Dunne, of H. L. Mencken, of Ring Lardner. Indeed, the whole spirit of democracy is that of satire; as Montaigne succinctly summed up the democratic faith: "Sit he on never so high a throne, a man still sits on his own bottom." Yet today American society can only be described as a pompous society, at least in its official manifestations. Early in 1958 Mort Sahl, the night-club comedian, made headlines in New York because he dared make a joke about J. Edgar Hoover! It was not an especially good joke, but the fact that he made it at all was an encouraging sign. One begins to feel that the American people can only stand so much reverence—that in the end our native skepticism will break through, sweep aside the stuffed shirts and the stuffed heads and insist that platitudes are platitudinous and the great are made, among other things, to be laughed at. Irony is good for our rulers; and it is even better for ourselves because it is a means of dissolving the pomposity of society and giving the individual a chance to emerge.

If irony is one source of spontaneity, art is another. Very little can so refresh our vision and develop our vision and develop our values as the liberating experience of art. The mass media have cast a spell on us: the popular addiction to prefabricated emotional clichés threatens to erode our capacity for fresh and direct aesthetic experience. Individual identity vanishes in the welter of machine-made reactions. But thoughtful exposure to music, to painting, to poetry, to the beauties of nature, can do much to restore the inwardness, and thereby the identity, of man. There is thus great hope in the immense cultural underground of our age—the paper-bound books, the long-playing records, the drama societies, the art festivals, the new interest in painting and sculpture. All this represents a disdain for existing values and goals, a reaching out for something more exacting and more personal, an intensified questing for identity.

And politics in a true sense can be a means of liberation—not the banal politics of rhetoric and self-congratulation, which aims at burying all real issues under a mass of piety and platitude; but the politics of responsibility, which tries to define the real issues and present them to the people for decision. Our national politics have become boring in recent years because our leaders have offered neither candid and clear-cut formulations of the problems nor the facts necessary for intelligent choice. A virile political life will be definite and hard-hitting, respecting debate and dissent, seeking clarity and decision.

As the American male develops himself by developing his comic sense, his aesthetic sense, and his moral and political sense, the lineaments of personality will at last begin to emerge. The achievement of identity, the conquest of a sense of self—these will do infinitely more to restore American masculinity than all the hormones in the test tubes of our scientists. "Whoso would be a *man*," said Emerson, "must be a nonconformist"; and, if it is the present writer who adds the italics, nonetheless one feels that no injustice is done to Emerson's intention. How can masculinity, femininity, or anything else survive in a homogenized society, which seeks steadily and benignly to eradicate all differences between the individuals who compose it? If we want to have *men* again in our theaters and our films and our novels—not to speak of in our classrooms, our business offices, and our homes—we must first have a society which encourages each of its members to have a distinct identity.

# Is History a Guide to the Future?

## Barbara Tuchman

The commonest question asked of historians by laymen is whether history serves a purpose. Is it useful? Can we learn from the lessons of history?

When people want history to be utilitarian and teach us lessons, that means they also want to be sure that it meets scientific standards. This, in my opinion, it cannot do, for reasons which I will come to in a moment. To practice history as a science is sociology, an altogether different discipline which I personally find antipathetic—although I suppose the sociologists would consider that my deficiency rather than theirs. The sociologists plod along with their noses to the ground assembling masses of statistics in order to arrive at some obvious conclusion which a reasonably perceptive historian, not to mention a large part of the general public, knows anyway, simply from observation—that social mobility is increasing, for instance, or that women have different problems from men. One wishes they would just cut loose someday, lift up their heads, and look at the world around them.

If history were a science, we should be able to get a grip on her, learn her ways, establish her patterns, know what will happen tomorrow. Why is it that we cannot? The answer lies in what I call the Unknowable Variable—namely, man. Human beings are always and finally the subject of history. History is the record of human behavior, the most fascinating subject of all, but illogical and so crammed with an unlimited number of variables that it is not susceptible of the scientific method nor of systematizing.

I say this bravely, even in the midst of the electronic age when computers are already chewing at the skirts of history in the process called

From *Practicing History*, by Barbara Tuchman. Copyright ©1981 by Alma Tuchman, Lucy T. Eisenberg, and Jessica Tuchman Matthews. Reprinted by permission of Alfred A. Knopf, Inc.

Quantification. Applied to history, quantification, I believe, has its limits. It depends on a method called "data manipulation," which means that the facts, or data, of the historical past—that is, of human behavior—are manipulated into named categories so that they can be programmed into computers. Out comes—hopefully—a pattern. I can only tell you that for history "data manipulation" is a built-in invalidator, because to the degree that you manipulate your data to suit some extraneous requirement, in this case the requirements of the machine, to that degree your results will be suspect—and run the risk of being invalid. Everything depends on the naming of the categories and the assigning of facts to them, and this depends on the quantifier's individual judgment at the very base of the process. The categories are not revealed doctrine nor are the results scientific truth.

The hope for quantification, presumably, is that by processing a vast quantity of material far beyond the capacity of the individual to encompass, it can bring to light and establish reliable patterns. That remains to be seen, but I am not optimistic. History has a way of escaping attempts to imprison it in patterns. Moreover, one of its basic data is the human soul. The conventional historian, at least the one concerned with truth, not propaganda, will try honestly to let his "data" speak for themselves, but data which are shut up in prearranged boxes are helpless. Their nuances have no voice. They must carry one fixed meaning or another and weight the result accordingly. For instance, in a quantification study of the origins of World War I which I have seen, the operators have divided all the diplomatic documents, messages, and utterances of the July crisis into categories labeled "hostility," "friendship," "frustration," "satisfaction," and so on, with each statement rated for intensity on a scale from one to nine, including fractions. But no pre-established categories could match all the private character traits and public pressures variously operating on the nervous monarchs and ministers who were involved. The massive effort that went into this study brought forth a mouse—the less than startling conclusion that the likelihood of war increased in proportion to the rise in hostility of the messages.

Quantification is really only a new approach to the old persistent effort to make history fit a pattern, but *reliable* patterns, or what are otherwise called the lessons of history, remain elusive.

For instance, suppose Woodrow Wilson had not been President of the United States in 1914 but instead Theodore Roosevelt, who had been his opponent in the election of 1912. Had that been the case, America might have entered the war much earlier, perhaps at the time of the *Lusitania* in 1915, with possible shortening of the war and incalculable effects on history. Well, it happens that among the Anarchists in my book *The Proud Tower* is an obscure Italian named Miguel Angiolillo, whom nobody remembers but who shot dead Premier Canovas of Spain in 1897.

Canovas was a strong man who was just about to succeed in quelling the rebels in Cuba when he was assassinated. Had he lived, there might have been no extended Cuban insurrection for Americans to get excited about, no Spanish-American War, no San Juan Hill, no Rough Riders, no Vice-Presidency for Theodore Roosevelt to enable him to succeed when another accident, another Anarchist, another unpredictable human being, killed McKinley. If Theodore had never been President, there would have been no third party in 1912 to split the Republicans, and Woodrow Wilson would not have been elected. The speculations from that point on are limitless. To me it is comforting rather than otherwise to feel that history is determined by the illogical human record and not by large immutable scientific laws beyond our power to deflect.

I know very little (a euphemism for "nothing") about laboratory science, but I have the impression that conclusions are supposed to be logical; that is, from a given set of circumstances a predictable result should follow. The trouble is that in human behavior and history it is impossible to isolate or repeat a given set of circumstances. Complex human acts cannot be either reproduced or deliberately initiated—or counted upon like the phenomena of nature. The sun comes up every day. Tides are so obedient to schedule that a timetable for them can be printed like that for trains, though more reliable. In fact, tides and trains sharply illustrate my point: One depends on the moon and is certain; the other depends on man and is uncertain.

In the absence of dependable recurring circumstance, too much confidence cannot be placed on the lessons of history.

There *are* lessons, of course, and when people speak of learning from them, they have in mind, I think, two ways of applying past experience: One is to enable us to avoid past mistakes and to manage better in similar circumstances next time; the other is to enable us to anticipate a future course of events. (History could tell us something about Vietnam, I think, if we would only listen.) To manage better next time is within our means; to anticipate does not seem to be.

World War II, for example, with the experience of the previous war as an awful lesson, was certainly conducted, once we got into it, more intelligently than World War I. Getting into it was another matter. When it was important to anticipate the course of events, Americans somehow failed to apply the right lesson. Pearl Harbor is the classic example of failure to learn from history. From hindsight we now know that what we should have anticipated was a surprise attack by Japan in the midst of negotiations. Merely because this was dishonorable, did that make it unthinkable? Hardly. It was exactly the procedure Japan had adopted in 1904 when she opened the Russo-Japanese War by surprise attack on the Russian fleet at Port Arthur.

In addition we had every possible physical indication. We had broken the Japanese code, we had warnings on radar, we had a constant flow of accurate intelligence. What failed? Not information but *judgment*. We had all the evidence and refused to interpret it correctly, just as the Germans in 1944 refused to believe the evidence of a landing in Normandy. Men will not believe what does not fit in with their plans or suit their prearrangements. The flaw in all military intelligence, whether twenty or fifty or one hundred percent accurate, is that it is no better than the judgment of its interpreters, and this judgment is the product of a mass of individual, social, and political biases, prejudgments, and wishful thinkings; in short, it is human and therefore fallible. If man can break the Japanese code and yet not believe what it tells him, how can he be expected to learn from the lessons of history?

Would a computer do better? In the case of Pearl Harbor, probably yes. If one could have fed all the pieces of intelligence available in November 1941 into a computer, it could have hardly failed to reply promptly, "Air attack, Hawaii, Philippines" and probably even "December 7." But will this work every time? Can we trust the lessons of history to computers? I think not, because history will fool them. They may make the right deductions and draw the right conclusions, but a twist occurs, someone sneezes, history swerves and takes another path. Had Cleopatra's nose been shorter, said Pascal, the whole aspect of the world would have been changed. Can a computer account for Cleopatra?

Once long ago when the eternal verities seemed clear—that is, during the Spanish Civil War—I thought the lessons of history were unmistakable. It appeared obvious beyond dispute that if fascism under Franco won, Spain in the foreshadowed European war would become a base for Hitler and Mussolini, the Mediterranean would become an Italian lake, Britain would lose Gibraltar and be cut off from her empire east of Suez. The peril was plain, the logic of the thing implacable, every sensible person saw it, and I, just out of college, wrote a small book published in England to point it up, all drawn from the analogy of history. The book showed how, throughout the eighteenth and nineteenth centuries, Britain had consistently interposed herself against the gaining of undue influence over Spain by whatever power dominated the continent. The affair of the Spanish marriages, the campaigns of Wellington, the policies of Castlereagh, Canning, and Palmerston all were directed toward the same objective: The strongest continental power must be prevented from controlling Spain. My treatise was, I thought, very artful and very telling. It did not refer to the then current struggle, but let the past speak for itself and make the argument. It was an irrefutable one—until history refuted it. Franco, assisted by Hitler and Mussolini, *did* win, European war *did* follow, yet unaccountably Spain remained neutral—at least nominally. Gibraltar did not fall, the portals of the Mediterranean did *not* close. I, not to mention all the other "premature" anti-fascists, as we were called, while morally right about the general danger of fascism, had been wrong about a particular outcome. The lessons of history I had so carefully set forth simply did not operate. History misbehaved.

Pearl Harbor and Spain demonstrate two things: One, that man fails to profit from the lessons of history because his prejudgments prevent him from drawing the indicated conclusions; and, two, that history will often capriciously take a different direction from that in which her lessons point. Herein lies the flaw in systems of history.

When it comes to systems, history played her greatest betrayal on Karl Marx. Never was a prophet so sure of his premises, never were believers so absolutely convinced of a predicted outcome, never was there an interpretation of history that seemed so foolproof. Analyzing the effects of the Industrial Revolution, Marx exposed the terrible riddle of the nineteenth century: that the greater the material progress, the wider and deeper the resulting poverty, a process which could only end, he decided, in the violent collapse of the existing order brought on by revolution. From this he formulated the doctrine of *Verelendung* (progressive impoverishment) and *Zusammenbruch* (collapse) and decreed that since working-class self-consciousness increased in proportion to industrialization, revolution would come first in the most industrialized country.

Marx's analysis was so compelling that it seemed impossible history could follow any other course. His postulates were accepted by followers of his own and later generations as if they had been graven on the tablets of Sinai. Marxism as the revealed truth of history was probably the most convincing dogma ever enunciated. Its influence was tremendous, incalculable, continuing. The founder's facts were correct, his thinking logical and profound; he was right in everything but his conclusions. Developing events did not bear him out. The working class grew progressively better, not worse, off. Capitalism did not collapse. Revolution came in the least, not the most, industrialized country. Under collectivism the state did not wither but extended itself in power and function and in its grip on society. History, ignoring Marx, followed her own mysterious logic, and went her own way.

When it developed that Marx was wrong, men in search of determinism rushed off to submit history to a new authority—Freud. His hand is now upon us. The Unconscious is king. At least it was. There are new voices, I believe, claiming that the Unconscious is a fraud—iconoclasm has reached even Freud. Nevertheless, in his effect on the modern outlook, Freud, I believe, unquestionably was the greatest influence for change between the nineteenth and twentieth centuries. It may well be that our time may one day be named for him and the Freudian Era be said to have succeeded the Victorian Era. Our understanding of human motivation has taken on a whole new dimension since his ideas took hold. Yet it does not seem to me that unconscious sexual and psychological drives are as relevant in all circumstances as they are said to be by the Freudians, who have become as fixed in their system as were the orthodox Marxists. They can supply historians with insights but not with guidance to the future because men *en masse* cannot be relied upon to behave according to pattern. All salmon swim back to spawn in the headwaters of their birth; that is universal for salmon. But man lives in a more complicated world than a fish. Too many influences are at work on him to make it applicable that every man is driven by an unconscious desire to swim back to the womb.

It has always seemed to me unfortunate, for instance, that Freud chose the experiences of two royal families to exemplify his concept of the Oedipus and Elektra complexes. Royalty lives under special circumstances, particularly as regards the issue of power between the sovereign and his heir, which are not valid as universal experience. The legend of Oedipus killing his father may have derived from the observed phenomenon that every royal heir has always hated his father, not because he wants to sleep with his mother but because he wants to ascend the throne. If the parental sovereign happens to be his mother, he hates her just as much. She will dislike him equally from birth because she knows he is destined to take her place, as in the case of Queen Victoria and her eldest son, who became Edward VII. That is not Freudian, it is simply dynastic.

As for Elektra, it is hard to know what to make of that tale. The House of Atreus was a very odd family indeed. More was going on there than just Elektra being in love with her father. How about Orestes, who helped her to kill their mother, or killed her himself, according to another version? Was not that the wrong parent? How come he did not kill his father? How about Iphigenia, the sister, whom Agememnon killed as a sacrifice? What is the Freudian explanation for that? They do not say, which is not being historical. A historian cannot pick and choose his facts; he must deal with all the evidence.

Or take Martin Luther. As you know, Professor Erik Erikson of Harvard has discovered that Luther was constipated from childhood and upon this interesting physiological item he has erected a system which explains everything about his man. This is definitely the most camp thing that has happened to history in years. It even made Broadway. Nevertheless I do not think Luther pinned the 95 Theses on the church door at Wittenberg solely or even mainly because of the activity, or inactivity rather, of his anal muscle. His personal motive for protest may have had an anal basis for all I know, but what is important historically is the form the protest took, and this had to do with old and deep social grievances concerned with the worldliness of the church, the sale of indulgences, corruption of the clergy, and so on. If it had not been Luther who protested, it would have been someone else; Protestantism would have come with or without him, and its causes had nothing whatever to do with his private physiological impediment. Professor Erikson, I am sure, was attempting to explain Luther, not Protestantism, but his book has started a fad for psycho-history among those without the adequate knowledge or training to use it.

Following Freud there flourished briefly a minor prophet, Oswald Spengler, who proclaimed the Decline of the West, based on an elaborate study of the lessons of history. Off and on since then people have been returning to his theme, especially since World War II and the end of colonialism. The rise of China and the rash of independence movements in Asia and Africa have inspired many nervous second looks at Spengler. Europe is finished, say the knowing ones; the future belongs to the colored races and all that.

People have been burying Europe for quite some time. I remember a political thinker for whom I had great respect telling me in the thirties that Europe's reign was over; the future belonged to America, Russia, and China. It was a new and awful thought to me then and I was immensely impressed. As I see it now, his grouping has not been justified. I do not think Russia and America can be dissociated from Europe; rather, we are extensions of Europe. I hesitate to be dogmatic about Russia, but I am certain about the United States. American culture stems from Europe, our fortunes are linked with hers, in the long run we are aligned. My impression is that Europe, and by extension the white race, is far from finished. Europe's vitality keeps reviving; as a source of ideas she is inexhaustible. Nuclear fission, the most recent, if unwanted, advance, came from the work of a whole series of Europeans: Max Planck, the Curies, Einstein, Rutherford, Fermi, Nils Bohr, Szilard. Previously the three great makers of the modern mind, Darwin, Marx, and Freud, were Europeans. I do not know of an original idea to have importantly affected the *modern* world which has come from Asia or Africa (except perhaps for Gandhi's concept of non-violent resistance or civil disobedience, and, after all, Thoreau had the same idea earlier).

It does not seem to me a passing phenomenon or an accident that the West, in ideas and temporal power, has been dominant for so long. Far from falling behind, it seems to be extending its lead, except in the fearful matter of mere numbers and I like to think the inventiveness of the West will somehow eventually cope with that. What is called the emergence of the peoples of Asia and Africa is taking place in Western terms and is measured by the degree to which they take on Western forms, political, industrial, and otherwise. That they are losing their own cultures is sad, I think, but I suppose it cannot be helped. The new realm is space, and that too is being explored by the West. So much for Spengler.

Theories of history go in vogues which, as is the nature of vogues, soon fade and give place to new ones. Yet this fails to discourage the systematizers. They believe as firmly in this year's as last year's, for, as

Isaiah Berlin says, the "obstinate craving for unity and symmetry at the expense of experience" is always with us. When I grew up, the economic interpretation of history, as formulated with stunning impact by Charles Beard, was the new gospel—as incontrovertible as if it had been revealed to Beard in a burning bush. Even to question that financial interests motivated our Founding Fathers in the separation from Britain, or that equally mercenary considerations decided our entrance into the First World War, was to convict oneself of the utmost naïveté. Yet lately the fashionable—indeed, what appears to be the required — exercise among historians has been jumping on Beard with both feet. He and the considerable body of his followers who added to his system and built it up into a dogma capable of covering any historical situation have been knocked about, analyzed, dissected, and thoroughly disposed of. Presently the historical establishment has moved on to dispose of Frederick Jackson Turner and his theory of the Frontier. I do not know what the new explanation is, but I am sure there must be some thesis, for, as one academic historian recently ruled, the writing of history requires a "large organizing idea."

I visualize the "large organizing idea" as one of those iron chain mats pulled behind by a tractor to smooth over a plowed field. I see the professor climbing up on the tractor seat and away he goes, pulling behind his large organizing idea over the bumps and furrows of history until he has smoothed it out to a nice, neat, organized surface—in other words, into a system.

The human being—you, I, or Napoleon—is unreliable as a scientific factor. In combination of personality, circumstance, and historical moment, each man is a package of variables impossible to duplicate. His birth, his parents, his siblings, his food, his home, his school, his economic and social status, his first job, his first girl, and the variables inherent in all of these, make up that mysterious compendium, personality—which then combines with another set of variables: country, climate, time, and historical circumstance. Is it likely, then, that all these elements will meet again in their exact proportions to reproduce a Moses, or Hitler, or De Gaulle, or for that matter Lee Harvey Oswald, the man who killed Kennedy?

So long as man remains the Unknowable Variable—and I see no immediate prospect of his ever being pinned down in every facet of his infinite variety—I do not see how his actions can be usefully programmed and quantified. The eager electronic optimists will go on chopping up man's past behavior into the thousands of little definable segments which they call Input, and the machine will whirr and buzz and flash its lights and in no time at all give back Output. But will Output be dependable? I would lay ten to one that history will pay no more attention to Output than it did to Karl Marx. It will still need historians. Electronics will have its uses, but it will not, I am confident, transform historians into button-pushers or history into a system.

# It Depends What You Mean By Violence

## Peter Jenkins

It is a temptation to lump all violence together. Mr Ian MacGregor, the
Coal Board chief, succumbed to it when in the aftermath of the Brighton
bombing he said: "The tragic thing about it is a projection of the violence
we have seen in other parts of the country."

Mr Neil Kinnock fell into the same trap, but from the other direction,
when in his speech to the Labour Party conference he said: "I condemn
violence. I do condemn the violence of despair, long-term unemployment,
the violence of loneliness and decay, ugliness and fear."

Then he went on, in the same breath, to condemn the violence of the
"stone-throwers and the battering ram carriers" and of "the cavalry charges
and the truncheon groups and the shield bangers".

To see all violence as one, as if a single contagion, is to exaggerate
the prevalence of violence. To link varieties of violence, real and metaphorical, is to sanitise actual physical violence. We are growing accustomed to Mr MacGregor's gaucheness and I don't suppose he intended
to put IRA terrorism on all fours with picket line violence, merely to express the familiar belief that one form of violence begets another.

Nor do I suppose that Mr Kinnock in his misuse of (or violence to?)
the language really intended to mean that there is nothing to choose
between loneliness, or ugliness, and grievous bodily harm. I am singling
the two of them out only because their words are illustrative of the ways
we tend to think about violence, and especially political violence.

Because we are frightened by violence and find it hard to comprehend, whether the gratuitous violence of the streets or more abstract acts

Peter Jenkins, "It Depends What You Mean by Violence," *Manchester Guardian Weekly*
(October 28, 1984).

of terrorism, we are prone to the idea that violence is some kind of epidemic, a pestilence sweeping through society like the Black Death. By the same manner of thought we imagine some earlier Golden Age in which the streets were safe, in which a Dixon of Dock Green pounded every beat and cloth-capped burglars from Hoxton gave themselves up with a cheerful "It's a fair cop, guv."

Yet it seems that each generation in its turn imagines itself to be afflicted by an unprecedented plague of violence. So we are told by Geoffrey Pearson in his book Hooligan—A History of Respectable Fears. Our belief that we live in a mounting wave of crime and juvenile delinquency, and the similar beliefs of previous generations, is more likely to do with changes in the reporting of crime, in rates of detecting or the attitudes of the courts.

It is not Pearson's intention to minimise the amount of violence with which we live and it is certainly not mine. The level of that violence is real enough: the point is that it may not be any greater or more real than at previous times. Are we to suppose that Mrs Thatcher's Britain is a more violent place than Mayhew's? To put violence in this better perspective is no consolation whatsoever to the victim of a mugging but is of some relevance to the shaping of social attitudes and the framing of public policy.

Much the same is true about collective or political violence. We are accustomed to seeing ourselves as a people of exceptional good temper, law-abiding and non-violent. Consequently, we are greatly shocked when Brixton and Toxteth burn as if Watts or Detroit and when hordes of miners clash with French-style riot police. Is this England?

Yes it is. It is the England, for example, in which in 1818 "two companies of troops with fixed bayonets had to be called in to suppress a rising of the pupils of Winchester. At Rugby, the pupils set fire to their books and desks and withdrew to an island, which had to be taken by assault by the army. There were similar incidents at Eton."

It is the England in which, as Disraeli in 1862 recalled, "Then arose Luddite mobs, meal mobs, farm riots, riots everywhere; Captain Swing and his rickburners, Peterloo 'massacres', Bristol conflagrations, and all the ugly sights and rumours which made young lads, thirty or forty years ago, believe (and not wrongly) that 'the masses were their natural enemies, and they might have to fight, any year or any day, for the safety of their property and the honour of their sisters'."

Later it became an England in which women (no, not Greenham women) "smashed windows, fired pillar-boxes, slashed pictures, threw things at MPs and even burned down churches and houses; in reply they were treated with great roughness by policemen and worse by crowds. They were kicked and beaten; their hair was pulled and their clothes half torn off; hatpins were pushed into them; they were knocked down and trampled upon".

I have taken those quotes from an essay by Professor Charles Tilley, commissioned by President Johnson's Commission on the Causes and Prevention of Violence which was set up in that violent of violent years 1968. Professor Tilley was intent on reminding Americans that if violence was as "American as apple pie" it was also as French as tarte de pommes or as English as steak-and-kidney pudding. He began with the words "As comforting as it is for civilised people to think of barbarians as violent and of violence as barbarian, Western civilisation and various forms of collective violence have always been close partners."

The twentieth century may seem to us, with good reason, to be a century which has succumbed extravagantly to barbaric violence. It had scarcely begun when James Joyce complained that history was a nightmare from which he was trying to awake. For Hegel, earlier, history was a "slaughter bench". For Albert Camus in the middle of the twentieth century it was a "charnel house". When Camus sat down to write The Rebel, he estimated that in the first half of this century 70 million people had been murdered. I have no idea what the score will be by the end of it. Shall we say a hundred million, a round average of a million murders a year?

How do we come to terms with such a toll of violence? I suppose in the same way as Thucydides did with the violence of his own age. He began by describing it and went on, in a famous passage:

"Human nature, always ready to offend even where laws exist, showed itself proudly in its true colours, as something incapable of controlling passion, insubordinate to the idea of justice, the enemy of anything superior to itself; for, if it had not been for the pernicious power of envy, men would not have so exalted vengeance above innocence and profit above justice."

Down the ages men have often felt themselves to be living in times such as ours.

So is there nothing to be done? After bloody terrorist murders is the only solace to be found in history books? I do not think so. For a start we can ensure that our perceptions of violence are not allowed to shape reality. For when the myth of violence takes hold societies are lost.

When bombs go up we call the bombers "cowards", I suppose because explosions are indiscriminate and, therefore, as acts of violence are more abstract. But I imagine that it takes much daring to carry out such acts of terrorism and requires moral courage of a kind to be responsible for such unselective and impersonal atrocities.

We would do better not to underestimate such an enemy. Listen to the chilling words of the IRA on Friday: "Today we were unlucky but remember, we have only to be lucky once. You will have to be lucky always." The enemy is fanatical and professional, but the enemy is few in number; the terrorist is not at large in society as is a phenomenon called "violence".

Violence in that general sense takes different guises, has different causes, exists in differing degrees. We resist violence, first, by calling it, and only it, by its name; we do not, by debasing the language, help violence to become the common currency. Apologists for violence do just this. Jean Genet for example. To speak of "consumer violence" is to promote the adman into an assassin and, by the same token, bring the assassin to the level of the adman.

It is no less scandalous, and inciteful to violence, to write as Edward Bond, the playwright, did in the Guardian earlier this year, comparing the 1983 General Election with "a chance to vote against the creation of Auschwitz or Belsen at the end of your street".

To provoke society into conformity with their sick and guilt-laden fascistic fantasies was the aim of Baader and Meinhoff. Violence which has irrational roots many yet still have rational ends. Proto-revolutionary violence may not bring down the government but it may succeed in drawing attention to the plight of Liverpool.

Riot more often results in reform than revolution. It is a misunderstanding, and an error, to deny violence its role: to assert that "democracy will prevail" is not sufficient, for if reform becomes the victim of violence and reaction the beneficiary, it ceases to be certain that democracy will prevail.

Violence prospers when one form of it is excused in terms of another. The violence of anti-colonial wars legitimises violence by the diminished proletariats of the developed, capitalist countries. This was what Sartre, Fanon, and Genet preached. "Violence," wrote Sartre, like Achilles's lance, can heal the wounds it has inflicted." Raymond Aron replied: "Only the reference to universality prevents (Sartre's) ethico-politics from sliding into the fascist cult of violence." The students of the Sorbonne wrote on their walls in 1968 "Better wrong with Sartre than right with Aron." No, always better right with Aron.

Violence can never be altogether suppressed, but it must never be legitimised. Nor must it be romanticised or aestheticised. It is, as Camus concluded, "both inevitable and unjustifiable." That is both an historical and moral view, spoken in the authentic voice of twentieth century experience. The task of government is to contain violence as best it can, always distinguishing one form from another, carefully weighing the price of violence against the price of its repression, and never permitting hysteria to take hold.

# The Intellectual and His World

## André Brink

(1980)

To say that the last quarter of the twentieth century presents us with a tough and practical world, with tough and practical demands on both society and the individual, is to state the obvious. Yet the obvious may require as much scrutiny as the cryptic or the arcane, since its very obviousness may tend to its being taken too much for granted. The result may be intellectual laziness and moral slackness. And this world of ours, provisionally described as tough and practical, demands above all a particular form of intellectual and moral courage—especially when it is approached from the perspective of the academic.

It has become customary to sneer at the impotence of the individual in general and the intellectual in particular. In a world overrun by masses and requiring, for its practical needs, ever-increasing common denominators, the individual appears a paltry and insignificant creature indeed, more often a hindrance than a help. And in a world demanding urgent solutions for problems like hunger, racism, exploitation, ideological and territorial expansionism, aggression and repression, the activity of the intellectual may appear not only futile but redundant, a luxury society can ill afford.

This is the context within which Lorca told his famous anecdote about the rich man and his peasant neighbour taking a stroll through a particularly scenic landscape: the rich man stopped in ecstasy every few minutes to exclaim with genuine appreciation: 'How beautiful!' But all the poor man could do in response was to clutch his belly and repeat: 'I am hungry, I am hungry, I am hungry!' Again, this is the context within which one encounters the accusation: 'No book and no thought can stop a bullet from a gun!' Or: 'I was suffering, and you offered me a theory of relativity.

Reprinted by permission of Faber and Faber Ltd. from *Mapmakers: Writing in a State of Siege* by André Brink.

I was oppressed, and you formed a Freedom and Justice Committee to debate the nature of oppression. I was put in jail and tortured by the Security Police, and you said liberty was a commendable thing.' It is the context within which a leading South African Sunday newspaper, reviewing the axing of staff and departments at a particular university, commented that this was only a logical and possibly even salutary step, in keeping with the practice in big business to eliminate non-profitable areas of production.

These arguments and accusations derive from a cartesian rigorism which divides thought and action into two separate categories divided by an either/or. In each group one finds thoroughly well-meaning persons condemning what they regard as their opposite group: 'You are being merely intellectual…'/'You are being merely practical…' There seems to be an unfortunate tendency in the West to think in these linear terms, these neat opposites. If you oppose the Government you are a communist; if you don't oppose it you're a fascist. And when an effort towards reconciliation is made, the solution usually seems to lie in creating a sliding scale containing thought on one end and action on the other, with the logical inference that the validity of thought lies in the measure in which it evolves into action, or prompts or promotes action. It seems to me an impoverishment of our experience to think in these terms. In fact, I would suggest that it is a line of thought which develops from either a misunderstanding or an obfuscation of the concepts 'thought' and 'action'; hence, of the concept 'intellectual'. It is the same sort of misunderstanding which, for such a long time, clouded the concepts of 'form' and 'content' in the arts.

Approached in one particular way one might suggest that 'thought' and 'action' are really two sides of the same coin, and that what matters is neither heads nor tails but the solid metal in between. In this context thought would be seen as interiorized action; action as expressive thought, or thought made visible. And neither can exist without the other: it is only in our impoverished interpretation of empirical processes that we fatefully separate them. But perhaps even the coin image is too mechanical: perhaps one should think in terms of an iceberg, with nine-tenths of thought submerged in order to allow one-tenth of action to protrude.

Although this may be a truer image, we are left with the situation I outlined at the beginning of my talk, in terms of which certain *kinds* of action seem to be preferable to others: preferable, at least, within the frameworks of the 'practical' demands of organized society. We are left, in other words, with the hungry man who cannot be fed on beauty; the jailed prisoner who cannot be freed through noble dictums; the company that cuts staff in order to 'rationalize' and which demands the same of universities. But in this situation, too, it seems to me that an either/or approach defeats the purpose and is too easy a way out. No one disputes that a hungry man should be fed, an unjustly imprisoned man freed, or an ailing company be made profitable. But having fulfilled all these obligations, would society then be a more just and free place to live in? Would people automatically be more fulfilled or the much vaunted 'quality of life' be enhanced *sans plus*? Put in the simplest possible terms: can man really live by bread alone? To take it one step further, remaining within the framework of our set examples: if Lorca's hungry man is given his daily bread, can one deny his well-fed neighbour his delight in something beautiful? Can a climate for justice, in which the unjustly jailed are set free, be created without the dedicated activity of those who insist on the basic requirement of justice in society? And once our company has been made profitable, is there not another set of rules to measure the 'profitability' of an institution for higher education? Balanced books are a good and honourable thing, but these do not rule out other kinds of books which create a balanced mind. 'Bread for one yen' says the Japanese proverb, 'For the other yen, white hyacinths.'

And so we are really back where we started: 'the intellectual and his world'. It may seem that we are now entitled to ask: What is the function of the intellectual in his world? But in Hamlet's words: *Madam, I know not 'seems'*. For it is, indeed, as unseemly a question as was the suggested dichotomy between 'thought' and 'action'. To pose this question would, after all, be to revive the dichotomy I have tried to discredit: it would imply a difference between an 'intellectual' and, say, an 'ordinary man', whatever either of these terms may mean. When I was caught up in the student protests in Paris in 1968 there was one particular march in which a million people took part, just after Daniel Cohn Bendit had been expelled from France, and a million voices shouted: 'We are all German Jews'—probably the only occasion in history when the French showed any liking for the Germans. But obviously nobody was so ridiculous as to take this in its literal sense. A form of poetry was on the streets that day; and a million people affirmed their common humanity and their common opposition to a system of laws and a pattern of society which denied or threatened that humanity. In this sense, we are all either 'ordinary men' or 'intellectuals'—or both: even though, in Orwell's immortal term, some may be more equal than others.

All I am trying to clarify is that asking about the function of the intellectual may be posing the wrong question. Let us rather, more cautiously, enquire about the function of that part in each one of us which is involved with intellectual activity: an enquiry which obviously has particular relevance within the framework of a university. For however 'modern' or 'practical' or 'pragmatic' or 'society-oriented' we may have become, I should still like to see, glimmering through the gloom, something of the original 'universality' in the word 'university': and if, as an institution, it is also becoming, through need and necessity, a career-orientated machine, it cannot *ever*, without denying itself, shed its function of shaping, broadening, stimulating and directing intellectual enquiry as the submerged nine-tenths of its unwieldy iceberg.

In thus directing my brief exploration towards the 'intellectual' half or nine-tenths of 'universal man', I accept, with Sir Herbert Read, that 'I am not concerned with the practicability of a programme. I am only concerned to establish the truth.' This is an ambitious activity into which one can enter only as an individual: thought is as exclusive to the individual as birth or death; and, I should like to think, as definitive. It is only natural that this activity of the individual should more often than not find itself in conflict with the accepted patterns of society: it is within this context that teaching has, rightly I think, been termed 'a subversive activity'. For in that territory of the mind where man is utterly and adventurously alone—even though he may assume responsibility for all men in what he undertakes (just as Sir Edmund Hilary, in a sense, climbed Everest for all mankind) the individual, putting everything at stake, can be guided only by the full and overwhelming reality of *that situation*, and not by general rules or by tradition. It is a religious solitude which can lead to perdition or redemption: but precisely because the stakes are so high it is an adventure unequalled by any other. To speak once again with Read:

'Life depends on the agitation set up by a few eccentric individuals. For the sake of that life, that vitality, a community must take certain risks, must admit a modicum of heresy. It must live dangerously if it would live at all.'

Or elsewhere:

'I realize that form, pattern, and order are essential aspects of existence; but in themselves they are the attributes of death. To make life, to ensure progress, to create interest and vividness, it is necessary to break down form, to distort pattern, to change the nature of our civilization.'

This seems a lofty and confused ideal. But it is possible to be more specific. I have no intention to be exhaustive in suggesting a few possibilities of intellectual action: only to venture a couple of yards across the border of this 'undiscover'd country' which differs from Hamlet's in that its travellers do survive to tell the tale.

'We must grasp what grips us,' said the literary theoretician Emil Staiger: a concept which may be broadened to intellectual activity as a whole. It is surely not part of our human condition simply to endure what happens: even in circumstances where it would appear impossible actively to influence the course of events the simple but momentous act of clarification—of establishing *what* is happening, and *why*—may become the starting point of significant social action. It works in two stages: informing oneself; and transmitting that information to others. The entire momentum of social action against authoritarian silence or authoritarian lies begins with the establishment of these two series of facts: what is happening; and why. No authority should be allowed to create a set of circumstances within which it becomes possible for anyone to say: *I didn't know*. What seems a very simple, basic procedure may, in societies like our own, prove to be an act of courage. It was the starting point of the Fischers and Mandelas in a struggle for a modicum of sanity in an insane structure. (Had the challenge of their intellectual enquiry been met instead of thwarted, violence could have been avoided.) It was the principle to which Beyers Naudé and the Christian Institute dedicated themselves. The Black Consciousness Movement, the Students' Council of Soweto, *The World*, Steve Biko, Donald Woods, and a fair percentage of the thousands of books banned in this country have been silenced in their various ways for this same basic reason: that truth is unbearable in a society which is built upon the lie. And only through the action of dedicated individuals, through the unflinching moral and intellectual enquiry of an independent mind, can silence and the lie be countered. We have an elemental need to know what grips us.

This enquiry is not directed exclusively towards a world of so-called external or social fact. The courage of the mind, which implies in our time Tillich's 'courage to be', demands also an enquiry of its own processes: of language, and of thought itself. We all know, when dealing with an estate agent, that 'charming' really means 'bloody awful', 'functional' means 'falling to pieces', and 'interesting view' means an unrestricted view of your neighbour's fence. But we also have to probe the language of authoritarianism: we have followed the semantic metamorphosis of 'apartheid' into 'separate development' into 'parallel development' into 'equal opportunity' into 'constellation of states'; of BOSS into DONS (a curious upgrading which the Mafia would appreciate), etc. But these are only the more glaring, obtrusive examples; and in an authoritarian society semantics is a very subtle game. We need only look at words like 'state security', 'law and order' and others to become aware of it. Among other processes one should be wary of the process of *definition*: our own society reveals startling similarities with that of Stalinist Russia described thus by Roland Barthes:

> In the Stalinist world, in which *definition*, that is to say the separation of Good and Evil, becomes the sole content of language, there are no more words without values attached to them, so that finally the function of writing is to cut out one stage of a process: there is no more lapse of time between naming and judging, and the closed character of language is perfected.

The search for truth, which is the search of the individual's intellectual activity, implies also an attack on facile polarities. In our dangerous society almost everything is experienced in terms of either/or. The most glaring: black/white; segregation/integration, etc....In such a closed situation, I suggest, intellectual activity can contribute to a defusing of the tension created by simplistic polarities by clarifying the complexity of the issues involved and by exploring other options.

In immediate, practical terms: several previously white-dominated societies on our borders have in recent years and even months demonstrated a variety of different options. On a limited scale it applies even to Namibia, where some white Afrikaners have scrapped laws and rules regarded by other white Afrikaners as guarantees of national identity. If Namibia can survive without pass laws, group areas or the relevant sections of the Immorality Act, why should we be the only country in the world to need them for our survival?

South Africa has entered an exciting period in which, for the first time in thirty years, a limited range of new possibilities is being debated and in which the word 'change' is no longer, in itself, anathema. Intellectual integrity would lie neither in summarily dismissing it nor in accepting it as sufficient in itself. Instead, the true adventure of the mind would ensure that the range of possibilities be expanded immeasurably both in width and in depth, and that not only matters of bread and of physical survival be explored but also, and above all, those matters of intellect and morality without which it would be presumptuous to claim for ourselves the name of *man*. Without quantity we may not be able to survive: without quality it would not be worth while to.

# White
# Lies

Robert Fulford

Canada is not a racist society, cannot possibly be a racist society—except in the sense that all societies are racist. It's true that opinion polls tell us that a good many Canadians believe Canada should remain predominantly white, but those people hold their views so diffidently or so timidly that they have almost no effect on public policy. Ever since the liberalization of immigration laws under the Pearson government in 1967, Canada has become increasingly a multiracial community, not by historic accident (like the United States) but by the conscious choice of a generally popular government. Currently about half of new immigrants are non-whites. If Canadians were racist in any serious sense they would force their members of parliament to force the government to reject Vietnamese, Indians, Pakistanis, West Indians, and other non-whites or "visible minorities," as the cant phrase describes them.

In truth, Canadian immigration policy is for all its faults as liberal as any on earth, far more liberal than the policies of most European countries, where "guest workers" are imported from poor countries and then sent home when no longer needed. Canadian policy, while it has drawn criticism from a few fringe groups, has not been seriously opposed by even one major national institution or public figure. This summer, at the Conservative convention, where right-wing views of almost every kind were being tossed around, the idea of white supremacy didn't make an appearance.

But Canadians, in this regard as in others, are a long way from being perfect. Like all other people, they have feelings of racism, and sometimes they express them. Non-whites particularly feel discriminated against in employment and housing, and organizations have sprung up to express their feelings. This problem, like so many others, has become a

Reprinted from *Saturday Night*, September, 1983.

subject for federal inquiry. In May, James Fleming, the minister responsible for multiculturalism and therefore the minister responsible for keeping minorities firmly at the side of the Liberal Party, announced plans for a seven-member all-party parliamentary committee on racism. The committee will travel across the country, hold public hearings, and listen to complaints from people who feel themselves victims of racism. After six months it will issue a report recommending ways to lessen intolerance.

Fleming, as he described his committee, noted that in various parts of Canada there have been outrageous incidents of racial discrimination, some of them violent. "The time is long past," he said, "when we can sit back and be comfortable with the thought that these incidents are aberrations....Parliamentarians, as the representatives of all Canadians, must acknowledge that we have wounds, and look for ways to heal those wounds."

What can the parliamentarians do? Until recently they might have acknowledged that visible minorities experience difficulty finding jobs and therefore recommended that Ottawa set an example of aggressive tolerance through an affirmative-action hiring programme. But, not long after Fleming's announcement, Ottawa declared that it was going in just that direction—although so far its programme encompasses only women, native people, and the handicapped. What, then, is left for this parliamentary committee? A kind of national teach-in, perhaps, an airing of grievances met by solemn promises to do better? At best this will be a media event, focussing the attention of television and newspapers on the views of racial minorities. For months people across the country will be talking, through the media, about racial issues. The committee will attempt to organize public opinion through mass communications. Not entirely a bad idea, but not so promising an idea as Fleming imagines.

Much of the research and writing on race centres on the mass media and their effects. The media are frequently blamed for creating or reinforcing stereotypes and frequently charged with the responsibility of reforming our attitudes. The media created this problem: let them solve it. That seems simple enough, but it may involve a mistaken view of both media and racism.

Marshall McLuhan made a remarkable career by demonstrating, among other things, that people do not take the media seriously enough. In the post-McLuhan era we may be committing the opposite error of taking them *too* seriously. An ignorant aloofness about the subject has been replaced, in many circles, by an ignorant dedication to the idea that the media are a kind of first cause, both the reason we are in trouble and the way we are going to get out of it. A recent issue of *Currents: Readings in Race Relations*, a magazine published in Toronto by the Urban Alliance on Race Relations, is devoted to the subject of the media and visible minorities. An editorial setting the tone for the issue attributes to the media powers that would be awe-inspiring if they in fact existed. "The media set norms, create stereotypes, build leaders, set priorities and educate the general public," the editorial says. "Mass media confer status on those individuals and groups they select for placement in the public eye, telling the viewer, or reader, who and what is important to know about, think about, and *have feelings about.* [Emphasis added.] Those who are made visible through the media become worthy of attention and concern; those whom the media ignore remain invisible."

This view, which is not atypical, seems to me outlandishly exaggerated. The persuasive powers of the media may be impressive, but they are not nearly so great as the editor of *Currents* and others like him imagine. We could argue, just as vehemently, that the media are remarkably impotent. For example, the national media concentrate much more of their attention on politics than on any other subject, implicitly urging us all to share this obsession. Yet a great many citizens remain entirely indifferent to politics; there are elections in which fewer than half of those eligible bother even to vote. Far from directing public opinion, the media seek frantically to keep up with it—witness the endless public-opinion polling conducted by the most powerful newspapers and television networks. If the media could tell us what to "have feelings about," they might well do so; but they cannot. TV and the newspapers may sometimes reinforce our feelings, but they cannot direct them. If they could, most readers of *The Toronto Star* would by now be dedicated supporters of Canadian nationalism, most readers of *The Globe and Mail* would be passionately concerned about civil liberties, all readers of Allan Fotheringham and Richard Gwyn would vote against the Liberals, and all children weaned on *Sesame Street* would be free of racial bigotry.

*Currents* argues that the media in general, and the movie industry in particular, "constantly portray racial and ethnic minorities in the most base and distorted characterizations." That's partly true, but the media also portray majorities—women, to start with—in distorted ways. Distortion of reality, which is also called drama, is a necessary characteristic of television, film, theatre, and fiction—a writer or a director or a network executive is not a human-relations counsellor or a statistician. It matters not at all whether we consider dramatic literature at the highest or the lowest level: we would not look to Shakespeare for a fair, balanced view of everyday life in Elizabethan England, any more than we would look to *Dallas* for an account of what actually happens in Dallas. Fiction and drama deal routinely in stereotypes, and only fools rely on fiction and drama for their view of the world. When race-relations experts—whose attitudes are accurately reflected by *Currents*—place this much emphasis on the media, they imply that the public in its deepest and most atavistic feelings is entirely malleable, that it drifts from attitude to attitude at the suggestion of the media. The parliamentary committee will be forced to rely on this same malleability in its earnest efforts to "heal these wounds."

"It is difficult to combat past stereotypes," says *Currents*, "if the most influential and pervasive medium of them all [television] continues to feature movies which originated those stereotypes." The implication is that TV should sanitize itself by discarding all those films of the 1930s and 1940s in which racial minorities are occasionally shown in ways that offend the values of the 1980s. That would result in a serious loss—in knowledge of film, in knowledge of the past, and in ordinary enjoyment. To jettison those movies would be to place a pious attitude toward racial feelings above all other values. It would also be to admit that the media are a major cause of the problem.

Are they? It could as easily be argued that the media have promoted good race relations. If we examine only North America, which has been subjected to more mass media than any other part of the world, we can see the rise of the mass media occurring simultaneously with a rise in racial tolerance. Certainly the residents of this continent were much more subject to bigotry in, say, 1910 (before mass media) than today. If the media have had an effect it is in the direction of opening up and enlarging our view of the human race. We begin to think differently about people of other races when we see them as actors, musicians, comedians, commentators—or as the subjects of documentaries. Northrop Frye has said: "Television does have a profoundly civilizing aspect in that it compels people to look like people. I think of what an abstract notion I had of Eskimos when I was a student at school, or even college, and how that simply disappeared as soon as one began seeing them on television....You have to start whittling away your stereotypes." Of course television will not automatically produce tolerant or understanding citizens. If one is predisposed to bigotry one may remain a bigot; if one is otherwise predisposed, one may be broadened by the images of minorities on TV and outraged when those images are limited to stereotypes. In any case, whatever the effect of TV in propagating the most famous media stereotypes (the "bad Indian" and the "good Indian" in westerns, for instance), there are other stereotypes that persist without the help of media. A veteran politician has told me that in rural Ontario the most persistent bigotry he encounters is against Roman Catholics, about whom the media have traditionally had little to say.

My own experience suggests that there are factors in everyone's life more important than either the exhortations of government bodies (even when conveyed through we're-all-in-this-together anti-racist advertising) or the routine bombardment of media images. Parental example, personal experience, religious training, the attitudes of peers—each of these separately, certainly all of them together, amount to much more than the larger and vaguer messages of government and media, whether those messages are clumsy and inadvertent or carefully shaped by propagandists. It is in the world of private experience, not the media or government, that racism persists and that racism may eventually be defeated. One does not hear Newfie jokes or Polish jokes on television; one hears them in private. Racism is given its power in our lives not by something seen on television but by something heard at the coffee machine in the office. And racism is stripped of its power every time someone of one race meets someone of another and finds the meeting engaging, or enjoyable, or enriching. The poetry of private life, the decency possible in ordinary relationships—these are the best and perhaps the only answer to racism.

A friend of mine, dealing in frustration with an incompetent black on the telephone, realized recently that he himself was—in one sense, at least — a racist. He wanted to say to her: "You black bitch, get moving on this." He has an extremely expensive education which should, theoretically, have rooted out the racism in his soul—an MD, a residency in psychiatry, a long practice in a multiracial city. But he remains, as he knew in that moment, a racist. He did not *utter* those words, being far too civilized, but he thought them, and in the process understood the persistence of his racism. He disapproves of this part of himself, and rightly so, but in thinking about him (and millions like him) we should understand that there are different forms of racism. There is a distinction between instinct and behaviour, between feelings and policy, and the distinctions are crucial.

In the 1940s my parents told me that racism (we called it "intolerance" or "discrimination" in those days) was evil, and I accepted their teaching. Ever since, I have tried not to be a racist. Yet I still find myself more comfortable with and more reliant on people of my own race or closely related races. Logic suggests that in my dealings I probably favour those like me. In a sense I am, therefore, a racist—and would distrust anyone, of any colour, who claimed that he or she was not. We can consciously affect our behaviour and policy; we are, for the most part, unable to change our instincts and feelings, however shameful we may think them.

This distinction is lost in much of the public discussion of racism. For example, a report on racism in Toronto—one of eleven regional reports released by James Fleming when he announced his parliamentary committee—declared that there had been a recent and obvious improvement in race relations and then quickly denied that any encouragement could be taken from that improvement. "It is generally agreed by both the minority communities and the civic authorities," the report said, "that acts of racism in the streets, transportation system and public places have decreased. Some believe, however, that prejudiced persons have learned to conceal their prejudice, and that those Torontonians who have been traditionally 'polite racists' are even more polite now." The implication is that, since all racism is bad (right), one form of it is as bad as another (wrong). The report seems to say that polite racism is no better than pushing people under subway trains or beating them with baseball bats. In fact, polite racism is an enormous improvement on the other kind: it indicates that those who hold racist feelings have been instructed (by their peers, by society, by the media, or some other force) that these feelings are despicable and like all despicable feelings should be held in private if they must be held at all. If people can understand that it is required of them to — as the report scornfully puts it — "conceal their prejudice," then enormous progress has been made. That may be all, in this unjust and imperfect world, that we can hope for.

# The Myth
# of
# Logic

## William Broad
## Nicholas Wade

Science is the distinctive enterprise of Western civilization in the twentieth century, and yet it is perhaps the least well understood. A major reason for this gap is that the philosophers of science, who have influenced the general conception of how science works, describe it as a purely logical process.

There is indeed a logical structure to the body of scientific knowledge, but the logic is often easier to see in retrospect, *after* the knowledge has been gathered. The way in which scientific knowledge is produced and disseminated is a wholly different matter. It is an activity in which nonrational elements such as creativity or personal ambition play conspicuous roles. Logical thought is of course a vital element in scientific discovery, maybe even more so than it is in poetry, art, or any other high exercise of intellect. But it is not the only element.

The myth of science as a purely logical process, constantly reaffirmed in every textbook, article, and lecture, has an overwhelming influence on scientists' perceptions of what they do. Even though scientists are aware of the nonlogical elements of their work, they tend to suppress or at least dismiss them as being of little consequence. A major element of the scientific process is thus denied existence or significance.

The prevalence of the myth of logic is due in large measure to an influential group of European philosophers. During the 1920's and 1930's the Logical Empiricists, also known as the Vienna Circle, constructed a powerfully attractive analysis of science. Scientific knowledge, in their view, is superior to all other kinds because it is empirically verifiable. Scientists

From *Betrayers of the Truth*. Copyright © 1982 by William Broad and Nicholas Wade. Reprinted by permission of Simon & Schuster, Inc.

propose hypotheses on the basis of inductive logic, and confirm or refute them by experimental test. From the hypotheses may be derived general principles about nature, known as scientific laws. The laws may be derived from or explained by the high-level cognitive structures known as theories. When old theories fail, new theories are proposed and adopted because of their greater explanatory power, and science thereby progresses another inexorable step toward the truth.

The Logical Empiricists deliberately ignored the historical context of science as well as psychological factors such as intuition, imagination, or receptivity to new ideas. Being more interested in science as a logical structure than in science as a process, they passed over the critically revealing subject of scientific change. Typical of the empiricist philosophers' abstractions is the doctrine of falsifiability propounded by Karl Popper of the University of London. A scientific theory, in Popper's view, can never be proved true, it can only be refuted, and once refuted in any serious way it is abandoned.

Popper's theory is at once profoundly true and profoundly absurd. No matter how well a theory is corroborated, it is always vulnerable to falsification at some time in the future, so maybe all scientific theories should be accepted only on the limited and pro tem basis that Popper prescribes. But that is not what happens in practice. Scientists will cling to a theory, no matter how damaging the counterevidence, at least until a better theory comes along and often for longer.

The Logical Empiricists' conception of science has impressed itself not just on the public but also on scientists as well. Researchers are imbued in their lengthy training with the notion that science is a realm of thought where logic and objectivity reign supreme. They are taught that science works just the way the philosophers say it should work. They learn the ideal as if it were reality. The myth has thoroughly pervaded even the central communications systems of science: it dictates with absolute authority the form in which all scientific articles and textbooks are written.

Considered as a literary form, a scientific paper is as stylized as a sonnet: if it fails to obey rigid rules of composition, it will simply not be published. In essence, the rules require that an experiment be reported *as if* every aspect of the procedure had been performed according to the philosophers' prescriptions. The conventions of scientific reporting require the writer to be totally impersonal, so as to give the appearance of objectivity.

Thus a scientist cannot describe the excitement of discovery, the false leads, the hopes and disappointments, or even the path of thinking that may have led him through the various steps of his experiment. Only in the most formalized way, usually by describing the current state of research in the field, may a scientist allude to his reasons for undertaking an investigation. Then comes a "materials and methods" section, where the ingredients and techniques are described in telegraphic form, supposedly so as to enable anyone in the world to repeat the experiment. The "results" section is a dry tabulation of the data produced by the given techniques. Last come the "conclusions," in which the researcher indicates how his data confirm, refute, or extend current theory, and what implications they may hold for future research.

The very nature of the scientific paper is profoundly antihistorical, because the guiding principle of scientific reporting demands that the historian's basic principles—who did what, why, and when—be jettisoned from the start. Because science aspires to be a universal truth, linked to neither time, place, or person, the iron dictates of scientific style demand that all reference to these particulars be omitted. In the name of objectivity, all purpose and motive must be suppressed. In the name of logic, the historical path to understanding must pass unmentioned. The literary framework of a scientific paper, in other words, is a fiction designed to perpetuate a myth.

Scientific textbooks are equally antihistorical, although in a different way. To the extent they refer to the past, they do so only to present it as reflecting the views or concerns of the present. All the false leads, fallible theories, and failed experiments which form so great a part of scientific endeavor are resolutely ignored: the textbooks portray the history of science as a straight line pointing inexorably forward. "From such references," notes the historian Thomas Kuhn, "both students and professionals come to feel like participants in a long-standing historical tradition. Yet the textbook-derived tradition in which scientists come to sense their participation is one that, in fact, never existed.…Partly by selection and partly by distortion, the scientists of earlier ages are implicitly represented as having worked upon the same set of fixed problems and in accordance with the same set of fixed canons that the most recent revolution in scientific theory and method has made seem scientific." The depreciation of historical fact, Kuhn believes, "is deeply, and probably functionally, ingrained in the ideology of the scientific profession."[1]

That ideology is seldom discussed or examined, yet it is all the more potent for being implicit. Most scientists would probably declare if asked that science has no ideology, that science itself is the opposite of ideology. But scientists in fact hold strong and definite views about their profession, about how it should operate, about what is a proper or improper procedure in terms of scientific methodology. These views amount to an ideology, because they are not derived solely from the facts but are shaped by preconceived ideals.

The ideology of the scientific profession has emerged from the writings of three groups of professional observers, the philosophers, historians, and sociologists of science. Each of these three groups has imposed its own professional biases on its descriptions of how science works. All have looked to science to embody the ideals so lacking in the real world. They have read into science the virtues of justice, of fairness, of lack of prejudice, of desire for the truth, of taking a man and his ideas on their merits alone regardless of his prestige or qualifications or status. They have described the scientific scene through spectacles made in Utopia.

Thus philosophers such as the Vienna Circle have explained science as a logical and purely empirical process. Sociologists have posited "norms" of the scientific ethos, contending that science is characterized by "organized skepticism," the acceptance of ideas on their merits, and the disinterested pursuit of truth. Historians, animated by the idea of progress of which scientific knowledge seems so shining an exemplar, have sought to portray scientific history in terms of its success, its great men, and its moral object lessons that show reason triumphing over superstition.

What philosophers, sociologists, and historians have had to say about science has been read and noted by scientists and adopted as the general basis of how they see themselves. The philosophers have said they are objective, so scientists strictly forbid any reference to subjective experience in the scientific literature. The sociologists have said they are disinterested, so scientists disdain any overt manifestation of competition or credit-seeking. The historians have said that science is the defense against unreason, so scientists deny with a passion that human passions have any place whatsoever in their work.

Robert Merton's influential essay describing the principles of the scientific ethos was written in 1942, under the shadow of the Second World War. The Vienna Circle formulated their views of science while Europe was sliding into economic and political chaos. They perhaps saw in science a way of dealing with facts, a rationality, a fairness and justice, that were so conspiciously absent in the real world around them. Here at least was a small enclave of human activity where men could be said to act by the pure light of intellect, not by the dark brutish forces then engulfing humanity.

History, said Edward Gibbon, "is, indeed, little more than the register of the crimes, follies and misfortunes of mankind." With what relief have many historians turned to the history of science, the single arena of human endeavor where it could invariably be reported that right had vanquished wrong, that truth had cast out error, that reason had prevailed over superstition and ignorance.

The high place that science holds in today's world, particularly among the educated, probably owes little to its practical accomplishments. If science is worshiped in Western societies, it is not because of the technological toys or comforts it may produce. It is for the far more fundamental reason that science seems to represent an ideal, a set of values, an ethical example of how human affairs could and should be conducted were reason to be man's guide. In the secular world of the twentieth century, science performs part of the inspirational function that myths and religions play in less developed societies.

It is because of this inspirational role that it is so difficult to see science as it really is. Scientists take it for granted that their way of thinking about the world—the "scientific method"—is different from everyone else's. But does the scientific method really exist? And if it does, do scientists always follow it?

The conventional ideology of science still retains a firm hold on the imaginations of both scientists and the public, but its basis long ago began to crumble among its formulators. The Logical Empiricists, despite the intellectual attraction of their analysis, left themselves vulnerable to criticism because of their deliberate neglect of the psychological and historical context of science. Among the most serious challenges was Thomas Kuhn's brilliant essay of 1962, entitled *The Structure of Scientific Revolutions.*[2] Though written by a historian of science, the book has had a profound influence on the philosophy of science because by looking at science as a changing, not a static, process it uncovered important general insights hitherto neglected by the philosophers.

Kuhn wastes little time on demolishing the Logical Empiricist view of science as an objective progression toward the truth. Instead he erects from ground up a structure in which science is seen to be heavily influenced by nonrational procedures, and in which new theories are viewed as being more complex than those they replace but not as standing any closer to the truth. "Objectivity and progress, the pride of traditional interpretations of science, have both been abandoned," was one critic's dismayed verdict.

Science, in Kuhn's view, is not the steady, cumulative acquisition of knowledge that is portrayed in the textbooks. Rather, it is a series of peaceful interludes punctuated by intellectually violent revolutions. During the interludes, scientists are guided by a set of theories, standards, and methods which Kuhn refers to as a "paradigm."

The paradigm is the basis of the research tradition. It defines which problems are interesting and which are irrelevant. During the paradigm-governed interludes, called periods of "normal science" by Kuhn, scientists essentially solve puzzles generated by the new paradigm. Study of mechanics after Newton's *Principia* is one example of a period of normal science; astronomy after Copernicus is another.

Nature is too complex to be explored at random; the paradigm is an exploration plan which both points to puzzles and guarantees that they are soluble. That is the reason for the rapid progress of the paradigm-based natural sciences compared with those in a pre-paradigm stage, such as the social sciences.

But the tranquillity of normal science does not last. Sooner or later, scientists trying to extend the paradigm find that there are puzzles they cannot solve. Often such anomalies were there from the outset but could be ignored during the heady process of paradigm explication. In fact, during normal science, scientists try to suppress novelties. Yet against the background of the paradigm the anomalies stand out with increasing prominence. The time comes when they can be ignored no longer. Then the field enters into crisis, such as befell earth-centered astronomy before Copernicus, or the phlogiston theory of burning before the understanding of oxygen.

During crises, scientists turn from puzzle-solving to worried discussion of fundamentals. A new paradigm may be proposed, its underlying discoveries almost always being made, Kuhn states, by men who are "either very young or very new to the field whose paradigm they change." But defenders of the old paradigm patch it up with ad hoc fixes, and battle is joined as the supporters of each paradigm compete for the allegiance of the community.

The means by which this battle is waged is of central importance: in Kuhn's view, nonrational factors play an essential role in the contest. Logic and experiment, says Kuhn, are not sufficient: "The competition between paradigms is not the sort of battle that can be resolved by proofs." In fact, a scientist's transfer of allegiance from one paradigm to another "is a conversion experience that cannot be forced." The grounds for conversion may include arguments that appeal to the individual's sense of the appropriate or the aesthetic, as well as faith that the new paradigm will be better able to resolve the anomalies that precipitated the crisis.

Why is logic alone not enough to resolve the competition between two paradigms? Because paradigms are logically incommensurable. Two paradigms may seem to use the same words and concepts, but in fact these elements are logically different. Mass, for example, is conserved in Newtonian physics but is convertible with energy in Einsteinian physics. Earth in pre-Copernican theory denoted a point of fixity. Proponents of rival paradigms are not speaking exactly the same language; they are bound to talk past each other because their terms of reference are not comparable.

The incommensurability of competing paradigms has another important consequence in the Kuhnian thesis. A new paradigm cannot build on the one it succeeds; it can only supplant it. Science is not the cumulative process portrayed in the textbooks; it is a succession of revolutions, in each of which one conceptual world view is replaced by another. But Kuhn sees no ground for believing that the new paradigm gives a *better* understanding of the world than did the old. The idea of progress in science can be conceded only in the relative sense that new paradigms can be recognized as being more evolved or more complex than those they replace. We may, says Kuhn, "have to relinquish the notion, explicit or implicit, that changes of paradigm carry scientists and those who learn from them closer and closer to the truth."

Kuhn did not deny the importance of logic and experiment in science; but he argued compellingly that nonrational factors are also important, and that scientific belief, particularly when in the traumatic conversion from one paradigm to another, has certain elements in common with religious belief.

An even more radical critic of Logical Empiricism is the Vienna-born philosopher Paul Feyerabend of the University of California, Berkeley. Feyerabend not only admits nonrational elements into the scientific process but sees them as dominant. Science, he says, is an ideology, completely shaped at any moment in time by its historical and cultural context. Scientific disputes are resolved not on their merits but by the theatrical and oratorical skills of their advocates, much as are legal cases. There is no one scientific method, good for all times and places; in fact, there is no such thing as scientific method. Despite scientists' claims, the rule in science is that "anything goes."

Since there is no one scientific method, success in science depends not only on rational argument but on a mixture of subterfuge, rhetoric, and propaganda, Feyerabend holds. He believes that the distinction commonly made between science and other modes of thought is unjustified, an artificial barrier erected by scientists to set them above their fellow citizens. "Those who do not like to see the state meddling in scientific matters should remember the sizeable chauvinism of science: for most scientists the slogan 'freedom for science' means the freedom to indoctrinate not only those who have joined them, but the rest of society as well....Combining this observation with the insight that science has no special method, we arrive at the result that the separation of science and non-science is not only artificial but also detrimental to the advancement of knowledge," states Feyerabend in his book *Against Method*.[3]

Is the scientific method merely an abstraction of philosophers? Do scientists deceive themselves in supposing logic alone to be their guide? Do rhetoric and propaganda play just as large a role in science as they do in politics, law, and religion? An interesting light on the problem comes from consideration of a quite regular phenomenon, the resistance of scientists to new ideas.

If science is a rational process, with logic its light and factual evidence its only guide, then scientists should quickly embrace new ideas and abandon old ones as soon as the evidence for the better idea has become reasonably convincing. But in fact scientists often cling to old ideas for long after they have been discredited. "The mere suggestion that scientists themselves sometimes resist scientific discovery clashes, of course, with the stereotype of the scientist as 'the open-minded man,' " notes sociologist Bernard Barber.[4] But history is replete with instances where open-mindedness and objectivity have failed. Tycho Brahe, the greatest observational astronomer of his time, resisted the theory of Copernicus to his dying day, and encouraged many other astronomers to do likewise. In the nineteenth century, Thomas Young's wave theory of light, Pasteur's discovery of the biological nature of fermentation, and Mendel's theory of genetics all met with dismissal or resistance from the professional scientists of the specialties concerned.

For any who might suppose that the twentieth century is immune to such foibles, consider the concept of continental drift, proposed by the German meteorologist Alfred Wegener in 1922. With one glance at the globe, a child can see the intuitive plausibility of Wegener's theory by noting how snugly the shoulder of South America tucks into the armpit of Africa. But it took geologists and geophysicists almost forty years, from 1922 to about 1960, to accept that the continents are in motion. Sometimes the excuse is offered that geologists knew of no mechanism by which the continents could be moved, but this is not so; a well-known article written by geologist Arthur Holmes in 1928 correctly advocated convection currents as the force that moves the continents.

It was the leaders of their profession, Harold Jeffreys in England and Maurice Ewing in the United States, who spearheaded the opposition. When in the 1960's geologists finally conceded that the earth's continents had moved, it was because the dating of the sediments on the sea floor provided incontrovertible evidence of the sort that compelled even the blind to see.

The reasons for scientists' resistance to new ideas are quite varied, and they have much in common with the reasons for which people in general resist giving up ideas they rely on or have grown comfortable with. Because of their own religious beliefs, scientists in the nineteenth century resisted both Darwin's theory of evolution and the findings of geologists that pointed to the great age of the earth.

The old commonly resist the young, and it is no different in science. "That academies and learned societies—commonly dominated by the older foofoos of any profession—are slow to react to new ideas is in the nature of things. For, as Bacon says, *scientia inflat*, and the dignitaries who hold high honors for past accomplishments do not usually like to see the current of progress rush too rapidly out of their reach," remarks biologist Hans Zinsser.[5] The same thought was expressed even more forcefully by the German physicist Max Planck, the originator of quantum theory, who in a famous passage proclaimed that old ideas in science die only with those who hold them: "An important scientific innovation rarely makes its way by gradually winning over and converting its opponents: it rarely happens that Saul becomes Paul. What does happen is that its opponents gradually die out and that the growing generation is familiarized with the idea from the beginning."[6] Evidently the height of intellectual resistance has been reached when death is the persuader: but of all the realms of human thought, why should science provide the example?

Despite the claim of science to be universal, social or professional standing can often influence receptivity to new ideas. If the originator of a revolutionary new concept either has low standing in the elite system of his own discipline or if he comes from outside the discipline, his ideas are particularly likely not to receive serious consideration: they will be judged on his perceived merits, not on their own. But it is just such people—the outsiders and the neophytes, neither of whom have been indoctrinated in the established dogmas of the discipline—who so often contribute the original ideas by which a discipline advances. That is why resistance to new ideas is such a constant theme in the history of science.

George Ohm, the nineteenth-century German who discovered the law of electrical resistance, was a math teacher at the Jesuit Gymnasium in Cologne; his ideas were ignored by scientists at German universities. Mendel's genetic laws were ignored by professionals in his field for thirty-five years, in part because, as an abbé with an experimental plot in his backyard, he seemed to be a mere amateur. The specialists' contempt for the outsider is evident in the geologists' attitude to Wegener, who was a meteorologist by training. The medical profession in particular has a long history of resisting scientific innovations from both without and within. Louis Pasteur met with violent resistance from doctors when he advanced his germ theory of disease; they regarded him as a mere chemist poaching on their scientific preserves. Joseph Lister's discovery of antisepsis was initially ignored in both England and the United States, in part because Lister, a doctor working in Glasgow and Edinburgh, was regarded as a provincial.

Few episodes in the illustrious annals of scientific progress are more striking than that of the nineteenth-century Hungarian physician Ignaz Semmelweis. He discovered that puerperal, or childbed, fever, then causing typically 10 to 30 percent mortality in maternity hospitals throughout Europe, could be virtually abolished by the simple expedient of having doctors wash their hands in a chlorine solution before examining the mother. In his division of the obstetric clinic in Vienna where Semmelweis first tried out his idea, the mortality rate dropped from 18 percent to 1 percent. By 1848 Semmelweis was losing not a single woman to childbed fever. But this experimental evidence failed to convince his superiors at the hospital.

Eighteen forty-eight was the year that a liberal political revolution swept Europe, and Semmelweis took part in the events in Vienna. His political activities only increased the resistance to his ideas. Dismissed from the clinic, he returned to Hungary and from his own obstetrical experience over the next ten years amassed copious evidence that antiseptic technique would prevent death from childbed fever. His findings were summarized in a book, published in 1861, copies of which he sent to medical societies and to the major obstetricians of Germany, France, and England.

The book was almost universally ignored by the medical profession, even though throughout Europe puerperal fever continued to ravage maternity hospitals. In Prague, 4 percent of the mothers and 22.5 percent of the babies died in 1861. In Stockholm in 1860, 40 percent of all women patients caught the fever and 16 percent died. In the General Hospital in Vienna, in the same ward where Semmelweis had shown twelve years earlier how the disease could be eradicated, 35 out of 101 patients died in the autumn of 1860.

Why did physicians and medical researchers ignore Semmelweis' theory? Even if they disagreed with the theory, why did they ignore his copious and undisputed statistics? Perhaps they found it hard to cope with the consequences of an idea which meant that each, with his own unwashed hands, had unwittingly sent many patients to their deaths. Then too, Semmelweis was not always as tactful as he could have been in trying to win acceptance for his ideas. His rhetoric was too strident. His propaganda was not sufficiently smooth and persuasive. Few facts could speak with greater emphasis and clarity than his did, but the facts were in no way sufficient to persuade physicians and medical researchers throughout Europe that their hands were spreaders of disease.

In the knowledge that many women were dying unnecessarily, and that no one would listen to his simple principles for preventing death, Semmelweis started cranking out somewhat hysterical letters. In an open letter of 1862 to professors of obstetrics, Semmelweis wrote: "If the Professors of Obstetrics do not soon comply by instructing their students in my doctrine...then will I myself say to the helpless public, 'You, father of a family, do you know what it is to summon an obstetrician or a midwife to your wife?...It is as much as to expose your wife and your yet unborn child to the danger of death. And if you do not wish to become a widower and if you do not wish that your still unborn child be inoculated with the germ of death, and if your children are not to lose their mother, then buy a single kreutzer's worth of chloride of lime, infuse it in some water, and do not allow the obstetrician and the midwife to examine your wife until they have washed their hands in the chlorine solution in your presence, and also do not permit the obstetrician and the midwife to make an internal examination until you have convinced yourself by touching their hands that the obstetrician and midwife have washed so long that their hands have become slippery.' "[7]

Semmelweis' mind began to wander. Some days he scarcely spoke at all; on others he would embarrass his colleagues by bursting out in a violent harangue. In 1865 he was induced by friends to visit a mental sanatorium. While the friends slipped out, he was forcibly restrained, confined to a straitjacket, and put in a dark room. He died two weeks later, on August 13, 1865. It was just one day earlier that Lister, whom Semmelweis had anticipated by a full fifteen years, first began to test the use of carbolic acid as an antiseptic agent. Once Lister had won his battle, and Pasteur had persuaded the medical profession that germs did really exist, then, some thirty years later than necessary, the doctors understood the *theory* by which they could make sense of the *facts* that said for them to wash their hands before undertaking obstetric examinations.

"But on principle it is quite wrong to try founding a theory on observ able magnitudes alone. In reality the very opposite happens. It is the theory which decides what we can observe." So wrote Einstein to Werner Heisenberg, a year before Heisenberg formulated his indeterminacy principle in 1927. "It is the theory which decides what we can observe"—that is the exact reverse of the test-theory-by-facts methodology by which the philosophers say science always proceeds. Einstein's observation emphasizes that for scientists, just as for others, it is ideas and theories that are important. Ideas explain facts, theories make sense of the world. A fact by itself is trivial; it is interesting only if it sheds light on some underlying principle or theory. On psychological grounds alone, it is not surprising that scientists should often continue to believe in a theory, even when it is contradicted by experimental fact.

Sometimes the belief in theory over fact proves erroneous; sometimes it is well founded, because the contradictions turn out to be apparent, not real. When the American Physical Society heard in 1925 from its president, D.C. Miller, that he had discovered evidence that contradicted the Special Theory of Relativity (a "positive effect" in the Michelson-Morley experiment), the audience should instantly have abandoned the theory or at least assigned it to provisional status. "But no," comments physicist Michael Polanyi, "by that time they had so well closed their minds to any suggestion which threatened the new rationality achieved by Einstein's world picture, that it was almost impossible for them to think again in different terms. Little attention was paid to the experiments, the evidence being set aside in the hope that it would one day turn out to be wrong."[8] True, Miller's work is now thought to have been flawed by subtle experimental effects, but for scientists simply to presume that awkward results will turn out to be incorrect is a mere act of faith.

Verification of a theory, Polanyi points out, in fact requires the same kind of intuition about nature as did the devising of the theory in the first place. Intuition, a nonrational factor, does not enter into the philosopher's accounts. When discussing the verification of scientific laws, the philosophers always choose as examples laws about which there is not any doubt. "They are describing the practical demonstration of scientific law, and not its critical verification. As a result we are given an account of the scientific method which, having left out the process of discovery on the grounds that it follows no definite method, overlooks the process of verification as well, by referring only to examples in which no real verification takes place."

The first historians of science tended to see their subject matter in much the same light as did the philosophers and scientists themselves — as a straight-line, objective progression toward the truth. More recently, historians have begun to doubt that scientists always behave in the strictly objective manner prescribed by the hypothetico-deductive system of the philosophers. Some historians of science, writes Stephen G. Brush, "have been moving toward another conception of their role, based on the notion that scientists often operate in a subjective way and that experimental verification is of secondary importance compared to philosophical arguments, at least in some of the major conceptual changes that have occurred in science."[9]

Brush's own conversion to this view stemmed from his analysis of three topics in nineteenth-century physics — the wave theory of heat, the kinetic theory of gases, and interatomic forces — where theoretical considerations were given primacy by scientists over direct experimental facts that contradicted them. "While these decisions were made in the first instance by individual scientists, their colleagues did not protest the irrationality of the decisions but simply followed the leader; hence these cases provide legitimate evidence for the behavior of the scientific community," notes Brush. On the basis of the examples he has studied, Brush concludes that "improper behavior is not peculiar to a handful of great scientists but is characteristic of a much larger group. Indeed, the burden of proof would seem to be on anyone who claims that a majority of scientists habitually use the hypothetico-deductive method in the strict sense (that is, rejecting a theory if it fails to agree with all experimental facts)."

The human mind has a well-known capacity for retaining political or religious beliefs well beyond the point at which reason suggests they should be modified or abandoned. The claim of science is that it differs fundamentally from other belief systems in that it rests demonstrably upon reason alone. But the claim must be modified in light of what historians have to say about scientists' resistance to scientific ideas and their penchant for seeing the world through the prism of their own theories.

The fact is that the way in which science actually works, the process by which the existing stock of scientific knowledge is extended or restructured, is not by any means an entirely rational process. A logical structure can be discerned, post facto, in the substance of received scientific knowledge. The existence of a logical structure in scientific knowledge has led to the assumption that the structure was logically built. But the process of doing science, as distinct from the body of scientific knowledge, is created and governed by a different set of principles. Logical inference and the intent of being objective are important among them. But rhetoric, propaganda, appeal to authority, and all the usual arts of human persuasion are also influential in winning acceptance for a scientific theory.

Even the apparently logical mechanisms to which the philosophers have devoted so much attention, such as verification and replication, are in practice subject to nonrational decisions. Verification, the critical feature of science, which in the Logical Empiricists' view raised it above all other forms of knowledge, is dominated by scientists' expectations, and the strength of their belief in the theory under test, as much as by the facts. Replication is not a normal scientific procedure; it is undertaken only in special circumstances, such as with results of unusual importance or when fraud is suspected on other grounds.

To say that the process of science includes nonrational elements is not to say that rationality is absent. Science is both logical and illogical, rational and irrational, open-minded and dogmatic. The exact proportions of each ingredient vary from one discipline to another, depending on time, cause, and place. The degree of nonrational elements in scientific thinking is doubtless less than in other belief systems, but perhaps not significantly less. The burden of proof must lie on those who make special claims for science and scientists.

Some of the nonrational elements that govern the scientific process, such as intuition, imagination, or attachment to particular theories, are ones that most working scientists readily acknowledge. But others, such as rhetoric and propaganda, are denied any official role in science by scientific ideology, despite the fact they can play major, sometimes decisive, roles in the acceptance or rejection of hypotheses. Precisely because scientists believe themselves immune to these forms of argument, they are the more susceptible.

It is only when the existence of nonrational elements in science is conceded that the phenomenon of scientific fraud can be understood. Conversely, the study of fraud sheds light on how the nonrational elements operate in the scientific process. Fraud gains entry into science along with the nonrational elements, and is often successful because the same elements work in its favor.

Acceptance of fraud is the other side of that familiar coin, resistance to new ideas. Fraudulent results are likely to be accepted in science if they are plausibly presented, if they conform with prevailing prejudices or expectations, and if they come from a suitably qualified scientist affiliated with an elite institution. It is for the lack of all these qualities that radical new ideas in science are likely to be resisted.

Only on the assumption that logic and objectivity are the sole gatekeepers of science is the prevalence and frequent success of fraud in any way surprising. Only on the assumption that replication is the inexorable test to which all results are submitted is the persistence of fraud difficult to understand. Like sin among the faithful, fraud should not exist, let alone thrive, within the community of science. That it does is because practice differs from ideology.

For the ideologists of science, fraud is taboo, a scandal whose significance must be ritually denied on every occasion. For those who see science as a human endeavor to make sense of the world, fraud is merely evidence that science flies on the wings of rhetoric as well as reason.

## Notes

[1]Thomas S. Kuhn, *The Structure of Scientific Revolutions*, 2nd ed. (University of Chicago Press, 1970).

[2]*Ibid.* Parts of this account of Kuhn's work are taken from Nicholas Wade, "Thomas S. Kuhn: Revolutionary Theorist of Science," *Science*, 197, 143-45, © 1977, American Association for the Advancement of Science.

[3]Paul Feyerabend, *Against Method* (Verso, London, 1975; distributed in U.S. by Schocken Books, New York).

[4]Bernard Barber, "Resistance by Scientists to Scientific Discovery," *Science*, 134, 596-602, 1961.

[5]Quoted in Barber, *ibid.*

[6]Max Planck, *The Philosophy of Physics* (George Allen & Unwin, London, 1936), p. 90.

[7]Frank G. Slaughter, *Immortal Magyar* (Collier, New York, 1950).

[8]Michael Polanyi, *Personal Knowledge* (University of Chicago Press, 1958), p. 13.

[9]Stephen G. Brush, "Should the History of Science Be Rated X?" *Science*, 183, 1164-1172, 1974.

# What Psychiatry Can and Cannot Do

## Thomas S. Szasz

Psychiatry today is in the curious position of being viewed simultaneously with too much reverence and with undue contempt. Indeed, thoughtful Americans can be roughly divided between those who dismiss all forms of psychiatric practice as worthless or harmful, and those who regard it as a panacea for crime, unhappiness, political fanaticism, promiscuity, juvenile delinquency, and virtually every other moral, personal, and social ill of our time.

The adherents of this exaggerated faith are, I believe, the larger and certainly the more influential group in shaping contemporary social policy. It is they who beat the drums for large-scale mental health programs and who use the prestige of a massive psychiatric establishment as a shield of illusion, concealing some ugly realities we would rather not face. Thus when we read in the paper that the alcoholic, the rapist, or the vandal needs or will be given "psychiatric care," we are reassured that the problem is being solved or, in any event, effectively dealt with, and we dismiss it from our minds.

I contend that we have no right to this easy absolution from responsibility. In saying this I do not, as a practicing psychiatrist, intend to belittle the help that my profession can give to some troubled individuals. We have made significant progress since the pre-Freudian era, when psychiatry was a purely custodial enterprise.

"What Psychiatry Can and Cannot Do," copyright © 1964 by Harper's Magazine, Inc. from *Ideology and Insanity* by Thomas Szasz. Reprinted by permission of Doubleday & Company Inc.

However, our refusal to recognize the differences between medicine and psychiatry—that is, between deviations from biological norms, which we usually call "illness," and deviations from psychological or social norms, which we often call "mental illness"—has made it possible to popularize the simplistic clichés of current mental health propaganda. One of these, for instance, is the deceptive slogan "Mental illness is like any other illness." This is not true; psychiatric and medical problems are fundamentally dissimilar. In curing a disease like syphilis or pneumonia, the physician benefits both the patient and society. Can the psychiatrist who cures a "neurosis" make the same claim? Often he cannot, for in "mental illness" we find the individual in conflict with those about him—his family, his friends, his employer, perhaps his whole society. Do we expect psychiatry to help the individual—or society? If the interests of the two conflict, as they often do, the psychiatrist can help one only by harming the other.

## II

Let us, for example, examine the case of a man I will call Victor Clauson. He is a junior executive with a promising future, a wife who loves him, and two healthy children. Nevertheless he is anxious and unhappy. He is bored with his job, which he believes saps his initiative and destroys his integrity; he is also dissatisfied with his wife, and convinced he never loved her. Feeling like a slave to his company, his wife, and his children, Clauson realizes that he has lost control over the conduct of his life.

Is this man "sick"? And, if so, what can be done about it? At least half a dozen alternatives are open to him: He could throw himself into his present work or change jobs or have an affair or get a divorce. Or he could develop a psychosomatic symptom such as headaches and consult a doctor. Or he could seek help from a psychotherapist. Which of these alternatives is the right one for him? The answer is not easy.

For, in fact, hard work, an affair, a divorce, a new job may all "help" him; and so may psychotherapy. But "treatment" cannot change his external, social situation; only he can do that. What psychoanalysis (and some other therapies) can offer him is a better knowledge of himself, which may enable him to make new and better choices in the conduct of his life.

Is Clauson "mentally sick"? If we so label him, what then is he to be cured of? Unhappiness? Indecision? The consequences of earlier, unwise decisions?

In my opinion, these are problems in living, not diseases. And by and large it is such problems that are brought to the psychiatrist's office. To ameliorate them he offers not treatment or cure but psychological counseling. To be of any avail, this process requires a consenting, co-operative client. There is, indeed, no way to "help" an individual who does not want to be a psychiatric patient. When treatment is imposed on a person, inevitably he sees it as serving not his own best interests, but the interests of those who brought him to the psychiatrist (and who often pay him).

Take the case of an elderly widow I will call Mrs. Rachel Abelson. Her husband was a successful businessman who died five years ago, bequeathing part of his estate of four million dollars to his children and grandchildren, part to charities, and one third to his wife. Mrs. Abelson has always been a frugal woman, whose life revolved around her husband. After he died, however, she changed. She began to give her money away —to her widowed sister, to charities, and finally to distant relatives abroad.

After a few years, Mrs. Abelson's children remonstrated, urging her to treat herself better, instead of wasting her money on people who had long managed by themselves. But Mrs. Abelson persisted in doing what she felt was "the right thing." Her children were wealthy; she enjoyed helping others.

Finally, the Abelson children consulted the family attorney. He was equally dismayed by the prospect that Mrs. Abelson might in this fashion dissipate all the funds she controlled. Like the children, he reasoned that if Mr. Abelson had wanted to help his third cousin's poverty-stricken daughters in Rumania, he could have done so himself; but he never did. Convinced that they ought to carry out the essence of their father's intention and keep the money in the family, the Abelson children petitioned to have their mother declared mentally incompetent to manage her affairs. This was done. Thereafter Mrs. Abelson became inconsolable. Her bitter accusations and the painful scenes that resulted only convinced her children that she really was mentally abnormal. When she refused to enter a private sanitarium voluntarily, she was committed by court order. She died two years later, and her will—leaving most of her assets to distant relatives— was easily broken on psychiatric grounds.

Like thousands of other involuntary mental patients, Mrs. Abelson was given psychiatric care in the hope of changing behavior offensive to others. Indeed, what was Mrs. Abelson's illness? Spending her money unwisely? Disinheriting her sons? In effect, recourse to psychiatry provided Mrs. Abelson's children with a socially acceptable solution for their dilemma, not hers. To an appalling degree, state mental hospitals perform a like function for the less affluent members of our society.

Out of all too many comparable cases, I will cite that of a man we may call Tim Kelleher, who worked steadily as a truck driver for forty years, supporting a wife and nine children. In his early sixties Kelleher found jobs getting scarcer. Now in his late seventies, he has not worked for over a decade. Since his wife died a few years ago, he has lived with one or another of his children.

For two years his daughter Kathleen, mother of four, has been caring for him. Because the old man has grown progressively senile and burdensome, Kathleen's husband wants to shift the responsibility to the other children, but they all feel they've done their share.

Mr. Kelleher's future depends on what his family decides to do with him. One of them may still be willing to take care of him, but, if not, he will be committed to a state mental hospital. His case will be diagnosed as a "senile psychosis" or something similar. More than a third of the patients now in our mental hospitals are such "geriatric" cases. This is how psychiatry meets a purely socioeconomic need.

If Mr. Kelleher or one of his children were even moderately wealthy, they could hire a companion or nurse to care for him at home, or they could place him in a private nursing home. There would be no need to label him a "mental patient" and confine him to a building he will never again leave, and where he will doubtless die within a year.

But, for the poor, the mental hospital is often the only way. Such is the plight of Mrs. Anna Tarranti (this is not her real name). At thirty-two—but looking ten years older—she has just been delivered of her seventh child. Her husband is a construction worker, sporadically employed, and a heavy drinker. After each of the last three babies was born, Mrs. Tarranti was so "depressed" that she had to stay in the hospital an extra week or more. Now she complains of exhaustion, cannot eat or sleep, and does not want to see her baby. At the same time she feels guilty for not being a good mother, and says she ought to die.

The fact is that Mrs. Tarranti is overwhelmed. She has more children than she wants, a husband who earns only a marginal living, and religious beliefs that virtually prohibit birth control. What should she do? She knows that if she goes home, she'll soon be pregnant again, a prospect she cannot endure. She would like to stay in the hospital, but the obstetrical ward is too busy to keep her long without a bona fide obstetrical illness.

Again psychiatry comes to the rescue. Mrs. Tarranti's condition is diagnosed as a "post-partum depression" and she is committed to the state hospital. As in the case of Mr. Kelleher, society has found no more decent solution to a human problem than confinement in a mental hospital.

In effect, psychiatry has accepted the job of warehousing society's undesirables. Such, alas, has long been its role. More than a hundred and fifty years ago, the great French psychiatrist Philippe Pinel observed, "Public asylums for maniacs have been regarded as places of confinement for such of its members as have become dangerous to the peace of society."[1]

---

[1]   Pinel, P.: *A Treatise on Insanity* (1801, 1809), transl. by D. D. Davis, facsimile of the London 1806 edition (New York: Hafner Publishing Co., 1962), pp. 3-4.

## III

Nor have we any right to comfort ourselves with the belief that in our enlightened age confinement in a mental institution is really the same as any other kind of hospitalization. For even though we show more compassion and understanding toward the insane than some of our forebears, the fact is that the person diagnosed as mentally ill is stigmatized—particularly if he has been confined in a public mental hospital. These stigmata cannot be removed by mental health "education," for the root of the matter is our intolerance of certain kinds of behavior.

Most people who are considered mentally sick (especially those confined involuntarily) are so defined by their relatives, friends, employers, or perhaps the police—not by themselves. These people have upset the social order—by disregarding the conventions of polite society or by violating laws—so we label them "mentally ill" and punish them by commitment to a mental institution.

The patient knows that he is deprived of freedom because he has annoyed others, not because he is sick. And in the mental hospital he learns that until he alters his behavior he will be segregated from society. But even if he changes and is permitted to leave, his record of confinement goes with him. And the practical consequences are more those of a prison than a hospital record. The psychological and social damage thus incurred often far outweighs the benefits of any psychiatric therapy.

Consider, for example, the case of a young nurse I will call Emily Silverman, who works in a general hospital in a small city. Unmarried and lonely, she worries about the future. Will she find a husband? Will she have to go on supporting herself in a job that has become drudgery? She feels depressed, sleeps poorly, loses weight. Finally, she consults an internist at the hospital and is referred to a psychiatrist. He diagnoses her trouble as a case of "depression" and prescribes "anti-depressant" drugs. Emily takes the pills and visits the psychiatrist weekly, but she remains depressed and begins to think about suicide. This alarms the psychiatrist, who recommends hospitalization. Since there is no private mental hospital in the city, Emily seeks admission to the state hospital nearby. There, after a few months, she realizes that the "treatment" the hospital offers cannot help solve her problems. She then "recovers" and is discharged.

From now on, Emily is no longer just a nurse; she is a nurse with a "record" of confinement in a state mental hospital. When she tries to return to her job, she will probably find it filled and that there are no openings. Indeed, as an ex-mental patient, she may find it impossible to obtain any employment in nursing. This is a heavy price to pay for ignorance, yet no one warned her of the hazards involved before she decided to enter the hospital for her "depression."

Because the therapeutic potentialities of psychiatry are consistently exaggerated and its punitive functions minimized or even denied, a distorted relationship between psychiatry and the law has evolved in our time.

Years ago some people accused of serious crimes pleaded "insanity." Today they are often charged with it. Instead of receiving a brief jail sentence, a defendant may be branded "insane" and incarcerated for life in a psychiatric institution.[2]

This is what happened, for example, to a filling-station operator I will call Joe Skulski. When he was told to move his business to make way for a new shopping center, he stubbornly resisted eviction. Finally the police were summoned. Joe greeted them with a warning shot in the air. He was taken into custody and denied bail, because the police considered his protest peculiar and thought he must be crazy. The district attorney requested a pretrial psychiatric examination of the accused. Mr. Skulski was examined, pronounced mentally unfit to stand trial, and confined in the state hospital for the criminally insane. Through it all, he pleaded for the right to be tried for his offense. Now in the mental hospital, he will spend years of fruitless effort to prove that he is sane enough to stand trial. If he had been convicted, his prison sentence would have been shorter than the term he has already served in the hospital.

## IV

This is not to say that our public mental hospitals serve no socially useful purpose. They do, in fact, perform two essential—and very different—functions. On the one hand, they help patients recover from personal difficulties by providing them with room, board, and a medically approved escape from everyday responsibilities. On the other hand, they help families, and society, care for those who annoy or burden them unduly. It is important that we sort out these very different services, for unfortunately their goals are not the same. To relieve people annoyed by the eccentricities, failings, or outright meanness of so-called mentally disturbed persons requires that something be done *to* mental patients, not *for* them. The aim here is to safeguard the sensibilities not of the patient, but of those he upsets. This is a moral and social, not a medical, problem. How, for example, do you weigh the right of Mr. Kelleher to spend his declining years in freedom and dignity rather than as a psychiatric prisoner, against the right of his children to lead a "life of their own" unburdened by a senile father? Or the right of Mrs. Tarranti to repudiate overwhelming responsibilities, against her husband's and children's need for the services of a full-time

2Szasz, T.S.: *Psychiatric Justice* (New York: Macmillan, 1965).

wife and mother? Or the right of Mrs. Abelson to give away her money to poor relatives, against her children's claim on their father's fortune?

Granting that there can often be no happy resolution to such conflicts, there is no reason to feel that we are as yet on the right road. For one thing, we still tolerate appalling inequities between our treatment of the rich and the poor. Though it may be no more than a dimly grasped ideal, both medicine and law strive to treat all people equally. In psychiatry, however, we not only fail to approximate this goal in our practice; we do not even value it as an ideal.

We regard the rich and influential psychiatric patient as a self-governing, responsible client—free to decide whether or not to be a patient. But we look upon the poor and the aged patient as a ward of the state—too ignorant or too "mentally sick" to know what is best for him. The paternalistic psychiatrist, as an agent of the family or the state, assumes "responsibility" for him, defines him as a "patient" against his will, and subjects him to "treatment" deemed best for him, with or without his consent.

Do we really need more of this kind of psychiatry?

# Terms and Topics

## TERMS

1. ***Vocabulary, Section III:*** aberrations, absolution, affluent, ameliorate, amenity, anathema, arcane, atavistic, banal, bolstered, cacophony, cajoled, capriciously, compendium, cryptic, debasing, derogatory, dichotomy, diffidently, disdain, emasculate, euphemism, exuberant, frugal, imbued, imminent, immutable, incarnation, incidence, incipient, incontrovertible, incurred, insuperable, irate, irrefutable, jeopardy, laudatory, lugubriously, metamorphosis, modicum, obeisance, obfuscation, obstreperous, paltry, panacea, pedagogical, penchant, perdition, pernicious, philological, pragmatic, precocious, ramparts, ranting, recalcitrant, repudiate, retrospect, ruminated, salutary, semantic, simper, simplistic, sporadically, stereotypes, stigmatized, stylized, succinctly, transcendent, trauma, unconscionable, utilitarian, vaunted, vehemently, virility, vogues, welter, wonky.

2. All kinds of writing use ***rhetorical devices***, though argument probably makes the greatest use of them. Prominent among them is the ***rhetorical question*** (see Terms, section I), whereby a speaker or writer implicitly invites readers to strengthen an argument by themselves supplying a supposedly obvious answer. ***Parallelism*** (see Terms, section II) could be thought of as another. ***Chiasmus*** is used in "A Note to the Reader." A similar device is ***antithesis***, a balanced structure whose two halves contrast, sometimes in parallel form and sometimes in the reverse order of chiasmus.

3. ***Metaphor*** and ***simile*** are defined in "A Note to the Reader," along with other terms. Are ***symbols*** and ***allusions*** also kinds of ***figurative language*** or ***figurative thought***? Differentiate between *figurative language* and *rhetorical devices*. For example, is ***paradox*** (see Terms,

277

section I) a figure of speech (or thought) or a rhetorical device, a figure of rhetoric? Is it, perhaps, a kind of *irony* (see Terms, section II)? Or can it be thought of as in a way all three?

4. *Analogy*　Reasoning from certain similarities between two things that they are alike in one or more other respects as well. For example, if one begins by assuming that a country is like a business in certain ways, one could then conclude, by analogy, that the qualities of a good business manager are the qualities needed in the leader of a country. Not all analogies are logically sound. Is this one?

5. *Denotation* and *connotation* are terms that it is important to understand and to keep in mind when deciding what words to use. *Denotation* is the literal, straightforward meaning of a word; *connotation* is what a word suggests or implies, sometimes by association of ideas or even of sound. For example, the words *fat, roly-poly, overweight, obese, chunky, heavy,* and *portly* all denote pretty much the same thing — but their connotations are quite different. Which do you think are negative? positive? neutral? What does *embonpoint* mean? What does it connote?

6. *Parody*　Imitation of a writer's style or of a specific work, either by exaggeration of style or by straightforward imitation of style with the subject altered — often to ridicule the original.

7. *Axiom*　A self-evident truth or established principle. How does an axiom differ from an *assumption* or a *presumption*? Distinguish between a *hypothesis* and a *theory*. Is there any place for *conjecture* in argumentative writing?

8. Distinguish between *journalism* and *journal*. What are the features of journalistic writing that make some people object to it? What are its advantages?

9. *Innuendo*　A usually derogatory suggestion or hint; an insinuation. Is an innuendo a kind of *allusion* (see "A Note to the Reader"), or not?

## TOPICS: On Individual Essays

PAULINE KAEL　"The Sound of..."

1. Identify these allusions: "the opium of the audience," "the best of all possible worlds." Is the allusion to Pavlov effective?

2. At the end of the review Kael says she is angry. Point out all you can find that makes her anger apparent throughout, long before she states it explicitly.

3. Is Kael guilty of using slanted or loaded diction in this review? Consider such forceful words as *cynical, purveyors, loathe, self-indulgent, imbeciles, shoddy, cant, sentimental.* Or does it depend on the

reader—that is, is she preaching to the converted? (The review appeared originally in *The New Yorker*.) What should a review do? Whom is it written for? Why might Kael's review appeal to or alienate particular kinds of readers? Do you think it could persuade someone who initially disagreed?

4. Using the appropriate indexes and other aids in your library, look up others' reviews of these films. Do any differ substantially from Kael in their assessments? If so, what are their reasons? Are you convinced that these two movies are bad, and do you therefore not want to see them? Or, if you have already seen one or both, do you agree with Kael's assessment? If you don't, compose a counter-argument.

5. Write a two- or three-page review of one or two movies or television programs you have seen recently and that you feel are bad for other than obvious or technical reasons—that is, not because of poor acting, script, direction, or photography, but because of their implicit assumptions or projected values. Try to convince your readers, not that they won't be entertained, but that they shouldn't foster, condone, or submit themselves to such programs or movies.

### FLANNERY O'CONNOR "Total Effect and the Eighth Grade"

1. Compose a sentence or two using *effect* as a verb.

2. From your own experience of reading fiction, both in and out of school, do you agree with O'Connor's assertions? Do you agree that a high-school student's taste, since it is in the process of being formed, should not be consulted? If so, at what point, if ever, should a student's taste be consulted?

3. In paragraph 6, is O'Connor correct, or fair, in using the word *stupid*? When she refers, near the end, to the high schools' "proper business of preparing foundations," is she *begging the question*—assuming as proved, or given, something that in fact needs to be proved? Who decides what is "proper," and on what grounds? What does "proper" mean? Try to defend her against the charge.

4. Pursue the ramifications of O'Connor's argument. Can you propose an acceptable counter-argument?

5. Write an essay in the form of a letter to a couple of cousins or other relatives two or three years your junior in which you tell them of several books you think they should read, and why you think they should. Would it be more difficult to tell them what you think they should *not* read? Try it.

### VIRGINIA WOOLF "Middlebrow"

1. At what level would you locate your own "brow"? Do you agree with Woolf's various definitions and assertions?

2. In a dictionary of quotations, find the line "The hungry sheep look and are not fed," and read at least the whole passage from which it comes. Does having done this help you understand Woolf's meaning? Can you find any other allusions and quotations in her letter?

3. Find at least half a dozen instances of irony in this piece, and explain how each works. Is Woolf at any point sarcastic, as opposed to merely ironic?

4. Near the end of her third paragraph Woolf says she always sits beside the conductor of an omnibus and tries "to get him to tell me what it is like—being a conductor." Compose a monologue as if spoken to Woolf by MacLennan's street-car conductor, telling her what it is like.

5. If Woolf never sent her letter, why did she write it? Write a letter to a public figure or to a newspaper or magazine protesting some statement or act or article or advertisement that you feel strongly about. Use all the irony you can muster, and allow yourself at least one good burst of outright sarcasm. Consider sending the letter.

**WILLIAM ZINSSER** "Nobody Here but Us Dead Sheep"

1. Note that Zinsser begins his article with three fragmentary or minor sentences. Effective? More such sentences occur farther on. Do the relatively short paragraphs work, or do they make the piece seem too choppy, too journalistic? (It first appeared in *Life* magazine, in a columnar format.)

2. Do the short sentences and paragraphs affect tone? Characterize Zinsser's tone, citing specific passages as examples. Does he seem to you to adopt any kind of mask or *persona*?

3. In a chapter on humour in his book *On Writing Well* (2nd edition [New York: Harper & Row, 1980], p. 159), Zinsser says that the "heightening of some crazy truth—to a level where it will be seen as crazy—is at the heart of what the serious humorist is trying to do." Does that describe what he is doing in this essay? How can one be a "serious humorist"? Is Zinsser serious when he refers to "one more joke"? Is the joke funny? Examine the function of irony in this essay. Is irony necessarily funny?

4. What audience is Zinsser addressing? Do you think his article would be a persuasive argument for one audience and not for another? Explain. In just what way can it be considered an argument at all?

5. Write an argument describing something going on in your vicinity that you think is patently absurd but that is nonetheless officially sanctioned. Try to use some humour and irony the way Zinsser does.

**JAMES THURBER** "The Psychosemanticist Will See You Now, Mr. Thurber"

1. Thurber wrote this essay in 1957: have things improved since then, or have they deteriorated? Cite some evidence to support your answer. Have any of the terms Thurber ridicules become more entrenched, even respectable? Can you think of any other terms besides "security" that have become "paralyzed"?

2. How important is the central medical metaphor that begins with the title and the opening paragraph? Is it carried through to the end? Is the military metaphor in the first paragraph also extended?

3. Thurber's essay is funny, but clearly has a serious point. How important is sarcasm as one of his argumentative weapons? Is he genuinely angry, or just having fun being critical? How can you tell? How would you characterize the tone of this essay?

4. Note Thurber's purposeful manglings of clichés and other familiar phrases. For example, what is the effect of "rears its ugly beat," "maul it over," and "full of sound and fury, dignifying nothing"? Can you find other examples? Would you call Thurber an unregenerate anti-cliché revitalizationist? What evidence is there that when he uses a cliché unchanged, like "cut off in the full flower of" in paragraph 5, he is doing so on purpose?

5. Point out some examples of Thurber's effective use of alliteration and other patterns of sound and rhythm.

6. Analyze the errors in Thurber's made-up ad at the end of the essay.

7. Point out examples of Thurber's using or coining terms that demonstrate the very point he's making, such as "double-jointedisms" and the portmanteau word "carcinomenclature" (see "the Timethod of wordoggle"). In effect Thurber is parodying or burlesquing the linguistic habits he is criticizing. Try that technique yourself: put in a few days or weeks of "purposeful listening…and reading" to see what verbal horrors you can come up with; then in a short essay focus on a few of them and imitate them to the point of ridiculousness.


**ELAINE MORGAN** "The Man-Made Myth"

1. Note how a recognizable argumentative tone and context is evident even in the kinds of terms Morgan uses—for example: *subtle underlying assumptions, distorted, eradicated, manifestly, conclusions, authoritative, homily, mistake, believe, theoretical, buttressed, authenticated, dispute the facts, ignore the facts, interpretation, ambiguous, prejudice, quibble, petulance, deduces, mesmerized, vitiated, specula-*

*tion, theory, rudiments, cursory, nonsense, postulate, doctrine, alleged, quandary, questions, incompatible.* Find some others.

2. As the opening chapter of a book, this piece is obviously not complete in itself; the main arguments and evidence are still to come. But note how deftly Morgan piques the reader's curiosity. Point out some places where she does this.

3. Morgan seems to deal fairly with the opposition, quoting at length from the books by Ardrey and Morris that constitute her principal targets. If you know their books, or even if you know only what Morgan quotes, do you agree, after reading this introductory chapter, that their explanations are on the face of it "ludicrous," logically absurd?

4. In paragraph 8 Morgan says that one "cannot avoid" using the word *man* for the species and that the generic pronoun *he* is "a simple matter of linguistic convenience." Is she correct? Have things changed since 1972? How important is this point as part of her argument?

5. Write an argument attacking some popular or widely distributed book or article that you believe to be illogical, dangerous, or otherwise wrongheaded — for example something about dieting, a piece of self-praise by some government or industry, an editorial on some feature of public policy. Use sound, clear, and hard-hitting logic, but use wit rather than table-pounding anger. And remember that if you call something outrageous or ludicrous, you are obliged to demonstrate that it is so.

## MARY MEIGS   "Pandora Was a Feminist"

1. Look up and read the stories of Eve, Pandora, Bluebeard, and Prometheus. What does *Prometheus* mean? Why doesn't Meigs mention that, as she does for *Epimetheus*? How did God test Job?

2. Are Meigs's curiosity, impatience, and hatred of suspense common traits among other people? More common among women than among men? Do you agree that "Pandora was right to open the box"? Would you, in Pandora's place, have opened the box? Do you have a "box of the secret self"? Are you afraid to open it? Can it be dangerous to know "too much" about oneself? Or do you agree with Meigs that it's best to know everything? How convincing is her argument on this point?

3. Is it fair of Meigs to emphasize that " 'plagues escaped to harass helpless *man*' "? What does the word *man* mean here? What does Meigs mean by referring to the reproduction of the sexes, in the myth of Deucalion and Pyrrha, "by a kind of parthenogenesis" as "another case of patriarchal wish-fulfillment"? Near the end Meigs says that Pandora had "the courage to show everybody what Zeus was up to," whereas earlier she follows the myth and calls it "curiosity." Is she

stretching a point for the sake of her argument, or has she successfully made the transition from one term to the other?

4. Find another classical myth that you can use in an essay to illustrate some truth about modern people. Use it.

**ARTHUR M. SCHLESINGER, JR.   "The Crisis of American Masculinity"**

1. Again note how some of the diction reveals the essay's argumentative nature: *evidence, pushed too far, fashionable answer, juridical, indictment, implication of the argument, spuriously, refutes, supposition, fundamental, plausibly, skepticism, platitudes, rhetoric.* Find other examples of the vocabulary of argument.

2. Look up as many as you need to of the many people—mostly authors—whom Schlesinger names.

3. This essay is dated 1958. Is it dated? In what ways is the story different today—if it is? Is there still a crisis? Is the plight of the individual even more critical now? Is (or was) what Schlesinger says of American men (and women) true also of Canadian men (and women)? Can you point to any significant differences?

4. Explain how *High Noon* can be seen "as an existentialist drama...or as a parable of McCarthyism."

5. Would you agree that "in the last part of the 19th century, women won their battle for equality"? Does Schlesinger agree with that assertion?

6. At the end of paragraph 6 Schlesinger uses the word "obviously"; is what he states there so obvious?

7. Do you think your identity is defined more by one or more groups to which you feel you belong than by yourself as an individual? If so, perhaps you could compose an argument defending that feature of your identity. Or write an essay agreeing with Schlesinger's contentions, using yourself as an illustrative example.

8. Write an essay suggesting other techniques besides art, satire, and politics (how well do you think they have worked?) that might liberate us from a "homogenized society."

**BARBARA TUCHMAN   "Is History a Guide to the Future?"**

1. Tuchman begins by using negative definition, saying what she thinks history is by saying what it is not: it is not sociology, it is not scientific, it is not quantification. Does her characterization of what sociologists do jibe with what you know about sociology? Is sociology a science? In the fourth and fifth paragraphs she points out some of the dangers and weaknesses of classification, or categorization, and of overdependence on machines such as computers. Now, twenty years later, would

you be inclined to try to refute her argument by pointing to the increasing use and usefulness of computers? Do you believe that one *can* quantify behaviour and use the data to predict, reliably? If you do, compose an argument with some examples as evidence to support your position.

2. In paragraph 10 Tuchman acknowledges, with some qualification, that history can teach us lessons. What do you suppose she thought history could have taught Americans about Vietnam? Does hindsight help?

3. When Tuchman says (paragraph 9) that "*too* much confidence *cannot* be placed on the lessons of history," does she really mean that "*too* much confidence *can* be placed on the lessons of history" or that "*not* much confidence can be placed on the lessons of history"? (Our emphasis.) Could such a minor slip be attributable to the piece's being first delivered as a speech, and therefore being somewhat informal?

4. Can you think of any "modern" ideas that *have* come from Asia and Africa?

**PETER JENKINS**   **"It Depends What You Mean by Violence"**

1. If you don't already know about them, use whatever reference books and informants you need to check out the following people and events that Jenkins refers to: the Black Death; the Golden Age; Dixon of Dock Green; Henry Mayhew; Brixton, Toxteth, Watts, and Detroit; Luddites, Captain Swing, the Peterloo massacre; Benjamin Disraeli; James Joyce; Georg Wilhelm Friedrich Hegel; Albert Camus; Thucydides; Jean Genet; Baader and Meinhoff; Jean Paul Sartre; Frantz Fanon; Raymond Aron; the Sorbonne and elsewhere in 1968 (note that Brink also refers to it, and that Arlen's essay in section VI is from that year).

2. This is an essay, but it is also journalism, and therefore arises from and comments on happenings of the day. It appeared in the *Manchester Guardian Weekly* of October 28, 1984. At the beginning Jenkins refers to several current or recent events: (a) Ian MacGregor, the head of Britain's National Coal Board, was set off against Arthur Scargill, the head of the National Union of Mineworkers. A bitter strike had been going on for more than six months over the issue of the government's wanting to shut down "uneconomic" pits. The strike, which finally ended in early March of 1985, after almost a year, had been marked, or marred, by frequent and sometimes bloody clashes between police and picketing miners, resulting in several deaths, hundreds of injuries, and thousands of arrests. Neil Kinnock, leader of the Labour Party, was necessarily sometimes uneasy about the tactics of Scargill and the NUM. (b) The Brighton bombing occurred in the

early hours of Friday, October 12, 1984, when the IRA (Irish Republican Army) exploded a bomb in the Grand Hotel, where Prime Minister Margaret Thatcher and other Conservative Party leaders were meeting. Four people were killed, thirty-two injured. (c) "Greenham women," later in the essay, refers to women who had for months been marching and otherwise protesting at the airfield at Greenham Common, near Newbury, in Berkshire, where American nuclear missiles were being installed.

3. What is the effect of Jenkins's title? Does it undercut any argumentative purpose? Is Jenkins arguing a general subjectivity (anything goes: all moral decisions are purely relative)? Or is he arguing that we should observe a legitimate and important differentiation, or hierarchy — that we should see things in proper perspective?

4. Would you call this essay pessimistic, or optimistic, or is it neither? What is its tone, and how can you determine it?

5. Do you consider Thucydides's view of "human nature" accurate? Does Jenkins?

6. How could violence be "romanticised"? Is a public demonstration "violent"? Is so-called "direct action"? An American presidential candidate once said (1964) that "Extremism in the defense of liberty is no vice." Is "extremism" a cover-word for *violence*? Recently someone said, about the assassination of Indira Gandhi, "That wasn't violence; that was revenge!" Is this merely semantic justification, a form of rationalization? Would Jenkins deny the claim of some that pornography and censorship are forms of violence? Is Brink in his essay calling for action, possibly some kind of intellectual violence? Is brainwashing a form of violence? Does the word "violence" *have* a clear meaning anymore? Look in some dictionaries of quotations to see what people have said about violence over the centuries. Write a report on your findings.

ANDRÉ BRINK   **"The Intellectual and His World"**

1. What is the difference between *practical* and *practicable*? What does *cartesian* mean? Who is Sir Herbert Read? Paul Tillich? Identify the allusions in "can man really live by bread alone?" and "some may be more equal than others." If you know *Hamlet*, you will recognize the particular appropriateness of Brink's allusion in connection with the supposed dichotomy between thought and action. If you don't, read Hamlet's well-known "To be or not to be" soliloquy, for starters.

2. What is the role of thought in the life of a thinking person? Do you consider yourself an intellectual?

3. What kind of audience is Brink talking to? Does that help account both for his subject and for what he does with it?

4. Is it true that "truth is unbearable in a society which is built upon the lie"?

5. Sir Herbert Read was, among other things, a philosophical anarchist. Does it surprise you, then, that he should have been knighted? Why does Brink quote so much from Read, and how and why does he finally separate himself from Read?

6. Write an essay focussing on the weakness of an *either-or, black-white* approach as it is manifested in some issue in your community. Is something being pushed because it is "practical" or denounced because it is "impractical"?

### ROBERT FULFORD "White Lies"

1. Define *racism*. What is "polite racism"? How can one know it's racism if it's completely concealed? How would you characterize the tone of the essay? Do you agree that most if not all of us are "in a sense" racists, that we each have our racial prejudices within us, however much we conceal them? Do you think it would be useful to you to talk or write about them? (Would Meigs argue that it would be?)

2. Did you grow up watching *Sesame Street*? What effects do you think it had on you? What role does or should education play in the matter of racism?

3. Note how at the end of paragraph 8 Fulford brings the discussion back to his central point, racism. Does that mean that what immediately precedes has been a digression?

4. Look up the letters to the editor that followed publication of this editorial in *Saturday Night* in September 1983. How valid are the responses to Fulford? Write either a counter-editorial or one that could follow Fulford's, explaining its ramifications, pushing the same subject further.

### WILLIAM BROAD and NICHOLAS WADE "The Myth of Logic"

1. Which of the following words from the essay would you call part of the vocabulary of argument: *disseminated, conspicuous, suppress, prevalence, hypotheses, inductive, elite, inexorable, vulnerable, implicit, ideology, potent, exemplar, disinterested, profound, cumulative, anomalies, explication, ad hoc, allegiance, incommensurable, chauvinism, detrimental, replete, advocated, neophytes, copious, strident, hysterical, harangue, primacy, post facto*? Do any have a distinct provocative edge to them?

2. Define *empirical, paradigm*, and *cognitive*. Write an extended definition of *progress*.

3. Although an argument, this is also a research essay. Note the various ways the authors introduce and otherwise handle the material they

use. Is it smoothly integrated? Do the examples they cite support their claim? What other internal strategies do they use? Analyze the structure of this extended argument. List the pros and cons: how are they organized? How do Broad and Wade handle their appeals to authorities like Kuhn and Feyerabend? Does the citation of Einstein's letter to Heisenberg work entirely in their favour? How well is their argument served by the discussion of D.C. Miller's supposed discovery? Do these instances demonstrate their evenhandedness? What authorities are Broad and Wade trying to refute? (Note: near the end they may seem to be shifting their focus to scientific fraud, but that is the central subject of their book, of which this piece is only one chapter.)

4. Describe the experience of someone you know—perhaps yourself— hanging on to a belief "well beyond the point at which reason suggests [it] should be modified or abandoned." Do you have any superstitions? Be honest with yourself.

### THOMAS S. SZASZ "What Psychiatry Can and Cannot Do"

1. Why has Szasz provided fictitious names for the patients he describes as examples? If he didn't want to use real names, why not simply refer to Mr. A., Mrs. B., and so on?

2. Why (in parts II and III) does Szasz put the words *depressed* and *depression* in quotation marks?

3. Szasz's essay is a relatively formally structured argument. Analyze its structure by writing out the opening sentence of each paragraph (sometimes an opening word or two will be enough to reveal the structure or movement).

4. Construct a formal argument about some social or other problem that you feel deeply about and about which you have some personal knowledge. Like Szasz, use some case histories to illustrate your points and support your proposition. And be sure to take into account the points your opponents would be likely to raise.

## TOPICS: General and Comparative

1. Consider the ubiquitous world of advertising.
   (a) What techniques do advertisers use to try to persuade us? Examine several magazines of different kinds. What audience does each appeal to? How does the advertising in each magazine appeal to its audience?
   (b) Write a paragraph of advertising copy for some fictitious product. Then write a brief analysis of the techniques you use. What kind of reader were you aiming at? Rewrite your ad for a markedly different audience.

(c) Translate or compose some real-estate ads according to Brink's suggestions about their real meaning. Do they use other misleading terms? Do other kinds of advertisements similarly twist language? How does one learn to decode them?

(d) What makes a television commercial good or bad? Write an argument for or against the control of advertising on television.

2. What different kinds of persuasion do the essays in this section represent? Which persuade logically and which try to persuade emotionally? Point out instances of emotional appeal being used in addition to logic. Does that make for a stronger argument? Can it make an argument more interesting?

3. Examine some of the techniques of argument that the authors in this section use:

(a) appeal to authority: Thurber (who is Eric Partridge?), Broad and Wade. Does Zinsser cite authority?

(b) analogy: Analogy is notoriously weak as an argumentative technique. How effective is the analogy at the end of Kael's third paragraph? Evaluate the logic of O'Connor's comparison of literature to algebra and irregular French verbs: is the analogy sound, or could it be argued that literature is significantly different? Does Brink use analogy less as an argumentative tool than to illustrate or clarify? Compare its use in other kinds of writing, for example in Dillard's essay in section I.

(c) wit and humor, ridicule: Kael, Woolf, Thurber, and Zinsser use irony. Zinsser writes of "the funny story"; what connection does he see between logic and the unreasonable? Unreasonable to whom? Is Kael ironic throughout or sometimes sarcastic? How can you distinguish? What is the effect of words and phrases like "twinkles," "operetta cheerfulness," "a spider on the valentine"? Is Woolf more sarcastic than ironic? Thurber and Zinsser use *argumentum ad absurdum*—exaggerating to demonstrate the absurdity of what they oppose. How effective you do find such methods?

(d) examples: Woolf, Zinsser, Tuchman, Broad and Wade, and Szasz all use sequences of examples to support their generalizations. Are these cumulatively effective? Thurber, Meigs, and Brink use little narratives and illustrative anecdotes. In what other essays do you find examples, including anecdotes?

(e) questions: Both Meigs and Szasz end with rhetorical questions. How effective are these endings? Why does Szasz use so many rhetorical questions? Do any essays *begin* with questions?

(f) Zinsser uses some statistics to bolster his points. How does Tuchman feel about statistics? What techniques does Morgan use? How does she debunk her opposition? By tone? logic? parody?

What axioms does she accept? How does she use syllogism? Point out syllogistic structures in other essays; write them out as bare syllogisms.

4.  For each of these essays, write down the *thesis*—or, for arguments, what is sometimes better thought of as the *proposition*. Which essays clearly state it? Which only imply it? Can an implied thesis or proposition sometimes be more forceful than a stated one? Where do you most often find them stated? How often do you find a thesis or proposition broken up into several parts stated at different places in an essay? Is Brink's epigrammatic final sentence part of his thesis? Is Schlesinger's thesis as simple, or simplistic, as you may have thought while reading the first half or so of his essay?

5.  To what degree does each of these arguments acknowledge the opposition and dispose of it? Are some fairer than others? Can you explain why? Is it sometimes a matter of audience? Are some more successful in rebuttal than others? What techniques seem to you to work best?

6.  Consider also the more prominent internal strategies of development used in some of these essays. Woolf, Thurber, Morgan, Jenkins, Brink, and Broad and Wade make use of *definition*. Woolf and Jenkins also use *classification*, which is often a way of defining. How does Fulford use classification? Who besides Jenkins uses *comparison and contrast*? Brink uses some *process analysis*; do Broad and Wade use process analysis in trying to explain how science works? Not surprisingly, *cause and effect* is common in the essays in this section, for it is basic to much argument; Kael, O'Connor, Thurber, Morgan, Schlesinger, Brink, and Fulford all use it—and is it there, perhaps less prominently, or even implicitly, in some of the other essays? Do you find much narration and description in these essays, other than in the illustrative anecdotes?

7.  Compare Morgan, Meigs, Schlesinger, McClung (section II), and Atwood (section IV) on the subject of gender. Compose an imaginary conversation between two of them—or between three or four or even all five of them. Would there be much if any basic disagreement?

8.  Brink, like Schlesinger, stresses the importance of the individual as opposed to the masses. Compare Schlesinger's reference to "the unendurable burden of freedom" and Brink's to "that territory of the mind where man is utterly and adventurously alone." Why are people afraid to be alone? Would Schlesinger agree that individuals are necessarily subversives? In your experience, is teaching a subversive activity? What connotation does the word *subversive* have for you? for others? for Brink? Compare Brink's quotation from Read about the need for eccentrics with Schlesinger's quotation from Mill. Would

Schlesinger and Brink agree that change, feared by so many, is not only desirable but necessary? When Schlesinger speaks of "prefabricated emotional clichés," is he pointing to the same thing as Kael is condemning? Is Kael's mention of "the lowest common denominator of feeling" getting at the same point as Brink's reference to "ever-increasing common denominators"?

9. What is "scientific method"? Look up the term in several reference books and textbooks. Does what they say conform to what Broad and Wade are attacking? Consider Szasz's essay and those by Roueché, Gould, and Lewis Thomas in section IV: are they logical? Define *science*. What does science mean to you? Write an essay on the relevance or irrelevance of biology, the function of physics, the joys or dangers of chemistry, or some such topic—something you have first-hand experience of and firm opinions about.

10. What can we know? What can we prove? Compare what Broad and Wade have to say with Berlin's essay (section IV). Is complete objectivity possible, or should one think only of degrees of objectivity? Could you write an objective paper, or could you only try to appear objective? How would you go about trying to be "totally impersonal"? How important is objectivity in argument?

11. Given what we learn about Wittgenstein from Davenport's essay (section II), does it make sense that he heavily influenced the Vienna Circle of logical positivists, whom Broad and Wade blame for much of the "myth of logic"? Wittgenstein's interest was largely in language. Would he have appreciated Trillin's playful attitude (section V) and Colombo's (section VI)? How similar are some of Thurber's concerns about language to those of Galbraith (section IV) and Hornyansky (section VI)? Who are the worst offenders against clarity and common sense in verbal communication? Thurber cites politicians, journalists, space-shows, evangelists, psychologists, advertisers, and doctors. Can you cite others? Would Mitford (section IV) add morticians? Try to find examples that will enable you to distinguish among some of the kinds of *jargon*, variously referred to as *gobbledygook, bafflegab, psychobabble, journalese, bureaucratese, sociologese, educationese,* and so on. Or do they all run together? What characteristics do they *share*? Note that Jenkins's essay also focusses on how language—the way one uses a word—can influence one's thought and behaviour. Does Thurber also make this point? In pursuing these matters, you may want to go further afield and look at another essay by Orwell, "Politics and the English Language," and his novel *1984*; for example compare what Brink and Barthes, whom he quotes, say about language and what Orwell says in his appendix on "Newspeak."

12. Is Brink suggesting that people too easily take the obvious for granted, accepting what "is" as a *fait accompli*, a norm? How much control

can we exercise over the way we interpret reality? Fulford says that "we are, for the most part, unable to change our instincts and feelings." Is this true, or is it rationalization? How important is the qualifying phrase "for the most part"? What are some possible exceptions that you know of? Why is the either-or dualism that Brink focusses on dangerous in contemporary society? Is it a matter of choosing between a closed and an open system? When Tuchman criticizes the use of a system, a single organizing idea, is she also attacking a simplistic either-or method? Is totalitarianism basically simplistic? Consider too that when confronted with an either-or choice—for example between two competing scientific paradigms or other logically opposed alternatives — to seek the ever-popular "happy medium" is not always the best solution: the phrase itself implies a willingness to be satisfied with mediocrity. It may represent a weak compromise, a cop-out. The best solution may for example lie much nearer one alternative than the other. Or it may lie entirely elsewhere, in some third alternative. Write a brief argument exposing the wrongheadedness of some local board or committee or governing body in settling for a "happy medium" as the solution to a seeming either-or dilemma.

13. Tuchman refers to propaganda and truth as mutually exclusive. Is this an example of either-or thinking? Fulford refers to "propagandists" shaping messages of government and media (see also the word "propagating," which he uses earlier). Compare these with the way Broad and Wade use the word *propaganda* (in their discussion of Semmelweis, and twice later near the end). Who is using it correctly? Is it a matter of connotation rather than denotation? Or is it not a question of being either right or wrong?

14. Fulford directly confronts the issue of the media's influence; the subject is also present in Jenkins's argument about the public's knowledge and fears and the meaning of violence; Dryden's image (section IV) is largely a product of it; and it is strongly implicit in Arlen's essay (section VI). Compose an argument for or against the proposition that the media—the mass media—influence us too much. Draw on your own experience, but consult some other printed sources as well. (Fulford mentions Marshall McLuhan's ideas about the media; and note that Arlen refers to "the global village"—one of McLuhan's key phrases. Do you feel that you're living in a "global village"?) Or investigate and report on the phenomenon yourself: For a week, watch two or more television news programs and listen to the news on two radio stations. Compare them for coverage and bias. (a) What is the effect of their priorities, their decisions about what to report and when to report it? (b) What is the effect of their choice of what to omit, as well as what to include? (c) How are their presentations tailored for their respective audiences (especially the radio programs—but per-

haps you'll monitor an early-morning television program as well as evening ones)? What other sources can you check these programs against?

15. Meigs discusses self-censorship. Brink refers to the banning of books in South Africa. Atwood (section IV) talks of some poetry being off-limits to students, of the banning of books in Canada, and of the dangers of self-censorship by writers. What are the implications for society of various kinds of censorship? Have women been more censored than men? Write an argumentative essay for or against some or all kinds of censorship.

16. Broad and Wade refer to "the historian's basic principles—who did what, why, and when"; relate these principles to what Tuchman says about the practice of historians. Would she agree with Gibbon, as quoted by Broad and Wade? Consider what Tuchman says about learning from the past in the light of what Jenkins says about every age's thinking itself a time of particular trouble and violence.

17. Examine the psychology of Meigs's essay. Examine the psychology of myth itself. What is myth? Broad and Wade title their chapter "The Myth of Logic." Jenkins refers to the destructive power of "the myth of violence." Are the different uses of the word related? Meigs is in effect decoding the myth of Pandora for her own purposes. Tuchman decodes the myths of Oedipus and Elektra in order to contradict the conventional Freudian readings of them. Schlesinger too refers to the myth or legend of Oedipus. In what sense is Morgan, in "The Man-Made Myth," also decoding a myth, and for what purpose? Are Jenkins and Broad and Wade also decoding myths, or just debunking them? Are *myth* and *truth* mutually exclusive? Or can a myth be thought of as embodying a kind of truth? Is the fable that Kingston recounts (section VI) in effect a myth that she intends us to decode?

18. Schlesinger calls the theatre "that faithful mirror of a society's preoccupations." Is it legitimate to use literature as a portrait of social reality? Is it logical to claim that popular plays reflect their audience's feelings and fears? Or is Fulford right when he refers to "distortion of reality, which is also called drama"? Take and defend a position on this issue. Need it be either one or the other?

19. Tuchman's piece was first delivered as a lecture, as were Brink's, Atwood's (section IV), and Stein's (section VI). Do any stylistic features mark these as different from those intended in the first place to be read rather than heard? Or is the range from colloquial to formal equally possible in both kinds?

20. "What we call justice derives from our uneasy recognition of a social paradox: that it is impossible to be fair, and possible only to enact the law." Discuss.

21. "Boredom is the source of more social disorder than malice is, just as fear is a greater source of prejudice than hate." Discuss.

22. "Education is another name for brainwashing." Write two essays, one arguing each side of this proposition. Then analyze your own argumentative techniques. In which essay are you more convincing? Why?

23. "There is no unemployment crisis. There is only a crisis in employers' imaginations. Greater flexibility in retirement age and greater use of part-time workers would resolve many of the problems young people currently face in obtaining jobs." Write a commentary on this view.

24. Write a political speech.

# IV
# Writing
# to
# Explain
# and
# Inform

In his essay in a book called *The Canadian Imagination*, Northrop Frye tells the story of a southern doctor travelling with an Inuit guide in the Arctic. When a blizzard blows up and they have to bivouac, the doctor panics and shouts aimlessly, "We are lost! We are lost!" The guide looks at him thoughtfully for a moment, and then observes: "We are not lost. We are here." Frye transforms the anecdote into a commentary on identity, probing the relation between geography and the imagination and exploring the force of the perspective one brings to the definition of cultural boundaries. Using an anecdote in this fashion, making it a functional part of a commentary rather than a simple narrative ornament, constitutes a characteristic feature of much exposition. The expository writer's aim is to make a subject clear, to take a body of information and arrange the details so that they make sense, to answer the questions *how* and *why* as lucidly as possible: to explain things. A concrete anecdote often helps to get the process started or to move it along.

Aside from the anecdote, two of the chief methods by which expository writing begins are *definition* and *classification*. One writer might restrict the meanings of certain terms at the outset. Another might set up categories in order to clarify the nature of a subject—and then further divide these categories into particular subsets: classifying, for example, by size or colour, source or function, quality or reliability. Exposition is writing that attempts to explain the steps in a process, the makeup of a pattern, the causes of an event or a set of circumstances, or the applications or implications of a body of data. Among the essays that follow, Child, Schneider, Mitford, and Roueché trace processes. Schneider, Baker, and Cole proffer systems of classification, Atwood and Baker effective analogies, Berlin an extended definition. And more than one employs an anecdote along the way.

Though exposition seems one of the most straightforward of prose forms, it is difficult to master. An intelligent simplicity is an elusive goal. Try, for example, to explain how to put on a coat—as though you were explaining to someone who couldn't differentiate between left and right—and then ask someone to try to follow your directions exactly. Or try to explain why three times four is twelve. To explain things adequately, expository writers must make use of internal definitions, helpful descriptions, comparisons, contrasts, analogies, anecdotal illustrations—in short, any techniques that will help them make their subjects clear. They try to lead their readers through snowstorms of complexity, adapting their anecdotes and analogies and other devices to the purpose at hand.

Expository essays are also to a degree attempts to persuade. But because their essential aim is to explain, a reader primarily expects information from them. And however much readers may appreciate an essayist's wit, grace, intelligence, and personality, they ultimately judge an expository essay by how much they have learned from it. As explanations, an unclear recipe and a set of inexact street directions are at the very least unhelpful. The people who try to follow them may not get lost, but they will not know exactly what they are doing or where they are. Sometimes such uncertainty turns out to be productive (can uncertainty be the mother of discovery?), but more often it simply proves confusing. And what holds for simple explanations also holds for more complex analyses and more abstract subjects. Lack of clarity dulls one's ability to absorb information and to discriminate among details; clear information, in whatever form it comes, can both stimulate and delight.

The essays in this section range, therefore, in subject, method, function, and tone. There are instructions to accompany a recipe, a piece of informative journalism, and a medical whodunit; there are magazine articles, informal reflections, and a formal cultural inquiry. As the subjects vary, so do the language and the authors' attitudes. For Roueché, Gould, and Thomas, a scientific vocabulary is a natural medium of expression; Galbraith defends the use of specialized occupational words; Dryden is colloquial, Baker metaphysical and whimsical, and Mitford chillingly factual.

But is Mitford neutral and objective? Is Galbraith? Atwood? Berlin? Is, in fact, complete objectivity ever possible? Are explanations inevitably governed by bias and point of view? It is true that the reporter who strives for neutrality differs in many ways from the editorial writer who strives to persuade readers to embrace a particular social or political doctrine. The disinterested scientist and the academic investigator (neither of whom, it must be added, is likely to be *un*interested) differ in many ways from the intellectual partisan. Exposition is not polemic. But the expository language of the scientist, like the argumentative language of the partisan, can also be slanted. It is open to misuse and subject to misinterpretation. It requires care. Even a formal researcher can distort matters in the process of communicating results (remember "The Myth of Logic" in section III), just as a writer drawing only on personal experience may communicate unconsciously held biases. Given such conditions, it is a wonder that writers and readers don't feel lost more often than they do, and throw their hands up in antic despair. Sometimes they feel secure. But sometimes, after struggling to express or interpret an idea, they must be pleased even if they know with only a modest certainty where it is that they stand.

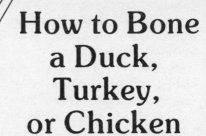

# How to Bone a Duck, Turkey, or Chicken

Simone Beck, Louisette Bertholle, and Julia Child

You may think that boning a fowl is an impossible feat if you have never seen it done or thought of attempting it. Although the procedure may take 45 minutes the first time because of fright, it can be accomplished in not much more than 20 on your second or third try. The object is to remove the flesh with the skin from the carcass bones without piercing the skin except at the back where the bird is slit open, and at the natural openings at the vent and neck. The skin is to serve as a container for the *pâté*. Laid flat on a board, the *pâté* mixture is heaped onto it, then the skin is folded over the *pâté* mixture and sewed in place. When baked in a *terrine* and unmolded, or baked in a crust, the sutures are on the bottom, and the *pâté* appears to be enclosed in an unbroken, browned casing—which is the skin. It is always an impressive sight. The important thing to remember is that the cutting edge of your knife must always face the bone, never the flesh, thus you cannot pierce the skin.

To begin with, cut a deep slit down the back of the bird from the neck to the tail, to expose the backbone. With a small, sharp knife, its edge always cutting against the bone, scrape and cut the flesh from the carcass bones down one side of the bird, pulling the flesh away from the carcass with your fingers as you cut. When you come to the ball joints connecting the wings and the second joints to the carcass, sever them, and continue down the carcass until you reach just the ridge of the breast where skin and

From *Mastering the Art of French Cooking*, by Julia Child, Simone Beck, and Louisette Bertholle. Copyright © 1961 by Alfred A. Knopf, Inc. Reprinted by permission of Alfred A. Knopf, Inc.

bone meet. Then stop. You must be careful here, as the skin is thin and easily slit. Repeat the same operation on the other side of the bird. By the time you have completed half of this, the carcass frame, dangling legs, wings, and skin will appear to be an unrecognizable mass of confusion and you will wonder how in the world any sense can be made of it all. But just continue cutting against the bone, and not slitting any skin, and all will come out as it should. When you finally arrive at the ridge of the breastbone on this opposite side, stop again. Then lift the carcass frame and cut very closely against the ridge of the breastbone to free the carcass, but not to slit the thin skin covering the breastbone. Chop off the wings at the elbows, to leave just the upper wing bones attached.

Then arrange this mass of skin and flesh on a board, flesh side up. You will now see, protruding from the flesh, the pair of ball joints of the wings and of the two second joints. Scrape the meat from the bones of the wings and pull out the bones. Repeat for the second joints, severing them from the ball joints of the drumsticks; the drumstick bones may be left in place if you wish. Discard any bits of fat adhering to the flesh, and the bird is ready to become a *pâté* or a galantine.

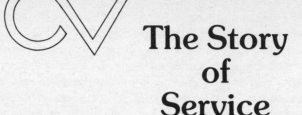

# The Story of Service

### Jessica Mitford

There was a time when the undertaker's tasks were clearcut and rather obvious, and when he billed his patrons accordingly. Typical late-nineteenth-century charges, in addition to the price of merchandise, are shown on bills of the period as: "Services at the house (placing corpse in the coffin) $1.25," "Preserving remains on ice, $10," "Getting Permit, $1.50." It was customary for the undertaker to add a few dollars to his bill for being "in attendance," which seems only fair and right. The cost of embalming was around $10 in 1880. An undertaker, writing in 1900, recommends these minimums for service charges: Washing and dressing, $5; embalming, $10; hearse, $8 to $10. As Habenstein and Lamers, the historians of the trade, have pointed out, "The undertaker had yet to conceive of the value of personal services offered professionally for a fee, legitimately claimed." Well, he has now so conceived with a vengeance.

When weaving in the story of service as it is rendered today, spokesmen for the funeral industry tend to become so carried away by their own enthusiasm, so positively lyrical and copious in their declarations, that the outsider may have a little trouble understanding it all. There are indeed contradictions. Preferred Funeral Directors International has prepared a mimeographed talk designed to inform people about service: "The American public receive the services of employees and proprietor alike, nine and one half days of labor for every funeral handled, they receive the use of automobiles and hearses, a building including a chapel

Copyright © 1963, 1978 by Jessica Mitford. Reprinted by permission of Simon & Schuster, Inc.

and other rooms which require building maintenance, insurance, taxes and licenses, and depreciation, as well as heat in the winter, cooling in the summer and light and water." The writer goes on to say that while the process of embalming takes only about three hours, yet, "it would be necessary for one man to work two forty-hour weeks to complete a funeral service. This is coupled with an additional forty hours service required by members of other local allied professions, including the work of the cemeteries, newspapers, and of course, the most important of all, the service of your clergyman. These some 120 hours of labour are the basic value on which the costs of funeral rests."

Our informant has lumped a lot of things together here. To start with "the most important of all, the service of your clergyman," the average religious funeral service lasts no more than 25 minutes. Furthermore, it is not, of course, paid for by the funeral director. The "work of the cemeteries" presumably means the opening and closing of a grave. This now mechanized operation, which takes 15 to 20 minutes, is likewise not billed as part of the funeral director's costs. The work of "newspapers"? This is a puzzler. Presumably reference is made here to the publication of an obituary notice on the vital statistics page. It is, incidentally, surprising to learn that newspaper work is considered an "allied profession."

Just how insurance, taxes, licenses and depreciation are figured in as part of the 120 man-hours of service is hard to tell. The writer does mention that his operation features "65 items of service." In general, the funeral salesman is inclined to chuck in everything he does under the heading of "service." For example, in a typical list of "services" he will include items like "securing statistical data" (in other words, completing the death certificate and finding out how much insurance was left by the deceased), "the arrangements conference" (in which the sale of the funeral to the survivors is made), and the "keeping of records," by which he means his own bookkeeping work. Evidently there is some confusion here between items that properly belong in a cost-accounting system and items of *actual* service rendered in any given funeral. In all likelihood, idle time of employees is figured in and prorated as part of the "man-hours." The up-to-date funeral home operates on a 24-hour basis, and the mimeographed speech contains this heartening news:

> The funeral service profession of the United States is proud of the fact that there is not a person within the continental limits of the United States who is more than two hours away from a licensed funeral director and embalmer in case of need. That's one that even the fire fighting apparatus of our country cannot match.

While the hit-or-miss rhetoric of the foregoing is fairly typical of the prose style of the funeral trade as a whole, and while the statement that 120 man-hours are devoted to a single man- (or woman-) funeral may be open to question, there really is a fantastic amount of service accorded the dead body and its survivors.

Having decreed what sort of funeral is right, proper and nice, and having gradually appropriated to himself all the functions connected with it, the funeral director has become responsible for a multitude of tasks beyond the obvious one of "placing corpse in the coffin" recorded in our nineteenth-century funeral bill. His self-imposed duties fall into two main categories: attention to the corpse itself, and the stage-managing of the funeral.

The drama begins to unfold with the arrival of the corpse at the mortuary.

Alas, poor Yorick! How surprised he would be to see how his counterpart of today is whisked off to a funeral parlor and is in short order sprayed, sliced, pierced, pickled, trussed, trimmed, creamed, waxed, painted, rouged and neatly dressed—transformed from a common corpse into a Beautiful Memory Picture. This process is known in the trade as embalming and restorative art, and is so universally employed in the United States and Canada that the funeral director does it routinely, without consulting corpse or kin. He regards as eccentric those few who are hardy enough to suggest that it might be dispensed with. Yet no law requires embalming, no religious doctrine commends it, nor is it dictated by considerations of health, sanitation, or even of personal daintiness. In no part of the world but in Northern America is it widely used. The purpose of embalming is to make the corpse presentable for viewing in a suitably costly container; and here too the funeral director routinely, without first consulting the family, prepares the body for public display.

Is all this legal? The processes to which a dead body may be subjected are after all to some extent circumscribed by law. In most states, for instance, the signature of next of kin must be obtained before an autopsy may be performed, before the deceased may be cremated, before the body may be turned over to a medical school for research purposes; or such provision must be made in the decedent's will. In the case of embalming, no such permission is required nor is it ever sought. A textbook, *The Principles and Practices of Embalming*, comments on this: "There is some question regarding the legality of much that is done within the preparation room." The author points out that it would be most unusual for a responsible member of a bereaved family to instruct the mortician, in so many words, to *"embalm"* the body of a deceased relative. The very term *"embalming"* is so seldom used that the mortician must rely upon custom in the matter. The author concludes that unless the family specifies otherwise, the act of entrusting the body to the care of a funeral establishment carries with it an implied permission to go ahead and embalm.

Embalming is indeed a most extraordinary procedure, and one must wonder at the docility of Americans who each year pay hundreds of millions of dollars for its perpetuation, blissfully ignorant of what it is all about, what is done, how it is done. Not one in ten thousand has any idea of what actually takes place. Books on the subject are extremely hard to come by. They are not to be found in most libraries or bookshops.

In an era when huge television audiences watch surgical operations in the comfort of their living rooms, when, thanks to the animated cartoon, the geography of the digestive system has become familiar territory even to the nursery school set, in a land where the satisfaction of curiosity about almost all matters is a national pastime, the secrecy surrounding embalming can, surely, hardly be attributed to the inherent gruesomeness of the subject. Custom in this regard has within this century suffered a complete reversal. In the early days of American embalming, when it was performed in the home of the deceased, it was almost mandatory for some relative to stay by the embalmer's side and witness the procedure. Today, family members who might wish to be in attendance would certainly be dissuaded by the funeral director. All others, except apprentices, are excluded by law from the preparation room.

A close look at what does actually take place may explain in large measure the undertaker's intractable reticence concerning a procedure that has become his major *raison d'être*. Is it possible he fears that public information about embalming might lead patrons to wonder if they really want this service? If the funeral men are loath to discuss the subject outside the trade, the reader may, understandably, be equally loath to go on reading at this point. For those who have the stomach for it, let us part the formaldehyde curtain....

The body is first laid out in the undertaker's morgue — or rather, Mr. Jones is reposing in the preparation room — to be readied to bid the world farewell.

The preparation room in any of the better funeral establishments has the tiled and sterile look of a surgery, and indeed the embalmer-restorative artist who does his chores there is beginning to adopt the term "derma-surgeon" (appropriately corrupted by some mortician-writers as "demi-surgeon") to describe his calling. His equipment, consisting of scalpels, scissors, augers, forceps, clamps, needles, pumps, tubes, bowls and basins, is crudely imitative of the surgeon's, as is his technique, acquired in a nine- or twelve-month post-high-school course in an embalming school. He is supplied by an advanced chemical industry with a bewildering array of fluids, sprays, pastes, oils, powders, creams, to fix or soften tissue, shrink or distend it as needed, dry it here, restore the moisture there. There are cosmetics, waxes and paints to fill and cover features, even plaster of Paris to replace entire limbs. There are ingenious aids to prop and stabilize the cadaver: a Vari-Pose Head Rest, the Edwards Arm and Hand Positioner, the Repose Block (to support the shoulders during the embalming), and the Throop Foot Positioner, which resembles an old-fashioned stocks.

Mr. John H. Eckels, president of the Eckels College of Mortuary Science, thus describes the first part of the embalming procedure: "In the hands of a skilled practitioner, this work may be done in a comparatively short time and without mutilating the body other than by slight incision—so slight that it scarcely would cause serious inconvenience if made upon a living person. It is necessary to remove the blood, and doing this not only helps in the disinfecting, but removes the principal cause of disfigurements due to discoloration."

Another textbook discusses the all-important time element: "The earlier this is done, the better, for every hour that elapses between death and embalming will add to the problems and complications encountered...." Just how soon should one get going on the embalming? The author tells us, "On the basis of such scanty information made available to this profession through its rudimentary and haphazard system of technical research, we must conclude that the best results are to be obtained if the subject is embalmed before life is completely extinct—that is, before cellular death has occurred. In the average case, this would mean within an hour after somatic death." For those who feel that there is something a little rudimentary, not to say haphazard, about this advice, a comforting thought is offered by another writer. Speaking of fears entertained in early days of premature burial, he points out, "One of the effects of embalming by chemical injection, however, has been to dispel fears of live burial." How true; once the blood is removed, chances of live burial are indeed remote.

To return to Mr. Jones, the blood is drained out through the veins and replaced by embalming fluid pumped in through the arteries. As noted in *The Principles and Practices of Embalming*, "every operator has a favorite injection and drainage point—a fact which becomes a handicap only if he fails or refuses to forsake his favourites when conditions demand it." Typical favourites are the carotid artery, femoral artery, jugular vein, subclavian vein. There are various choices of embalming fluid. If Flextone is used, it will produce a "mild flexible rigidity. The skin retains a velvety softness, the tissues are rubbery and pliable. Ideal for women and children." It may be blended with B. and G. Products Company's Lyf-Lyk tint, which is guaranteed to reproduce "nature's own skin texture...the velvety appearance of living tissue." Suntone comes in three separate tints: Suntan; Special Cosmetic Tint, a pink shade "especially indicated for young female subjects"; and Regular Cosmetic Tint, moderately pink.

About three to six gallons of a dyed and perfumed solution of formaldehyde, glycerin, borax, phenol, alcohol and water is soon circulating through Mr. Jones, whose mouth has been sewn together with a "needle directed upward between the upper lip and gum" and brought out slightly "for a more pleasant expression." If he should be bucktoothed, his teeth are cleaned with Bon Ami and coated with colorless nail polish. His eyes, meanwhile, are closed with flesh-tinted eye caps and eye cement.

The next step is to have at Mr. Jones with a thing called a trocar. This is a long, hollow needle attached to a tube. It is jabbed into the abdomen, poked around the entrails and chest cavity, the contents of which are pumped out and replaced with "cavity fluid." This done, and the hole in the abdomen sewn up, Mr. Jones's face is heavily creamed (to protect the skin from burns which may be caused by leakage of the chemicals), and he is covered with a sheet and left unmolested for a while. But not for long—there is more, much more, in store for him. He has been embalmed, but not yet restored, and the best time to start the restorative work is eight to ten hours after embalming, when the tissues have become firm and dry.

The object of all this attention to the corpse, it must be remembered, is to make it presentable for viewing in an attitude of healthy respose. "Our customs require the presentation of our dead in the semblance of normality...unmarred by the ravages of illness, disease or mutilation," says Mr. J. Sheridan Mayer in his *Restorative Art.* This is rather a larger order since few people die in the full bloom of health, unravaged by illness and unmarked by some disfigurement. The funeral industry is equal to the challenge: "In some cases the gruesome appearance of a mutilated or disease-ridden subject may be quite discouraging. The task of restoration may seem impossible and shake the confidence of the embalmer. This is the time for intestinal fortitude and determination. Once the formative work is begun and affected tissues are cleaned or removed, all doubts of success vanish. It is surprising and gratifying to discover the results which may be obtained."

The embalmer, having allowed an appropriate interval to elapse, returns to the attack, but now he brings into play the skill and equipment of sculptor and cosmetician. Is a hand missing? Casting one in plaster of Paris is a simple matter. "For replacement purposes, only a cast of the back of the hand is necessary; this is within the ability of the average operator and is quite adequate." If a lip or two, a nose or an ear should be missing, the embalmer has at hand a variety of restorative waxes with which to model replacements. Pores and skin texture are simulated by stippling with a little brush, and over this cosmetics are laid on. Head off? Decapitation cases are rather routinely handled. Ragged edges are trimmed, and head joined to torso with a series of splints, wires and sutures. It is a good idea to have a little something at the neck—a scarf or high collar—when time for viewing comes. Swollen mouth? Cut out tissue as needed from inside the lips. If too much is removed, the surface contour can easily be restored by padding with cotton. Swollen necks and cheeks are reduced by removing tissue through vertical incisions made down each side of the neck. "When the deceased is casketed, the pillow will hide the suture incisions...as an extra precaution against leakage, the suture may be painted with liquid sealer."

The opposite condition is more likely to present itself—that of emaciation. His hypodermic syringe now loaded with massage cream, the embalmer seeks out and fills the hollowed and sunken areas by injection. In this procedure the back of the hands and fingers and the under-chin areas should not be neglected.

Positioning the lips is a problem that recurrently challenges the ingenuity of the embalmer. Closed too tightly, they tend to give a stern, even disapproving expression. Ideally, embalmers feel, the lips should give the impression of being ever so slightly parted, the upper lip protruding slightly for a more youthful appearance. This takes some engineering, however, as the lips tend to drift apart. Lip drift can sometimes be remedied by pushing one or two straight pins though the inner margin of the lower lip and then inserting them between the two front upper teeth. If Mr. Jones happens to have no teeth, the pins can just as easily be anchored in his Armstrong Face Former and Denture Replacer. Another method to maintain lip closure is to dislocate the lower jaw, which is then held in its new position by a wire run through holes which have been drilled through the upper and lower jaws at the midline. As the French are fond of saying, *il faut souffrir pour être belle.*\*

If Mr. Jones has died of jaundice, the embalming fluid will very likely turn him green. Does this deter the embalmer? Not if he has intestinal fortitude. Masking pastes and cosmetics are heavily laid on, burial garments and casket interiors are color-correlated with particular care, and Jones is displayed beneath rose-colored lights. Friends will say, "How *well* he looks." Death by carbon monoxide, on the other hand, can be rather a good thing from the embalmer's viewpoint: "One advantage is the fact that this type of discoloration is an exaggerated form of a natural pink coloration." This is nice because the healthy glow is already present and needs but little attention.

The patching and filling completed, Mr. Jones is now shaved, washed and dressed. Cream-based cosmetic, available in pink, flesh, suntan, brunette and blond, is applied to his hands and face, his hair is shampooed and combed (and, in the case of Mrs. Jones, set), his hands manicured. For the horny-handed son of toil special care must be taken; cream should be applied to remove ingrained grime, and the nails cleaned. "If he were not in the habit of having them manicured in life, trimming and shaping is advised for better appearance—never questioned by kin."

---

\*In 1963 *Mortuary Management* reports a new development: "Natural Expression Formers," an invention of Funeral Directors Research Company. "They may be used to replace one or both artificial dentures, or over natural teeth; have 'bite-indicator' lines as a closure guide....Natural Expression Formers also offer more control of facial expression."

Jones is now ready for casketing (this is the present participle of the verb "to casket"). In this operation his right shoulder should be depressed slightly "to turn the body a bit to the right and soften the appearance of lying flat on the back." Positioning the hands is a matter of importance, and special rubber positioning blocks may be used. The hands should be cupped slightly for a more lifelike, relaxed appearance. Proper placement of the body requires a delicate sense of balance. It should lie as high as possible in the casket, yet not so high that the lid, when lowered, will hit the nose. On the other hand, we are cautioned, placing the body too low "creates the impression that the body is in a box."

Jones is next wheeled into the appointed slumber room where a few last touches may be added — his favourite pipe placed in his hand or, if he was a great reader, a book propped into position. (In the case of little Master Jones a Teddy bear may be clutched.) Here he will hold open house for a few days, visiting hours 10 A.M. to 9 P.M.

All now being in readiness, the funeral director calls a staff conference to make sure that each assistant knows his precise duties. Mr. Wilber Krieger writes: "This makes your staff feel that they are a part of the team, with a definite assignment that must be properly carried out if the whole plan is to succeed. You never heard of a football coach who failed to talk to his entire team before they go on the field. They have drilled on the plays they are to execute for hours and days, and yet the successful coach knows the importance of making even the bench-warming third-string substitute feel that he is important if the game is to be won." The winning of *this* game is predicated upon glass-smooth handling of the logistics. The funeral director has notified the pallbearers whose names were furnished by the family, has arranged for the presence of clergyman, organist, and soloist, has provided transportation for everybody, has organized and listed the flowers sent by friends. In *Psychology of Funeral Service* Mr. Edward A. Martin points out: "He may not always do as much as the family thinks he is doing, but it is his helpful guidance that they appreciate in knowing they are proceeding as they should.... The important thing is how well his services can be used to make the family believe they are giving unlimited expression to their own sentiment."

The religious service may be held in a church or in the chapel of the funeral home; the funeral director vastly prefers the latter arrangement, for not only is it more convenient for him but it affords him the opportunity to show off his beautiful facilities to the gathered mourners. After the clergyman has had his say, the mourners queue up to file past the casket for a last look at the deceased. The family is *never* asked whether they want an open-casket ceremony; in the absence of their instruction to the contrary, this is taken for granted. Consequently well over 90 per cent of all American funerals feature the open casket — a custom unknown in other parts of the world. Foreigners are astonished by it. An English woman living in San Francisco described her reaction in a letter to the writer:

> I myself have attended only one funeral here—that of an elderly fellow worker of mine. After the service I could not understand why everyone was walking towards the coffin (sorry, I mean casket), but thought I had better follow the crowd. It shook me rigid to get there and find the casket open and poor old Oscar lying there in his brown tweed suit, wearing a suntan makeup and just the wrong shade of lipstick. If I had not been extremely fond of the old boy, I have a horrible feeling that I might have giggled. Then and there I decided that I could never face another American funeral—even dead.

The casket (which has been resting throughout the service on a Classic Beauty Ultra Metal Casket Bier) is now transferred by a hydraulically operated device called Porto-Lift to a balloon-tired, Glide Easy casket carriage which will wheel it to yet another conveyance, the Cadillac Funeral Coach. This may be lavender, cream, light green—anything but black. Interiors, of course, are color-correlated, "for the man who cannot stop short of perfection."

At graveside, the casket is lowered into the earth. This office, once the prerogative of friends of the deceased, is now performed by a patented mechanical lowering device. A "Lifetime Green" artificial grass mat is at the ready to conceal the sere earth, and overhead, to conceal the sky, is a portable Steril Chapel Tent ("resists the intense heat and humidity of summer and the terrific storms of winter...available in Silver Grey, Rose or Evergreen"). Now is the time for the ritual scattering of earth over the coffin, as the solemn words "earth to earth, ashes to ashes, dust to dust" are pronounced by the officiating cleric. This can today be accomplished "with a mere flick of the wrist with the Gordon Leak-Proof Earth Dispenser. No grasping of a handful of dirt, no soiled fingers. Simple, dignified, beautiful, reverent! The modern way!" The Gordon Earth Dispenser (at $5) is of nickel-plated brass construction. It is not only "attractive to the eye and long wearing"; it is also "one of the 'tools' for building better public relations" if presented as "an appropriate noncommercial gift" to the clergyman. It is shaped something like a saltshaker.

Untouched by human hand, the coffin and the earth are now united.

It is in the function of directing the participants through this maze of gadgetry that the funeral director has assigned to himself his relatively new role of "grief therapist." He has relieved the family of every detail, he has revamped the corpse to look like a living doll, he has arranged for it to nap for a few days in a slumber room, he has put on a well-oiled performance in which the concept of *death* has played no part whatsoever—unless it was inconsiderately mentioned by the clergyman who conducted the religious service. He has done everything in his power to make the funeral a real pleasure for everybody concerned. He and his team have given their all to score an upset victory over death.

Dale Carnegie has written that in the lexicon of the successful man there is no such word as "failure." So have the funeral men managed to delete the word death and all its associations from their vocabulary. They have from time to time published lists of In and Out words and phrases to be memorized and used in connection with the final return of dust to dust; then still dissatisfied with the result, have elaborated and revised the lists. Thus a 1916 glossary substitutes "prepare body" for "handle corpse." Today, though "body" is Out and "remains" or "Mr. Jones" is In.

"The use of improper terminology by anyone affiliated with a mortuary should be strictly forbidden," declares Edward A. Martin. He suggests a rather thorough overhauling of the language; his deathless words include: "service, not funeral; Mr., Mrs., Miss Blank, not corpse or body; preparation room, not morgue; casket, not coffin; funeral director or mortician, not undertaker; reposing room or slumber room, not laying-out room; display room, not showroom; baby or infant, not stillborn; deceased, not dead; autopsy or post-mortem, not post; casket coach, not hearse; shipping case, not shipping box; flower car, not flower truck; cremains or cremated remains, not ashes; clothing, dress, suit, etc., not shroud; drawing room, not parlor."

This rather basic list was refined in 1956 by Victor Landig in his *Basic Principles of Funeral Service.* He enjoins the reader to avoid using the word "death" as much as possible, even sometimes when such avoidance may seem impossible; for example, a death certificate should be referred to as a "vital statistics form." One should speak not of the "job" but rather of the "call." We do not "haul" a dead person, we "transfer" or "remove" him—and we do this in a "service car," not a "body car." We "open and close" his grave rather than dig and fill it, and in it we "inter" rather than bury him. This is done not in a graveyard or cemetery but rather in a "memorial park." The deceased is beautified, not with makeup, but with "cosmetics." Anyway, he didn't die, he "expired." An important error to guard against, cautions Mr. Landig, is referring to "cost of the casket." The phrase, "amount of investment in the service," is a wiser usage here.

Miss Anne Hamilton Franz, writing in *Funeral Direction and Management,* adds an interesting footnote on the use of the word "ashes" to describe (in a word) ashes. She fears this usage will encourage scattering (for what is more natural than to scatter ashes?) and prefers to speak of "cremated remains" or "human remains." She does not like the word "retort" to describe the container in which cremation takes place, but prefers "cremation chamber" or "cremation vault," because this "sounds better and softens any harshness to sensitive feelings."

As for the Loved One, poor fellow, he wanders like a sad ghost through the funeral men's pronouncements. No provision seems to have been made for the burial of a Heartily Disliked One, although the necessity for such must arise in the course of human events.

# Programs as Essays

### Ben Ross Schneider, Jr.

When I consider the field of computing, two phenomena astonish me: that programmers aren't the best of writers, and that computer science has had to discover what the whole human race has known about the relative merits of chaos and order since God created the world in six days. I should have thought the discipline of programming would have made computer professionals the most polished group of writers in the country. But not only does the precision of programming fail to rub off on them, they have actually had to *invent* "structured programming" and *discover* the top-down approach, secrets quite obvious to writers—at least since Homer. I can't imagine how programmers went about their business before they, like Molière's Bourgeois Gentilhomme, suddenly discovered that they spoke prose.

There has been a failure of communication between writers and programmers, and this essay is an attempt to start a conversation.

Last fall I finally wrote a program. Although I have been computing since 1965 and have conducted three fairly horrendous computer projects, I have shied away from programming on the theory that it isn't a practical pursuit for a fellow who can't figure out in his head what day of the week it will be 10 days from now. But last fall, having some time on my hands and having been unable for some years to find a decent text formatter for my Centronics 737 printer (which, because its characters came in nine different widths, required special treatment), I decided to build my own formatter out of Microsoft BASIC. Progressing at a rate of about five good lines per day and 20 bad ones, in two months I produced a passable formatter, and proved two things to my own satisfaction: 1. I

Reprinted with permission of *Datamation* Magazine, © Copyright by Technical Publishing Company, A Dun & Bradstreet Company, (1984) — All rights reserved.

am indeed not cut out to be a programmer; 2. programming does indeed have close affinities to writing.

In the first place, the laws of programming seem to apply quite handily to writing as well. For bad writing is very like a program that doesn't work! Its GOTOs get lost, its GOSUBs overlap, its IFs have no THENs, its constants vary, its variables interlock. Consider, for example, the manual for a prominent text editor that I now have before me. It was shipped in 1981, and it may have improved considerably since then, but it will do for an example of bad writing.

*Its GOTOs get lost.* An early section of this manual sends us to Appendix A for instructions on customizing the editor. Appendix A informs us that "the enclosed 'Example Keyboard Layout' and the next section 'Running SETUP' give recommended values for every question" asked by the setup routine. "Enclosed" in what? The word suggests something loose, and there *was* a sort of handout in the package. There indeed we find, stapled in the middle of 10 other afterthoughts, a page called "Example Keyboard Layout." But we also find two other keyboard layouts that our GOTO never mentioned. And what about the "next section"? It isn't next to the sample keyboard layout, as strongly suggested; perhaps it's next to the original section. Sure enough, four pages further on, something approximately eligible does occur but not exactly what we expected, because it's called "Running SETUP or SETCRT." A good writer gives better addresses to other parts of his essay than this manual does, but he strives to avoid GOTOs altogether by collecting all the material on one subject in one place.

*Its GOSUBs overlap.* In this manual "Running SETUP" is a sort of subroutine whose purpose is to show us how to answer setup questions. But a considerable amount of discussion on this point has already occurred in a previous section, called "Getting Started," and there is a good deal more about it among the handouts. As a result, some of the advice is repeated several times and some of it doesn't agree. If the manual were a program, it would be inefficient in the first place, and unworkable in the second.

*Its IFs have no THENs.* On the first sheet of our handouts we are told to be sure that our package contains "Notes on Software License Agreement," "Software License Agreement," "Example Keyboard Layout," "Example Customization," "Software Update Option," and several other sheets. If this were a program, the author would have to tell us what to do if we don't find everything (proceed no farther?) and what to do if we do (sign license agreement and proceed with setup?); but it's a manual, and there's no further comment.

*Its constants vary.* Names change without warning. "Software Support Option" changes to "Software Update Option," "Auto Read/Write" changes to "Auto-Buffering," "text register" changes to "text save," "naming" a file switches to "opening" a file, and "eloquent" means "elegant." If this were a program it would soon fail to find a previously defined value and crash, just as most readers of this documentation do.

*Its variables interlock.* Categories aren't mutually exclusive. The system is said to have two modes, "Command Mode" and "Visual Mode," but both modes have commands. Nor does "Control Functions" gracefully divide into "Cursor Movement" and "Visual Functions," not only because apples don't divide into apples and oranges but also because in this case both categories have visual manifestations. The basis for comparison shifts in the very act of comparing, like that of the man who asked, "Do you walk to work or carry your lunch?" A programmer who defined his variables this sloppily would find them at variance in fatal dimensions. A reader is simply mystified.

Bad writing persists even in the unforgiving world of computers, I suppose, because we have come to depend on the human mind's marvelous power to make sense of a crazy, mixed-up world, which, not surprisingly, contains lots of crazy, mixed-up documentation. "Well, you know what I mean," the documentor says lazily. Programmers are friendly natives at heart. Perhaps if they thought of themselves as programming the user—which is exactly what they are doing—their writing would become friendly in deed as well as intent.

So much for the ways in which programming skills might help the writer. Let us now consider the ways in which writing skills might help the programmer. The computer does not forgive incoherence, but it does forgive lack of structure. The computer doesn't care about structure as long as the data paths are clear, but structure does make programs comprehensible to human beings who may need to know how they work. Into this category fall not just future programmers—enhancers, updaters, and debuggers—but also and especially the writer of the program himself, who adds more and more features and gets more and more confused.

Structure is the arrangement of parts; first of all, it involves recognizing the parts into which the material naturally divides, and second, it involves arranging these parts into a logical order that derives from the nature of the parts. Both writer and programmer have the problem of presenting a system of parts that is logically a tree but that must take the form of a list, and both use GOSUBs (and GOTOs) that patch the branches of the tree into the list. As they do so, they follow—or ought to follow—a few simple rules that maintain clarity.

*Never digress.* You know that your parts are in order when they march relentlessly forward to their final goal, glancing back occasionally (because of the tree), but never going back. The first principle of structure is to lay down at the beginning those definitions, facts, and assumptions that the rest of the work will take as given. We begin a program by setting parameters, those variables that remain constant during a given run. A storyteller that gets the cart before the horse can patch in a horse as an aside—"Oh, I forgot to tell you"—but that dulls the point of the story. When a programmer patches in a given as an afterthought, he spoils the structure of his program, increasing its obscurity.

*One thing at at time.* The second principle of structure is to define the parts so that you never have to cover the same topic twice. A certain amount of redundancy may be delightful in "Goldilocks and the Three Bears," but in expository prose or software it is a great bore, a waste of time, and a source of confusion. Our manual has three sections entitled "Getting Started," and all of them tell us something about keyboard layout; how much easier it would be for us if all the material were in one place! For the programmer, one thing at a time means defining subroutines so that they do not overlap.

*There must be a perceivable reason for the order of parts.* In an essay, we might move from familiar ground to the undiscovered country of the conclusion. In building my text formatter I discovered that I moved from setting parameters to a central branching point, after which I listed the subroutines according to the frequency with which they were used and the order in which they were used: first to last and general to particular.

The program starts by establishing margins, paragraph indentation, page length, and character widths; then it proceeds to measure out a string until it reaches the decision point—the string is long enough to be filled and printed, or a code embedded in the text requires special treatment. Next come the routines for chopping, filling, and printing lines that impinge on the right-hand margin; then the routines for lines that don't. These are followed by the paging routine, and finally the finishing-up routine. Because I had a systematic filing system, I knew where to find every routine, and because that system had something to do with dataflow, it helped me comprehend its operation.

My experience has been that in the search for structure, whether I am programming or writing, I discover things about my subject that I wouldn't otherwise have known. I discover, very simply, that I can't get from A to C without inventing B. That is why I would agree with those who say that structured programming increases programming efficiency.

I found that close line-by-line commentary also helped my comprehension. I'd get to a point where I'd added so many complexities I couldn't follow the program anymore, or to a point where my failure to understand *why* a routine happened to work caught up with me. Stopping to write in comments often got me out of the woods.

*Use commentary to explain branches.* A writer makes a big fuss about transitions, waving showy flags like "However," "Moreover," and "It follows" whenever he branches to a new part of his argument. I found it helpful in programming to mark every branch to a subroutine with words that highlighted why I branched and what subroutine I went to. I also decorated the subroutine itself, not only with an explanation of what it did, but what called it and what job it RETURNed to do. Rows of asterisks and other artistic devices also help, but commentary is the best way I know of to impose the actual tree structure on a listed presentation.

*Put an imperative verb in every comment.* A writer seeks as much precision as his topic allows. I found that a good way to increase the precision of my comments was to make sure that they always contained a verb, logically an imperative verb, because program statements are imperative. Don't say "output," say "print the line"; don't say "line length," say "calculate line length"; don't say "indent flag," say "set indent flag."

Modern American writing suffers in general from lack of verbs. We habitually compose sentences that consist mainly of strings of nouns, adjectives, and participles loosely connected by the verb "to be," our least dramatic verb. We say, "A main feature of X is its visual mode editing," instead of "X uses a crt screen to display changes in text as fast as the user makes them." I have added the verbs "use," "display," and "make," as well as some previously unstated subjects and objects that the verbs forced me to consider.

The avoidance of verbs in American speech and writing stems partly, I suppose, from laziness and partly from a wish to sound scientific. Scientific prose (quite hypocritically, I think) abhors the pronoun I. Many young people are prepared for college these days by being told never to use I in an essay. Avoiding I forces a writer to use passive verbs ("to be" plus past participle). The scientist says, "The telescope was pointed at Vega," instead of "I (We? They? My assistant?) pointed the telescope at Vega." Discourse in which nobody does anything sounds professional to us, and unfortunately it is. But when you avoid active verbs you avoid subjects and objects as well, and meaning and precision suffer. A line of programming code always acts; its commentary deserves an active verb.

*Imagine the user.* Writing is an activity of the imagination, and perhaps we have underestimated the degree to which this is also true of programming. Writing software appears at first glance to be an activity of reason, but when the programmer considers his "user interface" his imagination encounters a challenge. Too often we pick up documentation that on one page explains how to mount a floppy disk and on another expects the user to be able to count in hex. Or supposes that he can handle words like "iteration macro," but not "backup." What we have here is a failure to imagine the user's whereabouts. If we know our user, the task of reaching him reduces to choosing, from all the options open to us, the ones that suit him best. We have options both in the features we use and in the language that explains them, in design and in presentation.

No amount of good documentation will make a bad program good, because a good product begins with its basic design. If the software itself cannot serve the user's needs or match his capacities, documentation can do no more than show him the devious route by which he can reach his goals despite the dismaying complexity of the software. Thus dozens of handbooks surface when an essentially unfriendly piece of software happens to become the common default. The automotive industry, because it can imagine specific users, can design a car for a family, a sports buff, a commuter, a camper. But the computer industry has not progressed this far. A typical word processor today (to speak of what I know best) seems to be a helter-skelter assemblage of whatever features all the rest have plus a few bells and whistles of its own. If the designers of word processors really wanted to provide friendly systems, they would begin by scaling down to essentials.

"Simplify, simplify, simplify," said Thoreau. Get rid of the nonessential. The writer of a magazine article decides to avoid a section on whether or not Hitler died in his bunker, by simply assuming that he did. Why open that can of worms for a nonspecialist audience, as long as the consensus of specialists supports the assumption? Similarly, automobile manufacturers don't put a tachometer and a stick shift on a family car: families don't drive with that kind of precision. Nor does a family word processor need commands to set left margin, right margin, and standard indentation; let Mom, Dad, or Sonny state the width of his or her stationery—in inches—and let the word processor calculate good-looking values for the rest. The purpose of machines is to save labor, not increase it.

We are now finally facing the question of how to know this all-important user. Market research alone doesn't seem to do the trick. Back in 1975, market research couldn't have told anyone that personal computers were the world's greatest need. IBM, with its massive research and development spending, was sound asleep. If market research had asked the man on the street back then whether he wanted a computer, he would have said, "What for?" But Steve Jobs guessed that if he himself could afford a computer, anyone could, and he further guessed that anyone would find a use for it. He imagined the market. In his *Defence of Poetry* Shelley wrote, "A man, to be greatly good, must imagine intensely and comprehensively; he must put himself in the place of another and of many others; the pains and pleasures of his species must become his own."

It is not enough to want to be friendly; one must first know how, and imagination is the way. I do not equate imagination with inborn talent, genius, IQ, or romantic notions of "creativity." I think the imagination can be set in action by the will and that it can be trained. Shelley thought it could be trained with poetry, which "strengthens the imagination in the same way that exercise strengthens a limb." Let's say that a person who hungers and thirsts after knowledge develops, in due course, a strong imagination.

Few writers start to build on such flimsy foundations as programmers have been wont to use. We have perceived programming as a field sufficient unto itself, like mathematics, and we have sent programmers out into the dense jungle of whatever trade, profession, or business feels the need of automation, without any preparation for the perils they will assuredly encounter. While we wouldn't dream of appointing a programmer vice president for market research, we have had no qualms about assigning him the task of automating market research. On the face of it, his chances of success are about equal to those of a schoolboy asked to explain the causes of the Civil War.

If we really believed in top-down design we would give ultimate responsibility for automating market research to the vice president of marketing himself: his rank proves that he knows the territory; he knows what's essential; let him justify his salary. VisiCalc was the solution of a problem that conventional programming couldn't even define, let alone solve; it was not a programmer, but a student at Harvard Business School who imagined that program.

If Shelley is right about knowing the territory, programming should disappear as an isolated discipline, and take its place as an adjunct to the studies of any educated man or woman, like math, English composition, and foreign languages. Programming should never be anyone's primary course of study—or career.

Friendliness is not jocularity and stick figures: it is inherent clarity based on simplicity; it determines the essential through a sympathy with the user's needs that is established by an imaginative grasp of the territory he inhabits; it begins with clear design and ends with clear documentation.

# Three
# Sick
# Babies

Berton Roueché

Dr. Paul M. Taylor, an assistant professor of pediatrics at the University of Pittsburgh School of Medicine, left his office on the first floor of Magee-Womens Hospital, an affiliate of the medical school, and climbed the stairs to the premature-baby nursery, on the second floor. It was twenty minutes to eleven on the morning of July 12, 1965, a Monday, and this was his regular weekday round. He was, in a way, attending physician to all the babies in the nursery. Two pediatric residents were waiting for him in the gown room. That, too, was as usual, and while Dr. Taylor scrubbed and disinfected his hands and got into a freshly laundered gown, they gave him the customary nursery news report. The weekend had been generally uneventful. All but one of the twenty-six babies in the nursery were progressing satisfactorily. The exception was one of the smallest—a twenty five-day-old two-and-a-half-pound boy. He was in Room 227. Dr. Taylor nodded. He knew the one they meant. Well, early that morning, just after midnight, a nurse had noted that his breathing was unusually slow and his behavior somewhat apathetic. The resident on duty, seeing these signs as suggestive of septicemia, had treated the baby with penicillin and kanamycin, but he still looked and acted sick. It was probable that he would soon need artificial respiration. Meanwhile, the usual samples (blood, stool, mucus, spinal fluid) had been taken and sent along to the laboratory for culture and analysis.

Dr. Taylor heard his residents' review with no more than natural interest. Serious illness in a premature nursery is not an unusual occurrence, and a blood infection is only one of the many diseases that may afflict a

From *The Orange Man*. Copyright C 1968 by Berton Roueché. Reprinted by permission of Harold Ober Associates.

premature baby during its first days of life. Trouble is inherent in the phenomenon of prematurity. For the truth of the matter is that premature birth is itself a serious affliction. A premature baby is a baby born in the seventh or eighth month of pregnancy. Its birth weight is largely determined by its relative prematurity, ranging from around two to five and a half pounds. The average term (or nine-month) baby weighs around seven pounds at birth, and it generally comes into the world alive and kicking. Premature babies begin life almost incapable of living. There is nothing more frail and fragile. Many of them are too meagerly developed to maintain normal body temperature. One in three requires immediate, and often prolonged resuscitation, and about the same number are unable to nurse, or even to swallow. Some of them are even unable to cry. All of them are exquisitely susceptible to all infection. Mental and neurological defects are also common in premature babies. One of the commonest of these is cerebral palsy. About half of all victims of the affliction are of premature birth. As recently as twenty-five years ago, most premature babies died. The technological innovations of the postwar era have greatly improved that record, but the mortality rate among newborn premature babies is still high. In even the best hospitals, some ninety percent of all two-pound babies die. So do about fifty percent of those weighing two to three pounds, around ten percent of those weighing three to four pounds, and between five and eight percent of those weighing four to five pounds. Such babies are simply too fetal to survive outside the womb. There are many causes of premature birth (including falls and blows), but most current investigators think that malnutrition is perhaps the most important cause. Prematurity would thus seem to be a socioeconomic problem, and this supposition is confirmed by statistics. The great majority of premature babies are born to women too poor to buy the nutritious food they need.

Dr. Taylor tied up the back of his gown and led the way through an inner door to the central nursing station of the nursery. Room 227 was the second room on the right. The sick baby was one of five babies being cared for there. He lay on his side in his incubator bassinet with a stomach feeding tube in his mouth, and he looked even sicker than the resident had said. There was nothing, however, that Dr. Taylor could do that hadn't already been done. He confirmed the resident's course of treatment and agreed that a respirator would probably soon be required, and then moved on to the other babies in that and the other rooms. They were all, as far as he could read the almost imperceptible manifestations of the premature, in their usual precarious but normal condition. At the end of his rounds, Dr. Taylor had lunch, and after lunch he occupied himself with his other professorial duties. Before leaving for home, he put in a call to the nursery for a report on the sick baby. The report was not comforting. The baby's condition had continued to worsen, and he had been moved to Room 229, which is reserved for babies needing constant scrupulous care. Later that evening, on his way to bed, he called the nursery again. The nurse who picked up the telephone was able to answer his question. The sick baby from Room 227 was dead.

Dr. Taylor's Tuesday-morning round was much like that of Monday. The residents' gown-room report included another sick baby. It also contained a post-mortem note on the baby from Room 227. The hospital laboratory had confirmed the general diagnosis of septicemia. A microbial culture had been grown from a sample of the baby's blood and identified as bacteria of the gram-negative type. It was one of some twenty-five species of bacteria (among them the causative organisms of typhoid fever, brucellosis, whooping cough, plague, and gonorrhea) that react negatively to the standard staining test devised in 1884 by the Danish bacteriologist Hans Christian Joachim Gram. A more specific identification was promised for the next day. Meanwhile, of course, the laboratory had been supplied with diagnostic samples from the second sick baby. This baby, also a boy, was one of the babies in Room 229. He was a term baby, three days old, but had been assigned to the premature nursery directly from the delivery room because he required artificial respiration and other intensive care. Dr. Taylor remembered the baby when he saw him. He had begun life with a severe aspiration pneumonia, stemming from an original inability to breathe, but that had been quickly controlled with penicillin, kanamycin, and dexamethasone. His trouble now was diarrhea. Diarrhea in a newborn baby is not a common complaint, and Dr. Taylor wondered if this attack might be a septic aftermath of the earlier pneumonia. But that was a question that only the laboratory could readily answer. There was no doubt about the treatment the baby was receiving. That seemed to be entirely satisfactory.

The Wednesday-morning gown-room news review contained three major items. One was that still another baby boy had become seriously ill overnight. The next item was a preliminary laboratory report on the second sick baby, which identified the cause of his diarrhea as a gram-negative bacillus. The third item was a more or less definitive laboratory report on the dead baby. After forty-eight hours of growth, the gram-negative bacteria cultured from his blood presented the colonial configuration, the fluorescent yellow-green pigmentation, and the spearmint odor generally characteristic of the type known as Pseudomonas aeruginosa.

Dr. Taylor went to Room 229 for a look at the new sick baby. He was nine days old and weighed about three pounds. His illness appeared to be a pneumonia. This illness had come on abruptly, but, like so many other premature babies, he had never been really well. He had been unable at birth to breathe spontaneously and had spent the first five or six days of his life in a respirator. It was obvious to Dr. Taylor that the baby's condition was grave. It seemed equally clear, however, that he was receiving the best of care, and a conventional course of penicillin and kanamycin had been started. Dr. Taylor left the nursery in an uneasy state of mind. His uneasiness had to do with Room 229 and the sudden string of serious illnesses there. He was afraid that they might be more than merely coincidental.

Dr. Taylor was not kept in suspense for long. One of his fears was confirmed that afternoon by a call from the resident then on duty in the nursery. He called to report that the new sick baby—the three-pound nine-day-old—was dead. His illness had lasted a scant eight hours. The next morning brought another confirmation. There was a final laboratory report on the first sick baby: the cause of his death was definitely Pseudomonas infection. There was a forty-eight-hour report on the second sick baby: the gram-negative bacteria grown from his blood had all the important characteristics of Pseudomonas aeruginosa. There was a twenty-four-hour report on the third sick baby: cultures grown from his blood had been identified as gram-negative bacteria. And that was too much for coincidence. It meant—it could almost certainly only mean—that a Pseudomonas epidemic had struck the premature nursery.

Pseudomonas aeruginosa is one of a group of gram-negative pathogens that have only recently come to be seriously pathogenic. Other members of this group include Escherichia coli and the several species of the Proteus and the Enterobacter-Klebsiella genera. Their rise to eminent virulence is a curious phenomenon. These microorganisms regularly reside in soil and water, and in the gastrointestinal tracts of most (if not all) human beings. Their presence in that part of the body is normally innocuous. Healthy adults are impervious to the thrust of such bacteria. The victims of Pseudomonas (and E. coli and Proteus and Enterobacter) infections are the very old, the very young, and the very debilitated (the badly burned, the postoperative, the cancerous), and in almost every case they have been receiving vigorous sulfonamide or antibiotic or adrenalsteroid therapy. Most antimicrobial drugs have little destructive effect on bacteria of the Pseudomonas group. Just the reverse, in fact. Their action, in essence, is tonic. In people rendered susceptible to the gram-negative pathogens by age or illness, the result of chemotherapy is the elimination not only of the immediately threatening pathogens but also of the natural resident bacteria that normally hold further incursions of Pseudomonas (or E. coli or Proteus or Enterobacter) in check. The virulence of Pseudomonas and its kind is thus a wry expression of perhaps the most beneficent accomplishment of twentieth-century medicine.

It is also cause for some alarm. "One of the great changes wrought by the widespread use of antibacterial agents has been the radical shift in the ecologic relations among the pathogenic bacteria that are responsible for the most serious and fatal infections," the *New England Journal of Medicine* noted editorially in July of 1967. "Whereas John Bunyan could properly refer to consumption as 'Captain of the Men of Death,' this title, according to Osler, was taken over by pneumonia in the first quarter of this century. During the last two decades, it has again shifted, at least in hospital populations, first to the staphylococcal diseases and more recently to infections caused by gram-negative bacilli. Most of the gram-negative organisms that have given rise to these serious and highly fatal infections are among the normal flora of the bowel and have sometimes been referred to as 'opportunistic pathogens.' . . . Before the present antibiotic era, some of them, like Escherichia coli, although they frequently caused simple urinary-tract infections, only occasionally gave rise to serious sepsis. . . . Strains of Proteus or Pseudomonas did so very rarely, and those of Enterobacter were not even known to produce infections in human beings before the introduction of sulfonamide drugs. Of great importance are the facts that most of these opportunistic pathogens are resistant to the antibiotics that have been most widely used, and that the infections they produce are associated with a high mortality." This mortality is anachronistically high. It is roughly that resulting from the common run of pathogenic bacteria some thirty years ago—in the days when the best defense against the many Men of Death was a strong constitution.

The most conspicuously troublesome of these ordinarily unaggressive pathogens is E. coli. It has been implicated in some ninety percent of the urinary-tract infections caused by members of this group, and it is responsible for many of the more serious cases of bacteremia, gastroenteritis, and pneumonia. It is not, however, the most opportunistic. The organism best equipped to take advantage of almost any chemotherapeutic opportunity is the Pseudomonas bacillus. Pseudomonas aeruginosa is all but invulnerable to the present pharmacopoeia. Only two antibiotics—polymyxin B and colistin—are generally effective against most Pseudomonas strains. Moreover, both must be used with great discretion to prevent severe kidney side reactions. Ps. aeruginosa is also distinctively lethal. Its mortality rate, as numerous recent outbreaks (including that in Pittsburgh in 1965) have shown, may run as high as seventy-five percent.

An investigation into the source of the Pseudomonas infections in the premature nursery at Magee-Womens Hospital was started by Dr. Taylor on Friday morning, July 16. A forty-eight-hour report from the laboratory had by then established as Ps. aeruginosa the gram-negative bacteria that had been cultured from the blood of the third sick baby, and the presence of an epidemic was now beyond dispute. The investigation began with a survey to determine the scope of the trouble. There were at that time, in addition to the surviving (or diarrheal) sick baby, twenty-eight babies in the nursery. Samples of nose, throat, and stool material were taken from each, to be dispatched to the laboratory for culture and analysis. Dr. Taylor saw this work well under way, and then walked down to his office and put in a call to a colleague named Horace M. Gezon, at the Graduate School of Public Health. Dr. Gezon (at the time professor of epidemiology and microbiology at the University of Pittsburgh Graduate School of Public Health and now chairman of the Department of Pediatrics at the Boston University School of Medicine) is an authority on hospital infections, and

Dr. Taylor wanted his help. Dr. Gezon had two immediate suggestions. One was that the investigators meet at the hospital the following morning for an exchange of information and ideas. The other was that Joshua Fierer, of the Allegheny County Health Department, be invited to join the investigation. Dr. Fierer (now a postdoctoral fellow in infectious diseases at the University of Pittsburgh Department of Medicine) was an Epidemic Intelligence Service officer assigned to Allegheny County by the National Communicable Disease Center, in Atlanta.

"Dr. Taylor called me on Friday afternoon," Dr. Fierer says. "I know it was Friday, because that's when all investigations seem to begin—at the start of the weekend. I knew Dr. Taylor. I had met him with Dr. Gezon back in March—on a Friday in March. There had an outbreak of diarrhea in the premature nursery that they thought might be a viral disease, and they called the county because we had the only virus-diagnostic laboratory in the area. That case turned out to be nothing to worry about. It got the three of us together, though, and I guess that was what brought me to mind when this new problem came up. I was delighted to be asked to participate. Pseudomonas is a very interesting organism these days. But I had to tell Dr. Taylor that I couldn't make the Saturday-morning meeting. Or, if I could, I'd be late. I had a firm commitment at the Pittsburgh Children's Zoo on Saturday morning. They had a chimpanzee out there with hepatitis.

"I got to the hospital, but I was more than late. It was after lunch, and the meeting was over and everybody had gone. I looked around the nursery, feeling kind of foolish, and said hello to the nurses, and they told me who had been at the meeting. There were six in the group, including Dr. Taylor and Dr. Gezon. The others were the two residents, a study nurse of Dr. Gezon's, and an assistant professor of epidemiology at the School of Public Health named Russell Rycheck. Dr. Rycheck was a particular friend of mine. I went over to the school and looked him up, and he gave me a good report. The meeting had naturally concentrated on the nursery. The big question, of course, was: Where had the infection come from? How had Pseudomonas been introduced into the nursery? Well, Pseudomonas is a water-dwelling organism. It can live on practically nothing in the merest drop of water. That suggested water as the probable source of the trouble, and the nursery had plenty of such sources. There were thirty incubator bassinets equipped with humidifiers drawing on water reservoirs, and there were fourteen sinks—one in each of the ten baby rooms, three in the central nursing station, and one in the gown room. And then there were the usual jugs of sterile water for washing the babies' eyes and for other medicative purposes. Dr. Gezon arranged for water samples from every possible source. That included two samples from each sink—one from the drain and one from the aerator on the faucet. The screens that diffuse the water in an aerator can provide a water bug like Pseudomonas with an excellent breeding place. For good measure, he took a swab of the respirator used in the ward. Also, Dr. Rycheck said, Dr. Gezon arranged for throat and stool samples from the two residents and from all the nurses working in the premature nursery. And he had called another meeting for Monday morning. The laboratory findings would be ready for evaluation by then.

"I made the Monday meeting. The laboratory reports were presented, and then we tried to decide what they meant. The human studies made pretty plain reading. There were two sets—the nurses and residents, and the twenty eight seemingly well babies in the nursery. The laboratory eliminated the nurses and residents as possible carriers. Their cultured specimens were all negative for Pseudomonas. The reports on the babies confirmed what I think most of us had already suspected. This was a real epidemic. Twenty-two of the babies were negative for Pseudomonas, but six were positive. They weren't clinically sick. They didn't show any symptoms. They were, however, infected with Ps. aeruginosa. Why they weren't sick is hard to say. There were several possible explanations. The best one was that their exposure was relatively slight and their natural defenses were strong—they hadn't been weakened by antibiotics. The results of the environmental studies were very interesting. But they were also rather confusing. They showed five sink drains and three of the bassinet reservoirs to be contaminated. Everything else was negative for Pseudomonas—the water jugs, the respirator, the faucet aerators, and the other drains and bassinets. The contaminated drains were in Room 207, Room 209, Room 227, an unoccupied room, and the gown room. The contaminated bassinets were in 224, 227, and 229. All the infected babies were associated with just two rooms. They were, or had been, in either Room 227—the room where the first baby took sick—or Room 229, where he died and where the two other babies became sick. There was a contaminated sink in Room 227, but the sink in 229 was clean. There was a contaminated bassinet reservoir in each room, but only one of the bassinets was, or had been, occupied by an infected baby. There were no infected babies in two rooms—Room 209 and Room 207—that had contaminated sinks, and none in Room 224, which had a contaminated bassinet. It was all very peculiar. We had a lot of contamination and we had a lot of infected babies, but there didn't seem to be any connection between the two. The only link we could think of was the nurses. The babies had no contact with each other. The bassinets were self-contained, and none of the babies shared any equipment or medication. The nurses might have carried the infection on their hands. They could do that without becoming infected themselves. Healthy adults don't succumb to Pseudomonas. But why did they carry it only to the babies in 227 and 229?

"The meeting ended on that unsatisfactory note. Dr. Gezon was as puzzled as the rest of us. But, of course, this puzzling point was only part of the investigation. We still had an epidemic to contain. We didn't understand the mechanics of its spread, but we did know what it was, and we thought we had enough information to bring it under control. We knew who was sick and we knew that the nursery was contaminated at eight specific sites. By Monday night, the nursery was as clean as Dr. Gezon and the nursery staff knew how to make it. All the sinks were scrubbed with sodium-hypochlorite disinfectant. The bassinet reservoirs were emptied and disinfected with an iodophor, and only those in use were refilled. As a further precaution, that water was to be changed every day. Certain nurses were assigned to take exclusive care of the infected babies. Also, in the hope of dislodging their infection, all the infected babies were placed on a five-day course of colistimethate given intramuscularly, and colistin sulphate by mouth. It wasn't necessary to isolate the infected babies. They were already isolated. And it was arranged that specimens be taken every day from all the babies in the nursery, and from all the sinks and bassinets and so on. That would give us a constant focus on the course of the epidemic.

"I didn't participate in the sanitation program. They didn't need me. I would have been an extra thumb. I went back to my office and back to the regular Health Department routine, but part of my mind was still out there at the nursery, and I got to thinking about something I'd read a few months before. It was a report in the *Lancet* about an outbreak of Pseudomonas in an English nursery that was traced to a catheter used to relieve throat congestion in the babies. The source of the trouble eluded detection for almost a year. What I particularly remembered about the report was a description of a new system of microbial identification. There are several different types of Ps. aeruginosa, and this report told how they could be differentiated by a laboratory procedure called pyocine typing. Pyocine typing makes use of the fact that certain strains of Pseudomonas will kill or inhibit the growth of other Pseudomonas strains, and it's a complicated procedure. Well, it occurred to me that pyocine typing might help to clarify our problem. It could at least tell us if all the sinks and all the bassinets and all the infected babies were infected with the same strain of Pseudomonas. I thought about it, and finally I called up Dr. Gezon. He saw the point at once. But, as I say, pyocine typing was then very new, and we didn't know where to turn for help. It could be that the system was being used only in England. We talked it over and decided that the best place to begin was at the Communicable Disease Center, in Atlanta. If anybody was doing pyocine typing in this country, the people there would certainly know. That was Monday evening. On Tuesday morning, I got on the phone to Atlanta and talked to one of my friends at CDC and asked him what he knew about something called pyocine typing. 'Pyocine typing?' he said, 'Why, Shulman is working on that right now. I'll switch you over to him.' Shulman was Dr. Jonas A. Shulman, and a fellow Epidemic Intelligence Service officer. He's now assistant professor of preventive medicine at Emory University. I described the case to him and asked him if he could help us out, and he was more than willing. He was eager. He wanted all the work he could get. So as soon as we finished talking I arranged for specimens of all our isolates to be air-mailed down to Atlanta. Pyocine typing takes about two days. Shulman might have something for us by Thursday.

"Before I left the hospital, I went around to the premature nursery. That *Lancet* paper was still on my mind. Not pyocine typing. What interested me now was the source of the outbreak it described—that contaminated catheter. I looked up one of the pediatric residents and asked him what went on in the delivery rooms. I was thinking about contaminated equipment that the babies might have shared. For example, did they use a regular aspirator? The resident said no. The aspirators they used were all disposable and were discarded after each use. What about the resuscitators? Did they have humidifying attachments? A humidifier would mean water, and a possible breeding place for Pseudomonas. Another no. The resuscitators used in the delivery rooms were simply bags and masks attached to an oxygen line from the wall. I asked a few more questions along those lines and got the same kind of answers, and gave up. This wasn't a case like the *Lancet* case. So I was back in the nursery again. But the more I thought about those contaminated sinks and bassinets the less convinced I was that they were the source of our trouble. I just couldn't see any plausible link between those particular sites and those nine particular babies. But if the answer wasn't a piece of contaminated equipment, what else could it be? A contaminated person? And then I got a thought— maybe a contaminated mother. It sounded only too possible. A contaminated mother could very easily transmit an infection to her baby in the course of its birth. Childbirth is not a very tidy process.

"The next question was: Which mother? I thought I could answer that. It had to be the mother of the second sick baby. Not the baby in whom the infection was first diagnosed. The significant case was the second Pseudomonas baby—the term baby who came into the nursery with pneumonia and then developed diarrhea. The first sick baby had been healthy until the day before his death. He had been healthy for over three weeks. So he was actually No. 2. It wasn't hard to reconstruct the possible course of events. The infection was introduced into the nursery by the term baby and then spread to the other babies by the nurses. Pseudomonas is a difficult organism. You can't wash it off your hands with a little soap and water, the way you can the staphylococcus bug. To get Pseudomonas off, you have to scrub and scrub and scrub. And it's also extremely resistant to most disinfectants. But what made the infected-mother theory really attractive was that it seemed to explain what the environmental theory left unexplained. It explained why the infected babies were concentrated in Room 227 and Room 229. Both of those rooms were intensive-care rooms, and there was very little traffic between them and the other rooms. However, it was just a theory. It was based on the supposition that the diarrheal baby's mother was a Pseudomonas carrier. So the next thing to do was find out. The first thing I found was that the baby had been discharged on Saturday, and that he and his mother were now at home. I got the address, and Dr. Taylor and the baby's pediatrician gave me the necessary permission. I went out to the house and introduced myself, and the mother was nice and cooperative, and I got the specimens I needed and took them back to the Health Department Lab.

"She wasn't a carrier. The preliminary laboratory report on my specimens was negative for Pseudomonas. That was the following day—Wednesday afternoon. But by then it didn't matter. We had something much more interesting to think about. The way it happened was this. I was in the nursery that afternoon, and one of the residents came over and told me they had another infected baby. New babies had been coming along every day, of course, and this one was a term baby born on Monday and sent up to the premature nursery for special care. He had had trouble breathing at birth, and had required extensive resuscitation in the delivery room. Well, a routine nasopharyngeal culture taken when he was admitted to the nursery had just been found to be positive for Pseudomonas. I looked at the resident and the resident looked at me. This was real news. That baby could not possibly have been infected in the nursery. The laboratory samples had been taken before he was even settled there. He could have been infected only in the delivery room. And there were just two possible sources of infection there. His mother was one, and the other was some piece of contaminated equipment. My guess was naturally the mother. I found out what room the new baby's mother was in, and made the necessary arrangements, and went up and took the standard nose, throat, and stool samples, and arranged for the hospital laboratory to culture them. When I got back to the nursery, Dr. Gezon was there talking to the resident, and I could tell from the look on his face that he had heard the news.

"The three of us went down to the delivery suite. We found the nurse in charge and told her what we were doing. She was terribly upset. It was most distressing to her to have us arrive in her domain on such a mission. But she was a good nurse and she cooperated perfectly. The room where the baby had been born was not in use, and she took us in and showed us around. There was a delivery table in the middle of the room, and a row of scrub sinks along the left-hand wall. On the opposite wall was a resuscitator of the type described to me the day before. It consisted of a rubber face mask and a rubber Emerson bag enclosed in a cellophane casing, and it looked very neat and clean. But something made me take it down for a closer look. There was a little dribble of water in the bottom of the Emerson bag. I showed it to Dr. Gezon, and he raised his eyebrows and passed it on to the resident. The resident took a sample of the water. There were five other rooms in the delivery suite, and luckily none of them were in use. We checked the resuscitator in every room, and every one was wet. The question was: How come? The nurse explained the delivery suite cleaning procedure. There was one central wash sink, where all delivery-room equipment was washed. Everything was washed after every use, and then sterilized by steaming in an autoclave. Including the resuscitators? No—of course not. They were made of rubber, and rubber can't stand that kind of heat. The resuscitators were washed with a detergent, rinsed with tap water, and left on the drainboard to dry. It was possible, the nurse said, that they were sometimes returned to the delivery rooms before they were completely dry. We asked to see the wash sink. We were all beginning to feel sort of elated. I know I was. And when we saw the sink, that just about finished us. The faucet was equipped with an aerator—a standard five-screen water-bug heaven.

"It *was* a water-bug heaven. The laboratory cultured Pseudomonas from the swab samples we took from the aerator. It also cultured Pseudomonas from five of the six resuscitator samples. You can imagine how the delivery-suite nurses felt when those reports came down. They were crushed. Dr. Gezon was able to reassure them, though. He didn't consider them guilty of ignorance. They assumed, like almost everybody else, that city drinking water is safe. It is and it isn't. It's perfectly safe to drink, but it isn't absolutely pure. This is something that has only recently been recognized. There are water bugs in even the best city water. The concentrations are much too low in ordinary circumstances to cause any trouble, but a dangerous concentration can occur in any situation—like that provided by an aerator—that enables the bugs to accumulate and breed. An aerator is a handy device, but you'd probably be better off letting the water splash. It's certainly a device that a hospital can do without.

"The laboratory gave us three reports in all. The third was on the mother of the new baby. They found her negative for Pseudomonas, and that was welcome news. A positive culture from her would have been an awkward complication. Because everything else was very satisfactory. The contaminated resuscitators seemed to explain the concentration of infected babies in Room 227 and Room 229. Seven of the ten infected babies—including the diarrheal baby and the two that died—had received at least some resuscitation in the delivery room, and it was reasonable to suppose that the three others had got their infection from the resuscitated babies by way of the nurses. There's plenty of evidence for that in the literature. I remember one report that showed that nurses' hands were contaminated simply by changing the bedding of an infected patient. It was Dr. Shulman, however, who finally pinned it down. His pyocine typing confirmed the circumstantial evidence at every point. Shulman did two groups of studies of us—one on the original material I sent him, and then another on the new infected baby and the delivery-suite material. The results of his studies were doubly instructive. They identified the delivery-room resuscitators as the source of the epidemic, and they eliminated the contaminated sinks and bassinets in the nursery. The different pyocine types of Pseudomonas aeruginosa are indicated by numbers. The Pseudomonas strain cultured from the delivery-suite aerator was identified as Pyocine Type 4-6-8. So were the isolates from the resuscitator bags. And so were those of all of the infected babies. Type 4-6-8 was also recovered from two pieces of equipment in the nursery, but I think we can safely assume that they had been contaminated indirectly from the same delivery-room source. They were a bassinet used by an infected baby and the sink in Room 227. The other contaminations in the nursery were a wild variety of types—6, 4-6, 6-8, 1-2-3-4-6-7-8, and 1-3-4-6-7-8. And where they came from wasn't much of a mystery. There was only one possible explanation. They came out of the water faucets, too."

That was the end of the formal investigation. It wasn't, however, the end of the trouble. The pockets of contamination in the sinks and elsewhere in the nursery and in the delivery suite were eliminated (and a system of ethylene-oxide sterilization set up for all resuscitation equipment), but the epidemic continued. In spite of the most sophisticated treatment (first with colistimethate and colistin sulphate, and then with colistin in combination with polymyxin B), the infected babies remained infected. Moreover, in the course of the next few weeks twelve new infections were discovered in the nursery. In two of the new victims, the infection developed into serious clinical illness. It was not until the middle of September, when the remaining infected babies were moved to an isolated ward in another part of the hospital, that the epidemic was finally brought under control.

Hospital infections of any kind are seldom easily cured. Pseudomonas aeruginosa is only somewhat more stubborn than such other institutional pathogens as Staphylococcus aureus and the many Salmonellae. These confined and yet all but unextinguishable conflagrations are, in fact, the despair of modern medicine. They are also, as it happens, one of its own creations. The sullen phenomenon of hospital infection is a product equally of medical progress and of medical presumption. It has its roots in the chemotherapeutic revolution that began with the development of the sulfonamides during the middle nineteen-thirties, and in the elaboration of new life-saving and life-sustaining techniques (open-heart surgery, catheterization, intravenous feeding) that the new antibacterial drugs made possible, and it came into being with the failure of these drugs (largely through the development of resistance in once susceptible germs) to realize their original millennial promise. Its continuation reflects a drug-inspired persuasion that prevention is no longer superior to cure. "In the midst of the development of modern antibacterial agents, infection has flourished with a vigor that rivals the days of Semmelweis," Dr. Sol Haberman, director of the Microbiology laboratories at Baylor University Medical Center, noted. "It would appear that the long sad history of disease transmission by attendants to the sick has been forgotten again."

# By the Numbers

### K.C. Cole

*Mathematics is all well and good, but Nature keeps dragging us around by the nose.*
—Albert Einstein

One day last winter, MIT theoretical physicist Philip Morrison was talking about forces and particles, and in particular about those strange entities known as force particles. Finally Morrison said, "Look, forces and particles may not be appropriate ways to describe these things. If you read the *Physical Review*, you won't read about force particles. You'll read about Lagrangians."

A Lagrangian is not a physical thing; it is a mathematical thing—a kind of differential equation, to be exact. But physics and math are so closely connected these days that it is hard to separate the numbers from the things they describe. In fact, a month after Morrison's remark, Nobel Prize winner Burton Richter of the Stanford Linear Accelerator Center said something that eerily echoed it: "Mathematics is a language that is used to describe nature," he said. "But the theorists are beginning to think it *is* nature. To them, the Lagrangians are the reality."

Every high school student knows that nature and numbers go hand in hand. The exploration of the physical universe is open only to those who are willing to suffer total immersion in the abstract ideas of geometry and calculus. Science often deals with real things that people can see, hear,

K.C. Cole, "By the Numbers," ©*Discover* Magazine, 1-84, Time Inc.

feel, and wonder about: stars, pendulums, rainbows, sounds, cells, heat, earthquakes, and elements. It hardly seems right that the only route to learning about them should be by the numbers. Yet, says Caltech's Richard Feynman, "I am sorry, but this seems to be the case. It is impossible to explain honestly the beauties of the laws of nature in a way that people can feel, without their having some deep understanding of mathematics."

The belief that truth lies in numbers goes back at least as far as the sixth century B.C., when the philosopher Pythagoras went about making such statements as "Things are numbers." And later, "There are also numbers beyond things." Pythagoras was probably the first person to formulate a physical law mathematically: the harmonic combinations of sounds that are music to our ears are based on simple, whole-number relationships. The frequency ratio 2:1 corresponds to an octave; 3:2 to a fifth. Pythagoras believed that the planets were placed in the heavens in orbits that played similar but unheard harmonies. "There is music in the spacing of the spheres," he wrote.

The Pythagoreans saw in numbers a purity and perfection impossible to achieve amid the messy complexities of everyday life. Unfortunately, they soon discovered that numbers could be messy and complicated, too — even, it turned out, "irrational." An irrational number is one that cannot be expressed as a ratio of two whole numbers, like the never-ending decimal $\pi$ (3.14159...). Every soap bubble and every bit of ocean froth is built on irrational numbers. Yet the Pythagoreans were so shattered by their own discovery (was the world, at its root, irrational?) that they kept it a closely guarded secret. (It is probably just as well they did not know about "imaginary" numbers, such as the square root of minus 1, which are not only irrational but impossible.)

Several millennia later, the astronomer Johannes Kepler became so entranced by the Pythagorean ideal that he devoted his life to proving that the planets orbited in spheres enclosed in a stacking of five perfect solids. "Geometry existed before the Creation," said Kepler. "It is coeternal with the mind of God...Geometry is God himself." Even as recently as the nineteenth century, the discoverer of radio waves, Heinrich Hertz, wrote, "One cannot escape the feeling that these mathematical formulae have an independent existence and an intelligence of their own, that they are wiser than we are, wiser even than their discoverers..."

One cannot deny the astounding number of discoveries that have emerged from the mouths of equations: quarks, antimatter, even the fact that light is an electromagnetic wave. James Clerk Maxwell could not help noticing that the number $3 \times 10^{10}$ kept turning up in all his equations that contained an electric field on one side and a magnetic field on the other side. The number $3 \times 10^{10}$ is the velocity of light in a vacuum in centimeters per second. Even "imaginary" numbers turned out to be crucial to the theory of relativity: only through such a device could time be combined with the three dimensions of space to form a four-dimensional space-time continuum.

It should not be surprising, of course, that numbers turn up surprising relationships. Numbers *are* relationships. In fact, numbers may be one of the few ways of relating one thing to another that do not depend ultimately on sense perceptions. But if numbers reveal higher truths, they also reveal different kinds of truths from the ones we are used to. Or, as Einstein put it, "As far as the propositions of mathematics refer to reality they are not certain, and in so far as they are certain they do not refer to reality."

Strangely, however, this very quality seems to be the source of the strength in numbers. That is, mathematical descriptions do not, and cannot, exactly reflect reality. Reality is simply too complex. The glory of mathematics, on the other hand, "is that *we do not have to say what we are talking about,*" says Feynman. "The glory is that the laws, the arguments, the logic are independent of what 'it' is." (Bertrand Russell gave this same idea a slightly different shading: "Mathematics may be defined as the subject in which we never know what we are talking about, nor whether what we are saying is true.")

Mathematics is different from things; it is a way of thinking about things, a method of reasoning that takes you from one step to another. The mathematical language of science is not easily translatable into other languages because it is more than a language. It is language plus logic. It is a method of connecting things that has been coded in such a way that it can be reproduced and repeated by many different people following the same path. In a sense, it *is* the path.

So many of the puzzles that confront physicists are presented in the form of numbers. There is, for example, the unexplained ratio 1/137. This is a number that keeps popping up whenever the universal constants of nature (things like the natural unit of electric charge, the velocity of light, and "Planck's constant"—a kind of universal limit of smallness) are mathematically combined. The funny thing about 1/137 is that it is dimensionless. It is not 1/137 inches or grams or seconds (or even inch-gram–seconds). It comes out 1/137 no matter what kinds of measures you put into the equation (as long as the units are consistent). Another curious correlation emerges when you compare the ratio of the electric force to the gravitational force (the number 1 divided by $4.17 \times 10^{42}$) and the ratio of the diameter of a proton to the diameter of the universe (also the number 1 divided by a number containing 42 zeros). A funny coincidence? Perhaps. But it has set at least some physicists to thinking that if the diameter of the universe is increasing as the universe expands, then perhaps the "constant" force of gravity is changing, too.

Finally, there is the matter of mass numbers. That is why is the mass of an electron 2,000 times smaller than the mass of a proton or neutron—a relationship that fundamentally shapes the nature of the atom? Why are muons and tau particles, identical to electrons in other respects, vastly larger in their masses? "The most striking realm of ideas is where these mass numbers come from," says Feynman. "If we could find a theory to tell us where the numbers come from, then that same theory could give many other answers."

It is unlikely that these answers will come from experiments or observations of nature. The solutions must lie in the numbers. Indeed, not so long ago, Caltech theoretical physicist David Politzer told me that "all the recent inventions in the physics of the early universe are mathematical theorems."

Of course, searching for clues in numbers sometimes leads nowhere; Kepler's attempt to find geometrical order in the planetary orbits led to a dead end. At other times, the search is amazingly fruitful. But whether or not true knowledge of the physical world can be contained in mathematical theorems is yet another question. As Bertrand Russell suggested, "Physics is mathematical not because we know so much about the physical world, but because we know so little; it is only its mathematical properties that we can discover."

# The Purpose of Philosophy

## Isaiah Berlin

What is the subject-matter of philosophy? There is no universally accepted answer to this question. Opinions differ, from those who regard it as contemplation of all time and all existence—the queen of the sciences—the keystone of the entire arch of human knowledge—to those who wish to dismiss it as a pseudo-science exploiting verbal confusions, a symptom of intellectual immaturity, due to be consigned together with theology and other speculative disciplines to the museum of curious antiquities, as astrology and alchemy have long ago been relegated by the victorious march of the natural sciences.

Perhaps the best way of approaching this topic is to ask, what constitutes the field of other disciplines? How do we demarcate the province of, say, chemistry or history or anthropology? Here it seems clear that subjects or fields of study are determined by the kind of questions to which they have been invented to provide the answers. The questions themselves are intelligible if, and only if, we know where to look for the answers.

If you ask someone an ordinary question, say 'Where is my coat?', 'Why was Mr  Kennedy elected President of the United States?', 'What is the Soviet system of criminal law?', he would normally know how to set about finding an answer. We may not know the answers ourselves, but we know that in the case of the question about the coat, the proper procedure is to look on the chair, in the cupboard, etc. In the case of Mr Kennedy's election or the Soviet system of law we consult writings or specialists for the kind of empirical evidence which leads to the relevant

From Isaiah Berlin, *Concepts and Categories: Philosophical Essays* (London: Oxford University sity Press, 1980). Oxford Paperback edition. Originally published by Hogarth Press.

conclusions and renders them, if not certain, at any rate probable.

In other words, we know where to look for the answer: we know what makes some answers plausible and others not. What makes this type of question intelligible in the first place is that we think that the answer can be discovered by empirical means, that is, by orderly observation or experiment, or methods compounded of these, namely those of common sense or the natural sciences. There is another class of questions where we are no less clear about the proper route by which the answers are to be sought, namely the formal disciplines: mathematics, for example, or logic, or grammar, or chess or heraldry, defined in terms of certain fixed axioms and certain rules of deduction etc., where the answer to problems is to be found by applying these rules in the manner prescribed as correct.

We do not know the correct proof of Fermat's Theorem, for example, — no one is known to have found it — but we know along what lines to proceed: we know what kind of methods will, and what kind of methods will not, be relevant to the answer. If anyone thinks that answers to mathematical problems can be obtained by looking at green fields or the behaviour of bees, or that answers to empirical problems can be obtained by pure calculation without any factual content at all, we would today think them mistaken to the point of insanity. Each of these major types of questions — the factual and the formal — possesses its own specialised techniques: discoveries by men of genius in these fields, once they are established, can be used by men of no genius at all in a semi-mechanical manner in order to obtain correct results.

The hallmark of these provinces of human thought is that once the question is put we know in which direction to proceed to try to obtain the answer. The history of systematic human thought is largely a sustained effort to formulate all the questions that occur to mankind in such a way that the answers to them will fall into one or other of two great baskets: the empirical, i.e. questions whose answers depend, in the end, on the data of observation; and the formal, i.e. questions whose answers depend on pure calculation, untrammelled by factual knowledge. This dichotomy is a drastically over-simple formulation: empirical and formal elements are not so easily disentangled: but it contains enough truth not to be seriously misleading. The distinction between these two great sources of human knowledge has been recognised since the first beginning of self-conscious thinking.

Yet there are certain questions that do not easily fit into this simple classification. 'What is an okapi?' is answered easily enough by an act of empirical observation. Similarly 'What is the cube root of 729?' is settled by a piece of calculation in accordance with accepted rules. But if I ask 'What is time?', 'What is a number?', 'What is the purpose of human life on earth?', 'How can I know past facts that are no longer there — no longer where?', 'Are all men truly brothers?', how do I set about looking for the answer? If I ask 'Where is my coat?' a possible answer (whether correct or not) would be 'In the cupboard', and we would all know where to look. But if a child asked me 'Where is the image in the mirror?' it would be little use to invite it to look inside the mirror, which it would find to consist of solid glass; or on the surface of the mirror, for the image is certainly not on its surface in the sense in which a postage stamp stuck on it might be; or behind the mirror (which is where the image looks as if it were), for if you look behind the mirror you will find no image there—and so on.

Many who think long enough, and intensely enough, about such questions as 'What is time?' or 'Can time stand still?', 'When I see double, what is there two of?', 'How do I know that other human beings (or material objects) are not mere figments of my own mind?', get into a state of hopeless frustration. 'What is the meaning of "the future tense"?' can be answered by grammarians by mechanically applying formal rules; but if I ask 'What is the meaning of "the future"?' where are we to look for the answer?

There seems to be something queer about all these questions—as wide apart as those about double vision, or number, or the brotherhood of men, or purposes of life; they differ from the questions in the other basket in that the question itself does not seem to contain a pointer to the way in which the answer to it is to be found. The other, more ordinary, questions contain precisely such pointers—built-in techniques for finding the answers to them. The questions about time, the existence of others and so on reduce the questioner to perplexity, and annoy practical people precisely because they do not seem to lead to clear answers or useful knowledge of any kind.

This shows that between the two original baskets, the empirical and the formal, there is at least one intermediate basket, in which all those questions live which cannot easily be fitted into the other two. These questions are of the most diverse nature; some appear to be questions of fact, others of value; some are questions about words and a few symbols; others are about methods pursued by those who use them: scientists, artists, critics, common men in the ordinary affairs of life; still others are about the relations between various provinces of knowledge; some deal with the presuppositions of thinking, some with the nature and ends of moral or social or political action.

The only common characteristic which all these questions appear to have is that they cannot be answered either by observation or calculation, either by inductive methods or deductive; and, as a crucial corollary of this, that those who ask them are faced with a perplexity from the very beginning—they do not know where to look for the answers; there are no dictionaries, encyclopedias, compendia of knowledge, no experts, no orthodoxies, which can be referred to with confidence as possessing unquestionable authority or knowledge in these matters. Moreover some of these questions are distinguished by being general and by dealing with matters of principle; and others, while not themselves general, very readily raise or lead to questions of principle.

Such questions tend to be called philosophical. Ordinary men regard them with contempt, or awe, or suspicion, according to their temperaments. For this reason, if for no other, there is a natural tendency to try to reformulate these questions in such a way that all or at any rate parts of them can be answered either by empirical or formal statements; that is to say efforts, sometimes very desperate ones, are made to fit them into either the empirical or the formal basket, where agreed methods, elaborated over the centuries, yield dependable results whose truth can be tested by accepted means.

The history of human knowledge is, to a large degree, a sustained attempt to shuffle all questions into one of the two 'viable' categories; for as soon as a puzzling, 'queer' question can be translated into one that can be treated by an empirical or a formal discipline, it ceases to be philosophical and becomes part of a recognised science.[1] Thus it was no mistake to regard astronomy in, say, the early Middle Ages as a 'philosophical' discipline: so long as answers to questions about stars and planets were not determined by observation or experiment and calculation, but were dominated by such non-empirical notions as those, e.g., of perfect bodies determined to pursue circular paths by their goals or inner essences with which they were endowed by God or Nature, even if this was rendered improbable by empirical observation, it was not clear how astronomical questions could be settled: i.e. what part was to be played by observing actual heavenly bodies, and what part by theological or metaphysical assertions which were not capable of being tested either by empirical or by formal means.

Only when questions in astronomy were formulated in such a manner that clear answers could be discovered by using and depending on the methods of observation and experiment, and these in their turn could be connected in a systematic structure the coherence of which could be tested by purely logical or mathematical means, was the modern science of astronomy created, leaving behind it a cloud of obscure metaphysical notions unconnected with empirical tests and consequently no longer relevant to the new science, and so gradually relegated and forgotten.

So, too, in our own time, such disciplines as economics, psychology, semantics, logic itself, are gradually shaking themselves free from every-

[1] The claims of metaphysics or theology to be sciences must rest on the assumption that intuition or revelation are direct sources of knowledge of facts about the world; since they claim to be forms of direct experience, their data, if their existence is allowed, belong, for our purposes, to the 'empirical' basket.

thing that is neither dependent on observation nor formal; if and when they have successfully completed this process they will be finally launched on independent careers of their own as natural or formal sciences, with a rich philosophical past, but an empirical and/or formal present and future. The history of thought is thus a long series of parricides, in which new disciplines seek to achieve their freedom by killing off the parent subjects and eradicating from within themselves whatever traces still linger within them of 'philosophical' problems, i.e. the kind of questions that do not carry within their own structure clear indications of the techniques of their own solution.

That, at any rate, is the ideal of such sciences; in so far as some of their problems (e.g. in modern cosmology) are not formulated in purely empirical or mathematical terms, their field necessarily overlaps with that of philosophy. Indeed, it would be rash to say of any developed high-level science that it has finally eradicated its philosophical problems. In physics, for instance, fundamental questions exist at the present time which in many ways seem philosophical—questions that concern the very framework of concepts in terms of which hypotheses are to be formed and observations interpreted. How are wave-models and particle-models related to one another? Is indeterminacy an ultimate feature of sub-atomic theory? Such questions are of a philosophical type; in particular, no deductive or observational programme leads at all directly to their solution. On the other hand, it is of course true that those who try to answer such questions need to be trained and gifted in physics, and that any answers to those questions would constitute advances in the science of physics itself. Although, with the progressive separation of the positive sciences, no philosophers' questions are physical, some physicists' questions are still philosophical.

This is one reason, but only one, why the scope and content of philosophy does not seem greatly diminished by this process of attrition. For no matter how many questions can be so transformed as to be capable of empirical or formal treatment, the number of questions that seem incapable of being so treated does not appear to grow less. This fact would have distressed the philosophers of the Enlightenment, who were convinced that all genuine questions could be solved by the methods that had achieved so magnificent a triumph in the hands of the natural scientists of the seventeenth and early eighteenth centuries.

It is true that even in that clear day men still appeared no nearer to the solution of such central, indubitably philosophical, because apparently unanswerable, questions as whether men and things had been created to fulfil a purpose by God or by nature, and if so what purpose; whether men were free to choose between alternatives, or on the contrary were rigorously determined by the causal laws that governed inanimate nature; whether ethical and aesthetic truths were universal and objective or relative and subjective; whether men were only bundles of flesh and blood and bone and nervous tissue, or the earthly habitations of immortal souls; whether human history had a discernible pattern, or was a repetitive causal sequence or a succession of casual and unintelligible accidents. These ancient questions tormented them as they had their ancestors in Greece and Rome and Palestine and the medieval west.

Physics and chemistry did not tell one why some men were obliged to obey other men and under what circumstances, and what was the nature of such obligations; what was good and what was evil; whether happiness and knowledge, justice and mercy, liberty and equality, efficiency and individual independence, were equally valid goals of human action, and if so, whether they were compatible with one another, and if not, which of them were to be chosen, and what were valid criteria for such choices, and how we could be certain about their validity, and what was meant by the notion of validity itself; and many more questions of this type.

Yet—so a good many eighteenth-century philosophers argued—a similar state of chaos and doubt had once prevailed in the realm of the natural sciences too; yet there human genius had finally prevailed and created order.

> Nature and Nature's laws lay hid in night:
> God said 'Let Newton be!' and all was light.

If Newton could, with a small number of basic laws, enable us, at least in theory, to determine the position and motion of every physical entity in the universe, and in this way abolish at one blow a vast, shapeless mass of conflicting, obscure, and only half-intelligible rules of thumb which had hitherto passed for natural knowledge, was it not reasonable to expect that by applying similar principles to human conduct and the analysis of the nature of man, we should be able to obtain similar clarification and establish the human sciences upon equally firm foundations?

Philosophy fed on the muddles and obscurities of language; if these were cleared away, it would surely be found that the only questions left would be concerned with testable human beliefs, or expressions of identifiable, everyday human needs or hopes or fears or interests. These were the proper study of psychologists, anthropologists, sociologists, economists; all that was needed was a Newton, or series of Newtons, for the sciences of man; in this way, the perplexities of metaphysics could once and for all be removed, the idle tribe of philosophical speculators eradicated, and on the ground thus cleared, a clear and firm edifice of natural science built.

This was the hope of all the best-known philosophers of the Enlightenment, from Hobbes and Hume to Helvétius, Holbach, Condorcet, Bentham, Saint-Simon, Comte, and their successors. Yet this programme was doomed to failure. The realm of philosophy was not partitioned into a series of scientific successor states. Philosophical questions continued (and continue) to fascinate and torment inquiring minds.

Why is this so? An illuminating answer to this problem was given by Kant, the first thinker to draw a clear distinction between, on the one hand, questions of fact, and, on the other, questions about the patterns in which these facts presented themselves to us — patterns that were not themselves altered however much the facts themselves, or our knowledge of them, might alter. These patterns or categories or forms of experience were themselves not the subject-matter of any possible natural science.

Kant was the first to draw the crucial distinction between facts — the data of experience as it were, the things, persons, events, qualities, relations, that we observed or inferred or thought about — and the categories in terms of which we sensed and imagined and reflected about them. These were, for him, independent of the different cosmic attitudes — the religious or metaphysical frameworks that belonged to various ages and civilisations. Thus, the majority of Greek philosophers, and most of all Aristotle, thought that all things had purposes built into them by nature — ends or goals which they could not but seek to fulfil. The medieval Christians saw the world as a hierarchy in which every object and person was called upon to fulfil a specific function by the Divine Creator; He alone understood the purpose of the entire pattern, and made the happiness and misery of His creatures depend upon the degree to which they followed the commandments that were entailed by the differing purposes for which each entity had been created — the purposes that in fulfilling themselves realised the universal harmony, the supreme pattern, the totality of which was kept from the creatures, and understood by the Creator alone.

The rationalists of the eighteenth and nineteenth centuries saw no purpose in anything but what man himself had created to serve his own needs, and regarded all else as determined by the laws of cause and effect, so that most things pursued no purposes, but were as they were, and moved and changed as they did, as a matter of 'brute' fact.

These were profoundly different outlooks. Yet those who held them saw very similar items in the universe, similar colours, tastes, shapes, forms of motion and rest, experienced similar feelings, pursued similar goals, acted in similar fashions.

Kant, in his doctrine of our knowledge of the external world, taught that the categories through which we saw it were identical for all sentient beings, permanent and unalterable; indeed this is what made our world one, and communication possible. But some of those who thought about history, morals, aesthetics, did see change and difference; what differed was not so much the empirical content of what these successive civilisations saw or heard or thought as the basic patterns in which they perceived them, the models in terms of which they conceived them, the category-spectacles through which they viewed them.

The world of a man who believes that God created him for a specific purpose, that he has an immortal soul, that there is an afterlife in which his sins will be visited upon him, is radically different from the world of a man who believes in none of these things; and the reasons for action, the moral codes, the political beliefs, the tastes, the personal relationships of the former will deeply and systematically differ from those of the latter.

Men's views of one another will differ profoundly as a very consequence of their general conception of the world: the notions of cause and purpose, good and evil, freedom and slavery, things and persons, rights, duties, laws, justice, truth, falsehood, to take some central ideas completely at random, depend directly upon the general framework within which they form, as it were, nodal points. Although the facts which are classified and arranged under these notions are not at all identical for all men at all times, yet these differences—which the sciences examine—are not the same as the profounder differences which wearing different sets of spectacles, using different categories, thinking in terms of different models, must make to men of different times and places and cultures and outlooks.

Philosophy, then, is not an empirical study: not the critical examination of what exists or has existed or will exist—this is dealt with by commonsense knowledge and belief, and the methods of the natural sciences. Nor is it a kind of formal deduction as mathematics or logic is. Its subject-matter is to a large degree not the items of experience, but the ways in which they are viewed, the permanent or semi-permanent categories in terms of which experience is conceived and classified. Purpose versus mechanical causality; organism versus mere amalgams; systems versus mere togetherness; spatio-temporal order versus timeless being; duty versus appetite; value versus fact—these are categories, models, spectacles. Some of these are as old as human experience itself; others are more transient. With the more transient, the philosopher's problems take on a more dynamic and historical aspect. Different models and frameworks, with their attendant obscurities and difficulties, arise at different times. The case of contemporary problems in the explanatory framework of physics, already mentioned, is one example of this. But there are other examples, which affect the thought not just of physicists or other specialists, but of reflective men in general.

In politics, for example, men tried to conceive of their social existence by analogy with various models: Plato at one stage, perhaps following Pythagoras, tried to frame his system of human nature, its attributes and goals, following a geometrical pattern, since he thought it would explain all there was. There followed the biological pattern of Aristotle; the many Christian images with which the writings of the Fathers as well as the Old and New Testaments abound; the analogy of the family, which casts light upon human relations not provided by a mechanical model (say that of Hobbes); the notion of an army on the march with its emphasis on such virtues as loyalty, dedication, obedience, needed to overtake and crush the enemy (with which so much play has been made in the Soviet Union); the notion of the state as a traffic policeman and night watchman preventing collisions and looking after property, which is at the back of much individualist and liberal thought; the notion of the state as much more than this—as a great cooperative endeavour of individuals seeking to fulfil a common end, and therefore as entitled to enter into every nook and cranny of human experience, that animates much of the 'organic' thought of the nineteenth century; the systems borrowed from psychology, or from theories of games, that are in vogue at present—all these are models in terms of which human beings, groups and societies and cultures, have conceived of their experience.

These models often collide; some are rendered inadequate by failing to account for too many aspects of experience, and are in their turn replaced by other models which emphasise what these last have omitted but in their turn may obscure what the others have rendered clear. The task of philosophy, often a difficult and painful one, is to extricate and bring to light the hidden categories and models in terms of which human beings think (that is, their use of words, images and other symbols), to reveal what is obscure or contradictory in them, to discern the conflicts between them that prevent the construction of more adequate ways of organising and describing and explaining experience (for all description as well as explanation involves some model in terms of which the describing and explaining is done); and then, at a still 'higher' level, to examine the nature of this activity itself (epistemology, philosophical logic, linguistic analysis), and to bring to light the concealed models that operate in this second-order, philosophical, activity itself.

If it is objected that all this seems very abstract and remote from daily experience, something too little concerned with the central interests, the happiness and unhappiness and ultimate fate of ordinary men, the answer is that this charge is false. Men cannot live without seeking to describe and explain the universe to themselves. The models they use in doing this must deeply affect their lives, not least when they are unconscious; much of the misery and frustration of men is due to the mechanical or unconscious, as well as deliberate, application of models where they do not work. Who can say how much suffering has been caused by the exuberant use of the organic model in politics, or the comparison of the state to a work of art, and the representation of the dictator as the inspired moulder of human lives, by totalitarian theorists in our own times? Who shall say how much harm and how much good, in previous ages, came of the exaggerated application to social relations of metaphors and models fashioned after the patterns of paternal authority, especially to the relations of rulers of states to their subjects, or of priests to the laity?

If there is to be any hope of a rational order on earth, or of a just appreciation of the many various interests that divide diverse groups of human beings—knowledge that is indispensable to any attempt to assess their effects, and the patterns of their interplay and its consequences, in order to find viable compromises through which men may continue to live and satisfy their desires without thereby crushing the equally central desires and needs of others—it lies in the bringing to light of these models, social, moral, political, and above all the underlying metaphysical patterns in which they are rooted, with a view to examining whether they are adequate to their task.

The perennial task of philosophers is to examine whatever seems insusceptible to the methods of the sciences or everyday observation, e.g. categories, concepts, models, ways of thinking or acting, and particularly ways in which they clash with one another, with a view to constructing other, less internally contradictory, and (though this can never be fully attained) less pervertible metaphors, images, symbols and systems of categories. It is certainly a reasonable hypothesis that one of the principal causes of confusion, misery and fear is, whatever may be its psychological or social roots, blind adherence to outworn notions, pathological suspicion of any form of critical self-examination, frantic efforts to prevent any degree of rational analysis of what we live by and for.

This socially dangerous, intellectually difficult, often agonising and thankless, but always important activity is the work of philosophers, whether they deal with the natural sciences or moral or political or purely personal issues. The goal of philosophy is always the same, to assist men to understand themselves and thus operate in the open, and not wildly, in the dark.

# The Game

## Ken Dryden

Once I used to wait in line like everyone else. Then one day a bank teller motioned me out of the line, and I haven't been back in one since. I feel no small guilt each time; nonetheless I continue to accept such favours. For the tellers and me, it has become normal and routine. They treat me the way they think people like me expect to be treated. And I accept.

It is the kind of special treatment professional athletes have grown accustomed to, and enjoy. It began with hockey, with teenage names and faces in local papers, with hockey jackets that only the best players on the best teams wore, with parents who competed not so quietly on the side; and it will end with hockey. In between, the longer and better we play the more all-encompassing the treatment becomes. People give, easily and naturally. And we accept. Slippers, sweaters, plant holders, mitts, baby blankets, baby clothes sent in the mail. Paintings, carvings, etchings, sculptures in clay, metal, papier-mâché. Shirts, slacks, coats, suits, ties, underwear; cars, carpets, sofas, chairs, refrigerators, beds, washers, dryers, stoves, TVs, stereos, at cost or no cost at all. After all, a special person deserves a special price. A hundred letters a week, more than 3,000 a year—"You're the best," all but a few of them say. On the street, in restaurants and theatres, we're pointed at, talked about like the weather. "There he is, the famous hockey player," your own kids announce to their friends. In other homes, your picture is on a boy's bedroom wall. Magazines, newspapers, radio, TV; hockey cards, posters, T-shirts, and curios, anywhere, everywhere, name, face, thousands of times.

And we love it. We say we don't, but we do. We hate the nuisance and inconvenience, the bother of untimely, unending autographs, handshakes, and smiles, living out an image of ourselves that isn't quite real, abused if we fail to, feeling encircled and trapped, never able to get away.

From the *Saturday Night* adaptation of *The Game* by Ken Dryden. Reprinted by permission of Macmillan of Canada, a Division of Canada Publishing Corporation.

But we also feel special—head-turning, chin-dropping, forget-your-own-name special. What others buy Rolls-Royces and votes and hockey teams for, what others take off their clothes for, what others kill for, we have. All we have to do is play.

If exposure is the vehicle of celebrity, attention is what separates one celebrity from another. Guy Lafleur and Yvon Lambert are both celebrities, yet on the same ice, the same screen, Lafleur is noticed, Lambert is not. Lambert, methodical and unspectacular, has nothing readily distinctive about him. His image is passed over, his name unheard. Lafleur *is* distinctive. The way he skates, the sound of the crowd he carries with him, the goals he scores.

And so, too, others, for other reasons. Mario Tremblay, for his fiery, untamed spirit; Bob Gainey, for his relentless, almost palpable will; Tiger Williams, Eddie Shack, Ron Duguay, each colourful and exciting; and Dave Schultz, once king of the mountain. As sports coverage proliferates beyond games, as it becomes entertainment and moves to prime time, as we look for the story behind the story, off-ice performance becomes important. And so personas are born, and sometimes made, and cameras and microphones are there as it happens. The crazies, the clowns, the "sports intellectuals," the anti-jock rebels (Jim Bouton, Bill "Spaceman" Lee), the playboys (Joe Namath, Derek Sanderson), each a distinctive personality, each a bigger celebrity because of what he does away from the game.

TV has given us a new minimum off-ice standard. The modern player must be articulate (or engagingly inarticulate, especially southern style). It's not enough to score a goal and have it picked apart by the all-seeing eyes of replay cameras. A player must be able to put it in his own eloquent words. How did you do it? How did you feel? Live, on-camera words that cannot be edited for the morning paper.

Celebrity is a full, integrated life, earned on-ice, performed, sustained, strengthened, re-earned off-ice. As Roger Angell once put it, we want our athletes to be "good at life." Role models for children, people we want to believe earned what they have, every bit as good at things off the ice as on. If they're inarticulate, harsh and pejorative, they're suddenly just jocks. Merely lucky, less likable, less good at life, less celebrated; finally, they even seem less good *on* the ice.

At its extreme, the process creates the category of professional celebrity, people "famous for being famous," so accomplished at being celebrities that their original source of celebrity is forgotten. At the least, it encourages all celebrities to learn the *skills* of the public person. How to look good, how to sound modest and intelligent, funny and self-deprecatory, anything you want. It's a celebrity's short-cut to the real thing, but it works. Walter Cronkite *looks* trustworthy, Ronald Reagan *seems* like a nice guy. Denis Potvin *sounds* intelligent; or is he only articulate?

Good enough at something to be a public person, or simply a good public person? You'll never get close enough long enough to know.

All around us are people anxious to help us look better. Not just flaks and PR types but a whole industry of journalists, commentators, biographers, award-givers. Ghost-writers who put well-paid words under our names, then disappear; charity organizers, volunteers who give time and effort so that "honorary chairmen," "honorary presidents," and "honorary directors" may look even better. Children in hospitals, old folks in old-folks' homes—we autograph their casts, shake their hands, make them props to our generosity and compassion. And never far away, photographers and cameramen record the event. It is the bandwagon momentum of celebrityhood.

In the end, for us, is an image. After thousands of confused messages, we cut through what is complex and render it simple. One image, concrete and disembodied. What agents call "Ken Dryden."

Recently, I asked an executive at an advertising agency to pretend he was trying to persuade a client to use me as a commercial spokesman for his company. We'd met two or three times, several years before, so he knew me mostly as others do. He wrote the following memo to his client: "Historically I know you have had some concerns about using an athlete …either because of potential problems developing out of their careers and public life, or due to simply their lack of availability. I think Ken is quite different from the rest. He is known as a thoughtful, articulate and concerned individual. I think it would go without saying he would not participate in any endorsation unless he was fully committed to and satisfied with the product. (His Ralph Nader exposures would assure that.) He is serious, respected and appears to be very much his own man. I don't think we could ever consider using him in humorous or light approaches (like Eddie Shack) unless it would be by juxtaposition with another…actor or player. He has good media presence.…His physical presence is also commanding. He is quite tall and impressive… . Other encouraging things would be his intelligence and educational background. He would be more in tune with our target audience with his credentials as a college graduate (Cornell) and a fledgling professional person (law). Also, during production, I think this intelligence and coolness would help in case of commercial production as well as helping to keep costs under control due to mental errors.…"

So that's my image. Is it accurate? It doesn't matter. It's what people think, it presupposes how they'll react to me. And for the ad man and his client, how people will react is what matters.

If I don't like my image, I can do something about it. I can do things that are "good for my image." I can stop doing things that are "bad for my image." As actors remind us casually and often, I can do things to change my image. Is it too serious? If I run around the dressing room throwing water at the right moment, someone is bound to notice. A journalist with a deadline to meet and space to fill, a new angle, *news*— "Dryden misunderstood."

Want to be known as an antique collector? Collect an antique. A theatre-goer? Go. Once is enough. Tell a journalist, sound enthusiastic, and, above all, play well. Then stand back and watch what happens. Clipped and filed, the news spreads like a chain letter, to other journalists who don't have time to check it out. Presto, it's part of your standard bio. And your image.

If you substitute the word "reputation" for "image," as you might have done a few years ago, you'd have something quite different. A reputation is nothing so trifling or cynical. Like an old barge, it takes time to get going. It's slow and relentless, difficult to manoeuvre, even harder to stop. An image is nothing so solemn. It is merely a commercial asset, a package of all the rights and good-will associated with "Ken Dryden" —something I can sell to whomever I want.

But it's a sticky matter. For the image I'm selling is *your* image of me. The good-will, though it relates to me, is your good-will. Whatever commercial value there is in my name, my image, it's you who puts it there. You like me or trust me, and any prospective buyer of my image, anxious to put my name alongside his product, knows that and counts on it to make you buy his product. And you might, even though it may not be in your best interest. So by selling my name, I have perhaps taken your trust and turned it against you.

I did a commercial once, six years ago. I'd decided I never would, but this one was different enough to start a web of rationalizations until I forgot the point and accepted. A fast-food chain was looking for a winter promotion; Hockey Canada, the advisory and promotional body, wanted a fundraiser and a way to deliver the message to kids and their parents that minor hockey can be approached and played differently. The idea was a mini-book done by Hockey Canada, then sold through the restaurant chain. I was to be a collaborator on the book, and its public spokesman. But after doing the TV and radio ads (for the book, but with a corporate jingle at the end), and seeing the point-of-purchase cardboard likenesses of me in the restaurants, I realized my mistake.

Since then, I have turned down endorsements for, among other things, a candy bar ("The way I see it, a full body shot of you in the net, mask up, talking, then we draw in tight on your catching glove, you open it, the bar's inside...."), a credit card company ("You may not know me without my mask, but...."), and a roll-on deodorant that would also be promoted by several other people whose names begin with the sound "dry."

It's a game—an ad game, an image game, a celebrity game—that no one really loses. Everyone needs someone to talk about—why not about us? Everyone needs heroes and villains. We earn a little money, get some exposure. The commercials are going to be done anyway. Besides, it doesn't last long. A few years and images change, celebrity cools, it's over. It all evens out.

But it doesn't. We all lose, at least a little. We lose because you think I'm better than I am. Brighter than I am, kinder, more compassionate, capable of more things, as good at life as I am at the game. I'm not. Off the ice I struggle as you do, but off the ice you never see me, even when you think you do. I appear good at other things because I'm good at being a goalie; because I'm a celebrity; because there's always someone around to say I'm good. Because in the cozy glow of success, of good news, you want me to be good. It's my angle, and so long as I play well the angle won't change. I appear bright and articulate because I'm an athlete, and many athletes are not bright and articulate. "Like a dog's walking on his hind legs," as Dr. Johnson once put it, "it is not done well; but you are surprised to find it done at all."

But you don't believe that, just as I don't believe it about celebrities I don't know. They're taller, more talented, more compassionate. They glitter into cameras and microphones, give each other awards for talent and compassion, "great human beings" every one. Wet-eyed I applaud, and believe. And all of us lose. You, because you feel less worthy than you are. Me, because once, when I was twenty-three years old and trying to learn about myself, I wanted to believe I was, or soon would be, everything others said I was. Instead, having learned much and grown older, I feel co-conspirator to a fraud.

Professional athletes do exciting, sometimes courageous, sometimes ennobling things, as heroes do, but no more than you do. Blown up on a TV screen or a page, hyped by distance and imagination, we seem more heroic, but we're not. Our achievement seems grander, but it isn't. Our cause, our commitment, is no different from yours. We are no more than examples, metaphors, because we enter every home; we're models for the young because their world is small and we do what they do.

A few years ago, Joe McGinniss, author of *The Selling of the President, 1968*, wrote a book called *Heroes*. It sketches McGinniss's own tormented trail from being *the youngest*, to *the highly acclaimed*, to *the former*—all before he was thirty. At the same time, he ostensibly searches for the vanished American hero. He talks to George McGovern and Teddy Kennedy, General William Westmoreland, John Glenn, Eugene McCarthy, author William Styron, playwright Arthur Miller—some of them heroes of his, all of them heroes to many.

But it's like chasing a rainbow. He finds that, as he gets closer, his heroes disappear. In homes and bars, on campaign trails, they're distinctly, disappointingly normal. Not wonderfully, triumphantly, down-to-earth normal, but up-close, drinking-too-much, sweating, stinking, unheroically normal. And for heroes, normal isn't enough. We are allowed one image; everything must fit.

The Greeks gave their gods human imperfections. In the modern hero, however, every flaw is a fatal flaw. It has only to be found, and it *will* be. Moving from celebrity to hero is like moving from a city to a small town. In a city, the camera's eye, though always present, is distant. In a small town, there isn't that distance. There's no place to hide.

"Whom the gods would destroy," Wilfrid Sheed wrote in *Transatlantic Blues*, "they first oversell." Superficially created, superficially destroyed—for the hero, for the celebrity, it all evens out. Except a heavy price is paid along the way. We all lose again. You, because, saddened and hurt by heroes who turn out not to be heroes at all, you become cynical and stop believing. Me, because I'm in a box. What is my responsibility? Is it, as I'm often told, to be the hero that children think I am? Or is it to live what is real, to be something else?

Recently, a friend asked me to speak to his college seminar. Near the end of two hours, we began to talk about many of these questions. A girl raised her hand. She said that a year or two earlier, on the Academy Awards, she had seen Charlton Heston receive an award for his "humanitarian" work. Heston had made the point, the girl said, that thousands of volunteers had done far more than he, that they deserved the award.

I asked the class what that story told them about Charlton Heston. That he's even modest, they decided. A few of the students laughed; then, one by one, several others joined in.

# Witches

## Margaret Atwood

(1980)

When I was walking through the rain in Cambridge today, lugging a heavy bag of books, having been sent to the wrong place, it was hard for me to believe that almost 20 years had passed since I first walked through Cambridge in the rain, lugging a heavy bag of books, with the deep suspicion that I had been sent to the wrong place. I had ostensibly come to Radcliffe to study Victorian literature, and that part of it was all right, since one of my fellow Canadians was teaching it here. But underneath my Victorian exterior I fancied myself a poet, a fancy that—as anyone who has ever been a graduate studentess in English will know—it was death to admit. And all the modern poetry, as well as the devices for listening thereto, were locked in Lamont Library, which was restricted to students and banned to studentesses. Getting out a book of modern poetry required somewhat the same procedures as those needed to extract a book of pornography from the X section of the Widener Library, and, being of a retiring nature, I didn't want anyone to see me doing the former under the mistaken impression that I was doing the latter. To this fact I owe my ignorance of modern American poetry, as well as my Canadian nationalism—for the Canadian poetry was not kept with the *real* poetry, but was down with Canadiana in the bowels of the Widener, underneath Ethnology and Folklore, and freely accessible to students and studentesses alike.

Walking around Cambridge today, trying to find out what I was supposed to be doing—a continuation of a lifelong endeavour—I was reminded of many happy afternoons spent in the bathtub on the third floor of 6 Appian Way (which is, alas, no more), reading Charles Dickens, scribbling dismal poems, and listening to the rain and the pitter-patter of sexual perverts as they scampered up and down the fire escape. I was also

©Radcliffe College 1980. Reprinted with permission of the Radcliffe Quarterly.

reminded of those many nights when I sat up until dawn, popping No-Nods and trying to get my term papers finished on time—for I have to confess that I actually wrote this speech this afternoon in the Greenhouse Restaurant, over a Frogurt and a cup of Sanka. It is to my habits of procrastination in things academic that I owe my success as a writer, for if I had done scholarship true justice, how would I ever have had time to write? (I did, however, learn an important distinction in graduate school: a speculation about who had syphilis when is gossip if it's about your friends, a plot element if it's about a character in a novel, and scholarship if it's about John Keats.)

It was at Radcliffe, too, that I first heard about role models. The position of dean, or was it don, was open, and there was much discussion about who should fill it. "We need a good role model," someone said. "What's that?" I asked, being from Canada. It was explained to me that, for role-modelhood, even at a university, scholarship was not the only requirement. One also had to be punctual, clean behind the ears, a good mother, well dressed, and socially presentable.

I'm afraid I'm a bad role model, but then, I long ago decided that I could be either a good role model or a writer, and for better or worse I chose writing.

Which brings me to the title of my address, a title I plucked from the air when presented with the need for one, without having the least idea of what I was going to say. I did feel, however, that it was appropriate to talk of witches here in New England, for obvious reasons, but also because this is the land of my ancestors, and one of my ancestors was a witch. Her name was Mary Webster, she lived in Connecticut, and she was hanged for "causing an old man to become extremely valetudinarious." Luckily, they had not yet invented the drop: in those days they just sort of strung you up. When they cut Mary Webster down the next day, she was, to everyone's surprise, not dead. Because of the law of double jeopardy, under which you could not be executed twice for the same offence, Mary Webster went free. I expect that if everyone thought she had occult powers before the hanging, they were even more convinced of it afterwards. She is my favourite ancestor, more dear to my heart even than the privateers and the massacred French Protestants, and if there's one thing I hope I've inherited from her, it's her neck.

One needs a neck like that if one is determined to be a writer, especially a woman writer, and especially if you are good at it. After 10 years of the Women's Movement we like to think that some of the old stereotypes are fading, but 10 years is not a very long time in the history of the world, and I can tell you from experience that the old familiar images, the old icons, have merely gone underground, and not far at that. We still think of a powerful woman as an anomaly, a potentially dangerous anomaly; there is something subversive about such women, even when they take care to be good role models. They cannot have come by their power naturally, it is felt. They must have *got it from somewhere.* Women writers are particularly subject to such projections, for writing itself is uncanny: it uses words for evocation rather than for denotation; it is spell-making. A man who is good at it is a craftsman. A woman who is good at it is a dubious proposition. A man's work is reviewed for its style and ideas, but all too often a woman's is reviewed for the supposed personality of the author as based on the jacket photograph. When a man is attacked in print, it's usually for saying what he says; when a woman is attacked in print, it's often for being who she is.

Which brings me to the next unfortunate aspect of witches. Witches were consulted in private, but their only public role was to be persecuted; or, as we say, "hunted." And here, with brief mention of the fact that in the current wave of book banning taking place in Canada, all the most prominently publicized banned writers have been women, I'd like to switch from women writers—who, after all, have it rather soft in this century, on this continent, and whose necks are strong enough to survive a little name-calling whenever they stick them out—to a larger and more alarming picture.

Witch-hunting was probably always political in nature, an attempt by the powerful to control the potentially subversive, and it still is. The difference between witch-hunting and more conventional forms of justice and punishment is that in the latter you're supposedly being punished for what you've done, but in the former it's enough to be who you are. I'm a member of Amnesty International, and I read their monthly bulletins, which I would like to give *gratis*, a year's subscription, to the next literary critic who accuses my work of being unduly pessimistic. Political witch-hunting is now a worldwide epidemic. Torture for the purposes of extracting a confession, which will in turn justify the torture, is not a thing of the past. It did not end with racks, stakes, and Grand Inquisitors, or with Cotton Mather. It's here with us now, and growing. One of the few remedies for it is free human speech, which is why writers are always among the first to be lined up against the wall by any totalitarian regime, left or right. How many poets are there in El Salvador? The answer is none. They have all been shot or exiled. The true distinction in the world today is not between the so-called left and the so-called right. It's between governments that do such things as a matter of policy, or that wink at them when they are done, and those that do not. It would be simple stupidity to suppose that North America is by nature exempt. We've had witch-hunts before, and there is every indication that we're on the verge of having them again. When times are tough, when the Black Plague strikes or the economy falters and people get restless, those in authority start looking around for someone to burn.

When you are a fiction writer, you're confronted every day with the question that confronted, among others, George Eliot and Dostoevsky: what kind of world shall you describe for your readers? The one you can see around you, or the better one you can imagine? If only the latter, you'll be unrealistic; if only the former, despairing. But it is by the better world we can imagine that we judge the world we have. If we cease to judge this world, we may find ourselves, very quickly, in one which is infinitely worse.

# The Size
# of Thoughts

## Nicholson Baker

Each thought has a size, and most are about three feet tall, with the level of complexity of a lawnmower engine, or a cigarette lighter, or those tubes of toothpaste that, by mingling several hidden pastes and gels, create a pleasantly striped product. Once in a while, a thought may come up that seems, in its woolly, ranked composure, roughly the size of one's closet. But a really *large* thought, a thought in the presence of which whole urban centers would rise to their feet, and cry out with expressions of gratefulness and kinship; a thought with grandeur, and drenching, barrel-scorning cataracts, and detonations of fist-clenched hope, and hundreds of cellos; a thought that can tear phone books in half, and rap on the iron nodes of experience until every blue girder rings; a thought that may one day pack everything noble and good into its briefcase, elbow past the curators of purposelessness, travel overnight toward Truth, and shake it by the indifferent marble shoulders until it finally whispers its cool assent— this is the size of thought worth thinking about.

I have wanted for so long to own and maintain even a few huge, interlocking thoughts that, having exhausted more legitimate methods, I have recently resorted to theoretical speculation. Would it be possible to list those features that, taken together, confer upon a thought a lofty magnificence? What *makes* them so very large? My idle corollary hope is that perhaps a systematic and rigorous codification, on the model of Hammurabi's or Napoleon's, might make large thoughts available cheap, and in bulk, to the general public, thereby salvaging the nineteenth-century dream of a liberal democracy. But mainly I am hoping that once I can coax from large thoughts the rich impulses of their power, I will be able to think them in solitude, evening after evening, walking in little circles on the carpet with my arms outspread.

Nicholson Baker, "The Size of Thoughts," *The Atlantic Monthly* (March, 1983).

In my first attempt to find an objective measure for the size of thoughts, I theorized (as most of us have, I suppose) that I had only to mount the narrow stairs to my attic, stand in the hypotenuse of sunlight that passed through the window there in midwinter, and, concentrating, punch the thought in question once quite firmly, as if it were a pillow. The total number of tiny golden dust-monads that puffed forth from the thought's shocked stuffing would indicate, I believed, its eternal, essential size.

I found this to be a crude technique, and rejected it. Next, influenced by Sir John Eccles, the famous neurophysiologist, who used the axon of the giant-squid neuron to arrive at truths about the chemistry of human nerve fibers (small truths, needless to say: all scientific truths are small), I cast about for a suitably large thought existing in a form compact enough for me to experiment on it intensively. I tried a line of Wordsworth's,

> ...steps
> Almost as silent as the turf they
>     trod.

but it wasn't really big enough for my purposes. I tried

> O, for a beaker full of the warm
>     South,
> Full of the true, the blushful
>     Hippocrene...

but I wept every time I read it, and got nowhere. Finally I decided to think about Henry James's sentence "What is morality but high intelligence?" It came to seem so conveniently vast, so ideally ample, that I handled it for several days, as if it were some richly figured object carved in cool stone; and when it failed to relinquish the secret of its size after that period, I discovered that I had indirectly arrived at my first theorem regarding large thoughts, which was:

1) *All large thoughts are reluctant.* I don't think this is intentional on their part. It follows from the unhasty, liquid pace of human thinking. As an experiment, overturn half a glass of wine onto a newly starched tablecloth. Watch, wholly absorbed, as the borders of the stain search their way outward, plumping up each parched capillary of cotton, threadlet by threadlet, and then traveling on — a soundless, happy explosion, with no moving parts. Thought moves at the velocity of that stain. And since a large thought seems to wish to pierce and acknowledge and even to replenish many more shoots and plumules of one's experience, some shrunken from long neglect (for every thought, even the largest, tires, winds down, and hardens into a hibernating token of chat, a place-holder for real intellection, unless it is worried into endless, pliant movement by second thoughts, and by the sense of its own provisionality, passing and repassing through the hundreds of semi-permeable membranes that insu-

late learning, suffering, ambition, civility, and puzzlement from one another, and from their neighbors), its thrum of fineness will necessarily be delayed, baffled, and drawn out with numerous interstitial timidities—one pauses, looks up from the page, waits; the eyes move in meditative polygons in their orbits; and then, somehow, *more* of the thought is released into the soul, the corroborating peal of some new, distant bell—until it has filled out the entirety of its form, as a thick clay slip settles into an intricate mold, or as a ladleful of batter colonizes cell after cell of the waffle iron, or as, later, the smell of that waffle will have toured the awakening rooms of the house.

Yet I sensed that reluctance was insufficient. What else did a large thought have to have? Filled with an ambitious sort of wistfulness, I flung open the door of the island cottage where I was staying, nodded to the moon, and began to walk up the fairway of a golf course, repeating, to the pulse of my invisible feet, a large thought of Tennyson's on which I had decided to perform a few experiments:

> Witch-elms that counterchange the
> floor
> Of this flat lawn with dusk and
> bright…

The sand traps, ghostly objects shaped like white blood cells, floated slowly past. At last I reached the green, the moon-colored green, where a dark flag flapped, and looked out over the warm, white sea. I threw my arms wide, and waited. Right then my second theorem regarding large thoughts ought to have formed itself in silver characters on the far horizon, but, in fact, it reached me only some weeks later, in a public library:

2) *Large thoughts are creatures of the shade.* Not deep shade, necessarily, but the mixed and leafy shade at the floor of large forests. Small thoughts are happy to run around in their colorful swimwear under the brutallest of noons, but large thoughts really must have sizable volumes of cool, still air, to allow room for the approach and docking of their components of sadness. Nobody can frown intently at a delicate task sitting on the floor of a large forest, and large thoughts, too, evade the pointedness and single-purposiveness of a frown; instead, they assert with a general pressure, and avoid contentiousness, and limit themselves to the suggestion that not far off, not far off, there are wholly convincing marginalia of still-undiscovered feeling, stored like heaped tapestries in unlit vaults: they exhibit, then, a lush shadiness, as do the purple fastnesses in one's lungs, or the wrought, jewelled, dark interiors of water-resistant watches. All large thoughts are also patched and played over by leaf-shadows of slight hesitation and uncertainty: this tentativeness gives the thought just enough humility for it to be true. (All that is untrue is small.) I have found that dusk—the moment of planetary shade—is the most likely time to encounter large thoughts. Because, I suppose, of some power struggle between the retina's rods and cones brought on with the coming of darkness,

there is a quarter-hour or so when colors, though less distinct, seem superbly pigmented, and the important things, faces and especially the teeth of smiles, take on a soft, amiable light: it is then that large thoughts may best be observed, strolling on their somber porches, and reciting from their codices.

As you may imagine, by the time I had successfully formulated this second theorem regarding large thoughts, I was desperately tired of them. If I felt one looming up in a page of Tolstoy, I ran off; I hid. The party seemed over: Ed Peters and the band had packed up, and the deadened balloons scudded about the floor.

I slumped in a chair. More than anything else, I wished just then for the minty breath of a slighter, gentler truth or two in my ear. A minor botanical discovery concerning a rare species of fern, perhaps; a paradox or an aperçu would do; faint harpsichord music; tricks with coins or cards; witty biographies of peripheral Victorians. What was so very contemptible about small thoughts? Where, indeed, would we be without cornish game hens such as "It is one of the chief merits of proofs that they instill a certain skepticism about the result proved," which came to rest in Bertrand Russell's lucky mind one day? Or Charles Churchill's little two-step:

> With curious art the brain, too
> finely wrought,
> Preys on herself, and is destroyed
> by thought.

Or, finally, this bit from Pater: "There is a certain shade of unconcern, the perfect manner of the eighteenth century, which may be thought to mark complete culture in the handling of abstract questions": a thought that bounds beamingly, radiantly skyward for an instant, but is then, like many fine small thoughts, snuffed out on the second bounce by a bookish delegation of counterexamples. If we exiled all that is nifty, careless, wildly exaggerated, light-footed, vulnerable, or curiously spiced from our spiritual landscape, we would be in terrible shape. I became disgusted with myself for my callousness toward the small. "Refine all epics into epigrams!" I said. "I shall measure only the flares and glimmers of the world, thimbleful by peerless thimbleful; and I shall not grudge even the jingle of a light-bulb filament the silence of an enraptured continent."

But this extreme reaction missed the point, which was, as I found out not long afterward, that:

3) *Large thoughts depend more heavily on small thoughts than you might think.* Why does velvet feel smoother than chrome? Because smoothness is a secondary inference on the part of the confused fingertip, based on its perception of many extraordinarily fleeting little roughnesses running underneath it too quickly to be individually considered. This suggestion of resistance in all truly smooth surfaces, like the sense of ornamental insurrection in all truly graceful lines, is analogous to the profusion, the

anarchy, of lovely, brief insights that we often experience as we read or listen our way through a great work of the mind, a work that, once completed, will leave us filled with large, calm truths. I do not know how this happens, but it happens. The villi on the inside of our small intestine — dense groves of microscopic protuberances — constitute a total surface area dedicated to absorption of nutrients which, if flattened out, would rival the island of Manhattan in size, I am told. Large thoughts, too, disembellished and abstracted from the small thoughts that diversify their surface, become sheer and indigestible. Consider the infinitesimal hooks on the horsehairs that draw from the cello string its lavish tone; consider the grosgrain in silk; the gargoyles on a cathedral; the acanthus sprays or egg-and-dart molding along the tasteful curve of a chair; the lumps of potato that, by exception, prove the otherwise fine uniformity of a cream soup; consider the examples that enforce a moral essay; the social satire in a novel with a tragic ending; the sixteenth notes in a peaceful melody; the fanatically detailed foliage in a Dutch landscape; the incessant roadside metaphors in a work of philosophy — consider all the indefensible appliances, the snags, the friction, the plush, that seem to hinder the achievement of a larger purpose, but are, in fact, critical to it. Major truths, like benevolent madonnas, are sustained aloft by dozens of busy, cheerful angels of detail.

I have tested these three theorems — the theorem of reluctance, the theorem of shade, and the theorem of dependence — on as many of the artifacts of reason as I could while holding a steady job. My results may have a certain severe appeal. Few indeed are the hobbyists in human memory who have known the recondite craft of building a spacious, previously unthought thought of their very own: how to obtain, in arranging its long hallways and high, ornate rooms, that pull of an ever-riper deferment, by returning to it again and again, after some studied distraction — now full-face, now three-quarter view, now very near, now far off; how to gather in its huge, slow force with an encircling persistence that is three parts novelty, two parts confirming, strengthening repetition. I count Henry James, Brahms, Bellini. Burke, Bach, Pontormo. A mere eighty-six others. And now, in a mood of icy impartiality, I am going to test the size of the thought I am offering you right here, which I expect to see peter out very shortly with few surprises, wrapped up after another two or three breaths of the mind, extended perhaps by a last, gravelly spatter of instantiation, unless, O yearn! I just happen to happen upon that loose-limbed, reckless acceleration, wherein this very thought might shamble forward, plucking tart berries, purchasing newspapers, and retrieving odd bits of refuse without once breaking stride — risking a smile, shaking the outstretched hands of young constituents, loosening its tie! — no, that's all, I believe: this thought has rounded itself out, and ratified itself, despite all of its friendly intentions, as small.

# Our Allotted Lifetimes

## Stephen Jay Gould

J.P. Morgan, meeting with Henry Ford in E.L. Doctorow's *Ragtime*, praises the assembly line as a faithful translation of nature's wisdom:

> Has it occurred to you that your assembly line is not merely a stroke of industrial genius but a projection of organic truth? After all, the interchangeability of parts is a rule of nature....All mammals reproduce in the same way and share the same designs of self-nourishment, with digestive and circulatory systems that are recognizably the same, and they enjoy the same senses....Shared design is what allows taxonomists to classify mammals as mammals.

An imperious tycoon should not be met with equivocation; nonetheless, I can only reply "yes, and no" to Morgan's pronouncement. Morgan was wrong if he thought that large mammals are geometric replicas of smaller relatives. Elephants have relatively smaller brains and thicker legs than mice, and these differences record a general rule of mammalian design, not the idiosyncrasies of particular animals.

But Morgan was right in arguing that large animals are essentially similar to small members of their group. The similarity, however, does not reside in a constant shape. The basic laws of geometry dictate that animals must change their shape in order to work the same way at different sizes. Galileo himself established the classic example in 1638: the strength of an animal's leg is a function of its cross-sectional area (length x length); the weight that legs must support varies as the animal's volume (length x length x length). If mammals did not increase the relative thickness of

"Our Allotted Lifetimes" is reprinted from *The Panda's Thumb: More Reflections in Natural History* by Stephen Jay Gould, by permission of W.W. Norton & Company, Inc. Copyright © 1980 by Stephen Jay Gould.

their legs as they got larger, they would soon collapse (since body weight would increase so much faster than the supporting strength of limbs). To remain the same in function, animals must change their form.

The study of these changes in form is called "scaling theory." Scaling theory has uncovered a striking regularity of changing shape over the 25-millionfold range of mammalian weight from shrew to blue whale. If we plot brain weight versus body weight for all mammals on the so-called mouse-to-elephant (or shrew-to-whale) curve, very few species deviate far from a single line expressing the general rule: brain weight increases only two-thirds as fast as body weight as we move from small to large mammals. (We share with bottle-nosed dolphins the honor of greatest upward deviance from the curve.)

We can often predict these regularities from the basic physics of objects. The heart, for example, is a pump. Since all mammalian hearts work in essentially the same way, small hearts must pump considerably faster than large ones (imagine how much faster you could work a finger-sized, toy bellows than the giant model that fuels a blacksmith's forge or an old-fashioned organ). On the mouse-to-elephant curve for mammals, the length of a heartbeat increases between one-fourth and one-third as fast as body weight as we move from small to large mammals. The generality of this conclusion has recently been affirmed in an interesting study by J.E. Carrel and R.D. Heathcote on the scaling of heart rate in spiders. They used a cool laser beam to illuminate the hearts of resting spiders and drew a crab spider-to-tarantula curve for eighteen species spanning nearly a thousandfold range of body weight. Again, scaling is regular with heart rate increasing four-tenths as fast as body weight (.409 times as fast, to be exact).

We may extend this conclusion for hearts to a general statement about the pace of life in small versus large animals. Small animals tick through life far more rapidly than large animals—their hearts work more quickly, they breathe more frequently, their pulse beats much faster. Most importantly, metabolic rate, the so-called fire of life, increases only three-fourths as fast as body weight in mammals. To keep themselves going, large mammals do not need to generate as much heat per unit of body weight as small animals. Tiny shrews move frenetically, eating nearly all their waking lives to keep their metabolic fire burning at the maximal rate among mammals; blue whales guide majestically, their hearts beating the slowest rhythm among active, warm-blooded creatures.

The scaling of lifetime among mammals suggests an intriguing synthesis of these disparate data. We have all had enough experience with mammalian pets of various sizes to understand that small mammals tend to live for a shorter time than large ones. In fact, mammalian lifetime scales at the about the same rate as heartbeat and breath time—between one-fourth and one-third as fast as body weight as we move from small to large animals. (*Homo sapiens* emerges from this analysis as a very peculiar animal. We live far longer than a mammal of our body size should. In [another] essay I argue that humans evolved by an evolutionary process called "neoteny"—the preservation in adults of shapes and growth rates that characterize juvenile stages of ancestral primates. I also believe that neoteny is responsible for our elevated longevity. Compared with other mammals, all stages of human life arrive "too late." We are born as helpless embryos after a long gestation; we mature late after an extended childhood; we die, if fortune be kind, at ages otherwise reached by warm-blooded animals only at the very largest sizes.)

Usually, we pity the pet mouse or gerbil that lived its full span of a year or two at most. How brief its life, while we endure for the better part of a century. As the main theme of this essay, I want to argue that such pity is misplaced (our personal grief, of course, is quite another matter; with this, science does not deal). Morgan was right in *Ragtime*—small and large mammals are essentially similar. Their lifetimes are scaled to their life's pace, and all endure for approximately the same amount of biological time. Small mammals tick fast, burn rapidly, and live for a short time; large mammals live long at a stately pace. Measured by their own internal clocks, mammals of different sizes tend to live for the same amount of time.

We are prevented from grasping this important and comforting concept by a deeply ingrained habit of Western thought. We are trained from earliest memory to regard absolute Newtonian time as the single valid measuring stick in a rational and objective world. We impose our kitchen clock, ticking equably, upon all things. We marvel at the quickness of a mouse, express boredom at the torpor of a hippopotamus. Yet each is living at the appropriate pace of its own biological clock.

I do not wish to deny the importance of absolute, astronomical time to organisms. Animals must measure it to lead successful lives. Deer must know when to regrow their antlers, birds when to migrate. Animals track the day-night cycle with their circadian rhythms; jet lag is the price we pay for moving much faster than nature intended.

But absolute time is not the appropriate measuring stick for all biological phenomena. Consider the magnificent song of the humpback whale. E.O. Wilson has described the awesome effect of these vocalizations: "The notes are eerie yet beautiful to the human ear. Deep basso groans and almost inaudibly high soprano squeaks alternate with repetitive squeals that suddenly rise or fall in pitch." We do not know the function of these songs. Perhaps they enable whales to find each other and to stay together during their annual transoceanic migrations. Perhaps they are the mating songs of courting males.

Each whale has its own characteristic song; the highly complex patterns are repeated over and over again with great faithfulness. No scientific fact that I have learned in the last decade struck me with more force than Roger S. Payne's report that the length of some songs may extend for more than half an hour. I have never been able to memorize the five-minute first *Kyrie* of the B-minor Mass (and not for want of trying); how could a whale sing for thirty minutes and then repeat itself accurately? Of what possible use is a thirty-minute repeat cycle—far too long for a human to recognize; we would never grasp it as a single song (without Payne's recording machinery and much study after the fact). But then I remembered the whale's metabolic rate, the enormously slow pace of its life compared with ours. What do we know about a whale's perception of thirty minutes? A humpback may scale the world to its own metabolic rate; its half-hour song may be our minute waltz. From any point of view, the song is spectacular; it is the most elaborate single display so far discovered in any animal. I merely urge the whale's point of view as an appropriate perspective.

We can provide some numerical precision to support the claim that all mammals, on average, live for the same amount of biological time. In a method developed by W.R. Stahl, B. Günther, and E. Guerra in the late 1950s and the early 1960s, we search the mouse-to-elephant equations for biological properties that scale at the same rate against body weight. For example, Günther and Guerra give the following equations for mammalian breath time and heartbeat time versus body weight.

breath time $= .0000470 \text{ body}^{0.28}$
heartbeat time $= .0000119 \text{ body}^{0.28}$

(Nonmathematical readers need not be overwhelmed by the formalism. The equations simply state that both breath time and heartbeat time increase about .28 times as fast as body weight as we move from small to large mammals.) If we divide the two equations, body weight cancels out because it is raised to the same power in both.

$$\frac{\text{breath time}}{\text{heartbeat time}} = \frac{.0000470 \text{ body}^{0.28}}{.0000119 \text{ body}^{0.28}} = 4.0$$

This states that the ratio of breath time to heartbeat time is 4.0 in mammals of any body size. In other words, all mammals, whatever their size, breathe once for each four heartbeats. Small mammals breathe and beat their hearts faster than large mammals, but both breath and heart slow up at the same relative rate as mammals get larger.

Lifetime also scales at the same rate as body weight (.28 times as fast as we move from small to large mammals). This means that the ratio of both breath time and heartbeat time to lifetime is also constant over the entire range of mammalian size. When we perform a calculation similar to the one above, we find that all mammals, regardless of their size, tend to breathe about 200 million times during their lives (their hearts, therefore, beat about 800 million times). Small mammals breathe fast, but live for a short time. Measured by the internal clocks of their own hearts or the rhythm of their own breathing, all mammals live the same time. (Astute readers, after counting their breaths or taking their pulses, may have calculated that they should have died long ago. But *Homo sapiens* is a markedly deviant mammal in more ways than braininess alone. We live about three times as long as mammals of our body size "should," but we breathe at the "right" rate and thus live to breathe about three times as often as an average mammal of our body size. I regard this excess of living as a happy consequence of neoteny.)

The mayfly lives but a day as an adult. It may, for all I know, experience that day as we live a lifetime. Yet all is not relative in our world, and such a short glimpse of it guarantees distortion in interpreting events ticking on longer scales. In a brilliant metaphor, the pre-Darwinian evolutionist Robert Chambers wrote in 1844 of a mayfly watching the metamorphosis of a tadpole into a frog:

> Suppose that an ephemeron [a mayfly], hovering over a pool for its one April day of life, were capable of observing the fry of the frog in the waters below. In its aged afternoon, having seen no change upon them for such a long time, it would be little qualified to conceive that the external branchiae [gills] of these creatures were to decay, and be replaced by internal lungs, that feet were to be developed, the tail erased, and the animal then to become a denizen of the land.

Human consciousness arose but a minute before midnight on the geologic clock. Yet we mayflies try to bend an ancient world to our purposes, ignorant perhaps of the messages buried in its long history. Let us hope that we are still in the early morning of our April day.

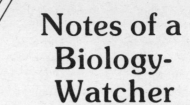

# Notes of a Biology-Watcher

## The Hazards of Science

### Lewis Thomas

The codeword for criticism of science and scientists these days is *hubris*. Once you've said that word, you've said it all; it sums up, in a word, all of today's apprehensions and misgivings in the public mind—not just about what is perceived as the insufferable attitude of the scientists themselves but, enclosed in the same word, what science and technology are perceived to be doing to make this century, this near to its ending, turn out so wrong.

Hubris is a powerful word, containing layers of powerful meaning, which is a peculiar thing when you consider its seemingly trivial history in etymology. It turned up first in popular English usage as a light piece of university slang at Oxford in the late 19th century, with the meaning of intellectual arrogance and insolence, applicable in a highly specialized sense to certain literary figures within a narrow academic community. But it was derived from a very old word, and as sometimes happens with ancient words it took on a new life of its own, growing way beyond the limits of its original meaning. Today, it is strong enough to carry the full weight of disapproval for the cast of mind that thought up atomic fusion and fission as ways of first blowing up and later heating cities, as well as the attitudes that led to strip-mining, off-shore oil wells, Kepone, food additives, SST's, and the tiny spherical particles of plastic recently discovered clogging the waters of the Sargasso Sea.

The biomedical sciences are now caught up with physical science and technology in the same kind of critical judgement, with the same pejorative

Lewis Thomas, "Notes of a Biology Watcher: The Hazards of Science" from *New England Journal of Medicine*, Feb. 10, 1977. Reprinted by permission of the author.

word. Hubris is responsible, it is said, for the whole biologic revolution. It is hubris that has given us the prospects of behavior control, psychosurgery, fetal research, heart transplants, the cloning of prominent politicians from bits of their own eminent tissue, iatrogenic disease, overpopulation and recombinant DNA. This last, the new technology that permits the stitching of one creature's genes into the DNA of another to make hybrids, is currently cited as the ultimate example of hubris. It is hubris for man to manufacture a hybrid, on his own.

This is interesting, for the word hybrid is a direct descendant of the ancient Greek word hubris. Hubris originally meant outrage; it was in fact a hybrid word from two Indoeuropean roots: *ud*, meaning out, and *gwer*, meaning rage. The word became *hydrida* in Latin, and was first used to describe the outrageous offspring from the mating of a wild boar with a domestic sow; these presumably unpleasant animals were, in fact, the first hybrids.

Since then the word hybrid has assumed more respectable meanings in biology, and also in literary and political usage. There have been hybrid plants and hybrid vigor, hybrid words and hybrid bills in parliament for several centuries. But always there has been a hidden meaning of danger, of presumption and arrogance, of risk. Hybrids are things fundamentally to be disapproved of.

And now we are back to the first word again, from hybrid to hubris, and the hidden meaning of two beings joined unnaturally together by man is somehow retained. Today's joining is straight out of Greek mythology: it is the combining of man's capacity with the special prerogative of the gods, and it is really in this sense of outrage that the word hubris is being used today. This is what the word has grown into, a warning, a code-word, a shorthand signal from the language itself: if man starts doing things reserved for the gods, deifying himself, the outcome will be something worse for him, symbolically, than the litters of wild boars and domestic sows were for the ancient Romans.

To be charged with hubris is therefore an extremely serious matter, and not to be dealt with by murmuring things about anti-science and anti-intellectualism, which is what many of us engaged in science tend to do these days. The doubts about our enterprise have their origin in the most profound kind of human anxiety. If we are right, and the critics are wrong, then it has to be that the word hubris is being mistakenly employed, that this is not what we are up to, that there is, for the time being anyway, a fundamental misunderstanding of science.

I suppose there is one central question to be dealt with, and I am not at all sure how to deal with it although I am certain about my own answer to it. It is this: are there some kinds of information leading to some sorts of knowledge, that human beings are really better off not having? Is there a limit to scientific inquiry not set by what is knowable but by what we ought to be knowing? Should we stop short of learning about some things, for fear of what we, or someone, will do with the knowledge? My own answer is a flat no, but I must confess that this is an intuitive response and I am neither inclined nor trained to reason my way through it.

There has been some effort, in and out of scientific quarters, to make recombinant DNA into the issue on which to settle this argument. Proponents of this line of research are accused of pure hubris, of assuming the rights of gods, of arrogance and outrage; what is more, they confess themselves to be in the business of making live hybrids, with their own hands. The mayor of Cambridge, Massachusetts, and the Attorney General of New York have both been advised to put a stop to it, forthwith.

It is not quite the same sort of argument, however, as the one about limiting knowledge, although this is surely part of it. The knowledge is already here, and the rage of the argument is about its application in technology. Should DNA for making certain useful or interesting proteins be incorporated into *Escherichia coli* plasmids, or not? Is there a risk of inserting the wrong sort of toxins, or hazardous viruses, and then having the new hybrid organisms spread beyond the laboratory? Is this a technology for creating new varieties of pathogens, and should it be stopped because of this?

If the argument is held to this level, I can see no reason why it cannot be settled, by reasonable people. We have learned a great deal about the handling of dangerous microbes in the last century, although I must say that the opponents of recombinant-DNA research tend to downgrade this huge body of information. At one time or another, agents as hazardous as those of rabies, psittacosis, plague and typhus have been dealt with by investigators in secure laboratories, with only rare cases of self-infliction of the investigators themselves, and none at all of epidemics. It takes some high imagining to postulate the creation of brand-new pathogens so wild and voracious as to spread from equally secure laboratories to endanger human life at large, as some of the arguers are now maintaining.

But this is precisely the trouble with the recombinant-DNA problem: it has become an emotional issue, with too many irretrievably lost tempers on both sides. It has lost the sound of a discussion of technologic safety, and begins now to sound like something else, almost like a religious controversy, and here it is moving toward the central issue: are there some things in science we should not be learning about?

There is an inevitably long list of hard questions to follow this one, beginning with the one that asks whether the mayor of Cambridge should be the one to decide, first off.

Maybe we'd be wiser, all of us, to back off before the recombinant-DNA issue becomes too large to cope with. If we're going to have a fight about it, let it be confined to the immediate issue of safety and security of the recombinants now under consideration, and let us by all means have regulations and guidelines to assure the public safety wherever these are indicated, or even suggested. But if possible let us stay off that question about limiting human knowledge. It is too loaded, and we'll simply not be able to cope with it.

By this time it will become clear that I have already taken sides in this matter, and my point of view is entirely prejudiced. This is true, but with a qualification. I am not so much in favor of recombinant-DNA research as I am opposed to the opposition to this line of inquiry. As a long-time student of infectious disease agents I do not take kindly the declarations that we do not know how to keep from catching things in laboratories, much less how to keep them from spreading beyond the laboratory walls. I believe we learned a lot about this sort of thing, long ago. Moreover, I regard it as a form of hubris-in-reverse to claim that man can make deadly pathogenic micro organisms so easily. In my view, it takes a long time and a great deal of interliving before a microbe can become a successful pathogen. Pathogenicity is , in a sense, a highly skilled trade, and only a tiny minority of all the numberless tons of microbes on the earth has ever involved itself in it; most bacteria are busy with their own business, browsing and recycling the rest of life. Indeed, pathogenicity often seems to me a sort of biologic accident in which signals are misdirected by the microbe or misinterpreted by the host, as in the case of endotoxin, or in which the intimacy between host and microbe is of such long standing that a form of molecular mimicry becomes possible, as in the case of diphtheria toxin. I do not believe that by simply putting together new combinations of genes one can create creatures as highly skilled and adapted for dependence as a pathogen must be, any more than I have ever believed that microbial life from the moon or Mars could possibly make a living on this planet.

But, as I said, I'm not at all sure this is what the argument is really about. Behind it is that other discussion, which I wish we would not have to become enmeshed in. And I will tell you why.

I cannot speak for the physical sciences, which have moved an immense distance in this century by any standard, but it does seem to me that in the biologic and medical sciences we are still far too ignorant to begin making judgments  about what sorts of things we should be learning or not learning. To the contrary, we ought to be grateful for whatever snatches we can get hold of, and we ought to be out there on a much larger scale than today's, looking for more.

We should be very careful with that word hubris and make sure it is not used when not warranted. There is a great danger in applying it to the search for knowledge. The application of knowledge is another matter, and there is hubris in plenty in our technology, but I do not believe that looking for new information about nature, at whatever level, can possibly be called unnatural. Indeed, if there is any single attribute of human beings, apart from language, that distinguishes them from all other creatures on earth, it is their insatiable, uncontrollable drive to learn things and then to exchange the information with others of the species. Learning is what we do, when you think about it. I cannot think of a human impulse more difficult to govern.

But I can imagine lots of reasons for trying to govern it. New information about nature is very likely, at the outset, to be upsetting to someone or other. The recombinant-DNA line of research is already upsetting, not because of the dangers now being argued about but because it is disturbing, in a fundamental way, to face the fact that the genetic machinery in control of the planet's life can be fooled around with so easily. We do not like the idea that anything so fixed and stable as a species line can be changed. The notion that genes can be taken out of one genome and inserted in another is unnerving. Classical mythology is peopled with mixed beings— part man, part animal or plant—and most of them are associated with tragic stories. Recombinant DNA is a reminder of bad dreams.

The easiest decision for society to make in matters of this kind is to appoint an agency, or a commission, or a subcommittee within an agency, to look into the problem and provide advice. And the easiest course for a committee to take, when confronted by any process that appears to be disturbing people or making them uncomfortable, is to recommend that it be stopped, at least for the time being.

I can easily imagine such a committee, composed of unimpeachable public figures, arriving at the decision that the time is not quite ripe for further exploration of the transplantation of genes, that we should put this off for a while, maybe until next century, and get on with other affairs that make us less uncomfortable. Why not do science on something more popular?

The trouble is, it would be very hard to stop once this line was begun. There are, after all, all sorts of scientific inquiry that are not much liked by one constituency or another, and we might soon find ourselves with crowded rosters, panels, standing committees, set up in Washington for the appraisal, and then the regulation, of research. Not on grounds of the possible value and usefulness of the new knowledge, mind you, but for guarding society against scientific hubris, against the kinds of knowledge we're better off without.

It would be absolutely irresistible as a way of spending time, and people would form long queues for membership. Almost anything would be fair game, certainly anything to do with genetics, anything relating to population control, or, on the other side, research on aging. Very few fields would get by.

The research areas in the greatest trouble would be those already containing a sense of bewilderment and surprise, with discernible prospects of upheaving present dogmas. I can think of several of these, two current ones in which I've been especially interested, and one from the remote past of 40 years ago.

First, the older one. Suppose this were the mid-1930's, and there were a Commission on Scientific Hubris sitting in Washington, going over a staff report on the progress of work in the laboratory of O.T. Avery in New York. Suppose, as well, that there were people on the Commission who understood what Avery was up to and believed his work. This takes an excess of imagining, since there were vanishingly few such people around in the 1930's, and also Avery didn't publish a single word until he had the entire thing settled and wrapped up 10 years later. But anyway, suppose it. Surely, someone would have pointed out that Avery's discovery of a bacterial extract that could change pneumococci from one genetic type to another, with the transformed organisms now doomed to breed true as the changed type, was nothing less than the discovery of a gene; moreover, Avery's early conviction that the stuff was DNA might turn out to be correct, and what then? To this day, the members of such a committee might well have been felicitating each other on having nipped something so dangerous in the very bud.

But it wouldn't have worked in any case, unless they had been equally prescient about bacteriophage research and had managed to flag down phage genetics before it got going a few years later. Science can be blocked, I have no doubt of that, or at least slowed down, but it takes very fast footwork.

Here is an example from today's research on the brain, which would do very well on the agenda of a Hubris Commission. It is the work now going on in several laboratories here and abroad dealing with the endorphins, a class of small polypeptides also referred to as the endogenous opiates. It is rather a surprise that someone hasn't already objected to this research, since the implications of what has already been found are considerably more explosive, and far more unsettling, than anything in the recombinant-DNA line of work. There are cells in the brain, chiefly in the limbic system, which possess at their surfaces specific receptors for morphine and heroin, but this is just a biologic accident; the real drugs, with the same properties as morphine, are the pentapeptide hormones produced by the brain itself. Perhaps they are switched on as analgesics at times of trauma or illness; perhaps they even serve for the organization and modulation of the physiologic process of dying when the time for dying comes. These things are not yet known, but such questions can now be asked. It is not even known whether an injection of such pentapeptides into a human being will produce a heroin-like reaction, but that kind of question will also be up for asking, and probably quite soon since the same peptides can be synthesized with relative ease. What should be done about this line of research—or rather, what should have been done about it two or three years ago when it was just being launched? Is this the sort of thing we are better off not knowing? I know some people who might think so. But if something prudent and sagacious had been done, turning off such investigations at an early stage, we would not have glimpsed the possible clue to the mechanism of catatonic schizophrenia, which was published just this month from two of the laboratories working on endorphins.

It is hard to predict how science is going to turn out, and if it is really good science it is impossible to predict. This is in the nature of the enterprise. If the things to be found are actually new, they are by definition unknown in advance, and there is no way of foretelling in advance where a really new line of inquiry will lead. You cannot make choices in this matter, selecting things you think you're going to like and shutting off the lines that make for discomfort. You either have science, or you don't, and if you have it you are obliged to accept the surprising and disturbing pieces of information, even the overwhelming and upheaving ones, along with the neat and promptly useful bits. It is like that.

And even if it were possible to call most of the shots in advance, so that we could make broad selections of the general categories of new knowledge that we like, leaving out the ones we don't have a taste for, there would always be slips, leaks, small items of shattering information somehow making their way through. I have an example of this sort of thing in mind, a small item largely overlooked in its significance, a piece of news to match in importance, for what it tells us about ourselves and our relation to the rest of nature, anything else learned in biology during the past century. This is the astonishing tale—astonishing to my ears anyway—of the true nature of mitochondria and chloroplasts.

Between them, these organelles can fairly be said to run the place. They are, from every fair point of view, in charge. The chloroplasts tap the energy of the sun, and the mitochondria make use of it. Without them we might still have a world of microbes, but we could not have eukaryotic forms of life, nor metazoans, nor any of ourselves. Now, as it turns out, both of these can be viewed as living entities, organisms rather than organelles. The mitochondria live in our cells, and the chloroplasts in the cells of plants, as symbiotic lodgers. They replicate on their own, independently of nuclear division, with their own DNA and RNA, their own ribosomes, their own membranes, and these parts are essentially similar to the corresponding parts of bacteria and blue-green algae from which they are now believed to have descended. They are, in fairness, the oldest living inhabitants of the earth, and the least changed by evolution.

Well, this is the sort of knowledge I would call overwhelming, even overturning, in its implications. It has not yet sunk in, really, but when it does it is bound to affect our view of ourselves as special entities, as selves, in charge of our own being, in command of the earth. Another way to put it is that what we might be, in real life, is a huge collection of massive colonies of the most primitive kind of bacteria, which have adapted themselves for motile life in air by constructing around themselves, like a sort of carapace, all the embellishments and adornments of the modern human form. When you settle down to think a thought, you may think it is all your own idea, but perhaps it is not so. You are sharing the notion around, with more creatures than you could count in a lifetime, and they are the ones that turned the thought on in the first place. Moreover, there is more than a family resemblance, maybe even something like identity, between the mitochondria running your cells and those in control of the working parts of any cloud of midges overhanging a summer garden, or of seagulls, or the mouse in the basement, or all the fishes in the sea. It is a startling relationship, of such strange intimacy that none of us could have counted on before the facts began coming in. Would you prefer not to know about this? It is too late for that. Or would you prefer to stop it here and learn no more, leaving matters where they stand, stuck forever with one of the great ambiguities in nature, never to know for sure how it came out?

The only solid piece of scientific truth about which I feel totally confident is that we are profoundly ignorant about nature. Indeed, I regard this as a major discovery of the past 100 years of biology. It is, in its way, an illuminating piece of news. It would have amazed the brightest minds of the 18th-century enlightenment to be told by any of us how little we know, and how bewildering seems the way ahead. It is this sudden confrontation with the depth and scope of ignorance that represents the most noteworthy contribution of 20th-century science to the human intellect.

We are, at last, facing up to it. In earlier times, we either pretended to understand how things worked or ignored the problem, or simply made up stories to fill the gaps. Now that we have begun exploring in earnest, doing serious science, we are getting glimpses of how huge the questions are, and how far from being answered. Because of this, these are hard times for the human mind, and it is no wonder that we are depressed. It is not so bad being ignorant if you are totally ignorant; the hard thing is knowing in some detail the reality of ignorance, the worst spots and here and there the not-so-bad spots, but no true light at the end of the tunnel nor even any tunnels that can yet be trusted. Hard times, indeed.

But we are making a beginning, and there ought to be some satisfaction, even exhilaration, in that. The method works. There are probably no questions we can think up that can't be answered, sooner or later, including even the matter of consciousness. To be sure, there may well be questions we can't think up, ever, and therefore limits to the reach of human intellect that we will never know about, but that is another matter. Within our limits, we should be able to work our way through to all our answers, if we keep at it long enough, and pay attention.

I am putting it this way, with all the presumption and confidence that I can summon, to raise another, last question. Is this hubris? Is there something fundamentally unnatural, or intrinsically wrong, or hazardous for the species, in the ambition that drives us all to reach a comprehensive understanding of nature, including ourselves? I cannot believe it. It would seem to me a more unnatural thing, and more of an offense against nature, for us to come on the same scene endowed as we are with curiosity, filled to overbrimming as we are with questions, and naturally talented as we are for the asking of clear questions, and then for us to do nothing about it, or worse, to try to suppress the questions. This is the greater danger for our species, to try to pretend that we are another kind of animal, that we do not need to satisfy our curiosity, that we can get along somehow without inquiry and exploration, and experimentation, and that the human mind can rise above its ignorance by simply asserting that there are things it has no need to know. This, to my way of thinking, is the real hubris, and it carries danger for us all.

# The Language
# of
# Economics

## John Kenneth Galbraith

Among the Social Sciences, and indeed among all reputable fields of learning, economics occupies a special place for the reproach that is inspired by its language. The literate layman regularly proclaims his discontent with the way in which economists express themselves. Other scholars emerge from the eccentricities of their own terminology to condemn the economist for a special commitment to obscurity. If an economist writes a book or even an article in clear English, he need say nothing. He will be praised for avoiding jargon—and also for risking the rebuke of his professional colleagues in doing so. And economists themselves, in their frequent exercises in introspection, regularly wonder whether they are making themselves intelligible to students, politicians and the general public. Committees are occasionally impaneled to consider their communication with the world at large. Invariably they urge improvement.

My purpose in this essay is to go into these charges and assess their substance. My ambition is to put a period, or at least semicolon, to this discussion. For I hope to show that the transgressions of the economists in transmitting their knowledge, though some must be conceded, are not remarkable. Some of the fault lies in the attitudes, including the insufficient diligence, of those who lead the attack. Some is in the sociology of the subject and is not wholly peculiar to economics.

The language of economics is commonly indicted on three different counts. It is of some importance that these charges, which often are mixed together, be kept separate. They are:

"The Language of Economics" from *Economics, Peace and Laughter* by John Kenneth Galbraith. Copyright ©1971 by John Kenneth Galbraith. Reprinted by permission of Houghton Mifflin Company.

1. That the ideas and terminology of economics are complex and artificial and exceedingly confusing to the layman.
2. That economists are bad writers. And it is said that proficiency in obscure and difficult language may even enhance a man's professional standing.
3. That arcane concepts and obscure language are the symptoms of a deeper disorder. So far from seeking communication with the world at large, the tendency of economics is to divorce itself therefrom and construct an unreal universe of its own.

I shall take up these several charges in turn. Each calls for a progressively more detailed examination.

## II

That economics has a considerable conceptual apparatus with an appropriate terminology cannot be a serious ground for complaint. Economic phenomena, ideas and instruments of analysis exist. They require names. No one can reasonably ask a serious scholar in the field to avoid reference to index numbers, the capital gains tax, the consumption function, acceleration effects, circular money flows, inflation, linear programming, the progressive income tax, the pure rate of interest or the European Common Market. Nor should he be expected to explain what these are. Education in economics is, in considerable measure, an introduction to this terminology and to the ideas that it denotes. Anyone who has difficulties with the ideas should complete his education or, following an exceedingly well-beaten path, leave the subject alone. It is sometimes said that the economist has a special obligation to make himself understood because his subject is of such great and popular importance. By this rule the nuclear physicist would have to speak in monosyllables.

A physician, at least in the United States, does not tell you that a patient is dying. He says that the prognosis as of this time is without significant areas of encouragement. The dead man becomes not that to his lawyer but the decedent. Diplomats never ask. They make representations. Economists have similar vanities of expression and an accomplished practitioner can often get the words parameter, stochastic and aggregation into a single sentence.[1] But it would be hard to prove that the working terminology of the subject is more pretentious or otherwise oppressive than that of jurisprudence, gynecology or advanced poultry husbandry. One indication that it is not is the speed with which the really important words and ideas—gross national product, compensatory fiscal policy, GATT, interna-

---

[1]Arcane terminology and esoteric concepts do play a certain role in the prestige system of the subject to which I shall return.

tional liquidity, product differentiation, balance of payments deficit—pass into general use.

I turn now to the quality of writing in economics.

## III

Anyone who wished to contend that economists are bad writers is faced with the fact that no learned discipline unconnected with literature or the arts has had such distinguished ones. Everyone has his own test of good writing. I would urge a multiple test for economists in which particular excellence in one respect is allowed to offset lesser achievement in others.

Thus power and resourcefulness of language are important, as is purity of style. Style means that the writing is identified with personality—that it does not have the rigid homogeneity sometimes associated with scientific prose. Nor should it. Language has many dimensions. It does not convey meaning better or more accurately by being flat and colorless.

Good writing, and this is especially important in a subject such as economics, must also involve the reader in the matter at hand. It is not enough to explain. The images that are in the mind of the writer must be made to reappear in the mind of the reader, and it is the absence of this ability that causes much economic writing to be condemned, quite properly, as abstract.

Finally, I doubt that good economic writing can be devoid of humor. This is not because it is the task of the economist to entertain or amuse. Nothing could be more abhorrent to the Calvinist gloom which characterizes all scientific attitudes. But humor is an index of man's ability to detach himself from his subject and such detachment is of considerable scientific utility. In considering economic behavior, humor is especially important for, needless to say, much of that behavior is infinitely ridiculous.

The writing of an impressive number of English-language economists qualifies by these standards. At the head of the list, I would put the work of Adam Smith. In purity and simplicity of style, and certainty in his command of language, he is inferior to John Stuart Mill. But he is more resourceful than Mill and much more amused by his subject. Smith sensed that a trip into the pin factory to see the division of labor in operation would establish the importance of the phenomenon for good. Pins, "a very trifling manufacture," were also an excellent selection; had the product been more portentous it would have competed with the process by which it was made. In competition with pins, the division of labor could not be less than triumphant. Similarly a less amused man would have stressed the penchant of businessmen for getting together to fix prices. (A halfway decent modern scholar would have isolated an instinct for antisocial behavior.) The businessmen would then have defended themselves, not without indignation. As the men of influence and admitted respectability, their views would have prevailed; Smith would have been dismissed as anti-business. Or, more likely, he would have been ignored. Instead, in one brilliant sentence, he noted that, "People of the same trade seldom meet together, even for merriment and diversion, but the conversation ends in a conspiracy against the public, or in some contrivance to raise prices."[2] Though the tendency is wholly innocent and convivial, the impulse to wickedness is overpowering. Neither anger nor reproach is in order; only sorrow at the inability to resist an improper penny. So expressed, the indictment has never been lifted. To this day, in the United States at least, anyone observing an exchange of words between two competitors assumes it is costing the public some money. Those so engaged feel obliged to make some embarrassed comment to the same effect when they are finished. Such craftsmanship was far beyond the reach of Mill.[3]

Mill, of course, was a greatly talented writer, a standard by which others have long been judged. And to the list I would add the name of Thorstein Veblen. In one sense it is hard even to think of him in the same terms as Mill; his prose, unlike Mill's, is involuted and pretentious. One reads Veblen with the constant impression of a struggle for effect. But few men have ever so resourcefully driven home a point. What had always seemed commonplace and respectable became, after Veblen, fraudulent, ridiculous and (a favorite word of his) barbaric. This is high art. The American rich never recovered from the sardonic disdain with which Veblen analyzed their behavior. The manners of an entire society were altered as a result. After he made the phrase "conspicuous consumption" a part of the language, the real estate market in Newport was never again the same. What had been the biggest and best was henceforth the most vulgar. "Conspicuous leisure" made it difficult even for the daughters of the rich to relax. Their entertainment had thereafter to be legitimatized by charitable, artistic or even intellectual purpose or, at minimum, sexual relief. Here is Veblen's account of the effect of increasing wealth on behavior:

> . . .Since the consumption of these more excellent goods is an evidence of wealth, it becomes honorific; and conversely, the failure to consume in due quantity and quality becomes a mark of inferiority and demerit.
>
> This growth of punctilious discrimination as to qualitative excellence in eating, drinking, etc. presently affects not only the manner of life, but also the training and intellectual activity of the gentleman of leisure. He is no longer simply the successful, aggressive male—the man of strength,

---

[2]Adam Smith, *Wealth of Nations* (New York, Modern Library, 1937), p. 128.

[3]I have always been enchanted by another observation of Smith's: "The late resolution of the Quakers in Pennsylvania to set at liberty their negro slaves, may satisfy us that their number cannot be very great." Adam Smith, *Wealth of Nations*, Book 3 (New York: Modern Library, 1937), chapter 2.

resource, and intrepidity. In order to avoid stultification he must also cultivate his tastes, for it now becomes incumbent on him to discriminate with some nicety between the noble and the ignoble in consumable goods. He becomes a connoisseur in creditable viands of various degrees of merit, in manly beverages and trinkets, in seemly apparel and architecture, in weapons, games, dancers, and the narcotics. This cultivation of the aesthetic faculty requires time and application, and the demands made upon the gentleman in this direction therefore tend to change his life of leisure into a more or less arduous application to the business of learning how to live a life of ostensible leisure in a becoming way.[4]

The list of good if less than inspired writers—the elder Mill, Thomas Malthus, Henry George, Alfred Marshall and (subject to some reservations to be mentioned presently) John Maynard Keynes—is also an impressive one. So it would be difficult, on the general evidence, to find fault with the literary qualifications of the English-writing economists.

## IV

Perhaps, however, this does not quite settle things. It will be said that when economists have gone to the technical heart of the matter, as did Ricardo in *Principles*, or as they have come up against the full complexity of modern economic problems, as did Keynes in *The General Theory*, they have become less than lucid and accessible. Some will surely think it significant that the best writer by my accounting was so nearly the first. Were Smith or Mill writing about the economy today, they would, it will be said, be either as incomprehensible or as condescending in their prose as their contemporaries.

This confuses the problem of complex exposition or scientific perception with bad writing. Ricardo's problems were no more difficult than those which were lucidly discussed by Malthus or Mill and he did not go into them very much more deeply. Ricardo's reputation as a bad writer is greatly deserved. He was, in addition, an unscientific one. His prose was awkward, uncertain and unpredictable as to meaning conveyed, and it was his habit to state strong propositions and then qualify them to possible extinction. His natural price of labor was such as to "enable laborers, one with another, to subsist and perpetuate their race." But within a page or two the application of this heroic (and historic) law was suspended in "improving" societies, of which contemporary England was obviously one as were all others to which he had relevance. The notion of subsistence was simultaneously enlarged to include conveniences, these being any luxuries

---

[4]Thorstein Veblen, *The Theory of the Leisure Class* (New York: Macmillan, 1912), pp. 74-75.

to which the worker had become or might become accustomed. And the population theory on which the proposition depended was modified to exclude Englishmen although it was deemed to have full force and effect for the Irish. This is neither good writing nor good scientific method. It is bad writing based on incomplete thought.

The writing in Keynes's *General Theory* justifies similar if somewhat less severe comment. Keynes has been widely acclaimed as a master of English prose. A good part of this applause has come from economists who are not the best of judges. Much of it approved his criticism of the Versailles Treaty, or Winston Churchill, or his pleasant memoirs on academic contemporaries. But the real test of a writer is whether he remains with a difficult subject until he has thought through not only the problem but also its exposition. This Keynes did not do. *The General Theory* is an acrostic of English prose. The fact that it was an important book should not cause anyone to say that it was well written. In a real sense it was not even finished. Though new, the ideas were not intrinsically more complex than those presented with competence by A. C. Pigou and a certain churchly eloquence by Alfred Marshall. Other writers—Mrs. Joan Robinson, Professors Hansen, Harris and Samuelson—turned Keynes's ideas into accessible English, thus showing that it could be done. A better writer—patience has a certain notoriety as a component of genius—would have done the job himself.[5] The ideas of *The General Theory* could have been stated in clear English.

The influence of this book, combined with its unintelligibility, does bring up another question. It is whether clear and unambiguous statement is the best medium for persuasion in economics. Here, I think, one may have doubts.

## V

Had the Bible been in clear, straightforward language, had the ambiguities and contradictions been edited out and had the language been constantly modernized to accord with contemporary taste, it would almost certainly have been, or have become, a work of lesser influence. In the familiar or King James version it has three compelling qualities. The archaic constructions and terminology put some special strain on the reader. Accordingly, by the time he has worked his way through, say, Leviticus, he has a vested interest in what he has read. It is not something to be dismissed like a col-

[5]Those who think this underestimates the difficulty of the ideas with which Keynes was dealing will do well to notice the carelessness of his nontechnical expression in this volume. The following is from a summary of his position in an early chapter: "The celebrated optimism of traditional economic theory, which has led to economists being looked upon as Candides who, having left this world for the cultivation of their gardens, teach that all is for the best in the best of all possible worlds provided we will let well enough alone, is also to be traced, I think, to their having neglected to take account of the drag on prosperity which can be exercised by an insufficiency of effective demand." *The General Theory of Employment Interest and Money* (New York: Harcourt, Brace, 1936), p.33.

umn by Alsop or even Lippmann. Too much has gone into understanding it.

The contradictions of the Old Testament also mean that with a little effort anyone can find a faith that accords with his preferences and a moral code that is agreeable to his tastes, even if fairly depraved. In consequence, dissidents are not extruded from the faith; they are retained and accommodated in a different chapter.

Finally, the ambiguities of the Scriptures allow of infinite debate over what is meant. This is most important for attracting belief, for in the course of urging his preferred variant on a particular proposition, the disputant becomes committed to the larger Writ.

Difficulty, contradiction and ambiguity have rendered precisely similar service in economics. Anyone who has worked his way through Ricardo, Marx or Keynes needs to feel that he has got something for such an effort. So he is strongly predisposed to belief. Ricardo is sufficiently replete with qualification and Marx with contradiction so that the reader can also provide himself with the interpretation he prefers.[6] All three lend themselves marvelously to argument as to what they mean. Thousands read these authors less for wisdom than because of need to participate in a suitably impressive way in arguments over what they said.

The case of Keynes is especially interesting because prior to the publication of the immensely difficult *General Theory*, he had advocated its principal conclusion—fiscal policy as an antidote for depression—in clear English in both the United States and Great Britain. He had not been greatly influential. Then in *The General Theory* he involved economists in a highly professional debate on technical concepts and their interpretation. His practical recommendations were not central to this discussion. But the participants carried his practical program to Washington and Whitehall. Would a simple, clearly argued book such as later produced by (among others) Professor Alvin Hansen have been as influential? My reluctant inclination is to doubt it.

Yet ambiguity is a tactic which not everyone should try. Economists will seize upon the ill-expressed ideas of a very great man and argue over what he had in mind. Others had better not run the risk.

## VI

So far I have been dealing with (by broad definition) classical rather than contemporary writing in economics. The time has come to consider the

---

[6]No great figure since Biblical times has lent himself to such varied interpretation as Marx. This arises partly from the manner of expression, partly from the contradiction inherent in some of the ideas and partly from the fact that so much of his work was uncompleted at his death and conflicts that might otherwise have been cleared up by revision or deletion were carried into print. It is for this reason that the interpretation and re-interpretation of Marx has been not a scholarly pursuit but a profession.

complex language and the difficult mathematics of the current contributions not only to *Econometrica* and *The Review of Economic Studies* but also of many of the articles in *The Economic Journal* and *The American Economic Review*. And here the question ceases to be purely one of language. These articles are obviously beyond the reach of the intelligent layman. Is it possible that they are also out of touch with reality and that it is the ambition of some scholars to construct a world of their own choosing and exclusive understanding? Doubt is not confined to noneconomists. Professor Samuelson, in his presidential address to the American Economic Association several years ago, noted that the three previous presidential addresses had been devoted to a denunciation of mathematical economics and that the most trenchant had encouraged the audience to standing applause. Once when I was in Russia on a visit to Soviet economists, I spent a long afternoon attending a discussion on the use of mathematical models in plan formation. At the conclusion an elderly scholar, who had also found it very heavy going, asked me rather wistfully if I didn't think there was still a "certain place" for the old-fashioned Marxian formulation of the labor theory of value.

What is involved here is less the language of economics than its sociology. Once this is understood, the layman can view what he does not understand with equanimity.

Professional economists, like members of city gangs, religious congregations, aboriginal tribes, British regiments, craft unions, fashionable clubs, learned disciplines, holders of diplomatic passports and, one is told, followers of the intellectually more demanding criminal pursuits, have the natural desire of all such groups to delineate and safeguard the boundary between those who belong and those who do not. This has variously been called the tribal, gang, club, guild, union or aristocratic instinct.

The differentiation of those who belong from those who do not is invariably complemented by a well-graded prestige system within the tribal group. And—a vital point—the two are closely interdependent. If the members of the tribal group are sufficiently conscious of the boundary that separates them from the rest of the world, the tribe becomes *the* world to its members. Its limits and the mental horizons of its members are coterminous. This means, in turn, that the prestige system of the tribe is the only one that has meaning to a member and it is all important. The most honorific position in the tribal group then becomes the most honorific position in the universe. If the school is all that counts, then the head boy is a person of the greatest possible grandeur. In the Barchester Close the eminence of the Bishop was absolute because no one took cognizance of the world beyond. Similarly those who are privileged to the secrets of the CIA or who work in the White House. In each case, everything within depends on the exclusion of what is without.

The prestige system of economics is wholly in accord with these principles. It assigns, and for good reason, the very lowest position to the man who deals with everyday policy. For this individual, in concerning himself with the wisdom of a new tax or the need for an increased deficit, is immediately caught up in a variety of political and moral judgments. This puts him in communication with the world at large. As such, he is a threat to the sharp delineation which separates the tribal group from the rest of society and thus to the prestige system of the profession. Moreover, his achievements are rated not by his professional peers but by outsiders. This causes difficulty in fitting him into the professional hierarchy and argues strongly for leaving him at the bottom.[7,8]

A very low position is also assigned to economists who, even though forswearing any interest in practical affairs, occupy themselves with related disciplines—urban sociology, education, the social causes of poverty or juvenile delinquency. The reason is the same. These men are also inimical to the tribal delineation for their achievements depend on the judgment of noneconomists and thus cannot be integrated into the established scale. They are assumed by their colleagues to be escaping the rigors of their own subject.

At the higher levels, economics divorces itself fully from practical questions and from the influence of other fields of scholarship with the exception of mathematics and statistics. One can think of the full prestige structure of the subject as a hollow pyramid or cone, the sides of which, though they are transparent and with numerous openings at the base. become increasingly opaque and impermeable as one proceeds to the apex. Positions near the apex are thus fully protected from external communication and influence. Work here is pure in the literal sense. Questions of practical application are excluded as also the influence of other disciplines. And this being so, tasks can be accommodated to the analytical techniques which the scholar wishes to use. These techniques may not be

[7]In the United States, at least, a similar disposition is made of members who, being good teachers, are accorded the approval of their students.

[8]Thus during his life Keynes was held in rather low regard. In his *History of Economic Analysis*, which he intended to be an authoritative view of professional precedence. Professor Schumpeter affirms this judgement and bases his disapproval on Keynes's unscholarly preoccupation with useful and practical matters. He condemns Ricardo on similar grounds.

At the time of his election to the United States Senate, Professor Paul Douglas had a very high position in the prestige system of the profession and. indeed. had just completed his term as President of the American Economic Association. While economists continued to take pride in his accomplishments. and especially welcomed his demonstration of the versatility of their craft, no grave professional importance could any longer be attached to his writing or his stand on technical issues. From being a leading economist, he became the leading economist in politics. This resolution of the matter, no doubt, is a sensible one. To fit a United States Senator into the prestige system of the profession would be very difficult. Better to compromise on purely nominal rank.

mathematical but the absence of extraneous practical considerations is conducive to mathematical techniques. Needless to say, communication is closely confined to those within the pyramid and advancement to higher levels within the pyramid is exclusively by the agency of the other occupants. The standards of accomplishment which lead to recognition are thus self-perpetuating. It is no criticism of this work that is unrelated to the real world. Such divorce is its most strongly intended feature.[9]

## VII

It is not part of my present task to pass judgment on this prestige structure or to compare it with that of other learned disciplines. In a world where for pedagogic and other purposes a very large number of economists is required, an arrangement which discourages many of them from rendering public advice would seem to be well conceived. Otherwise there would be more such advice than could possibly be heard let alone used. Much of the discussion in the upper reaches of the pyramid is idle—economic models unrelated to reality are constructed, criticized, amended, on occasion commended and then, alas, completely forgotten. But, as often happens, there is no ready way of separating valueless work here from the possibly valuable and any effort to do so would be intrinsically damaging. And it is the good fortune of the affluent country that the opportunity cost of economic discussion is low and hence it can afford all kinds. Moreover, the models so constructed, though of no practical value, serve a useful academic function. The oldest problem in economic education is how to exclude the incompetent. A certain glib mastery of verbiage—the ability to speak portentously and sententiously about the relation of money supply to the price level—is easy for the unlearned and may even be aided by a mildly enfeebled intellect. The requirement that there be ability to master difficult models, including ones for which mathematical competence is required, is a highly useful screening device.[10]

What is clear from this brief excursion into the sociology of economics, and this is the matter of present importance, is how the intelligent layman or the scholar from another discipline should regard contemporary economic writing. Its relevance to the real world is not great. Much of it, and more

[9]This explains why professional economists of the highest standing often come forward with proposals—for the abolition of corporations or trade unions, the outlawing of oligopoly, the enforcement of free competition, therapeutic unemployment, cathartic deflation, elimination of central banks, ending of income taxes—of the most impractical sort with no damage whatever to their reputations. No store is set by ability to assess such measures in their political and social context. On the contrary, such preoccupation is discrediting.

[10]There can be no question, however, that prolonged commitment to mathematical exercises in economics can be damaging. It leads to the atrophy of judgement and intuition which are indispensable for real solutions and, on occasion, leads also to the habit of mind which simply excludes the mathematically inconvenient factors from consideration.

especially that exchanged in the upper levels of the pyramid, is not meant to be. So it may be ignored.[11] It being designed to exclude practical questions, there is no practical loss. It being designed to exclude the outside scholar, the outsider may safely take the hint. The work at the less prestigious lower edges, since it must take account of information from other disciplines and also take account of political reality, does not lend itself to highly technical and mathematical treatment. This is the part that is important to the outsider. While he may not find it easy, he is not excluded.

None of this excuses anyone from mastering the basic ideas and terminology of economics. The intelligent layman must expect also to encounter good economists who are difficult writers even though some of the best have been very good writers. He should know, moreover, that at least for a few great men ambiguity of expression has been a positive asset. But with these exceptions he may safely conclude that what is wholly mysterious in economics is not likely to be important.

[11]The layman may take comfort from the fact that the most esoteric of this material is not read by other economists or even by the editors who publish it. In the economics profession the editorship of a learned journal not specialized to econometrics or mathematical statistics is a position of only moderate prestige. It is accepted, moreover, that the editor must have a certain measure of practical judgement. This means that he is usually unable to read the most prestigious contributions which, nonetheless, he must publish. So it is the practice of the editor to associate with himself a mathematical curate who passes on this part of the work and whose word he takes. A certain embarrassed silence covers the arrangement.

# Terms and Topics

## TERMS

1. **Vocabulary, Section IV:** abolition, adjunct, anarchy, arduous, attributed, attrition, beneficent, callowness, cognizance, conflagrations, convivial, demarcate, denizen, disparate, docility, enraptured, entailed, entity, equably, equivocation, extraneous, extricate, forswearing, frenetically, glib, imperious, impinge, inference, inherent, insufferable, intractable, introspection, keystone, laity, lucid, lush, mandatory, pejorative, perplexity, perverts, prerogative, prescient, presuppositions, procrastination, proliferates, proponents, qualms, relegated, revamped, sagacious, sardonic, speculative, sullen, torpor, transgressions, transient, trenchant, viable, virulence, wont.

2. **Satire** Ridicule of something, supposedly in order to reform it. *Satire* could also be applicable to section V, since it is often humorous. Or it could be applicable to section III, since it is a kind of criticism, or argument. Do any of the essays in this section (IV) use satire?

3. **Exposition** One of the four traditional modes of discourse, the other three being **narration**, **description**, and **argument**. In a literary context, *exposition* refers to the providing of essential data, the who-what-where-when-why of a story. The essential meaning is the same in both instances: providing information, explaining, *exposing* the facts.

4. **Rhetoric** The art or craft of using words effectively, whether in speaking or in writing. All of the techniques and strategies represented and discussed in this book are *rhetorical* techniques and strategies. The word *rhetoric* has also come to mean "*mere* rhetoric," empty, artificial, showy, exaggeratedly elaborate style—but that popular meaning does not apply in the context of the study of the principles of effective writing.

5. What is **language**? Consult a variety of sources for definitions (dictionaries, encyclopedias, handbooks, linguistic glossaries, and the like). You will likely find a variety of definitions. Then write a one- or two-page extended definition of the term.

6. **Jargon** Strictly speaking, the specialized language of a particular occupation. Compare it in this respect to the terms **slang**, **cant**, and **argot**. The term *jargon*, however, is commonly broadened to mean any artificially or unnecessarily complex, fuzzy, wordy, or otherwise incomprehensible diction or style. One synonym is *gibberish*. (See quotation number 6 in the "Introduction: Audience and Purpose," and see general and comparative topic number 11 in section III.)

7. **Ambiguity** Multiple meaning. An *ambiguous* statement is one that can be understood in more than one way. *She struck the man with the stick*, for example, or *The sparrow looked longer than the owl*, can be understood in two different ways. Poets and other writers will sometimes purposely create ambiguity, thereby forcing the reader to juggle two appropriate meanings at once. Jargon and other sloppy uses of language, however, can produce unintentional and befuddling ambiguity. Look for ambiguity in the things you read—whether in this book or elsewhere, and whether creative or unintentional. In what kinds of essay is intentional ambiguity most likely to be found? Try composing some ambiguous sentences.

## TOPICS: On Individual Essays

SIMONE BECK, LOUISETTE BERTHOLLE, and JULIA CHILD   "How to Bone a Duck, Turkey, or Chicken"

1. The principal obligation of an instructional process is to be clear. Are these directions clear? With them before you, could you approach the task with at least a small degree of confidence? Note how the authors begin by trying to overcome the natural diffidence of a novice ("You may think"), then state the object, provide some incentive ("impressive sight"), add a specific caution ("the important thing to remember"), and only then give the actual steps ("To begin with," etc.); they conclude by pointing to the usefulness of the process, indicating the elegant and tasty result. Do they omit anything that you would like to know about—for example what kind of knife to use—or do they assume a basic culinary competence on the part of the reader?

2. Write a set of instructions for some process of similar complexity that you know well, first for a reader of your own age and experience, then again for a child of about nine. What does the change in audience force you to do?

JESSICA MITFORD   **"The Story of Service"**

1. Why does Mitford begin unfolding the "drama" with the words "Alas, poor Yorick!"? Who was Yorick? Why does she call it a "drama"? Where else does she play on this metaphor? What other metaphors does she use?

2. This piece constitutes Chapter 5 of Mitford's 1963 book *The American Way of Death.* What is the effect of the title of the book? of the title of this chapter? Are they in any way ironic?

3. To what extent is this an argument? How would you describe Mitford's overall purpose? What internal strategies or techniques of development does she use besides the major one of process analysis?

4. Point out some of the many instances where Mitford's style takes on a tone of barbed irony or sarcasm, and where her diction becomes decidedly loaded. (Would you call her wit, as displayed in this piece, *mordant?*) Is this the kind of moderate and objective tone that is supposedly most effective in persuasive writing? Or is it a matter of audience? Whom is she writing *for?* Whom is she writing *against*— that is, who constitutes her opposition? How does she deal with that opposition?

5. Early on, Mitford refers to the "hit-or-miss rhetoric" of a passage she quotes, and disparages "the prose style of the funeral trade as a whole" (N.B. "trade," not "profession"), but she doesn't explain. Taking your cue from the few places where she does single out specific details for criticism, write an essay analyzing the prose style of some or all of the many passages she quotes in this chapter. Are her own language and tone, and her concern about language, comparable to those of Thurber in his essay in section III?

6. Using Mitford's chapter as a model, write a revealing explanation of some other process, step by step and detail by detail. How is commercial ice-cream made? How is sugar refined? How is ketchup made? How is fast-food hamburger meat prepared? How are hot-dogs made? What goes on in a slaughter-house? How are chickens raised for market? What is shock therapy? How does aversion therapy work?

BEN ROSS SCHNEIDER, JR.   **"Programs as Essays"**

1. Play with and freshen some other clichés the way Schneider does the one about putting the cart before the horse—perhaps such similarly horsy ones as changing horses in midstream, closing the barn door after the horse is stolen, looking a gift horse in the mouth, or being a horse of a different colour.

2. Point out some of Schneider's many other uses of colloquialisms and clichés. Is this kind of familiar style appropriate for his subject? for his

audience? Would you call this essay user-friendly? How about the literary references (Homer, Molière, Thoreau, Shelley)?

3. What other internal strategies does this process analysis use? It is full of details, of course, used as examples and illustrations. How much of a role do classification and division play? How would you describe the way he handles the two large parts of his subject, the writing of computer programs and the writing of essays?

4. As an instructional process, Schneider's essay should follow its own precepts, for example about structure. Analyze it to see if it does.

5. The next time you write an essay, especially a long and complicated one, carefully apply Schneider's advice: about structure (digression, repetition, reasonable order), transitions, active verbs (other than *be*), knowing your user (audience, real or imaginary), getting rid of nonessentials, and, overall, clarity, including documentation.

6. "The purpose of machines is to save labor, not increase it." Use this as the thesis for an essay. Will the essay necessarily be argumentative, or can it be simply explanatory, informative, expository? Think carefully about the internal strategies you will want or need to use.

**BERTON ROUECHÉ  "Three Sick Babies"**

1. Who is John Bunyan? Who is Osler? Semmelweis you will recognize if you've read Broad and Wade's essay in section III.

2. Note how Roueché begins with narrative (though it contains information, or "exposition"), somewhat in the manner of a police story, and then in the second paragraph shifts to almost pure exposition, background information readers need in order to understand what's going on. What is the effect of this pattern? Does it continue?

3. After Dr. Fierer comes on the scene we get continuous direct quotation until the final two paragraphs. Does Fierer in a sense, then, become the author of the essay? Considering this and the information Roueché gives about Dr. Taylor, does this essay differ significantly in kind from Cameron's interview with Davies (section II)? Does Roueché have greater control over what he reports?

4. Do you think Roueché intends a kind of situational irony or irony of fate when he tells us that Dr. Fierer was delayed by "a chimpanzee... with hepatitis"? Is the effect heightened by the fact's being disclosed at the end of a paragraph?

5. The Communicable Disease Center (CDC) in Atlanta is now known as the Centers for Disease Control (CDC). What do you suppose was the reason for the change in name (and for the retention of the initials)?

6. Does having read this essay make you feel less secure or more secure

about the prospect of going into hospital? Do you think Rouché had one or the other of these results in view? Compare his intent with that of Orwell (section II). If you have had experience as a patient in a hospital, try writing an essay directed at a general audience in which you explain what it was like. Make your *primary* purposes those of explaining and informing, rather than merely relating, describing, or revealing; and try to keep anything argumentative out of it altogether.

### K.C. COLE  "By the Numbers"

1. Do some research into the Pythagorean theory of numbers or into Bertrand Russell's work with mathematics.
2. Is mathematics a science? Russell was a philosopher—is mathematics a· philosophy, a way of looking at things? (Note that Berlin in his essay discusses Fermat's Theorem. Could Cole have brought that into his essay too? Should he have?) Is mathematics a kind of language? "Numbers *are* relationships," says Cole: irrationality, regularity, order, motion, speed—all are forms of relations or movement that numbers represent. How does language do the same thing?
3. Did *you* know that "nature and numbers go hand in hand"? Can you think of any exceptions to this general principle?
4. Explain Einstein's statement that Cole quotes halfway through the essay.
5. Write a short essay about the importance or unimportance of numbers in your life. Write an essay about "5½."
6. According to Galileo, "To understand the universe, you must understand the language in which it is written." Use this quotation as the beginning of an essay. It need not be about mathematics. Might it be about music? Might it be about art, as suggested in the second section of Colombo's essay (section VI)?

### ISAIAH BERLIN  "The Purpose of Philosophy"

1. What is Fermat's Theorem? What is the Enlightenment? Who gave it that name? What poem is Berlin quoting in paragraph 20?
2. Note the close similarity in form of the semantically diverse words *causal* and *casual*, which Berlin uses in one sentence in paragraph 18. Can you think of any other such pairs? Use each pair in a sentence.
3. To help yourself understand this essay, construct a detailed and coherent sentence outline for it.
4. Berlin's is essentially an essay in definition. What other methods or strategies does he use to define "philosophy"? The most prominent one is of course classification; in a sense his whole subject is classification (see for example paragraph 31). Explain in your own terms the two kinds of classification or categorization he points to in paragraph

30. What is he classifying, and what are the classes he decides on? Does he acknowledge that settling on the two categories is in a sense to commit the either-or fallacy that Brink criticizes (section III)? Is the setting up of a third or "intermediate basket" still perhaps an over-simplification? What are Kant's categories? Do we in the twentieth century still have our set or sets of "category-spectacles"? Do you? Should you?

5. Almost any paragraph in Berlin's essay is pregnant with possibilities for further thought. Grab one or two of his pronouncements to examine in an essay of your own. Be sure to supply concrete and specific details to clarify and support your abstractions and generalizations.

### KEN DRYDEN   "The Game"

1. What is the origin of the saying that begins "Whom the gods would destroy"?

2. If Dryden's essay is explanation, what is he explaining? Is it a work of definition?

3. Is Dryden "articulate"? Do you infer that he is also "intelligent"? Is he "modest"? Do you think he used a ghost-writer? Do you think the "image" he presents in this essay is "accurate"? If, as he says, "it doesn't matter," how can he be "his own man"—or is that his para-doxical point: he can be, because he accepts his image for what it is? When he says of a self-deprecating remark, "But you don't believe that," do you believe him? Is he genuinely "self-deprecatory"? After reading this piece, do you consider Dryden in any way a victim of his own "image"? How is his "reputation" different from his "image"—or is it, since he refused to play the "game" after doing only one com-mercial? Look and listen for other instances of "the game" and "playing the game" used metaphorically in contemporary rhetoric—for example "the game of life," with its "winners and losers."

4. If you're among those who attend to the "image" of sports heroes, do you feel that you've had a "fraud" perpetrated on you?

5. Do you discern any irony, of whatever kind, in this essay? What is the effect of the closing anecdote?

6. Many a hero in the great literature of the past supposedly possessed a "tragic flaw" which brought about his downfall—for example Oedi-pus and Othello. Do modern heroes, including sports heroes, have tragic or fatal flaws? In an essay, explore the nature of modern hero-ism, perhaps by comparing a modern hero or heroine with some from the past.

7. Write an essay in which you explain how some other public figures can be thought of as "metaphors."

### MARGARET ATWOOD "Witches"

1. Why do you suppose modern poetry in the library should have been off-limits to female students? And why should Canadian poetry have been exempt from this restriction?

2. How important is irony in this piece? Point out instances of Atwood's verbal and other witticisms. What is their function? Do they merely help to establish a tone, a *persona*? Do they make a point, or several points? Is Atwood weaving a spell?

3. To what degree is this piece feminist? From the whole talk, how much can you infer about the sort of audience she was speaking to?

4. Write an essay about "role models" in your life. Are you a role model for anyone?

5. Write a short essay that begins with a personal anecdote about revisiting a place after several years and then moves on to discuss some topic growing out of that experience.

### NICHOLSON BAKER "The Size of Thoughts"

1. Did you find Baker's vocabulary intimidating? How many of these words did you have to look up: *nodes, corollary, codification, relinquish, replenish, intellection, thrum, interstitial, contentiousness, fastnesses, codices, aperçu, peripheral, insurrection, profusion, recondite*? What do such words contribute to the tone and texture of this essay? Which of them do you want in your working vocabulary? What is the effect of terms like *nifty* and *peter out* occurring among the others?

2. Who was Hammurabi? What is the point of the reference to "the nineteenth-century dream of a liberal democracy"? What poet does Baker quote after Wordsworth?

3. Baker divides thoughts into three classes, by size; then he focusses on one of the categories, large thoughts, and defines them in terms of three criteria. What other internal strategies does he use?

4. But of course thoughts do not, literally, have size, physical bulk. Baker is using *synesthesia*, metaphorically mixing the senses, as when one speaks of the taste of defeat or the smell of victory. Try classifying and defining the colours of anger, the dimensions of pain, the taste of numbers, the smells of sorrow, the textures of prose, the colour or touch of sounds, the sounds of colours. Write an essay categorizing thoughts according to their colours.

5. What are Brahms, Bellini, Bach, and Pontormo doing among the builders of large thoughts? Who might some of the "mere eighty-six others" be? Is Baker serious here? Is it likely that your or anyone else's list would coincide or even overlap much with his? Or are his three criteria personal, subjective? Is objectivity possible with this sub-

ject? How do the lines from Tennyson qualify as a "large thought" according to Baker's criteria? As evidenced here, are some of Baker's own thoughts large? Or is he content with thinking small ones?

6. What does Baker mean by saying "(all scientific thoughts are small)" and "(All that is untrue is small)"? Why does he put these statements in parentheses?

7. This essay is so complexly rich with figurative language that it both invites and defies comment. Try taking one section—a sentence or two, for example the image of the spreading wine-stain—and analyzing as thoroughly as you can how its metaphors work. Then write a brief speculative or metaphysical piece of your own in which you try to use language as imaginatively as he does.

### STEPHEN JAY GOULD   "Our Allotted Lifetimes"

1. What are the principal internal strategies Gould uses? Does he classify? define? compare and contrast? provide examples and illustrations? Does he rely only on scientific evidence, or does he explain his point in other ways as well? Does the analogy between heart and bellows (paragraph 5) help you understand the point he is making?

2. Does the essay flow smoothly? Examine each paragraph to see if its beginning provides a transitional hook to the preceding paragraph or refers to the overall topic, or both. Do any paragraph openings lack one or both of these devices? If so, what then maintains coherence and unity?

3. Does the fact that Gould concludes with the mayfly, which is not a mammal, damage either the consistency or the structural integrity of his essay? Or does it usefully broaden the perspective—as well as provide him with an effective metaphor to end on?

4. Compare the ways in which scientist Gould and nonscientist Dillard (section I) approach nature.

5. Build the beginning of your next essay around a longish quotation— dialogue or not—from some published work.

### LEWIS THOMAS   "Notes of a Biology Watcher: The Hazards of Science"

1. Thomas begins almost as if his main interest were in the history of the words *hubris* and *hybrid*. Browse in an etymological dictionary until you find two or three interesting words that are similarly related etymologically but whose current meanings do not at first glance appear related (for example *savour, savant; safe, salute; grammar, glamour*). Then write a short essay tracing the history of their meanings.

2. If Thomas thinks that "the question about limiting human knowledge" is "too loaded" (paragraph 14), why does he later turn to a direct discussion of it and give an extended answer to it? Is this an example

of artful artlessness? Analyze the structure and strategy of Thomas's whole extended beginning.

3. Read Milton's *Paradise Lost*, Book VII, lines 5-38, 66ff., 167-68, and Book XII, lines 553-87, and write an essay discussing the statements of Raphael, Michael, and Adam alongside those of Thomas.

4. Imagine yourself a non-scientist member of a "Hubris Commission." Four cases are put before you:

   (1) A team of scientists seem to be on the verge of discovering a way to convert lead into gold. How would you react?

   (2) A scientist is experimenting with ants—enormously strong creatures for their size—in an attempt to breed larger ones to serve as "workhorses" and thus conserve energy. Should he be allowed to continue?

   (3) A parapsychologist claims to have proof that a human being, properly trained, can appreciably raise the temperature of objects hundreds of miles away. Should he be locked up?

   (4) A medical institute conducting research on aging wants a huge grant, claiming to be hot on the track of a way to double or even triple human life-expectancy. Should they get the money, or should they be turned off?

   Write a brief brief on one of these cases for presentation to the committee.

JOHN KENNETH GALBRAITH   **"The Language of Economics"**

1. If Galbraith's vocabulary sent you to the dictionary unusually often, is that a good thing or a bad thing? Here are a few of his larger words: *portentous, involuted, punctilious, stultification, equanimity, coterminous, honorific, inimical, sententiously, esoteric.* Do you want any of these in your working vocabulary? Which of them are now in your recognition vocabulary?

2. Is part II, in its brevity, sufficient to accomplish its purpose? Try putting the words *parameter, stochastic* and *aggregation* into a single sentence (not, of course, the way Galbraith does, or we do here).

3. Explain in your own words what Galbraith finds so good about the two statements he quotes from Adam Smith in part III (one in footnote 3).

4. Need Galbraith have used so many and such long discursive footnotes? Are they in themselves an element of his style in this essay? Using Galbraith's announced principles, analyze his own prose style.

5. In part V, is Galbraith's analogy between the Bible and the writings of economists clear and valid? What does it suggest about modern economic theory?

6. In parts VI and VII, is Galbraith being intentionally ironic in spots? If

so, where did the irony begin? What is the final, overall tone of this essay?

7. Veblen may have dealt what he called "conspicuous consumption" a heavy blow, but it did not disappear. Write an essay on one or more kinds of conspicuous consumption in today's society. Or write a confessional essay about conspicuous consumption's part in your own behavior (you may wish to be ironically self-mocking—remember Forster's essay in section I). Or write an argumentative essay in which you try to justify at least some forms of conspicuous consumption.

8. Write an essay anatomizing a passage of prose from some professional journal. Evaluate the necessity and effectiveness of the language and style of the passage.

## TOPICS: General and Comparative

1. What is the thesis of each essay in this section? What is each writer trying to explain? What for example is Baker's purpose? Are any theses implied rather than stated? Note also where theses are stated. Does Roueché's thesis appear only at the end? Are some stated—in different form—both near the beginning and near the end? Note how Gould calls attention to his "main theme"—but not until almost halfway through the essay; is that actually his thesis? Note that Thomas, like Forster in section I, puts his thesis in the form of a question which he then proceeds to answer. In your own essays, think carefully about the form and the placement of your thesis.

2. Consider the tone of the essays in this section. Atwood is informal and partly ironic; Roueché is objective and intense; Berlin is formal; Baker is openly subjective and playful—but is he also quite serious? Is Galbraith formal and academic as well as wry? How would you characterize Cole's tone? Try ordering these essays on a scale running from formal to informal or colloquial, on another running from objective to subjective, and on yet another running from sober to sardonic. What is the effect of each tonal choice? What do Beck, Bertholle, and Child do to keep their set of instructions from sounding utterly dry and mechanical?

3. These essays are expository—written to explain and inform. But expository writing is often also argumentative, at least implicitly if not explicitly. Even the set of instructions on boning a fowl are trying to convince you that it's not so difficult a process as you might think, to persuade you to give it a try, and also to convince you that the process as described is the proper or best or only way to do it. But of course it is not argumentative in tone. Mitford is openly, even blatantly argumentative. Gould says he wants to "argue" his "main theme";

but is his essay primarily argumentative? Galbraith makes clear at the beginning that his essay is argument as well as exposition; analyze its argumentative structure. Clearly Thomas's essay is not only informative but also argumentative: compare his rhetorical techniques with those of one or more of the other essays in this section that are written to persuade; then compare them with the techniques of the essays in section III. Is there anything argumentative about Schneider's essay? Cole's? Berlin's?

4. Because they deal with something that takes place during a period of time, process essays often use narrative; they also often use cause and effect. Examine the first four essays in this section to see how much and in what ways and for what reasons they use narrative and cause-and-effect techniques.

5. Could Dryden's essay just as well be in the "Writing to Reveal" section as here? What, if anything, gets revealed, as opposed to explained? Is Atwood's intention partly to reveal something about herself? How about Baker, Thomas, and Galbraith? What is Mitford striving to reveal? How does she accomplish the revelation?

6. How important are titles? What should a title do? Evaluate the titles of the essays in this section—and in the other sections too. How effective are they? How are they effective? Try classifying them according to their kinds and the way they work. Does Cole's title constitute an allusion, or is it just a conveniently familiar phrase? Do you believe that Atwood "plucked" her title "from the air" before she'd even planned her talk? How effective does her title turn out to be? In how many ways does she apply it? Try the tactic yourself: find a title at random (perhaps by sticking your finger into a dictionary or other book with your eyes closed, or arranging a pile of letter-tiles from a word game) and see if from it, by processes of association and the like, you can generate material for a short essay.

7. Do Thomas and Gould write the way you would expect scientists to write? Do they write the way Broad and Wade (in section III) say scientists write? How *should* scientists write? Does it depend on their audience on a given occasion? Do you feel legitimately included in their audiences here? Faced with the complexities of subjects like medicine, biology, mathematics, and economics, how do writers strive to be clear? Does their use of a technical vocabulary help, or does it hinder? Does the medical terminology Rouché uses annoy you or does it add authenticity? Does Berlin help you understand the function of philosophy? How does his purpose differ from that of Davenport in section II? Are Cole and Galbraith intent on getting you to understand mathematics and economics, respectively, or are they content with more modest aims? Galbraith tries to distinguish between

the clarity of a necessary technical language and the ambiguity that much jargon creates. How effective is he? Is the distinction valid? Write a short informative essay on a technical subject. Don't shy away from technical terminology, however; use it so that it will help rather than hinder non-specialist readers.

8. Eiseley (section I) mentions "the passion of modern men for the precision of machines" and their dislike of "vagueness of any sort." Cole refers to numbers as different from "the messy complexities of everyday life" and Broad and Wade refer (section III) to Merton and the Vienna Circle latching onto science amid times of chaos. Is mathematics always true, certain, dependable? How does what Cole says about numbers and truth accord with what Broad and Wade call "the myth of logic" in science? Do "irrational" numbers fit into the myth of logical science? How can mathematicians talk, rationally, about "imaginary" or "impossible" numbers? Would it have bothered Wittgenstein (see Davenport in section II)? How might a mathematician answer Berlin's question, "What is a number?" Try answering it yourself. Is it a "philosophical" question, according to Berlin's definition? Do some of the questions Berlin uses as examples sound similar to those of Wittgenstein? How central is *language* to the problems of philosophy that Berlin discusses (see for example paragraph 22)?

9. Compare what Berlin says about "the history of thought" being "a long series of parricides" to what Broad and Wade (section III) say scientific progress amounts to. Are they making a similar point? Berlin outlines history as a succession of patterns, models, categories. How would such a view sit with Tuchman (section III)? Would she find such a view too neat and tidy? Or is Berlin's view really neat and tidy at all? Note that she cites him in support of her position. Does his essay reveal the same attitudes or assumptions as appear in what she quotes from another of his works?

10. Explain the difference between a base-3 number system and a base-10 number system. Are there advantages to each? Or explain the differences between a diatonic scale, a 12-tone scale, a pentatonic scale, and a chromatic scale.

11. Classify the books in your own or a friend's personal collection. What does the classification reveal? Or write an essay classifying your closest friends and acquaintances. Decide on what criteria you will use—gender, age, size, intelligence, interests, national or ethnic background, and so on. Which scheme of classification yields the most interesting or useful results?

12. Write an essay defining happiness, courage, romance, friendship, or some other abstract idea. If necessary divide your topic into parts and focus selectively. Provide plenty of examples and illustrations.

13. Write an essay explaining the causes of a particular election result, of the outcome of a particular battle, of a notable athletic victory or defeat, or of some similar event. Choose an event small enough to be manageable. Do whatever research is necessary. You will probably need to use some narration.

14. Write an essay interpreting a body of statistics. Consider such topics as the differences in the cost of food from place to place, ethnic distribution in your area over a twenty-year span, the unemployment figures for your province during the last decade, or the spread and control of an epidemic disease.

15. If you know how to tie flies, write a brief instructional process essay on how to tie a particular kind—perhaps a Harger's Orange? Or explain how to make spaghetti sauce; how to fix the gears on a ten-speed bike; how to play soccer; how to get from Winnipeg to Thunder Bay; how to drink soup through a straw; how to tie shoes; how to fly a kite; how to peel a tomato; how to play dominoes; how to throw a frisbee; how to write a good paragraph; how to eat grapefruit; how to darn stockings; how to beat inflation; how to tune a guitar; how to use dental floss; how to prune a fruit tree; how to make an omelette; how to analyze a poem; how to polish brass; how to polish apples; how to win friends and influence people; how to use a dictionary; how to re-pot a root-bound plant; how to eat an artichoke; how to make croutons; how to change a spark-plug; how to trim a moustache; how to give up smoking; how to sew on a button; how to.... Consider beginning your essay with "It's not so difficult to...," or words to that effect.

# V
# Writing
# to
# Amuse

In an essay called "Humour as I See It," published in 1916 in *Further Foolishness*, Stephen Leacock reflects characteristically on his own craft:

> Until two weeks ago I might have taken my pen in hand to write about humour with the confident air of an acknowledged professional. But that time is past. Such claim as I had has been taken from me. In fact I stand unmasked. An English reviewer writing in a literary journal, the very name of which is enough to put contradiction to sleep, has said of my writing, "What is there, after all, in Professor Leacock's humour but a rather ingenious mixture of hyperbole and meiosis?"
>
> The man was right. How he stumbled upon this trade secret I do not know. But I am willing to admit, since the truth is out, that it has long been my custom in preparing an article of a humorous nature to go down to the cellar and mix up half a gallon of meiosis with a pint of hyperbole. If I want to give the article a decidedly literary character, I find it well to put in about half a pint of paresis. The whole thing is amazingly simple.*

Writing humorously, he underlines the difficulties that exist in writing about humour: the almost overwhelming impulse to become solemn, the easy reliance on categories of humorous techniques, the temptation to cap the humorist's jokes with other jokes that usually fall flat. There are good reasons why one should not write about humorous writing at all, but instead just sit back and enjoy it.

Yet humour often has serious implications, and writers of humour do use various techniques, and there is an art to good storytelling: all of these subjects are worthy of comment. Involved in good storytelling are such matters as a writer's control over intonation, careful pacing, and use of dramatic pauses. Because intonation is particularly important in a work striving to amuse, it is necessary for a writer to orchestrate a written work so that readers can adequately gauge the tone. The techniques of hyperbole (exaggeration) and meiosis (understatement) will both work to this end. But not always. A writer, or even a speaker, must place some trust in a reader's or an audience's ability to adjust to changes in tone, and such trust is often betrayed. Humourless persons often fail to perceive a speaker's ironic tone or ironic intent. Responding literally is the surest way to kill the humour of a situation, and literal (often outraged) responses are usually out of all proportion to the original comment. "Letters to the Editor" columns frequently fill up with such misspent energy. And readers who fail to find a written work funny—if indeed it is funny—have

---

*From *Further Foolishness* by Stephen Leacock, reprinted by permission of The Canadian Publishers, McClelland and Stewart Limited, Toronto.

often, like those mistaken listeners, simply failed to *hear the voice*—to catch the cadence and intonations—of the speaker who transcribed his ironic observations onto the page.

People use several different terms when talking about events or things that amuse, and the terms are often confused. Here are some of them:

> *humorous* (How neutral a term is this?)
> *funny* (Why does this word imply both simple amusement and strangeness?)
> *ironic* (Are there any limits to this term?)
> *comic* (Has this term become codified by modern criticism?)
> *laughable* (Does this imply any humour at all?)
> *witty* (Does this imply intellectual enjoyment only?)
> *amusing* (Does this imply distant superiority?)
> *wry* (In what way does this suggest emotional release?)
> *sardonic* (Does this differ from *wry*?)
> *smart* (Is this a culturally biased word?)
> *whimsical* (Is this word socially biased?)
> *facetious* (Has this word become a slur?)
> *capricious* (How does this relate to humour or enjoyment?)
> *farcical* (Why is this word associated with drama?)
> *droll* (Does this word now sound oddly archaic?)
> *sarcastic* (What does this imply that *ironic* does not?)
> *satiric* (Is humour a necessary element here?)

There are other terms as well, all of which imply different variations of response. And we have to be careful to distinguish among these differences. People often confuse *sarcastic* (which means "flesh-tearing") with *ironic*, even though irony need not be aggressive. *Comic*, similarly, is synonymous with neither *ironic* nor *satiric*, nor even with *witty*. Whereas *wit* usually involves verbal cleverness (not necessarily with intent to amuse), *comic*—like some of the other terms on the list—can refer to visual incongruity rather than verbal, or in a much more general way to a genial acceptance of the complexities and possibilities of life.

When one tries to distinguish *comedy* from *irony* and *satire*—either in substance and intent or in form—other problems arise, and still more literary categories spring into being. Irony and sarcasm can be formal techniques in the context of satiric writing, which many critics think of as essentially reformative. So can innuendo. So can burlesque, parody, and travesty. But irony can also refer to a whole attitude of human expectations, a shrugging resignation in the face of the difference between human desires and the way things are.

To contemplate theories of humour is to encounter further disagreement. A number of theorists see *wit*, for example, as a kind of indirect savagery, and they define both satiric humour and humour of the farcical, slipping-on-a-banana-peel kind as psychological sublimation of violence. These writers stress the implicit viciousness of humorous writing. By contrast, someone like Leacock, who in "A, B, and C" expresses a sympathy (not unalloyed) for human fallibility, stresses how humour emerges from our awareness of the close relation between sorrow and joy. Some people call humour elitist or escapist; others claim that it is necessary for sanity, for survival, for openness, for flexibility, and for the ability to deal sensibly with reality. All of these are large claims, and perhaps no single theory adequately explains why people find things funny or why they laugh.

Whatever the impulse behind it, humorous writing—whether reformative or reflective in nature, whether sympathetic or angry—will work only when the writer carefully controls what he or she has to say. Letting things get out of hand—letting more anger than amusement show, pushing the ridiculous too hard or for too long—will get in the reader's way. Uncontrolled invective will simply appear frivolous—laughable rather than mirthful—or else vicious or simply embarrassing. Sometimes the reformative impulse of humour has to declare itself, of course. Thomas Chandler Haliburton, in his 1836 work *The Clockmaker*, notes that "When reason fails to convince, there is nothin' left but ridicule." Ritter's wry amusement at contemporary urban pretensions, Murdoch's stylized annoyance with cliché, Beerbohm's impatience with the manual-writer's unrealistic assumptions about people: these represent various shades of attack. But how closely, how *literally*, can one accept what these essays say? Possibly not at all. Humour works at tangents, works with two levels of reality in mind. The humour derives from our sense of an author's control over such disparity and from our sense of an author's engaging eye for incongruities in language, form, and human behaviour. Because language is often the medium for such incongruities, it is also a frequent topic of humour as well. Trillin's reflections on the pain of living literally, Thurber's joyful exposé of the clichés of French westerns, and Beerbohm's pastiche of letter-writing all take language comically—in order, one might say, to take language (and life) seriously. Through humour they find a way of dealing with life's absurdities and ironies, and enduring. Through burlesque and exaggeration, through puns and ironic asides, they probe cultural values, social attitudes, and the idiosyncrasies of character. They also amuse.

# Bicycles

## Erika Ritter

It wasn't always like this. There was a time in the life of the world when adults were adults, having firmly put away childish things and thrown away the key.

Not any more. The change must have come about innocently enough, I imagine. Modern Man learning to play nicely in the sandbox with the other grown-ups. Very low-tension stuff.

Now, in every direction you look, your gaze is met by the risible spectacle of adults postponing adolescence well into senility by means of adult toys: running shoes, baseball bats, roller skates, and—bicycles!

But the attitude is no longer the fun-loving approach of a bunch of superannuated kids, and I'm sure you can envision how the evolution occurred. Jogging progressed from a casual encounter with the fresh air to an intensive relationship, attended by sixty-dollar jogging shoes and a designer sweatband. Playing baseball stopped being fun unless you had a Lacoste (as opposed to low-cost) tee-shirt in which to impress your teammates. And where was the thrill in running around a squash court unless it was with a potentially important client?

As for bicycles—well, let's not even talk about bicycles. On the other hand, maybe we *should* talk about them, because there's something particularly poignant about how it all went wrong for the bicycle, by what declension this once proud and carefree vehicle sank into the role of beast of burden, to bear the weight of sobersided grown-ups at their supposed sport.

First, there was the earliest domestication of the North American bicycle (*cyclus pedalis americanus*) in the late Hippie Scene Era of the 1960s. This was the age of the no-nuke whole-grain cyclist, who saw in the bicycle the possibility of Making a Statement while he rode. A statement about pollution, about materialism, about imperialism, about milita-

From Erika Ritter, *Urban Scrawl: The World as Seen Through the Bemused Eyes of Erika Ritter* (Toronto: Macmillan of Canada, 1984).

rism, about—enough already. You get the picture: two wheels good, four wheels bad.

Thus it was that the basic bicycle gradually evolved into a chunky three-speed number from China, bowed down under a plastic kiddie carrier, army surplus knapsacks, and a faded fender-sticker advising Make Tofu, Not War. And a rider clad in a red plaid lumber-jacket, Birkenstock sandals, and an expression of urgent concern for all living things.

Once the very act of bicycle riding had become an act of high moral purpose, it was an easy step to the next phase of the bicycle's journey along the path of post-Meanderthal seriousness.

I'm speaking of the era of the high-strung thoroughbred bicycle, whose rider had also made advances, from pedalling peacenik to a hunched and humorless habitué of the velodrome, clad in leather-seated shorts, white crash helmet, and fingerless gloves, whizzing soundlessly, and with no hint of joy, down city streets and along the shoulders of super-highways, aboard a vehicle sculpted in wisps of silver chrome. A vehicle so overbred, in its final evolutionary stages, that it began to resemble the mere exoskeleton of a conventional cycle, its flesh picked away by birds of carrion.

Having been stripped of any connection with its innocent and leisurely origins, the bicycle now no longer bore the slightest resemblance to the happy creature it once had been. And in the mid-Plastic Scene Era, another crippling blow was struck by the upscale name-brand cyclist, who came along to finish what the fanatical velodromist had refined. Namely, the complete transformation of an ambling and unhurried mode of transit into a fast, nerve-wracking, expensive, and utterly competitive display of high speed, high technology, and high status.

The Upscale Cyclist was looking for a twelve-speed Bottecchia that matched his eyes, something that he'd look trendy upon the seat of, when riding to the office (the office!), and he was ready to pay in four figures for it.

Not only that, he was also prepared to shell out some heavy bread for those status accessories to complete the picture: the backpack designed by the engineers at NASA, the insulated water-bottle to keep his Perrier chilled just right, the sixteen-track Walkman that would virtually assure him the envy of all his friends.

So much for the cyclist. What of his poor debased mount?

Not surprisingly, amongst the breed of bicycle, morale is currently low, and personal pride all but a thing of the past. And yet…and yet, there are those who say that *cyclus pedalis americanus* is an indomitable creature, and that it is the bicycle, not its rider, who will make the last evolution of the wheel.

In fact, some theorize that the present high incidence of bicycle thievery, far from being evidence of crime, is actually an indication that the modern bicycle has had enough of oppressive exploitation and man's joyless ways, and is in the process of reverting to the wild in greater and greater numbers.

There have always remained a few aboriginal undomesticated bicycles—or so the theory goes—and now it is these free-spirited mavericks, down from the hills at night, who visit urban bike-racks, garages, and back porches to lure tame bicycles away with them.

Costly Kryptonite locks are wrenched asunder, expensive accoutrements are shrugged off, intricate gear systems are torn away, and lo—look what is revealed! Unadorned, undefiled *cyclus* in all his pristine glory, unfettered and unencumbered once more, and free to roam.

A wistful fantasy, you might say? The maundering illusions of someone who's been riding her bicycle too long without a crash helmet? I wonder.

Just the other day, there was that piece in the paper about a bicycle that went berserk in a shopping centre, smashing two display windows before it was subdued. And did you hear about the recent sighting of a whole herd of riderless bicycles, all rolling soundlessly across a park in the night?

It all kind of gets you to thinking. I mean, do *you* know where your ten-speed is tonight?

# Literally

## Calvin Trillin

September 12, 1981

My problem with country living began innocently enough when our well ran dry and a neighbor said some pump priming would be necessary.

"I didn't come up here to discuss economics," I said. Actually, I don't discuss economics in the city either. As it happens, I don't understand economics. There's no use revealing that, though, to every Tom, Dick and Harry who interrupts his dinner to try to get your water running, so I said, "I come up here to get away from that sort of thing." My neighbor gave me a puzzled look.

"He's talking about the water pump," Alice told me. "It needs priming."

I thought that experience might have been just a fluke—until, on a fishing trip with the same neighbor, I proudly pulled in a fish with what I thought was a major display of deep-sea angling skill, only to hear a voice behind me say, "It's just a fluke."

"This is dangerous," I said to Alice, while helping her weed the vegetable garden the next day. I had thought our problem was limited to the pump-priming ichthyologist down the road, but that morning at the post office I had overheard a farmer say that since we seemed to be in for a few days of good weather he intended to make his hay while the sun was shining. "These people are robbing me of aphorisms," I said, taking advantage of the discussion to rest for a while on my hoe. "How can I encourage the children to take advantage of opportunities by telling them to make hay while the sun shines if they think that means making hay while the sun shines?"

Copyright ©1982 by Calvin Trillin. From *Uncivil Liberties* published by Ticknor & Fields.

"Could you please keep weeding those peas while you talk," she said. "You've got a long row to hoe."

I began to look at Alice with new eyes. By that, of course, I don't mean that I actually went to a discount eye outlet, acquired two new eyes (20/20 this time), replaced my old eyes with the new ones and looked at Alice. Having to make that explanation is just the sort of thing I found troubling. What I mean is that I was worried about the possibility of Alice's falling into the habit of rural literalism herself. My concern was deepened a few days later by a conversation that took place while I was in one of our apple trees, looking for an apple that was not used as a *dacha* by the local worms. "I just talked to the Murrays, and they say that the secret is picking up windfalls," Alice said.

"Windfalls?" I said. "Could it be that Jim Murray has taken over Exxon since last time I saw him? Or do the Murrays have a natural-gas operation in the back forty I didn't know about?"

"Not those kinds of windfalls," Alice said. "The apples that fall from the tree because of the wind. They're a breeding place for worms."

"There's nothing wrong with our apples," I said, reaching for a particularly plump one.

"Be careful," she said. "You may be getting yourself too far out on a limb."

"You may be getting yourself out on a limb yourself," I said to Alice at breakfast the next morning.

She looked around the room. "I'm sitting at the kitchen table," she said.

"I meant it symbolically," I said. "The way it was meant to be meant. This has got to stop. I won't have you coming in from the garden with small potatoes in your basket and saying that what you found was just small potatoes. 'Small potatoes' doesn't mean small potatoes."

"Small potatoes doesn't mean small potatoes?"

"I refuse to discuss it," I said. "The tide's in, so I'm going fishing, and I don't want to hear any encouraging talk about that fluke not being the only fish in the ocean."

"I was just going to ask why you have to leave before you finish your breakfast," she said.

"Because time and tide wait for no man," I said. "And I mean it."

Had she trapped me into saying that? Or was it possible that I was falling into the habit myself? Was I, as I waited for a bite, thinking that there were plenty of other fish in the sea? Then I had a bite—then another. I forgot about the problem until after I had returned to the dock and done my most skillful job of filleting.

"Look!" I said, holding up the carcass of one fish proudly, as Alice approached the dock. "It's nothing but skin and bones."

The shock of realizing what I had said caused me to stumble against my fish-cleaning table and knock the fillets off the dock. "Now we won't have anything for dinner," I said.

"Don't worry about it," Alice said. "I have other fish to fry."

"That's not right!" I shouted. "That's not what that means. It means you have something better to do."

"It can also mean that I have other fish to fry," she said. "And I do. I'll just get that other fish you caught out of the freezer. Even though it was just a fluke."

I tried to calm myself. I apologized to Alice for shouting and offered to help her pick vegetables from the garden for dinner.

"I'll try to watch my language," she said, as we stood among the peas.

"It's all right, really," I said.

"I was just going to say that tonight it seems rather slim pickings," she said. "Just about everything has gone to seed."

"Perfectly all right," I said, wandering over toward the garden shed, where some mud seemed to be caked in the eaves. I pushed at the mud with a rake, and a swarm of wasps burst out at me. I ran for the house, swatting at wasps with my hat. Inside, I suddenly had the feeling that some of them had managed to crawl up the legs of my jeans, and I tore the jeans off. Alice found me there in the kitchen, standing quietly in what the English call their smalls.

"That does it," I said, "We're going back to the city."

"Just because of a few stings?"

"Can't you see what happened?" I said. "They scared the pants off me."

# A, B, and C

## The Human Element in Mathematics

## Stephen Leacock

The student of arithmetic who has mastered the first four rules of his art, and successfully striven with money sums and fractions, finds himself confronted by an unbroken expanse of questions known as problems. These are short stories of adventure and industry with the end omitted, and though betraying a strong family resemblance, are not without a certain element of romance.

The characters in the plot of a problem are three people called A, B, and C. The form of the question is generally of this sort:

"A, B, and C do a certain piece of work. A can do as much work in one hour as B in two, or C in four. Find how long they work at it."

Or thus:

"A, B, and C are employed to dig a ditch. A can dig as much in one hour as B can dig in two, and B can dig twice as fast as C. Find how long, etc., etc."

Or after this wise:

"A lays a wager that he can walk faster than B or C. A can walk half as fast again as B, and C is only an indifferent walker. Find how far, and so forth."

The occupations of A, B, and C are many and varied. In the older arithmetics they contented themselves with doing "a certain piece of work." This statement of the case, however, was found too sly and mysterious, or possibly lacking in romantic charm. It became the fashion to define the job more clearly and to set them at walking matches, ditch-digging, regattas, and piling cord wood. At times they became commercial and entered into partnership, having with their old mystery a "certain"

From *Literary Lapses* by Stephen Leacock, reprinted by permission of The Canadian Publishers, McClelland and Stewart Limited, Toronto.

capital. Above all they revel in motion. When they tire of walking-matches —A rides on horseback, or borrows a bicycle and competes with his weaker-minded associates on foot. Now they race on locomotives; now they row; or again they become historical and engage stagecoaches; or at times they are aquatic and swim. If their occupation is actual work they prefer to pump water into cisterns, two of which leak through holes in the bottom and one of which is water-tight. A, of course, has the good one; he also takes the bicycle, and the best locomotive, and the right of swimming with the current. Whatever they do they put money on it, being all three sports. A always wins.

In the early chapters of the arithmetic, their identity is concealed under the names John, William, and Henry, and they wrangle over the division of marbles. In algebra they are often called X, Y, and Z. But these are only their Christian names, and they are really the same people.

Now to one who has followed the history of these men through countless pages of problems, watched them in their leisure hours dallying with cord wood, and seen their panting sides heave in the full frenzy of filling a cistern with a leak in it, they become something more than mere symbols. They appear as creatures of flesh and blood, living men with their own passions, ambitions, and aspirations like the rest of us. Let us view them in turn. A is a full-blooded blustering fellow, of energetic temperament, hotheaded and strong-willed. It is he who proposes everything, challenges B to work, makes the bets, and bends the others to his will. He is a man of great physical strength and phenomenal endurance. He has been known to walk forty-eight hours at a stretch, and to pump ninety-six. His life is arduous and full of peril. A mistake in the working of a sum may keep him digging a fortnight without sleep. A repeating decimal in the answer might kill him.

B is a quiet, easy-going fellow, afraid of A and bullied by him, but very gentle and brotherly to little C, the weakling. He is quite in A's power, having lost all his money in bets.

Poor C is an undersized, frail man, with a plaintive face. Constant walking, digging, and pumping has broken his health and ruined his nervous system. His joyless life has driven him to drink and smoke more than is good for him, and his hand often shakes as he digs ditches. He has not the strength to work as the others can; in fact, as Hamlin Smith has said, "A can do more work in one hour than C in four."

The first time that ever I saw these men was one evening after a regatta. They had all been rowing in it, and it had transpired that A could row as much in one hour as B in two, or C in four. B and C had come in dead fagged and C was coughing badly. "Never mind, old fellow," I heard B say, "I'll fix you up on the sofa and get you some hot tea." Just then A came blustering in and shouted, "I say, you fellows, Hamlin Smith has shown me three cisterns in his garden and he says we can pump them until tomorrow night. I bet I can beat you both. Come on. You can pump in your rowing things, you know. Your cistern leaks a little, I think, C." I heard B growl that it was a dirty shame and that C was used up now, but they went, and presently I could tell from the sound of the water that A was pumping four times as fast as C.

For years after that I used to see them constantly about town and always busy. I never heard of any of them eating or sleeping. Then owing to a long absence from home, I lost sight of them. On my return I was sur-prised to no longer find A, B, and C at their accustomed tasks; on inquiry I heard that work in this line was now done by N, M, and O, and that some people were employing for algebraical jobs four foreigners called Alpha, Beta, Gamma, and Delta.

Now it chanced one day that I stumbled upon old D, in the little garden in front of his cottage, hoeing in the sun. D is an aged labouring man who used occasionally to be called in to help A, B, and C. "Did I know 'em, sir?" he answered. "Why, I knowed 'em ever since they was lit-tle fellows in brackets. Master A, he were a fine lad, sir, though I always said, give me Master B for kindheartedness-like. Many's the job as we've been on together, sir, though I never did no racing nor aught of that, but just the plain labour, as you might say. I'm getting a bit too old and stiff for it nowadays, sir—just scratch about in the garden here and grow a bit of a logarithm, or raise a common denominator or two. But Mr. Euclid he use me still for them propositions, he do."

From the garrulous old man I learned the melancholy end of my former acquaintances. Soon after I left town, he told me, C had been taken ill. It seems that A and B had been rowing on the river for a wager, and C had been running on the bank and then sat in a draught. Of course the bank had refused the draught and C was taken ill. A and B came home and found C lying helpless in bed. A shook him roughly and said, "Get up, C, we're going to pile wood." C looked so worn and pitiful that B said, "Look here, A, I won't stand this, he isn't fit to pile wood to-night." C smiled feebly and said, "Perhaps I might pile a little if I sat up in bed." Then B, thoroughly alarmed, said, "See here, A, I'm going to fetch a doctor; he's dying." A flared up and answered, "You've no money to fetch a doc-tor." "I'll reduce him to his lowest terms," B said firmly, "that'll fetch him." C's life might even then have been saved but they made a mistake about the medicine. It stood at the head of the bed on a bracket, and the nurse accidentally removed it from the bracket without changing the sign. After the fatal blunder C seems to have sunk rapidly. On the evening of the next day, as the shadows deepened in the little room, it was clear to all that the end was near. I think that even A was affected at the last as he stood with bowed head, aimlessly offering to bet with the doctor on C's laboured breathing. "A," whispered C, "I think I'm going fast." "How fast do you think you'll go, old man?" murmured A. "I don't know," said C, "but I'm going at any rate."—The end came soon after that. C rallied for a moment and asked for a certain piece of work that he had left downstairs. A put it in his arms and he expired. As his soul sped heavenward A watched its flight with melancholy admiration. B burst into a passionate flood of tears and sobbed, "Put away his little cistern and the rowing clothes he used to wear. I feel as if I could hardly ever dig again."—The funeral was plain and unostentatious. It differed in nothing from the ordinary, except that out of deference to sporting men and mathematicians, A engaged two hearses. Both vehicles started at the same time, B driving the one which bore the sable parallelopiped containing the last remains of his ill-fated friend. A on the box of the empty hearse generously consented to a handicap of a hundred yards, but arrived first at the cemetery by driving four times as fast as B. (Find the distance to the cemetery.) As the sarcophagus was lowered, the grave was surrounded by the broken figures of the first book of Euclid.—It was noticed that after the death of C, A became a changed man. He lost interest in racing with B, and dug but languidly. He finally gave up his work and settled down to live on the interest of his bets.—B never recovered from the shock of C's death; his grief preyed upon his intellect and it became deranged. He grew moody and spoke only in monosyllables. His disease became rapidly aggravated, and he presently spoke only in words whose spelling was regular and which presented no difficulty to the beginner. Realising his precarious condition he voluntarily submitted to be incarcerated in an asylum, where he abjured mathematics and devoted himself to writing the History of the Swiss Family Robinson in words of one syllable.

# Wild Bird Hickok and His Friends

## James Thurber

In one of the many interesting essays that make up his book called 'Abinger Harvest,' Mr. E. M. Forster, discussing what he sees when he is reluctantly dragged to the movies in London, has set down a sentence that fascinates me. It is: 'American women shoot the hippopotamus with eyebrows made of platinum.' I have given that remarkable sentence a great deal of study, but I still do not know whether Mr. Forster means that American women have platinum eyebrows or that the hippopotamus has platinum eyebrows or that American women shoot platinum eyebrows into the hippopotamus. At any rate, it faintly stirred in my mind a dim train of elusive memories which were brightened up suddenly and brought into sharp focus for me when, one night, I went to see *The Plainsman*, a hard-riding, fast-shooting movie dealing with warfare in the Far West back in the bloody seventies. I knew then what Mr. Forster's curious and tantalizing sentence reminded me of. It was like nothing in the world so much as certain sentences which appeared in a group of French paperback dime (or, rather, twenty-five-centime) novels that I collected a dozen years ago in France. *The Plainsman* brought up these old pulp thrillers in all clarity for me because, like that movie, they dealt mainly with the stupendous activities of Buffalo Bill and Wild Bill Hickok; but in them were a unique fantasy, a special inventiveness, and an imaginative abandon beside which the movie treatment of the two heroes pales, as the saying goes, into nothing. In the moving from one apartment to another some years ago, I somehow lost my priceless collection of *contes héroïques du Far-Ouest*,

Copyright © 1937 James Thurber. Copyright © 1965 Helen W. Thurber and Rosemary Thurber Sauers. From *Let your Mind Alone*, published by Harper & Row. Originally printed in *The New Yorker*.

but happily I find that a great many of the deathless adventures of the French Buffalo Bill and Wild Bill Hickok remain in my memory. I hope that I shall recall them, for anodyne, when with eyes too dim to read I pluck finally at the counterpane.

In the first place, it should perhaps be said that in the eighteen-nineties the American dime-novel hero who appears to have been most popular with the French youth—and adult—given to such literature was Nick Carter. You will find somewhere in one of John L. Stoddard's published lectures—there used to be a set in almost every Ohio bookcase—an anecdote about how an American tourist, set upon by *apaches* in a dark *rue* in Paris in the nineties, caused them to scatter in terror merely by shouting '*Je suis Nick Carter!*'· But at the turn of the century or shortly thereafter, Buffalo Bill became the favourite. Whether he still is or not, I don't know—perhaps Al Capone or John Dillinger has taken his place. Twelve years ago, however, he was going great guns—or perhaps I should say great dynamite, for one of the things I most clearly remember about the Buffalo Bill of the French authors was that he always carried with him sticks of dynamite which, when he was in a particularly tough spot—that is, surrounded by more than two thousand Indians—he hurled into their midst, destroying them by the hundred. Many of the most inspired paperbacks that I picked up in my quest were used ones I found in those little stalls along the Seine. It was there, for instance, that I came across one of my favourites, *Les Aventures du Wild Bill dans le Far-Ouest*.

Wild Bill Hickok was, in this wonderful and beautiful tale, an even more prodigious manipulator of the six-gun than he seems to have been in real life, which, as you must know, is saying a great deal. He frequently mowed down a hundred or two hundred Indians in a few minutes with his redoubtable pistol. The French author of this masterpiece for some mysterious but delightful reason referred to Hickok sometimes as Wild Bill and sometimes as Wild Bird. '*Bonjour, Wild Bill!*' his friend Buffalo Bill often said to him when they met, only to shout a moment later, '*Regardez, Wild Bird! Les Peaux-Rouges!*' The two heroes spent a great deal of their time, as in *The Plainsman*, helping each other out of dreadful situations. Once, for example, while hunting Seminoles in Florida, Buffalo Bill fell into a tiger trap that had been set for him by the Indians—he stepped onto what turned out to be sticks covered with grass, and plunged to the bottom of a deep pit. At this point our author wrote, ' "*Mercy me!*" *S'écria Buffalo Bill.*' The great scout was rescued, of course, by none other than Wild Bill, or Bird, who, emerging from the forest to see his old comrade in distress, could only exclaim, '*My word!*'

It was, I believe, in another volume that one of the most interesting characters in all French fiction of the Far West appeared, a certain Major Preston, alias Preeton, alias Preslon (the paperbacks rarely spelled anyone's name twice in succession the same way). This hero, we were told when he was introduced, 'had distinguished himself in the Civil War by capturing Pittsburgh,' a feat which makes Lee's invasion of Pennsylvania seem mere child's play. Major Preeton (I always preferred that alias) had come out West to fight the Indians with cannon, since he believed it absurd that nobody had thought to blow them off the face of the earth with cannon before. How he made out with his artillery against the forest skulkers I have forgotten, but I have an indelible memory of a certain close escape that Buffalo Bill had in this same book. It seems that, through an oversight, he had set out on a scouting trip without his dynamite—he also carried, by the way, cheroots and a flashlight—and hence, when he stumbled upon a huge band of redskins, he had to ride as fast as he could for the nearest fort. He made it just in time. 'Buffalo Bill,' ran the story, 'clattered across the drawbridge and into the fort just ahead of the Indians, who, unable to stop in time, plunged into the moat and were drowned.' It may have been in this same tale that Buffalo Bill was once so hard pressed that he had to send for Wild Bird to help him out. Usually, when one was in trouble, the other showed up by a kind of instinct, but this time Wild Bird was nowhere to be found. It was a long time, in fact, before his whereabouts were discovered. You will never guess where he was. He was 'taking the baths at Atlantic City under orders of his physician.' But he came riding across the country in one day to Buffalo Bill's side, and all was well. Major Preeton, it sticks in my mind, got bored with the service in the Western hotels and went 'back to Philadelphia' (Philadelphia appears to have been the capital city of the United States at this time). The Indians in all these tales—and this is probably what gave Major Preeton his great idea—were seldom seen as individuals or in pairs or small groups, but prowled about in well-ordered columns of squads. I recall, however, one drawing (the paperbacks were copiously illustrated) which showed two *Peaux-Rouges* leaping upon and capturing a scout who had wandered too far from his drawbridge one night. The picture represented one of the Indians as smilingly taunting his captive, and the caption read, '*Vous vous promenez très tard ce soir, mon vieux!* ' This remained my favourite line until I saw one night in Paris an old W. S. Hart movie called *Le Roi du Far-Ouest*, in which Hart, insulted by a drunken ruffian, turned upon him and said, in his grim, laconic way, '*Et puis, après?* '

I first became interested in the French tales of the Far West when, one winter in Nice, a French youngster of fifteen, who, it turned out, devoted all his spending money to them, asked me if I had ever seen a 'wishtonwish.' This meant nothing to me, and I asked him where he had heard about the wishtonwish. He showed me a Far West paperback he was reading. There was a passage in it which recounted an adventure of Buffalo Bill and Wild Bill, during the course of which Buffalo Bill signalled to

Wild Bird 'in the voice of the wishtonwish.' Said the author in a parenthesis which at that time gave me as much trouble as Mr. Forster's sentence about the platinum eyebrows does now, 'The wishtonwish was seldom heard west of Philadelphia.' It was some time—indeed, it was not until I got back to America—before I traced the wishtonwish to its lair, and in so doing discovered the influence of James Fenimore Cooper on all these French writers of Far West tales. Cooper, in his novels, frequently mentioned the wishtonwish, which was a Caddoan Indian name for the prairie dog. Cooper erroneously applied it to the whip-poor-will. An animal called the 'ouapiti' also figured occasionally in the French stories, and this turned out to be the wapiti, or American elk, also mentioned in Cooper's tales. The French writer's parenthetical note on the habitat of the wishtonwish only added to the delightful confusion and inaccuracy which threaded these wondrous stories.

There were, in my lost and lamented collection, a hundred other fine things, which I have forgotten, but there is one that will forever remain with me. It occurred in a book in which, as I remember it, Billy the Kid, alias Billy the Boy, was the central figure. At any rate, two strangers had turned up in a small Western town and their actions had aroused the suspicions of a group of respectable citizens, who forthwith called on the sheriff to complain about the newcomers. The sheriff listened gravely for a while, got up and buckled on his gun belt, and said, '*Alors, je vais demander ses cartes d'identité!*' There are few things, in any literature, that have ever given me a greater thrill than coming across that line.

# On Pioneering

## Walter Murdoch

Hail, ye faithful, much-enduring readers!. . .But perhaps I had better explain. I spent a vacation recently in reading nearly three hundred Odes to Western Australia; and I wonder whether anybody ever spent a vacation in this way before, since the world began. I am now convalescent, thank you; except that I find a certain difficulty in not beginning sentences with "Hail!" the symptoms of odeshock have practically disappeared.

They mostly began with "hail" or "all hail" and many of them threw in an extra "hail" whenever their feelings got the better of them or the metre seemed to call for an extra syllable. They hailed everything and everybody; they hailed the country, they hailed the centenary, they hailed our wool, our wheat, our gold, our pearling industry, our wildflowers, the men of a century ago and the generations yet unborn. One of them exhorted his readers, at intervals, to "shout a loud hooray," and the variation was so pleasing that I felt inclined to take him at his word. Another invited us all to "shout and sing, and make the welkin blithely ring," but most of them were content with something less noisy than this. They were satisfied with hailing.

Of the earnest patriotism of these poets there can be no question; they have boundless faith in their land. We are a young people—"the debutante of nations," one of our singers calls us; and another, whose grammar is his servant, not his master, says, "the youngest of all thy fair sisters art thee"—and, being young, we are apt to be shy and to have too much respect for our elders. Our poets teach us a truer faith,

> Hail, beauteous land! hail, bonzer West Australia;
> Compared with you, all others are a failure.

"On Pioneering" by Walter Murdoch, reprinted from *Speaking Personally*, by permission of Angus & Robertson Publishers, Sydney. Copyright © Walter Murdoch 1930. © Barbara Murdoch 1970.

That is the kind of thing, and it undoubtedly warms the cockles of the heart, though some may object to the rhyme—but then Western Australia is a puzzling name to fit into rhyme; one minstrel ingeniously solves the problem by turning it round:

> Hail, Groperland! Australia West!
> Of earth's fair places thou art best.

There is no doubt about the fervour of this; and most of these poems are fervid. We are the salt of the earth; other people are its scum. We inhabit the loveliest of lands; other countries are more or less blots on the landscape. Even the size of our State comes in for its meed of praise:

> Hail to Westralia!
>   Hail to its bigness!
> Hail to its motto
>   "Cygnis insignis."

We have done wonderful things—especially Lord Forrest, who comes into scores of odes; this, for instance is the country

> Where the purest water flows up-hill
> In accordance with Lord Forrest's will.

Wonderful man! wonderful country! wonderful poets! Hail, every one of you! All hail, in fact.

But what most of these bards praise most loudly and continuously is the character and achievements of the men of a century ago—the pioneers. So far as I am concerned, the net result is that I never want to hear another word about pioneers as long as I live. That being so, you may object, why write an essay about them?—but I hope this essay will turn out before it is done, not to be about the pioneers at all, but about a quite different subject. Anyhow, I am tired of them,

> Those souls of priceless rarity,
>   Pioneers of our State,

who seem to have been physically almost as remarkable as they were in soul:

> Lean they were, with eyes aflame,
> These strong and sturdy men from hame.

"From hame" does not mean that they came from Scotland; it only means that the bard was bothered for a rhyme. (But what was the matter with "they came"?) When I try to discover from the odes what, exactly, these persons with flaming eyes and priceless souls did when they arrived, I get no very adequate account of their achievements. One poet does, indeed, endeavour to describe their doings with some exactness.

> They stopped at Mount Eliza,
> They camped beneath a tree,
> They said to one another,
> "This is good enough for me."

But I rather doubt the accuracy of this; the idiom has a too modern sound. It is wiser, perhaps, to keep to general statements, such as—

> They founded here a mighty State,
> On January 26th, 1828.

I suppose this is substantially true, though the poet seems to have antedated the event; and I suppose it is also true that they came to an inhospitable land, where—

> The native with his waddy, his boomerang and spear
> Held sway o'er its vast spaces by ignorance and fear.

And they got the better of him. At all events, whatever they did and whatever they were, it is in their honour that most of the odes beat the big drum.

> Then give to them the honour,
> For that they well deserve,
> And do your best endeavour
> To hand on the preserve.

By all means. Give them the honour they deserve; and give others the honour they, in their turn, deserve. The centenary celebrations are not to be arranged, I take it, for the glorification of the passengers on the *Parmelia* or of Thomas Peel's syndicate, but rather for public rejoicing that Western Australia has reached a certain stage in her journey—that she has survived the teething troubles (or weathered the storms, if that seems a more dignified way of putting it) of her first century; and for public thankfulness to whatsoever powers, human or divine, have guided her steps so far. Why anybody should pick out for special gratitude the men and women who happened to be the first on the spot it is a little difficult to see. We might as well go farther back and sing paeans of praise to the Angles and Saxons and Jutes, calling them souls of priceless rarity. Or why not sing hymns in honour of Adam, with eyes aflame, and also Eve, his beauteous dame?

The men and women who first came to settle in Australia were of British stock, and of an honourably adventurous strain. They came here to better their fortunes, lured by fantastic accounts of the country (Fraser's report dwelt on the "superiority of the soil"—and also on its "permanent humidity," a feature not conspicuous in my garden). Captain Stirling described it as "the land, out of all that I have seen in various quarters of the world, that possesses the greatest natural attractions." Vast tracts of this land were to be granted to each settler for next to nothing, and they were to cultivate cotton, tobacco, sugar and flax, to rear horses for the East Indian trade, and to establish large herds of cattle and swine for the supply of salt junk to His Majesty's shipping. They were to make fortunes easily and quickly. The land did not come up to their expectations, and they had but a thin time of it for many years after their arrival.

I do not wish to say a word against them; only, I do not see why special praise is due to them. They showed a spirit of adventure, which is the common birthright of our race—and of other races. They showed great courage in coming out to a remote and unknown world; courage, thank Heaven, is not an uncommon virtue. Are we not all born of women who have sailed gallantly into the perilous sea of marriage and faced death to bring us into the world? Everywhere in our country to-day, not only in remote and lonely places in the backblocks, but in the heart of our cities, too, men and women are confronting their fate with a high courage worthy of all honour. Those pioneers endured many hardships without whimpering; all praise to them for that; but why not praise also the innumerable persons who in our midst today are enduring hardships without whimpering, and who, because they do not whimper, are unhonoured and unsung? To single out the pioneers for special glorification is to libel humanity; it is to imply that virtue has been lost. The world is as full today as ever it was of the shining virtues of courage in danger and fortitude in adversity. Did the war show that our nation—or any nation—had lost its ancient hardihood? It is impossible to read the newspapers intelligently without being proud to belong to the indomitable human race; but the best examples do not get into the newspapers. They are to be found in all sorts of odd places; in the lonely bush and in the crowded slum; the heroic is everywhere at home.

Of course if, misled by the glamour of the past, you like to talk nonsense about the pioneers, and represent them as souls of priceless rarity stalking about with eyes aflame, I suppose no great harm is done. They were probably decent people, of average intelligence, fairly industrious and not without grit and resourcefulness; very like the normal Australian of to-day. The mistake made by the writers of some of these odes was to suppose that, to write poetry, you must talk nonsense. It is not so. Poetry and nonsense are incompatible. And this nonsense about pioneers gets, after a time, on one's nerves; hence this protest. The world is young; and we are all pioneers.

# How
# Shall I
# Word It?

## Max Beerbohm

It would seem that I am one of those travellers for whom the railway bookstall does not cater. Whenever I start on a journey, I find that my choice lies between well-printed books which I have no wish to read, and well-written books which I could not read without permanent injury to my eyesight. The keeper of the bookstall, seeing me gaze vaguely along his shelves, suggests that I should take *Fen Country Fanny*, or else *The Track of Blood* and have done with it. Not wishing to hurt his feelings, I refuse these works on the plea that I have read them. Whereon he, divining despite me that I am a superior person, says 'Here is a nice little handy edition of More's *Utopia*' or 'Carlyle's *French Revolution*' and again I make some excuse. What pleasure could I get from trying to cope with a masterpiece printed in diminutive grey-ish type on a semi-transparent little grey-ish page? I relieve the bookstall of nothing but a newspaper or two.

The other day, however, my eye and fancy were caught by a book entitled *How Shall I Word It?* and sub-entitled 'A Complete Letter Writer for Men and Women'. I had never read one of these manuals, but had often heard that there was a great and constant 'demand' for them. So I demanded this one. It is no great fun in itself. The writer is no fool. He has evidently a natural talent for writing letters. His style is, for the most part, discreet and easy. If you were a young man writing 'to Father of Girl he wishes to Marry' or 'thanking Fiancée for Present' or 'reproaching Fiancée for being a Flirt', or if you were a mother 'asking Governess her Qualifications' or 'replying to Undesirable Invitation for her Child', or indeed if you were in any other one of the crises which this book is designed to alleviate,

From *And Even Now* by Max Beerbohm, London: William Heinemann Ltd. (1920). Reprinted by permission of Mrs. Eva Reichmann.

you might copy out and post the specially-provided letter without making yourself ridiculous in the eyes of its receiver—unless, of course, he or she also possessed a copy of the book. But—well, can you conceive any one copying out and posting one of these letters, or even taking it as the basis for composition? You cannot. That shows how little you know of your fellow-creatures. Not you nor I can plumb the abyss at the bottom of which such humility is possible. Nevertheless, as we know by that great and constant 'demand', there the abyss is, and there multitudes are at the bottom of it. Let's peer down. . . . No, all is darkness. But faintly, if we listen hard, is borne up to us a sound of the scratching of innumerable pens—pens whose wielders are all trying, as the author of this handbook urges them, to 'be original, fresh, and interesting' by dint of more or less strict adherence to sample.

Giddily you draw back from the edge of the abyss. Come!—here is a thought to steady you. The mysterious great masses of helpless folk for whom *How Shall I Word It?* is written are sound at heart, delicate in feeling, anxious to please, most loth to wound. For it must be presumed that the author's style of letter-writing is informed as much by a desire to give his public what it needs, and will pay for, as by his own beautiful nature; and in the course of all the letters that he dictates you will find not one harsh word, not one ignoble thought or unkind insinuation. In all of them, though so many are for the use of persons placed in the most trying circumstances, and some of them are for persons writhing under a sense of intolerable injury, sweetness and light do ever reign. Even 'yours truly, Jacob Langton', in his 'letter to his Daughter's Mercenary Fiancée', mitigates the sternness of his tone by the remark that his 'task is inexpressibly painful'. And he, Mr. Langton, is the one writer who lets the post go out on his wrath. When Horace Masterton, of Thorpe Road, Putney, receives from Miss Jessica Weir, of Fir Villa, Blackheath, a letter 'declaring her Change of Feelings', does he upbraid her? No, 'it was honest and brave of you to write to me so straightforwardly and at the back of my mind I know you have done what is best. . . . I give you back your freedom only at your desire. God bless you, dear.' Not less admirable is the behaviour, in similar case, of Cecil Grant (14, Glover Street, Streatham). Suddenly, as a bolt from the blue, comes a letter from Miss Louie Hawke (Elm View, Deerhurst), breaking off her betrothal to him. Haggard, he sits down to his desk; his pen traverses the notepaper—calling down curses on Louie and on all her sex? No; 'one cannot say good-bye for ever without deep regret to days that have been so full of happiness. I must thank you sincerely for all your great kindness to me. . . . With every sincere wish for your future happiness,' he bestows complete freedom on Miss Hawke. And do not imagine that in the matter of self-control and sympathy, of power to understand all and pardon all, the men are lagged behind by the women. Miss

Leila Johnson (The Manse, Carlyle) has observed in Leonard Wace (Dover Street, Saltburn) a certain coldness of demeanour; yet 'I do not blame you; it is probably your nature'; and Leila in her sweet forbearance is typical of all the other pained women in these pages; she is but one of a crowd of heroines.

Face to face with all this perfection, the not perfect reader begins to crave some little outburst of wrath, of hatred or malice, from one of these imaginary ladies and gentlemen. He longs for—how shall he word it?—a glimpse of some bad motive, of some little lapse from dignity. Often, passing by a pillar-box, I have wished I could unlock it and carry away its contents, to be studied at my leisure. I have always thought such a haul would abound in things fascinating to a student of human nature. One night, not long ago, I took a waxen impression of the lock of the pillar-box nearest to my house, and had a key made. This implement I have as yet lacked either the courage or the opportunity to use. And now I think I shall throw it away. . . . No, I shan't. I refuse, after all, to draw my inference that the bulk of the British public writes always in the manner of this handbook. Even if they all have beautiful natures they must sometimes be sent slightly astray by inferior impulses, just as are you and I.

And, if err they must, surely it were well they should know how to do it correctly and forcibly. I suggest to our author that he should sprinkle his next edition with a few less righteous examples, thereby both purging his book of its monotony and somewhat justifying its sub-title. Like most people who are in the habit of writing things to be printed, I have not the knack of writing really good letters. But let me crudely indicate the sort of thing that our manual needs. . . .

### LETTER FROM POOR MAN
### TO OBTAIN MONEY FROM RICH ONE

[*The English law is particularly hard on what is called blackmail. It is therefore essential that the applicant should write nothing that might afterwards be twisted to incriminate him. —Ed.*]

Dear Sir,

To-day, as I was turning out a drawer in my attic, I came across a letter which by a curious chance fell into my hands some years ago, and which, in the stress of grave pecuniary embarrassment, had escaped my memory. It is a letter written by yourself to a lady, and the date shows it to have been written shortly after your marriage. It is of a confidential nature and might, I fear, if it fell into the wrong hands, be cruelly misconstrued. I would wish you to have the satisfaction of destroying it in person. At first I thought of sending it on to you by post. But I know how happy you are in your domestic life; and probably your wife and you, in your perfect mutual trust, are in the habit of opening each other's letters. Therefore, to avoid risk, I would prefer to hand the document to you personally. I will not ask you to come to my attic, where I could not offer you such hospitality as is due to a man of your wealth and position. You will be so good as to meet me at 3.0 A.M. (sharp) to-morrow (Thursday) beside the tenth lamp-post to the left on the Surrey side of Waterloo Bridge; at which hour and place we shall not be disturbed.

> I am, dear Sir,
> Yours faithfully,
> James Gridge.

### LETTER FROM YOUNG MAN
### REFUSING TO PAY HIS TAILOR'S BILL

Mr. Eustace Davenant has received the half-servile, half-insolent screed which Mr. Yardley has addressed to him. Let Mr. Yardley cease from crawling on his knees and shaking his fist. Neither this posture nor this gesture can wring one bent farthing from the pockets of Mr. Davenant, who was a minor at the time when that series of ill-made suits was supplied to him and will hereafter, as in the past, shout (without prejudice) from the house-tops that of all the tailors in London Mr. Yardley is at once the most grasping and the least competent.

### LETTER TO THANK AUTHOR
### FOR INSCRIBED COPY OF BOOK

Dear Mr. Emanuel Flower,

It was kind of you to think of sending me a copy of your new book. It would have been kinder still to think again and abandon that project. I am a man of gentle instincts, and do not like to tell you that 'A Flight into Arcady' (of which I have skimmed a few pages, thus wasting two or three minutes of my not altogether worthless time) is trash. On the other hand, I am determined that you shall not be able to go around boasting to your friends, if you have any, that this work was not condemned, derided, and dismissed by your sincere well-wisher, Wrexford Cripps.

### LETTER TO MEMBER OF PARLIAMENT
### UNSEATED AT GENERAL ELECTION

Dear Mr. Pobsby-Burford,

Though I am myself an ardent Tory, I cannot but rejoice in the crushing defeat you have just suffered in West Odgetown. There are moments when political conviction is overborne by personal sentiment; and this is one of them. Your loss of the seat that you held is the more striking by reason of the splendid manner in which the northern and eastern divisions of Odgetown have been wrested from the Liberal Party. The great bulk of the newspaper-reading public will be puzzled by your extinction in the midst of our party's triumph. But then, the great mass of the newspaper-reading public has not met you. I have. You will probably not remember me. You are the sort of man who would not remember anybody who might not be of some definite use to him. Such, at least, was one of the impressions you made on me when I met you last summer at a dinner given by our friends the Pelhams. Among the other things in you that struck me were the blatant pomposity of your manner, your appalling flow of cheap platitudes, and your hoggish lack of ideas. It is such men as you that lower the tone of public life. And I am sure that in writing to you thus I am but expressing what is felt, without distinction of party, by all who sat with you in the late Parliament.

The one person in whose behalf I regret your withdrawal into private life is your wife, whom I had the pleasure of taking in to the aforesaid dinner. It was evident to me that she was a woman whose spirit was well-nigh broken by her conjunction with you. Such remnants of cheerfulness as were in her I attributed to the Parliamentary duties which kept you out of her sight for so very many hours daily. I do not like to think of the fate to which the free and independent electors of West Odgetown have just condemned her. Only, remember this: chattel of yours though she is, and timid and humble, she despises you in her heart.

> I am, dear Mr. Pobsbury-Burford,
> Yours very truly,
> Harold Thistlake.

### LETTER FROM YOUNG LADY IN ANSWER
### TO INVITATION FROM OLD SCHOOL MISTRESS

My Dear Miss Price,

How awfully sweet of you to ask me to stay with you for a few days but how *can* you think I may have forgotten you for of course I think of you so very often and of the three ears I spent at your school because it is such a joy not to be there any longer and if one is at all down it bucks one up derectly to remember that *thats* all over atanyrate and that one has enough food to nurrish one and not that awful monottany of life and not the petty fogging daily tirrany you went in for and I can imagin no greater thrill and luxury in a way than to come and see the whole dismal grind still going on but without me being in it but this would be *rather* beastly of me wouldn't it so please dear Miss Price dont expect me and do excuse mistakes of English Composition and Spelling and etcetra in your affectionate old pupil,

Emily Thérèse Lynn-Royston.

ps, I often rite to people telling them where I was edducated and highly reckomending you.

### LETTER IN ACKNOWLEDGMENT
### OF WEDDING PRESENT

Dear Lady Amblesham,

Who gives quickly, says the old proverb, gives twice. For this reason I have purposely delayed writing to you, lest I should appear to thank you more than once for the small, cheap, hideous present you sent me on the occasion of my recent wedding. Were you a poor woman, that little bowl of ill-imitated Dresden china would convict you of tastelessness merely; were you a blind woman, of nothing but an odious parsimony. As you have normal eyesight and more than normal wealth, your gift to me proclaims you at once a Philistine and a miser (or rather did so proclaim you until, less than ten seconds after I had unpacked it from its wrappings of tissue paper, I took it to the open window and had the satisfaction of seeing it shattered to atoms on the pavement). But stay! I perceive a possible flaw in my argument. Perhaps you were guided in your choice by a definite wish to insult me. I am sure, on reflection, that this was so. *I shall not forget.*

Yours, etc.,
Cynthia Beaumarsh.

PS. My husband asks me to tell you to warn Lord Amblesham to keep out of his way or to assume some disguise so complete that he will not be recognised by him and horsewhipped.

PPS. I am sending copies of this letter to the principal London and provincial newspapers.

### LETTER FROM . . .

But enough! I never thought I should be so strong in this line. I had not foreseen such copiousness and fatal fluency. Never again will I tap these deep dark reservoirs in a character that had always seemed to me, on the whole, so amiable.

# Man, Bytes, Dog

## James Gorman

Many people have asked me about the Cairn Terrier. How about memory, they want to know. Is it I.B.M.-compatible? Why didn't I get the I.B.M. itself, or a Kaypro, Compaq, or Macintosh? I think the best way to answer these questions is to look at the Macintosh and the Cairn head on. I almost did buy the Macintosh. It has terrific graphics, good word-processing capabilities, and the mouse. But in the end I decided on the Cairn, and I think I made the right decision.

Let's start out with the basics:

MACINTOSH:
  Weight (without printer): 20 lbs.
  Memory (RAM): 128 K
  Price (with printer): $3,090

CAIRN TERRIER:
  Weight (without printer): 14 lbs.
  Memory (RAM): Some
  Price (without printer): $250

Just on the basis of price and weight, the choice is obvious. Another plus is that the Cairn Terrier comes in one unit. No printer is necessary, or useful. And—this was a big attraction to me—there is no user's manual.

Here are some of the other qualities I found put the Cairn out ahead of the Macintosh:

PORTABILITY: To give you a better idea of size, Toto in "The Wizard of

Reprinted by permission; ©1984 James Gorman. Originally in *The New Yorker*.

Oz" was a Cairn Terrier. So you can see that if the young Judy Garland was able to carry Toto around in that little picnic basket, you will have no trouble at all moving your Cairn from place to place. For short trips it will move under its own power. The Macintosh will not.

RELIABILITY: In five to ten years, I am sure, the Macintosh will be superseded by a new model, like the Delicious or the Granny Smith. The Cairn Terrier, on the other hand, has held its share of the market with only minor modifications for hundreds of years. In the short term, Cairns seldom need servicing, apart from shots and the odd worming, and most function without interruption during electrical storms.

COMPATIBILITY: Cairn Terriers get along with everyone. And for communications with any other dog, of any breed, within a radius of three miles, no additional hardware is necessary. All dogs share a common operating system.

SOFTWARE: The Cairn will run three standard programs, SIT, COME, and NO, and whatever else you create. It is true that, being microcanine, the Cairn is limited here, but it does load the programs instantaneously. No disk drives. No tapes.

Admittedly, these are peripheral advantages. The real comparison has to be on the basis of capabilities. What can the Macintosh and the Cairn do? Let's start on the Macintosh's turf—income-tax preparation, recipe storage, graphics, and astrophysics problems:

|           | Taxes | Recipes | Graphics | Astrophysics |
|-----------|-------|---------|----------|--------------|
| Macintosh | yes   | yes     | yes      | yes          |
| Cairn     | no    | no      | no       | no           |

At first glance it looks bad for the Cairn. But it's important to look beneath the surface with this kind of chart. If you yourself are leaning toward the MacIntosh, ask yourself these questions: Do you want to do your own income taxes? Do you want to type all your recipes into a computer? In your graph, what would you put on the $x$ axis? The $y$ axis? Do you have any astrophysics problems you want solved?

Then consider the Cairn's specialties: playing fetch and tug-of-war, licking your face, and chasing foxes out of rock cairns (eponymously). Note that no software is necessary. All these functions are part of the operating system:

|           | Fetch | Tug-of-War | Face | Foxes |
|-----------|-------|------------|------|-------|
| Cairn     | yes   | yes        | yes  | yes   |
| Macintosh | no    | no         | no   | no    |

Another point to keep in mind is that computers, even the Macintosh, only do what you tell them to do. Cairns perform their functions all on their own. Here are some of the additional capabilities that I discovered once I got the Cairn home and housebroken:

WORD PROCESSING: Remarkably, the Cairn seems to understand every word I say. He has a nice way of pricking up his ears at words like "out" or "ball." He also has highly tuned voice-recognition.

EDUCATION: The Cairn provides children with hands-on experience at an early age, contributing to social interaction, crawling ability, and language skills. At age one, my daughter could say "Sit," "Come," and "No."

CLEANING: this function was a pleasant surprise. But of course cleaning up around the cave is one of the reasons dogs were developed in the first place. Users with young (below age two) children will still find this function useful. The Cairn Terrier cleans the floor, spoons, bib, and baby, and has an unerring ability to distinguish strained peas from ears, nose, and fingers.

PSYCHOTHERAPY: Here the Cairn really shines. And remember, therapy is something that computers have tried. There is a program that makes the computer ask you questions when you tell it your problems. You say, "I'm afraid of foxes." The computer says, "You're afraid of foxes?"

The Cairn won't give you that kind of echo. Like Freudian analysts, Cairns are mercifully silent; unlike Freudians, they are infinitely sympathetic. I've found that the Cairn will share, in a nonjudgmental fashion, disappointments, joys, and frustrations. And you don't have to know BASIC.

This last capability is related to the Cairn's strongest point, which was the final deciding factor in my decision against the Macintosh — user friendliness. On this criterion, there is simply no comparison. The Cairn Terrier is the essence of user-friendliness. It has fur, it doesn't flicker when you look at it, and it wags its tail.

# Terms and Topics

## TERMS

1. ***Vocabulary, Section V:*** abjured, accoutrements, amiable, archetype, blatant, boisterous, blustering, cater, dallying, decorum, demeanour, deranged, diversion, eponymously, err, forbearance, garrulous, incarcerated, indomitable, insinuation, lamentable, lapse, maundering, mavericks, mitigates, parsimony, pecuniary, pettifoggery, plaintive, precarious, pristine, purging, revel, reverting, risible, servile, superseded, sybil, tyranny, unencumbered, unfettered, unostentatious, unpalatable, veritable, wrangle.

2. ***Meiosis*** (see the introduction to this section) and ***litotes*** (see "A Note to the Reader"), two forms of understatement, are also kinds of ***irony*** (see Terms, section II). Is ***hyperbole*** (overstatement, exaggeration) also a kind of irony? What is ***paresis***?

3. Differentiate among the terms in each of the following groups: (a) witty, comic, humorous; (b) caricature, burlesque, parody, travesty, satire, lampoon; (c) adage, aphorism, axiom, epigram, maxim, motto, proverb, saw, saying.

4. Find out the meanings of ***spoonerism*** and ***malapropism*** and record several examples of each. Why are spoonerisms and malapropisms funny, whereas ordinary solecisms usually are not?

5. ***Invective*** Direct verbal abuse; vituperation. Explain the difference between invective and sarcasm. Can invective be called a kind of satire?

6. ***Pun*** Wordplay that depends on a word's having two different meanings or on two words having similar sounds but different meanings. For example, one could say of inflation that "it never reigns but it

poors." Consult a good dictionary or glossary of literary terms to find out about the various kinds of puns. Puns are usually considered a product of wit; but wit is not always humorous. Are puns always humorous? A pun is a figure of speech. Can a pun also be a kind of *allusion* (see "A Note to the Reader")?

7. What do the terms *pacing* and *cadence* mean when applied to prose? Are they just other words for *rhythm* (see "A Note to the Reader"), or do they rather refer to certain *features* of rhythm?

## TOPICS: On Individual Essays

**ERIKA RITTER   "Bicycles"**

1. Is this piece meant merely to amuse? Or is Ritter using humour to score a point or few? If it is satiric, is it narrowly aimed, or more like scatter-shot? Does its world of allusions—to designer sweatbands, tofu, Perrier, and so on—make it a comedy of middle-class fads? What are some of her other allusions? What is Kryptonite? What does *upscale* mean? What is the point of the terms "Hippie Scene Era," "post-Meanderthal," and "mid-Plastic Scene Era"?

2. Is this essay a "wistful fantasy"? If so, or partly so, what prompts the wistfulness? What is the point of the three short opening paragraphs? Is their implication borne out by the rest of the piece? Does Ritter mean that bicycles are "childish things"? Is she focussing on a contrast between past and present, or between adults and children? Compare what she is saying in this regard with other essays in this book, for example Fisher and White (section I) and Schlesinger (section III).

3. Write a short essay in which you personify or animate some familiar object, as Ritter does with bicycles. Does such a technique automatically lead to humour?

4. Write an essay on the proposition "Inflation is good only for the bicycle industry."

**CALVIN TRILLIN   "Literally"**

1. Does Trillin's sketch have any serious purpose, or is it purely a *jeu d'esprit*? Do you believe that something even a little like this actually happened, or do you think Trillin is making up the whole thing? Do some of the instances of verbal confusion he describes seem more likely than others?

2. The word *literally* is often used when *figuratively* would be correct. For example someone says, "He literally blew his top!" Unless the *he* in question is Mt. St. Helens or its like, this should be something like "Figuratively speaking, he blew his top." Is Trillin perhaps satirizing

this colloquial tendency? That is, one could say of a diligent farmer, "He literally makes hay while the sun shines," and mean it—literally. Would it also be true figuratively?

3. Metaphors are much more common in our language than most people might think. Analyze your own everyday speech or something informal you've recently written (a letter?) for metaphors you've used without consciously realizing you were being metaphorical. If you refer to the *leg* of a table or an *arm* of the sea, are you being metaphorical? Is a dead metaphor nevertheless still a metaphor? Bring some dead or moribund metaphors back to life.

4. From various reference books, draw up a list of metaphorical aphorisms, proverbs, saws, even appropriate clichés and slang expressions. Then create a narrative context in which several of them can be intended or interpreted literally instead of (or as well as) figuratively. Are you necessarily limited to rural or nature-oriented expressions? Why does Trillin choose that kind?

**STEPHEN LEACOCK**  "A, B, and C: The Human Element in Mathematics"

1. In the third paragraph from the end Leacock splits an infinitive ("to no longer find"). Is this necessary?

2. Point out some instances of wordplay in Leacock's essay.

3. By means of a humorous excess of imagination, Leacock makes fun of the apparent lack of imagination of those who set mathematical problems. Write a brief essay satirizing some similar unimaginativeness that you find in one of your textbooks. Or write a sketch in which, like Leacock, you personify some abstract concepts or labels—perhaps some other mathematical concepts, or the symbols of some elements or chemicals, or a few acronyms, or even punctuation marks. Use your imagination.

4. Retell some familiar fable or fairy tale in words of one syllable. Or write a narrative or descriptive paragraph of 100-200 words using only monosyllables. Try to keep it from sounding artificial.

5. Write an essay on one of the following topics: "The Human Element in Concrete Design," "The Human Element in F# Minor," "The Human Element in Cobalt Blue," "The Human Element in Garbage."

**JAMES THURBER**  "Wild Bird Hickok and His Friends"

1. Analyze and discuss the various ways in which Thurber makes this piece amusing. Pay attention to even the smallest details. How much of the humour depends on the phrases in French? Note also how often Thurber uses an aside, a parenthetical insertion usually set off with either parentheses or dashes. Are these always funny? Compose some sentences of that kind yourself.

2. From your own experience—including your reading—find a subject having to do with cultural and linguistic mistranslation and misunderstanding, and write a humorous sketch about it. Aim, as Thurber does here, not for the guffaw and the thigh-slapper but for the gentler humour arising from the innocently erroneous and incongruous.

3. Write the opening paragraph of a Harlequin Romance. Then write a parody version of the paragraph. (You'll have to give your hero, heroine, and villain unexpected qualities or incongruous things to say—but what will be incongruous in this context?)

### WALTER MURDOCH "On Pioneering"

1. Is Murdoch's title at first partly misleading? How long was it before you realized how broadly it applies?

2. Have you recently suffered an affliction similar to Murdoch's "ode-shock"? *Adshock*, perhaps, from perusing glossy magazines or spending an evening watching television? Or *edshock*, from reading too many Letters to the Editor or from overexposure to Educationists' jargon? Or *idshock*, from listening to some fanatically Freudian friends? Using Murdoch's essay as a model, write a short essay satirizing something of this sort. You may wish, like Murdoch, to delay your full thesis until near the end.

3. Murdoch ends by turning his satire into a serious statement about everyday human beings. Write a short essay praising some similarly "unhonoured and unsung" people from everyday life—perhaps streetcar conductors? (See MacLennan, section I, and Woolf, section III.) Perhaps you would also like to try your hand at composing an ode to them.

### MAX BEERBOHM "How Shall I Word It?"

1. What mask or *persona* does Beerbohm adopt for the purpose of this essay? What is the tone? Analyze a dozen or so sentences in order to point out significant characteristics of his style. How much does the humorous effect depend on stilted diction and syntax? Is Beerbohm just having fun, or is he also criticizing the social custom of hypocritical politeness?

2. Write a letter of the sort you imagine Beerbohm to have found in the book of samples; then rewrite it in the vein of the samples he himself offers. Or write a humorous short essay (also titled "How Shall I Word It?") about the problems you might face when writing a letter asking a favour of someone you dislike, or a letter applying for a job for which you are totally unqualified, or…

3. Satirize à la Beerbohm some other kind of "How to" manual that you find both monotonous and unrealistically incomplete.

**JAMES GORMAN**   **"Man, Bytes, Dog"**

1. Is the allusiveness of the title in any way functional, or is it just witty, amusing?

2. This piece is a model of one kind of comparison-and-contrast essay, or report, in which the overall purpose is to demonstrate the superiority of one thing over one or more other similar things. The seemingly absurd disparity between the two things Gorman is comparing, however, suggests that his main purpose is to entertain. But see if you can construct a serious thesis statement that would fit this piece. Is Gorman indulging in satire? If so, does he possibly have more than one target?

3. Write a humorous comparative evaluation of two widely different kinds of things—much more different than the proverbial apples and oranges or bananas, each of which is a fruit, after all. Compare peanut butter with a lawnmower, a grandmother with a guitar, a Shakespeare sonnet with a sports car, a...but you can think up your own unlikely pairing. Does the comparison lead you to any serious implications about one or both of your items? Devise an inventive title for your essay.


# TOPICS: General and Comparative

1. How do writers of humour establish and control a desired tone? Point out examples in the essays in this section. How would you characterize the tone of each? How soon does the tone of each essay become clear?

2. How do other writers in this book use humorous techniques or establish an ironic frame of reference? Consider for example the ironic understatement of MacLennan's essay (section I), the puns in the essays by Haig-Brown (section I) and Colombo (section VI), the exaggerated punctuation at the beginning of Lewis Thomas's essay in section VI, Frayn's use of parodic form (section VI), the tone of the essays by Dylan Thomas, White, and Forster (section I), Lane (section II), Morgan (section III), and Hornyansky (section VI), the irony and sarcasm in the essays by Woolf (section III), Mitford, and Atwood (section IV). In what way might Davenport's essay (section II) be considered humorous?

3. A common theory of humour claims that it depends on *incongruity* of some kind. Test this idea against each of the essays in this section. Consider for example Ritter's exaggeration, Leacock's absurdly reductive literal-mindedness, Beerbohm's techniques of digression and burlesque, Gorman's understatement. In what way are puns and iro-

ny examples of incongruity? Can you suggest any other constant or frequent ingredients of humour?

4. To what extent is humour culturally, economically, or otherwise biased? Consider for example the essays by Thurber and Ritter. Does some humour depend on intellectual or social differences?

5. Note that much humour depends to some degree on language as subject matter. Does Trillin's essay—whether it has any overtly serious purpose or not—make you think about some of the oddities of our language, or of the way we use it? Thurber's essay in section III focusses on shoddy English; his essay in this section looks at peculiar translations from English to French. Compare Trillin's, Beerbohm's, and Murdoch's attitudes toward language with those of Galbraith (section IV), Hornyansky, and Stein (section VI).

6. How do people respond to humour? Can one take any of the essays in this section *literally*? How do you recognize irony? Why is much humour not simply dismissed as "lying"?

7. Consider humour as a weapon. In his book *Writing Well*, Zinsser says that "Humor is the secret weapon of the nonfiction writer. It is secret because so few writers realize that it is often their best tool—sometimes their only tool—for making an important point" (p. 158). Why is humour (satire, jokes, cartoons) a way of dealing—even from inside—with a society that, like the one Brink describes in section III, "is built upon the lie"? Note that Schlesinger (section III) lists satire and irony first among the "techniques of liberation." Is Zinsser in his own essay (section III) using satire and irony in that way? What other writers in this book use humour to make serious and important points?

8. Compare Leacock's use of caricature with that of Dylan Thomas (section I) or Lane (section II). Compare it with the creation or rendition of *character* in the pieces by Johnston, Fisher, and Mukherjee (section I).

# VI
# Choosing
# a
# Form

The eight examples in this last section constitute a varied group. By turns expository and argumentative, humorous and narrative, they reveal the virtues (some would say vices) of a number of stylistic idiosyncrasies, and they therefore draw attention to the personality of literary form. Writing is not a mechanical act but a practised art, and the skilled writer to a degree invents his way into a new subject, breaking standard rules of order and syntax, developing other standards, honing fresh combinations of words and fresh ways to communicate. This observation does not mean that standards are pointless, that mechanics do not matter, or that every pretense at style should be tolerated. Indeed, Hornyansky's essay reads as a powerful tribute to the meanings that people should remember to respect in the words they use. Yet it is by no means stylistically staid. In method and in intent, it champions clarity and vigour together.

Other approaches to language and usage, possibly less conventional but not intrinsically more vital, emerge in the essays by Colombo, Stein, Frayn, and Arlen. Colombo cleverly defines form; Hornyansky discusses it. Frayn plays with it, both musically and visually, in the process of writing what starts out to be a film review (what does it end up as?). Kingston and MacEwen probe the further reaches of the essay form by putting what they have to say in the shape of fable and story. Thomas wittily demonstrates the virtues of punctuation; and the concrete poems that Colombo examines emphasize the power that language can have when people actually see words — as visual objects — as well as when they decode, by the ordinary process we call "reading," what words more conventionally have to say. (A novelist once asked one of us if the word *castle* would be as interesting if it had no *t* in it; for him, it wouldn't, for lodged visually in the *t* were the crenellated walls and turrets of the castles of his imagination.) And in Stein's lecture and Arlen's reflections on, or of, the medium of television there sounds another inflection of the art of communication: they rely heavily for their meaning on cadence and oral association. The reader of these essays has to think aurally. Voice matters. And the page, in a curious way, intervenes.

Everyone knows that words, whether lodged on the page or freed from it in some sort of utterance, have the capacity to convey meaning. But good writers also know that words are not the sole agency for conveying meaning, that good writing often borrows from other modes of expression for some of its finest effects. Music is one such mode, and there are also the visual arts, including film; and there is even mathematics. How the borrowing takes place is another question. It has become a commonplace for critics to praise "musical" and "cinematic" and "visual" literary styles — though it is not always easy to know what they mean. Or to recognize the criteria that elicit their praise. For example, critics laud rhythmic prose — and in this might be praising "musicality" — but they condemn overly apparent metrical patterns and disconcertingly obvious rhymes. Not all sound patterns prove laudable. Clearly it is the intrusiveness that bothers the critics, not the rhythm per se. They are uneasy whenever any single pattern of sound or structure takes over; they will be equally bothered by clusters of words ending in *-tion*, by strings of prepositional phrases, by monotonously similar sentence lengths, and by excessive alliteration. A good writer, however, might still be able to take any one of these flaws and turn it, in a special context, into a stylistic strength.

Music has long been an obvious analogy for writers and critics to use. It has led them to think of rhythm as a product of movement and sound, providing ways to talk about the aural effects of language and ways to produce these effects on the page. More recently, film has provided a related analogy, one that adds the element of visual perspective to those of sound and movement, that transforms rhythm into a visual notion, and that makes *leitmotif*, for example, a visual as well as a musical technique. (Think of the sound patterns in Prokofiev's *Peter and the Wolf*; think of the light patterns in the film *Doctor Zhivago*.) And though there has not yet appeared a "scientific" ("mathematical"? Certainly not "formulaic"!) school of prose style, the division between the sciences and the art of writing is not necessarily greater than that between writing and the other arts. Science, indeed, may be among the most potent contributors to current stylistic change. Explications of entropy and quantum physics have already had some effect on literary style—most evident so far, perhaps, in interrupted, nonlinear fictional forms—and the influence might go further and deeper than many humanities-trained critics now realize.

But there remains a difficulty of interpretation and assessment. How can one validly distinguish between faddishness and creative experiment? For conservative critics there is no problem here: they see no distinction. But not many writers can accept that judgment. Casual reflection might suggest that *topic* determines *style*, and that to talk about a chaotic universe would require a kind of linguistic chaos. Yet even the essays collected here would say otherwise. Hornyansky, conservative by persuasion, is at least relaxed and idiomatic if not actually radical in style. And Stein, the most idiosyncratic stylist, is discussing what many would consider a commonplace. Possibly by refashioning the commonplace, her style freshens it as well. Possibly, too, by opting for a relatively conservative style before he innovates with form, Colombo gives an illusion of familiarity to the subject of experimental literary form.

The point is that writing depends on sound and sight and texture and movement as well as on grammar and syntax and vocabulary; the overall form an idea takes in speech and writing is as great a part of its meaning as the sum of the definitions a reader or listener attaches to a series of separate words. Good writers, knowing enough about the ordinary rules of coherent discourse to know when to break them to gain an effect, choose their form. It is not accidental. It is personal. And it is clear enough in execution to be shared.

Matters of time, taste, and fashion affect the distinctions we make among personal styles. Every writer, moreover, has to guard against defending quixotic notions and idiosyncratic styles simply on the grounds of "personality." Solipsism is not a literary virtue, if it is a virtue of any sort at all. And time often modifies the enthusiasms of fashion and taste. But over time, and transcending the individuality of style, the virtues of vitality and clarity persist. If writers begin with a subject to talk about and the intelligence to deal with it, then the two problems they face are these: how to present their subject so that it is fresh and alive, and how to make it clear. Vitality. Clarity. The trouble with an experimental style is that it often sacrifices clarity, and the trouble with a conventional style is that it often sacrifices vitality. Writers who claim, in the name of the other virtue, that they must make such sacrifices—that they can be vital only by being obscure, or be clear only by being conventional—are rationalizing, not excusing or explaining their act. Vitality and clarity are not mutually exclusive. Balance is all.

We know that poets, of all writers, squeeze the maximum of meaning from the words they bring together, which might suggest that the kind of balance they achieve could prove instructive for essayists as well. We do not ask essay-writers to be poets. Yet many of the techniques poets use, once (and by some critics still) considered out of bounds for the essayist, have become widely acceptable in prose, even praiseworthy. Puns, echoes, creative ambiguities, and the resuscitation of obscure or archaic meanings in the context of the contemporary and everyday: these are not the standard equipment of explication. Yet a stylist with a particular subject might find them appropriate. What is praiseworthy is a writer's ability to use any technical means available to make a subject clearer than it was before, to help a reader understand it better. Fiction included. Experiments, of course, are not intrinsically more valuable than standard forms. Indeed, writing obscurely on the grounds that a subject is dense and therefore requires it is as wrongheaded as assuming a difficult idea can be made simple by ignoring its complexities.

Good writers do not make such mistakes. Instead, they address the problem they are trying to solve. They neither underestimate its difficulty nor inflate it; they neither impose rigid and simplistic solutions upon it nor allow it to dissipate in clouds of generalization. They keep in mind, rather, that they must direct their words in an appropriate manner to the audience they want to reach. At the same time, they bring to their subject the range of their personal understanding and the force of their personal style. Good writers invest themselves in their words, and shape ideas the way they choose. They often make "unsafe" choices—choices that force readers to adjust their stylistic expectations. But "safe" writers often commit far more grievous assaults on the language: they uncritically adopt the evasive passive voice, as bureaucratese does; they equate length of word with height of style, and sound like a thesaurus in search of meaning; they parrot jargon in an attempt to feather themselves in the colour and prestige of the sciences; they confuse effusive writing with emotional commitment, pedantic writing with accuracy, mechanical and predictable writing with openness. Writers who follow such practices shirk their obligation to convey meaning. By contrast, good writers, who say what they mean and mean what they say, assert themselves validly and reach their chosen audiences. In the process of communicating, they call attention to the rewards to be gained, by writer and reader alike, from actually learning the craft.

# Communicating through Form

## John Robert Colombo

### What We Mean by Form

Form follows function.
Content has its own shape.
"Good form" versus "bad form".
Form versus content.
Manner or matter.
Substance or style.
Formal, informal; material, immaterial.
Chaos, cosmos; chance, control.
Form as a vessel; content as a liquid.
Freedom regardless of form; the freedom to conform.
A matter, question, problem, possibility of form.
The necessity of form; the irrelevancy of form.
A formula; a formlessness.
Transcendental form; immanent form.
"The earth was without form."

These are only a few of the phrases we regularly use when we talk about form. There are many more, but most of these concepts cancel each other (if not themselves) out. The alleged dichotomy between form and content, which is one of the hoariest of metaphysical problems, has puzzled philosophers down through the ages, and there is no reason to believe

From *A Media Mosaic*, ed. Walt McDayter, Holt, Rinehart & Winston of Canada Limited, 1971.

that it will ever be solved. In fact, there is no reason to believe that it is even a "problem". Perhaps it is only an issue—a platform on which you take a stand and defend it whether you actually believe in it or not. It has been argued, quite convincingly, that the words "form" and "content" have no meaning whatsoever.

One difficulty facing anyone making an inquiry into the meaning of form is that we think with words (or, at the very least, we formulate and communicate our thoughts using words to help us along). But like children with an unlimited supply of lettered blocks, we raise up immense and often shaky structures which spell out imponderables and then topple of their own weight. Some of these constructions have no obvious relation to reality and are of various orders of complexity.

At random: We can have pure forms that are antilogies, like the phrase "a formless form". We can have nonexistent things (about which we know a great deal), like "unicorns". We can have impossible things, like "phlogiston" and "sky hooks". We can have no-longer-existing things, like Napoleon I and the dodo. And we can have things like "god" and "angel" and "sin" and "grace", which may or may not have any objective meaning. Is our concept of form one of these? And if it is, which one?

No definition of "form" will be found in this essay. Everyone has his own rule-of-thumb meaning, and we all know we can recognize a single shape or a recurring pattern or an ordering principle when we see one. More general inquiries into form in reading matter are helped along not by narrowing down the concept but by expanding it as much as possible. Instead, what will be found in this essay are instances of infracted forms. Forms are not as much seen as over-seen. A form is exposed when another is imposed upon it, with a moiré screen. The patterned lines of such a screen, when placed over another pattern of lines, "generate" a third pattern. This is purely an optical illusion. The pattern does not exist, except perceptually, and what exists objectively are the two parents of that illusion, the two original patterns. The "third thing" is an interesting distortion, a child with a subjective existence only. This applies to many of the instances discussed in this essay.

Much modern art has the perception of pattern or the hunt for meaning as its organizing principle. As Paul Valery wrote, "I write half the poem, the reader writes the other half." There are numerous essays and books that discuss the serious arts, and the reader has only to turn to authors like Harold Rosenberg (*The Anxious Object* and *The Tradition of the New*) to fit many of these ideas into their proper perspective. But there are nooks and crannies that have not been swept clean and which, to my knowledge, have not been examined from the point of view of form and the new directions contemporary art is taking. The instances of violated forms I will be discussing are all literary and, in the main, poetic. But the inquiry could quite easily be extended to the other arts as well, music and painting and cinema in particular, and even into modern social concerns.

## Art and the Environment

My starting point is that, strictly speaking, there is no content in art that is separate from the world. All art is entirely formal. By this I mean that art is an attitude to life and that the object of this attitude is life itself. To some extent, to be a human being one must be something of an artist. And to be an artist, one must work in the public, accessible world of people and their perceptions. At various times art has been other and different things. In fact, there is no single "art" but many "arts". At one point in history, art was craftsmanship and little more. The English word "art" derives from this sense of the artist as artisan or artificer. Art was something well done. At various other points in history, art (even the artist) was equated with expression, communication, madness, divine inspiration, problem-solving, information-accumulation, or what-have-you. Usually it was a number of these combined. Today it is perfectly possible for the artist to create works of art that are co-extensive with the world itself. It is, in a parallel fashion, perfectly possible for the art-fancier to react to the world as if it were a work of art itself. Was it Claes Oldenburg, the pop artist, who signed the southern-most tip of Manhattan Island, as he would a canvas, to "aesthetically claim" both this object and this way of seeing things?

With art so fully an attitude to life, everything that exists can be declared to be a work of art. Not all works are good ones, of course, but with this environmental approach as a background, it is possible to criticize one part of the ecology along aesthetic lines and retain some standard of objectivity. The Vancouver painter, Iain Baxter, photographs cityscapes and landscapes and then labels them. Bad views are marked "ART"—Aesthetically Rejected Things. Good views are stamped "ACT"—Aesthetically Claimed Things. Behind this seemingly facile gesture lies a deep and overwhelming idea: that the world itself is a single work of art. This is, at core, a religious notion. The world is not "the work of God" so much as the "the artwork of God". In a small way this has been recognized with landscapes. A brilliant sunset is called "a lovely Turner", a gentle countryside "a fine Constable". Nature imitates art, as Oscar Wilde observed, but in even more fundamental a sense than he imagined.

The "deep focus" of art may thus include all reaction, since nothing is exclusive to the aesthetic experience. The American composer, John Cage, has a composition called "4′ 33″" which is four minutes and 33 seconds of silence. He "performs" this composition at the keyboard. At the premiere, his audience was first surprised, then moved to irritation, and finally taken to a state of self-knowledge. The realization slowly dawned on those present that the random noises which accompany a musical concert in a hall—the shuffling of feet, coughing, etc.—are an accepted part of the auditory experience and can, as such, for a short while anyway, be contemplated singly.

This view, that art is co-extensive with the environment, that the artist is in a sense the "stage-manager of reality", is sometimes called Expanded Art.

It is close to the positions taken by Susan Sontag, with her stress on surface value and "against interpretation"; Andy Warhol, whose Campbell's soup labels are not representational so much as presentational; and Marshall McLuhan, who sees art as an anti-environment which exposes the invisible "wrap-around" of the environment. Expanded Art gives a rationale for such contemporary art movements as underground films, camp, happenings, environmental sculptures, endless paintings, interminable poems, sidewalk theatre, dance as movement, etc. Various phrases are commonly used to identify these contemporary artistic tendencies: Ecological Art, Environmental Art, Conceptual Art, Earth Art, and so on.

One of the pleasures of this new approach to art is that one can respond to a work (or a nonwork) on the simplest of levels. In fact, one's response is often joyous, and incredibly naive. It is like the nursery rhyme about the man and woman who live in Fife.

> In a cottage in Fife
> Lived a man and his wife,
> Who, believe me, were comical folk;
> For, to people's surprise,
> They both saw with their eyes,
> And their tongues moved whenever they spoke!
> When quite fast asleep,
> I've been told that to keep
> Their eyes open they could not contrive;
> They walked on their feet,
> And 'twas thought what they eat
> Helped, with drinking to keep them alive!

## Reading Forwards, Backwards, Up or Down

One way in which we too are "comical folk" is that we accept all our conventions, and work within them. We seldom make fun of them, or if we do, we consider this "bad form". One convention of literacy in the Western world is that, without blinking or appearing to notice it, you are reading this page from the left-hand margin to the right-hand margin, moving from line to line in a downward direction. Why not read from right to left, as the Hebrews do? Or down rather than across, as the Chinese do? What difference does it make? Little, really, except that Westerners are inclined to "scan" the world in a similar fashion, and look at reality from left to right, from top to bottom, "placing" things in this total form. For the eye, focussed on the printed page, at least half of the movement is wasted effort. Our eyes "scan" across the page, taking in information, and then sweep back, disregarding the information that is available on the return leg of the round trip. The ancients, who read less than we do, were more concerned about this than we are, and some ancient inscriptions are carved into rock both forwards and backwards in alternate lines, just as a field is ploughed. The Greek word for "the turning of an ox" is *boustrophedon*, and boustrophedonic writing is prose which appears in this backwards-and-for-wards, continuous fashion. Strictly speaking, alternate "return" lines should appear in a second set of characters in which the actual letter-forms are reversed. (Many of these matters are discussed in Herbert Spencer's *The Visible Word* [London: Lund Humphries, 1968].) But making do with the standard set of characters, here are the first four lines of Lincoln's "Gettysburg Address" in a boustrophedonic treatment.

> Fourscore and seven years ago our fathers brought forth
> dna ytrebil ni deviecnoc noitan wen a tnenitnoc siht no
> dedicated to the proposition that all men are created
> gnitset raw livic taerg a ni degagne era ew woN .lauqe

Why resurrect a form of writing as weird as boustrophedon? No one practises it today. Since it was once a form of writing, at variance with our own practice, why not reuse it if it can be made to serve a useful purpose? What follows is a found poem (a free-verse arrangement of a passage of someone else's prose) that has been given a semi-boustrophedonic treat-ment—"semi" because, given the difficulty the eye encounters when forced to read a line backwards, the line has been arranged to be read in the standard way but with the words in the backwards order. Thus only the word order is boustrophedonic. One hold-over of this principle today is the Hungarian custom of referring to an individual by his last name first. (In English, this is customary only with alphabetical listings.) Thus, in Hungarian, the former Prime Minister of Canada is "Diefenbaker John". The found poem "Budapest" grew out of this convention.

BUDAPEST
> day present the to time that from
> from that time to the present day
> capital hungarian the of record the
> the record of the hungarian capital
> advance uninterrupted of one been has
> has been one of uninterrupted advance
> as such externals in merely not
> not merely in externals such as
> town the of reconstruction the slums of removal the
> the removal of slums the reconstruction of the town
> trade and industry communications of development the
> the development of communications industry and trade
> buildings public important of erection the and
> and the erection of important public buildings
> elevation physical and moral mental the in also but
> but also in the mental moral and physical elevation
> inhabitants the of
> of the inhabitants
> gain important another besides
> besides another important gain

statesman hungarian the of view of point the from
from the point of view of the hungarian statesman
improvement and increase progressive the namely
namely the progressive increase and improvement
population the of element magyar the of status of
of status of the magyar element of the population

The text of "Budapest" was given in—or taken from—the Eleventh Edition of the *Encyclopaedia Britannica*. The same 1911 edition supplies texts for the four found poems that follow. (They form part of a group, called *The Great Cities of Antiquity*, which treats each of 76 ancient cities mentioned in the *E.B.* in a characteristic style.) What is more appropriate for the capital of Japan than a (found) haiku?

KIOTO

Clear water
ripples everywhere
throughout the city.

For such a picturesque place as the capital of Thailand, only a delicate and romantic form like the (found) triolet would do.

BANGKOK

The climate has without a doubt
In occupation of Siam
Becoming king it was chosen
The climate has without a doubt
It was seized by the warrior
Become hotter and less humid
The climate has without a doubt
In occupation of Siam

Since the ancient capital of Persia, now Iran, is a closed book, archaeologically and historically, only a short poem is necessary. The entry in the *E.B.* begins and ends with the two words which open and close this brief poem. Luckily they happen to be evocative words.

PERSEPOLIS

Persepolis
ruins.

Two words are used to recreate the rise and fall of Persepolis, and only two words, united in a single graphic design, are needed to dramatize the fate of Pompeii in 79 A.D. This poem is both "found" and "concrete", and shows how Expanded Art can combine two modes of poetry and two types of art—graphics and poetry—to make a singleness of effect. (For those unused to "reading" this kind of poetry, the "X" might be seen as lava.)

                    POMPEII
                      X
                     VES
                    UVIUS
                   POMPEII
                 XXXXXXXXX

## Oddities of Shape

One difference between prose and poetry is that prose runs to the edge of the page and poetry does not. Purely typographical considerations play a large role in our appreciation of a passage of writing, and poets have occasionally given their poems typographical "shapes" consistent with the subjects or themes of their poems. The original inspiration might be derived from inscriptions in books and on monuments. "Emblematic poems" were popular in the late-sixteenth century, and the practice has persisted as a minor genre until our time. "Shaped whimseys" were very popular in the late-nineteenth century, and Carolyn Wells has collected a number of these in *A Whimsey Anthology* (New York: Charles Scribner's Sons, 1906). The ones reproduced here are oddities, perhaps, but Stéphane Mallarmé and Apollinaire both took the conceit and raised it from a curiosity to a cultural product. George Herbert, John Donne, Dylan Thomas, Edward Lear, John Hollander—all have tried their hand at "Shaped poems". "The Wine Glass" is based on Proverbs xxiii: 29-30.

              THE WINE GLASS
        Who hath woe? Who hath sorrow? Who
          hath contentions? Who hath wounds
            without cause? Who hath redness
             of eyes? They that tarry long
              at the wine! They that
               go to seek mixed wine!
               Look not thou upon the
              wine when it is red,
                when it giveth
                  its colour
                   in the
                    cup,
                  when it
               moveth itself
                  aright.
                   At
                the last it
             biteth like a serpent
          and stingeth like an adder!

"The Wine Glass" is a kind of collaboration between the author of Proverbs (said to be Solomon himself) and the anonymous nineteenth-century poet or designer or scribe who first gave the passage its picturesque shape. A characteristic of "Shaped poetry" is that it is impossible to read such poems without experiencing both a perception and an apperception. The reader experiences both the poem and his consciousness of experiencing the poem. Such experiments encourage self-awareness, self-consciousness. This response is close to the Distancing Effect discussed by the German playwright, Bertolt Brecht.

The following poem is an original, rhymed composition set in the shape of a sinister creature. A Stegomyia is a genus of mosquito, one variety of which carries Yellow Fever. Certainly the point of "The Stegomyia" is a moralistic one: Wash up, kiddies, or you will suffer!

THE STEGOMYIA

I
t
s

b
i
l
l

is
long
and wick-
ed, and
is
filled
with deadly

juice                    and                    you
needn't try         to dodge         it      for      it
won't                    be                   any use;
it
will
chase
you up
and catch
you and
with woe will
fill your cup;
oh, the steg-
omyia'll get
you if you
don't clean
up
!

Even if "Avoirdupois" is not strictly a poem, it is a fine example of the way in which an argument can be typographically visualized and given a concrete form. The poem could, as well, be presented orally. A stand-up comedian would give each line a different vocal emphasis—the lightness of the ashes, the monstrous size of the bill. The form seems to mirror the content. Or is it *vice versa*?

AVOIRDUPOIS

The length of this line indicates the ton of coal as dug by the miner.
This one indicates the ton shipped to the dealer.
The small dealer gets a ton like this.
This is the one you pay for.
This is what you get.
The residue is:
Cinders and
Ashes.
And this line will give you some conception of the size of the BILL.

## Tricks and Teasers

Moving into the area of the poem-as-puzzle, we have "Greetings, in Season". The poem is more than the letters of the alphabet arranged in an aesthetically pleasing pattern. Examine the anonymous composition closely and you will find that a letter is missing. Which one? The point of the poem turns on a pun that identifies the missing letter. A clue: It's a Christmas greeting. (The answer is given at the end of this essay.)

GREETINGS, IN SEASON

A B C D E
F G H I J
K M N O P
Q R S T U
V W X Y Z

During the Victorian Era, versifiers by the hundreds tried their hands at typographical extravagances like "O I C". The title, and indeed the whole poem, must be sounded phonetically. These verses have to be "worked out". As constructions, they differ from rebuses only in that a rebus actually introduces a tiny picture of what the substituted word means, whereas a typographical poem uses symbols instead of signs.

O I C

I'm in a 10der mood today
& feel poetic, 2;
4 fun I'll just—off a line
& send it off 2 u.

> I'm sorry you've been 6 O long;
> Don't B disconsol8;
> But bear your ills with 42de,
> & they won't seem so gr8.

Perhaps the most unusual novel ever written is a book called *Gadsby*, published in 1939. The author was Ernest Vincent Wright, who subtitled his work "A Story of Over 50,000 Words Without Using the Letter E." The ingenious and industrious author decided to write a work which avoided the most common letter in the English alphabet—e. He tied down the e-key on his typewriter, and avoided "the" and "ed" endings and hundreds of other everyday words and phrases. He wrote what must be the longest lipogram ever created. (A lipogram is a work so constructed that a single letter has been consistently avoided.) Imagine the problems that Wright faced. Why, even this sentence alone contains six! David Kahn, in *The Code-Breakers: The Story of Secret Writing* (London: Weidenfeld and Nicholson, 1967), goes into further details about the significance of Wright's experiment, and he reproduces the opening paragraph:

> Upon this basis I am going to show you how a bunch of bright young folks did find a champion; a man with boys and girls of his own; a man of so dominating and happy individuality that Youth is drawn to him as is a fly to a sugar bowl. It is a story about a small town. It is not a gossipy yarn; nor is it a dry, monotonous account, full of such customary "fill-ins" as "romantic moonlight casting murky shadows down a long, winding country road". Nor will it say anything about twinklings lulling distant folds; robins carolling at twilight, nor any "warm glow of lamplight" from a cabin window. No. It is an account of up-and-doing activity; a vivid portrayal of Youth as it is today; and a practical discarding of that worn-out notion that " a child don't know anything".

Works which can be read every-which-way to yield differing meanings have been dubbed "Jesuitical verses". The work that follows is the "all-around platform", and was popular in the 1860s in the United States when the Secessionists and the Abolitionists were arguing it out. For the Secessionist view, read the first column down. For the Abolitionist view, read the second column down. For the Democratic platform, read everything all together.

THE PLATFORM
(Read down or across)

| Hurrah for | The old Union |
|------------|---------------|
| Secession  | Is a curse    |

| | |
|---|---|
| We fight for | The Constitution |
| The Confederacy | Is a league with hell |
| We love | Free speech |
| The rebellion | Is treason |
| We glory in | A free press |
| Separation | Will not be tolerated |
| We fight not for | The negro's freedom |
| Reconstruction | Must be obtained |
| We must succeed | At every hazard |
| The Union | We love |
| We love not | The negro |
| We never said | Let the Union slide |
| We want | The Union as it was |
| Foreign intervention | Is played out |
| We cherish | The old flag |
| The stars and bars | Is a flaunting lie |
| We venerate | The habeas corpus |
| Southern chivalry | Is hateful |
| Death to | Jeff Davis |
| Abe Lincoln | Isn't the Government |
| Down with | Mob law |
| Law and order | Shall triumph. |

From works so formed that three points of view are simultaneously meaningful, it is not much of a leap to a work with a point of view that is logically impossible. "Resolutions Passed by the Board of Councilmen, Canton, Mississippi" pops up time and time again in different places. The former premier of Ontario, Mitch Hepburn, used to tell the same tale but in terms of a jail rather than a school. Here the form of the work is a series of mutually dependent propositions. The form of the syllogism is preserved, but the spirit is violated in intent.

1. Resolved, by this Council, that we build a new Jail.
2. Resolved, that the new Jail be built out of the materials of the old Jail.
3. Resolved, that the old Jail be used until the new Jail is finished.

## Juggling the letters

Out of the twenty-six letters of the English alphabet, a million books could be constructed. Out of a half-a-dozen letters, what can be made? A word, a short phrase perhaps. With some juggling, the letters could be arranged and rearranged to make different words and phrases, different meanings. This accounts for the perpetual fascination of the anagram. An anagram is a word or phrase that has been transformed into another by the simple transposition of letters. For instance, "Evangelists" can be perversely rearranged without loss or substitution or addition of letters into "Evil's Agents".

Here are some others. "The Mona Lisa" may be altered into the following comment: "No hat, a smile."

To the anagramist, "Nova Scotia and Prince Edward Island" presents intriguing possibilities, including "The Canadian Provinces: Lands I Dread!"

Even the word "Anagrams" itself can be so treated. It becomes "Ars Magna", Latin for "Great Art."

Creating anagrams is a test of patience and wit. C. C. Bombaugh, in *Oddities and Curiosities of Words and Literature* (New York: Dover Publications, 1961), edited by Martin Gardner, takes anagrams a step further, into the area of magic squares, and writes:

> This word, Time, is the only word in the English language which can be thus arranged, and the different transpositions thereof are all at the same time Latin words. These words, in English as well as in Latin, may be read either upward or downward. Their signification as Latin words is as follows: Time—fear thou; Item—likewise; Meti—to be measured; Emit—he buys.

T I M E<br>I T E M<br>M E T I<br>E M I T

A cousin of the anagram is the palindrome. In the anagram, the letters are reordered to create a different sense. In the palindrome, the letters are merely read backwards to repeat the same sense. This often results in such awkward English that the reader might confuse it initially with doubletalk. Take these two examples:

> Trash? Even interpret Nineveh's art.
> Red root put up to order.

Both sound preposterous, and as imponderable as the predictions of Nostradamus. Not all palindromes are laughable, for a few have a poetic quality that lends them memorability and has ensured their survival through the years. There is no basis for the following palindromes in the Bible, but there is a popular tradition that maintains the following conversation took place in Eden. Adam's first words to Eve were:

> Madam, I'm Adam.

And Eve's reply? This too is palindromial and has been preserved:

> Name no one man.

In the same fashion, Napoleon's last words—spoken in English!—are reputed to be:

> Able was I ere I saw Elba.

Thousands of palindromes have been written. There is something uncanny about them, almost magical.

### Concrete Poetry

"The only unfortunate thing about concrete poetry," Emmet Williams once said, "is the phrase concrete poetry. The word 'concrete' is misleading. The stress should be on the word 'poetry'." Williams is the editor of *An Anthology of Concrete Poetry* (New York: Something Else Press, 1967) and a world authority on the subject. Even he would balk at defining this fairly recent development in contemporary art. "The medium is the message" might well have been coined to answer the question, "What is concrete poetry?"

In any discussion of form in art, the work of the Brazilian poet Pedro Xisto is of particular interest. The two examples of his work that follow come from Xisto's *Logogrammes*, or word-forms, published in 1966.

At first glance, "Epithalamium II" looks like a corporate symbol. In fact, it is a simple poem of great subtlety. It is also quite memorable and mnemonic; once seen, it is unlikely to be soon forgotten. As well, Xisto's poem has the virtues of brevity and wit. The theme of the poem is one's interpretation of it. The "h" can represent "he" or "homo", man. The "e" can represent "Eve" or "elle". The "s" surely represents the uniting of the two figures in a forceful yet graceful way. It is also a serpent, perhaps, and is the poem "set" in the Garden of Eden? Together, the man and the woman are united in a sexual union. Do they become a she? Is there a female child of the union? Or is this another incarnation of the Eternal Feminine? Whatever the poet intended, all these (and many more) are valid readings of this simple-seeming concrete poem.

The second poem is a "logogram", and a splendid, classical one at that. The image is one of solid repose. It could be looked upon as many

```
                        l           e
                        o         e
              l     l   o   v   e
                    o       e   v   o   l
          l   l   o   v   e       o
                    e   v   o   l
              e           o
          e               l
```

* Concrete poem "Blues" by bpNichol. Used by permission of the author. (From New Direction in Canadian Poetry, Holt, Rinehart and Winston of Canada, Limited, 1971.)

things, including an Art Deco design, a geometric construction, or rafters against a wall. In actual fact, the title of the poem is a dead giveaway. It is called "Zen", and this word can be traced continuously throughout the composition. Less is more.

David Kahn writes in *The Code-Breakers*:

> Three-quarters of English text is "unnecessary". English could theoretically express the same things with one-quarter its present letters if it were wholly non-redundant. A literary curiosity demonstrates graphically how a few letters carry most of the information of a text while the others are redundant.

DEATH AND LIFE

|  | cur | f | w | d | dis | and p |
|---|---|---|---|---|---|---|
| A | sed | iend | rought | eath | ease | ain. |
|  | bles | fr | b | br | and | ag |

## A New Category for Artists

Today, in the West, the artist is regarded as now a craftsman, now a creator, but seldom as a realizer. Some of the newer art forms, like film, suggest that this new category of "realizer" should be created for the artist. In what way is a film director a creative artist? All the elements he works with—the script, the dialogue, the setting, the story, the actors, even the camera work—are the contributions of other individuals, often interpretative artists of the highest calibre. But with the *auteur*, or "author", theory, the director is the one who gives the film its final stamp. He imposes his personality on all its parts and makes them work together as a single whole—the artist is the "entrepreneur of reality", whose task it is to reveal aesthetic possibilities within situations or with objects not always of his own making.

The anthropologist Edmund Carpenter has described how the Eskimo sculptor does not carve his stone into the shape of a seal but, by cutting away, "releases" the seal from the stone. Chinese artists have made "natural stone paintings" which involve finding suitable rocks and then cutting them to reveal previously existing patterns. Perhaps the best-known Western expression of this search for a naturally satisfying form is the taste for driftwood. This is "low art", perhaps, and appropriate for living room tables and mantles. Found "high art" is the *objet trouvé*, the discovery of Dada that any object, taken from its original context and placed in another, acquires new and interesting aesthetic possibilities.

Word-plays like the ones that follow must be low on any artistic totem-pole. But if nothing else, these one-liners are interesting examples of juggled forms, "realized" possibilities. Placing one word within another is like injecting one form into another:

PREJEWDICE

Disguising a given formal order by giving it the trappings of another period is another way of having fun with forms. (This example comes from the first edition of the *Encyclopaedia Britannica*, 1768.)

Miffiffippi

Making a word reflexive—that is, making it comment upon itself—can be the operative device behind any number of word-plays:

CXNSXRSHXP

They can get quite short:

Ha!t

They can imitate natural objects:

mountAin

They can look pretty:

sn*w

Occasionally an innocent typo can subtly shift letters to bring home a different message:

UNITED STATES OF AMERCIA

This is not a misspelling of "AMERICA" but a way of drawing attention to the fact that the "CIA" is a part of American life and "deforms" the very symbol of the country. Finally, finding one complete word within another is a kind of punning that is especially appropriate in an essay on Expanded Art:

E(ART)H

So the search for form is an on-going process, and one that will never end—as long as there is a human being with an interest in art alive in the world. Man may think he imposes his "sense of form" on the world, but the chances are fifty-fifty that the world imposes its "sense of form" on him too.

---

* [Note. The poem "Greetings, In Season" is missing the letter L. There is no L. Noel.]

# Is Your English Destroying Your Image?

Michael Hornyansky

When I let it slip among ordinary company that I'm a professor of English, you can guess what the reaction is: "Oh-oh," they say with nervous smiles, "I'd better watch my language." No use explaining that I don't teach composition. If English professors hit the front page, or confront public awareness at all, it's not when they have had profound or brilliant ideas about literature, but when they are testily muttering that their latest crop of freshmen can neither read nor write. And the truth is, of course, that we are—we must be—concerned with language. It is the medium both of the works we study, and of our attempts to teach it. If language should decay far enough, the study of literature becomes difficult or impossible. I won't play for headlines by pretending this is the condition we have reached; but such a condition is at least imaginable, as things are going. So I worry a good deal about language, myself. And I think the most useful way to put my worries before you is to pursue that automatic reaction: "Oh-oh, I'd better watch my language."

It's a touchy area. People are as anxious about the impression their words make as they are about their clothes or their faces or their waistlines. If you catch someone in an error, he is mortified. If you suggest he doesn't speak well, you wound his vanity as sharply as if you claim he has no sense of humour. Sniping at other people's mistakes is a favourite sport of those who write letters to the *Globe and Mail*; and there are always other correspondents to jeer at the snipers. And even when there are no English

"Is English Destroying Your Image?" by Michael Hornyansky from *In the Name of Language* edited by Joseph Gold. Reprinted by permission of Macmillan of Canada, a Division of Canada Publishing Corporation.

teachers (official or amateur) within earshot, private citizens go on fretting over what words to use, and whether they're using them properly. I know of a group which spent hours wrangling over whether a certain person should be described as *responsible* for the task assigned to him, or whether that didn't seem to wag the finger at him needlessly. They finally settled on *accountable* instead—a word in fashion these days, but one which to my mind conveys a good deal less personal dignity and freedom than *responsible* does. That's how it often goes: the questions we're least certain about are the ones that arouse our stronger feelings. And when it comes to language, most of us are uncertain. The frequency of little check-up phrases in our normal speech—"you know? eh? like? see what I mean?"—is a symptom not so much of sloppiness, but of concern about whether we're getting through.

This is why I thought of offering some helpful hints. I don't aim to give you a lessson in grammar. Think of this chapter as an essay in linguistic psychology, not in rules. Remember my title: "Is your English destroying your image?" I put it that way not to be cute or disarming, but because that's the form our anxiety takes. I shall be asking not just what errors we make, but why we make them, and how they affect our view of each other; and after that, how to set about improving matters. To tell you that this is Right and that is Wrong (even if I had the confidence to do so) wouldn't be much help, anyway. Far better in the long run to try to understand why some things work and others don't—so we can judge for ourselves instead of carrying around a list of lapses. I say "we" because I talk for a living, and I am reminded daily of how my words can undermine rapport, or on good days virtually magic people into understanding me. I dare to advise you not because I'm a professor, but because I've been there, and I have some practical knowledge of what can go wrong and how to cure it.

If I am to write about mistakes in our use of language, I had best begin by establishing what makes a mistake—what standards to measure by. There are two possible misconceptions here. At one extreme is the idea of Correctness. Some people still hold to the notion that there is such a thing as Correct English: the King's English, possibly the Queen's, existing as a heavenly paradigm to which only educated people and professors have access. (Francophones are even more prone to think of Correct French, because they have an official Academy to act as its guardian and legislator; but as they are beginning to discover, their hopes are misplaced.) There are several reasons why this mystical notion won't do. One is that educated people—even teachers; even, heaven knows, Her Majesty—do not always speak well. How can we be certain when to follow them? Worse still, the belief that a correct pattern exists can become, in a curious way, a cause of errors: for the people who most firmly believe in the King's English are usually hazy about *what precisely it is*, and in their anxiety to be proper they lean over backwards, into slips that would not befall a more natural stance. No, the idea of Correct English has at best a social validity. By speaking like the Queen you may prove your loyalty and your place in society, but you do not exempt yourself from error. In fact there is no enduring pattern of correctness. As most people have come to realize, language changes, constantly and irresistibly—and correctness, if it's a workable idea at all, must change too. The purists are remembered as quaint defenders of the last ditch: like Jonathan Swift, rejecting the uncouth expression "mob," because all right-speaking people knew it should be *mobile vulgus*. (Swift also won a few, however. See Dwight Macdonald, *Against the American Grain*, Vintage, 1962, p. 323.) Or like the person who answers the telephone with "Hello: it is I, Clifton Webb."

At the other extreme is the notion that since language constantly changes, then anything goes—there are no rules at all, Usage is king. It will not be so easy to persuade you that this too is a misconception. The barometer of our times is set at Change. A recent letter to the *Globe* condemns the declared policy of Ontario's Minister of Education to return to the 3 R's: "[he] invites our children to take firm, confident steps backward into the future. Pity." (Ray MacLain, *Globe*, 25 Feb. 1975.) The CBC's news-readers, once modestly reliable (meaning they could be counted on to apologize for errors), have lost their supervisor of broadcast language, and now commit cheerfully such barbarisms as "It sounds like he's going to reform." This is the age of Humpty Dumpty, who claimed that words meant what he wanted them to mean; it was simply a question of who was to be master. You will recall what happened to Humpty Dumpty. But his fragmented soul is still with us: it lives on in the third edition of Webster's *New International Dictionary* (1961), which makes no attempt to distinguish acceptable usage from colloquial, slang, or illiterate. "If it is used, it is usage": that is Webster's principle in a nutshell—and a nutshell is where it belongs. To see the enterprise mercilessly analysed, read Dwight Macdonald's patient and savage review called "The String Untuned." (Reprinted in *Against the American Grain*, p. 289.)

Those who appeal to usage as the final arbiter seem to march under the banners of Life and Progress. In fact they are making a mystique of change, supposing that since it is normal it must also be good. Happily, the letter columns of the newspaper do feature other correspondents, who realize that change may be not growth but decay, and that mere growth is not always welcome, in language as in life.

> It is fatuous (publicists please note: this word does not yet mean stout or plump) to argue that the language is undergoing positive and dynamic change in the hands of our public figures. Only fools would unreservedly maintain so.
>
> (C.C.J. Bond, *Globe*, 17 Feb. 1975)

(I expect a later correspondent observed that it wasn't their *hands* but their mouths that did the damage.) Not all change is progress. Some of it has to be resisted, and when possible reversed. If the last ditch needs defending, I'll take my place alongside Sam Johnson:

> If the changes we fear be thus irresistible, what remains but to acquiesce with silence, as in the other insurmountable distresses of humanity? It remains that we retard what we cannot repel, that we palliate what we cannot cure.

> (Preface to the *Dictionary*)

That final sentence, by the way, is a grand example of how to project the image of Doctor Johnson.

But I don't think the situation's quite so desperate. One can take account of a flood without drowning in it or becoming flotsam. Call me Noah. I think that even for a language in flux, certain firm criteria can be proposed. They are based on this assumption: *that language is a means of giving a precise pattern to thought and feeling, and a means of conveying that pattern to other people.* I do not claim this is the only assumption possible. Language is commonly used for several other purposes. It is used to make up for, or disguise, the absence of thought, and to mask one's feelings; and it may communicate nothing more than a soothing assurance of togetherness. But for this purpose, as politicians (and some married couples) know, almost any noise will do: there is no question of Good Usage, or Correctness. Language can also be used deliberately to deceive. Here the question is skill, not usage. An assumption more likely to mislead us is one I've already alluded to: that language is above all a badge of social position. Here usage does matter. But which usage is socially acceptable (and that is the criterion, even though it may be called "proper"; for instance, there was a time not long ago when saying *ain't* and droppin' your final g's were the signals of aristocratic talk)—that is a question that varies rapidly with time and place, so that no general criteria can be proposed. One has to play it by ear, or find a member of the desired club who knows the passwords and is willing to tell, like Nancy Mitford or Henry Higgins.

My concern, however, is language that communicates thought and feeling—the kind I am trying to use now. This is where it makes some sense to apply standards of proper, or good, usage. And the standards I propose are these three: *Clarity, Impact,* and *Idiom.* (Not *correctness,* as you see, but bases upon which we can decide what *is* correct, or at least what is preferable.) *Is it clear? Does it hit home? Is it English?* These are the only reasonable standards I can find; and since they apply, so far as I can see, to a language at any time, they need not be surrendered under the pressure of change.

*Clarity* is of course what we aim at when we want to express thoughts with cool precision: *easy* to talk about, hard to achieve. It will govern our choice of words, the design of our sentences and arguments. It is the standard that causes Humpty Dumpty to fall, or at least to remain babbling to himself in a private lingo: for we all should know from experience that if we use words arbitrarily, instead of in their agreed senses, we will not make contact. Clarity also governs the gradual smoothing out of inflections (that is, variations in the form of a word according to its grammatical function, like *who/whose/whom*). Presumably it was in the interest of clarity that primitive tongues established remarkably complex systems of inflection (and of syntax generally); but as the history of our language shows, the complicated patterns that make French or German (or Latin) hard for us to learn have not proved necessary for speakers of English. Indeed, if clarity were our sole guide, we might wind up saying *he loves she*, or *you did hurt I*—in fact we're well on the way to that. But I proposed three standards, not one.

The second of them, *Impact*, is our aim when we want to persuade or impress rather than to inform; when instead of taking our cue from logicians or astronauts, we speak like witch doctors, advertising men, or poets. We know that by choosing certain words over others (not because they're more exact, but because they're fresh, arresting, expressive of likeness not essence) and by combining them in unexpected ways, we can charge our speech, and make it strike home as clarity alone would never do. We say, "John's a tiger." In point of literal fact, John is a featherless biped rather short on hair; but one simple and over-used metaphor conveys more about how he *strikes* us than would paragraphs of careful analysis. Again, however, impact by itself is not a sufficient guide. Without clarity squeezing the brakes, impact may run riot and collapse into nonsense or mumbo-jumbo— as poetry has been known to do, or advertising slogans, or slang. And there is no dull thud to compare with yesterday's impact: I mean, *lamp the frail with the solo cheater, will ya? Bro-ther, she just don't connect.* And neither do you, I imagine—though thirty years ago you would have followed me without trouble.

The mention of slang brings us at once to my third criterion, the tricky one: *Idiom*. I might have defined idiom as "the sense of linguistic fitness possessed by one who has grown up speaking a language"—I might have defined it so, if I hadn't learned better from experience. For I teach third- and fourth-generation Canadians who have spoken English (sort of, you know?) since the crib, yet who have no more sense of English idiom than a recent arrival from the Old Country.

You might suspect that under the mask of idiom I am actually dragging correctness in through the back door. Not so. By asking "Is it English?" I do not mean to ask, is it *proper* English—but whether it is English rather than Transylvanian or Tagalog. Thus, we accept as idiomatic "That's all right by me," but do not (yet) accept "By me you are lovely" (which is fine in German). This also demonstrates that idiom is not equivalent to usage: for there are some usages which although clear, and even fashionable for a while, are ultimately rejected as unidiomatic. By idiom in general, then, we mean the ground rules or *customs* of a particular language, developed over the centuries—no matter whether all its speakers know them or not. These rules (like those that distinguish Canadian football from the American and the British games) set limits to the ways in which a given language works, the kinds of "play" that are legitimate—limits that may have little connection with clarity or force; indeed, they almost set up an independent standard for clarity and force. I would suppose that idiom arises from the same motive as slang: a sense of clubbiness, of "the way we do things" (as against the way outsiders—aliens and foreigners—handle them). The difference is that in slang the club is narrower, the motive keener and more restless, so that fashions in slang change very swiftly—as I shall be noting later on. Idioms do change, but not too far and not too fast, for the club they signify is the main coherent body of speakers of a language; and the changes are not mindless accidents (as the proponents of Usage seem at times to suggest) but organic and adaptive. We may be able to explain why particular idioms arise; but they are unlikely to be logical or even grammatical, even in French. In short, idiom is the human side of language, balancing between the poles of emotion and reason (as we ourselves do). The idiomatic speaker recognizes that his language has a living identity. He will be so intimately acquainted with its every nerve and fibre that he knows instinctively how it prefers to behave, and will not force it into unnatural postures.

You see that these three standards of good usage are flexible, not absolute. I trust you will find them reasonable, not arbitrary. And you will realize that they work together in odd and unpredictable ways, so that we cannot apply them unimaginatively or with stickling accuracy. It should also be even clearer why I have chosen to discuss not "the mistakes we make in grammar," but (using the adman's idiom) the linguistic images we project: there are territories where grammar has little relevance. I shall assume that for the most part we *hope* to project the image of educated people—an image of clear thought, charged only with the emotion we consciously intend, and conveying by the way a perfect familiarity with the structure and temperament of our language. In short, the picture of people in control of themselves. But the fact is that we very easily go wrong, in the sense of transmitting unexpected and damaging pictures of ourselves, because our language is not wholly under our control. My main concern, therefore, will be the images we actually do project without intending them.

I'll start with a group of images that convey—well, I was going to say Ignorance, which has a nice honest ring to it; but it's not quite adequate, because in a way all the faulty images involve some ignorance. Let's try a few, and see what they have in common. First, the image of the Illiterate (the uneducated, the rube, the rough diamond). It is the most obvious, and should be the simplest to avoid; yet even in the guarded speech of Academe you may catch such expressions as *irregardless*, *equally as good as*, *a little ways further on*, *with regards to*, *anyways*, *most everyone*. I do not include in this category expressions which are linguistically O.K. but socially taboo, like *ain't*. I am pointing only at those which violate one or more of my three criteria, principally the test of clarity. For instance, *with regards to* is unclear because it's ambiguous; it belongs at the end of a letter—with regards to Auntie May, Uncle Harry, and Roger the dog—whereas *with regard to* is rather pompous but clear enough. A complaint about *how bad prisoners are treated* (on CBC Viewpoint, 17 March 1975) leaves us confused between bad prisoners and bad treatment. Or take the formula beloved of the newspaper reader: "Hey, I see where René Lévesque's been elected." *Where?* Well, in his constituency; where else?

These are the obvious errors, the ones that schoolteachers have hammered away at for years. Then why are they as common as ever? Partly carelessness, no doubt, and partly, yes, ignorance, for education of any kind is the perpetual caulking of a leaky boat. But I think there is another reason, much stronger than these: inverted snobbery, the wish not to seem better than anyone else. Illiteracy is an image often assumed for this purpose. When a mechanic reports that "she's runnin' real good," it takes a pretty stuffy professor to reply that "it is indeed running rather well." Instead, with tact and democratic sympathy, he agrees that she sure is running purty smooth, by the sound of her. For he knows that grammar varies inversely as virility; and that if you *continue on* down to the stadium, you'll find that nobody there plays well. He-men play *good*. In that quaint dream of pioneer society to which we North Americans so desperately cling, careful speech is the mark of the sissy or the dude or the schoolmarm (who isn't even a Real Woman until she takes off her glasses and drops her g's). Fluency is suspect, suggesting a flim-flam man at work: which is one reason why our politicians burble, haw, and drone.

As I shall bear witness, I have every sympathy with changing your tune to fit your environment. Boswell's memory of Dr. Johnson, addressing a baffled stable-boy as if he were a meeting of the Royal Society, should be a warning to us all. By all means let us keep up the fiction that we're all simple country folk—if it makes us talk simply, it can't be all bad. But there are times in the real world when talking like Gary Cooper does not meet the necessities of the situation. Another risk: if we don't watch what we're doing, our assumed illiteracies may become chronic, and we'll find ourselves (at a Home and School meeting, say) unable to shift gears. For instance, in the past ten years it has become chic among fairly well-educated British journalists and authors to imitate the laxer kind of Americanism—at first in a campy way, half-sneering, but then trendily, and at last unconsciously. So that now you find columnists in the London *Observer* "spending money like it was going out of style" (as it is, of course; but the locution doesn't harmonize with the rest of their column), and authors, *veddy* conservative and precise by nature, striving for the Chandler image and descending to vilely un-British depths:

> This man had hooked her *helplessly*. Who now talked *like*
> he did and sometimes more wildly. (My italics)

That's from a thriller by William Haggard (*The Bitter Harvest*, Cassell, 1971, p. 142), whose normal style is literate and careful. By odd contrast, I find two American authors of fast, tough thrillers being surprisingly choosy. Ross Macdonald has his hero (Lew Archer, in *The Moving Target*) announce that he's the "new-type detective," and soften the illiteracy by carefully putting in the hyphen. John D. MacDonald (in the Travis McGee books) is liberal with illiteracies, but uses *horrid* either in the British slang sense or, it may be, in the original Latin sense.

All right: I've oversimplified the North American scene. Pioneer simplicity is not our only dream, or even the dominant one. We have a strong contrary tendency, to inflate and load down our language with impressive sonorities: to talk like judges and senators rather than cowboys. And for this too there is a trap. It's a subspecies of Illiteracy: call it the image of a *narrow education*—specifically, an education short on etymology in Latin, Greek, or even English. I am not saying educated people all ought to know Latin or Greek (though I opine wistfully that if they knew one or the other, preferably a bit of Latin, they would use English in a less wooden way). I am saying that when English words are imported from those tongues, it is useful to know what they've brought with them. The expression *continue on*, for example, occurs even in ivied towers; but it doesn't take a classical education to know that *continue* means to *go on*, not just *go*. The word *major* is generally believed to be a powerful synonym for *big* or *important* or *significant*, so that one hears visiting pundits speak continually of Very Major Problems. At the risk of offending them, let me spell it out: *major* began life as a Latin comparative, and the comparative flavour is still there—it means either *bigger* or *rather big*. And neither a "very bigger problem" nor a "very rather big" one makes much sense. Or take four common words which afford a handy test of a man's breadth of education: *phenomenon, criterion, stratum,* and *medium.* Two are Greek, two are Latin; and they behave accordingly when they become plural. Yet I have heard a respected literary scholar in a national broadcast refer to "an interesting phenomena"; to appreciate the full effect of this, imagine hearing it in the voice of W.C. Fields. *Criteria* and *strata* are likewise frequently used as if they were singular. They were not; they are not. And everyone these days knows (without pausing to think about it) that *a media* is something you communicate to the masses with. In fact there is only one Media: it's where the Medes came from.

Now I grant you there is a line past which this sort of objection becomes precious. But I think we ought to draw that line with care. For instance, the spelling (and pronunciation) *chaise lounge* is a peculiarly insensitive gaffe to allow ourselves in a country with Francophone leanings. And on our own monoglot ground, "between the three of us" should sound wrong (to the idiomatic ear) not because grammarians say so, but because *between* was once *bi tweyen*, or *by two*. "By two the three of us" becomes a study in vulgar fractions. Keep *between* for intimate moments *à deux*; it was made for you and me.

Pretentiousness in our speech is bedevilled by other dangers. Consider the image of Fogginess, shrouding the speaker who would like to make clear distinctions but has forgotten how. He says, "To me this is a semantic problem in that the confusion centres around a verbal misunderstanding." Sounds impressive at first; but there are three dead give-aways. *Semantic* is a favourite word with people who can't convey their meaning and want to shift the blame. *In that*, as my students seem to know by instinct, is a dandy way of implying a subtle connection when you are actually going to repeat the identical idea in different words. And *centres around*, as the critics have pointed out long ago, betrays a confusion in basic geometry. Nothing centres *around* anything. Things may *revolve around*, if they must, but if they centre at all, they centre *on*.

A frequent cause of fog is choosing the wrong word in a pair: *continual* for *continuous*, *differential* for *different*, *lie* for *lay*, and so on. (For a charmingly outdated list, see Fowler's *Dictionary of Modern English Usage* under "Pairs and Snares.") The normal result is haziness of outline, but at times it may be something more risky: "Oh, I was just laying around." One of Richard Needham's correspondents cripples his indignation with this kind of error:

> When the Government takes over Bell Canada—as *regret-*
> *fully* they will one day—does anyone seriously think that
> either service or costs will improve?
>
> (Needham, *Globe*, 25 Feb. 1975; my italics)

*Regretfully* imputes an emotion to the government which does it too much honour. And come to think of it, what does a cost do when it improves? *Nutritional*, much in people's mouths lately, is either ambiguous or an unnecessary variant of *nutritious*. And *disinterested* has virtually lost its useful idiomatic meaning of "impartial." I have had people tell me no thanks, they were disinterested in football—the perfect qualification for a referee, but I was looking for someone to use the other ticket. The most common confusion is that of *infer* with *imply*. I am quite aware that even a good dictionary gives *imply* as one meaning of *infer*. That simply proves you cannot always trust dictionaries. The words are so obviously meant for each other as opposites (the speaker *folding in* an extra meaning, the listener *taking it in*) that I mistrust the judgment of a person who mixes them up. Perhaps the most noticeable symptom of the foggy speaker, or woofer, is an addiction to *facts* and *factors*. He speaks of a *fact* when he means an opinion, a risk, or a possibility; and he says *factor* when he senses that something is important but doesn't know how or why. Allow me to offer you a brief cautionary tale about factors. Originally, you recall, factors were the men in charge of trading posts for the Hudson's Bay Company; but they proved to be such willing workers that when the Company retrenched, the factors went forth and multiplied—and became factotums.

Remember that I am speaking of inadvertent fogginess. Conscious or deliberate blurring of outlines belongs to propaganda. No doubt we condition ourselves to be its victims if we use, or even listen to without comment, such expressions as "the military *internationalization* of Arab oil" (proposed in a bloodless way by a U.S. commentator not long ago). Others have pointed out that the use of woolly abstractions (*defoliation* being one of the mildest) to disguise ugly particulars is one of the sorry consequences of the war in Vietnam. A senior American journalist (Edwin Newman, in *Strictly Speaking*, Bobbs-Merrill, 1974) has been so appalled by it as to cry out against the murder of the language; once *that* murder is accomplished, it makes others easier to excuse or condone. I think it is fair to describe this as the Nazification of English. It is the process that caused George Steiner virtually to give up on language altogether (see *Language and Silence*, Atheneum, 1967). I shall content myself with this brief reminder that the seemingly trivial effects which I am discussing do border on sombre realities; and that if I choose to play it light, that's because lightness makes for more clarity than does indignation.

Close kin to fogginess is the image of what appears to be the absent mind—which cannot remember how it started, three words ago. It goes to pieces over what the grammarian calls Agreement, because it forgets both the person and the number of what it was talking about. Try this: "Bell Canada refunds your money without question if you tell *them* you reached a wrong number." How many Bells are ringing here, and for whom? Or this advice from a TV golfer: "*a person* of short stature should take care in grasping *their* club. *He (or she)* should grasp *their* club firmly..." Who grasps whose club, exactly? Does the owner know? But I'm being unfair. The difficulty in both cases has to do with pronouns which won't do precisely the job we intend. For one thing, speakers of English feel the lack of a genuinely impersonal pronoun like *on* in French: the nearest we can come to *on dit* is "they say," or "it is said." Actually *on* derives from *homo*, the Latin word for *man*—just as the impersonal *man* in German is connected with the masculine *Mann*—but in French the derivation is so masked by time that I doubt if most French speakers recognize it. Our convention in English is that *he* does duty for both *he* and *she*, and can be used impersonally. Evidently this was felt to be awkward or misleading even before the voice of women was heard, and so it has been replaced by something even more awkward, the explicit *he or she*, or in some places *s/he*. English does have the alternative *one*: "one should grasp one's club. . . ." But one hesitates to do much of this, largely because the British are prone to use *one* as a coy or playful self-effacement for *I* and *me*. Perhaps you recall the courtship of Princess Anne, when in interviews with the press Captain Phillips proved far too well-bred to draw attention to himself, and therefore became *oneself:* one belonged, one gathered, to the nation. . . . When the princess replied in kind, the two dear things practically faded from sight.

In such a cleft stick, what is the average speaker to do? I'd advise him to rely on *they*, and to avoid awkwardness by carrying the plural through: for instance "When you tell *them*, Bell Canada *refund* your money." Besides, it's good psychology to treat corporate entities like Bell or the government as plurals rather than monoliths; it helps remind us they're made of people, and can be reached. Another device is to stop being so impersonal, and use *you* instead: "If you're short, grasp your club." And try to stay out of ambiguous situations like "Everybody thinks they're in charge."

There are clearer test cases for this image (the absent or sieve-like mind). One is the formula so many people find irresistible, especially politicians talking to us on television: *as far as [X] is concerned. . .* By beginning the formula, one stands pledged to follow through, eventually, with the rest of it. But usually the windbag who starts out with a really big X, "as far as low-rental housing developments and their location within the metropolitan area within the foreseeable future, by which I mean until the next election, ah. . . "—well, such a man is lost. He's forgotten his launch platform, and we could wait for weeks without hearing a whisper of *concern*. Strip it down, and he's left with a silly dangle—"as far as housing." (If this is your problem, let me recommend some safe and easy alternatives, like *as for, as to, concerning,* or even *with regard to.* You might play it Edward G. Robinson style: "You wanna know about housing? Okay, I'll tell ya.") The other telltale habit is the mixed metaphor, as in "We promise to *harness* those *bottlenecks*," or (to quote an Ontario cabinet minister) "One bad apple can give the whole thing a black *eye*." Perhaps it is too kind to blame these unconscious jokes on forgetfulness. A truer explanation may be that such speakers are totally deaf to metaphor, and largely deaf to wit as well. A *bad apple* no longer carries for them any memory of fruit, it's just a phrase filed under Crook or Rascal (in the same fashion, I suspect, as jokes are filed under subject headings and "injected" into their speeches at apt moments).

More seductive (and for the discriminating judge, more damaging) is the image of would-be elegance, which produces Genteelisms, like *between you and I*. A little grammar is a dangerous thing. The cause of trouble is something I've already mentioned: a misplaced faith in the King's English, a striving to be correct at any cost. The effect is the same as lifting one's pinkie at a formal teacup—exaggerated propriety, more ludicrous than honest ignorance. (The British used to have a word for such behaviour: *refained*. The Refained Speaker is so anxious not to sound like a Cockney—"the rine in Spine styes minely in the pline"—that he converts *all* his i's to a's; so he cannot even say *refined*.) The psychology of such errors is plain enough. Because one got scolded as a child for saying "Us kids are going to the store" or "Me and Jimmy got whipped," one assumes that *us* and *me* are always wrong. The result is Refained Grammar, like *between you and I*. Educated people, I suppose because they are conscious of having to set an example, are specially prone to this trick. I have heard my own colleagues say, "This report was prepared by Professor Perkins and I." If they reversed the order and said "by I, and Professor Perkins" they might notice the error—but they wouldn't do that, it would be impolite to put themselves first. Or take "you must be tolerant with *we* ordinary mortals": that came from an instructor in English. (No, an English department does not have faultless speakers; what makes it unusual is that the mistakes are more likely to be noticed.) A brilliant philosopher of my acquaintance will construct noble sentences rotten at the core: "Distinctions of this order are of major importance to he who cares about logic." *Him who cares about his image, I bid take note.* And then there is the *whom* problem, which the *New Yorker* used to love so well. "The lady in question, whom our informants advise us is known as Lou . . ." Whom is? Well, in my view *whom* is a booby trap. My advice is to drop it. It's on the way out, and the tactful speaker may avoid it even when it's technically correct. A question like "Whom do you mean?" really deserves the answer it gets from Pogo: "*Youm*, that's whom."

Now for a cluster of images which offend chiefly against Idiom. In doing so they also becloud clarity and muffle impact, for my three criteria intertwine so subtly that to hurt one is to hurt all. This fact strikes me as good presumptive evidence of having hit upon the right criteria.

The image which I confess most quickly riles me is that of the Pseudo-Immigrant—the speaker who blurs or disfigures the native idiom. The irony here, as I've already suggested, is that this speaker has known no other idiom since birth. *Genuine* foreigners who learn our language from the ground up can, of course, put him to shame—as Conrad and Nabokov have demonstrated for the written word. It is not always easy to decide what is idiomatically wrong, and what is merely illiterate or malaprop. What to do with this sentence, spoken by an old friend of mine: "We are enough individuals that we could never expect unanimity"? *Hein?* Does he mean, "There are so many of us that somebody is bound to vote No," or does he mean, "We're so different we'll never agree completely"? I suspect, but I can't be sure. What I do feel sure of is that he's not at home in the language. And that's what he has in common with the speaker who gets his meaning across but sounds all wrong: "If you would have broken that tackle, you may have gone all the way." A clear case of the conditional so *imperfect* as to be totally loused up; and a very common blooper among sports announcers and "colour commentators."

The most treacherous ground of all may be the use of prepositions, for it is here that English idiom hits a peak of unreason. Small wonder that they drive foreigners to despair; but a daily wonder that they also baffle a great many native high-school graduates, who speak of having *a preference to blondes* (or sometimes *an attraction for blondes,* lucky them), *an interest for snowmobiles* (let the finance company handle that one), or *an insight of the problem* (part of the problem being that they will spell "insight' with a C). And the chances are strong that they will compound the crime by leaning significantly on the faulty preposition: "an insight OF the problem." That's a habit they learn from their elders, who may choose the right prepositions but then try to project an image of profound deliberation by weighing them down: "I don't have detailed data ON that, Chief, but my office can get the figures FOR you." A clear and simple case of lead-swinging.

The pseudo-foreign flavour comes back strong with the unidiomatic choice of tenses, as in "Did you have dinner yet?" Did I have dinner yet: let a man ask me that but once, and his image by me is irreparably flawed. A host who understood English idiom (and human feelings) would ask, "Have you had dinner?"— by which he would delicately but unmistakably convey that there was (yet) more in the kitchen. By replying, "No, I haven't," I would likewise convey implicitly that although I had not dined up to that moment, I lived in hopes. That is what is so perfectly splendid about the Present Perfect. But our Alien wouldn't understand; in his world, I eat or I ate. And if I reply in the only language he knows, "No I didn't," it's all over and done with—dinner has fled, there is nothing but bleakness and starvation. I've *had it.*

This did-you-have-dinner-yet is the thin end of a great clumsy wedge. Pretty soon we'll be saying things like "Are you in this country since long?" and "Yes, my god, I was here since I am a child." It's full of rich ethnic flavour, no doubt, the stuff of which warm situation comedies are made, but it sticks in my craw. Why should I have these uncouth alien notions of time and sequence thrust upon me, when English idiom allows me to specify time within time, before time, and after time with infinite subtlety and satisfaction? Take for example this snatch of song from *Camelot:*

> If ever you would leave me,
> It wouldn't be in springtime.

I object to Mr. Lerner's lyrics because they warp idiom, and therefore wreak confusion. What he means, in his schmaltzy Transylvanian heart, is, "If ever you *should* leave me"—that is, it hasn't happened so far, and with luck it may not happen at all. But he says instead, "If ever you *would* ", which conveys something precise but quite different. To the idiomatic ear, it suggests a pitiable stretch of Time Past (*not* time to come), during which You were accustomed in a habitual and rather heartless way to leave Me—though not (one infers) for very long at a time, and never (one knows) between March and June. Given that opening clause, the verse ought really to unfold like this:

> If ever you would leave me
> I knew you had a reason—
> Like wishing to deceive me,
> Or wild duck's being in season.

Another form of idiom-smashing that attracts educated people is what I call Literalism. This is the habit of using a word for what it looks as if it should mean, rather than what idiom has brought it to mean. The most familiar example is *presently.* A man who asks me for a job, and says he is *presently completing* his thesis, already has one strike against him. Sure, to a foreign eye it appears to mean "at present." But as speakers of English we inherit the English genius for delay (as Samuel Johnson observes, "languages are the pedigree of nations"), and when we say "any moment now" we mean tomorrow. Once upon a time there was a good old four-letter word, *anon,* which meant *in one, at once;* but it soon became clear that you couldn't trust a tapster who said "anon, anon, sir," so somebody introduced the precise Latin word *presently* to mean *now,* and all was plain for a while. But the barman dragged his heels again, and *presently* became *some other time.* Now, if you want prompt action, you must specify *immediately,* or *on the double.* And if you mean *at present,* why not say it? It takes not one millisecond longer.

A slightly different case is presented by *momentarily* and *hopefully.* The idiomatic meaning—the only meaning given in a reliable Scottish dictionary, *Chambers's*—of *momentarily* is "for a moment, briefly," as in the poignant phrase, "momentarily she was mine; then, alas, she slipped through my fingers and was gone." (Feminist readers will substitute *he.*) So the fellow who says, with eyes aglow, "She will be mine momentarily," may be in for a big disappointment—and anyone who talks that way deserves it. He means *in a moment.* Other people abuse the word to mean *at the moment.* Thornton Wilder has even used it to mean *by the moment,* or *moment by moment*—and he does it in a stage direction, so there's no way out:

> The children lean forward and all watch the funeral in silence
> growing *momentarily* more *solemnized.*
> (*The Long Christmas Dinner*, Harper and Row, 1963, p. 95)

He wrote that in 1931. *Solemnized* is a bonus boner, which happily hasn't caught on. It will do fine as a reminder that if we wish to keep our language undefiled, we cannot always trust reputable authors.

As for *hopefully*, it appears to be a more recent immigrant from Germany by way of New York. But in German it was *hoffentlich*, and meant "hopingly": a detached, impersonal adverb that English hasn't invented yet—because English has other ways of being impersonal. If we want to say "hopingly" we can use *I hope, one hopes*, or even *it is to be hoped*, which ought to be impersonal enough for anybody. When we say *hopefully*, we mean in our idiomatic way that whoever is speaking or acting is *full of hope*. A famous example: "it is better to travel hopefully than to arrive." The man who tells us "She will be mine, hopefully, within the week (*ja*)" may thus be a decent modest fellow by German standards; but in English he's taking an awful lot for granted, for he implies that it's *she* who is so keen. And when the Hon. John Turner advertises in a British newspaper that his four children "require a kind and loving nannie [sic], *hopefully* with previous experience," any nanny worth her salt will perceive that it isn't only the children who need her help.

*Momentarily*, then, is misused through literalness and unawareness of idiom, as is *presently* (examples of what *Chambers's Dictionary* calls folk-etymology, or "popular unscientific attempts at etymology"). But the case of *hopefully* suggests an additional dimension, at least to my sensibilities. I connect it first with other personal adverbs misapplied in a general, impersonal way—*regretfully* instead of *regrettably*, maybe *pitifully* a while ago. What's happening here is the transfer of a private emotion to "the public sector," so that its source can no longer be traced. No wonder these usages prevail among businessmen and politicians. *Who* is full of hope, or regret, or pity? Not me, not you, not anyone: it has been shifted into a quality of the objective environment, as if there were a something, a process out there which had taken on sentience. Is it fanciful to connect this with other hints of personal abdication, such as is implied by *a decision-making process?* If a process can feel hope or regret, it can surely make decisions. And when decisions are made by a process, no single person can be held responsible; it *happens*, objectively and inexorably, like the march of history. No doubt, the original motive for the phrase was to imply (without promising) the breaking down of tyranny, the sharing of decisions by a number of persons (as in *participatory democracy*). In practice, however, both phrases are cop-outs, and in neither case does anything get decided or done. These are the phrases of people who have no policies, no self-reliance, no confidence—and who deserve none. The only way to bring about decisions and actions is to find some *person* who can *decide*, and *act*.

What disturbs me more than the standard lies and distortions of such propaganda language is this curious appearance of an inexorable process *out there*, because in common parlance we do not merely take part in a *decision-making process*, we are *plugged into it*. Immediately I am reminded of other locutions with the same metallic flavour: "This really turns me on, you know?" and, "Man, she turns me off" (which isn't an action by "her," exactly, nor yet a response by "me"). Who, or what, is speaking? *Where is the switch?* The image I detect here is Mechanism—half surrender to, half propitiation of the great, half-glimpsed machine which we half adore, half fear. By using the language of machines to describe our hopes, actions, reactions, by transferring to a humming external process what was once our private domain of striving, do we placate the Computer Politic, the World Machine, or do we program ourselves for sacrifice? Machines, as I understand them, have languages but no idioms. What I am expressing is not the modern fear that the robots are coming, but the fear that we are *robotizing*, *dehumanizing*, *depersonalizing* ourselves through words as ugly as the process they describe.

Another troublesome question under the general head of idiom has to do with the set of sub-idioms we call Slang. There are two opposite causes of concern: whether it is proper to use slang at all, or more commonly the question of *which* slang is fashionable or "in." The motive in both cases is *togetherness* (a piece of manufactured slang which never quite made it), the wish to confirm one's belonging to a group: in the first case the large group, the great club of all those who Speak Properly (and whose slang is called idiom); in the second case the small exclusive group, the tribe of the elite who share a secret attitude (and whose exclusiveness must be assured by continual changes in the password), like adolescents or pop musicians or anglers or astronomers. To those who ask the first question I reply cheerfully, "Yes, by all means use slang—if you know the risks." Those who worry about the second are not likely to ask me, because I am obviously no swinger; all the same, one or two of my random reflections may prove edifying.

Those who ask whether slang is permissible in polite society are really preoccupied with correctness, on which I've already offered my view. Applying my kind of standards, I would repeat that in our democratic, colloquial society you are more likely to be censured for using no slang at all. But of course there are risks in using it too. Some sober groups may find your flip ways unacceptable; argot that suits one milieu may draw sneers in another. My own preference for the simple and colloquial as salt to my discourse leads many of my colleagues to dismiss me as frivolous, unscholarly, simple-minded—a reflection to which I shall return. And slang of all kinds is in constant danger of not being clear, because impact, not clarity, presides at its birth. A current fad leans heavily but ambiguously on the simple word *to*. "To me, he's a wonderful person." (Great, but how does he behave to others?) "To the majority of immigrants, their perception of education is quite different from our own" (a spokesman for the Toronto Board of Education, quoted by Canadian Press, 17 Feb. 1975). Here *to* implies a perception *of a perception*. He means "most immigrants look on education in a way native Canadians don't," but he says, "most immigrants don't look at their perceptions as we would look at *their perceptions*"—which is true, perhaps, but not useful. A short way off is the modish use of *into*: "Yeah, I'm into the hard stuff," "I'm into medieval studies," "I'm into people." The obvious risk is that the literal meaning may overturn the slang one, as with the earnest boy who confides that he's really getting into girls now. Or take the curious American insistence on *human beings* as if they were a species of achievement. "Bruce is a superb human being," they affirm glowingly. (The hell you say; and here I was, expecting a stoat.)

This approaches the image of the Hopeless Square, who keeps treading on verbal land-mines because he is unaware of slang meanings. Scientific colleagues have complained to me of inexplicable merriment in their classes when they speak of a *crude model;* and we all recall the visiting Britisher who apologizes for *knocking up* his hostess at 2 a.m. Words like *cool* and *hot* have a perpetual but fluctuating slang sense: so that Marshall McLuhan's attempt to give them specific content with regard to the media runs into difficulties. The other way to look hopelessly square is to use argot that is out of date (or *old hat,* if you get me). For instance, a few years back *no way* was the all-purpose surfboard of the young, until like so many other passwords it sank from sight. But it did not quite disappear, for adults (in those days when youth could do no wrong) snatched at it eagerly, and have never let go—with the result that instead of being in the swim as they hoped, they are now quaintly stranded on an antique beach.

On the other hand, I observe with an agreeable sense of irony how the whirligig of time brings back the exile. *Groovy,* which I helped to bury 30 years ago, is suddenly alive and well. *Chap,* which in those early days was laughably British and probably a bit effeminate, is now a perfectly normal fella, even in New York. And although *gay* is at the moment unfit for any but its slang use, a fact I deplore, it seems possible that at last *queer* can be reinstated—and perhaps *fruit* as well.

One particular area which I would hesitate to call trendy in itself has undeniably provoked trendy convulsions in language: I mean of course the movement to liberate women. It took me a long time to realize that *consciousness raising* was not a phase of transcendental meditation but a specific manoeuvre in the feminist campaign. And I doubt that *chauvinism* will be fit for its original duty in my lifetime. But the silly edge of this argot shows when the new consciousness starts in on the unsexing of *métiers*. The *Globe* for Valentine's Day carried advertisements for "a Bodyman-woman, a Foreperson and, the most intriguing of all, a Parts man-woman." (Quoted in Letters, 18 Feb. 1975.) Richard Needham notes other transformations: cowboy into cattleperson, bus boy into dining-room attendant, governess into child mentor. Everyone keeps his own list. And because this kind of neurotic fiddling quickly invites a backlash, as we say, everyone keeps a list of put-downs. I have already demonstrated my impartiality, I hope, in various ways. So let me register my objection to the plague of *persons* where hateful sexist English reads -*man*. In *spokesman*, *chairman*, *barman*, and so on we don't even pronounce it "man," but "mun." I am reminded of a special British expression in which *person* is not neutral but insulting: "She's more of a *person*, really..." I am also reminded of the ultimate achievement in desexing language, the invention of a columnist that would replace *human* with the triumphant neuter *hu-person*. (And *Mädchen* is neuter, I recall. Do liberated Ger-persons object?)

Trendiness annoys me above all not merely because it is seductive and always has been, but because it seduces us back into the screwloose religion of change. The man who deplores a return to the 3 R's as a step back toward the cave is suffering from delirium *trendens*. He belongs to the McLuhanite fringe who scream that print is dead, the book is buried, and citizens of the global village must be expert in the new mysteries of film and tape and incantation. I never know how much to blame on the ancient sage himself, because I'm never sure what he means or how serious he is. But risking naiveté, let me suggest, to his disciples at least, that if the universe around the corner is electronic all the way, then we've got to find someone else who can write the *script*, and someone who can read it, and someone else who can use the camera properly (the emptiness of hand-held scriptless impromptu inaudible film happenings having at last registered on the most glazed watcher).

Are we lapsing into barbarism? Will we soon be unable to communicate except by coos and grunts and formulas? I don't really think so—though there are portents, dammit: such as my wife's hitchhiker, a braw school-leaver of nineteen, personable and polite. When she asked him to find out what was causing the noisy rattle he checked, diagnosed, and reported, "The uh thing...is, like...Uhhh..." Aghast, she conferred: did he mean the back door on the wagon was not properly shut? He heaved a great smiling sigh of relief. "Yuh," he said, having got through. No, what I fear is that well before that, we shall have lost touch with the past. That is the other purpose and glory of language, which the usage-mongers and the progress-peddlers and the flux-worshippers forget. The gift of my tongue does not merely enable me to "interrelate" with my contemporaries; it makes me a citizen of the entire human commonwealth, of an empire across time. I will not exchange that for a wilderness of global villages.

I remember that when I sang "We Three Kings" as a child I repeated the line, "Star with royal beauty *dight*," as generations of children had done before me. Later I learned with pleasure the ancient words to "This Endris Night." But I am hard put to excavate them now. Within one generation *dight* has vanished, replaced by "royal beauty *bright*." And in "Jingle Bells"—now sanctified as a *carol*, together with "Silver Bells"—who sings now of a one-horse open *shay*? (But it's still listed, glory be, in the *Dictionary of Canadian English* as a by-form of *chaise*.) How much longer before the only readers capable of grasping ancient documents (like *Sunshine Sketches of a Little Town* or *The Great Gatsby*) are eccentric antiquarians? You zealots of the flood, explain to me how it is that words can be preserved intact through the centuries, down the ringing grooves of change, and crumble only within our own half-life? I can guess. It is because, through the efforts of traditionalists and tories and purists who refused, God bless them, to believe that all our yesterdays were irrelevant, the barbarous babble current at any one time in the past was not allowed to prevail or prescribe. *Barbarous:* a good honest word. In Greek it meant "stammering," and they used it of foreigners' talk. We should know better. We know that stammering begins at home; and that barbarism begins inside the citadel.

To return, more calmly, from sermon to images. Let me round off my survey by asking what we should project, instead of all these inadvertent and regrettable images. I wonder how many readers will agree with my suggestion that there is no single answer, no proper image for all seasons. There is a whole range of good, desirable, effective impressions we can make with our words. It is our business to choose among them, and the one we choose should depend on the job we want to do and the audience we address. You can see the truth of this when it comes to accent. Only a very narrow-minded speaker would claim that the proper way to pronounce your English is the way they do it in Aburrdeen, or Suhhbiton, or Long Guyland, or Arnpryre. I propose quite seriously that the same is true for grammar, within limits, and above all for style. The style, or *register*, which you use to a bridge partner is not appropriate when you address a tax consultant or a bus driver—though each style may be free of errors. I remember a lady who taught grade nine, and told me of a boy who told her: "Look, I talk the way my father talks. What does my father *do?* He drinks. If I talked the way *you* talk, I'd get beat to a pulp." That boy was *right.* I suspect he was also clever enough to be leading a double or triple life by now, with a perfectly idiomatic language for each (as butlers used to do in England).

But let's take an example closer to hand. I wouldn't mind a small bet that some of you think there is such a thing as a Professorial Style—correct, dignified, formal, impressive, like a god talking. There is, of course; I've put in some examples of it myself, just to prove I can. But what I'd bet on is that you have a sneaky feeling that it's *the* proper style—that we should all aim to talk or write that way, and that when I depart from it (as I do) my image suffers. This is where people go wrong—professors most of all. That formal, god-like style is only too easy to reach; and if reached too often it becomes no style at all, but a disease. This is where Humpty Dumpty's remark does make sense. The question is who is to be master—you, or the style. A man at the mercy of his own style is as comic, and as much to be pitied, as a man at the mercy of drink. Your style ought to express *what you are*, and you are not the same person on all occasions, in every company. If you seem to be, you are a bore.

I see where I am heading. The image which I have really been deploring all along, an image which embraces all the unhappy ones I've described, is the image not of the Poor Boob, but of the Zombie. What I mourn over is not the mistakes, but the *numbness*, to every aspect of language, which they imply. I regret the sort of mind that measures sense by the syllable, and accepts as oratory flannel a yard wide. To such a mind, ideas expressed in a simple, playful way are (necessarily) simple and obvious ideas, not worth having. I regret likewise the mind that must cloak metaphors in prose, apparently believing that naked metaphor is indecent—the progeny of Knowlton Nash, those newsmouths that say "climb off his *legislative* high horse," or "this promises to become a *political* hot potato." I regret above all the mind insensitive to humour and wordplay of all kinds—not just the reflex groan at a bad pun, but the total inability to grasp a good one. I regret the mind which wears a superior smile when you play with a deliberate error (for instance, a friend of mine habitually says, "Oh, it was a congenital evening," and people exchange secret smiles because they think *he's* slipped). I regret, in sum, the mind to which all languages are dead languages, including its own.

# Notes on Punctuation

## Lewis Thomas

There are no precise rules about punctuation (Fowler lays out some general advice (as best he can under the complex circumstances of English prose (he points out, for example, that we possess only four stops (the comma, the semicolon, the colon and the period (the question mark and exclamation point are not, strictly speaking, stops; they are indicators of tone (oddly enough, the Greeks employed the semicolon for their question mark (it produces a strange sensation to read a Greek sentence which is a straightforward question: Why weepest thou; (instead of Why weepest thou? (and, of course, there are parentheses (which are surely a kind of punctuation making this whole matter much more complicated by having to count up the left-handed parentheses in order to be sure of closing with the right number (but if the parentheses were left out, with nothing to work with but the stops, we would have considerably more flexibility in the deploying of layers of meaning than if we tried to separate all the clauses by physical barriers (and in the latter case, while we might have more precision and exactitude for our meaning, we would lose the essential flavor of language, which is its wonderful ambiguity)))))))))))).

The commas are the most useful and usable of all the stops. It is highly important to put them in place as you go along. If you try to come back after doing a paragraph and stick them in the various spots that tempt you you will discover that they tend to swarm like minnows into all sorts of crevices whose existence you hadn't realized and before you know it the whole long sentence becomes immobilized and lashed up squirm-

From *The Medusa and the Snail* by Lewis Thomas. Copyright © 1979 by Lewis Thomas. Reprinted by permission of Viking Penguin Inc.

ing in commas. Better to use them sparingly, and with affection, precisely when the need for each one arises, nicely, by itself.

I have grown fond of semicolons in recent years. The semicolon tells you that there is still some question about the preceding full sentence; something needs to be added; it reminds you sometimes of the Greek usage. It is almost always a greater pleasure to come across a semicolon than a period. The period tells you that that is that; if you didn't get all the meaning you wanted or expected, anyway you got all the writer intended to parcel out and now you have to move along. But with a semicolon there you get a pleasant little feeling of expectancy; there is more to come; read on; it will get clearer.

Colons are a lot less attractive, for several reasons: firstly, they give you the feeling of being rather ordered around, or at least having your nose pointed in a direction you might not be inclined to take if left to yourself, and, secondly, you suspect you're in for one of those sentences that will be labeling the points to be made: firstly, secondly and so forth, with the implication that you haven't sense enough to keep track of a sequence of notions without having them numbered. Also, many writers use this system loosely and incompletely, starting out with number one and number two as though counting off on their fingers but then going on and on without the succession of labels you've been led to expect, leaving you floundering about searching for the ninethly or seventeenthly that ought to be there but isn't.

Exclamation points are the most irritating of all. Look! they say, look at what I just said! How amazing is my thought! It is like being forced to watch someone else's small child jumping up and down crazily in the center of the living room shouting to attract attention. If a sentence really has something of importance to say, something quite remarkable, it doesn't need a mark to point it out. And if it is really, after all, a banal sentence needing more zing, the exclamation point simply emphasizes its banality!

Quotation marks should be used honestly and sparingly, when there is a genuine quotation at hand, and it is necessary to be very rigorous about the words enclosed by the marks. If something is to be quoted, the *exact* words must be used. If part of it must be left out because of space limitations, it is good manners to insert three dots to indicate the omission, but it is unethical to do this if it means connecting two thoughts which the original author did not intend to have tied together. Above all, quotation marks should not be used for ideas that you'd like to disown, things in the air so to speak. Nor should they be put in place around clichés; if you want to use a cliché you must take full responsibility for it yourself and not try to job it off on anon., or on society. The most objectionable misuse of quotation marks, but one which illustrates the dangers of misuse in ordinary prose, is seen in advertising, especially in advertisements for small restaurants, for example "just around the corner," or "a good place to eat." No single, identifiable, citable person every really said, for the record, "just around the corner," much less "a good place to eat," least likely of all for restaurants of the type that use this type of prose.

The dash is a handy device, informal and essentially playful, telling you that you're about to take off on a different tack but still in some way connected with the present course — only you have to remember that the dash is there, and either put a second dash at the end of the notion to let the reader know that he's back on course, or else end the sentence, as here, with a period.

The greatest danger in punctuation is for poetry. Here it is necessary to be as economical and parsimonious with commas and periods as with the words themselves, and any marks that seem to carry their own subtle meanings, like dashes and little rows of periods, even semicolons and question marks, should be left out altogether rather than inserted to clog up the thing with ambiguity. A single exclamation point in a poem, no matter what else the poem has to say, is enough to destroy the whole work.

The things I like best in T.S. Eliot's poetry, especially in the *Four Quartets*, are the semicolons. You cannot hear them, but they are there, laying out the connections between the images and the ideas. Sometimes you get a glimpse of a semicolon coming, a few lines farther on, and it is like climbing a steep path through woods and seeing a wooden bench just at a bend in the road ahead, a place where you can expect to sit for a moment, catching your breath.

Commas can't do this sort of thing; they can only tell you how the different parts of a complicated thought are to be fitted together, but you can't sit, not even take a breath, just because of a comma,

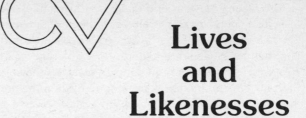

# Lives
# and
# Likenesses

## Michael Frayn

Mr. Ken Russell seems to have hit upon a simple but important new biographical principle in his films for "Monitor" on B.B.C. Television. According to sympathetic critics, he makes each film in the style of the artist it is about.

Thus, according to Peter Black, "his Elgar was straightforward and sentimentalised, his Debussy misty and complex." His Douanier Rousseau, similarly, was naïve and primitive. In fact it was considerably *more* naïve and primitive than Rousseau. It takes a real hardened professional to get as naïve and primitive as that. These amateur innocents like Rousseau never knew the tricks of the trade.

Writers have obviously been missing an opportunity. In fact, it's rather presumptuous, when you come to think about it, for old Strachey to have written "Queen Victoria" in his own style and not Queen Victoria's. And why didn't Mr. Alan Bullock couch his study of Hitler rather more in the familiar Nuremberg vein? A touch of egomania here?

Now Mr. Russell has shown the way, no doubt the idea will be taken up. Here are trailers for one or two biographies I hope to be seeing in the book-shops soon.

Firstly I should like to say this—and I make no apology for mentioning it: Harold Wilson was born—and I choose that word advisedly—on the eleventh of March 1916. Not on the tenth, or the twelfth, as some people would like you to believe—and here I intend no disrespect to the many men and women up and down the country who I know *were* born on the tenth or the twelfth, and who have given loyal and unstinting service to

From Michael Frayn, *The Original Michael Frayn* (London: The Salamander Press, 1983). © The Observer Ltd. 1967.

the community, and whose special needs—I say this to them now—have not been forgotten.

But—and it's a big but—if this book is to make any real headway, if we're really going to bring it up to date, we simply cannot afford—and this cannot be said too often—we simply cannot afford to sit back and rest content with our progress so far. Because make no mistake—and there's none of us who doesn't make mistakes at times—if we're forced to go on breaking off like this for modifications, concessions, and reassuring asides, we shan't reach Mr. Wilson's first birthday until about Chapter 23.

A (indef. art.) man who might with some justice be called the
AARDVARK (noun) of English letters, whose
AARONIC (adj.) pronouncements upon anything from the
AASVOGEL (noun) to the
ABACA (noun) often took his companions
ABACK (adv.), and frequently caused them to
ABANDON (verb) themselves to mirth, Dr. Johnson was never known to let anyone
ABASE (verb) or
ABASH (verb) him, and would wallow agreeably
ABASK (adv.) in what others might have found to be a veritable conversational
ABATTOIR (noun).

### Mozart:
### Chapter No. 21 in D Minor

In 1779 Mozart returned to Salzburg. In the year 1779 Mozart returned to Salzburg. Back to his native city in the year after 1778 Wolfgang Amadeus Mozart came.

And was made court organist, was appointed organist at the court, the organ-player at the court he was created. Having come back to Salzburg in 1779 he became court organist, the court organist is what he became after his return to Salzburg in 1779.

He was oppressed with debts. He owed money. Goods and services had been credited to him for which he had not yet paid. He was oppressed with debts, debts weighed him down. Money was outstanding. He owed. Money was what he owed.

In 1779 Mozart returned to Salzburg. Back to his home town came he. And was appointed court organist.

To Salzburg, the well-known town in Austria. That was where, in 1779, Mozart returned.

*A Life of T.S. Eliot:*
*Acknowledgments*

How can I begin to thank
Professor Pomattox, or Doctor Frack,
The Misses Fischbein, or Monsignor Blum?
Words lose their meaning, and grow slack.

Some typed upon Remingtons in obscure rooms.
Some made suggestions.
Some read the proofs. Some wept. One smiled:
"The world is full of questions."

Mrs. Crupper came and went
With tiny jars of liniment.

The finished pages flutter to the floor.
La lune éternue et s'endort.
All this, and so much more,
And so much more.

# Composition
# as
# Explanation

## Gertrude Stein

There is singularly nothing that makes a difference a difference in beginning and in the middle and in ending except that each generation has
something different at which they are all looking. By this I mean so simply
that anybody knows it that composition is the difference which makes each
and all of them then different from other generations and this is what
makes everything different otherwise they are all alike and everybody
knows it because everybody says it.

It is very likely that nearly every one has been very nearly certain that
something that is interesting is interesting them. Can they and do they. It is
very interesting that nothing inside in them, that is when you consider the
very long history of how every one ever acted or has felt, it is very interesting that nothing inside in them in all of them makes it connectedly different. By this I mean this. The only thing that is different from one time to
another is what is seen and what is seen depends upon how everybody is
doing everything. This makes the thing we are looking at very different and
this makes what those who describe it make of it, it makes a composition, it
confuses, it shows, it is, it looks, it likes it as it is, and this makes what is
seen as it is seen. Nothing changes from generation to generation except
the thing seen and that makes a composition. Lord Grey remarked that
when the generals before the war talked about the war they talked about it
as a nineteenth century war although to be fought with twentieth century
weapons. That is because war is a thing that decides how it is to be when it
is to be done. It is prepared and to that degree it is like all academies it is
not a thing made by being made it is a thing prepared. Writing and painting

From *What Are Masterpieces?* by Gertrude Stein, London: Chatto and Windus Ltd.
Reprinted by permission of David Higham Associates Limited.

and all that, is like that, for those who occupy themselves with it and don't make it as it is made. Now the few who make it as it is made, and it is to be remarked that the most decided of them usually are prepared just as the world around them is preparing, do it in this way and so I if you do not mind I will tell you how it happens. Naturally one does not know how it happened until it is well over beginning happening.

To come back to the part that the only thing that is different is what is seen when it seems to be being seen, in other words, composition and time-sense.

No one is ahead of his time, it is only that the particular variety of creating his time is the one that his contemporaries who also are creating their own time refuse to accept. And they refuse to accept it for a very simple reason and that is that they do not have to accept it for any reason. They themselves that is everybody in their entering the modern composition and they do enter it, if they do not enter it they are not so to speak in it they are out of it and so they do enter it; but in as you may say the non-competitive efforts where if you are not in it nothing is lost except nothing at all except what is not had, there are naturally all the refusals, and the things refused are only important if unexpectedly somebody happens to need them. In the case of the arts it is very definite. Those who are creating the modern composition authentically are naturally only of importance when they are dead because by that time the modern composition having become past is classified and the description of it is classical. That is the reason why the creator of the new composition in the arts is an outlaw until he is a classic, there is hardly a moment in between and it is really too bad very much too bad naturally for the creator but also very much too bad for the enjoyer, they all really would enjoy the created so much better just after it has been made than when it is already a classic, but it is perfectly simple that there is no reason why the contemporaries should see, because it would not make any difference as they lead their lives in the new composition anyway, and as every one is naturally indolent why naturally they don't see. For this reason as in quoting Lord Grey it is quite certain that nations not actively threatened are at least several generations behind themselves militarily so aesthetically they are more than several generations behind themselves and it is very much too bad, it is so very much more exciting and satisfactory for everybody if one can have contemporaries, if all one's contemporaries could be one's contemporaries.

There is almost not an interest.

For a very long time everybody refuses and then almost without a pause almost everybody accepts. In the history of the refused in the arts and literature the rapidity of the change is always startling. Now the only difficulty with the *volte-face* concerning the arts is this. When the acceptance comes, by that acceptance the thing created becomes a classic. It is a natural phenomena a rather extraordinary natural phenomena that a thing accepted becomes a classic. And what is the characteristic quality of a classic. The characteristic quality of a classic is that it is beautiful. Now of course it is perfectly true that a more or less first rate work of art is beautiful but the trouble is that when that first rate work of art becomes a classic because it is accepted the only thing that is important from then on to the majority of the acceptors the enormous majority, the most intelligent majority of the acceptors is that it is so wonderfully beautiful. Of course it is wonderfully beautiful, only when it is still a thing irritating annoying stimulating then all quality of beauty is denied to it.

Of course it is beautiful but first all beauty in it is denied and then all the beauty of it is accepted. If every one were not so indolent they would realize that beauty is beauty even when it is irritating and stimulating not only when it is accepted and classic. Of course it is extremely difficult nothing more so than to remember back to its not being beautiful once it has become beautiful. This makes it so much more difficult to realise its beauty when the work is being refused and prevents every one from realising that they were convinced that beauty was denied, once the work is accepted. Automatically with the acceptance of the time-sense comes the recognition of the beauty and once the beauty is accepted the beauty never fails any one.

Beginning again and again is a natural thing even when there is a series.

Beginning again and again and again explaining composition and time is a natural thing.

It is understood by this time that everything is the same except composition and time, composition and the time of the composition and the time in the composition.

Everything is the same except composition and as the composition is different and always going to be different everything is not the same. Everything is not the same as the time when of the composition and the time in the composition is different. The composition is different, that is certain.

The composition is the thing seen by every one living in the living they are doing, they are the composing of the composition that at the time they are living is the composition of the time in which they are living. It is that that makes living a thing they are doing. Nothing else is different, of that almost any one can be certain. The time when and the time of and the time in that composition is the natural phenomena of that composition and of that perhaps every one can be certain.

No one thinks these things when they are making when they are creating what is the composition, naturally no one thinks that is no one formulates until what is to be formulated has been made.

Composition is not there, it is going to be there and we are here. This is some time ago for us naturally.

The only thing that is different from one time to another is what is seen and what is seen depends upon how everybody is doing everything. This makes the thing we are looking at very different and this makes what those who describe it make of it, it makes a composition, it confuses, it shows, it is, it looks, it likes it as it is, and this makes what is seen as it is seen. Nothing changes from generation to generation except the thing seen and that makes a composition.

Now the few who make writing as it is made and it is to be remarked that the most decided of them are those that are prepared by preparing, are prepared just as the world around them is prepared and is preparing to do it in this way and so if you do not mind I will again tell you how it happens. Naturally one does not know how it happened until it is well over beginning happening.

Each period of living differs from any other period of living not in the way life is but in the way life is conducted and that authentically speaking is composition. After life has been conducted in a certain way everybody knows it but nobody knows it, little by little, nobody knows it as long as nobody knows it. Any one creating the composition in the arts does not know it either, they are conducting life and that makes their composition what it is, it makes their work compose as it does.

Their influence and their influences are the same as that of all of their contemporaries only it must always be remembered that the analogy is not obvious until as I say the composition of a time has become so pronounced that it is past and the artistic composition of it is a classic.

And now to begin as if to begin. Composition is not there, it is going to be there and we are here. This is some time ago for us naturally. There is something to be added afterwards.

Just how much my work is known to you I do not know. I feel that perhaps it would be just as well to tell the whole of it.

In beginning writing I wrote a book called *Three Lives* this was written in 1905. I wrote a negro story called *Melanctha*. In that there was a constant recurring and beginning there was a marked direction in the direction of being in the present although naturally I had been accustomed to past present and future, and why, because the composition forming around me was a prolonged present. A composition of a prolonged present is a natural composition in the world as it has been these thirty years it was more and more a prolonged present. I created then a prolonged present naturally I knew nothing of a continuous present but it came naturally to me to make one, it was simple it was clear to me and nobody knew why it was done like that, I did not myself although naturally to me it was natural.

After that I did a book called *The Making of Americans* it is a long book about a thousand pages.

Here again it was all so natural to me and more and more complicatedly a continuous present. A continuous present is a continuous present. I made almost a thousand pages of a continuous present.

Continuous present is one thing and beginning again and again is another thing. These are both things. And then there is using everything.

This brings us again to composition this the using everything. The using everything brings us to composition and to this composition. A continuous present and using everything and beginning again. In these two books there was elaboration of the complexities of using everything and of a continuous present and of beginning again and again and again.

In the first book there was a groping for a continuous present and for using everything by beginning again and again.

There was a groping for using everything and there was a groping for a continuous present and there was an inevitable beginning of beginning again and again and again.

Having naturally done this I naturally was a little troubled with it when I read it. I became then like the others who read it. One does, you know, excepting that when I reread it myself I lost myself in it again. Then I said to myself this time it will be different and I began. I did not begin again I just began.

In this beginning naturally since I at once went on and on very soon there were pages and pages and pages more and more elaborated creating a more and more continuous present including more and more using of everything and continuing more and more beginning and beginning and beginning.

I went on and on to a thousand pages of it.

In the meantime to naturally begin I commenced making portraits of anybody and anything. In making these portraits I naturally made a continuous present an including everything and a beginning again and again within a very small thing. That started me into composing anything into one thing. So then naturally it was natural that one thing an enormously long thing was not everything an enormously short thing was also not everything nor was it all of it a continuous present thing nor was it always and always beginning again. Naturally I would then begin again. I would begin again I would naturally begin. I did naturally begin. This brings me to a great deal that has been begun.

And after that what changes what changes after that after that what changes and what changes after that and after that and what changes and after that and what changes after that.

The problem from this time on became more definite.

It was all so nearly alike it must be different and it is different, it is natural that if everything is used and there is a continuous present and a beginning again and again if it is all so alike it must be simply different and everything simply different was the natural way of creating it then.

In this natural way of creating it then that it was simply different everything being alike it was simply different, this kept on leading one to lists. Lists naturally for a while and by lists I mean a series. More and more in going back over what was done at this time I find that I naturally kept simply different as an intention. Whether there was or whether there was not a continuous present did not then any longer trouble me there was or there was, and using everything no longer troubled me if everything is alike using everything could no longer trouble me and beginning again and again could no longer trouble me because if lists were inevitable if series were inevitable and the whole of it was inevitable beginning again and again could not trouble me so then with nothing to trouble me I very completely began naturally since everything is alike making it as simply different naturally as simply different as possible. I began doing natural phenomena what I called natural phenomena and natural phenomena naturally everything being alike natural phenomena are making things be naturally simply different. This found its culmination later, in the beginning it began in a center confused with lists with series with geography with returning portraits and with particularly often four and three and often with five and four. It is easy to see that in the beginning such a conception as everything being naturally different would be very inarticulate and very slowly it began to emerge and take the form of anything, and then naturally if anything that is simply different is simply different what follows will follow.

So far then the progress of my conceptions was the natural progress entirely in accordance with my epoch as I am sure is to be quite easily realised if you think over the scene that was before us all from year to year.

As I said in the beginning, there is the long history of how every one ever acted or has felt and that nothing inside in them in all of them makes it connectedly different. By this I mean all this.

The only thing that is different from one time to another is what is seen and what is seen depends upon how everybody is doing everything.

It is understood by this time that everything is the same except composition and time, composition and the time of the composition and the time in the composition.

Everything is the same except composition and as the composition is different and always going to be different everything is not the same. So then I as a contemporary creating the composition in the beginning was groping toward a continuous present, a using everything a beginning again and again and then everything being alike then everything very simply everything was naturally simply different and so I as a contemporary was creating everything being alike was creating everything naturally being naturally simply different, everything being alike. This then was the period that brings me to the period of the beginning of 1914. Everything being alike everything naturally would be simply different and war came and everything being alike and everything being simply different brings everything being simply different brings it to romanticism.

Romanticism is then when everything being alike everything is naturally simply different, and romanticism.

Then for four years this was more and more different even though this was, was everything alike. Everything alike naturally everything was simply different and this is and was romanticism and this is and was war. Everything being alike everything naturally everything is different simply different naturally simply different.

And so there was the natural phenomena that was war, which had been, before war came, several generations behind the contemporary composition, because it became war and so completely needed to be contemporary became completely contemporary and so created the completed recognition of the contemporary composition. Every one but one may say every one became consciously became aware of the existence of the authenticity of the modern composition. This then the contemporary recognition, because of the academic thing known as war having been forced to become contemporary made every one not only contemporary in act not only contemporary in thought but contemporary in self-consciousness made every one contemporary with the modern composition. And so the art creation of the contemporary composition which would have been outlawed normally outlawed several generations more behind even than war, war having been brought so to speak up to date art so to speak was allowed not completely to be up to date, but nearly up to date, in other words we who created the expression of the modern composition were to be recognized before we were dead some of us even quite a long time before we were dead. And so war may be said to have advanced a general recognition of the expression of the contemporary composition by almost thirty years.

And now after that there is no more of that in other words there is peace and something comes then and it follows coming then.

And so now one finds oneself interesting oneself in an equilibration, that of course means words as well as things and distribution as well as between themselves between the words and themselves and the things and themselves, a distribution as distribution. This makes what follow what follows and now there is every reason why there should be an arrangement made. Distribution is interesting and equilibration is interesting when a continuous present and a beginning again and again and using everything and everything alike and everything naturally simply different has been done.

After all this, there is that, there has been that that there is a composition and that nothing changes except composition the composition and the time of and the time in the composition.

The time of the composition is a natural thing and the time in the composition is a natural thing it is a natural thing and it is a contemporary thing.

The time of the composition is the time of the composition. It has been at times a present thing it has been at times a past thing it has been at times a future thing it has been at times an endeavour at parts or all of these things. In my beginning it was a continuous present a beginning again and again and again and again, it was a series it was a list it was a similarity and everything different it was a distribution and an equilibration. That is all of the time some of the time of the composition.

Now there is still something else the time-sense in the composition. This is what is always a fear a doubt and a judgement and a conviction. The quality in the creation of expression the quality in a composition that makes it go dead just after it has been made is very troublesome.

The time in the composition is a thing that is very troublesome. If the time in the composition is very troublesome it is because there must even if there is no time at all in the composition there must be time in the composition which is in its quality of distribution and equilibration. In the beginning there was the time in the composition that naturally was in the composition but time in the composition comes now and this is what is now troubling every one the time in the composition is now a part of distribution and equilibration. In the beginning there was confusion there was a continuous present and later there was romanticism which was not a confusion but an extrication and now there is either succeeding or failing there must be distribution and equilibration there must be time that is distributed and equilibrated. This is the thing that is at present the most troubling and if there is the time that is at present the most troublesome the time-sense that is at present the most troubling is the thing that makes the present the most troubling. There is at present there is distribution, by this I mean expression and time, and in this way at present composition is time that is the reason that at present the time-sense is troubling that is the reason why at present the time-sense in the composition is the composition that is making what there is in composition.

And afterwards.

Now that is all.

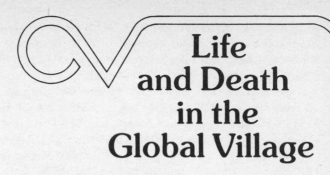

# Life and Death in the Global Village

## Michael J. Arlen

He was shot in secrecy, away from cameras. No strange slow-motion scenes, as when the young Japanese student, sword in hand, rushed across the stage to lunge at a Socialist politician, or when Verwoerd, the South African, was shot at and for whole crazy moments (it seems so long ago; so many people shot at since then) the cameras swirled and danced around the tumbling, stampeding bodies of the crowd—and then John Kennedy was killed, his life made to disappear right there before us, frame by frame, the projector slowing down, s-l-o-w-i-n-g d-o-w-n, s—l—o—w—i—n—g   d—o—w—n, as we watched (three consecutive days we watched), gathered in little tight-gutted bands around the television set, meals being cooked somehow, children put to bed, sent out to play, our thoughts of abandonment and despair and God knows what else focusing on the images of the television set, television itself taking on (we were told later) the aspect of a national icon, a shrine, an exorciser of grief; we were never so close (we were told later) as in those days just after Dallas. It could not have been quite close enough, it seems, or lasted long enough. The man who was shot in Memphis on Thursday of last week was standing on a second-floor balcony of a motel, the Lorraine, leaning over the railing of the balcony in front of his room, which was No. 306. (We have been told it was No. 306.) He was shot once and killed by a man who fired his rifle (a Remington 30.06), apparently, from inside a bathroom window of a rooming house some two hundred feet away. The address of the rooming house is 420 South Main Street. There was no film record of the act, no attendant Zapruder to witness for us the body falling and other memorabilia, but most of us found out about it by televi-

From *Living-Room War* by Michael J. Arlen. Copyright ©1966, 1967, 1968, 1969 by Michael J. Arlen. Reprinted by permission of Candida Donadio & Associates, Inc.

sion, and it is by television that most of us have been connected with whatever it is that really happened, or is happening now. Television connects—the global village. We sit at home—We had been out, actually, a party full of lawyers, and had come back early and turned on the eleven-o'clock news. "I have a dream…" young Dr. King was chanting, "that one day on the red hills of Georgia…" CBS's Joseph Benti said that Dr. King had been shot and killed, was dead. The President was speaking. "I ask every citizen to reject the blind violence that has struck Dr. King, who lived by non-violence," he said. They showed us pictures of Dr. King in Montgomery. They showed us pictures of the outside of the Lorraine Motel.

The telephone rang. A friend of my wife's. "Have you heard?" she said. I said we'd heard. "It's so horrible," she said. And then, "I can't believe it." And then, "I feel we're all mad." I held the phone against my ear, mumbling the usual things, feeling, in part, her grief, her guilt, her sense of lunacy—whatever it was—and, in part, that adrenalin desire we strangers have who have been separate in our cabins all the long sea voyage to somehow touch each other at the moment that the ship goes down. She talked some more. "I'm keeping you from watching," she said at last. I mumbled protests, and we said good-by and disconnected. We will all meet for dinner three weekends hence and discuss summer rentals on the Vineyard.

All over the country now the members of the global village sit before their sets, and the voices and faces out of the sets speak softly, earnestly, reasonably, sincerely to us, in order once again (have four and a half years really gone by since Dallas?) to bind us together, to heal, to mend, to take us forward. The President appears. His face looks firmer, squarer, straighter now than it has looked in months. "We can achieve nothing by lawlessness and divisiveness among the American people," he says. "It's only by joining together and only by working together we can continue to move toward equality and fulfillment for all of our people." The Vice-President speaks. "The cause for which he marched and worked, I am sure, will find a new strength. The plight of discrimination, poverty, and neglect must be erased from America," he says. Former Vice-President Richard Nixon is expected to release a statement soon. There are brief pictures of a coffin being slid onto a plane. The Field Foundation, one hears, has just undertaken to donate a million dollars to the civil-rights movement. Dr. Ralph Bunche asks for "an effort of unparalleled determination, massiveness, and urgency to convert the American ideal of equality into reality."

The television sets hum in our midst. Gray smoke, black smoke begins to rise from blocks of buildings in Washington and Chicago. Sirens whine outside our windows in the night. The voices out of Memphis seem to be fainter now; the pictures of that little nondescript motel, the railing, the bathroom window are already being shown to us less frequently today. Down below us on the sidewalk, six blue-helmeted policemen are gathered in a group. Three police cars are parked farther down the street. The television beams out at us a Joel McCrea movie. Detroit and Newark have been remembered. Responsible decisions have been made in responsible places. The President is working now "to avoid catastrophe." The cartoons are on this morning. The air is very bright outside. The day is sunny. All day long the sirens sound. The television hums through its schedule. There is a circus on Channel 4. Back from the dime store, my daughter asks one of the helmeted policemen if anything has happened. He seems surprised. No, nothing, he says. A squad car drives slowly, slowly by. A bowling exhibition is taking place on Channel 7. Another movie — and then the news. Great waves of smoke, clouds, billowing waves are suddenly pouring out of buildings. The sounds of bells and sirens. Mayor Daley speaks. Mayor Daley declares a curfew. Six Negro boys are running down a street, carrying armfuls of clothes. Police cars steak by. More smoke. The news is over. We are re-enveloped in a movie. We sit there on the floor and absorb the hum of television. Last summer it inflamed our passions, did it not? This time the scenes of black men running past the smoking buildings of Chicago are handled briefly, almost dreamily — a light caress by cameras and announcers. The coffin — one wonders where the coffin is at present, who is with it. Boston University announces that ten new scholarships for "underprivileged students" have just been created. The Indian Parliament pays tribute. The voices of reason and reordering rise out of the civic temples of the land and float through the air and the airwaves into our homes. Twenty-one House Republicans have issued an "urgent appeal" for passage of the new civil-rights bill. "With whom will we stand? The man who fired the gun? Or the man who fell before it?" Senator Edward Brooke, of Massachusetts, asks. The City Council of Chicago meets and passes a resolution to build a "permanent memorial." Senator Robert Kennedy deplores the rise in violence.

There was a moment the other evening when (just for a few seconds) everybody stopped talking, when (just for a few seconds) the television stopped its humming and soothing and filling of silences and its preachments of lessons-we-have-just-learned and how we-must-all-march-together — and (just for a few seconds) Mrs. King appeared; she was speaking about her husband, her dead husband. She spoke; she seemed so alive with him — it's marvelous how that sometimes happens between people; he really had been alive, and one knew it then — and for a few scant moments, just at that time, and afterward, sitting there looking at the set, that very imperfect icon, that very imperfect connector of people (will somebody really have the nerve to say this week that we are a nation "united in grief"?), one could almost hear the weeping out there, of real people in real villages, and the anger, this time, of abandonment.

And then the sounds came back—the sounds of one's own life. The weather man came on. A Negro minister on Channel 13 was talking about the need to implement the recommendations of the President's new Commission on Civil Disorders. He *had* been alive...hadn't he? Later that night, one could hear the sirens—very cool and clear—and, somewhere nearby (around the corner? blocks away?), the sounds of footsteps running.

# On Mortality

## Maxine Hong Kingston

As you know, any plain person you chance to meet can prove to be a powerful immortal in disguise come to test you.

Li Fu-yen told a story about Tu Tzu-chun, who lived from A.D. 558 to 618, during the Northern Chou and Sui dynasties. Tu's examiner was a Taoist monk, who made him rich twice, and twice Tu squandered his fortune though it took him two lifetimes to do so. The third time the Taoist gave him money, he bought a thousand li of good land, plowed it himself, seeded it, built houses, roads, and bridges, then welcomed widows and orphans to live on it. With the leftover money, he found a husband for each spinster and a wife for every bachelor in his family, and also paid for the weddings. When he met the Taoist again, he said, "I've used up all your money on the unfortunates I've come across."

"You'll have to repay me by working for me," said the Taoist monk. "I need your help on an important difficult task." He gave Tu three white pills. "Swallow these," he said, pouring him a cup of wine. "All that you'll see and feel will be illusions. No matter what happens, don't speak; don't scream. Remember the saying 'Hide your broken arms in your sleeves.'"

"How easy," said Tu as he swallowed the pills in three gulps of wine. "Why should I scream if I know they're illusions?"

Level by level he descended into the nine hells. At first he saw oxheads, horsefaces, and the heads of generals decapitated in war. Illusions. Only illusions, harmless. He laughed at the heads. He had seen heads before. Soon fewer heads whizzed through the dark until he saw no more of them.

Suddenly his wife was being tortured. Demons were cutting her up into pieces, starting with her toes. He heard her scream; he heard her

From *China Men*, by Maxine Hong Kingston. Copyright ©1977, 1978, 1979, 1980 by Maxine Hong Kingston. Reprinted by permission of Alfred A. Knopf, Inc.

bones crack. He reminded himself that she was an illusion. *Illusion*, he thought. She was ground into bloodmeal.

Then the tortures on his own body began. Demons poured bronze down his throat and beat him with iron clubs and chains. They mortar-and-pestled and packed him into a pill.

He had to walk over mountains of knives and through fields of knives and forests of swords. He was killed, his head chopped off, rolling into other people's nightmares.

He heard gods and goddesses talking about him, "This man is too wicked to be reborn a man. Let him be born a woman." He saw the entrance of a black tunnel and felt tired. He would have to squeeze his head and shoulders down into the enclosure and travel a long distance. He pushed head first through the entrance, only the beginning. A god kicked him in the butt to give him a move on. (This kick is the reason many Chinese babies have a blue-gray spot on their butts or lower backs, the "Mongolian spot.") Sometimes stuck in the tunnel, sometimes shooting helplessly through it, he emerged again into light with many urgent things to do, many messages to deliver, but his hands were useless baby's hands, his legs wobbly baby's legs, his voice a wordless baby's cries. Years had to pass before he could regain adult powers; he howled as he began to forget the cosmos, his attention taken up with mastering how to crawl, how to stand, how to walk, how to control his bowel movements.

He discovered that he had been reborn a deaf-mute female named Tu. When she became a woman, her parents married her to a man named Lu, who at first did not mind. "Why does she need to talk," said Lu, "to be a good wife? Let her set an example for women." They had a child. But years later, Lu tired of Tu's dumbness. "You're just being stubborn," he said, and lifted their child by the feet. "Talk, or I'll dash its head against the rocks." The poor mother held her hand to her mouth. Lu swung the child, broke its head against the wall.

Tu shouted out, "Oh! Oh!"—and he was back with the Taoist, who sadly told him that at the moment when she had said, "Oh! Oh!" the Taoist was about to complete the last step in making the elixir for immortality. Now that Tu had broken his silence, the formula was spoiled, no immortality for the human race. "You overcame joy and sorrow, anger, fear, and evil desire, but not love," said the Taoist, and went on his way.

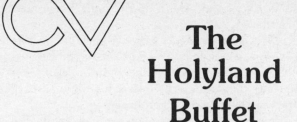

# The Holyland Buffet

## Gwendolyn MacEwen

'The most amazing thing I saw in all my travels,' Kali was saying, 'was that streetcar in Cairo.'

'I thought you never travelled,' said Ibrahim the Syrian, who was sitting across the table from her in a new vegetarian restaurant called Mythological Foods. 'When you get mad, you always swear that you're going to pack up and go to India. But you never go, so I assumed you never travel.'

'Ah but I have, you know. I have been to two holy lands—Israel and Egypt. I have also been to Greece, which is not really a holy land. But to get back to that streetcar—'

'Tell me about Israel,' Ibrahim said. 'I want to comprehend the enemy.'

'On my first day there I took a walk alone along the beach at Jaffa, which means *The Beautiful*. Some boy about eleven or twelve came up and asked me the time—everybody there asks you the time, don't ask me why—and when I told him he attacked me and threw me to the ground and starting punching me all over. We punched and kicked for a while until he finally got bored and walked away. I never knew what it was all about, except that because I was wearing shorts I probably offended him.'

'Bloody aggressive Israelis,' Ibrahim said. 'That's all they know, how to punch and kick their way through the world.'

'The boy was a Palestinian Arab,' Kali said. 'He thought *I* was an Israeli.'

'Then the story is entirely different,' said Ibrahim. 'It needs re-examining.'

From *Views from the North*, ed. Karen Mulhallen (Erin, Ont.: Porcupine's Quill, Inc., 1984).

The mythological food arrived at their table and they dug in. Ibrahim showed her how to eat a dish of dark brown powder with an indescribable smell.

'This is *zaatar*,' he said. 'We've been eating it for centuries in the East. You dip the bread first in the olive oil to moisten it, then into the *zaatar*— so.' He popped a piece into her mouth. 'Jesus Christ ate this all the time,' he said. 'Him and his disciples. This is the bitter herbs they wrote about. Anyway, tell me more about Israel.'

'It's really the streetcar I want to talk about,' Kali said.

'Never mind the streetcar.'

'Well I was walking through this village called Lifta, outside Jerusalem, and I was wearing shorts again, so I looked like a *sabra* again, and a whole tribe of little Arab boys came screaming up the mountain path toward me and started pelting me with stones. Stoned outside of Jerusalem, can you imagine, in the twentieth century, and me a Kanadian. In the clinic they put something called a spider clamp into my head where the worst wound was, and covered it with bandages that looked like a turban. They said now I looked like an Arab, and told me not to do anything exciting for a few days. I tried not to do anything exciting, but the Israelis are hooked on speed—I mean anything that goes fast, the faster the better. So I had this wild motorcycle ride with a guy who thought he was doing me a favour by giving me a ride up to Tiberias, and every moment I thought I was going to die, which was of course the whole point, the thrill. Then I walked around Tiberias with the spider clamp rusting in my skull, holding my thoughts together as it were, keeping my head from flying apart in a hundred directions; then I brooded and felt biblical in a small hotel, and the next day another guy offered me a ride in his motor-boat in Lake Tiberias. I should have known better. He rode at top speed to the middle of the lake and informed me that now, two minutes either way, meant the difference between Israel and Jordan, life or death. Then he laughed and laughed like a madman and started going around in crazy wild circles. Can you imagine—this maniac in the middle of the Sea of Galilee and us going round and round and the laughter so loud they could probably hear it on both shores....'

'Bloody insane Israelis,' said Ibrahim, and passed her a plate of ripe green figs.

'Well all the guys are on the make over there,' Kali said, 'and I was a female tourist travelling alone, so what could I expect? Come on, it would be the same in your country.'

Ibrahim addressed his full attention to the figs.

'Oh wait,' Kali remembered, 'I knew I forgot something, I forgot to tell you about the Holyland Buffet....'

'*What?*'

'The Holyland Buffet. It was this crazy little place at the foot of the

Mount of Loaves and Fishes. Nothing more than a little shack, really, with a counter in the front and a few shelves behind full of orange drinks and cigarettes and halvah bars. I must have been the first person the owner had seen for days, because —'

'Wait!' Ibrahim cried. 'Wait wait wait! I have a cousin in Jordan who has a place called the Holyland Buffet, just outside of Bethlehem!'

'Well this one was in Israel.'

'It's impossible that there are two!' Ibrahim cried, his face getting very red. 'It's just impossible!'

'Well, I didn't know if the guy who ran this one was Arab or Israeli. Anyway, as I was saying, I must have been the first person or maybe just the first woman he'd seen for days because he leaned over the counter after he served me my drink and clutched my wrists and pleaded *Come with me to Haifa! The lights, the cabarets, the people!* I said that I couldn't, and I didn't even know him. He said that didn't matter, we'd have a wonderful time anyway. *To Haifa, to Haifa together!* I wonder where he is today; what a beautiful man....'

'There can't be two Holyland Buffets,' Ibrahim said, and proceeded not to listen to her as she went on.

'And then there was old Ephraim, the painter who lived in the old village of Safed in the mountains. He wanted to seduce me too, although he went on for hours about Eisenstein and Isadora Duncan and Stanislavsky and all the others he had known who were black-listed in the States. Now in Israel the tourist bureau warned tourists against having their portraits done by the infamous communist Ephraim, so he ended up with more business than anyone....'

'Let's change the subject,' said Ibrahim, dejectedly sipping a Turkish coffee. 'What about Egypt?'

'At last we're getting to what I wanted to tell you in the first place. The streetcar —'

'Who cares about a streetcar? What happened in Egypt?'

'Well of course, it's even worse there for a woman to walk around alone. When I went every day to the museum in Cairo because there was so much to see, the guards thought I must have been playing some really sexy game with them; it was inconceivable that I would go alone to a museum every day—why? What was my *real* reason? I could not possibly have travelled half-way around the world to stare at statues and mummies of the dead lords of Egypt, the gold of Tutankhamon, the most exquisite sculpture imaginable. No, I was indeed a tart, a slut, a whore. So they kept plying me with sugary tea and cigarettes, and they smiled and joked among themselves, and when I didn't want more sugary tea they offered me *Misra-Cola* and more cigarettes and endless offers of escorted tours around Cairo. Within a few days I had acquired a reputation of being one of the loosest women in the city, a tramp, an easy lay;

and of course each one of them boasted to the others of his conquest of this piece of garbage, this foreigner. I don't know how I got to actually see what I wanted to see in the museum, but somehow I did.'

'Would you like some *halvah*?' Ibrahim asked. 'It's the lovely kind with chocolate marbled all through it. Here, have some.' And he popped a piece into her mouth. 'Now, what else?'

'The pyramids,' Kali said. 'Not the pyramids themselves—what can one say? But the washrooms, the horrible little washrooms that had no doors on the cubicles and no doors closed to the outside, and you had to pay the guard—a man—to go and pee, and you sat there in the shameless light of day staring at the Great Pyramid of Giza from the vantage point of a toilet seat, for Christ's sake. I remember it well; I have tried to forget.'

The waiter at Mythological Foods produced the bill for the meal, and Ibrahim frowned darkly as he checked it over.

'It's amazing and disgusting what they think they can charge for food that has been eaten since before Jesus Christ walked the earth, before Ulysses set sail from Ithaca, before there even was a Holy Land,' he said.

He paid, and they left. Outside the sky was a frail blue, the colour of Roman glass.

'But you come back from these travels, and it's wonderful,' Kali mused. 'You come back to Kanada, and the jet going from East to West interferes with the world's turning. You realize there are other times, arrested sunsets, moments that go on forever, cities whose walls trap time....'

'That bill was too high,' Ibrahim muttered. 'We'd have gotten a better meal at the Holyland Buffet. The one my cousin owns. In Jordan.'

They waited for a streetcar; they were both going in the same direction.

'*Now* will you listen to my story, the one I was going to tell you in the first place? Kali asked.

'All right, but make it fast.'

'Well there I was, standing in the middle of Cairo one afternoon, hot, mad, and completely disoriented, with people screaming all around me and donkeys braying and a chaos that exists nowhere else in the world—when what should I see?'

'I don't know. What did you see?'

'What should I see, coming toward me with the slowness and grace of a dream, its colours an unmistakable dark-red and yellow, the sign on its metal forehead a magic name recalling a distant, mythic land....'

'What did you *see*?' Ibrahim's mood was black.

'*A King Street streetcar.*'

'A what?'

'A King Street streetcar. From Toronto, Kanada. The city gives old ones away to Egypt and I guess other places, when they're too worn out to use here. There it was, coming toward me, this great, fabulous beast. Try to imagine it, Ibrahim, try to imagine what I felt.'

But Ibrahim was too angry about the meal, about the bill, about the second Holyland Buffet which was in the country of the enemy, and about the coldness of the day in this country of his exile, to pay much attention to what she said.

# Terms and Topics

## TERMS

1. ***Vocabulary, Section VI***: abdication, arbiter, arbitrary, chic, condone, criterion, deploying, disarming, edifying, evocative, extrication, fatuous, flim-flam, gaffe, hoariest, immanent, imputes, imponderables, indolent, inexorable, inflection, memorabilia, metaphysical, milieu, monoliths, mortified, mystical, mystique, nondescript, palliate, propitiation, pundits, rapport, rube, sanctified, schmaltzy, sombre, tack, testily, uncouth, unethical, unstinting, wallow, zealots.

2. What is a concrete poem? What is meant by ***concrete language***? (See "A Note to the Reader.") Does a concrete poem have to use concrete language?

3. Distinguish between the words ***simplistic*** and ***solipsistic***. How does *simplistic* differ from *simple*? How does *solipsistic* differ from *personal, private,* or *subjective*?

4. What is the difference between a ***motif*** and a ***leitmotif***? What are some other terms that, like *leitmotif*, literary criticism has adopted from the visual and plastic arts and from music?

5. ***Metre, alliteration, assonance, consonance*** and ***rhyme*** are defined in "A Note to the Reader." They are all common devices in poetry. How much can a writer of prose use such devices? Are there some kinds of essays in which a writer should avoid them all, others where they can be used in a limited way, and others where they can be used with abandon? Carefully examine several essays of different kinds in this book to determine to what extent these devices are present tin them. What are the differences between poetry and prose? See if you

500

can find one or more pieces of writing (not in this book) that it would be difficult if not impossible to classify as either poetry or prose. Write a paragraph of prose—perhaps describing a scene or an action—in which you make deliberate use of metre, alliteration, assonance, consonance, and rhyme. Are you tempted to think of the result as poetry? or at least poetic prose?

6. What does the term **reading** mean? What is the relation between reading and writing? Should readers try to reproduce in themselves the experience the writer had while writing? How important is it that readers "hear" an essay that is written down? Should writers always read aloud what they have written? Do you make it a practice to read your essays aloud—whether anyone else is around or not—before you consider them finished? How can readers learn to be conscious of *voice* in what they read? What exactly is *voice*? How much attention should readers pay to the *appearance* of an essay on the page? How can a reader "read" a concrete poem?

## TOPICS: On Individual Essays

JOHN ROBERT COLOMBO   **"Communicating through Form"**

1. What is Dada? What is Art Deco? Prepare a research report on one of these or some other movement in twentieth-century art.

2. Explain in your own words, with concrete examples, the difference between *perception* and *apperception*. What is the difference between a *symbol* and a *sign*?

3. Advertising often picks up innovations in the arts. Find several ads that make use of the kinds of "infracted forms" Colombo discusses. Write an essay exploring "violated forms" of other than a literary kind, for example in music, painting, photography, or film. How could they exist also in "modern social concerns," as Colombo says they do?

4. Colombo says that "today it is perfectly possible...to react to the world as if it were a work of art itself." Possible, yes—but, considering what the word *art* means, is it legitimate to do so, to adopt "this way of seeing things"? Compose an argument answering this question.

5. Try making an anagram of your own name.

6. Write a lipogram of at least one hundred words avoiding one of the vowels. Then write one avoiding *r*, *s*, or *t*. Write a paragraph in which each word contains an *a*, then one with each word having an *e*; an *i*; a *t*; an *o*; an *n*. Write five univocalic sentences—each using only one of the five vowels; for example: Jack has a swayback nag that balks at a caravan march.

7. Compose a concrete poem.

## MICHAEL HORNYANSKY  "Is Your English Destroying Your Image?"

1.  Identify the literary allusions in "Call me Noah" and "A little grammar is a dangerous thing." Are these allusions amusing? Point out and explain some of Hornyansky's many other allusions.

2.  In the fourth paragraph Hornyansky clarifies the meaning of "mistake" as he wants it understood. What other terms does he find it necessary to define? Show how he uses classification in this essay.

3.  This is a long essay. Examine Hornyansky's topic sentences to see how well each also works transitionally, helping to maintain coherence between paragraphs.

4.  Do you agree that "lightness makes for more clarity than does indignation"? Why should this be so? Which would make for more *impact*? Is Hornyansky correct when he says that his three criteria are always subtly intertwined?

5.  Hornyansky says he likes to use "the simple and colloquial as salt to my discourse." Point out several examples of his doing that, and evaluate the overall effectiveness of the technique. Examine also his use of metaphors.

6.  In the third paragraph Hornyansky uses *magic* as a verb—which ordinarily it isn't—thereby adding vigour and freshness to the sentence. Compose half-a-dozen sentences using nouns as verbs, then another half-dozen using adjectives as verbs. You may then want to try building paragraphs around one or more of the sentences.

7.  From your everyday reading and listening, gather more words and phrases that create images of Fogginess and Mechanism. Find some examples—perhaps in your textbooks—of the "Professorial" or "Godlike" style that Hornyansky calls a "disease." Can you think of any other "images" to add to those he lists?

8.  Keep score for a week, recording the number of times you see or hear *hopefully* misused. Compare several dictionaries to see what, if anything, they say about the usage of such terms as *ain't, like* as a conjunction, *disinterested, due to, irregardless, good* as an adverb, *media, infer, hopefully, presently, momentarily.* Write a brief report on your findings. You may want to classify the various dictionaries according to how they treat such matters.

9.  Hornyansky doesn't refer to passive voice. Show how passive voice is often weak in the same way that such phrases as "a decision-making process" are weak. Does Hornyansky use much passive voice?

10. Do you agree that *whom* is best avoided? If not, construct a brief argument for its retention. Or try an ironic argument, if you agree with Hornyansky.

11. Write a persuasive essay either agreeing or disagreeing with Hornyansky's stand on "sexist English."

### LEWIS THOMAS   "Notes on Punctuation"

1. Is there a significant difference between *precision* and *exactitude* as Thomas uses them at the end of his first paragraph?
2. How can one use a comma "with affection"? Do you agree with Thomas's preference for the semicolon over the colon? Why or why not?
3. Thomas is a scientist (see his essay in section IV); why should he be writing about punctuation? And discussing poetry?
4. Is this essay argumentative? Is Thomas trying to convince his readers that punctuation is important, that it shouldn't be considered as something accidental or added on but rather as part of *what* is being said because it tells readers *how to read* what is being said? If so. does he succeed? Does he also communicate the *pleasures* of punctuation?
5. Apply Thomas's advice to your own writing. For practice, compose sentences—preferably many of them—that experiment with each of the marks in the various ways suggested by Thomas's remarks and examples. Could a single sentence contain all the marks?

### MICHAEL FRAYN   "Lives and Likenesses"

1. What signs indicate the original occasion for this essay? What differentiates it as a review from that of Kael in section III? Is Frayn's piece also argumentative?
2. Are the examples Frayn offers examples of different things, or is it all one essay? If it is all of a piece, what holds it together? Show how the *forms*—the patterns and the organization—of the sentences in each example are related to what that example is saying.
3. When do you first know that this is going to be a humorous essay? The subtitle of the collection from which it comes is "Satirical Essays by Michael Frayn." What or whom is this essay satirizing?
4. Frayn's use of *form* as part of *content*—the *how* as part of the *what*—is obvious. For fun, try devising an appropriate form to tell part of the life of a famous media personality, sports star, politician, or artist—someone identified with a particular form (Bogart? Ali? Lévesque? Nixon? Picasso? Tom Thomson? Schoenberg?). Or write a book review (would it have to be a negative one?) that parodies the style or some of its mannerisms, or a gossip column in the form of a dialogue over the back fence or by the office water-cooler, or a piece on a famous cook or on dieting in the form of a recipe, or....But you can probably find a better subject yourself.

### GERTRUDE STEIN   "Composition as Explanation"

1. Analyze the reflexive quality of this essay, the way it turns in upon itself, uses itself as part of its own subject. Discuss the effect of the

"constant recurring and beginning" Stein refers to and makes much use of. What is the function of all the repetition? Is there any pattern to it? What does it have to do with what she says about time? Try your own hand at writing a paragraph that conveys the feeling of a "continuous present." Perhaps make it a portrait, a description of someone you know well.

2.  Try to explain how *romanticism* and *war* function in this discussion of composition. What does Stein mean by "the authenticity of the modern composition"? What exactly does she mean by "composition"?

3.  Does Stein adequately define *distribution* and *equilibration*? Define them yourself in order to help explain what she means.

4.  Stein uses the word *phenomena* as both a singular noun and a plural noun. Is this deliberate, or a careless or carefree handling of the language?

5.  Some of Stein's sentences at first sound like nonsense, but if you read them over and over again they begin to make a kind of sense that would be impossible with more conventional sentences. Analyze two or three sentences to show how this happens. How does her style force a reader to look closely at individual words and at the specific functions of parts of speech?

**MICHAEL J. ARLEN   "Life and Death in the Global Village"**

1.  The book in which this and other of Arlen's columns from the late 1960s are collected is called *Living-Room War*. In his introduction to the book, many of whose pieces are about the war in Vietnam and its daily exposure on television, Arlen says he doesn't fully agree that the war is "necessarily made 'real' " to viewers by being brought into their living rooms, claiming that it is "also made less 'real' — diminished," because it is seen on a small screen with its "picture of men" three inches tall shooting at other men three inches tall, and trivialized, or at least tamed, by the enveloping cozy alarums of the household." How does this idea help you appreciate the way he treats the assassination of Martin Luther King as he saw it reported on television?

2.  At the end of the fourth paragraph Arlen reports that "Robert Kennedy deplores the rise in violence." Consider the adventitious irony and poignancy accruing to this remark from the fact that only two months later Kennedy himself was assassinated in Los Angeles.

3.  What is the effect of the ending, his reference to "the sounds of footsteps running"?

4.  Consider the *form* or style Arlen chooses to write in: it is marked by (among other things) the play with "slowing down," the many ellipses and parentheses, the short and sometimes fragmentary sentences and quotations (as well as a few unusually long ones, such as the first).

How does such a style help convey not only the nature of the event itself but also the way the event was perceived by him and millions of others? What effect do cadence and movement have on meaning?

5. Make your medium your message. Compose an essay about commercial television's news coverage of some major event—not necessarily a violent one. Use judicious amounts of direct quotation from reporters and commentators as well as interviewees. And find some way to incorporate (perhaps parenthetically?) words, phrases, and sentences from the commercials that occur before and after parts of the news stories, especially if (as often happens) the juxtaposition makes the commercial appear in some way ironic or otherwise relevant to the news, or just outrageously inappropriate. That is, create your own juxtapositions for the effects you want. And try mixing present tense in, as Arlen does, for a sense of immediacy.

### MAXINE HONG KINGSTON  "On Mortality"

1. A *fable* is a brief story told to make a moral point or to illustrate something about human nature; the point is usually stated explicitly at the end. What other characteristics do fables sometimes have? How does a *parable* differ from a fable? How do these forms work? Compare Kingston's fable with others you know, such as Aesop's or Thurber's, and perhaps with Christ's parables in the Bible. Would it be accurate to call all of these *allegorical?* How is a fable or a parable different from a *myth* or *legend* or *folktale* or *fairy tale?*

2. What does Kingston's piece suggest about the nature of *illusion?* What does it suggest about the need for *perspective*, for seeing something from another's point of view—namely that of the opposite sex?

3. The original form of the story was obviously not the same as that in which Kingston relates it. For one thing, it wasn't in English. Do you think she has done much more than simply translate it? What else might she have changed, or added—and why? Do you believe that Tu actually lived from A.D. 558 to 618? What is the effect of Kingston's use of such a matter-of-fact tone for the recounting of such extravagant and horrific events? Do you find yourself virtually compelled to seek significance beyond the literal level?

### GWENDOLYN MacEWEN  "The Holyland Buffet"

1. This piece appears in a book descriptively subtitled *An Anthology of Travel Writing*, which also includes straightforward accounts, extracts from journals (including Johnston's; see section I), poetry, impressionistic prose-poems, and photographs. A note tells us that "The Holyland Buffet" is "from a new book of short stories" by MacEwen, but adds that "all of the events" in it "are true and happened to her."

Is it then fiction, or fact? Is it an imaginative autobiographical narrative cast in the *form* of a third-person short story? Or is it a "story"? Does it differ essentially in kind from, say, White's "Once More to the Lake" (section I)? Does it have a plot? Does it have a thesis? Compare it as travel writing with some of the other pieces in this book. Is White's essay (story?) in any sense travel writing? Mukherjee's (section I)? How about Huxley's and Orwell's essays (section II)?

2. Analyze this work as a story—that is, in terms of plot, character, setting, style, and structure. Is the narrative point of view (a) omniscient, (b) limited to one of the characters, or (c) objective, "dramatic"? Who is the protagonist? Does it contain any elements of what you might call fantasy? Does it use conversation to *reveal*, in the manner of some of the essays in section II?

3. Why "Mythological Foods"? Why "Kanada" and "Kanadian" with a *K*? Why the name "Kali"? *Is* there a "Mount of Loaves and Fishes"? If not, what might MacEwen be suggesting by the name? *Are* there two Holyland Buffets? How many "Holylands" are there? Why might Greece be, to some, "really a holy land"?

4. As has often been said, "It all depends on your point of view." Explain how this piece dramatizes that truism. One of Rooney's bits of advice (section II) reads: "You aren't the only one who doesn't understand the situation in the Middle East." Is MacEwen's intention partly to illustrate such a point?

5. Write a "story," a fictionalized account, in the third person, based on your own personal experience—perhaps about something that happened to you while you were travelling. What do you find yourself doing differently than you would if you were writing a straightforward first-person report?

## TOPICS: General and Comparative

1. Colombo says he will provide no definition of the word *form*. What is your own "rule-of-thumb meaning" for it? How does your dictionary define it? How could it possibly be argued that *form* and *content* "have no meaning whatsoever," as Colombo in his first paragraph says it has been? Are *form* and *content* in the arts inseparable in the same way Brink at the end of his fourth paragraph says *thought* and *action* are (section III)? Test his analogy. Consider the question of form with respect to other essays in this book—and not just those in section VI. To what degree is *method* part of *meaning*? The meaning of Arlen's narrative comes largely through the way he delivers it, and Frayn in his biographical sketches clearly uses form—*style*—to echo the content of what he says. Do Davenport and Lane (section II)

manipulate meaning through the style they use? Does Ludwig (section II)? How does Thurber in his essay in section III make style match substance? How do White's diction and syntax (section I) reflect his shifting point of view?

2. Consider punctuation: it is part of form. It is most often simply a visual sign of an author's intended aural pacing, but it can be crucial. Some of the oddity of Stein's prose is due simply to the absence of conventional punctuation. Since it was originally given as a lecture, try reading a paragraph or two aloud, several times: does oral delivery make it clearer? Try supplying the punctuation necessary to make it more like conventional writing. Does that make it clearer? If so, however, given her idiosyncratic style and what she is using it to say, is anything lost by adding punctuation? (For fun, listen to a record of Victor Borge's comic skit on "oral punctuation.") At the other extreme, Lewis Thomas offers good advice about the different punctuation marks, and in each instance he uses the particular mark in the process of saying something about it. That is, he adopts—or constructs—a *form* of expression that enables him to illustrate the point he is making while he is making it. Form joins function. When he seems to overdo it, for example with parentheses, is it for humour or emphasis rather than because he is insensitive to the nuances of punctuation? Examine the punctuation of other writers to see if they punctuate as Thomas recommends. Try to evaluate and explain any notable departures from the principles he outlines.

3. Hornyansky, like Thurber (section III), sometimes demonstrates the very fault he is discussing. Write a short paragraph discussing some weakness or error of style in which you add to the point by purposely committing the error or weakness yourself. Then write another paragraph in which you use the same technique to demonstrate a stylistic or rhetorical strength. That is, give some advice about writing in such a way that you demonstrate what you're writing about while you're writing about it. Some possible subjects: sentence length or variety, passive voice, placement of topic sentences, vigorous verbs, clichés, slang, wordiness, rhetorical questions, metaphors—perhaps even punctuation.

4. Narration is often used for exposition. Arlen's essay, for example, is overall a narrative. How, within that mode, does he engage your interest in and attention to other matters than the mere sequence of events? That is, how does he make it *expository*? Kingston's fable is itself expository, and appears inside an essay form; MacEwen's story is expository, as are the narratives of personal experience by White and others in section I. Rouechés essay (section IV) is largely narrative; Brink's essay (section III) includes a fable, and Atwood (section IV), Hornyansky, and others use anecdotes to help make their exposi-

tory points. Examine the way these writers use narrative (and descriptive) elements in their essays. How do they introduce them? How do they comment on them?

5.   Note how some writers use graphic devices to help control the structure of their essays. Colombo, for example, uses boldface headings, or subtitles, for the sections of his essay. Galbraith (section IV) uses Roman numerals, as do Szasz (section III) and Eiseley (section I). Schneider (section IV) uses italicized opening sentences. Baker (section IV) numbers his three criteria. Which writers in this book use simply a little extra white space to mark a break or division? Is that method equally effective but less obtrusive? Are numerals somehow more formal? Does it depend on the length or complexity of the essay?

6.   Write an essay about violence and the media. Many different approaches are possible. Explore the dual subject until you find a focus that appeals to you. Take into account not only Arlen's essay but also those by Jenkins, Zinsser, Fulford, and Brink in section III, and possibly other sources as well. Plan carefully: decide on your overall purpose and your major internal strategies, and draw up an outline. If your essay is to be at all long or complex, consider dividing it into sections, whether numbered or not.

7.   Hornyansky refers to the word *togetherness*, saying he's glad it didn't succeed in becoming established. Kael uses the word scornfully in her review (section III). Note also what Schlesinger (section III) says about *togetherness*. Would he agree with Hornyansky, or is he concerned only with the concept? Is Hornyansky also concerned with the concept, or only with the word? How do you feel about the word—and the concept? Are the two separable?   Write a short expressive essay on the subject.

8.   In the next essay you write, make a conscious effort to introduce rhythm and sound patterns. How far dare you go? What considerations seem to determine how far you can go?

9.   Choose a subject that interests you, such as athletics, home movies, blackberrying, Cézanne, dog shows, English kings, forensic medicine, snowmobiles, *Genesis*, whole numbers, sound waves, or seismography. First define your subject closely, narrowing it to a topic that can be handled in a short essay. Then cast yourself in a range of writer's roles, and write a series of short essays, say two or three pages each, all on the same subject, but varying in emphasis and approach as you alter your purpose and your audience in the following ways:

(a)  *Relate and describe.* Write a personal narrative which illustrates your involvement with the subject, but keep your emphasis on the subject rather than on yourself. Build descriptive elements into your story in such a way that they add to, but do not overpower, the narrative itself. Use some metaphorical language.

(b) *Reveal.* Interview several people about your subject, taking notes. Then use some or all of your notes in an essay which explores the subject but also reveals aspects of personality—either your own or that of the person or persons who supplied the most striking perspective.

(c) *Persuade.* Treat your subject argumentatively. Perhaps try to convince a reader of its virtues or shortcomings, or try to defend it against some attack which you can imagine being mounted against it. In any event, be sure to take into account what an opposing argument might say. If your subject is suitable, you might try writing an extended advertisement for it. Don't be afraid to use satire or irony if they are appropriate to your intentions.

(d) *Explain and inform.* Explain some particular feature of your subject. Use descriptive and narrative elements if they help you to be clear about the point you are trying to elucidate, but keep them minimal. Do not let yourself be drawn into an argumentative stance; be as objective as possible.

(e) *Amuse.* Treat your subject humorously. (Your central point can be serious, but the tone should be light.) Decide in advance which devices of humour will be appropriate to your purpose, but don't therefore automatically discard other promising ideas that inspiration gives you as you write.

When you have finished these essays, look back over them and consider the differences among them. To what audience does each essay appeal? Which essays are the most (and least) successful? Why? How and why have you varied their form? Have you been technically experimental? Where? Why? Now write one more essay, one in which you analyze your own writing style (as these five short essays reveal it) and explore how and why your style varies.

# Notes on Authors
# and Sources

ARLEN, MICHAEL J. (b. 1930).   English-born writer and television critic; author of *Exiles*, *The Camera Age*, and *Passage to Ararat*, which won a National Book Award in 1976. "Life and Death in the Global Village" first appeared in *The New Yorker* and was collected in *Living-Room War* in 1969.

ATWOOD, MARGARET (b. 1939).   Canadian poet and writer of novels, stories, and criticism; *The Circle Game* won a Governor General's Award. Among her novels are *Surfacing* and *Bodily Harm*. "Witches" was collected in *Second Words: Selected Critical Prose* (1982).

BAKER, NICHOLSON (b. 1957).   American writer, contributor to *The Little Magazine*, *Story Quarterly*, *The New Yorker*, and *The Atlantic*, where "The Size of Thoughts" appeared in March 1983. His story "K.590" was included in *The Best American Short Stories, 1982*.

BECK, SIMONE, and LOUISETTE BERTHOLLE.   *See* Child, Julia.

BEERBOHM, SIR MAX (1872-1956).   English novelist, essayist, and caricaturist, perhaps best known for his novel *Zuleika Dobson* and for *Seven Men*. "How Shall I Word It?" is from the 1920 collection *And Even Now*.

BERLIN, SIR ISAIAH (b. 1909).   Latvian-born British teacher, philosopher, and writer—often about political theory and the history of ideas. Among his better known works are *The Hedgehog and the Fox: An Essay on Tolstoy's View of History* and *Four Essays on Liberty*. "The Purpose of Philosophy" first appeared in *Insight* in 1962 and was collected in *Concepts and Categories: Philosophical Essays* (1978).

BRINK, ANDRÉ (b. 1935).   South African novelist, playwright, and essayist; author of *A Chain of Voices*, *Looking on Darkness*, and *A Dry White Season*. "The Intellectual and His World," the 1980 Graduation address, University of the Witwatersrand, was collected in *Mapmakers: Writing in a State of Siege* (1983).

BROAD, WILLIAM (b. 1951).   American journalist, science reporter with *The New York Times*; author of articles in *Science* and *New Scientist*. With Nicholas Wade wrote *Betrayers of the Truth* (1982), of which "The Myth of Logic" is Chapter 7.

CAMERON, SILVER DONALD (b. 1937).   Canadian freelance writer and founder of *The Mysterious East*; author of *Faces of Leacock* and other books, including *Conversations with Canadian Novelists* (1973), from which his interview with Davies is taken.

CHILD, JULIA (b. 1912).   California-born chef and writer on culinary arts, and star of the television programme "The French Chef"; collaborated with French cooking teachers Simone Beck and Louisette Bertholle to produce *Mastering the Art of French Cooking* in 1965 (from which come the instructions on boning a fowl), and with Simone Beck to produce a second volume in 1970; and since then has written *Julia Child and Company* and other books as well as starred in another television series.

COLE, K.C. (b. 1946).   American magazine editor and free-lance writer. Among his books are *Visions: In the Eye of the Beholder*, *Order in the Universe*, and *Between the Lines*. "By the Numbers" first appeared in *Discover* magazine in January 1984.

COLUMBO, JOHN ROBERT (b. 1936).   Canadian poet, translator, and anthologist, compiler of *Colombo's Canadian Quotations*, and devotee of "found poetry." "Communicating Through Form" appeared in *A Media Mosaic*, ed. Walt McDayter, in 1971.

DAVENPORT, GUY (b. 1927).   American teacher, poet, and critic. "Wittgenstein" was collected in *The Geography of the Imagination* (1981).

DILLARD, ANNIE (b. 1945).   American essayist who often writes about herself and nature; author of *Living by Fiction*, *Pilgrim at Tinker Creek* (which won a Pulitzer Prize in 1975), and *Teaching a Stone to Talk*, in which "Living Like Weasels" was collected in 1982.

DRYDEN, KEN (b. 1947).   Canadian hockey star, now retired; played 1030 NHL games. "The Game," adapted from his 1984 book *The Game*, appeared in *Saturday Night* magazine.

EISELEY, LOREN (1907-1977).   American anthropologist; author of *The Firmament of Time*, *The Immense Journey*, and several other books on nature and modern life. "The Creature from the Marsh" is taken from *Night Country* (1971).

FISHER, M.F.K. (b. 1908). American writer, principally about gastronomy and travel; author of *How to Cook a Wolf*, *The Gastronomical Me* (which includes "A Thing Shared"), and *An Alphabet for Gourmets*, which were collected with two other works in 1954 as *The Art of Eating*.

FORSTER, E.M. (1879-1970). English novelist and critic, best known for *A Passage to India*, *The Celestial Omnibus*, and *Aspects of Fiction*. "My Wood" appeared in *Abinger Harvest*, a collection of his essays, in 1936.

FRAYN, MICHAEL (b. 1933). English columnist, novelist, and dramatist; author of *The Russian Interpreter*. His plays include *Noises Off* and *Benefactors.* "Lives and Likenesses" first appeared in *The Observer* and was collected in 1983 in *The Original Michael Frayn*.

FULFORD, ROBERT (b. 1932). Canadian journalist and (under the pseudonym Marshall Delaney) film critic; author of *Crisis at the Victory Burlesk* and other books. Since 1968 he has been the editor of *Saturday Night*, where "White Lies" appeared in September 1983.

GALBRAITH, JOHN KENNETH (b. 1908). Canadian-born U.S. diplomat and economist; author of *The Scotch* and *The Affluent Society*. "The Language of Economics" appeared in *Fortune* magazine (December 1962), and was republished in *Economics, Peace & Laughter*, ed. Andrea D. Williams, in 1971.

GORMAN, JAMES (b. 1949). American writer of humorous pieces and of pieces about science — sometimes of humorous pieces about science; author of a humorous column in *Discover* magazine and of *First Aid for Hypochondriacs* (1982). "Man, Bytes, Dog" appeared in *The New Yorker* July 2, 1984.

GOULD, STEPHEN JAY (b. 1941). American teacher and frequent writer about geology, paleontology, and evolution; author of *Ever Since Darwin* and *Hen's Teeth and Horse's Toes*. He has won awards for *The Mismeasure of Man* and for *The Panda's Thumb*, from which "Our Allotted Lifetimes" comes.

HAIG-BROWN, RODERICK (1908-1976). English-born Canadian essayist, novelist, and magistrate; author of several books for children, including *Saltwater Summer*, and a number of books on the art of fishing, including *Fisherman's Fall* (1964), from which "Behind the Salmon" is taken.

HORNYANSKY, MICHAEL (b. 1927). Canadian folklorist, children's writer (*The Golden Phoenix*) and professor of English. His essay on usage appeared in *In the Name of Language!*, ed. Joseph Gold, in 1975.

HUXLEY, ALDOUS (1894-1963). English satirist, essayist, and novelist, long a United States resident; best known for his moral fable *Brave New*

*World* and novels like *Point Counter Point* and *Island.* "Usually De-stroyed" was collected in *Adonis and the Alphabet* (1956), called *Tomorrow and Tomorrow and Tomorrow* in the American edition.

JENKINS, PETER (b. 1934).   English journalist; since 1974, Political Com-mentator and Policy Editor for *The Guardian*; Granada TV Journalist of the Year in 1978. Author of the play *Illuminations* (1980) and *The Battle of Downing Street* (1970). "It Depends What You Mean by Violence" appeared in the *Manchester Guardian Weekly* of October 28, 1984.

JOHNSTON, GEORGE (b. 1913).   Canadian poet and internationally known authority on Old Norse and the Icelandic sagas. His books include *Happy Enough, The Saga of Gisli*, and *Rocky Shores: An Anthology of Faroese Poetry.* "The Site at Kvivik" appeared in *Views from the North: An Anthology of Travel Writing*, ed. Karen Mulhallen, in 1984.

KAEL, PAULINE (b. 1919).   Widely printed American film critic; author of *Kiss Kiss Bang Bang* (1968), in which her comments on *The Sound of Music* were collected, and other works, including *Going Steady* and *Reeling.*

KINGSTON, MAXINE HONG (b. 1940).   American writer and English teacher, of Chinese ancestry; author of the award-winning books *The Woman Warrior: Memoirs of a Girlhood among Ghosts* (1976) and *China Men* (1980), from which "On Mortality" comes.

LANE, MARGARET (b. 1907).   English reporter, novelist, and biographer of Beatrix Potter, Edgar Wallace, Charlotte Brontë, and other literary figures. "The Ghost of Beatrix Potter" appeared in her *Purely for Pleasure* (1966).

LEACOCK, STEPHEN (1869-1944).   Canadian humorist and professor of economics and political science; widely known as a humourous lec-turer and as the author of *Sunshine Sketches of a Little Town* and other works. *Literary Lapses*, in which "A, B, and C" appeared, was first published in 1910.

LUDWIG, JACK (b. 1922).   Canadian novelist, professor, and sports observer, now resident in New York; his works include a novel, *Above Ground*, and a book of essays, *Games of Fear and Winning* (1976), which included his comments on the Calgary Stampede.

MacEWEN, GWENDOLYN (b. 1941).   Canadian poet, dramatist, and fiction writer; among her books are *The Shadow-Maker*, winner of a Gover-nor General's Award in 1969, *Magic Animals*, and *The Fire-Eaters.* "The Holyland Buffet" first appeared in *Views from the North: An Anthology of Travel Writing*, ed. Karen Mulhallen, in 1984.

MacLENNAN, HUGH (b. 1907).   Canadian novelist (*Barometer Rising, The Watch That Ends the Night, Voices in Time*) and essayist. "The Street-Car Conductor" appeared in his *Thirty and Three* (1955).

McCLUNG, NELLIE (1873-1951).  Canadian novelist and polemicist, often advocating temperance and women's rights. Among her books are *Sowing Seeds in Danny* and the autobiography *Clearing in the West.* "A Gentleman of the Old School" is Chapter XIII of *The Stream Runs Fast: My Own Story* (1945).

MEIGS, MARY (b. 1917).  American-born writer now resident in Canada; author of *The Medusa Head* and *Lily Briscoe.* "Pandora Was a Feminist" appeared in *Women and Words: The Anthology  Les Femmes et les Mots; Une Anthologie,* in 1984.

MITFORD, JESSICA (b. 1917).  Member of a well-known English family, long resident in the United States; author of many books and articles, including *Kind and Usual Punishment: The Prison Business* and *Poison Penmanship: The Gentle Art of Muckraking.* Her first major success was *The American Way of Death* (1963), in which "The Story of Service" is the fifth chapter.

MORGAN, ELAINE (b. 1920).  Welsh playwright, feminist sociological writer, and author of *Falling Apart.* "The Man-Made Myth" is the opening chapter of *The Descent of Woman* (1972).

MUKHERJEE, BHARATI (b. 1940).  Bengali-born Canadian novelist; author of *The Tiger's Daughter* and *Wife.* "Intimations" is part of the section she wrote for *Days and Nights in Calcutta,* an autobiographical account of a year in India which she wrote in collaboration with her husband, Clark Blaise.

MURDOCH, WALTER (1874-1970).  Australian newpaper essayist. "On Pioneering" appeared in *Speaking Personally* in 1930, and again in his *Collected Essays* in 1941.

O'CONNOR, FLANNERY (1925-1964).  American novelist and short story writer; author of *Wise Blood* and *Everything that Rises Must Converge.* Her essay on education appeared in *Mystery and Manners,* ed. Sally and Robert Fitzgerald, in 1969.

ORWELL, GEORGE (1903-1950).  pseud. of ERIC BLAIR. English novelist, essayist and cultural observer; author of *Animal Farm* and *1984,* and several collection of essays. "How the Poor Die" first appeared in *Now* in the 1940s, and was collected in his *Shooting an Elephant* (1950).

RITTER, ERIKA (b. 1948).  Canadian dramatist and humorist; author of *Automatic Pilot* (a play that won the 1980 Chalmers award) and *The Passing Scene.* "Bicycles" was collected in *Urban Scrawl* in 1984.

ROONEY, ANDREW A. (b. 1919).  American columnist and television writer, producer, and performer. His television essays have been collected in *A Few Minutes with Andy Rooney;* his newpaper columns are collected in *And More by Andy Rooney* and *Pieces of My Mind,* which includes "A Penny Saved Is a Waste of Time".

ROUECHE, BERTON (b. 1911). American medical journalist; author of *Eleven Blue Men*, *The Incurable Wound*, and other "narratives of medical detection." "Three Sick Babies" appeared in his *The Orange Man* in 1971.

SCHLESINGER, ARTHUR M., JR. (b. 1920). American teacher and historian; among his works are *The Age of Roosevelt*, *The Politics of Freedom*, and *A Thousand Days* (National Book Award 1966). "The Crisis of American Masculinity" first appeared in *Esquire* in 1958 and was collected in *The Politics of Hope* in 1962.

SCHNEIDER, BEN ROSS, JR. (b. 1920). American teacher and literary scholar who also writes about computers; author of *Wordsworth's Cambridge Education* and *Travels in Computerland*. "Programs as Essays" appeared in *Datamation* magazine in 1984.

SHEEHAN, LAURENCE (b. 1940). American writer on sports and other subjects; his "The Christmas Tree Lot Murders" was among the *Best Detective Stories of the Year* in 1977; co-author of *Home Gardening at Its Best*; other pieces, often humorous, have appeared in *Harper's*, *New England Monthly*, *Golf Digest*, *Tennis*, and other magazines. "How to Play Second Base" first appeared in the *Atlantic Monthly* in September 1974.

STEIN, GERTRUDE (1874-1946). American writer, trained in psychology and medicine, who became a literary leader among the exiles who settled in Paris in the 1920s; author of *The Autobiography of Alice B. Toklas* and other works. "Composition as Expanation," first delivered as a lecture, was first published in 1926 in *What Are Masterpieces?*

SZASZ, THOMAS S. (b. 1920). American psychiatrist and author of *The Myth of Mental Illness*, *Ceremonial Chemistry*, and other books on psychiatry and public attitude. "What Psychiatry Can and Cannot Do" appeared in *Harper's Magazine* in 1964, and in his *Ideology and Insanity* (1970).

THOMAS, DYLAN (1914-1953). Welsh poet, scriptwriter (*Under Milk Wood*), and story writer. "Memories of Christmas" was first broadcast by the BBC Welsh Home Service in 1945 and printed in *The Listener*, and collected in *Quite Early One Morning* in 1954.

THOMAS, LEWIS (b. 1913). American medical doctor, director of the Memorial Sloan-Kettering Cancer Center in New York; author of *The Lives of a Cell*, which won a 1974 National Book Award, *The Medusa and the Snail*, from which "Notes on Punctuation" comes, and *Late Night Thoughts on Listening to Mahler's Ninth Symphony*. His "Notes of a Biology Watcher: The Hazards of Science" first appeared in the *New England Journal of Medicine*, 10 February 1977.

THURBER, JAMES (1894-1961).   American cartoonist, humorist, journalist, and playwright, long a staff member of *The New Yorker;* among his many works are *The Seal in the Bedroom, Fables for Our Time,* and *The Wonderful O.* "Wild Bird Hickok and His Friends" (also published as "The French Far West") appeared in *Let Your Mind Alone* in 1937; "The Psychosemanticist Will See You Now, Mr. Thurber" appeared in *Alarms and Diversions* in 1957.

TRILLIN, CALVIN (b. 1935).   American reporter and columnist; author of *An Education in Georgia, U.S. Journal, American Fried: Adventures of a Happy Eater,* and *Killings.* "Literally" is from *Uncivil Liberties,* a 1982 collection of his columns from *The Nation,* where it appeared on September 12, 1981.

TUCHMAN, BARBARA W. (b. 1912).   American historian; winner of Pulitzer Prizes for *The Guns of August* and *Stilwell and the American Experience in China;* author also of *The Proud Tower* and *A Distant Mirror.* "Is History a Guide to the Future?" was collected in *Practicing History* (1981).

UPDIKE, JOHN (b. 1932).   American writer of novels, short stories, poems, and essays; among his many works are *Rabbit, Run, Pigeon Feathers, The Centaur,* and *The Coup.* In 1982 his novel *Rabbit Is Rich* won a Pulitzer Prize and two other awards. "Central Park," which originally appeared in *The New Yorker,* was collected in *Assorted Prose* in 1965.

WADE, NICHOLAS (b. 1942).   English-born American science writer, editorial writer for *The New York Times;* author of *The Ultimate Experiment* and many magazine articles. (*See* Broad, William.)

WHITE, E.B. (1899-1985).   American poet, essayist, letter writer; author of *Charlotte's Web* and other books for children as well as of numerous collections of essays and letters. "Once More to the Lake," written in 1941, appeared in *One Man's Meat* (1944) and was reprinted in *Essays of E.B. White* (1977).

WOOLF, VIRGINIA (1882-1941).   English novelist and essay writer, best known for *To The Lighthouse, Mrs. Dalloway, The Waves,* and *A Room of One's Own.* "Middlebrow," written but never sent to *The New Statesman,* was printed in *The Death of the Moth* (1942).

ZINSSER, WILLIAM (b. 1922).   American feature writer, editor, and teacher; author of *On Writing Well, Pop Goes America,* and *Writing with a Word Processor.* "Nobody Here but Us Dead Sheep" first appeared in *Life* magazine, 22 August 1969.

# Index of Terms